Alcon Laboratories

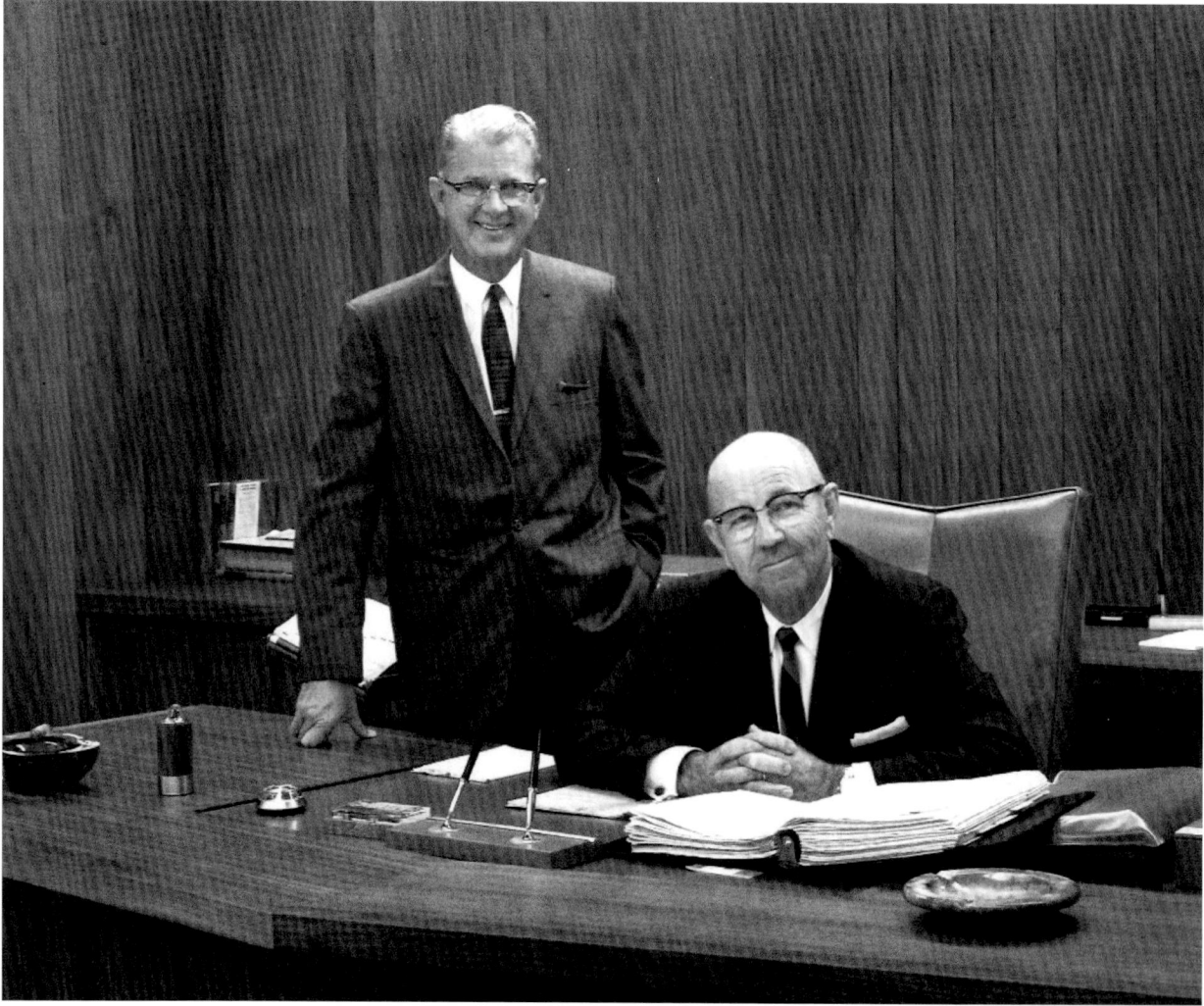

Alcon Laboratories

A Vision Fulfilled, 1947–1997

By Thomas O. McDonald

TCU
Press

Fort Worth, Texas

Library of Congress Control Number: 2024057608

TCU
Press

TCU Box 298300
Fort Worth, Texas 76129
www.tcupress.com

DEDICATION

Alcon Family—Past, Present, Future

Preface

I joined Alcon Laboratories on Monday, December 13, 1965, in the Research and Development Division (R&D). Seven days later, the R&D vice president was fired, and the division entered a rudderless period until 1968. Nevertheless, it was a heady time for a twenty-three-year-old scientist who worked full-time while earning a master's degree from Texas Christian University (TCU). The acumen of the company's two founders, Robert "Bob" D. Alexander and William "Bill" C. Conner, intrigued me. I was introduced to Conner during my first week when he made his Friday afternoon rounds of the laboratories and offices. As I listened to Ruby Zellers, my laboratory colleague who had been with Alcon since 1956, reminisce with Conner about the company's foundational years, I was captivated.

My interest grew after meeting C. Harold Beasley, an ophthalmologist and member of Alcon's board of directors. Luckily, I was assigned to a project proposed by him, one that developed a successful product, Miostat. He became my mentor and colleague until he died in 1999. Beasley suggested research projects to fill the specific needs of eye care specialists. On Wednesday afternoons, he taught ophthalmology to young scientists and regaled us with stories about Alcon's founding and its role in the ophthalmic industry. I was fascinated.

After thirty-nine years in Alcon R&D, I gravitated toward historical research after I retired in October 2004. My initial foray into history was not related to Alcon. As a seventh-generation Texan, my first book, *Texas Rangers, Ranchers, and Realtors* (University Oklahoma Press, 2021), paid tribute to the state's early settlers. As I was finishing the manuscript, I picked up Edgar "Ed" H. Schollmaier, Alcon's second CEO, to attend a lunch with retired R&D executives. While I was amusing my friends with the challenges of historical publication, Schollmaier suggested I write a history of Alcon's first fifty years. I am grateful to have had a continued dialogue with

Schollmaier as the narrative evolved. Sadly, he did not live to see the final manuscript; he died in September 2021.

In one respect, historians and scientists are similar. Both analyze records and documents to construct an interpretative narrative. In this regard, my four decades as an Alcon R&D scientist prepared me for historical research. Moreover, I am an intrinsic part of the history of Alcon. In my role as head of toxicology beginning in 1972 and as head of the Clinical Science group since 1980 (after I received my PhD), I signed every clinical protocol and report. As a member of R&D management, I knew each product R&D developed and the trials and tribulations encountered. I was privy to the marketing and sales techniques used for these new products; many set sales records. In writing this history, I did not rely on just my personal recollections to document Alcon's first fifty years. Instead, I sifted through countless archived sources; all are noted in the endnotes and the bibliography.

Most of the sources for this book are held in four archives: Alcon Laboratories Inc. Collection, Tarrant County Archives; Alcon Materials, Special Collections, Mary Couts Burnett Library, TCU; Alcon Historical Records, Alcon Laboratories; and the Bob Alexander Family Papers. I made digital copies of virtually everything I encountered; most of these I placed in Alcon Materials at the TCU library or the Alcon Collection at the Tarrant County Archives.

In 2004 Alcon's CEO Timothy "Tim" R. G. Sear had copies of early Alcon records, annual reports, and the company magazine, *Alcon World News*, deposited in the Tarrant County Archives. I arranged for these to be digitized and made available online at https://www.tarrantcountytx.gov/en/tarrant-county-archives/holdings/named-collections/a/alcon-laboratories-inc.html. Sear also organized an oral history project to preserve the recollections of numerous retirees. I tracked down the original recordings and transcripts and placed all in the Alcon Materials at the TCU library under the names of the interviewers, Dean Cobb and Loral Cobb (MS 232-2021-011).

When I contacted a member of the Alcon Family for an interview, I asked to see any documents or memorabilia they had. Schollmaier gave me his collection, and one of the unusual items acquired was a set of artificial eyes donated by Bob Grantham. Helmut Horchler donated his privately published book, *A Journey Well Traveled* (2005), an extensive discourse about his nearly thirty-five years at Alcon. Few of the Alcon materials at TCU are digitized, though some are to be made available online. My personal sets are being curated by archivists at the TCU library and the Tarrant County Archives.

Before embarking on this venture, I discussed my plans with the surviving Alexander and Conner family members. They were generous with their time, sitting for interviews and responding to countless emails and phone calls requesting clarification on specific events and people. I was fortunate the Conner and Alexander families read drafts of the manuscript; they corrected factual errors and added new perspectives, giving the narrative an authentic depth.

After Schollmaier's death, his son, Taylor, provided access to additional Alcon records and his family's legacy photos. Taylor's interview afforded additional insight into his father's personality and attitudes toward Alcon and its employees.

I am indebted to the current leadership of Alcon for its cooperation, in particular CEO David Endicott and chief legal counsel Royce Bedward, as well as Tad Heitmann, who was my contact within the company. I was granted access to Alcon's Historical Records, which had been collected since the 1980s under the guidance of Schollmaier, Sear, and Richard "Dick" H. Sisson. The documents, photos, reports, magazines, product samples, and so forth were placed at my disposal in a secure room along with a high-speed copier. As noted earlier, these digital copies are now being curated by archivists.

Alcon produced several company periodicals. One was the *Alcon-o-Gram*, which I located in the Alexander Family Papers and the Alcon Historical Records. The most complete set of the second publication, *Spectrum*, which later became R&D's newsletter, was compiled and saved by Barry Schlech, the head of microbiology in R&D. Schlech also kept other company publications and several videos, now deposited at the TCU library. Beginning in 1980, Schollmaier inaugurated the *Alcon World News*. Published quarterly, it is a key source for descriptions of important events in Alcon's history. Every issue featured an employee, giving depth to the role of the Alcon Family in the company's success. The marketing and sales groups of the Ophthalmic and Vision Care Divisions and the Surgical Division had their own publications, *Scope* and *Surgical Journal*. Both are found in the Alcon Historical Records. All these magazines were major resources for reconstructing the history of Alcon's first fifty years. During the years it was a public company listed on the stock exchange, Alcon also published annual reports; these are found in the Alcon Collection at the Tarrant County Archives and in the Alcon Historical Records.

When Nestlé bought Alcon in 1977, Alcon ceased to be a public company. I am grateful to Nestlé's archivist Albert Pfiffner, who gave me access to Nestlé's files on Alcon. He also sent me digital copies of Nestlé's annual reports. The story of Nestlé acquiring Alcon is best told from these records. Jacqualyn Fouse, former Nestlé treasurer and Alcon CFO, put me in contact with Pfiffner and translated the records from French into English. My good luck continued when I was granted interviews with Pierre Vogel and José Daniel, both of whom were responsible for shaping the unique and productive relationship between Alcon and Nestlé.

A major source of information and perspective came from nearly seventy-five oral histories I collected from Alcon retirees, whose recollections provide the most vibrant outlook of how people shaped Alcon. The list of names is too extensive to include here but is cited in the endnotes. I chose these participants from all divisions. I knew all from my years with the company, and I trusted them to be frank and expansive in our recorded discussions. A gigantic thanks to all of you: this narrative would not have been possible without your contributions. It was a huge joy to hear your stories, and I hope our discussion rekindled fond memories of your Alcon service.

I discovered other Alcon material at the Smithsonian Institution; Special Collections, Central Library, University of Texas at Arlington; and the Baker Library, Bloomberg Center, Harvard Business School (HBS). I used three Alcon case studies, two from the HBS and the other from the International Institute for Management Development in Lausanne, Switzerland. The latter is unpublished and commissioned by Nestlé, so its inclusion rounds out Alcon's story from the perspective of its parent company.

Throughout my career, I wrote scientific and regulatory dossiers. Writing a historical manuscript requires a different skill set. I had the good fortune and pleasure to engage three professional editors who shaped my words into this coherent, readable manuscript. To say thank you is inadequate to describe how much Jenny Luke, Bonnie Lovell, and Richard B. McCaslin contributed to the project. It was also a pleasure for me to introduce them to Alcon's story.

The manuscript was exposed to critical comment. I asked several people, mostly Alcon retirees, to read various chapters. The Alexander and Conner siblings and Taylor Schollmaier read every chapter; I came to depend upon their forthright assessment, which corrected errors and gave extra depth to my text. Many thanks to Denny Alexander, Lane Anne Kimzey, Anita Taylor, Halden Conner, Debbie Norris, and Taylor Schollmaier. It is only fitting that your fathers' accomplishments be recorded for posterity. I selected Alcon retirees to critique my text who I knew would be unstintingly frank, as they had been during their careers. I was not disappointed. My sincere appreciation to Jerry Cagle, Helmut Horchler, James Arno, Allen Baker, Howard Luttrell, Giorgio Vescovo, André Bens, Daryl Dubbs,

Carlos Coscia, Gregg Brown, Sandy Howell, Jerry Stein, Dilip Raval, Don Lobdell, Robert Stevens, Cary Rayment, and Bill Burns. I also depended on Alcon's review of the manuscript to make sure I did not inadvertently reveal any proprietary information.

The narrative mostly follows Ed Schollmaier's "Alcon Story," preserved in Special Collections at TCU. As such, it concentrates on Science and Technology and the importance of power marketing and selling. Though other segments of the company are less discussed, this does not diminish their pivotal roles for Alcon's success. We were all the Alcon Family.

I also want to thank TCU Press and its director Dan Williams for their support and patience. Considering TCU and Alcon are Tarrant County institutions, and given the close association between the two, it is only fitting that Alcon's story be published by TCU Press.

The Alcon Family is a major theme in the company's history. Throughout the writing process, I reflected on the character of the people who worked at Alcon and the growth of its incredibly constructive corporate culture. I have no doubt that the many people who thrived at Alcon selectively hired new employees who possessed similar traits. It was one reason why we worked together so effectively. Therefore, I must acknowledge that my success was in large part due to those colleagues who surrounded me. Being fortunate does not adequately convey how I benefited from their talents. I just know my life was and is richer due to having worked with them, many of whom I continue to call my friends.

Working closely with the same individuals every day over a period of years gives rise to close relationships, and many of us found soulmates at Alcon. I did when I met my wife, Shinko, in the Alcon organization in Japan. She is a gem and willingly supported me throughout my career and continued to do so as I morphed into a grassroots Texas historian, while establishing herself as a premiere English/Japanese interpreter.

Finally, I want to acknowledge my responsibility for the content of this book. Although I relied on many individuals to complete the project, any errors are mine.

Introduction

Fort Worth, Texas, is known more for cattle drives and cowboys than being the home of a world-renowned ophthalmic specialty company. From its meager beginnings in 1947 to its current role as a global leader in vision care and eye surgical devices, Alcon Laboratories has become a prominent part of Fort Worth's history. The company's founders and executives consolidated this relationship by creating public and private spaces, endowments, libraries, and scholarships in the city. Alcon's founders, Bob Alexander and Bill Conner, had the vision to create an "ophthalmic house" and the entrepreneurial courage to set Alcon on a course to global dominance. Of the twenty-five or so ophthalmic specialty companies founded around the world after World War II, Alcon was unique in its level of success. This narrative explores the first fifty years of Alcon's history, examining the accomplishments and failures that led to this remarkable achievement.

From its inception in 1947 to the fifty-year mark in 1997, Alcon grew from two founding partners to employing over 10,500 people; from one building in Fort Worth to over one hundred around the world, including modern manufacturing plants and the world's largest ophthalmic Research and Development laboratory; from one product to several thousand; and from annual sales of $45,000 to $2 billion. Three themes explain Alcon's success: the Alcon Family, Alcon products, and Alcon leadership.

People make an organization successful. Alexander and Conner, who coined the phrase "Alcon Family," understood this. They created an environment where work was intellectually and financially rewarding and personally enjoyable. The nucleus of the Alcon Family comprised employees who spent their entire working life, or a good portion of it, at Alcon—those who began working there in the late 1950s through the 1970s. Many retired with thirty to forty years of service. This nucleus mentored the next generations, who joined in the 1980s and 1990s, and instilled in them the company's core values. Members of the Alcon Family dominate the narrative, some named, some only featured in the accompanying photographs, but all an integral part of the Alcon Story. Individuals in the Alcon Family have a common work ethic and similar personality traits, and evidence suggests that about one-fifth of employees remained with the company for their entire career. The Alcon Family is an extraordinary, and essential, feature of the Alcon story.

Ophthalmic pharmaceuticals, as well as vision care and surgical products, are not developed, manufactured, marketed, or sold by mere chance. Their availability to eye care specialists results from the intellectual and physical efforts of multitalented people found in the Alcon Family. New products are developed in response to the evolution of science and technology surrounding ophthalmic medical and surgical practices. Alcon led trends in innovation and research to develop, manufacture, market, and sell an expanding selection of breakthrough products. From its earliest years, Alcon took pride in assuring customers that its quality products were compounded exactly as stated. It was the first ophthalmic company to make such guarantees. This narrative is crowded with the remarkable journeys taken by many Alcon products as they progressed from early research and development, to final government approval, through manufacturing, and lastly innovative marketing and sales.

Successful organizations require leaders with vision, articulating viable strategic and tactical plans. Executive leadership must have the ability to motivate a broad spectrum of personalities to competently implement these plans. The Alcon story highlights leaders who, possessing both that essential quality of effective leadership and management skills, learned from successes and mistakes. Conner was the epitome of an entrepreneurial visionary, and Alexander was the consummate salesman, and their skill sets were thoroughly complementary. They selected and mentored leaders who were central to the growth and eventual dominance of Alcon. Among these were George F. Leone, Edgar "Ed" H. Schollmaier, Richard "Dick" H. Sisson, John W. Spruill, Keith Lane, Frank X. Buhler, Theodore "Ted" C. Fleming, Dilip N. Raval, Timothy "Tim" R. G. Sear, Allen Baker, and Robert R. Montgomery. How they created a dynamic and a productive leadership team is a compelling story and remarkable achievement.

Effective medical industry leadership manages not only people but also facilitates changes while navigating an evolving market in an ever-changing scientific environment. Alcon leaders demanded the highest standards from all employees, in all endeavors. If any single word encapsulated Alcon leadership's secret to success it is *focus*. Alcon's success was due to a determined focus on providing, and anticipating, the needs of the global eye care specialist community. Whenever Alcon expended resources outside ophthalmology, it began to falter, a lesson Schollmaier learned early when Alcon faced bankruptcy in 1961. Crucial to Alcon's success was a continuity of management philosophy. The company had only two CEOs in its first fifty years, bringing an unusual degree of stability. This, along with a stable, increasingly experienced workforce, created an institutional knowledge of strategies, goals, products, and customer needs. From its inception, Alcon leaders followed their frugal instincts, keeping costs low and increasing profits, which were spent on growth. Alcon mostly developed its executives internally and rounded out their skills in management programs at renowned business schools, most notably Harvard. Alcon's leadership style encouraged optimum performance across the organization, creating a juggernaut of an ophthalmic specialist company with no rival on the global stage.

This book explores the Alcon story chronologically, devoting a chapter to each of the first five decades, a reflection of how the Alcon Family understands its own history. The complexity of the organization grew in response to the rapid development of ophthalmic science and the corresponding technical sophistication of the industry. Thus, each successive chapter increases in complexity, scope, and length. Examining various seminal events important to Alcon's history reveals how the company globally expanded its presence among eye care specialists.

Alexander and Conner decided by 1949 to concentrate on the ophthalmic market. This commitment was reinforced in 1953 when Alexander invented the revolutionary Drop-tainer, a plastic eye drop dispenser that transformed the industry. Alcon and its competitors still use a modification of Alexander's invention. In the 1950s, Alcon created a series of prescription eye drop products for the Drop-tainer. In 1961, a misguided marketing program nearly led to bankruptcy but pushed Schollmaier to develop the first long-term strategic plan, focused on the "strength of power selling" to eye doctors. Conner hired Buhler in 1962 to establish Alcon throughout the world, the first such push for an eye specialty company. From 1962 until 1972, Alcon dabbled in diversification by acquiring other medical specialty companies, though diversifying was internally debated. These acquisitions defocused resources and set the company on the road to chaos and an unproductive R&D division. Schollmaier took charge in 1972 and divested non-ophthalmic assets to refocus Alcon as a single-specialty company. This development is historically important as a business case study, the result being a company with a unique centralized organizational technology division and decentralized marketing and sales.

Leone created the Science and Technology Division composed of Research & Development (R&D), Regulatory Affairs (RA), Manufacturing/Engineering, and Quality Assurance (QA); at the head of each was an experienced leader. In a key strategic move, Alcon decided against becoming a chemical synthesis house that designed new medical molecules; rather, it depended on licensing new therapeutic compounds and surgical devices. This shift placed the scientists in R&D at the center of licensing pharmaceutical molecules and surgical devices, which drove research and innovative product development. With various exceptions, by 1997 most of the new ophthalmic, vision care, and surgical products resulted from this licensing effort. The 1973 fiasco of the United Kingdom manufacturing inspection is an example of how Alcon responded constructively to a significant setback. The failed inspection resulted in the building of improved production facilities and the integration of QA into a critical role in manufacturing facilities and processes. The International Division at the same time bought several companies for their market share and in the process acquired manufacturing plants in South America and Europe. By 1997 Alcon's facilities in the United States and overseas were state-of-the-art production plants run equally by QA and manufacturing personnel.

Schollmaier divided marketing and sales into Domestic and International Operations; he functioned as the bridge between these and S&T. In effect, he was the chief marketing officer. Sisson was in charge of the Ophthalmic and Vision Care Divisions, Spruill ran the Surgical Division, Lane led the Dermatology Division, and later Sear took over the International Division. Sisson created a dynamic marketing and sales organization that was renowned for its product launches. Spruill's audacious mentoring and strategic acquisitions led his division to produce one-half of Alcon's sales by 1997. Sear energized his division with a new marketing department located in Fort Worth that supported three geographic regions: EURMEA—Europe/Middle East/Africa; LACAR—Latin America and the Caribbean; and CAFE—Canada, Asia, and the Far East. By 1997 the International Division contributed 44 percent of Alcon's total revenues.

Alcon was listed on the New York Stock Exchange in 1971, only the second company founded in Tarrant County to achieve this goal. Perhaps the most consequential event in Alcon's history was its purchase by Nestlé in 1977. Nestlé made strategic investments in Alcon's infrastructure and was a source of funds for important acquisitions, the most significant being CooperVision in 1989. This gave Alcon access to novel technologies and competent scientists, prompting a slew of new surgical products. Of these, an innovative intraocular lens, AcrySof, became a keystone product for Alcon.

By 1997 Alcon sat at the pinnacle of the ophthalmic industry with annual sales of $2 billion. Its portfolio rested upon three pillars: ocular prescription medicines, vision care products, and ophthalmic surgical devices. Marketed and sold by seasoned, enthusiastic teams, three R&D-developed products—Betoptic, Opti-Free, and AcrySof—accounted for 25 percent of the $2 billion. Moreover, Alcon contributed 4.6 percent of Nestlé's global sales and an extraordinary 12 percent of its profits. This alone proves the sagacity of Nestlé's investment strategy and Alcon's success in its industry.

From a two-man, Fort Worth–based company, Alcon became the global leader in ophthalmic pharmaceutical, vision care, and ocular surgical products, an achievement of which the Alcon Family can be incredibly proud. The Alcon story is integral to the evolution of the American pharmaceutical and ophthalmic industries and should be preserved. Moreover, the accomplishments of its first fifty years are a unique chapter in Fort Worth, Tarrant County, and Texas history and worthy of acknowledgment. And finally, the Alcon story is another important chapter in the history of Texas's shift from an agricultural to an industrial economy during the twentieth century. Oil began the shift from the deep-rooted focus on cotton and cattle, but the explosion of science and technology in the Lone Star State after World War II added a key component to the modern economy. Alcon was a leader among many corporations that transformed Texas, and thus the world, forever. Arguably, no one did it better.

Chapter 1

"Become an Ophthalmic House Someday"

1907–1947

Allied victories in 1944 meant peace was inevitable, and Americans began to consider a future beyond World War II. One such American was William "Bill" Clarence Conner, a district manager for Wyeth Pharmaceutical Company, who was about to set in motion a life-changing plan. As he backed his sedan out of the driveway of his Dallas home and headed for Fort Worth, he contemplated his options. He was on his way to meet a member of his sales team to discuss a proposal that would change both of their futures.[1]

Robert "Bob" Denzil Alexander, a member of Lake Worth Sailing Club, had agreed to take his boss, Bill, sailing as an opportunity to talk confidentially. Bob lived in north Fort Worth and, driving up the Jacksboro Highway to the lake, he watched the military aircraft land and take off from the US Army Air Corps field, not realizing how much his life was about to change. At this meeting on a breezy North Texas lake, Bob and Bill laid the groundwork that ultimately established the largest and most influential ophthalmic specialty company in the world.[2]

Bill was born into modest circumstances on April 30, 1907, in Hamilton County, Texas. His parents, James Clarence and Laura Edna (née Brock) Conner, were locals (fig. 1.1). James was a farmer and mechanic and Laura operated a laundry and worked as a secretary. Religion was the bedrock of the Conner household, and the young minister of the local Christian Church, Granville T. Walker, became an important figure in Bill's young life; they would reconnect when Bill was an adult. Though Bill spent most of his childhood in Hamilton County, eventually the family moved to nearby San Saba County, where he graduated from high school in 1925.

In school, Bill was well-rounded, playing on the football team and in the band. For football games he ran on the field with the team, changed clothes at halftime and played the

FIG 1.1
James Clarence Conner (1884–1960) and Laura Edna Conner (1886–1966), Hamilton County, Texas, ca. 1906 (William Clarence Conner Alcon Collection [WCCP], TCU)

FIG 1.2
Robert Otto Alexander (1891–1958),
Alma Sarah Hilburn Alexander (1895–1961),
and Robert Denzil Alexander (1912–1985), Fort
Worth, ca. 1929 (Courtesy of the
Alexander Family)

Robert Otto Alexander
(1891-1958)
about 1929, age 38

Alma Sarah Hilburn Alexander
(Mrs. Robert Otto)
(1895-1961)
about 1929, age 34

Robert Denzil Alexander
(1912-1985)
about 1929, age 17

trombone, and suited up once more to finish the game. Even as a high school student, Bill was a volunteer fireman. He effortlessly interacted with everyone, and his "warm, jolly" personality made him popular. These teenage habits were a prelude to his adult personality—he never forgot a name or a face, he was an extrovert extraordinaire, and he felt compelled to be involved with people and organizations.

His parents also left an imprint on his character. His mother was a forceful, assertive, determined person and effortlessly moved from one endeavor to another. She seldom took "no" for an answer, even from her husband, and impatience forced her to complete tasks left unfinished by others. Bill's father was contemplative, reserved, and wise, and he spoke with an authority. He was the only person Bill ever obeyed without question. After graduating from high school, Bill joined his father in the fields, but he was determined to find his own life without the backbreaking work of a Texas farmer.[3]

Bill admired the family physician, Robert A. Kooken, an eye, ear, nose, and throat specialist who practiced in Fort Worth before settling in Hamilton. Bill considered applying to medical school before realizing the cost was beyond his family's means. One day his mother sent him to the local pharmacy to retrieve a prescription, and after being charged seventy-five cents for the medicine, she exclaimed, "Bill, that's the business you ought to be in!" So, determined to escape the farm, Bill secured a job at the local drugstore, learning to clerk, "jerk" sodas, and stock shelves. It did not take long for him to recognize that being a pharmacist offered the career opportunity he sought. A friend told him about the Danforth School of Pharmacy in Fort Worth, so he sent an inquiry. In a short time, an application, a postcard, arrived in the mail. He was accepted for the thirteen-week course to become a licensed pharmacist, and in September 1927, he moved to Fort Worth to begin his studies.[4]

Bob was born in Tanglewood, Lee County, Texas, on April 14, 1912. Tanglewood was a bustling cotton-farming community, but as the 1920s began, the population began to decline, forcing Bob's parents, Robert Otto and Alma Sarah (née Hilburn), to move to Fort Worth (fig. 1.2). The family settled in the Rosen Heights neighborhood in north Fort Worth. Otto labored at the Armour meatpacking plant, then for watchmaker John G. Berger, and finally, beginning in 1923, for the Fort Worth Power and Light Company's Northside plant, where he became the turbine operator, a responsibility that he discharged for the next thirty-five years. These were not high-paying jobs; Otto earned $1,340 in 1940, and Alma worked occasionally in a fabric store.[5]

North Fort Worth became a vibrant working-class neighborhood where young Texan families, like the Alexanders, merged with other migrants. There were enclaves of Austrian, Serbian, Italian, Russian, Greek, Romanian, Jewish, Czech, Slavic, Polish, and Yugoslavian immigrants, and of course Hispanics from elsewhere in Texas or Mexico. Bob and his younger brother, Charles Lester, had typical boyhoods; they once received a scolding from their mother for ruining their brand-new pants by sliding down their roof. The Armour and Swift meatpacking companies, the stockyards, grain companies, and a myriad of small businesses offered employment. Churches sprang up, and the Alexanders likely went to the Chestnut Avenue Christian Church. Despite many job opportunities, money was scarce, and on one occasion their church brought food for the family. These life lessons remained with Bob; he supported the local church even after he moved his membership, and when able, he "paid cash for everything." Moreover, he absorbed from his parents the values of "humbleness, quietness, and honesty."[6]

Bob graduated from North Fort Worth High School in May 1930. Demonstrating his strong work ethic, Bob worked at Leonard Brothers, the largest grocery and department store in Fort Worth, and at the stockyards. Bob recalled transferring goods from railroad cars to the store and its discount affiliate, Everybody's. He also clerked in the Leonard Brothers pharmacy before he started pharmacy school, which may have provided him with the impetus to apply in 1933 to the Danforth School of Pharmacy.[7]

Little is known about the Danforth School of Pharmacy. Newspaper archives reveal its graduates served as pharmacists in numerous Texas counties from the 1920s through the twentieth century. Notably, William James Danforth, born May 17, 1887, in New York, left an indelible footprint in Tarrant County. He was a graduate of Boston College and obtained his PhD in pharmacy from American University in Washington, DC. Before World War I, he taught and worked as a chemist and pharmaceutical salesman. During the war, he served in the Thirtieth Infantry Division of the US Army, which fought on the Western Front. Back in the United States, Danforth remained in the army at Camp Pike in Arkansas until 1921, when he was discharged. Afterward, he operated the Little Rock School of Pharmacy. Realizing that most of the school's attendees were Texans, he and his wife, Marion, moved to Fort Worth in November 1924 and established the Danforth School of Pharmacy in the Oil Operators Building, which stood at Fifth and Calhoun Streets. The space was previously occupied by the Fort Worth School of Pharmacy, so presumably he inherited functioning classrooms and laboratories.[8]

Danforth participated in the Lions Club and the American Legion. He traveled on behalf of both organizations and promoted his school while doing so. The school's reputation reached well beyond Texas. The winter class of 1925 included sixty-five students from eight southern states. Danforth asserted that his school brought almost "250 students to Fort Worth" each year. His wife made special efforts to recruit women. She claimed that "because they are usually serious minded about their work—they are 'better students' as a whole than men." Seven women enrolled in the fall of 1926 and four for the spring of 1927.[9]

Danforth's courses followed the most current pedagogical methods and emphasized individual instruction. Subjects included materia medica, practical and theoretical pharmacy, advanced and elementary chemistry, botany, posology, toxicology, bacteriology, pharmaceutical Latin, pharmaceutical arithmetic, and drugstore management. The students could opt for a short thirteen-week term or a longer course of study of up to two years. Throughout, Danforth maintained an unusual daily schedule. Classes met in the morning and evening, allowing for a dedicated study period in the afternoon. With its extensive list of courses and long days, the school must have had other teachers besides Danforth and his wife, but none have been discovered. The semesters were timed to end immediately before the Texas State Board of Pharmacy examinations. Danforth asserted that 90 percent of his students passed these exams. The board met twice annually, to conduct examinations and attend to other business, at various places that coincided with the regional and state druggist association conferences, where Danforth often spoke.[10]

Bill had what it took to succeed, including a mother determined to see her son reach his full potential. She pawned her wedding ring to pay his tuition, travel, and living expenses. He arrived in Fort Worth in September 1927 and entered the thirteen-week semester at the Danforth School of Pharmacy. The term's end coincided with the Texas State Board of Pharmacy licensing examination, but Bill had to wait until the following May to take it. The minimum age for taking the exam was twenty-one, which he reached on April 30, 1928.[11]

The board met on May 15, 1928, at the Stephen F. Austin Hotel in Austin, to administer the North American Pharmacist Licensure Examination prepared by the National Association of Boards of Pharmacy to 189 applicants. The practical and oral examinations were conducted in the Pharmacy Laboratory of the University of Texas. Only 62 applicants, including Bill, passed the examination and received certificates. The failure of almost two-thirds indicates that the test was not easy; furthermore, of the 127 failures, only 91 got the opportunity to retake it. Bill's grades reflect the difficulty: chemistry, 75; pharmacy, 80; practical, 75; pharmacognosy, 75; and physiology, 75. Thus, "William C. Connor," R.Ph., received license no. 7982 on June 30, 1928. In later years, when showing his license to others, Bill would note that his last name had been misspelled—Connor instead of Conner.[12]

Renfro Drugs, "the busiest prescription counter in Fort Worth," hired Bill for $100 a month (fig. 1.3). His hours were long, often from six thirty in the morning until sometime in the evening. Realizing the most senior Renfro pharmacist earned only $150 per month, Bill began looking for other opportunities and by 1930 relocated to Skillern and Sons drugstore in Dallas. At about this time, he married Viola Genevieve Halden, better known as BeBe. The Halden family had lived next door to the Conners in San Saba County, where Roger Goodhue Halden was a mail carrier, and Margaret Dama Halden (née McNatt) taught the piano. BeBe was born on October 8, 1908, in Richland Springs, and excelled at the piano at a young age. She studied at the Lamont School of Music in Denver, graduating with her teacher's diploma on June 20, 1929. Seven months later, on February 18, 1930, Bill and BeBe married in Dallas County.[13]

FIG 1.3
William C. Conner (*5th from right*),
pharmacist at Renfro Drugs no. 2,
Fort Worth, 1929 (WCCP)

The young couple settled at 3545 Granada, which was convenient for Bill's work at Skillern's no. 17. He became the store manager and pharmacist. As an example of his entrepreneurial talent, he convinced the Skillern family to allow him to stock general merchandise, which proved to be successful. Bill and BeBe had their first child, Claire Crystelle, in March 1936. To advance his career, the family moved to Longview, Texas, and Bill worked at Oliver's Drug Store (fig. 1.4). By the end of 1936, though, he was "frustrated but did not know why."

Thankfully, a new opportunity presented itself. Bill became a traveling salesman for the Wyeth Pharmaceutical Company. His territory covered sixty-five counties west of Fort Worth, so the Conners returned to Fort Worth. There is no record, but an educated guess suggests that the sales area more or less encompassed the counties west of present-day I-35 to Abilene, south as far as the Colorado River, and north to the Red River. In the year before he took the job, annual sales in the territory were lackluster at $250, but Bill soon had annual sales of $6,000. He built a relationship with every pharmacist and doctor in his territory, never forgetting a face or name. Talking and salesmanship suited him perfectly. Later, Bill recalled, "I found out what I liked to do. It was pleasant, delightful—and I felt I was contributing to an education in a sense."[14]

Bill and BeBe also soon found new friends: Bob and his wife, Catherine Melba Alexander (née Roseberry). Bob had taken a one-year course of study at the Danforth School of Pharmacy, beginning in September 1933. He worked at Everybody's to pay his tuition. His friend Cody H. Wheeler, a Dallas fireman, also gave him money. Bob rode the streetcar from Rosen Heights to downtown Fort Worth, but later he owned a small coupe. He lived at home initially but moved southwest of downtown on Park Avenue.

Near the end of the spring semester in 1934, Bob was ready to take the Texas licensing examination but encountered a major obstacle. The legislature had enacted a law requiring new applicants to the Texas State Board of Pharmacy to have completed studies at an accredited four-year institution. Danforth School of Pharmacy was not a four-year institution, nor was it accredited. The board also ruled that a person with out-of-state credentials had to work as a pharmacist for one year in that state before becoming eligible for reciprocity in Texas. Having thus lost its clientele, the Danforth School of Pharmacy was out of business and Bob was seemingly out of luck. Ever resourceful, he discovered he could take the exam given by the New Mexico Board of Pharmacy. With money given to him and the loan of a car by his friend Cody, he drove to Santa Fe, took the test on May 21, 1934, and passed with

W. C. CONNER
Oliver's Drug Store
Longview, Texas

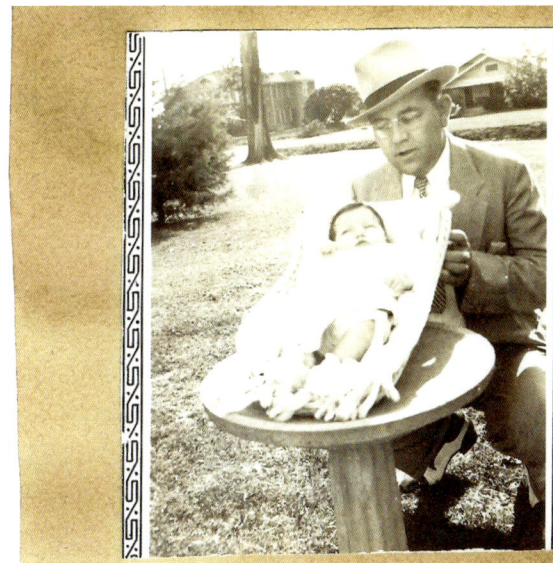

Southwestern Drug Trade News for the month of July, 1936

FIG 1.4
Left, W. C. Conner, pharmacist, Oliver's Drug Store, Longview, Texas; *right*, Conner holding daughter, Claire Crystelle, Dallas, 1936 (*Southwestern Drug Trade News*, July 1936) (WCCP)

an overall score of 78. On the individual exams, Bob's grades were pharmacy, 87; chemistry, 60; New Mexico medical law, 85; math, 83, and the oral exam, 75. On June 1, 1934, he received his New Mexico pharmacist license. Fortunately, five months later, in November, the Texas State Board of Pharmacy eliminated the residency requirement for out-of-state pharmacists. So, Bob applied in Texas and was issued his Texas license, no. 10,010, on January 22, 1935. He began his tenure as a Texas pharmacist at a Ben Weeks Pharmacy on Camp Bowie in Fort Worth.[15]

Bob was an avid dancer. In the depths of the Depression, swing music dominated the scene and young folks flocked to dance halls. Bob, tall, lanky, and personable with an engaging smile, frequented several in Fort Worth. The Casino Ballroom, on the shore of Lake Worth, became a popular destination. There, in the summer of 1933, a friend introduced Bob to Catherine, a feisty young woman. They danced once and she left an indelible impression on Bob, although Catherine later said she never remembered him or that dance. When winter arrived, dancers crowded into the Top of the Texas Ballroom in Fort Worth's Texas Hotel, and the couple met again. Catherine later explained, "He danced with me every chance he got that night. . . . Well, next day's Sunday and I got a call from him and he asked me for a date. So, I had a date with him Sunday afternoon and ... that was it. I never dated anyone after that."[16]

Three years younger than Bob, Catherine was an only child of a single mother, Irene Dunn, who remarried Lane M. Roseberry, a car salesman in Waco, Texas. By 1930 the Roseberry family had moved to the south side of Fort Worth, where Catherine attended Central High School. After graduation, she worked at the fabric counter at the Montgomery Ward on Seventh Street. Her marriage to Bob was announced in the *Fort Worth Star-Telegram*, but their wedding was unconventional. Sick at home from work that day, after a tiff, Bob picked up Catherine "to talk about it." After hours of discussion, they decided to marry that night despite facing hurdles and issues, not the least of which was the disappointment their elopement would cause her parents. Since Texas required a blood test for marriage, they went to Oklahoma, the closest place that would marry them. Catherine wanted a white satin dress from a dress shop, and Bob's white shirt was at his parents' home. They retrieved the clothes, Bob bought shoes, hose, and a purse for Catherine, and a friend bought a $10 wedding ring from Leonard's. On the way out of Fort Worth, they stopped by the pharmacy to tell a friend what was happening, and he insisted Bob should take his new Buick for the trip. It was a stormy, muddy night as they drove to Marietta, just across the state line. Arriving late, they had to wake up a justice of the peace to perform the ceremony. Though

FIG 1.5
Robert Alexander, pharmacist,
Ben Weeks Pharmacy, Fort Worth,
ca. 1938 (AFP)

FIG 1.6
Robert and Catherine Alexander
sailing on *Bob Kat*, Lake Worth, Texas,
ca. 1937 (AFP)

disappointed their daughter did not have a conventional wedding, Catherine's welcomed Bob into the family.[17]

Catherine quit her job while Bob continued to work at Ben Weeks Pharmacy (fig. 1.5). Initially, they lived with his parents but as Bob circulated through Weeks's pharmacies, they leased small apartments nearby. Money was tight, but they budgeted prudently, with the conservative financial acumen that characterized their entire lives. They were even able to buy a new Plymouth and with another couple journeyed to Monterrey, Mexico, on vacation. Bob became the manager of the pharmacy on Camp Bowie, and Catherine worked there, too. Managing the store provided Bob with a strong foundation to his career. He was forced to be self-sufficient as Weeks proved an unreliable boss. It was during this time that Bill and Bob met. They instantly liked each other, and their business relationship flourished into a friendship between their families. Catherine even babysat Crystelle, BeBe and Bill's first child.[18]

Working for Weeks meant long hours for Bob and Catherine, but in their limited spare time, they joined the Lake Worth Sailing Club, and Bob bought a kit to build his own sailboat, which they named *Bob Kat* (fig. 1.6). Sailing became their passion, a source of relaxation, and a pastime that lasted their entire lifetime. Between work and sailing, their days were full. Moreover, their combined income was a modest $2,294 in 1940. Bob was dissatisfied with his income, given the hours he had to work, much as Bill had been when he became a Wyeth salesman. Bob saw that Bill worked a five-day week and usually an eight-hour day. When Bill was offered the position as Wyeth's district manager, he hired Bob to replace him. It was just what Bob was looking for. He began his work in the pharmaceutical business with a month's training at Wyeth's company headquarters in Philadelphia. It was 1941, and war was on the horizon; with Catherine pregnant and Bob covering a large sales territory, they moved back in with his parents.[19]

During the war years, Bob honed his selling skills, calling on pharmacies, drug wholesalers, and physicians in the sixty-five counties west of Fort Worth. He was a natural salesman and productive as well. With a manageable work schedule and increased income, Bob and Catherine expanded their family. Lane Anne was born on June 13, 1942, Anita on March 23, 1944, and Robert Denny on January 29, 1946. The house on Roosevelt was crowded until Bob's parents moved to Lake Worth. Bebe and Bill moved back to Dallas; they now had a second child, a son, William Halden, born in May 1940. The couples visited often and developed a close, supportive friendship. Their photograph at a Wyeth employee event in September 1943 is revealing (fig. 1.7): the Conners and Alexanders relaxing in fashionable clothes demonstrate a sense of comfort and confidence (fig. 1.8). To both men's good fortune, their division manager was William Henry Westphal, a seasoned sales executive, who had established Wyeth's sales training program during the 1930s. No doubt Westphal's influence refined Bob's and Bill's management skills, an influence that served them well. Bob and Bill also talked about their future. Bill later told others that he and Bob had some of these discussions while fishing or on Bob's sailboat.[20]

FIG 1.7
Wyeth Laboratory function,
Dallas, Sept. 1943. See detail below. (AFP)

FIG 1.8
Left to right: Bob Alexander,
Catherine Alexander, Bill Conner,
and BeBe Conner at Wyeth function, Sept.
1943 (AFP)

FIG 1.9
Bill Conner and Bob Alexander standing at the entrance to the Alcon Prescription Laboratory, 1945 (Courtesy of Alcon Historical Records, Alcon, Fort Worth)

FIG 1.10
Business card announcing the opening of the Alcon Prescription Laboratory, 1945 (AFP)

ROBERT D. ALEXANDER AND WILLIAM C. CONNER

REGISTERED PHARMACISTS

ANNOUNCE THE OPENING OF

ALCON PRESCRIPTION LABORATORY

610 WEST 7TH STREET   FORT WORTH, TEXAS

TELEPHONE: 2-9366

FORMERLY WITH WYETH INCORPORATED

Bill and Bob both registered for the draft. Danforth, their pharmacy school mentor, chaired the Tarrant County draft board. Likely because of their ages, thirty-three and twenty-eight respectively, and professions, both received a deferment, but in the spring of 1945 the board notified Bill to prepare for induction as a pharmacist's mate in the US Navy. The notice was rescinded once Germany surrendered, and the two men proceeded with their plan: they were going to establish a prescription pharmacy in Fort Worth. Bob resigned from Wyeth in July 1945, effective September 15, and Bill left at about the same time. Westphal wrote to Bob, "Here's wishing you the very best of success in your new venture," adding, "we know you will make as good as you have with Wyeth Incorporated." Westphal's additional comment gave some insight into Bob's sales acumen: "You have always done a swell job & we are going to miss seeing those nice orders." In September, Bob and Bill established Alcon Prescription Laboratory. It was Catherine who suggested merging the first letters of their last names.[21]

Bob and Bill considered buying a Fort Worth pharmacy, but decided the $40,000 price was too steep, so they started their own. The two men selected Fort Worth since they knew many of the physicians there and a prime location in downtown Fort Worth was available. The triangle-shaped property stood at the convergence of West Sixth and West Seventh Streets and across from the largest physician's office building in Tarrant County, the Medical Arts Building. They leased the western half of the single-story structure, reconfigured it for a pharmacy, and used the facility's shape and location to have drive-up windows on two sides, the first pharmacy drive-thru in Tarrant County (fig. 1.9). Each man contributed $3,000; Bob sold his war bonds, and Bill, his house in Dallas. After stocking the store and buying a branch pharmacy on Camp Bowie in Arlington Heights, they were in debt $25,000. Nevertheless, in September 1945 Alcon Prescription Laboratory was in business (fig. 1.10).

Upon opening their pharmacy, Bob and Bill told Fort Worth citizens that "Alcon Prescription Laboratory was founded with the owners' pledge to devote their entire efforts to supporting the physician and to fill his prescriptions with scientific accuracy and with the highest quality drugs." Their business model was innovative and simple—"they chose to open a professional pharmacy limited to filling prescriptions and supplying sickroom needs." They sold no consumer products and did not install a soda counter, a typical component of Texas drugstores until the 1960s.[22]

Later, Bill told a reporter that they might have done better if they had bought Weaver's Pharmacy, considering their investment almost equaled the asking price. In any case, their experience as pharmacists, drugstore managers, and pharmaceutical salesmen was invaluable; they outfitted both of their new stores with counters, prescription and over-the-counter (OTC) medicines, pharmaceutical compounds, printed material, and rubber mats for the comfort of pharmacists' feet. They kept the first one hundred checks to remind them of this financially daunting time. Besides filling prescriptions, the two pharmacists made sterile, injectable vitamins they sold during visits to physicians. Bill borrowed his wife's electric mixer to stir the formulas, and Bob used his mother's pressure cooker as an autoclave. Soon they added a few oral preparations. The men's wives, and even in-laws, helped with manufacturing.[23]

Just a month after opening, they employed their first salesman, Harold C. Johnson (fig. 1.11). Born in Iowa in 1908, Harold was in West Texas by 1935, working as a radio announcer. Bill met him while traveling as a Wyeth salesman, and then again in Paris, Texas, when Harold was stationed there with the army and Bill was selling to the local military hospital. Despite having no knowledge of pharmaceuticals, Harold accepted a sales position with Alcon Prescription Laboratory in September 1945. He recalled Bill saying at the time, "Hopefully, someday we'll get into manufacturing, too." That aspiration was soon fulfilled.[24]

The earliest surviving financial record for Alcon Prescription Laboratory is a statement of profits and losses ending on December 31, 1946. In the previous three months, the downtown drugstore had made a profit of $9,832.62 on sales of $27,119.94, but during a five-month period, the Arlington Heights branch had lost $1,951.06 on sales of $2,759.73.

FIG 1.11
Beulah and Harold Johnson,
Chicago, ca. 1958 (AFP)

There was the unexpected cost of burglary, too. An attempt at the main store was foiled in May, but twice in August burglars broke into the Arlington Heights branch and stole narcotics. Bob and Bill did not take a paycheck until after four months, when it became necessary, according to Bob, for both men to "draw $100 per month in order to satisfy our families' peculiar addiction for food." However, by the end of 1946, each man was drawing about $330 a month. Both pharmacies operated from seven in the morning to ten at night, and the payroll suggests they had seven or so employees, including a pharmacist or two. From all appearances, as 1947 began, Bob and Bill owned a budding pharmacy business, but the manufacturing and sale of therapeutic products to physicians had captured their entrepreneurial imagination and absorbed more of their time.[25]

Through March 1947, Alcon Prescription Laboratory in Arlington Heights lost money. Thereafter, no financial records remain for the branch, so presumably it closed. The downtown store continued to be profitable, but it still owed a considerable amount in outstanding notes, including $3,000 to Bill's father-in-law. Convinced that manufacturing pharmaceuticals was more lucrative than operating a pharmacy, Bob, Bill, and Harold decided to form a new corporation, Alcon Laboratories, Inc. Incorporation papers were signed on May 14, 1947, and filed two days later with the Tarrant County clerk. The trio issued 150,000 shares of common stock, with Harold getting 10 percent and the other two splitting the remainder evenly. Bob and Bill transferred $516 in cash and assets from Alcon Prescription Laboratory in the form of merchandise, personal property, accounts receivable, trademarks, and formulae valued at $16,984. Harold contributed $7,500. Bill held the office of president, Bob was vice president, and Harold became secretary-treasurer—and initially they were the only members of the board of directors. Nine physicians in Fort Worth and one each in Dallas and Hamilton purchased 1,375 preferred shares at $20 a share for a total of $27,500. The Fort Worth investors were Noel W. Bailey, John W. Garnett, Frank W. Halpin, Wesley N. Jenkins, Walter R. Lenox, DeWitt Neighbors, David M. "Mal" Rumph, Walter B. West, and John A. Wiggins Jr. James N. Walker lived in Dallas and Robert A. Kooken Jr., the son of the doctor whom Bill admired when he was a child, lived in Hamilton. Thus, in May 1947, Alcon Laboratories, Inc., was in business.[26]

The incorporation documents list the products Bob and Bill had developed since their partnership twenty months earlier: six vitamin formulations, two local anesthetics, and two feminine products. Alcon would later become a global name in eye care products, but in May 1947 it had developed only one ophthalmic and one nasal product. The manufacturing operation, led by Bill, separated from the pharmacy by moving a few blocks away to a facil-

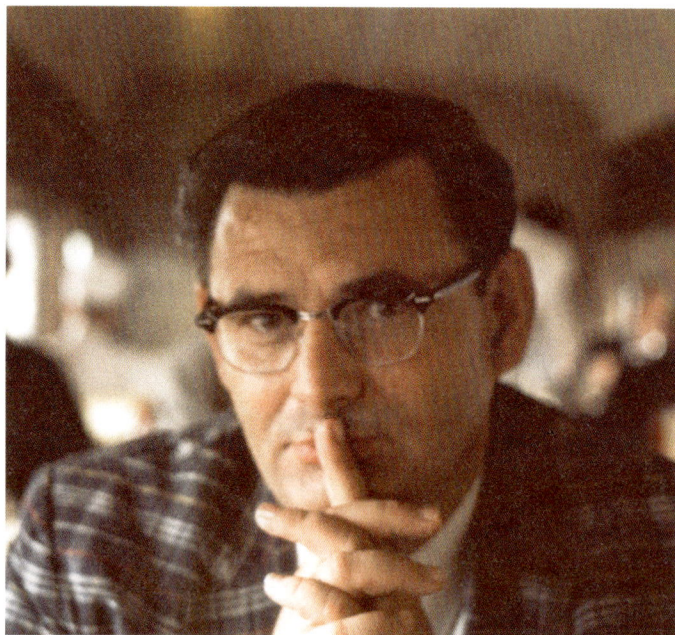

FIG 1.12
Dave Merrill, ca. 1957 (AFP)

ity on Burnet Street; Bob managed the pharmacy on West Seventh. When Bill's secretary left, he hired Betty Newton; she would work for Alcon for twenty-five years.[27]

Bob and Bill continued to expand their product list but needed help in the testing and development of new ideas. In the fall of 1947, hearing a job might be available, twenty-seven-year-old Navy veteran David "Dave" Ledrick Merrill (fig. 1.12), a Texas Christian University student with a double major in chemistry and physics and a double minor in mathematics and microbiology, visited Bill in the manufacturing facility. Merrill recalled the entrance to the facility was between a barbershop and cafe, and the room itself was not more than five hundred square feet with two desks, several chairs, four filing cabinets, a safe, a typewriter, a heater, a fan, and a Dictaphone and transcriber. Bill communicated with almost everyone by memos. In a short conversation with Merrill, Bill reported that Alcon had two unique products, Alconefrin, a nasal decongestant, and Zincfrin, a soothing eye astringent. He added that his firm hoped "to become an ophthalmic house someday," but admitted they had "a long way to go." Getting to the point, Bill presented the latest problem to Merrill: a cocoa butter–based rectal suppository for asthma patients sometimes would not melt when inserted. If Merrill could find a solution, he could have a job.

Taking five pounds of cocoa butter to experiment with, Merrill discovered that Bill's process elevated the cocoa butter's melting temperature. Therefore, the suppository required a temperature higher than body temperature to melt. He had solved the problem, so he was hired to perform all chemical analyses. Merrill requested expensive equipment to effectively fulfill his duties, but he soon learned that Bill and Bob were tightfisted. It took until 1953 to convince them that the expenditure was necessary. Other employees also recall the two men's frugal habits. Merrill's monthly salary was $220 for thirty hours weekly of work in manufacturing, analyzing, and shipping products; he received an extra dollar each week for handling the mail. He was outspoken, sarcastic, and not easily intimidated, making his relationship with Bill contentious, but Merrill was the right person with the right skills at the right time, and in this regard Bob and Bill were fortunate.[28]

The two formulations that Bill mentioned during his interview with Merrill, Alconefrin (fig. 1.13) and Zincfrin, were exceptional products that established the foundation for their company. Both contained the vasoconstrictor phenylephrine. Technical challenges in

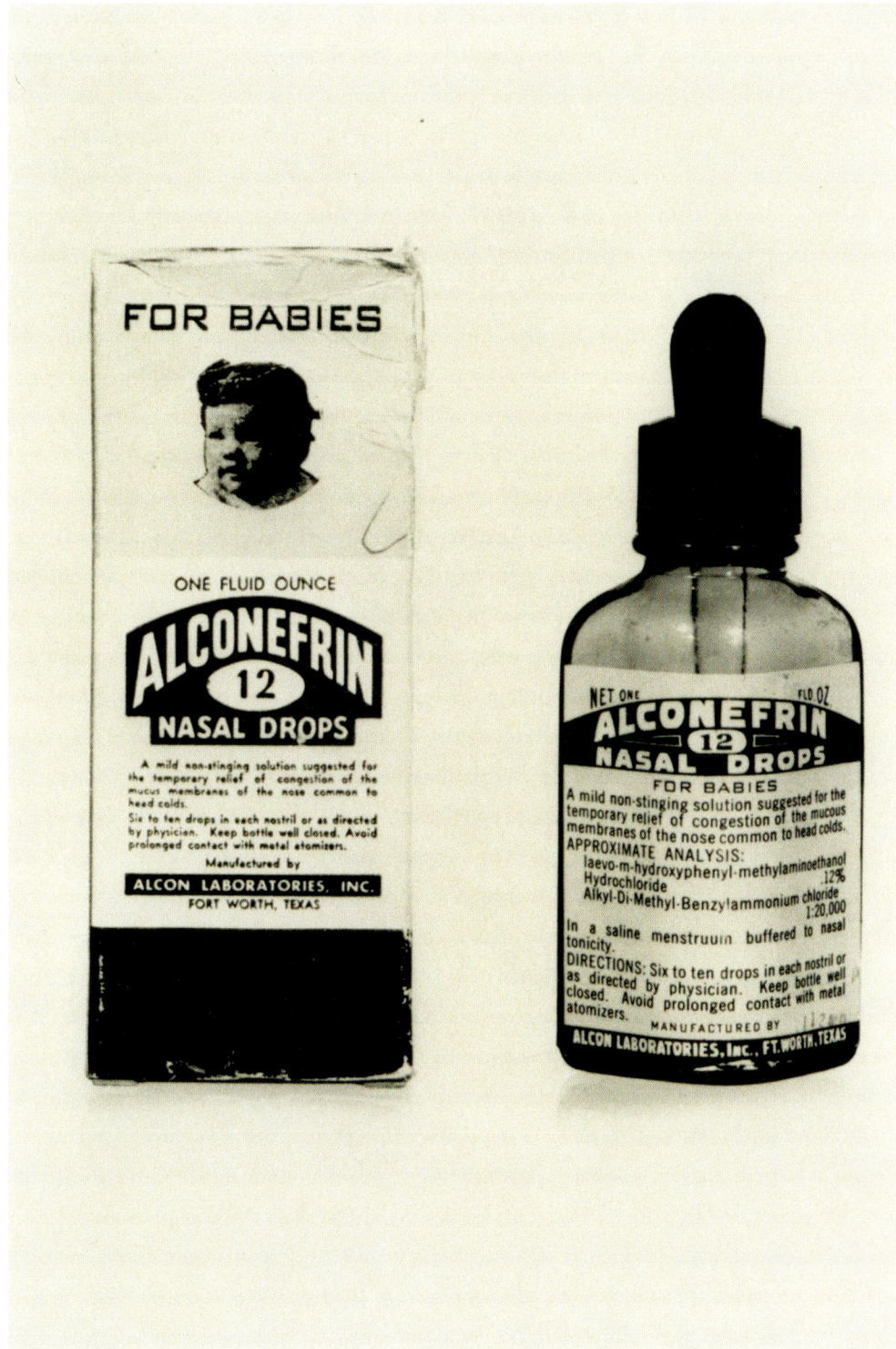

FIG 1.13
Alconefrin 12 Nasal Drops,
first packaging for the baby nose
drop product, ca. 1946. The baby
pictured is Conner's daughter,
Claire Crystelle. (AHR)

developing a comfortable buffered solution of the two products were considerable, and yet in 1947, using basic scientific knowledge learned from Danforth, Bill and Bob made a significant leap forward in their pharmaceutical formulation. While they solved the chemistry of creating unique formulations, their achievement also illustrates another key facet in the long-term success of Alcon—listening to timely advice from creative scientists and physicians. In the case of Alconefrin, James N. Walker, the Dallas pediatrician who had bought stock in Alcon, proposed the therapy concept to Bill and Bob. They took the idea, solved the technical problems, and marketed it successfully.[29]

Medical compounds are inherently unstable in water and generally prefer an aqueous solution that is somewhat acidic. However, most sting when dropped on the surface of the eye. Moreover, prescription solutions for the eye made at the bench by a pharmacist at that time had two other major drawbacks—the drugs were imprecisely measured, and they were not sterile. Bob and Bill set about to eliminate these hurdles. To minimize variations in concentrations of active ingredients, Alcon manufactured Zincfrin in big batches that were analyzed to ensure the correct therapeutic concentration, which was zinc at 0.25 percent and phenylephrine at 0.12 percent. The manufacturing tank, filling lines, and glass containers and droppers in which the solution was packaged were sterilized with high-pressure steam, much like a pressure cooker, in an autoclave. Some solutions were sterilized by ultrafiltration, and sterility was assured by adding a preservative before bottling. To make the drops comfortable to the eye, solutions were buffered with other chemicals, so they were neutral, not acidic or basic, and near the pH of tears. A final problem was stability. Sitting on the shelf, the product needed to be stable; that is, the dissolved chemical should not degrade, crystallize, or precipitate. Then, as now, making sterile, safe, stable, comfortable ophthalmic solutions is an experimental learning process. Fortunately for Bob and Bill, Zincfrin contained two easily formulated compounds, zinc and phenylephrine. Yet they embarked on a development process that created a juggernaut of expertise in ophthalmic formulation that within fifty years discouraged pharmaceutical companies from developing their own eye medications. This in-house expertise also created opportunities when Alcon later sought to license compounds from non-ophthalmic pharmaceutical companies.[30]

The advances made in preparing compounds did not immediately result in financial gains for Alcon. At the end of 1947, sales totaled $16,378.68 for Alcon Laboratories, Inc., and the company was in debt $9,367.03. However, Bob and Bill were a powerful team, with a partnership that would allow their common vision to become a reality. Having complementary personalities was instrumental in their success. One person who knew both men well was Granville T. Walker of the University Christian Church in Fort Worth. He had been Bill's minister in Hamilton. Walker asserted that Bob "was quiet, even self-effacing, meticulous in his recollections and approaches," but at the same time he was "indefatigable … undyingly persistent … and determined to conserve what gains there [were] to be had in any operation." Bill, on the other hand, was "the epitome of the hard-driving, free-enterprising entrepreneur." His "venturesome spirit" reflected an "optimism and victorious" attitude. Walker concluded that Bill had "the ability to see problems in their total perspective" and could "make a decision and stay with it." These qualities would be called upon to ensure the success of Alcon as 1948 began.[31]

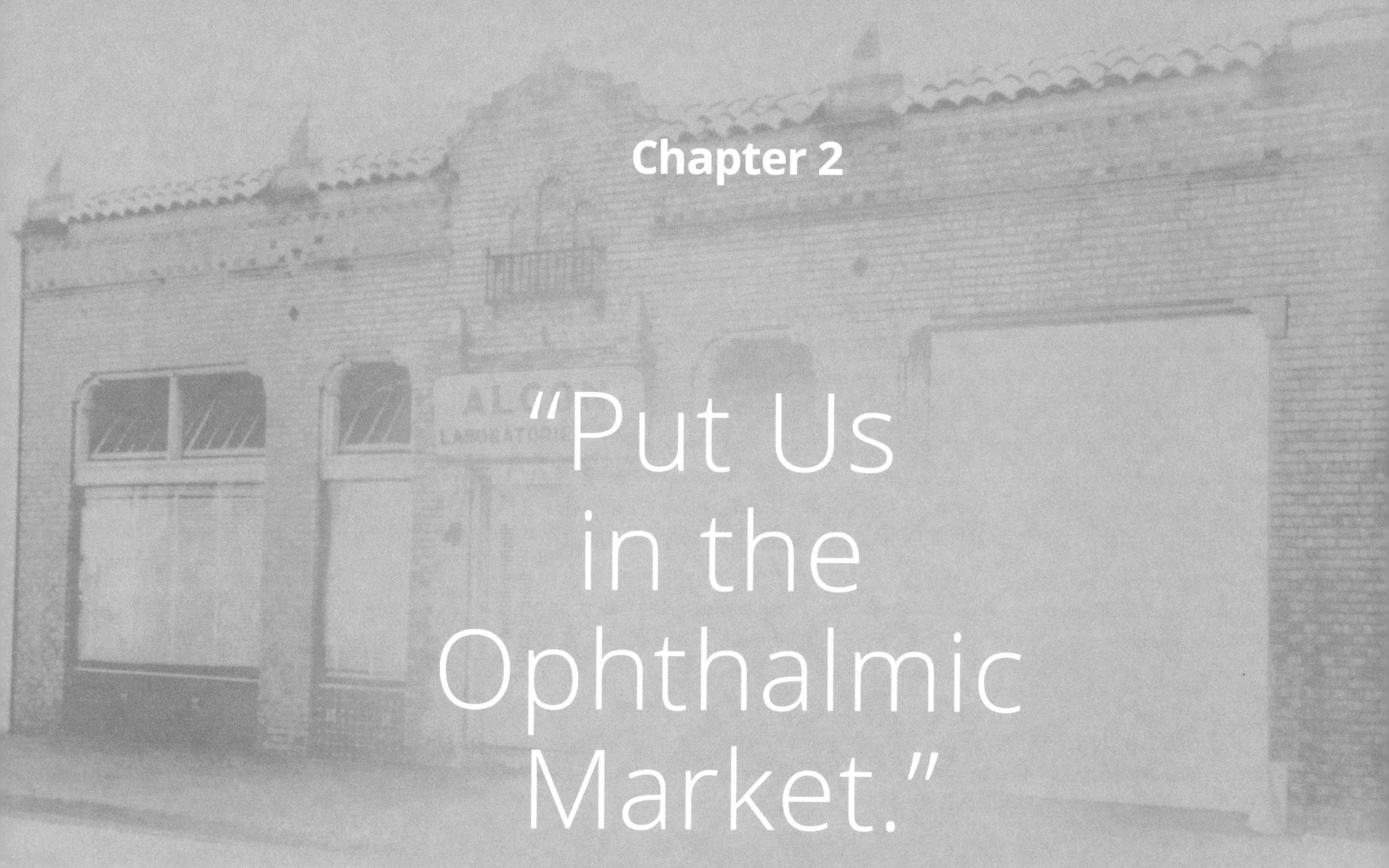

Chapter 2

"Put Us
in the
Ophthalmic
Market."

1948–1957

n the summer of 1953, Bob Alexander drove into Amarillo to call on physicians and pharmacists. With an economy built on oil, cattle, grain, and helium, it seemed an unlikely place for Alcon to take another giant step toward world dominance in the ophthalmic pharmaceutical industry. But it was. A suggestion by a local doctor led Alexander to create the Drop-tainer (fig. 2.1), the small, squeezable plastic bottle that dispenses drops of eye medications. Alcon's innovation replaced clumsy glass bottles and droppers, revolutionizing the packaging, delivery, and instillation of eye drops. Its product line proliferated, and sales started to increase by almost 40 percent every year.[1]

In 1948 Alcon Prescription Laboratory reported annual sales of $77,365.52 and a net profit of $6,450.39. Net income decreased to nearly $1,000 in 1949 but then rebounded to almost $4,000 in 1950. Clearly, the pharmacy was not the secure financial enterprise both men had envisioned. Meanwhile, Alexander and Bill Conner refocused their attention on their manufacturing business, Alcon Laboratories Inc. (hereafter Alcon). Alexander split his time in 1948 but worked full-time in the facility on Burnet Street in 1949.[2]

With Alexander and Conner concentrating on Alcon, their other business, Alcon Prescription Laboratory, needed a pharmacist to manage it. They settled on John Ralph Gibson, the manager of a Renfro pharmacy. Born in adjacent Parker County in 1904, Gibson received his Texas pharmacist license in September 1929 and worked in Tarrant County. On June 8, 1949, the Texas secretary of state granted a charter to Alcon Prescription Laboratory with Gibson as president; Alexander, vice president; and Conner, secretary. The firm moved to a modern air-conditioned building at 661 Fifth Avenue, one block north of Harris Memorial Methodist Hospital. The pharmacy stocked prescription drugs, OTC

FIG 2.1
Drop-tainer (AHR)

medicines, and other medical products but no consumer goods. In printed advertisements, the pharmacy encouraged patients to have their doctor call in a prescription so they could use the drive-up window for convenient service. It also boasted "FAST City-Wide Delivery." Gibson opened the pharmacy at seven in the morning, Monday through Saturday, and closed between nine and ten at night. Four pharmacists worked there, with at least one on duty until closing.[3]

By the end of April 1954, sales for Alcon Prescription Laboratory reached $138,765.22, up from $21,095.63 in April 1950. However, net profits continued to be inconsistent, fluctuating from $795.14 to $6,207.10. Meanwhile, Alcon, the manufacturing business, experienced a sevenfold sales increase, from $45,345 in 1948 to $311,972 in 1954. Alexander and Conner intentionally reinvested the profits into their enterprise. By their assessment, their economic future looked more promising with manufacturing than with the pharmacy. So, in April 1954 they sold their shares of Alcon Prescription Laboratory to Gibson for $25,136.94. Gibson agreed to change the corporate name and merged with William Ray "Bill" Whitten's store, operating as Gibson-Whitten Pharmacy until Gibson died in 1963.[4]

Focusing on Alcon Laboratories allowed Alexander and Conner to complete a decade of strong sales growth, from $45,345 in 1948 to $980,140 in 1958. As it began, the two men and Harold C. Johnson were enthusiastic but lacked a market strategy. Using company cars, Conner, Alexander, and Johnson called on physicians, pharmacists, and drug wholesalers. David "Dave" L. Merrill developed and manufactured products. Conner's secretary, Betty Newton, worked as bookkeeper, office manager, and mail clerk and sometimes filled bottles in the manufacturing room. Newton later explained, "The main job for me in those days was to get out as many promotional letters as I could to as many doctors as I could to let them know we were in business." The company's three unique products, focusing on the eye, ear, nose, and throat (EENT), were marketed to physicians. Alconefrin, Op-thal-Zin, and Zincfrin sales increased monthly and were almost half of the total sales by December 1948. Alcon was also the sole Texas distributor of Walker Vitamins. But while sales for the year totaled $45,345, there was a net loss of $15,108. Conner, Alexander, and Johnson drew $450-per-month salaries in 1948. Adding to the laboratory-size autoclave acquired in 1947, the company acquired more improvements, including filtering and filling machines, growing as a pharmaceutical manufacturing enterprise.[5]

Until the summer of 1948, Alcon distributed products only in Texas, but an unexpected event led Conner and Alexander to make sales calls in New Mexico, Arizona, and Southern California. Conner belonged to Kiwanis International, and in 1948 the Fort Worth Club

FIG 2.2
Left to right, Bill Conner,
Catherine Alexander, and
BeBe Conner, on trip from
Fort Worth to Los Angeles,
1948 (AFP)

gave him $200 to be its representative at the annual convention in Los Angeles. Both men and their wives loaded up the company's Studebaker (fig. 2.2) and hand-delivered samples to "every eye specialist from Fort Worth to Los Angeles." They also left literature profiling Alcon's prepackaged products as sterile with accurately measured ingredients. Alexander and Conner discovered eye specialists were being overlooked by pharmaceutical companies. Conner wrote, "In this way we became specialists in the ophthalmologists' field. We learned the needs of just one kind of doctor, and now we could concentrate our efforts in marketing and research upon a smaller field. ... and cut our competition in a highly competitive industry down to size." Alcon thus defined its market; now it needed a strategy and products for that market.[6]

What did Conner mean by "specialists in the ophthalmologists' field"? Ophthalmology began in ancient Egypt about 2500 BC. The study of ocular anatomy during the Greek and Roman periods led to the earliest descriptions of ocular diseases, the two most common being trachoma and cataracts. During medieval times, oculists in the Arab world defined the optics of vision, knowledge later used by an English monk in the eleventh century to describe lenses, which in turn led to spectacles. Ocular surgery began early, but it was not until the 1700s that rudimentary cataract extraction began. About the same time, high eye pressure was discovered to be the cause of glaucoma. Ophthalmologic advancements accelerated in the 1800s. Cocaine was found to anesthetize the eye for surgery. The origination of the ophthalmoscope for examining the retina began the history of treating retinal diseases. Pharmacologic drugs that decreased intraocular pressure were soon discovered.

At the beginning of the twentieth century, improvements in ophthalmology accelerated. The slit-lamp biomicroscope was invented, allowing for magnified observation of eye tissues. Studies of the ocular pathologies of the living eye followed. Ocular surgery techniques for corneal transplants, retinal detachment, glaucoma, and others evolved, and surgeons designed numerous surgical tools and sutures. The operating microscope, which magnified the ocular surgeons' field of view, appeared. As World War II ended, early prototypes of contact lenses and intraocular lenses were designed. Advances in understanding the pharmacology of numerous classes of drugs for systemic diseases facilitated their application for eye diseases. Just as antibiotics revolutionized treating systemic infections, their role in ophthalmology proved to be no less revolutionary.[7]

When Alexander and Conner returned to Fort Worth, they contemplated what segment of the eye specialist's world Alcon should focus on. Ophthalmologists prescribed glasses, which were made by opticians. Exacting ophthalmic surgical tools were made by skilled craftsmen, like watchmakers. Examination tools—the ophthalmoscope, slit-lamp, and so forth—required engineered designs, expensive components, and optical technicians. Pharmacists compounded prescriptions sent by ophthalmologists, who asked for drugs recommended by ophthalmic researchers and other clinicians. But some pharmaceutical companies had begun making and distributing prepared medicines. Alexander and Conner understood the business of pharmacies and selling pharmaceuticals. Thus, Alcon focused on manufacturing and selling eye medicines. But neither Conner and Alexander, nor anyone, knew the potential of the ophthalmic pharmaceutical market. They would help define it.

With a focus on eye care specialists, 1949 became a transitional year. Except for Alconefrin, Pentam Suppositories, and Walker Vitamins, by the end of the year Alcon's non-ophthalmic products had been discontinued. Alexander divided sales efforts into three territories. When the year ended, Alcon's net sales had more than doubled, to $99,166, with the annual loss reduced to $3,751. Alcon products, principally Alconefrin, Op-thal-Zin, and

Zincfrin, accounted for 53 percent of annual sales. The 1949 postage cost of $1,611 suggests that Newton could have mailed as many as fifty thousand advertisements. While the true number of bottles filled are not known, Merrill was in charge of production and shipping, and he hired a group of women part-time to meet the increased demand. He explained, "I singled out the woman who usually told the others what to do and asked her if she wanted to be manager and foreman. She said, 'Yes.' So I'd call her up when we needed some bottling done and she would round up the necessary number of persons needed. All we did was bottle the products, put the labels on them and take them over to the shipping area."[8]

Based on their reception during their West Coast trip, Conner and Alexander decided to exhibit Alcon's products at the October conference of the American Academy of Ophthalmology and Otolaryngology (AAOO), which met annually at the Palmer House in Chicago. Four to five thousand EENT specialists attended, which gave Alcon national exposure. They contacted the AAOO secretary, who responded, "Send me your products. I've never heard of you." After receiving a formal invitation, Alexander, Conner, and Johnson packed a company car with Alconefrin, Op-thal-Zin, and Zincfrin, strapped a homemade display on top, and drove to Chicago (fig. 2.3). Physicians attending the conference instilled drops of Alcon medications into their own eyes and, according to Conner, the products "were held in acclaim and demanded." Flush with success, the men drove back to Fort Worth via Detroit, Columbus, Dayton, and Indianapolis. Once home, they shipped samples of all three products to every drug wholesaler in the United States. Conner later recalled, "We sent them a bill for the products—even though they had never heard of them. Ultimately, they all paid us." Alexander and Conner looked for similar long-term investments. The first occurred in 1949 when Alcon funded a $1,200 fellowship in the College of Pharmacy of the University of Texas to support research in ophthalmic formulation. This is an early example of an investment by Alcon in relations with university pharmacy departments and pharmacists.[9]

When Alexander and Conner incorporated Alcon in 1947, they sold preferred stock to eleven doctors. They unwittingly violated state laws by not informing the Texas Security Commission (TSC). In 1950 the TSC asked for an explanation. Conner consulted one of Fort Worth's top law firms, Holloway, Crowley & Hudson, and was introduced to Edgar H. Keltner Jr. Wounded at Saint-Lô after the Normandy invasion in June 1944, Keltner left the army in 1946 and completed his law degree in 1947 at the University of Texas. Keltner accompanied Alexander and Conner to Austin. He explained to the TSC that Alexander and Conner acted in "good faith and they had no idea that they were violating the law." The

FIG 2.3
Bob Alexander, Harold Johnson, and Bill Conner, driving to Alcon's first exhibit at the AAOO in Chicago, 1949 (AFP)

TSC accepted the explanation and said the matter would be resolved if they offered rescission rights to the eleven doctors. They did, no doctor returned his stock, and Keltner joined Alcon's board of directors, serving through 1968.[10]

With annual sales of $112,130 in 1950, Alcon made a profit for the first time—$2,147. Alcon product sales were 60 percent of this total and accounted for the entire profit since Walker Vitamins lost $743. For the first time, Alcon prepared a budget and sales plan and set a goal for the next year: annual sales of $173,429 with a profit of $15,535. The three company officers paid themselves collectively $550 per month. Salesmen's salaries and commissions averaged $1,309 per month. Overall, Alcon's financial future seemed solid. Having recently sent sales representative Richard Lowrance to the West Coast, the Alcon team searched for a salesman to cover the lucrative East Coast, where the largest number of ophthalmology institutions were located. They selected George F. Leone, a New Yorker whose wife had relatives in Texas and who was unhappy working as a chemist at Lederle Laboratories. Leone and his wife were visiting her relatives in Fort Worth when Alcon hired him.[11]

It was a good match for Leone and Alcon. Leone had a long career, spanning thirty-five years. Upon his retirement, Alcon's CEO claimed that "without George there would be no Alcon." He added that Leone was an intellectual and a voracious reader of scientific literature, but unlike most intellectuals, he dealt with "simple concepts" by "eliminating the static and distortions and focusing on the real issues." He was a devotee of raja yoga, and although he rarely exposed his mysticism, he believed in focus and asserted, "Knowing takes focus, and it takes a lot of concentration before you truly grasp an idea." Leone's strength was in strategic thinking, and working with him was intense, exhilarating, and productive.[12]

Like many early Alcon employees, Leone had served in the military during World War II. Born in 1926 in Queens, New York, he left school and joined the US Navy when he turned eighteen. Sent to Fort Worth for training as a corpsman and pharmacist's mate, he met and married Mary Louise Potts, a "Texas gal." After his discharge, Leone completed high school and graduated from Texas Wesleyan College in 1949 with a double major in chemistry and mathematics. He returned to New York and worked for Lederle Laboratories. He noticed that management drove new cars, while chemists drove used ones. On vacation in the summer of 1950, Leone contacted his college friend, Richard Lowrance, who arranged a meeting with Conner. Leone recalled, "Bill was a very visionary kind of guy, and I was young then, very susceptible to his vision. His vision was that he was going to build an ophthalmic specialty company."

As Alcon's East Coast salesman, Leone was responsible for a territory stretching from Maine to Georgia, and he was paid a commission with a $400-per-month guarantee. His training consisted of two days with Alexander and one with Johnson, and both emphasized what set Alcon apart from its competition: Alcon's products could be relied upon to be sterile, buffered, with measured and analyzed ingredients. Leone found it hard to sell to pharmacists, who had to give up lucrative compounding for prepackaged and more costly prescriptions. Ophthalmologists were more receptive, though one asked, "You don't expect to make a living at this, do you?" Leone persevered; it took four years for his territory to make a profit. He covered the large area in about three months by packing his car with product samples and plenty of salami and crackers! He proved to be a remarkable salesman and seldom left a client without an order. He was likeable and had a booming voice, and his small stature and habit of wearing a black shirt with a red bow tie made him even more memorable. Indeed, Alcon had found a salesman extraordinaire.[13]

By 1951 Alcon had sixteen employees, of whom eight were salesmen: Conner, Alexander, Johnson, Lowrance, Leone, Griffith, and newcomers M. D. Herrick and John Fulford. Merrill continued to direct manufacturing, while Newton was company secretary. The names of the others are unknown, but they could have been women who worked part-time for Merrill. Over the holidays, Conner leased a building at 1109 North Main in Fort Worth and told Merrill to build a laboratory, create a shipping and receiving area, and install a production line (fig. 2.4). Except for paying a carpenter $24 to construct the storage room, Merrill did this single-handedly. Alcon had its first bona fide manufacturing, quality control, and research and development facility. Conner also leased the second floor of the Fort Worth Public Market building (fig. 2.5) at 1400 Henderson Street to house the administrative department; there was a butcher shop on the first floor. Alcon was beginning to resemble a typical pharmaceutical company, though small in scale.[14]

FIG 2.4
Alcon's first manufacturing facility, 1109
North Main, Fort Worth, 1950 (AHR)

FIG 2.5
Alcon's offices (1950–1960),
Fort Worth Public Market building,
1400 Henderson, Fort Worth, 2013 (Courtesy of John Roberts, AIA,
www.fortwortharchitecture.com)

Alcon product sales increased 58 percent in 1951 to $176,548, slightly more than the budget forecast of $173,429. Annual sales did not include $15,485 earned for distributing Walker Vitamins. The profit of $15,782 also slightly exceeded the forecast. For the first time, the annual statement included manufacturing costs—$112,846. Production runs had grown significantly and required more laboratory analyses, so Merrill hired chemist Robert "Bob" Willis Carter, a US Navy veteran. One longtime employee, Oleta Whitt, later recalled that the "production line consisted of nine assembly people and one labeler sitting on wire 'ice cream parlour' chairs" (fig. 2.6). Selling expenses, mostly salaries and commissions, increased by almost 65 percent to $45,633, and administrative costs, principally company officers' salaries, came to $15,842. Alconefrin, Op-thal-Zin (fig. 2.7), and Zincfrin (fig. 2.8) constituted approximately two-thirds of the sales. Alcon profiled these products at the AAOO meeting that year (fig. 2.9). By any measure, these results justified prior investments. Moreover, they validated Alcon's strategy of increasing its focus on the eye care specialists.[15]

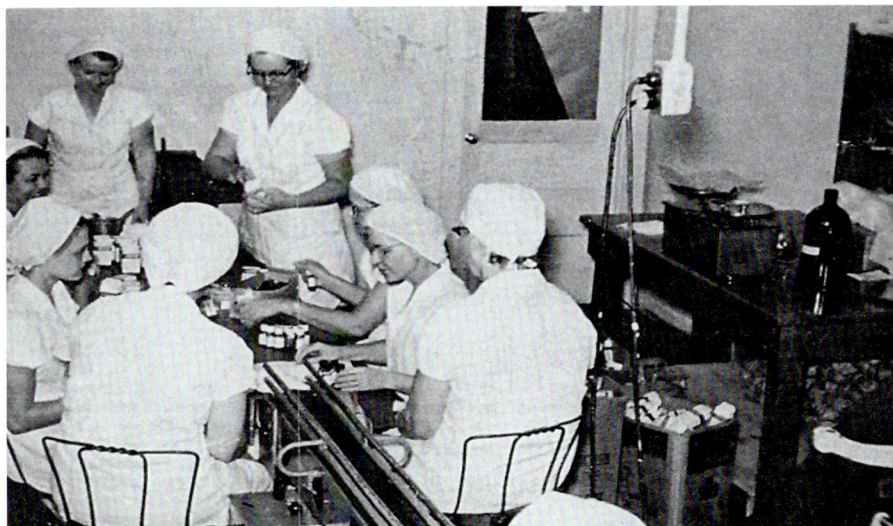

FIG 2.6
Production crew labeling a product in glass bottles, North Main manufacturing facility, ca. 1952. This room also served as the compounding space; notice the analytical scales to the right. (AHR)

With several salesmen in the field, Alexander and Conner had a variety of compensation plans. Leone, Lowrance, and Herrick worked on a commission of "25% for the first $2,000 and 15% for all in excess of $2,000." The three men got $250 to $450 each month, chargeable against commissions. Griffith received a monthly salary of $450 and a 10 percent commission for sales over $54,000. Fulham was paid $400 with a 10 percent commission when his sales exceeded $36,000. Travel expenses were reimbursed weekly. Alcon designed its compensation plan to incentivize sales. Although not confirmed, it is likely the pay schemes resembled what Conner and Alexander had at Wyeth.[16]

In 1951 Dr. Clifford Harold Beasley joined Alcon's board of directors, beginning a significant association that lasted until his death in 1999. Mostly unknown and unheralded, Beasley counseled Alcon's management to focus on the needs of ophthalmologists and taught ophthalmology to many Alcon R&D scientists. He provided medical advice and served as a medical monitor, the latter a unique concept in the pharmaceutical industry and developed by Alcon. Born in 1916 in Heber Springs, Arkansas, Beasley funded his medical

FIG 2.7
Op-thal-Zin, manufactured
ca. 1952 (AHR)

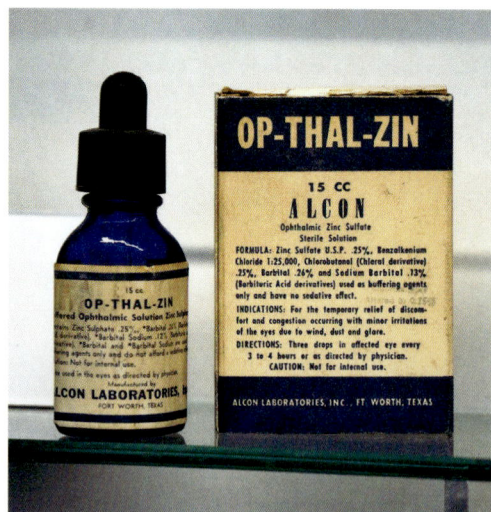

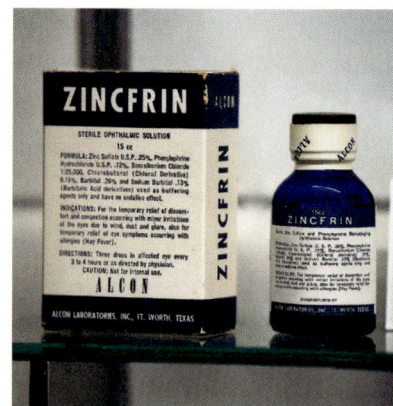

FIG 2.8
Zincfrin, manufactured
ca. 1952 (AHR)

FIG 2.9
Alcon exhibit, AAOO,
Chicago, 1951 (AFP)

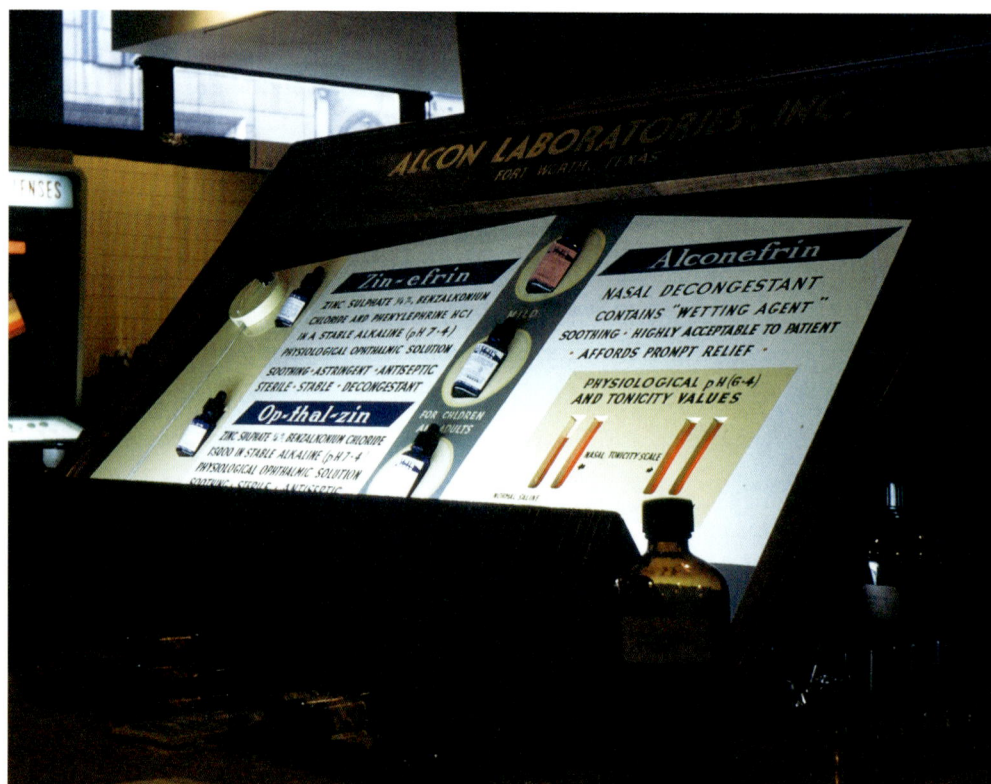

education by flying in the National Guard. After serving as a flight surgeon in World War II, he completed his residency in ophthalmology at Washington University and Barnes Hospital in St. Louis and established a practice in 1950 in Fort Worth. Beasley and Conner were neighbors; naturally, their conversations turned to ophthalmology, and Conner invited Beasley to join Alcon's board. Unassuming and soft-spoken, Beasley was always concise and frank; moreover, his advice was valued by those whose careers he influenced. Alcon was privileged to have his wise counsel for almost fifty years, a factor that contributed to Alcon's dominance in the ophthalmic pharmaceutical world.[17]

In February 1952 Alcon selected the first recipient of Alcon's fellowship at the University of Texas School of Pharmacy. William Jackson Campbell of Wichita Falls received $1,200 from Conner during a presentation in Austin. Alcon's sales continued to grow at a rate of 24 percent (to $216,540), which slightly exceeded expectations. However, a decline in net profits to just $1,062, due to investing profits in people and equipment to meet emerging government regulations, meant Alcon struggled. Nevertheless, Alcon had a viable message for customers: its ophthalmic products could be trusted to be exactly what the label said. Chemists analyzed samples from each production batch to confirm this. That being said, Alcon continued to invest in high-quality people and products.

Until 1952 Alcon's leadership had a short-term mindset, increasing sales goals one year at a time, but a longer-term strategy was emerging. Alcon was not alone. In California, Gavin Herbert Sr.'s company, Allergan, had similar ideas, as did Harry Hind with his firm, Barnes-Hind. Moreover, after World War II, other ophthalmic companies appeared in the United Kingdom, Germany, Spain, Mexico, Japan, and South America. In one way or another, each of these ophthalmic pharmaceutical businesses evolved as government regulations changed and scientific knowledge progressed. In the United States, the Food and Drug Administration (FDA) issued regulations after passage of the 1951 Durham-Humphrey Amendment that codified prescription drugs and OTC medicines. Moreover, the FDA announced in the *Federal Register* that ophthalmic solutions had to be sterile with a preservative. Alcon was uncertain how these regulations might affect Alconefrin, Op-thal-Zin, or Zincfrin, and, furthermore, it had no experience functioning under the surveillance of a federal agency. However, work in the laboratory by Merrill and his fellow scientists was underway to mitigate these issues, and a series of new products was imminent.[18]

The minutes of the stockholders meeting in June 1952 provide an in-depth view of Alcon's status. Conner may have been frustrated sales had missed the $400,000 target; he believed "the business was there" but Alcon lacked the "executive ability and organization" to tap into the market. Looking at the year ahead, Conner noted that Alexander and Johnson had "very carefully prepared a budget … right down to budgeting the men's time and their own time." Theirs was a top-down process where objectives and how to achieve them came from the home office. The budget review ended with the hope that new cost accounting procedures would help the cash flow. Next, reviewing the small contribution to profits by Walker Vitamins, the stockholders decided to terminate their arrangement in December. Looking ahead, Conner projected the next year's sales to be $301,600 but admitted he had not found a formula to predict profits. It is clear that Alcon's managers and investors were optimistic about long-term prospects. However, the company's fiscal vulnerability was apparent, and the stockholders recognized the potential risks of investing for the future with inexperienced managers at the helm.[19]

All of these concerns paled in comparison to the family tragedy that struck in September. On Labor Day, returning from a visit to his parents, Conner, his wife BeBe, and her parents drove north into Fort Worth on US Highway 18 (present-day I-35W). Traffic was stopped due to blinding rain when a fierce gust of wind ripped off the nearby roof of a construction shed, sending it through the top of Conner's car. BeBe was killed. She was forty-three years old. Conner and his in-laws were hospitalized with injuries, but BeBe's death was devastating for Conner since she "was a major part of his strength." Their daughter, Crystelle, then sixteen, took charge of the household while her father adjusted to being a widower. It was difficult. His son, Halden, who was eleven at the time, recalled, "I think it was obvious to Crystelle more than me, but it was even obvious to me, that if he didn't find somebody to live with and take care of him emotionally, as well as otherwise, he was going to go nuts."[20]

It is unclear how engaged Conner was for the rest of the year, but in January 1953 he signed revised contracts for the sales team. Alexander and Johnson still handled sales in Texas and surrounding states, Leone remained responsible for the Northeast, Herrick sold in Wisconsin and Ohio, and Lowrance worked the West. Two new men joined Alcon: Emmett Beaven was assigned to the Upper Midwest and Charles G. Rohrer got the Southeast. Rohrer, Beaven, and Lowrance received monthly salaries of $400 and 10 percent commissions for sales over $36,000, and each man got a company car with expenses paid monthly. Company cars came with a stick shift and no radio, so Leone and Herrick continued to use their own vehicles, for which mileage and expenses were reimbursed. Due to Conner's distraction, changes in personnel, and inexperience at marketing, sales that year missed the goal of $301,600, increasing just $8,424 from 1952 to $225,368, with a loss of $10,114.[21]

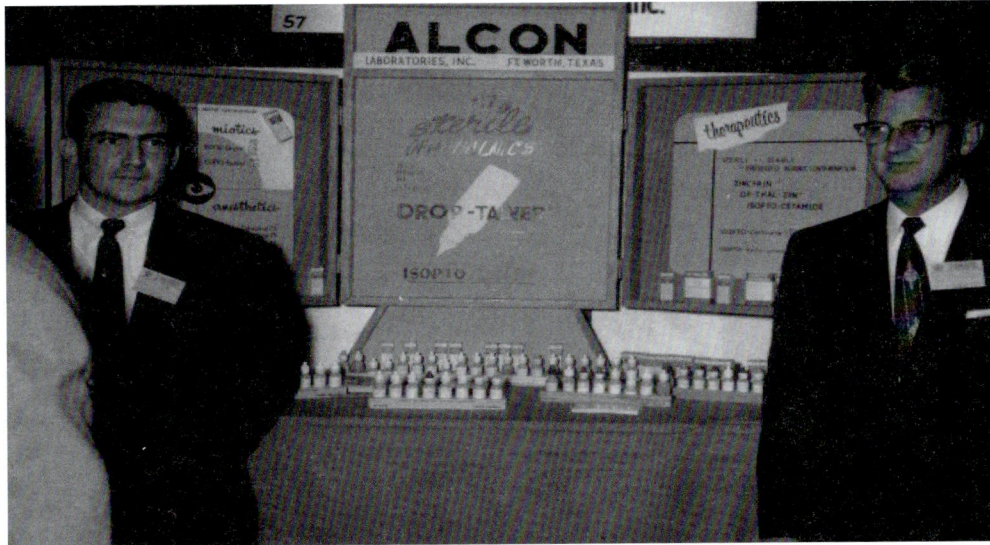

FIG 2.10
Drop-tainer products introduced at the AAOO, Chicago, 1953. *Left*: Emmett Beaven; *right*: Robert Alexander. (AFP)

Alexander and Conner realized Alcon's finances needed improvement. How to achieve this was the main topic at the June 1953 stockholders meeting. Alexander and Conner had obviously discussed options and inquired about loans. They decided that placing the company's entire future on the uncertain footing of a loan that could be called at any time was not viable. Believing that Alcon needed a reserve of $30,000 to survive the year, Alexander and Conner proposed that the company issue $30,000 in bonds at a 5 percent interest rate, due after two years. The bonds, offered first to stockholders and employees, could be converted to common stock after two years. Alexander and Conner agreed to sell to the corporation sufficient common stock, at fifty cents per share, to execute this agreement. Both men received a five-year promissory note at 5 percent. The proposal was approved at a special stockholder meeting on July 7, 1953, and the $30,000 reserve was quickly raised.[22]

Merrill's development program, started in 1951, resulted in fifteen new products, each clinically tested and approved by the FDA. They were groundbreaking, and Conner excitedly claimed, "We now have something that will definitely put us in the ophthalmic market." The new products contained an important ingredient, hydroxypropyl methylcellulose (HPMC), which increased viscosity and prolonged the medication's time on the eye. Merrill had been inspired to incorporate HPMC into his formulations after reading studies by Dr. Kenneth C. Swan of the University of Oregon Medical School. Alcon trademarked the word Isopto® to signify that a formulation contained HPMC and introduced the new products at the AAOO in October 1953 (fig. 2.10).

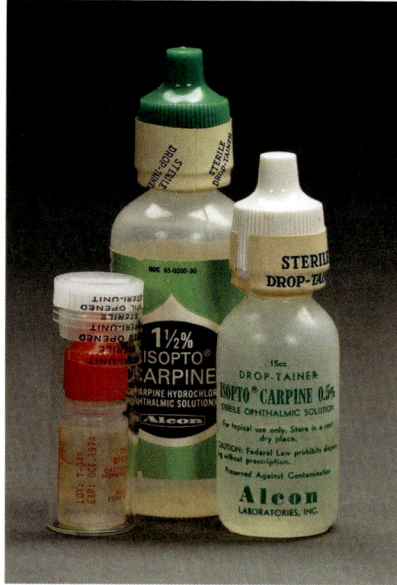

FIG 2.11
Isopto Carpine, ca. 1956 (AHR)

Merrill used mainstream drugs prescribed by ophthalmologists for his innovations. He buffered them, often to a neutral pH, then preserved formulations with thimerosal, chlorobutanol, or benzalkonium chloride, common preservatives at that time. The products included Isopto Carpine (fig. 2.11), Isopto Carbachol, Isopto Atropine, Isopto Homatropine, Isopto Hyoscine, Isopto Alkaline, Isopto Plain, Isopto Tears, Isopto Frin, Isopto Cetapred, and Isopto Cetamide. Merrill used the Zincfrin preparation, with the zinc removed, as the vehicle to prepare the new formulations. He merely added the active ingredient and HPMC. For example, solutions of pilocarpine and carbachol were mainstream therapies for glaucoma, while sodium sulfacetamide (Isopto Cetamide) was used for ocular infections. By today's standards, his effective approach was unsophisticated.[23]

Alcon made changes to meet regulations the FDA implemented in December 1952. The mandates for sterility meant Alcon needed more chemists and equipment. Merrill told Conner, "We have to build a sterile fill room, buy sterile filters and a tank that could be sterilized and connect them through stainless steel pipes. It is going to be expensive." The frugal Conner cautioned Merrill to keep costs low. Merrill hired William "Bill" A. Padgett in 1952 to help. After serving as a Marine in the South Pacific during World War II, Padgett had enrolled as a chemistry major at Texas Wesleyan College. Alberta Renick, a fellow student, was hired by Merrill on Padgett's suggestion. Renick helped to construct Alcon's first sterile manufacturing room, which they "cleaned up and put an ultraviolet light in there for sterility and everybody had to dress in white sterile clothes and sterile boots." Padgett and Renick made bulk batches of each product by measuring ingredients, placing each in a large stainless steel vat containing water, and then mixing them together. Each glass container filled by gravity as the formula flowed from the metal vat. Samples were chemically analyzed and released for shipping when the product met specifications. The chemistry lab had one hood with an exhaust fan, one analytical balance scale, and a very limited amount of glassware. Renick recalled, "We really just had the bare necessities."[24]

In March 1953 a glass container of Isopto Alkaline was discovered to be contaminated with a bacterium. The FDA required the contaminated batch to be recalled from pharmacies. This was Alcon's first recall. At the June stockholders meeting, Conner presented a plan to prevent a recurrence. During an inspection, the FDA had identified an area where contamination might occur, and Alcon subsequently hired its first microbiologist, Charles Evans Dickey (fig. 2.12), a veteran of the US Army's Pacific campaigns during World War II. He had completed a master's degree in microbiology in 1951 from North Texas State College (today the University of North Texas). Hired by Merrill in July 1953, Dickey revised the manufacturing procedures and established sterility testing protocols.

Dickey joining Alcon was fortuitous because one month later Alexander presented the Drop-tainer, an eye drop–dispensing bottle. Working with a local company, Alexander refined the specifications for the plastic components (bottle, plug, and cap), and manufacturing began. Since steam cannot sterilize plastic, Alcon's scientists designed a long, enclosed chute with a conveyor belt that was bathed in ultraviolet light (UV) and flooded with ozone, both effective surface disinfectants. After a thorough washing and drying, the Drop-tainer components were placed on the belt for a prolonged period. The bottles were aseptically filled from the large steel tank, the plugs inserted, and the caps tightened. All steps were done by hand. Line handlers glued on preprinted labels and packed the units in cardboard boxes for shipping. Dickey selected thimerosal, chlorobutanol, and benzalkonium chloride, then common preservatives, for products packaged in Drop-tainers. He asserted that "the 20 products placed on the market in the fall of 1953 were all very successful, without complaint or contamination."[25]

By nature, Conner enjoyed people and being involved, but after BeBe's death, loneliness overwhelmed him. At the time of the accident, as a supporter of Dwight D. Eisenhower's campaign for the presidency, he had just been elected chairman of the Tarrant County Republican Party. He was active in various civic organizations, including Kiwanis International. Even with these outside interests and being president of Alcon, Conner sought companionship. A friend, Teeny Bates, director of the local John Robert Powers Modeling School, set up a blind date with Mary Frances (née Guthrie) Scobee. Mary Frances, born in Austin in 1917, graduated from Sunset High School in Dallas in 1935. She enrolled in the Harris College of Nursing in Fort Worth and met Dr. Richard Gordon Scobee. They married in 1941. After his military service, the couple moved to St. Louis, Missouri, where he joined the Department of Ophthalmology at Washington University Medical School and Barnes Hospital. Scobee died on June 22, 1952. Mary Frances and her two children moved back to

FIG 2.12
Charles Dickey, ca. 1961 (AHR)

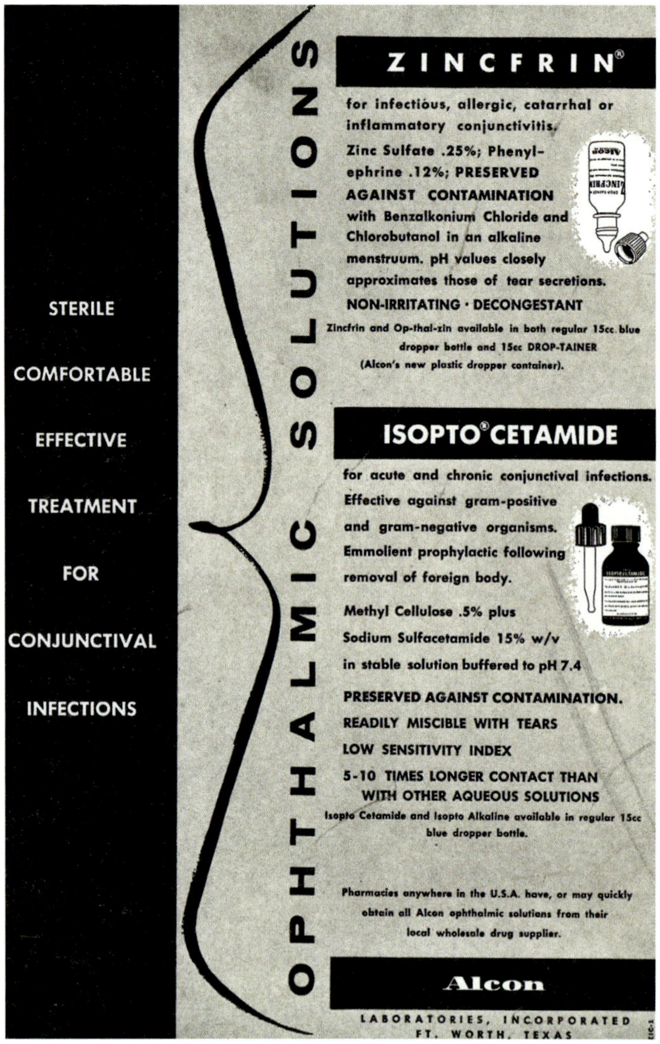

FIG 2.13
Alcon's advertisement in ophthalmic journals, 1954 and 1955 (AHR)

Fort Worth, where she resumed her nursing career.

After Bill's first date with Mary Frances, he was smitten. They married on March 12, 1953. Mary Frances exuded an ambience of elegance and determination. Though she and Bill often differed about raising their children, they enjoyed each other's company. Bill did not relish traveling alone, so Mary Frances frequently joined him on domestic and international business trips, and he insisted the children come along with their schoolwork. Just like the Alexanders, the Conners became synonymous with the Alcon brand.[26]

By July 1953 Alcon had forty employees. Merrill's new products packaged in Alexander's Drop-tainers became the center of Alcon's exhibit at the 1953 fall AAOO meeting (fig. 2.10). Doctors were impressed and the sales for 1954 increased 38 percent, to $311,972, while the annual net income of $14,905 was the best ever. Alexander, in charge of promotion and advertising, had flooded EENTs with mailings and began advertising in ophthalmic journals (fig. 2.13), and his effort paid off.[27]

While Alexander focused on promotion, Johnson managed the sales team as well as selling in his own territory. His August 2, 1954, memo, encouraging the sales force to meet their quotas, is revealing. He asserted that Alcon's increased prestige among the EENT specialists, and also with pediatricians and general practitioners, improved the salesmen's chances to achieve their quotas. He emphasized that their job was aided by the increased number of products, expanded advertising and direct mailing programs, and growth of the sales force and its experience. Each man in the field submitted a daily report, which the home office used to create monthly summaries. Thus, each salesman could see his performance in comparison to the others (fig. 2.14). Alexander and Conner likely adapted this sales criteria they experienced at Wyeth. The metrics shed light on Alcon's expectations; to achieve their goals, each salesman called on six to seven doctors and three to four pharmacies each day. This resulted in impressive sales figures for August 1954: $84,702.83. For comparison, the annual sales total in 1948 was $99,166. The sales force increased from six to nine members during 1954, the last to join being James Howard Clemmons, who would have an illustrious career at Alcon. In lieu of a sales meeting in Fort Worth each year, Alexander and

Conner used the AAOO as a substitute. In addition to manning the sales booth, the sales team met doctors from their territory, conducted training sessions, and socialized among themselves and with physicians (fig. 2.15).[28]

At a special meeting of the Alcon board of directors on December 17, 1953, Alexander and Conner recommended a change in the charter. They proposed increasing the authorized number of common stock to 475,000 shares. Existing common stockholders received two shares for every one that they currently owned. Each preferred share was exchanged for forty common shares. Every $100 bond was converted to two hundred shares of common stock. Approximately eighty thousand shares were sold or offered as stock options to employees and officers. This action gave Alcon the flexibility to raise funds by selling shares as sales increased due to the success of the Drop-tainer and a growing product line.[29]

By 1954 Alcon had progressed from its origins as a small pharmacy in Fort Worth. But its managers had greater visions. They had learned how to survive and prosper in the competitive arena of ophthalmic pharmaceutical marketing. Now they planned to finish their first decade by reaching the key milestone of $1 million in annual sales.

Continued sales growth placed an increased burden on the manufacturing process. Although production numbers are unavailable, given sales of $311,972 in 1954, a reasonable estimate is that Alcon produced approximately 1.2 million units that year. Most Alcon products retailed for fifty cents to one dollar, so the wholesale price was about twenty cents. Given their projected sales increase, Alexander and Conner realized their manufacturing facilities would soon become inadequate. Moreover, Alcon's organization had grown in complexity. Not only did it have more salesmen, but more personnel were hired for administrative needs, such as accounting and advertising, and also in the laboratory and manufacturing. These changes demanded more sophisticated management skills. Both men had extensive contacts within Fort Worth's business community, and their stockbroker offered pertinent advice. Earle Shields, the local director for Merrill Lynch, told Alexander and

September 17, 1954

SUMMARY OF DAILY REPORTS FOR AUGUST, 1954

	R.G. Terrell	Terr. #101	Terr. #102	Terr. #103	Terr. #105	Terr. #106	Terr. #107	Terr. #106-X
Working Days	22	22	22	22	22	22	22	22
Days Reported Calls	20	12	16	14	12	20	21	22
Medical Meetings	0	0	0	0	0	0	0	0
Illness	0	0	0	0	0	0	0	0
Unreported	2	0	0	0	0	0	1	0
Other	0	10	6	8	10	2	0	0
Doctor Calls per Month	90	92	99	69	107	166	139	146
Drug Calls per Month	74	42	60	78	57	46	48	20
Turn-over Orders perMO.	28	2	23	51	10	31	26	5
Direct Orders per Mo.	5	5	10	7	4	7	1	0
Average Daily Dr. Calls	4.5	7.5	6.0	4.92	8.9	8.3	6.6	6.6
Average Daily Drug Calls	3.07	3.5	3.75	5.57	4.75	2.3	2.28	0.9

Total Sales Per Month: $84,702.73

Terr. #101 - E. A. Beaven - $ 9,816.70
Terr. #102 - Russ Kerr - 4,651.38
Terr. #103 - D. H. Smith - 4,183.66
Terr. #105 - G. F. Leone - 8,131.77
Terr. #106 - M.D. Herrick - 10,696.21
Terr. #107 - Wm. Johnson - 8,927.01
Terr. #106X - A. T. Kish - 1,746.04
$48,152.77

Terr. #100 $29,158.70
Terr. #104 7,391.26

Total all Territories $84,702.73

FIG 2.14
Monthly summary of salesmen's daily reports, August 1954 (AFP)

FIG 2.15
Alcon management and salesmen, AAOO, 1954. *Back row, left to right*: George Leone, Dave Smith, Royce Crain, Charles Rohrer, Emmett Beaven;
front row, left to right: Harold Johnson, Bill Conner, Bob Alexander, Mike Herrick. (AFP)

Conner that they were pharmacists, not businessmen, and that they had no idea of how to organize and manage a fast-growing enterprise. Shields suggested they attend the Advanced Management Program (AMP) at the Harvard Business School. Thus, 1954 ended with sales booming, a stock offering in the future, and both men exploring new horizons.[30]

Johnson's efforts bore fruit as Alcon's advertising and mailing promotions, along with the reinforced sales force, supercharged sales in 1955. Net sales reached $495,995, an increase of $184,023 over the previous year. This 59 percent growth was three times greater than the company's annual goal of 20 percent. Net profits increased 42 percent, to $20,140. Obviously, everyone was elated but this also stretched Alcon's resources, and for the first time the company implemented a long-range plan. On February 14, Alcon offered twenty thousand shares at $3 per share to current stockholders and employees, and it tendered another ten thousand shares two weeks later. These thirty thousand shares would raise $90,000. At a special meeting on March 1, the stockholders authorized Alcon to purchase 84.1 acres six miles south of downtown Fort Worth on the east side of the North–South Freeway (today

1955 and 1956 Sales by Product

Product	1955 Sales	% Sales	1956 Sales	% Sales
Alconefrin	$166,317	33.0	$189,470	25.8
Zincfrin	$120,763	23.9	$163,436	22.4
Isopto Carpines	$68,400	13.6	157,041	21.5
Isopto Cetamide	$35,619	7.1	$58 113	7.9
Isopto Frin	$8,921	4.7	$25,062	3.5
Others	$103,858	17.7	$138,985	18.9
Total	$503,878		$732,107	

TABLE 2.1
1955 and 1956 sales by product (AHR)

I-35W). The property cost $92,000 and encompassed part of a small private airfield, Russell Airport. Alcon intended to build manufacturing, administration, and laboratory facilities on ten to twenty acres, leaving sixty acres for expansion or to sell. In a newspaper interview, Alexander and Conner explained that the manufacturing plant was designed "for the highly specialized production of sterile drug preparations for the use in the eye, ear, nose, and throat." They added that the state-of-the-art building would be air-conditioned and free of both dust and bacteria.[31]

After ending its relationship with Walker Vitamins, Alcon sold only its own products. The nasal decongestant Alconefrin was the top seller, and the combined sales of the four most popular ophthalmic products were about 45 percent of the total revenues (table 2.1). Both Alexander and Johnson continued to focus on the sales team, providing additional training and developing an understanding of the challenges of selling. These endeavors and increased advertising and selling expenditures for the year paid off. One unique investment was a medical film whose use is somewhat obscure. In addition to the AAOO, Alcon dispatched sales representatives to other conferences, one being the Texas Medical Association.[32]

Revised cost accounting procedures implemented in 1953 and 1954 provided new tools for management and more detailed financial records. Costs of manufacturing averaged $18,000 per month, R&D, $3,000, advertising and promotion, $8,600, and sales, $13,500. The cost for the medical film—$11,137—was particularly high. The company spent $13,600 monthly for salaries and commissions, with manufacturing and R&D accounting for 45 percent of the total. Alexander, Conner, and Johnson split $2,170 every

FIG 2.16
Howard Clemmons, Alcon exhibit,
AAOO, Chicago, 1956 (AFP)

month. Manufacturing disbursed almost $12,100 monthly for raw materials and packaging. Travel expenses for the salesmen were around $3,400 per month. With these data, Conner began estimating profits for the annual budgets, and Alcon started keeping track of monthly finances in a manner consistent with standard accounting practices.[33]

Alcon by 1955 sold twenty-two ophthalmic products and one nasal and one suppository product. Some were offered with the active ingredient at more than one concentration. Typically, a Drop-tainer contained 15 milliliters, but for the first time one product came in a 5 milliliter Drop-tainer. Merrill's R&D team released nine new products: topical anesthetics (Butacaine 2%, Phenacaine 1%, Tetracaine ½%), diagnostic (Fluorescein 2%), anti-inflammatories (Isopto Cortisone ½%, 2½%, Isopto Hydrocortisone ½%, 2½%), pupil-dilating mydriatics (Isopto Eucatropine, Isopto Phenylephrine 2%, 10%), and Benzalkonium solution. Hydrocortisone and tetracaine were relatively new, but most of these drugs were being prescribed by ophthalmologists and compounded by pharmacists. However, one aspect set Alcon apart: it was the only ophthalmic pharmaceutical firm with national distribution of an extensive product line that fit the needs of eye specialists. The AAOO exhibit in 1956 emphasized Alcon's broad spectrum of eye and nasal medications (fig. 2.16). The development, testing, and approval of nearly twenty products over a four-year period was a remarkable accomplishment for Merrill and his small R&D staff. However, formulation problems related to storage life and stability had appeared, some products became discolored, and cortisone and hydrocortisone, both insoluble in water, settled and hardened in the solutions.[34]

With sales booming, Leone convinced Alexander and Conner to add another salesman for his territory, and he became Alcon's first district manager. Until then, Leone had used his car and claimed expenses, but his new contract was different and became a template for other district managers. Alcon increased his salary 44 percent to $650 per month, with a 5 percent commission for sales over $100,000 in his territory. He was given a company car. Importantly, the company agreed to set aside one thousand shares, for which Leone would pay with his commission. These moves indicated Alcon's intention to offer its products to a wider set of ophthalmologists and EENTs, as well as to fairly compensate sales representatives that had a proven record. Allowing Leone to hire a new salesman left him free to conduct sales training and take on a supervisory role. On January 1, 1955, Leone hired Vincent Juliano to cover parts of New York.[35]

Alcon's original investors were Alexander, Conner, Johnson, and eleven physicians. The change in Alcon's charter in 1953 increased the total shares and offered opportunities for additional stockholders, including employees. Buying land for future growth did the same, and Alexander and Conner relinquished some of their shares. Thus, by mid-1955, the roster of stockholders had changed greatly. Alexander took a rough account of stockholders who attended the June meeting and found that of 475,000 authorized shares, 444,461 had been issued (fig. 2.17). Of the issued shares, Conner possessed 144,537, Alexander 125,370, and Johnson 40,000. Eight of the original investing doctors together had 79,290 shares. Eight newly investing doctors had 14,406 shares, and Beasley controlled 6,800 shares. Four employees—Carter, Dickey, Newton, and Merrill—had been given or purchased 3,493 shares. The number of investors had increased from the original fourteen to over thirty. Thus, by June 1955 Alcon had broadened the scope of its investors to include key employees but still had 30,539 unissued shares. While a closed investment, Alcon was primed to be listed on an exchange.[36]

Alcon again had its best sales ever in 1955. Manufacturing increased, nearing capacity and stretching personnel thin. Merrill assigned Carter as the first full-time manager of the manufacturing group and plant. Alexander, Conner, and Johnson faced circumstances that pushed their management and leadership skills. After lengthy negotiation with Harvard, Conner and Alexander enrolled in the school's AMP, with each to attend one session in

Jesse

```
STOCKHOLDERS ATTENDING

    MR. W. C. CONNER                              126,350
    MR. R. D. ALEXANDER                           125,300
    MR. HAROLD C. JOHNSON                          40,000
    MR. DAVE PITTS                                    100
    JOHN A. WIGGINS, M. D.                         10,400
    A. E. JACKSON, MD.                              1,000
    JERRELL BENNETT, M. D.                            113
    W. N. JENKINS M. D.                             6,450
    WALTEN H. MCKENZIE, M. D.                       6,860
    MR. HOMER L. BAUGHMAN, JR.                        500
    MRS. ROBERT NEWTON, JR.                         1,350
    MR. CHARLES E. DICKEY                             700
    MR. ROBERT W. CARTER                            2,081
    RONALD SMITH, M. D.                               350
    JAMES N. WALKER, M. D.                         13,600
    C. KEITH BARNES, M. D.                            500
    WALTER WEST, M. D.                              5,440
    J. FRANKLIN CAMPBELL, M. D.                     1,000
    MR. NORRIS G. NODURFT                             500
    JOHNNIE MONAGHAN, JR., M. D.                    3,750
    W. P. ANTHONY, M. D.                              333
    JULIUS TRUELSON                                   335
    MR. GUY M. KELLEY, JR.                          1,200
    DEWITT NEIGHBORS, M. D.                        10,000
    HAROLD BEASLEY, M. D.                           4,500
    MRS. MARY F. CONNER                               700
    NOEL L. BAILEY, M. D. ( Also signed a proxy)   23,500
    JOHN W. GARNETT, M. D. ( Also signed a proxy )  4,700

       MAL RUMPH, M. D.                             4,000
                                                 _____
                                                  395,112

STOCKHOLDER PROXIES
    WALTER WEST, M. D.                              1,000
    MR. R. D. ALEXANDER                                70
    HAROLD BEASLEY, M. D.                           2,300
    DEWITT NEIGHBORS, M. D.                           200
    MR. D. L. MERRILL                                 362
    MR. W. C. CONNER                               18,187

       MR. CHARLES DICKEY                             500
                                                 _____
                                                   22,619
```

Total Stock 444,461

FIG 2.17
"Names of Alcon stockholders attending the stockholders meeting and stockholder proxies," June 1955 (AFP)

1956. Traditionally, attendees were senior executives in large companies or government agencies, not entrepreneurial leaders from small, emerging companies, much less an ophthalmic specialty house in Fort Worth, Texas. Nonetheless, as the year ended, Conner prepared to go to Harvard.[37]

Other changes were afoot as well. The first documented contribution to the United Fund by Alcon employees was reported in the firm's monthly newsletter, the *Alcon-o-Gram*, in 1955. The United Fund began in the early 1950s when several charitable agencies joined in a single campaign for funds. President Eisenhower, like many civic and political leaders, encouraged people to support the organization. In 1952 Fort Worth joined the campaign, and local businesses became advocates during the annual fall donation drive. Alcon was no exception and, while its contribution was small in the beginning, over time Alcon became one of the Tarrant County's largest contributors, thanks to the generosity of its employees. A vocal leader for United Fund, Johnson spearheaded Alcon's initial participation, encouraging employees to donate a "fair share" to United Fund. In 1955, 24 percent of the employees gave to the United Fund, rising the next year to 46 percent.[38]

Conner attended Harvard's spring 1956 AMP session, January to May, and Alexander went to the fall session, September to December. They had never been among such a diverse group with so much experience; each group of about 150 attendees included executives from a gamut of industries and several senior military officers. Their fields of study included finance, economics, labor relations, marketing, advertising, administrative practices, and business policy. They also had practical case studies related to project management, management by objectives, salesmen compensation, employee participation, acquisitions, and hiring and firing. About his experience, Conner admitted, "We began to get a little more sophisticated in our management methods." Crammed into twelve weeks, the AMP programs did not allow time for attendees to work on their own company's business. In Conner's absence, Alexander as the acting president conducted the monthly directors' meetings. Sales equaled $303,601, an insignificant $1,503 less than planned, and expenses were 9 percent less than planned. Comments from the board members and Alcon staff present at the meetings indicate the problems and solutions during the months Alexander was in charge were typical of prior years. For example, Alcon had planned to launch Isopto P H N and expected FDA approval in the usual sixty-to-ninety-day time frame, but FDA approval came late in the year.[39]

Even without its two senior executives for most of 1956, Alcon's sales, manufacturing, and advertising groups maintained a remarkable pace. Sales in 1956 increased 45 percent to $717,265, bringing in a net income of $24,171. Alconefrin remained the top seller, though marginally, and for the first time the top four ophthalmic products cornered 55 percent of sales (table 2.1). Notably, sales of Isopto Carpine more than doubled due to promotion and ophthalmologist-driven glaucoma screening efforts. The manufacturing plant increased its capacity by spreading into the space formerly occupied by the shipping department, which moved to another building nearby. According to Alcon's first compounder, Joe Lutteringer, manufacturing now had "a 100-gallon glass lined tank, a 55-gallon plastic drum, and two 30-gallon plastic drums," and it produced 12,888 units daily with a night shift required to meet production goals. At this time, the process was still manual, beginning with compounding in the large steel vats and continuing with filling, plugging, and capping each Drop-tainer. Products were scheduled a few weeks in advance, based upon sales predictions by marketing and sales staff.

Success brought additional challenges. With more employees working in the administrative building, space was at a premium there. While R&D, advertising, and administrative expenses marginally increased, selling costs doubled. During a four-month period from late 1955 into early 1956, Alcon added nineteen salesmen, bringing the total to thirty. Clemmons became a district manager when new salesmen were assigned to his territory—Texas, New Mexico, Colorado, Oklahoma, Arkansas, and western Tennessee. With investment in sales pushing growth, district managers held their first sales meeting, while 650 physicians registered with Alcon at the AAOO convention, where the company debuted a twenty-foot display. The total number of Alcon employees reached almost ninety. Clearly, Alcon had entered a new phase in its growth, not only in physical space but also in demands on staff and management. For example, since overseas sales increased—principally to Canada but also to Colombia, Venezuela, El Salvador, Ecuador, Peru, Hong Kong, and Puerto Rico—Alcon had to establish an export unit that operated through an international trade consultant in Chicago.[40]

R&D released seven new products in 1956, leading Alcon to boast it was "the only manufacturer with a full line of eye preparations." Two were novel concepts, Steri-units and a steroid-antibiotic combination, which would be springboards for future products. Alcon created the steroid-antibiotic therapy with Isopto Cetapred, a mixture of prednisolone and sulfacetamide. For decades afterward, Alcon dominated this sector of the ophthalmic market by developing a series of improved formulations. Development began for Isopto P H N, which became the second-generation steroid-antibiotic combination. For this therapy, Dickey, Merrill, and Theodore "Ted" Carl Fleming combined hydrocortisone (0.5% and 1.5%) with antibiotics, polymyxin and neomycin. This combination gave ophthalmologists a means to treat ocular inflammations and infections with the convenience of only one drop. Designed for single use, the Steri-unit filled a need of the ocular surgeon. A sterile 2 milliliter Drop-tainer was aseptically filled with the formulation, then put in a sterile outer clear plastic container and sealed. In the surgery room, a technician unsealed the outer container and let the Drop-tainer slide onto the sterile surgical instrument tray. Thus, surgeons had a sterile medication they could use during and after the procedure. Pilocarpine HCL 2% was the first Steri-unit product. Sales representatives profiled the product as the "Drop-tainer® S, a single-dose unit with pre-sterilized outer surface as well as contents, another new concept in ophthalmic medication, [and] a new measure of safety and convenience where aseptic procedure had to be rigorously followed."[41]

Fleming, an army veteran of World War II, had earned a master's degree in microbiology and biochemistry from the University of Texas. Joining Alcon on January 3, 1956, he played a key role in developing new products and establishing stability, safety, and efficiency protocols. His benchmarks led to more technically sophisticated procedures developed later by second- and third-generation scientists at Alcon. Working with Merrill and Dickey, Fleming was the primary developer of Isopto P H N. In its first formulation, the ingredients began to deteriorate over time, but he discovered that at pH 5 the preparation could be buffered and remain stable. Merrill and Fleming wrote a pamphlet illustrating their discovery for the sales representatives to use in convincing ophthalmologists to prescribe the product.[42]

Stability problems continued to appear in some of the earliest Isopto products. For ¼% and 3% Isopto Carpine, substituting another preservative for chlorobutanol improved the formulations' comfort. Scientists also modified the ingredients in Isopto Cetamide, eliminating clumping and improving suspendability. Other products were adjusted as formulation problems arose.[43]

When management, department heads, and key employees met in 1956 to plan and budget for the next year, the session was an overnight affair. The prime subject was Alcon's profit-sharing trust (PST), today known as a 401(k) plan. It turned out to be among the most generous, if not the most generous, in the United States: an Alcon employee could save up to 5 percent of their salary and the company would match $2 for each employee's $1. A committee, composed of representatives from various departments, oversaw the investment, usually a balanced fund. However, Alcon had to make a gross (before taxes) profit of $40,000 before its profit-sharing commitment kicked in. Each employee had to work for Alcon for twenty years in order to be vested, meaning they owned the company's share deposited in their name. If a person quit before then, their company share was divided among the active participants. A twenty-year-old who joined Alcon in 1956 could anticipate retiring as a millionaire. This plan enhanced employee commitment and created a cadre of long-term experienced employees. The latter point became crucial in Alcon's success. Moreover, employees expected Alcon management to be a prudent steward of resources. In 1956 Alcon had a gross profit of $43,997.37, so it contributed $3,997.37 to the employees' PST.[44]

The influence of Harvard's AMP on Conner, Alexander, and indeed Alcon itself, cannot be overstated. For Alexander, the experience was life-changing, both professionally and personally. His daughter, Lane Anne Kimzey, recalled, "We started having business meetings, a family business meeting. I can't remember how often, but we would gather around the kitchen table and sometimes he'd have a blackboard up. And, we had business meetings." Denny, his son, noted how the experience affected Alexander professionally, how it shaped his view of education, management principles, and values. This is evident in his interaction with Alcon district managers in 1957. Alexander was particularly inspired by two articles used by the Harvard Business School to promote its case study process—"Because Wisdom Can't Be Told" and "Teachers Must Also Learn." He carried copies and gave one to almost everyone he met. The most significant outcome was Alexander meeting Edgar "Ed" Hans Schollmaier, which resulted in Schollmaier joining Alcon a year later. This chance meeting led to a transformation of Alcon's future.[45]

Unlike Alexander's daughter, Halden Conner concluded that his father's Harvard experience "didn't change him very much." If it did not change him as a father, it certainly altered his vision for Alcon's future. As an adult, Halden asked Leslie Rollins, then the head of admissions at Harvard, what Conner had learned at Harvard that fundamentally changed his approach. Rollins responded, "He learned that nobody up here had any answers either." His point is valid, yet it understates the value of case studies. All problems have solutions, but many are imperfect, and leaders use all available resources to discover the best outcome. Conner's first application of principles learned in the AMP was placing Alexander in charge of sales and moving Johnson to advertising. He realized Alcon needed new and different talents to manage future complexities, and in the years following he hired several top-notch executives, many with MBAs. Conner was not reluctant to put his new knowledge into action as he juggled problems, concerns, and decisions.[46]

Alcon by 1957 had around thirty-five products marketed by a larger sales force and promoted by robust direct mailing and advertising campaigns. Two Alcon-produced short films, *Ocular Biomicroscopy* and *Ocular Bacteriology*, were used as selling tools. Sales not surprisingly increased by 45 percent that year, but Alconefrin lost its dominance to ophthalmic medications. At 23.9 percent of the company's sales, the Isopto Carpine franchise eclipsed Alconefrin's 22.6 percent share, which was followed by Zincfrin at 18.9 percent. For the first time, Alcon had a second-generation therapy, the steroid-antibiotic combination Isopto P H N, to complement the original Isopto Cetapred. Moreover, the novel Steri-units were widely used by surgeons. In another first, R&D produced publications, some internal and others in scientific journals, supporting Alcon's products. All of this required more manufacturing capacity. Under Conner's guidance, the complex in south Fort Worth moved closer to reality. In every aspect, Alcon was poised to achieve another record-setting year operating, as predicted by Conner, as an "ophthalmic house."[47]

Total sales reached $999,320 in 1957, though profits remained almost unchanged at $18,308. Alcon's ophthalmic therapies (Isopto Carpine, Zincfrin, Isopto P H N, and Isopto Cetamide) amounted to 45 percent of the total, Although Alcon tabulated sales by product name, it also revolutionized the ophthalmic market by categorizing products by therapeutic purpose—anti-glaucoma, dry eye, anti-inflammatory, and anti-infective. It was a useful stratification, and Alcon's competitors soon followed suit. Exports grew fivefold, to $15,000. In addition to Canada, products went to ten countries, including Thailand, the Philippines, and several countries in South America. After several years of discussions, Venezuela approved Isopto Carpine 4 percent, Isopto Frin, and Alconefrin. Negotiations began for licensing Alcon products to a distributor in Mexico, and preparations commenced for establishing an Alcon company in Canada. Expenses increased commensurate with sales. The cost of goods totaled $308,694, while selling expenses were $324,693, advertising/promotion/administration, $300,861, and R&D, $65,072. Profit before taxes was a disappointing $27,640, resulting in no company contribution to the employees' PST. For the first time in several years, Alcon increased the price for twelve products. A new market opened with the Department of Defense after the surgeon general of the Air Force required that ophthalmic medicines be packaged in Drop-tainer–type bottles. Conner later claimed, "We are doing a pretty good business with the armed forces right now." By the end of the year, Alcon marketed forty-three products and manufactured an average of 11,500 units each day. Automation and modernization also came to the accounting department with the installation of an IBM 402, which created a new job—keypunch operator.[48]

When Alexander returned from his AMP course, he traded responsibilities with Johnson, who attended the AMP in spring 1957. Thus, in 1957 Alexander became the director of sales, and Johnson took over advertising and promotion. When that same year Alcon approached the $1 million milestone in sales, Alexander was managing the salesmen and ready to put his AMP know-how into action. District manager Clemmons hired rookie salesman John Woodruff Spruill, a larger-than-life character destined to pioneer Alcon's Surgical Division. Both Alexander and Conner, as well as the board, expressed concern that of the twenty-seven salesmen, only two-thirds were paying their way—selling enough to offset their expenses. Alexander set a goal: either the problem would be fixed by the end of March 1957 or the weakest would be let go. To begin, he visited each of the district managers, starting with Beaven on January 28. His twenty pages of notes illustrate how the AMP course had affected his behavior and attitude. Alexander outlined three key points: "I. What we in Ft. Worth want, expect, and when. II. How this may be accomplished. III. Immediate creative, detailed sales plan for action on 1. Steri-units, 2. Isopto P H N, 3. other products." Next came a list of ideas for managers to implement, emphasizing responsibilities, communications, and sales training, all designed to achieve one goal—selling Alcon products.

In June 1957 the four district managers came to Fort Worth to discuss an agenda Alexander had developed from his initial points. Beginning December 16 the four and Alexander met again at the Worth Hotel in downtown Fort Worth. This time it was the managers' turn to lead the discussion. Alexander wanted to know what they needed to meet his objectives and how the home office could help. The long list of topics included increasing sales, long-range planning, selecting new salesmen, delegating responsibility, salesmen accepting more responsibility, weekly and monthly reporting criteria, performance standards, and expense guidelines. One specific outcome was the designation of a training manager for each district. Alexander's approach sought to involve the district managers as partners, with increased sales from their territory being the measure of their success.[49]

Meanwhile, Johnson hired Joseph Parker Floyd to grow Alcon's advertising program and promotional materials. Together, they produced a sophisticated brochure, with photo-

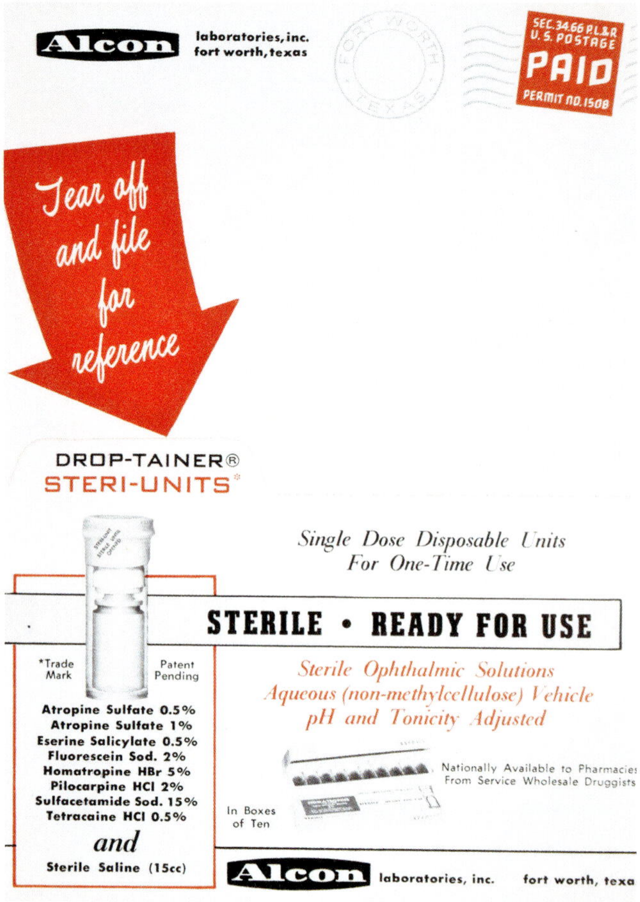

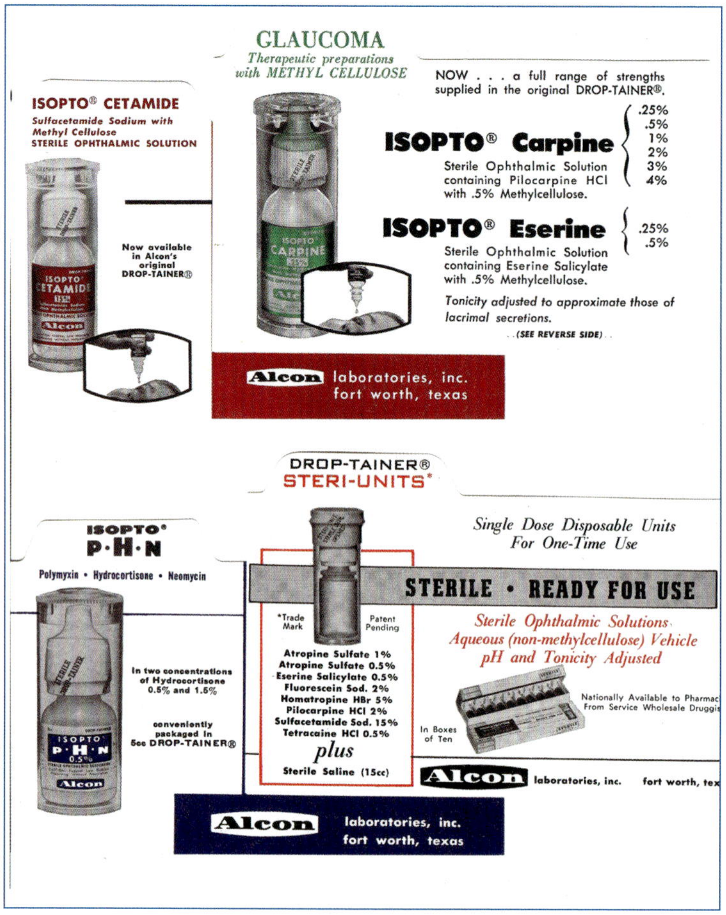

FIG 2.18
Drop-tainer Steri-units promotional material (AHR)

FIG 2.19
Mailing profiling Isopto Cetamide, Isopto Carpine, Isopto Eserine, Isopto P H N, and Drop-tainer Steri-units sent to ophthalmologists, 1957 (AHR)

graphs and captions, profiling Alcon's research, packaging, products, and medical meetings and services. The brochure included a series of mailings and preprinted index cards outlining each product (figs. 2.18, 2.19). Since its earliest days, mailings to physicians had remained an integral feature of Alcon's promotional campaigns and the brochure, also distributed at the AAOO, provided a multipurpose promotional tool to build on that success.[50]

Alcon continued its strategy of selling small tranches of shares to retire the note on the land in south Fort Worth and fund capital expenses for the planned manufacturing building. As 1957 commenced, fifty-two individuals owned Alcon shares. With this number of stockholders, Alcon had to notify the TSC of any future sale. Conner began the process in January and secured permission for the sale of 17,397 shares at $5 each, raising $86,985. Alcon made the third payment of $15,655 on the note for the land, leaving a considerable cash reserve.[51]

In 1957 Alcon personnel attended twenty-eight medical conferences to promote products. The list highlighted the impressive scope of the company's market: Georgia Society of Ophthalmology and Otolaryngology, American Academy of General Practice, Industrial Health Conference, Texas Medical Association, New Mexico Medical Society, Louisiana-Mississippi Ophthalmology and Otolaryngology Society, Pennsylvania Academy of Ophthalmology and Otolaryngology, Osteopathic College of Ophthalmology and Otolaryngology, Texas Academy of General Practice, American Academy of Pediatrics, and Southern Medical Association. Four new displays augmented the existing exhibits, while interchangeable panels provided the flexibility to focus on a particular product (fig. 2.20). A large contingent represented Alcon at the AAOO and, to celebrate Alcon's ten-year anniversary, Conner, Alexander, Johnson, and their wives, plus thirteen employees, attended. Over eight hundred physicians visited the Alcon booth, many of whom had developed a close relationship with the company over the last decade.[52]

FIG 2.20
Modular displays for medical meetings (AHR)

Alcon's bylaws required key decisions to be made by the stockholders. While it was a small company with only a few investors, this was rational and practical. As the number of stakeholders increased, this process became unwieldy. Alcon's legal counsel, Keltner, proposed changing the by-laws by transferring authority from the stockholders to the board of directors. Four subjects stimulated this conversation: authority to borrow money, the number of directors, titles of employees, and executive compensation. At the annual meeting, the stockholders amended the by-laws so that the number of directors would be no fewer than five and no more than twenty-five. Conner recommended, and the board appointed, Karl E. Rotegard, Dr. DeWitt Neighbors, and Dr. James N. Walker to formulate a broad policy for executive compensation. The committee returned in August with a comprehensive salary and bonus plan, which was adopted with the proviso that it would be revisited in five years. It is unclear if, or how much, Conner or Alexander influenced this. However, the process for establishing an executive compensation scheme was a classic Harvard Business School approach. After Conner and Alexander attended the AMP, they circulated the

Harvard Business Review among their directors. Moreover, Rotegard had graduated from the Harvard with an MBA in 1949.[53]

Financing the construction of the new plant on the South Freeway became a top priority. By July 1957 management had agreed on the plans for the manufacturing building. Numerous changes led to a revision of the drawings, requiring a new cost estimate, so the board told the architect to proceed with drilling test holes to complete the topography survey. Meanwhile, Alexander and Conner initiated discussions with Southwestern Life Insurance Company and Prudential Life Insurance Company to fund construction. To complicate matters, two companies inquired about acquiring Alcon. Hoping to license products or compounds to develop, Alexander and Conner visited with executives of Schering Corporation, who asked if Alcon was for sale. A representative of the Vick Chemical Company came to Fort Worth and asked Conner the same question. Told no, the discussion turned to licensing products, but nothing materialized. Two years later, Vick introduced Vicks Sinex Nasal Spray, a product similar to Alconefrin. When the board discussed both events, the consensus was that Alcon should remain independent for many more years.[54]

A new tradition was started at Christmas in 1957—a company party for Fort Worth employees and spouses (fig. 2.21). Over one hundred people attended. Conner's speech recognized the family spirit at Alcon and thanked all for making 1957 the best year ever. Furthermore, by Christmas, 75 percent of Alcon employees had donated to the United Fund. Conner also announced that the company had established major medical and hospital insurance coverage for its employees. Johnson recalled that at the first Christmas party, "Alcon discovered local restaurants would not allow an integrated party. The event moved to Fort Worth's railroad depot so all employees could attend." In subsequent years, Alcon's Christmas celebrations became legendary and spread beyond just a single night. Every employee of those days has a vivid recollection of one or more. Conner's idea that Alcon was a family was never epitomized in any better manner than by its Christmas parties.[55]

By the end of its tenth year, Alcon achieved a major milestone—$1 million in sales and around 3 million units manufactured. Alcon at that time marketed forty-three products—with the exception of one, all were eye medications—and the company had a reputation for credibility and reliability. Funding growth, Alcon management had reinvested profits, and Alexander and Conner continued to search for additional financing to cover the cost of the new complex. Beyond the physical structure, Alcon had outgrown its original business structure, and so the reorganized board of directors approved a compensation plan for the company's top eight executives. Emphasizing their role for Alcon's future, after the presi-

dent, the directors of sales and R&D were the highest-paid positions. Its new Christmas tradition, company medical insurance, and commitment to profit sharing made Alcon employees feel connected to the company's success. It is no surprise that when two competitors made overtures to acquire Alcon, both offers were rejected.

Many metrics can define the success of an organization; the pharmaceutical industry commonly uses annual sales. By this measure, Alcon clearly succeeded, hitting $1 million in sales in its tenth year (fig. 2.22). With their initial investment of $6,000, Alexander and Conner established a neighborhood pharmacy but then had the wherewithal to transform their vision to fit the emerging market, creating an ophthalmic pharmaceutical company. It is not generally recognized, though it is significant, that the key figures in Alcon's early years were veterans of the US military during World War II. The discipline and organization they experienced in the military created a mindset that benefited Alcon. Moreover, each took advantage of the GI Bill to obtain a university education. Several hired to work in the laboratory had master's degrees, giving the company a higher level of expertise that was crucial

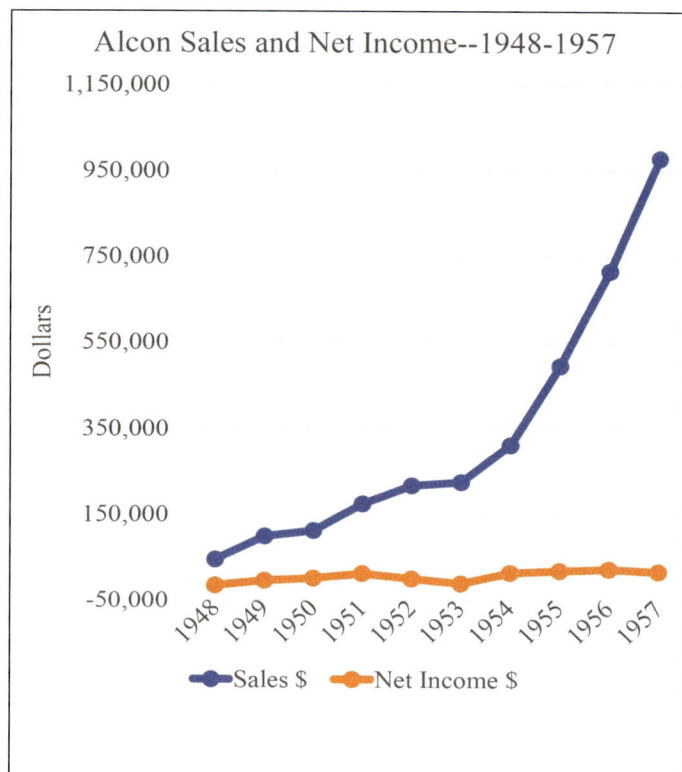

Alcon Sales and Net Income--1948-1957

FIG 2.22
Alcon sales and net income,
1948–1957 (TOM, AM)

to its survival. Alcon's early scientists laid the foundation for future generations of Alcon leaders.

* * *

Dominance in the pharmaceutical industry occurs through technical innovation and ingenious marketing and sales. Alexander's Drop-tainer is the number one packing invention that transformed instillation of eye drops. It made the process effortless and successful. Alexander's design still dominates the ophthalmic industry today. Its contribution to Alcon's growth cannot be overstated. Applying academic scientific observations, Merrill added HPMC to formulations and gave them the name of Isopto. These products were more viscous and remained on the eye longer, thereby having a greater therapeutic effect. They were an easier sale for the marketing team that turned Alcon products into recognizable brand names. The one truly unique new product was the steroid-antibiotic combination Isopto P H N. To reinforce Alexander and Conner's focus on product sterility and preservation, Merrill built a UV- and ozone-flooded production line that sterilized Drop-tainers. Alcon was ready when the FDA required both for ophthalmic medications.

Finding top-notch salesmen was always a challenge, but after ten years of trial and error, three members of the team stood out—Leone, Clemmons, and Beaven. They became the core regional managers as Alcon expanded nationwide. The truly successful salesmen overcame the reluctance of pharmacists to dispense prepackaged ophthalmic medications. Alexander began to comprehend that managing a sales organization was not a top-down process, and he shared responsibility with district and regional managers.

By 1954 Alexander and Conner realized their small company had the potential for a larger future, one that would require more sophisticated business acumen. Heeding the advice of Shields from Merrill Lynch, they attended Harvard's AMP. Their experiences were transformative, and the influence of the Harvard concepts can be seen in many aspects of Alcon's philosophy and development. Alexander took charge of the sales organization, and Conner began to explore future needs for production, R&D, and administration. Alcon's plans for its future campus began to take shape and company loyalty was enhanced with a generous profit-sharing program and health insurance.

Given Alcon's success, Alexander and Conner's relationship is relevant. The latter was a hard-driving risk-taker; the former, methodical and cautious. In some ways, their relationship was an extension of what it was at Wyeth Pharmaceutical Company, where Conner was a district manager and Alexander was his territory salesman. Conner became the public persona of Alcon, though physicians knew Alexander equally well. During Alcon's first decade, the two collaborated, and they shared personal costs and benefits equally. It is also important to note that Conner and Alexander did not manage the company alone but instead relied on capable directors. Drs. Beasley, Wiggins, West, Neighbors, and Walker invariably attended the monthly meetings, actively participated, and critiqued outcomes.

In the various forums where Alexander or Conner spoke or left a written record, neither used the word *focus*. Nevertheless, what evolved from the first days of Alcon Prescription Laboratory into Alcon Laboratories, Inc., can be summarized in a single word—*focus*. They focused on providing eye specialists with what they needed. In turn, ophthalmologists prescribed Alcon's therapies, which drug wholesalers stocked and pharmacists dispensed. Remaining focused on this seemingly simple objective would turn out to be more complicated in the future.

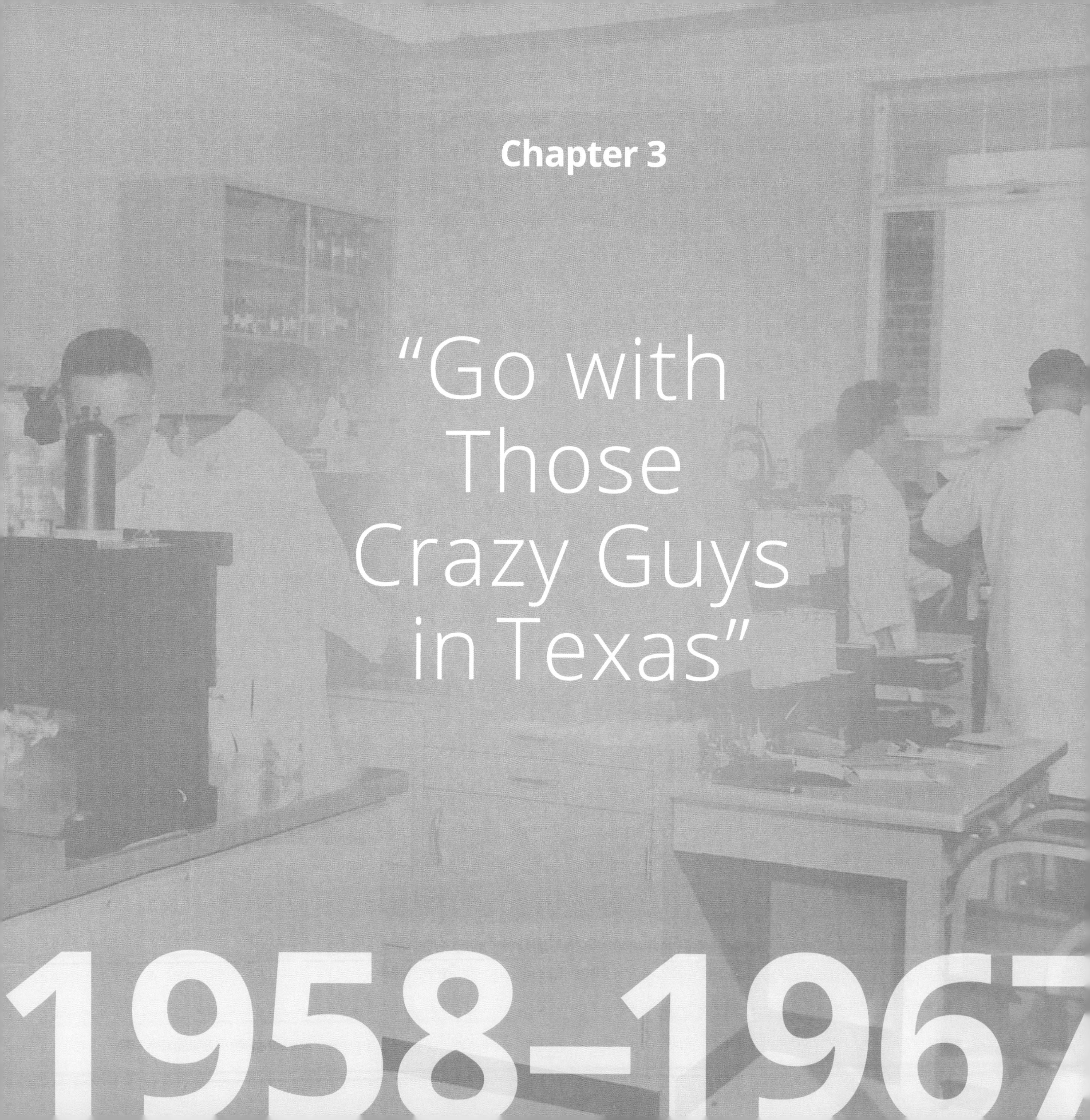

Chapter 3

“Go with Those Crazy Guys in Texas”

1958–1967

While attending the AMP at Harvard, Bob Alexander spoke to the New Enterprise Club about Alcon's history. A young MBA student, Edgar "Ed" Hans Schollmaier, was sitting in the audience wondering why Alexander, from a small startup pharmaceutical company in Texas, had enrolled in a course typically filled with experienced executives from major international firms. Twenty months later, Alexander hired Schollmaier as a sales representative; three years after that, he brought him to Fort Worth as a division manager. They worked closely for almost ten years, although Alexander's contemplative style sometimes clashed with Schollmaier's more direct approach. On one occasion, Alexander said, "Let's slow down a little and try to help each other. After all, neither one of us knows what he's doing. I haven't done this before, and I know for a fact that you haven't either." His philosophy resonated with those who chose a career at Alcon. Often, we did not know what we were doing, and we knew it, but with teamwork and patience we found solutions and, in the process, gained invaluable experience. This is one of several reasons for Alcon's success.[1]

Alcon in late 1957 produced two distinctly different publications. The first, *Proposed New Facilities, Alcon*, began with a drawing of the planned complex (fig. 3.1). The brochure highlighted Alcon's scientific expertise and its accomplishments in developing almost forty ophthalmic products over the past decade. Stressing Alcon's mission, the brochure guaranteed the quality of every ingredient, the accuracy of composition, and the sterility of the final product. Products were branded as sterile, stable, preserved, isotonic, pH neutral, and comfortable. Those containing HPMC, with the brand name Isopto, were featured because their prolonged time on the eye increased efficacy. The brochure highlighted the Drop-tain-

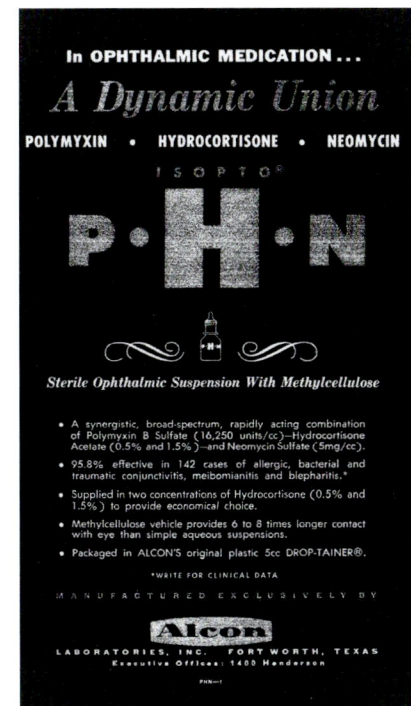

FIG 3.2
Isopto P H N, advertisement (AFP)

FIG 3.1
First architectural drawing of the
future Alcon campus, 1957 (AFP)

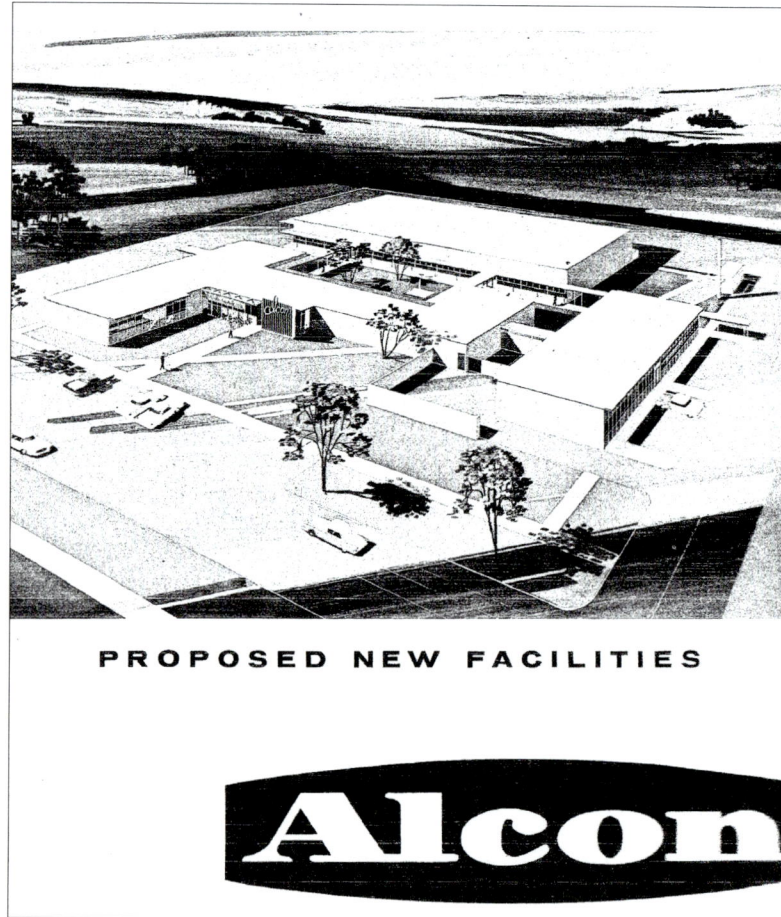

PROPOSED NEW FACILITIES

er, which demonstrated innovation in packaging and merchandising, while Steri-units were an example of Alcon's commitment to ophthalmic surgeons. Particularly eye-catching was the description of Isopto P H N (fig. 3.2), which reflected increased sophistication in marketing, advertising, and promotion. Alcon boasted about creating mailing lists based on salesmen's daily reports, with five hundred thousand mailings each year. While Alcon distributed this brochure to physicians, it also had the components of an annual report and was likely used to promote Alcon elsewhere.[2]

The second publication, *Profile and Prognosis*, released on January 15, 1958, was billed as a strategic study of Alcon and the dynamics of the ophthalmic market. More important, it was an initial effort at market research created by the market research and financial groups. Mainly authored by Harvey Andrews, Alcon's first chief financial officer, it summarized Alcon's history, declaring it to be the "only manufacturer of such a specialty line with national distribution." Alcon boasted a phenomenal 49 percent average increase in annual sales during its first decade, five times greater than the increase in all prescriptions in the United States and three times more than that for ophthalmic prescriptions. The brochure emphasized Alcon's managerial philosophy to reinvest profits in "growth and enhanced market position" and asserted that growth could continue without sacrificing profits. Alcon controlled about 8 percent of the ophthalmic market and was poised to dominate subsets such as glaucoma and steroid-antibiotic combinations. Alconefrin ranked eighth nationwide among nasal spray medicines, so while it was sold in a few regional markets, it had great potential. Such optimism was based upon external factors, too: population growth, an expanding national economy, an increase in health insurance plans, a global rise in the standard of living, increasing world trade, and continued progress in developing medicines. Alcon's sales were projected to surpass $6 million in five years, with a profit of $1 million.[3]

Earle Shields never expected how his advice would transform Alcon when he suggested that Bill Conner attend AMP. While Conner may have later said that he learned that Harvard did not have all the answers, his actions in this and the next decade belie his wry assertion. He wasn't the only one to bring Harvard's influence to Alcon. Army veteran Harvey Andrews graduated cum laude from the University of Pittsburgh and received a Harvard MBA in 1957, when he was recruited by Conner. Andrews began as Alcon's comptroller, and in his first month attended a Chicago symposium on the pharmaceutical industry and assessed Alcon's export potential. Andrews and his Harvard classmates were among the first to practice management accounting, which emphasized using financial information to shape managers' actions. In his first board meeting on April 30, 1958, Andrews presented a new budget concept: "responsibility performance." In his second board meeting on August 29, his accounting mindset was reflected in the scope and content of information Alcon released. His views influenced several tactical and strategic decisions affecting Alcon's future.[4]

Conner also recruited another Harvard MBA in 1957, Herbert J. Kleiman, to work as a salesman under district manager George Leone. Andrews hired Fredrick W. Lyons Jr. after he earned his MBA from Harvard in 1959. William R. Glover Jr., a 1961 Harvard MBA, joined the finance department, and Conner's son-in-law, Robert T. Rapp, a 1964 Harvard MBA, became a member of the marketing group. Alcon also sent its three senior managers to the AMP: Dave Merrill (1958), George Leone (1959), and Bob Carter (1961). From all this Harvard talent, however, Schollmaier emerged as the most significant. After attending Alexander's presentation to the New Enterprise Club, the intrigued Schollmaier told Alexander over cocktails, "I've never been to Texas and I'm going to check you out in two years

FIG 3.3
Ed Schollmaier and his mother, Else, August 1946 (Courtesy of Taylor Schollmaier)

when I graduate." Alexander replied, "You do that."[5]

Like Alexander and Conner, Schollmaier became linked to Alcon's success, serving as its president and CEO for the second half of its first fifty years. As he said in 2004, "In many ways, Alcon's history is my history." He added, "I was the one who came near the beginning, who orchestrated our decades of growth, who helped correct the problems, who developed the strategies—the wrong ones as well as the right ones—and who basically led the company for 25 years. This is very unusual. If you do a five-year stint as president of a company, it's considered a lot. I had the opportunity to do it for five times that long."[6]

Schollmaier was the son of German immigrants. His parents first met in Cincinnati, where his father worked in construction. Born in 1933 during the Depression, Schollmaier had a stark childhood but, thanks to his mother's keen insight, plans to return to Nazi Germany in 1936 were canceled. His parents opened a grocery and delicatessen that his mother operated after being widowed in 1944 (fig. 3.3). An only child, Schollmaier was close to his parents and shared a love of baseball with his father. Once, after a Cincinnati Reds game, his father introduced him to the players, and he dreamed of becoming a television baseball announcer. In 1950, during his senior year in high school, his mother died. The school principal had an acquaintance arrange for Schollmaier to meet Jim Shouse, the president of the local television station. When Schollmaier said he wanted to be a well-known local sportscaster, Shouse replied, "It will never happen." He went on to explain that the path for success in the television industry, and life in general, was liberal arts education, advice Schollmaier followed. At eighteen, he enrolled as a television studies major at the University of Cincinnati and worked part-time at the local television station. Later, he admitted that Shouse gave him "life-changing, meaningful advice."[7]

Schollmaier discovered the television industry was not for him. He struggled in his freshman year and would have failed had it not been for an English course, where he won high praise from the professor. In the same class, he met Rama Lee Skinner, better known as Rae, a brilliant woman with a "bubbly personality." During his junior and her senior year, they married (fig. 3.4). Schollmaier acknowledged that "her interest in me helped me focus and started getting my feet under me." Like her father, Rae was a teacher, and she supported

Schollmaier while he finished his education. Things began to click for him in a sophomore economics class, and soon he was an economics major and an A student. Following the advice of a professor who saw his potential, he successfully applied to Harvard.

Schollmaier recalled that his "Harvard experience was absolutely wonderful. ... Every one of the professors was brilliant, outstanding." Most important was the case study system, which trained students to analyze problems, a process Schollmaier intuitively grasped and used throughout his career. He was also exposed to a variety of bright, creative personalities with a mixture of experience and expertise. It was a dynamic and transformative period, and he thrived. The tuition took a large chunk of the $20,000 his mother left him, and although Rae's teaching salary and income from his summer employment kept them afloat, they were $8,000 in debt when he graduated in 1958.[8]

In October 1956, one month into his MBA program, Schollmaier attended the lecture by Alexander. At that time, Alcon had one nasal and several ophthalmic products, and it had reached almost $750,000 in sales. Schollmaier had briefly been a sales representative in the summer for William S. Merrell pharmaceutical company. Two years later, having chosen to enter the pharmaceutical industry, he secured interviews with five companies and sent a letter to Alcon. Conner invited him to visit with the proviso that trip expenses would be shared between other companies. Schollmaier arrived at the Public Market building and found Alcon's office upstairs. He had to wait while Conner cleared debris from his desk left over from when Fort Worth–based Air Force bombers rattled downtown. While waiting, he visited Andrews, whom he knew from Harvard. Andrews showed him fiscal records and explained how Alcon had recently averted bankruptcy by changing its bank. Once free, Conner proudly directed Schollmaier's attention to the drawing for Alcon's planned manufacturing complex displayed in his office. He boasted, "That's where we're going to be in three years." When asked if he had financing for the project, Conner pointed to a sales chart with a line going straight up and confidently declared that Alcon would grow sufficiently to ensure monies would be available. Taken on a tour of the existing premises, Schollmaier saw one large room with a manufacturing line around its perimeter. He visited the small, poorly equipped R&D building, where he found microscopes, homemade rabbit hutches, and

FIG 3.4
Ed Schollmaier and Rae Skinner, engagement, 1956. Ed is wearing in his US Coast Guard uniform.
(Courtesy of Taylor Schollmaier)

FIG 3.5
Ed Schollmaier with his first Alcon
company car, a VW Bug, 1958
(Courtesy of Taylor Schollmaier)

three men drinking coffee, so he joined them! As he left Alcon, Schollmaier decided that he had found the real world of new enterprise, and he departed from Fort Worth "brimming with excitement."[9]

Eager to hear about her husband's trip, Rae met him at the Boston airport, where he gave her his impression of Alcon. He had planned to consider each company's offer before they jointly made a decision, but Rae declared, "None of that is necessary … You've already decided … You are going to go with those crazy guys in Texas." Schollmaier rationalized that in sales you encountered reality, so in short order he would know if Alcon was viable or not. He accepted a salary of $5,400 and, because Alcon salesmen normally made only $4,800, agreed to keep the amount confidential. This situation rankled Alexander's secretary, Beverly Lasher, who refused to pay the higher amount until Alexander intervened. Consistent with Alcon's tightfisted policy, Schollmaier got a Volkswagen as his first company car (fig. 3.5). Requesting the most difficult territory, he was assigned western Pennsylvania under Leone, where fellow Harvard graduate Kleiman trained him. Schollmaier quickly learned real-world lessons that paid dividends for him and Alcon in the future.[10]

It is uncertain when Conner and Alexander first conceived Alcon's future campus for manufacturing, laboratories, and administration. By the time Conner showed architectural drawings of the new facility to Schollmaier, the vision was at least three years old (fig. 3.1). Alcon and two physicians purchased 175 acres of land south of downtown Fort Worth in 1955, and by 1958 architect John W. Floore had revised the plans three times. Company officials claimed Alcon grew "so fast that that the two earlier sets of Floore's plans were outmoded before construction could begin." Site surveys at Mead Johnson, Eli Lilly, and G. D. Searle by Carter, Floore, Joe Luttringer, and Dwight L. Deardorff, Alcon's consultant in pharmacy manufacturing, also brought improvements. Floore received $23,000, and Alcon signed a $1 million contract with Baughman Construction Company to build a three-building complex in phases—first, manufacturing; next, laboratories; then, administration.

Construction of the manufacturing plant was budgeted at $350,000. At a breakfast on June 14, 1958, the Fort Worth Chamber of Commerce recognized Alcon's achievements. That afternoon, Mayor John McCann and Chamber president Clay Berry joined Conner and Alexander in a groundbreaking ceremony for the twenty-thousand-square-foot building (fig. 3.6). Construction moved along uneventfully until December 1, when undefined problems arose with Baughman; Conner reported to his board that the situation was "quite grim." Alcon cancelled the existing contract and signed another with General Engineering Corporation of Fort Worth for an additional cost of $11,298. Amazingly, construction was completed on February 15, 1959, and after trial production runs, the new plant became operational on April 20 (fig. 3.7). The final cost totaled $405,000. During the dedication ceremonies on June 20 and 21, more than six hundred employees and guests toured the modern facility.[11]

The new building housed two production lines, a labeling area, warehouse, and shipping center. Alcon declared it to be "one of the nation's finest pharmaceutical manufacturing facilities of its kind." The production room walls were covered in ceramic tile to facilitate cleaning, sterilization, and maintenance. Westinghouse's Precipitron equipment in the air-conditioning and ventilation system used an electrostatic process that ionized particles, making the air in the production room free of dust, smoke, and bacteria. Alcon in-

FIG 3.6
Groundbreaking, manufacturing
building, June 1958 (CFP)

FIG 3.7
Alcon's new manufacturing
building, 1959 (AFP)

stalled a commercial-size steam and ethylene oxide gas sterilizer for bottles, Drop-tainers, equipment, and chemical compounds. It was the first sterilizer of its type in the Dallas–Fort Worth area. Initially, one of the production lines remained a manual operation, but the other was fully automated. The latter was designed so that hands touched Drop-tainers only twice while they were sorted, air-cleaned, sterilized, filled, plugged, capped, labeled, placed in vials, and packed in shipping cartons (figs. 3.8, 3.9). Drop-tainers were still sterilized by UV irradiation. The conveyor belt would weave back and forth under a clear plastic hood for thirty minutes in the sterilization room until the Drop-tainers passed into the filling room. Since it was located adjacent to a hallway lined with windows, visitors could see the automated line in operation, and many were brought to observe Alcon's state-of-the-art production.[12]

FIG 3.8
State-of-the-art filling machine designed by Alcon for Drop-tainer products, 1960 (AFP)

Carter collaborated with consulting engineers from Lyttleton Packaging Machinery Company, of Houston, and firms across the United States designed and manufactured components of the automated Drop-tainer production line: bottle sorter by US Engineering in Long Island; bottle cleaner, sterilizer, and filler by Karl Kiefer Machine Company in Cincinnati; plug inserter and capper by Consolidated Packaging Machinery in Buffalo; cellulose bander by Gisholt Machine Company in Madison; lateral-curve conveyor by Island Equipment Company in Miami; dryer by Miskella Infra-Red in Cleveland; and a thermoplastic labeler by New Jersey Machine Company in Newark. Drop-tainers were made of polyethylene by Plax in Hartford and Service Engineers in Fort Worth. Lone Star Plastics, also in Fort Worth, and Service Engineers supplied the polystyrene vials and caps. Coordinating these different sources must have been a great challenge. Nevertheless, all the equipment arrived on time and was installed more or less as planned.

With new technology came new problems. Drop-tainers tended to tip over when dropped onto the filling line, and the speed varied on the conveyor belt; nonetheless, oper-

FIG 3.9
Equipment to heat-shrink the cellulose seals of Drop-tainers, 1960 (AFP)

ators became adept at developing solutions to glitches. Sterility concerns surfaced periodically and were resolved after the air-conditioning system was modified. Luckily, Carter had anticipated troubles and ramped up production at the North Main facility so that by early 1959 there was a three-month surplus of inventory. In fact, it took two years to solve all problems, but once the system worked, fifty-five thousand units rolled off the line each day. For two decades, the Drop-tainer production line remained the crown jewel demonstrated during visitor tours (figs. 3.8, 3.9).[13]

In 1964, after continued sales growth, Alcon installed an automated line for Steri-units. Not only did output increase and cost decrease, Alcon improved quality. By now, more production lines, warehouse capacity, and loading docks were needed. Thus, construction commenced on April 15, 1964, expanding the facility from twenty thousand to thirty-six thousand square feet. The area used for labeling and storage was converted into zones for compounding, filling, and packaging. The new addition held quarantine space, a warehousing and shipping area, and loading docks with levelers and truck shelters. One key addition was a production line for ointments, since products were being developed in this format. Ointment manufacturing required specialized equipment for grinding, mixing, and blending ingredients, and extruding tools for filling the small tin tubes. An area with controlled-access quarantine space was partitioned into domestic and international sections to prevent mixing of products labeled in different languages. When the expansion was completed in mid-1965, Alcon stated that it would suffice for four to five years. However, in 1966 Alcon produced the Cryophake, a plastic device to freeze cataracts for easy removal. This unique ophthalmic surgical tool required a special area to be hand-assembled, sterilized, and packaged, so the manufacturing building was reconfigured again.[14]

In only eight years, from groundbreaking in 1958 to remodeling in 1966, Alcon's manufacturing capacity and sophistication increased exponentially. For about a $2.5 million investment, it had six automated lines—four for Drop-tainers, one each for Steri-units and ointments—and a special manual assembly system for the Cryophake. In total, a daytime crew working five days per week could produce about seventy million units each year.

In February 1959 Floore submitted drawings for laboratory and administration buildings, retaining the theme of a campus-like environment. He initially estimated construction costs at $400,000. However, Conner and others doubled the size of the laboratory to twelve thousand square feet, and by the time a cafeteria, large meeting room, and several more offices were added, the administration building measured twenty-two thousand square feet. Alcon selected Fort Worth's Porter Construction Company for the project. The total cost eventually grew to over $1 million dollars.

The changes delayed the groundbreaking for the laboratory building until February 16, 1960, and construction began in May. The specifications for each laboratory were challenging; each required access to water, natural gas, filtered compressed air, electricity, and a vacuum system. Some units needed extraction hoods vented to the exterior, while others required hoods equipped with laminar flow positive pressure air to prevent air from escaping. This prevented contamination and vented noxious substances to the exterior. Countertops had to be resistant to chemicals, and sturdy steel cabinets were needed (fig. 3.10). These requirements affected the foundation, floor coverings, ceilings, and exterior and interior walls. Additionally, animal rooms had special requirements for waste disposal and hygiene established by the US Department of Agriculture. The laboratory had only two ways to

FIG 3.10
Alcon R&D and QC laboratory, 1961
(AFP)

enter and exit, so the windows were designed to be easily pushed outward for emergency evacuation.

The laboratory was close to completion by January 1961; however, opening was delayed because the steel cabinets were backward and had to be remade before installation. Scientists finally relocated from the North Main facility in March (fig. 3.11). Despite the changes to the plans, the laboratory became inadequate within three years, so fourteen temporary buildings were positioned to the east. Each was about twenty-five feet long and ten feet wide and mostly housed pharmacologists, toxicologists, and administrative staff. By 1967, a new $1.5 million, 50,000-square-foot addition to the laboratory was being planned. To break ground on May 16, Conner, Alexander, and Dr. Earl Maxwell, Alcon's medical director, set off a small dynamite explosion. The enlarged facility, known as the Science and Technology Building contained quality control (QC) and R&D.[15]

The administration building was built at the same time as the laboratory (fig. 3.11). It was designed to house marketing, sales, and finance departments, as well as administrative personnel. One wing held executives' offices and the boardroom (fig. 3.12). The mahogany-paneled walls earned this area the nickname of "Mahogany Row," while the

boardroom had small, backlit cupboards that displayed art by Emil G. Bethke. Because of the remoteness of the campus and the lack of nearby restaurants, a cafeteria was added, and immediately behind it a very large meeting room. Along the northern perimeter, a large room with an elevated floor housed Alcon's IBM 407 and IBM 1400s, to which access was controlled. These stood about six feet tall and generated excessive heat, so they needed additional air-conditioning. There were three garden areas. Two lined both sides of the executive wing and were accessible by sliding glass doors. Bordering the entrance atrium to the west and computer room to the south, the architects laid out a twenty-yard square for a landscaped garden (fig. 3.13). Once established, mature trees shaded benches inside ivy-clad walls. Floore created a very functional, architecturally significant design in the mid-century modern style that at the time was recognized as a local treasure. That being said, Alcon's new, modern facilities belied the fact that the company's future was in jeopardy.[16]

Alcon had borrowed money and sold company stock to fund the almost $2 million spent on the new campus, but a debt of $600,000 remained. Sales for 1960 and 1961 were

FIG 3.12
First directors meeting in new boardroom, administration building, 1961. Note the Emil G. Bethke paintings inset in the wall. *Left to right:* Bob Alexander, James Walker, Walter West, Bill Connor, DeWitt Neighbors, Ed Keltner, Harold Johnson, Harold Beasley. (AFP)

FIG 3.13
Landscaped garden, administration building, 1961 (AFP)

stagnant at $3 million, and other financial indices were not reassuring. Working capital had decreased from $532,000 to $186,000 and cash on hand from $355,000 to $119,00, while accounts payable grew from $80,000 to $194,000 and accounts receivable plus inventories totaled $589,000 and $661,000. The current ratio (the ability to generate cash to pay debts) of 1.3:1 in 1961 was the lowest since the company's early years. Moreover, in nine of the ten districts, sales fell precipitously by the start of 1961. A new approach to marketing Alconefrin had led salesmen to quit in frustration and wholesalers to return Alcon products. Disaster loomed.[17]

From the beginning, Alconefrin had been the company's top seller but it was regionally distributed and competed in a crowded market. Harold Johnson and Alcon's advertising manager, Joseph P. Floyd, hired the Chicago agency of Jordan, Sieber & Corbett to propose a marketing campaign for the product. Their plan shipped family packs of Alconefrin to wholesalers and directed salesmen to ignore ophthalmologists and focus on pediatricians and general practitioners. Skilled at distribution, the sales force jammed the wholesalers with Alconefrin, but the plan was not as successful with doctors or pharmacies. Schollmaier explained, "Of course, calling on the pediatricians and GPs was tough. First, they didn't know us. Second, they had too many reps calling on them. Then, when we did get in to see them, they didn't have any use for what we had. The last thing in the world they wanted was to be detailed on another nose drop." Moving Alconefrin to pharmacy shelves was equally frustrating. Sales representatives were soon exhausted, physically and mentally. Several quit.[18]

After Schollmaier spent eleven months in western Pennsylvania, Alcon sent him to California to boost struggling sales there. He quickly made an impact and in May 1960 became the district manager for California, Oregon, Utah, and Washington. Early the next year, he was promoted again, to division manager, and asked to relocate to Fort Worth. The day he checked in, Lasher told him Alexander would be unavailable for a few days due to meeting with Conner. She gave him documents to review that were astounding: "Things at Alcon were going to hell in a handbasket. The company was really hitting the wall." Nine of the ten districts reported sales decreases, yet expenses were climbing. Only when Schollmaier finally talked to Alexander did he understand: the new directives for Alconefrin sales were destroying the company, and Alexander and Conner did not agree on how to solve the problem. Alexander wanted to abandon the program; Conner thought it might still work.

Schollmaier got to work. First, he addressed the demands of wholesalers, who wanted to return surplus stock but had been ignored by Alcon. He negotiated with them and reported to Alexander, telling him that Alcon *had to* focus on ophthalmologists and cut expenses. Given ten minutes to present his case to Conner, Schollmaier emphasized, "We're losing the great momentum we've gained with the ophthalmologists. Sir ... we are going to hit the wall at full speed." The conversation reveals the path for Alcon's future success. Conner said, "You'd get right back to the ophthalmologists, would you. ... I guess we could start adding them right away." Schollmaier responded, "No sir, when we go back, we should *only* go to ophthalmologists. That has to be defined as the business of the company."[19]

Shortly thereafter, Conner scheduled a meeting at the historic Baker Hotel in Mineral Wells, sixty miles west of Fort Worth. Conner, Alexander, Floyd, Merrill, Carter, Andrews, and Maxwell met there one Friday; Schollmaier was also invited. The meeting had no agenda, and the discussion initially drifted. Unable to contain his emotions, Schollmaier blurted, "Look, I don't even know why I'm here but I've got to tell you what I'm thinking. Let's cut all this crap about getting along. I'm going to assume that we're going to try to get along. But we've got to do the right things and face this issue of hitting the wall and dramatically cutting expenses. We've got to redirect the sales force. We have to know how many salesmen we can afford and then we've got to pay them right." That evening, Conner asked Schollmaier to join him on a stroll, during which he peppered the younger man with questions. Conner concluded, "Okay. Joe Floyd and Harold Johnson are gone. I'm going to direct Bob Alexander to immediately instigate a program to work ophthalmologists only and to stabilize the sales force." Alcon's Black Friday ended its precipitous tumble.[20]

Alexander ordered Schollmaier back to California to temporarily replace Dave Smith, who had been fired. He and Bill Darling, the Southern California district manager, fired the nine salesmen in the Los Angeles area. The two of them then called on ophthalmologists and wholesalers and, in the process, Schollmaier worked out a new sales program to promote each Alcon product. With the approval of Alexander and Conner, he developed another plan to train and supervise the sales force as it rebuilt. Meanwhile, regional managers replaced poorly performing salesmen and district managers. Alcon's procedures revitalized the sales hierarchy, from regional managers to district managers to sales representatives.

Although the regional managers were excellent salesmen, Schollmaier saw flaws in how they transmitted information to their teams. Emmett Beaven and his Midwest team were the first to have Schollmaier attend their meeting. Conner and Alexander came, too. Beaven led a disorganized meeting, and after a couple of hours Alexander and Conner determined that Schollmaier had to chair the proceedings. Alexander called the eastern regional manager, Leone, and Howard Clemmons, who ran the southern region, and informed them Schollmaier would also chair their meetings (fig. 3.14). Over two weeks, Alcon entirely reoriented to concentrate on ophthalmologists. Recalling 1961, Leone admitted, "Before we had weathered the storm, the company was in real danger of collapsing." The recollection of Richard "Dick" H. Sisson was vivid: "Alcon was very lucky it didn't go under. Knowing what I know today, the chances of Alcon making it couldn't have been more than 25 percent."[21]

Schollmaier's refocusing program quickly proved effective: annual sales in 1962 grew by 27 percent ($825,497) to $3,882,896. New York sales representative Andrew "Andy" A. Lubrano is a good example. As a top producer in 1961, he sold $8,000 in products, but his 1962 sales to-

FIG 3.14
Ed Schollmaier after Black Friday, leading the discussion at a district meeting, 1961 (AHR)

taled $38,000. Alcon's dire straits never became public. Nevertheless, the 1960 and 1961 annual reports reveal the magnitude of the threat. On May 1, 1961, sales, trade relations, and advertising were consolidated into a single marketing and sales department under Alexander, with Schollmaier reporting to him. In looking back over the first fifty years of Alcon, one can see events that truly affected the company. Black Friday is one—Alcon averted disaster by refocusing on ophthalmologists.[22]

Alcon's directors periodically considered the value of the firm's stock. In 1955 Alcon sold three hundred thousand shares at three dollars each to raise money to buy the property south of Fort Worth. Conner proposed issuing additional shares to fund construction. Until May 1958 he found buyers for shares sold by the company or individual investors, but this took much of his time. On January 27, 1958, he proposed that Alcon sell enough stock to raise $68,000, then borrow $550,000 and immediately issue more shares. He mentioned one hundred thousand shares as a possible issue, but because Alcon was limited by the state to no more than eighty investors, he admitted that might be too ambitious. Alcon worked with a local broker to sell new OTC shares and the existing stock of current investors. By May 1958 Barron McCulloch of Fort Worth, a member of the Investment Bankers

Association of America, began OTC trading of Alcon stock. Newspapers such as the *Fort Worth Star-Telegram* posted daily share prices for "Alcon Lab." The first was $5 offered and $5.50 asked. Thus, Alcon directors now had a real sense of the value of their shares. In July, Alexander sold twenty-five hundred shares through Barron McCulloch, while the board gave Conner the authority to sell ten thousand of his shares in small lots to keep the OTC market alive.[23]

Seeking funds to construct the new manufacturing plant, Conner met in 1958 with Kidder Peabody & Company of Chicago. Their proposal was to (1) borrow $350,000 on a twenty-year note at 5¾ percent interest; (2) sell 20,000 shares at $5 per share; and (3) issue $100,000 in debentures that could be converted to approximately 18,182 shares ($5.50 per share). The TSC approved this proposal in September. Kidder Peabody actually oversubscribed, selling twenty-eight thousand shares for $140,000 and raising $110,000 from the debentures, and negotiated a $325,000 loan from the American National Life Insurance Company. In June the stockholders authorized amending Alcon's charter to issue one million shares at a par value of fifty cents and to allow existing shares to be exchanged on a one-to-one basis. This gave Alcon flexibility to raise money by selling or trading stock. In order to establish a national market for Alcon shares, the board authorized management to issue three thousand to five thousand shares every six months. Conner predicted the first tranche would sell for $5 per share; with good sales and profits, the price would rise to $10 in two years and $20 by five years. Members of the board agreed to periodically send Kidder Peabody a few hundred of their shares to be sold OTC. Initially, the stock's value hovered at about $5 per share, and it remained between $15 and $31 through 1966. By the end of 1967, investors had driven the price up to $51 per share.[24]

Alcon did not have a formal employee or executive stock option plan. With Alcon shares being sold OTC in late 1958, the board considered an employee and executive stock option plan. The matter resurfaced in March 1959 and, after much discussion, the board agreed to offer executives and department heads two hundred shares, and twenty-five to one hundred shares to all other employees who were on the payroll as of May 4. The plan was delayed while the TSC approved it. During this period, the directors debated the offer price as the share value had appreciated to $12. Eventually, a maximum of twelve thousand shares at $8 each was set aside for employees to buy with funds withheld from their paychecks. The plan began in 1960, when 9,865 shares were distributed.

Alcon by 1960 had several possibilities for funding the $1 million construction cost of their new facility: a loan, selling OTC equity, employee stock options, or profits. The board also considered creating the Alcon Park Company, of which Alcon would own 37 percent and John A. Wiggins Jr., a director and physician, and his partner would hold the other 63 percent. This land development entity could borrow money to construct buildings and lease to Alcon. Fortunately, Alcon cobbled together funding from employee stock options and profits, thus avoiding additional debt. Stock options continued annually; by 1967 the company had offered options for almost one hundred thousand shares. If a person bought one thousand shares at $8 each in 1960, their value appreciated to $50,000 by the end of 1967. When Alcon decided to double its manufacturing space and install more filling and labeling lines, it funded a portion of the almost $2 million expense from profits and stock sales, including to employees. Additionally, the company planned to fund the expansion of its laboratory facility without borrowing. By the close of 1967, Alcon's long-term debt stood at a manageable $198,000.[25]

Immediately following Black Friday, Conner became uncharacteristically reflective and spent a few weeks walking the beaches near Galveston. Alcon had committed to becoming a powerhouse in the ophthalmic pharmaceutical business, but the pace needed to accelerate. He returned to Fort Worth determined to acquire other medical specialty companies, which Andrews supported since acquisitions would immediately increase sales. In a September 1961 letter to stockholders, Conner explained the new strategy: "This is the first move under a 10-year plan developed by your directors in recent months and adopted late in August. Even as expansion of our present interests continues, we are initiating this new plan for additional growth through acquisition of a number of existing enterprises. Considered for acquisition will be companies whose technology and marketing requirements overlap Alcon's present operations and know-how."[26]

One acquisition avenue emerged from Johnson's promotion efforts before his departure. Johnson had presented Alcon's eye medications at veterinary meetings and sent product information on possible uses to graduating veterinarians, giving each a copy of the Alcon-published *Canine Ophthalmology*, by Russell J. Beamer, a Texas A&M University professor. Globe Laboratories, a forty-year-old veterinary pharmaceutical company with annual sales of about $2 million, had its facilities on the north side of Fort Worth. Conner had it in his sights when, in August 1961, Pfizer Pharmaceutical Company announced plans to buy it in exchange for 45,000 shares. On September 18, a few days before Globe's stockholders meeting, Alcon offered 120,000 shares worth $2.4 million. Pfizer matched Alcon's bid and bought Globe. While this first attempt failed, the episode indicated Conner's newfound zeal to acquire companies.[27]

Service Engineers, founded in 1946 in Midland, moved its operations in 1960 to Fort Worth, where it developed and manufactured plastic products for pharmaceutical and cosmetic industries. It used injection blow molding technology to produce a precise dimension for the neck of polyethylene containers, like the Drop-tainer. Plax Corporation, a DuPont subsidiary, was Alcon's main supplier of bottles and plugs for Drop-tainers, but once manufacturers began selling liquid soap in plastic bottles, Alcon found that Plax and other vendors rejected their small orders. Acquiring a plastic company appeared to be the best option, leading Alcon to buy Service Engineers in February 1962 for $325,000 (12,550 shares at $26 per share). It seemed an ideal partnership. Alcon now owned a reliable source for a key component, and Service Engineers had a diverse product line for other industries. Service Engineers operated as a wholly owned subsidiary of Alcon and kept its own identity and management.[28]

The purchase also seemed propitious for another reason. On October 10, 1962, President Kennedy signed the Kefauver-Harris amendments to the Food, Drug, and Cosmetic (FD&C) Act. Of the new requirements for registering and selling a new drug in the United States, one instructed the FDA to "conduct a retrospective evaluation of the effectiveness of drugs approved for safety—but not for effectiveness—between 1938 and 1962." This applied to all Alcon products. Emerging in the scientific literature at the time were studies on the interaction of drugs with plastic containers, specifically the mold release agent zinc stearate. This meant Alcon R&D had to acquire new analytical technology and hire chemists, formulators, packing engineers, and toxicologists in a long-term reformulation program. The new regulations also extended to plastic companies such as Service Engineers. Thus, in 1963 Service Engineers embarked on its own R&D program. For a few years it remained Alcon's sole supplier of the Drop-tainer, but Alcon also collaborated with other manufacturers in the United States.[29]

Service Engineers endeavored to expand its product lines to larger-size plastic containers and bought new equipment for that purpose. This enhanced capability proved invaluable when Alcon developed and launched the Cryophake, a cataract extraction device. This handheld appliance consisted of two polypropylene halves clamped together. Service Engineers made the two halves, and the instrument was assembled in Alcon's manufacturing plant. According to Alcon's annual reports, Service Engineers struggled to grow, which forced a leadership change in January 1966. In the hope of expanding distribution, in December 1966 Service Engineers purchased Polyco from Scientific-Atlanta. An Atlanta- and New Orleans-based company, Polyco manufactured plastic containers larger than those produced by Service Engineers.[30]

In the same request to the TSC to use shares to buy Service Engineers in 1962, Alcon also sought permission to issue seventy-five thousand shares at $26 per share to purchase Chicago Pharmacal. Conner flew to Chicago in February and signed the almost $2 million deal. Founded in 1855, Chicago Pharmacal sold urological pharmaceuticals domestically and abroad. Because it formulated unique medicines for individual physicians to prescribe, the firm had over five hundred products in its inventory. Alexander devised a marketing plan, but within a year it was clear several products had to be discontinued to enhance profits. Alexander and Ted Fleming reduced the product line to one hundred. Later, Fleming, working with FDA guidelines and a urologist, cut that number to ten, including the leading seller, Urised, a medicine that treated urinary infections. Urised tablets contained methylene blue, hyoscyamine, atropine, methenamine, phenyl salicylate, and benzoic acid. This combination was anticholinergic, anti-infective, and analgesic and was useful during pregnancy. Alcon also initiated a urological R&D program and improved quality by buying new manufacturing equipment. In 1964 Alcon changed the name of Chicago Pharmacal to Conal, introduced a new logo, and created a smaller sales force. The next year, Lyons was relocated from Fort Worth to be the Conal general manager, extending reforms, further rationalizing products, and initiating programs in advertising and training. Conal then launched four new products, including Cystospaz.[31]

New product sales did not influence the overall figures for 1965 as anticipated, but Alcon's 1966 annual report was more optimistic. Sales for Urised, "a familiar standby for many years," increased. Urologists' reluctance to accept Conal faded as the sales force concentrated on attending medical meetings, much like Alcon had done in the 1950s. According to Alcon's 1967 annual report, "Intensified marketing efforts, better training of salesmen, and continued support of urologists' professional organizations all combined to make the year Conal's most successful." This optimistic statement belies the significant challenges that Lyons and Conal had encountered. Anestacon, a local anesthetic designed for easy delivery into the urethra, was launched with the expectation it would become one of Conal's leading therapeutics. The complex manufacturing process required an experienced hand, so Floyd Powell, a manager in Alcon's production facility, was sent to Conal to take charge of their plant. Transferring Alcon's winning strategy for ophthalmology to the urology specialists proved difficult, but Urised, which Powell accurately identified as "the big one," became the product that sustained Conal.[32]

Buoyed by the success of new products (Zolyse, Cryophake, and BSS) for ophthalmic surgeons, Alcon searched for an acquisition opportunity to augment its surgical line. The quest ultimately led to Lawton Company of New York. In late 1967 Alcon purchased the closely held company for $2 million plus twelve thousand shares, planning to operate it as a wholly owned subsidiary. Lawton imported precision stainless-steel surgical instruments manufactured in Europe, mainly by artisans in Germany. Some of these were used by ocular surgeons, but most of the instruments listed in the Lawton catalog were designed for other surgical specialties. In their 577-page 1967 catalog, only eighty-three pages listed instruments for the eye surgeon.[33]

As noted earlier, Conner's decision to expand Alcon included a shift in the board of directors. When Alcon was incorporated in 1947, there were fourteen investors—Conner, Alexander, Johnson, and eleven medical doctors. As president, Conner organized a board meeting almost every month. Transcripts reveal the collegial nature of these. Conner set the agenda, but discussions often included many other issues. The original board was composed of the initial investors, but in 1950 the core membership of Drs. James N. Walker, Walter B. West, DeWitt Neighbors, and John A. Wiggins Jr. expanded to include Dr. C. Harold Beasley as ophthalmology consultant and Ed Keltner Jr. as Alcon's legal counsel. Prominent local businessmen Karl E. Rotegard and Bernard P. Rosen joined the board for short terms. Keltner fondly recalled, "It was a very close-knit group. Our board meetings were fun: there was a lot of give and take. The doctors were excited about Alcon's prospects and the atmosphere was buoyant. Those were happy days."[34]

From 1959 through 1967, Conner, Alexander, Beasley, Wiggins, Neighbors, and Keltner served continuously on the board. Andrews joined as Alcon's CFO, as did Glenn M. Wilkins, the vice president of administrative affairs. But when OTC trading began in 1958, a more formalized election of members was mandated by law, and the board shifted from being a collegial group of peers into a more typical panel of experienced business executives or educators acting as advisors. Gene E. Engleman, chair of the board of the Texas Consumer Finance Corporation, began his term with Alcon in 1961. He described himself as a "professional director and consultant to top management." An active participant in Fort Worth's civic and social scene, D. O. Tomlin, CEO of the Acme Brick Corporation and the First Worth Corporation, joined Alcon's board with Engleman. John D. Glover, on the Harvard faculty, represented academia. His focus was strategic management and corporate administration. Time at Harvard was a common factor of board members; Engleman and Tomlin were both graduates. In fact, of the 1967 board, six of the eleven had attended Harvard. While this gave the board some continuity in thought, the fact that six of the eleven directors had served continuously from 1950 added stability. And the few meeting minutes that survive from this decade indicate that the dominant voice remained Conner's.[35]

The sales force underwent a similar transformation. Alexander supervised sales in 1958, giving much freedom and responsibility to the division managers. There were four: Leone managed Division A, the northeastern United States down through North Carolina; Beaven handled Division B, the Midwest; Clemmons led Division C, Texas and the South; and Smith supervised Division D, Colorado to the Pacific Ocean. Each trained his own team, but on occasions salesmen attended training seminars in Fort Worth. Some of Alcon's sales representatives were pharmacists, and most had a university degree. Alcon training began with calling on ophthalmologists. Provided with product information, the salesman had three minutes to convince the doctor to prescribe the medication. Salesmen were also responsible for ensuring that wholesalers and pharmacies were fully stocked with products. In addition, they were expected to call on hospitals and fill their dispensaries. In Leone's thickly populated territory, Lubrano visited the large hospitals in New York City.

In April 1958 in a new special program, salesmen became the middlemen between pharmacies and wholesalers. They called on pharmacies to obtain orders, which they took to wholesalers. Each sale was recorded in a Kardex system kept in the home office. It was a valuable resource for monitoring product users, buying habits, back-ordered items, and returned goods. With such information, the sales force could react to market shifts. Alcon always recognized its best sales representatives with bonuses for increased sales. However, in 1959, Alcon introduced "Operation Red Carpet," whereby the top sales performer in each division and their spouse enjoyed a weeklong Caribbean cruise.[36]

Even the best sometimes struggled. Schollmaier gave a frank account of his first attempt at the three-minute sales pitch:

> Herb Kleiman came in to train me after I'd been in the territory a couple of weeks. I'd been studying some anatomy and other things to try to get myself trained, but I was still very, very green. We called on a doctor, a really nice guy. … I gave him the best sales pitch I could. I used one single-page, laminated visual aid, and I gave him a very bad presentation. That was the best I could do! Kleiman and I went to lunch and he said, "Tell me where you failed in that doctor call." I said, "Herb, I want to tell you something. As bad as that call was, I didn't fail." "Why not?" "Because the guy liked me and he realized I was doing the best I could do. He's going to give us some business." Kleiman reacted like, *"How am I going to train you if you're such an idiot?"*

In California, Schollmaier did better by keeping his speech brief:

"I'm not going to spend a lot of time on the product line now—I'll give you a listing of the products—but let me feature just one detail for you." And I pulled out a bottle of Isopto Carpine. I said, "See this green cap?" And I unscrewed it. It had a green plug. I put it back in my pocket and got another. Isopto Atropine. It had a red cap and a red plug. Then I said, "Why do we do this? We do this so some idiot in the pharmacy can't mix them up. Thank you very much for your time and I hope we might have a few minutes to visit next time."

Impressed, the doctor invited Schollmaier into his office and, after a short talk, agreed to prescribe Alcon's products. Alcon had configured the Drop-tainer package as a safety valve for the patient, pharmacist, and doctor, and this facilitated Schollmaier's three-minute sale.[37]

New sales representatives were hired nearly every month in 1958, 1959, and 1960, so that by January 1961 there were nearly one hundred in the field, almost a threefold increase from thirty-seven in April 1959. Many of these stayed a long time. One of Schollmaier's hires, Sisson, developed an effective strategy for selling to pharmacies. He would gain access to the storage shelves where he removed out-of-date medications, crediting their cost, and updated the inventory, giving the pharmacist information on the latest marketing program. He usually sold twelve to fifteen products on each call.[38]

Until December 1959 sales meetings were held by region, with Alexander traveling between them. Often, someone from advertising and promotion joined these sessions, described products to be emphasized, and discussed materials to be used. This practice changed with Alcon's first national sales conference, which took place December 13–19, 1959, at Fort Worth's legendary Western Hills Hotel. Eighty-three sales representatives heard a program from advertising manager Floyd. The salesmen role-played as one method of implementing the new program. Sisson, who had been an employee for one month before the conference, recalled, "I had never seen such a motley crew of guys in my life. I just wondered where in the world did they get these people? I couldn't believe it. Everything was pretty chaotic because a lot of people at that meeting had just been hired, so they didn't know a thing about Alcon or any of Alcon's products. Of the 65 people I bet 35 or 40 were brand new." Nevertheless, Conner and Alexander considered the meeting to be a success, claiming that "by bringing together all field personnel and home office staff personnel, a new awareness of mutual resources, needs and responsibilities had been brought about." The conference concluded with Alcon's annual Christmas party. To accommodate more than two hundred people, it was held at the Glen Garden Country Club. Henceforth, national sales meetings were held annually, mostly in Fort Worth.[39]

Black Friday in 1961 resulted in almost 40 percent of Alcon's sales force resigning or being terminated. Smith was fired, leaving Darling and Schollmaier to reorganize Division D, reducing it by nine salesmen. The largest wholesaler in the territory threatened to return $20,000 of Alcon products. Schollmaier and Darling negotiated one month in which to restart the flow of prescriptions from ophthalmologists. Within weeks, the warehouse was depleted of several products, resulting in Alcon's largest invoice to date, for $20,000. This success was more or less repeated nationwide. In 1962 sales for ophthalmic medications increased 27 percent ($825,497), and the sales force was back to about eighty men by the end of the year. About Black Friday, Leone remembered, "That was a very bad mistake and I attribute that they didn't have a sophisticated enough board to know what the hell they were getting into in the field." With western sales stabilized, Schollmaier returned to Fort Worth and placed in charge of marketing, and Leone came to Fort Worth and became national sales director in 1963. Alexander continued to supervise both operations.[40]

Leone ran a "tight ship" and upon arrival got rid of several "dunderheads." He had attended the AMP in 1959, which influenced his strategy. He kept the four existing geographic regions, each overseen by a regional manager who supervised two or three district managers. Each district had six or so medical sales representatives (MSRs), a new title for salesmen. He moved the regional managers to Fort Worth to help him prepare annual plans and set long-term strategies. In addition to supervising district managers and creating training programs, district managers hired, supervised, and trained MSRs, who called on physicians, pharmacies, hospitals, and wholesalers. Regional managers coordinated with marketing on product launches and programs. This included Alcon's presence at medical and pharmacy conferences (fig. 3.15), the most important remained the annual meeting of the AAOO. Leone's core strategy was creating demand, getting ophthalmologists to prescribe more of Alcon's products. Conversely, Schollmaier, in marketing, stressed the importance of distribution to wholesalers and pharmacies. Leone and Schollmaier saw their collaborations as a win-win, and their professional and personal relationship thrived. In fact, Alcon's sales organization from 1963 through 1967 became a case study at Harvard.[41]

In addition to rebuilding and reorienting Alcon's sales force, Leone faced what he considered to be an unacceptably high rate of MSR turnover; one year, it reached 42 percent. District managers spent much time recruiting, leaving little time for training or supervising.

FIG 3.15
Alcon MSRs and product displays
at a medical meeting, 1957 (AFP)

Medical Meetings

About thirty national and regional medical meetings help constantly widen interest in Alcon's Rhinologic and Sterile Ophthalmic Specialties.

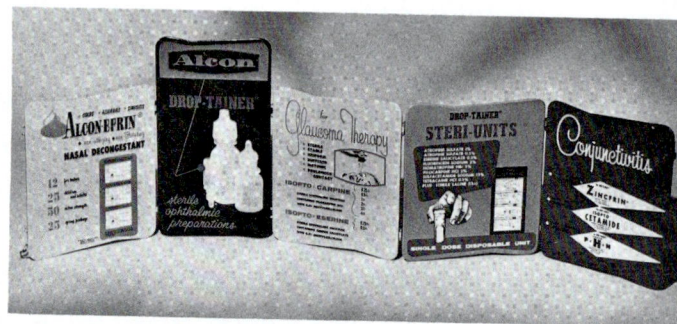

Special portable displays are used in hospitals and small group meetings.

In 1964 Alcon created the Advanced Development Program, a self-study available to any district manager or MSR. The success of the program became clear in 1967, when Leone reported that four of the best district managers were products of the training. He also examined the MSR compensation package and over the years substantially increased base salaries to be more in line with other pharmaceutical companies. Alcon's long-standing commission policy for MSRs was modified, making it more equitable for those with large territories. Nevertheless, Leone commented that 20 percent of the sales force earned 80 percent of the commissions, meaning that one-fifth of the MSRs produced the best sales results. By 1967, thirty-eight MSRs had been hired and retained, reflecting the success of Leone's changes and stabilizing the sales force.[42]

Selling pharmaceuticals is difficult, as documented by the recollections of Schollmaier, Leone, Sisson, and others. Since a physician does not buy a product directly from Alcon, the satisfaction of a sale does not occur in the doctor's office. It is only later, when distributors orders and reorders a product, that an MSR knows they succeeded. Many of the best MSRs were promoted to Alcon's headquarters. Among those in 1967 were Keith A. Lane Jr., William "Roy" M. Buchanan, Ralph L. Bunker, Andy Lubrano, Glenn E. Rickey, John W. Spruill, and Norbert J. Walter. Others stayed in the field for their entire Alcon career. These included Robert W. Ritchey, John A. Mercer, Albert A. Sims, John A. Fitch Jr., Reginald O. Jennings, John Mrozek, Jerold I. Nisenbaum, Samuel Vicari, and Dennis R. Cavanaugh. Working the same territory for twenty-five years or more and building relationships made these MSR's highly productive, and their value cannot be overstated.[43]

Schollmaier's marketing department evolved from the advertising group after Floyd and Johnson left. Initially, he profiled each product for Conner, Alexander, and the division managers; then he did the same in a series of public posters sent to over five thousand pharmacies. In one, he described the disease and symptoms of glaucoma. In 1962 he expanded this into Alcon's first *Product Reference Guide*, a small, twenty-nine-page booklet. Each product's main attribute was stated in one sentence, followed by summaries of the drug's advantages, indications, compositions, cautions, dosages, availability, and references. One, for example, was an insert for Alcon's new anti-inflammatory therapy, Maxidex. Reproduced by the thousands, the booklet was given by MSRs to doctors, hospitals, pharmacies, and wholesalers, and distributed at medical and scientific conferences. It was also a handy training and reference tool for Alcon's staff. The marketing department updated the guide in 1964 but kept the eye-catching blue cover of the first edition. It is worthwhile noting that this distinctive shade of blue became the Alcon blue in letterheads, advertisements, the company logo, and anywhere its name appeared.[44]

Schollmaier contracted with a new advertising agency—Kallir, Philips, Ross. John Kallir had brought his experience in pharmaceuticals to Gerald "Jerry" Philips and Warren Ross when he joined their organization shortly before meeting Schollmaier. Schollmaier recalled, "We were their first client. They were brilliant, a breath of fresh air in contrast to the idiots we had worked with before who had gotten the company all screwed up." Ross personally worked on Alcon's campaigns: "Those were great years. There were fine new products, successful campaigns, productive meetings, good people to work with—we all had fun." He credited Schollmaier for team spirit and for treating him and his partners as equals. Kallir, Philips, Ross remained the Ophthalmic Division's advertising agency until 1980. To illustrate his importance, Ross was inducted into Alcon's Hall of Fame in 1988.[45]

Reporting to Schollmaier were product managers responsible for preparing visual and printed materials and organizing marketing campaigns for each product. Len Schweitzer became Alcon's first product manager in 1963. His employment interview was typical of many at the time. An Army veteran and graduate of City College of New York, Schweitzer had advertising experience with Ross Laboratories. Laid off, he interviewed with Kallir, Philips, Ross, who gave his name to Schollmaier. A few days later, Schollmaier invited him to Fort Worth. Despite the hot July day, he was impressed by Alcon's "beautiful, contemporary, fairly new building." After a day and half, which included an interview with Conner, Schweitzer, awestruck by Alcon and Schollmaier, accepted a job. His first assignment was a promotion for Alcon's premier glaucoma therapy, Isopto Carpine. Howard F. Fleischer and Norman R. Dewar, a 1960 Harvard graduate and Pfizer advertising manager, joined the marketing group in 1964.

Working with Kallir, Philips, Ross, in 1965 Alcon's marketing department devised a program book for the launch of Maxitrol, a steroid-antibiotic therapy. For fifteen weeks, Maxitrol was the first product profiled to ophthalmologists in MSRs' three-minute pitch. The naming of Maxitrol began a trend; it was among the first of many brand names that Schollmaier conceived, and the product paved Alcon's way into markets all over the world. It also received a substantial portion of the company's advertising budget. In 1964 an innovative marketing scheme used the Excerpta Medica Foundation in the Netherlands to distribute the Alcon-sponsored *Glaucoma Review*, published six times per year. In 1966 all Alcon's glaucoma products were packaged together, and the "Glaucoma Therapy Tray" was delivered by MSRs to ophthalmologists. Schollmaier sensed that the global glaucoma market would soon become the largest segment in the ophthalmic therapeutic arena.[46]

Alcon periodically used competitions as a means of encouraging MSRs and engaging ophthalmologists. The Caribbean cruise for the best salesman was an example. More commonly, rewards comprised everyday items such as typewriters, coffee makers, briefcases, clock radios, and cameras. Cash, usually twenty dollars, was awarded for providing the best answer to a "Detailing Dilemma." Having a product prescribed was the goal with ophthalmologists, and Alcon kept a list of physicians with contact information for award offers. More unique programs included the Maxitrol photograph contest and golf benefit. Not only were Maxitrol-embossed golf balls and other equipment distributed, the winner was brought to Fort Worth to attend the Colonial Country Club tournament and a $300 donation was made to a medical institution in the winner's name. Smaller donations were also made in the names of the second, third, and fourth runners-up. All participating physicians received preprinted Maxitrol prescription pads.[47]

A year after Schollmaier and Leone settled at Alcon's new campus, the board appointed the former as general manager of Alcon, responsible for domestic marketing and sales and coordination with the medical and laboratory departments. Thus, Leone reported to Schollmaier. In 1967 Schollmaier appointed Leone as the director of marketing and sales, and Clemmons replaced Leone as national sales manager. As a consequence, beginning in 1964 and continuing for a few years, marketing and sales merged into the same group. One feature of Alcon was that its organization was fluid, adjusting to needs, personalities, and events. From this era, the marketing staff who stayed at Alcon for the duration of their careers included Schollmaier, Leone, Sisson, Schweitzer, Fleischer, Clemmons, Richard J. Hedlund, Martha Calkins, Jo Kent, Edward A. Paule, and James Bond.[48]

Since arriving in 1957, Harvey Andrews had participated in many corporate and board decisions. He became vice president for finance and a director in 1965. Andrews managed billing, payroll, personnel, the PBX (Alcon's private telephone network), computer systems, treasurer functions, the mailroom, and other duties. He had expanded the finance department, bringing in William R. Glover Jr. in 1960, Wayne McDonald and Milton Barley in 1962, and Charles R. Oster in 1965. Lyons joined the group in 1959. McDonald, Barley, and Oster made a career at Alcon. They formed the nucleus of the finance department and spread into numerous subsidiaries, plants, and countries. By 1966 several others in the department played key roles in finance or other parts of the company: Sandy Howell, Marva Clynch, Pat Cameron, Joyce Moore, Diane Stegall, Elva Wells, and Barbara Alice Williford. The entire workforce relied on these long-term employees; after all, their paychecks depended on them.[49]

Andrews established Alcon's first computer systems department, today known as information technology (IT). University of Texas at Arlington computer science student George A. Kuras set up Alcon's first IT department and, after he graduated in 1960, became its manager. IT analyst Johnny W. Hammonds kept the mainframe computers operating. At the Henderson Street office building, Alcon installed a punch-card-reading IBM 402 and IBM 407 in 1960. The latter was big, so the roof had to be partially removed to put it on the second floor. Wells used both to process orders and invoices. Computer-generated sales data, inventories, and cost reports replaced the monthly drudgery of typing tables. Kuras and Lyons, of the finance department, collaborated with architects in designing a computer room for the new administration building. It had high ceilings and an elevated floor; removable floor tiles allowed for servicing and expanding communication cables and electrical circuits. Alcon used its modern computer system for many financial functions, and Lyons worked with Carter in manufacturing to overcome production glitches. Alcon's first-generation IT system in the "old computer room" remained functional until it was updated with an IBM mainframe 370-148 in the mid-1970s.[50]

The executive department emerged in February 1966 when Alcon hired Glenn M. Wilkins as administrative corporate vice president, joining Conner and Alexander as executives. A Coast Guard veteran and SMU graduate, Wilkins had spent time with nonprofit organizations; for the previous seven years he had been executive director of Tarrant County's United Way. Schollmaier recalled that Conner wanted someone to relieve him of many administrative duties. Wilkins, who joined the board of directors, managed Alcon's external public relations and regulatory affairs.[51]

Vincent Juliano, the first salesman hired by Leone, became Alcon's first full-time employee outside the United States. In May 1958 Alexander brought five salesmen to the North Main facility in Fort Worth, where each met separately with him and Conner. Alexander asked them about their interest in working in Canada. Juliano was interested but asked for time to call his wife before he committed to a start date. Returning from the call, Juliano said he could be there in two weeks, which stunned Conner and Alexander since the other men would only commit to being there in a few months. Alcon approved Juliano's $23,000 plan, and he moved his family to Don Mills, a Toronto neighborhood, in the first week of June. Alcon authorized Juliano and his wife to sign checks on the company account at Canadian banks. Juliano registered Alcon's products in Canada and began calling on ophthalmologists, pharmacies, and wholesalers. Driving a six-cylinder station wagon with a stick shift and no radio, he visited "720 ophthalmologists spread across 4,300 miles." He made the round trip two or three times a year, leaving his wife to ship orders from their basement. "It was like the wild west, but the people were great," Juliano recalled, with wholesalers in sparsely populated areas letting him stay in their homes. When Juliano was only six months into the new job, Conner praised him to the board.[52]

By May 1958 Alcon was selling products in fifteen countries. One of Andrews's first assignments in 1958 was to assess the international consignee in Chicago. He recommended that Alcon use a new individual, Charles E. Weston, formerly of G. D. Searle, to be Alcon's director of overseas operations. By 1960 overseas shipments had increased to justify a full-time person to manage exports from the Chicago consignee. The process was complicated as labels had to be prepared in foreign languages, and shipping documents for each country varied from almost none to dozens of pages. Moreover, Alcon products had to be registered with overseas governments, another complex process. Conner's active participation in the Pan-American Association of Ophthalmology (PAAO) led to the creation of Alcon Laboratories International C.A., in 1960. Chartered in Venezuela, it facilitated distribution in South and Central America, where Alcon established an MSR training program, and the next year a Panamanian warehouse was opened. Alcon products were generally sold by distributors who arranged for advertising in local ophthalmic journals. Colombia was particularly important as its most prestigious ophthalmic institute, the Instituto Barraquer de América, dominated ophthalmology in South America and published the leading journal on ophthalmology, *Archivos de la Sociedad Americana de Oftalmologia y Optometria*, in which Alcon's distributor advertised in 1962 (fig. 3.16).[53]

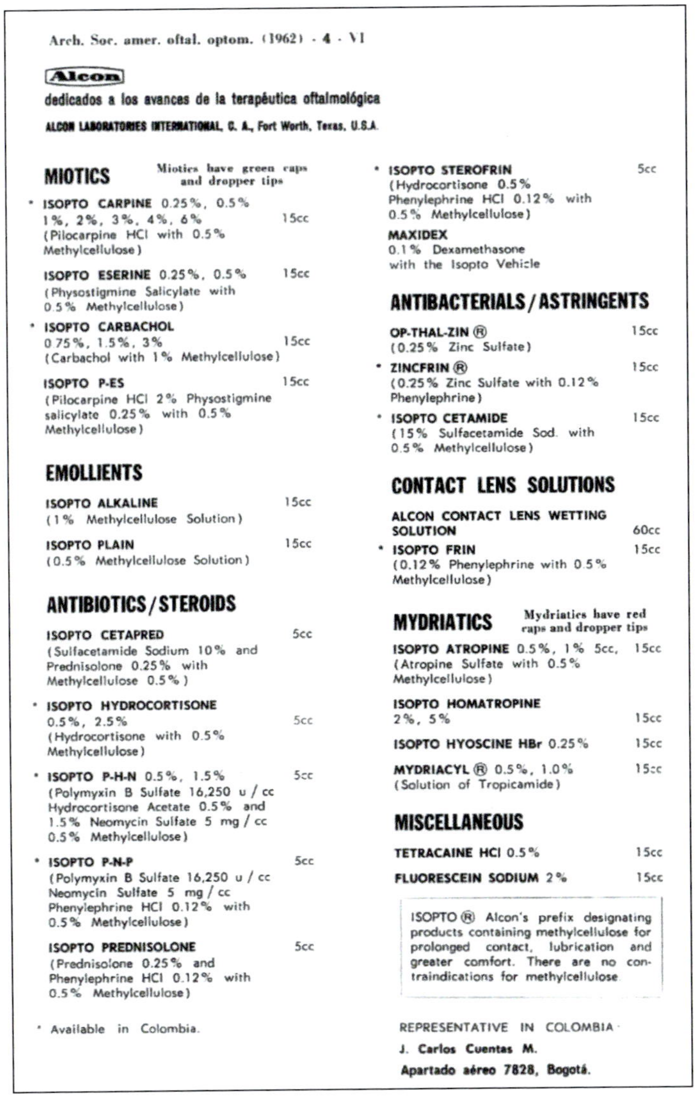
Arch. Soc. amer. oftal. optom. (1962) - 4 - VI

Alcon

dedicados a los avances de la terapéutica oftalmológica

ALCON LABORATORIES INTERNATIONAL, C. A., Fort Worth, Texas, U.S.A.

MIOTICS Miotics have green caps and dropper tips

* ISOPTO CARPINE 0.25%, 0.5% 1%, 2%, 3%, 4%, 6% — 15cc
(Pilocarpine HCl with 0.5% Methylcellulose)

ISOPTO ESERINE 0.25%, 0.5% — 15cc
(Physostigmine Salicylate with 0.5% Methylcellulose)

* ISOPTO CARBACHOL 0.75%, 1.5%, 3% — 15cc
(Carbachol with 1% Methylcellulose)

ISOPTO P-ES — 15cc
(Pilocarpine HCl 2% Physostigmine salicylate 0.25% with 0.5% Methylcellulose)

EMOLLIENTS

ISOPTO ALKALINE — 15cc
(1% Methylcellulose Solution)

ISOPTO PLAIN — 15cc
(0.5% Methylcellulose Solution)

ANTIBIOTICS/STEROIDS

ISOPTO CETAPRED — 5cc
(Sulfacetamide Sodium 10% and Prednisolone 0.25% with Methylcellulose 0.5%)

* ISOPTO HYDROCORTISONE 0.5%, 2.5% — 5cc
(Hydrocortisone with 0.5% Methylcellulose)

* ISOPTO P-H-N 0.5%, 1.5% — 5cc
(Polymyxin B Sulfate 16,250 u / cc Hydrocortisone Acetate 0.5% and 1.5% Neomycin Sulfate 5 mg / cc 0.5% Methylcellulose)

* ISOPTO P-N-P — 5cc
(Polymyxin B Sulfate 16,250 u / cc Neomycin Sulfate 5 mg / cc Phenylephrine HCl 0.12% with 0.5% Methylcellulose)

ISOPTO PREDNISOLONE — 5cc
(Prednisolone 0.25% and Phenylephrine HCl 0.12% with 0.5% Methylcellulose)

* Available in Colombia.

* ISOPTO STEROFRIN — 5cc
(Hydrocortisone 0.5% Phenylephrine HCl 0.12% with 0.5% Methylcellulose)

MAXIDEX
0.1% Dexamethasone with the Isopto Vehicle

ANTIBACTERIALS/ASTRINGENTS

OP-THAL-ZIN ® — 15cc
(0.25% Zinc Sulfate)

* ZINCFRIN ® — 15cc
(0.25% Zinc Sulfate with 0.12% Phenylephrine)

* ISOPTO CETAMIDE — 15cc
(15% Sulfacetamide Sod. with 0.5% Methylcellulose)

CONTACT LENS SOLUTIONS

ALCON CONTACT LENS WETTING SOLUTION — 60cc

* ISOPTO FRIN — 15cc
(0.12% Phenylephrine with 0.5% Methylcellulose)

MYDRIATICS Mydriatics have red caps and dropper tips

ISOPTO ATROPINE 0.5%, 1% 5cc, 15cc
(Atropine Sulfate with 0.5% Methylcellulose)

ISOPTO HOMATROPINE 2%, 5% — 15cc

ISOPTO HYOSCINE HBr 0.25% — 15cc

MYDRIACYL ® 0.5%, 1.0% — 15cc
(Solution of Tropicamide)

MISCELLANEOUS

TETRACAINE HCl 0.5% — 15cc

FLUORESCEIN SODIUM 2% — 15cc

ISOPTO ® Alcon's prefix designating products containing methylcellulose for prolonged contact, lubrication and greater comfort. There are no contraindications for methylcellulose.

REPRESENTATIVE IN COLOMBIA
J. Carlos Cuentas M.
Apartado aéreo 7828, Bogotá.

FIG 3.16
List of Alcon products sold in Colombia (*Archivos de la Sociedad Americana de Oftalmologia y Optometria*, 1962) (AHR)

By 1962 Alcon was shipping products to thirty countries. The strategy was to sign agreements with local companies to distribute products made by contracted manufacturers. To ensure these followed Alcon procedures and quality standards, Charles Dickey supervised the initial production runs. Tolid Daru in Tehran, Iran, was the first plant outside the United States to manufacture Alcon products. Next, one of the largest pharmaceutical companies in Brazil, Daveres S.A., not only manufactured Alcon products but marketed them. In 1964 Alcon founded a subsidiary in Toronto, with its own manufacturing plant and a marketing and sales force. The creation of a joint venture with a French company, Laboratoires Jouveinal, established more manufacturing and sales organizations. Manufacturing agreements were also signed with pharmaceutical companies in Mexico and Colombia. In 1966 Conal products were added to international sales and an ophthalmic sales group was set up in West Germany. The next year Alcon entered the Japanese ophthalmic market after signing a distribution agreement, and another Mexican pharmaceutical company started producing Alcon's products. In South Africa, Alcon signed a manufacturing agreement with a local company. By the decade's end, Alcon had its own plant in Canada and agreements to produce products in more than a half-dozen countries. The International Division brought its top twelve market managers and sales supervisors to Fort Worth in June 1965 for its first international conference. In annual sales reports, Conner reported that international sales were growing nearly as fast as sales in the United States.[54]

These achievements did not occur without the participation of a dedicated, experienced team, some of whom, like Juliano, were colorful characters. A key player who joined Alcon in 1962 was the charismatic, Swiss-born Frank Xavier Buhler. A graduate of Lucerne's School of Commerce and Université Catholique de Lyon, he came to the United States in 1949 to study at Columbia University. Initially hired by Pfizer, Buhler joined Abbott Laboratories in 1954 and began a career in the international pharmaceutical business in Mexico, Cuba, and South America. Contacted by a recruiting agency on behalf of Alcon, Buhler visited Fort Worth three times before he was convinced by Conner's vision. When he arrived in June 1962, Alcon's international sales were $127,000. Buhler recalled that the first year or so was "far from easy." On his way to Venezuela in 1963, he confided to Schollmaier that he might quit. Conner arranged for the premier Venezuelan ophthalmologist to escort Buhler during his visit, and the doctor spoke in such glowing terms about Alcon and its potential that Buhler returned from the trip invigorated and committed to the company. He concentrated on distributorships in Latin America. Convinced Buhler was crucial to Alcon's future, Conner sent him to the AMP in 1966, and by 1967 Buhler's effort, vision, and staff grew Alcon's international sales to about $1.5 million.[55]

In addition to finding cooperative distributors and manufacturing partners, Buhler used his contacts within the international pharmaceutical industry to locate people with the skills needed for the International Division to thrive. For Latin America, Buhler needed a native Spanish speaker on his team. He invited Juana Rosa Lorenzo (now Lorenzo-Daniell), whom he knew from Abbott, to Fort Worth. Sent by her mother from Cuba in 1960, Lorenzo had settled with her brother in Chicago and worked for Buhler as a bilingual secretary at Abbott. Convinced of Alcon's future, she joined Buhler in 1963 for $350 per month, which she described as being "extremely well-paid." Most of Buhler's efforts required corresponding in Spanish, and Lorenzo also prepared distribution agreements. She later recalled that in addition to being "hard-working, dedicated, and driven," Buhler also "believed in watching pennies and not wasting money."[56]

Looking to expand to Europe and the Far East, Buhler hired two men in 1965. His search in Europe eventually led to Frans Van Kets. On the eve of World War II, Van Kets's parents fled from Belgium to South Africa; as an adult he went to the Congo as an MSR for Eli Lilly until political instability drove him and his wife back to Belgium. Van Kets worked as a Lilly MSR in Geneva, Austria, and Paris until he accepted Buhler's offer to open Alcon's first European office, which he organized in his bedroom. He traveled throughout Europe, registered Alcon's products, introduced them to ophthalmologists, and established a distribution system. When Van Kets needed help, he hired fellow Belgian Jacques Van Damme in August 1965. Within a year, the multilingual Van Damme established his role as a customer service specialist; he would spend his entire career with Alcon. Lorenzo enjoyed working with Van Kets, who was "full of energy and creativity—it was contagious." So, she eagerly agreed to work in the Belgium office in 1967. That same year Edmond De Vos and Marie-Christiane Stevens became regional managers for Europe. Alcon's Antwerp headquarters managed operations in EURMEA: Europe, the Middle East, and Africa. By the end of 1967, the sales for EURMEA totaled nearly $1 million.[57]

As the decade continued, Alcon continued to expand sales in new markets. Geoffrey C. Crewe came by way of other pharmaceutical corporations. Born in Brazil to expatriate English parents in 1927, he enrolled in Eastern Illinois University and graduated from Indiana University. Upjohn hired him to manage its Caribbean and Puerto Rico markets, where he met Buhler. Crewe worked for the Pitman-Moore pharmaceutical company in 1958 and, when it was acquired by Dow Chemical, was assigned to expand its markets in the Far East, Europe, and Latin America. Seven years later, he was invited to Fort Worth, where Conner, Alexander, and Buhler convinced him that Alcon was the "right place" for him. Buhler challenged Crewe to build Alcon's profile in the Far East, where it was only a $40,000 business, and also to manage Canada, where a manufacturing plant had just opened. Crewe recalled that "he quickly learned what made Alcon so special." Buhler gave him a one-way economy class airplane ticket for his first trip to the Far East in 1966 and told him he could buy his return ticket after he sold enough products. Crewe was away for six weeks, in his first introduction to Buhler's penny-pinching. In 1967 Crewe negotiated an agreement with a Japanese company to distribute Cryophake, Cryoceps, and the Alcon Sterilizer. Setting the stage for growth, Crewe hired Thomas P. Grant, an Irishman living in Vancouver, and assigned him to Australia, where Alcon soon gained prominence.[58]

As Alcon expanded overseas, working through an agent in Chicago became untenable. Conner's presence at the annual conference of the PAAO boosted Alcon's profile with Latin American ophthalmologists, but deals with scattered distributors reflected a piecemeal approach that would not work in the long run. Placing Juliano as MSR in Canada proved to be effective, but assigning a representative to every country was not an option. Conner found the right person in Buhler to oversee the International Division. However, he and Juliano did not agree on how to manage Canada, leading Juliano to resign. Crewe found managing Canada uncomplicated, but the Far East proved to be a challenge. In Latin America, Buhler continued to juggle a disparate set of countries and did not find a suitable person to organize and manage a cohesive strategy. Nevertheless, at the end of 1967, international sales were 10 percent of Alcon's total, a remarkable start in the global marketplace.[59]

From Alcon's inception, Merrill had been in charge of the laboratory. His group developed products, established valid testing procedures, managed quality control testing, conducted clinical studies, and registered products with the FDA. Dr. Earl Maxwell became Alcon's first medical director when Conner hired him in October 1958. A graduate of Tulane University and Washington Medical School in St. Louis, Maxwell had served in the Air Force for twenty-one years and retired as a brigadier general. His Alcon responsibilities included relations with ophthalmologists, promoting ocular disease awareness, creating and handling an employee health care program, and managing clinical studies. He made scientific presentations and attended conferences. In 1960 he organized Alcon's first medical symposium, which was reported in the 1961 issue of *Highlights of Ophthalmology*. Maxwell was instrumental in developing three therapies—Zolyse for cataracts, Lyophrin for glaucoma, and Dendrid for herpes simplex ocular infections.

Maxwell organized Alcon's first formal clinical testing group, and by 1965 the group consisted of three experienced scientists on the Fort Worth campus. In 1966 Alcon's directors promoted Maxwell to vice president, director of research and medical affairs. In that role, he joined Conner and Alexander in 1967 in setting off a dynamite blast during ground-breaking for the Science and Technology Building extension (fig. 3.17). He became one of the three original trustees for the Alcon Eye Research Foundation and, like Catherine and Bob Alexander, served on the board of directors for the Texas Society to Prevent Blindness. Alcon's medical missions began in 1964 when Dora Moody, Maxwell's secretary, arranged for a donation of Alcon glaucoma products to the SS *Hope*, a hospital ship that extended American medical practices to the world. Word spread, and Medical Assistance Programs in Wheaton, Illinois, and Surgical Eye Expeditions, of Santa Barbara, California, asked for donated supplies. Unused stability samples of manufactured lots were usually discarded, so Moody asked if they could be donated. By 1967 Maxwell's influence was pervasive.[60]

With the medical responsibilities passed to Maxwell, Merrill focused on the laboratory. In July 1963 Conner announced that Alcon had hired Osgood Daniel Priddle Jr. as the director of research, reporting to Merrill, the laboratory director and a vice president. Strangely, no one ever remembered interviewing Priddle. Richard D. Poe, the head of analytical chemistry, believed that Conner could be enthralled by a person's resumé, and Priddle's was impressive. He had a doctoral degree in pharmacology from the University of Indiana, a stint at Johnson & Johnson Laboratories, postgraduate work at the Mellon Institute of Industrial Research, and six years of experience in opening a medical and graduate school in Pakistan. He had never developed a drug approved by the FDA, much less one for the eye, but his organizational skills were good and he convinced Conner to increase the budget for scientists and equipment to such an extent that fourteen temporary buildings were required to contain the laboratory. In a short time, the research staff more than doubled, with technicians, pharmacologists, microbiologists, chemists, toxicologists, pharmacists, and support staff.

Priddle proved to be controversial and not well liked. His office in Temporary Building no. 1 was the farthest from the laboratory building, just enough to allow warnings to spread that he was approaching the main laboratory building. He always disagreed with someone,

FIG 3.17
Left to right: Dr. Earl Maxwell, Bob Alexander, Bill Conner, Science & Technology building groundbreaking, 1967 (AHR)

mostly Merrill and his staff, or marketing folks. Contemporaries claim that Priddle fabricated stories and made promises he never kept. Certain technicians rankled him, and he threatened to fire them whenever he saw them. To say the least, there was turmoil in the research department, no new products were developed during his tenure, and product support efforts were in disarray. Why this was permitted to continue is uncertain, but Conner was absent for some time because of ill health so perhaps the situation was just not addressed. Priddle attended the 1965 spring AMP, but this did not solve the problem. Matters came to a head in the boardroom. In front of Conner and other executives, Priddle told Merrill that he had installed an atomic absorption analytical device. But he did not have one; it was on order. Merrill, surely with Conner's blessing, fired Priddle on December 20, 1965. Maxwell was placed in charge of research with operations managed by John D. Mullins, an experienced pharmaceutical scientist with a doctoral degree in his field.[61]

All this turmoil occurred just as the FDA was implementing the Kefauver-Harris amendments to the FD&C Act, which required reregistration of every Alcon product. The first step was to revise the formulation of more than forty products. All preservatives except benzalkonium chloride were discarded, and many inactive ingredients had to be modified to ensure each formulation was stable. Specifications for raw materials and finished products were revised. This meant additional documentation and validation of analytical and bacteriological procedures, and every product had to undergo toxicology tests. Once a formulation passed all the tests, manufacturing processes, first designed in the laboratory, were scaled up in a process facility before trial runs were made in manufacturing.

Problems occurred. The analytical assays procedure for benzalkonium chloride turned out to be different for every product. Ed Dorsey, the chemist in charge, said he became exhausted doing so many. In addition, bacteriological preservative test results also varied. Some of the issues were traced to the mold release chemical in the Drop-tainers. New regulations required testing for the leaching of minute amounts of chemicals from Drop-tainers into a product. Implantation toxicology studies had to demonstrate the safety of the plastic resin, with and without contact to the final product. Often a formulation passed these laboratory tests but glitches were found in manufacturing, so much had to be redone. New guidelines required stability tests to be conducted at various temperatures and humidities, with and without light, so the number of samples grew exponentially. In addition to chemical assays and bacteriology tests, pH, viscosity, sedimentation, and color were measured. Anita Tippett, who joined Alcon in 1962, spent her career as the go-to expert on these stability tests.

R&D leaned on marketing to rationalize the product line and set priorities, since everything required by the Kefauver-Harris amendments could not be done simultaneously. This sparked debate. The steep learning curve continued for several years, but the long-term consequences later brought huge benefits. One positive outcome of Priddle's expansion was the number and quality of scientists who joined R&D. Most remained with Alcon for their entire careers; thus, the firm never lost the institutional knowledge gained during this time. Cross-training resulted. Department heads learned about project management, and marketing folks began to grasp the complexity of a modern R&D organization tasked with delivering a continuous stream of new products. Another legacy of Priddle's tenure was the creation of the first organic synthesis group. Satoru Numajiri, who had a master's degree in chemistry from TCU, sought to synthesize pilocarpine, which was extracted from the *Pilocarpus microphyllus* (jaborandi) plant found in the upper Amazon River Basin. Pilocarpine was the prime glaucoma therapy, a market Alcon came to dominate. All these factors placed Alcon in a position to capitalize on the development and marketing of novel products that began in the 1970s.[62]

After the medical and R&D functions had been separated from the original laboratory group, it was renamed Quality Control (QC). Its responsibility was to test the manufactured batches of each product. If a lot did not meet sterility or chemical assay standards, it was rejected and destroyed. When the FDA approved a product, R&D transferred to manufacturing the written procedures for making each lot. QC also received the validated microbiology and chemical assay procedures and specifications. Validation is a key concept, meaning procedures or assays are repetitively performed to demonstrate that results are reproducible. Inevitably, problems arose with some assays transferred from R&D. Scaling up a new or revised manufacturing process introduced uncertainties that could affect the results. R&D and QC worked together, much of the interaction was informal, and problems were resolved at the laboratory bench.

In the QC group, Ted Fleming (fig. 3.18) and Lloyd G. Hodgkins were experienced and knew Alcon's products. That proved fortunate, since stability tests of manufactured lots were now required, increasing the number and scope of assays. Furthermore, in 1963 the FDA promulgated its first Good Manufacturing Practices (GMP), which affected R&D and QC as much as manufacturing plants. These required that chemical raw materials, active and inactive, had to be produced under GMP guidelines and assayed against known standards.[63]

The growth of Alcon created conflict as departments grew and split. For Merrill, whose

FIG 3.18
Ted Fleming, ca. 1965 (AHR)

role in establishing the Alcon product line cannot be overstated, it was a difficult time, and his relationship with Conner became contentious. Fleming worked with Merrill and described him as "a very strong-willed person" who had definite views about people, processes, and organization. Conner's hiring Priddle as director of research irked Merrill, and his assigning the medical group to Maxwell created frustration. Carter remembered that Merrill and "Conner had their ups and downs. ... They both had strong personalities." Ultimately, their relationship fractured. Poe recalled, "I had no problem with Dave Merrill. He was a good old boy. But in 1967... Dave resigned and left the company. I don't know why Dave left the company, but I suspect it was because he and Bill Conner had a personality conflict."

What prompted Merrill's departure was not a long-term personality clash but a specific event. Alcon had purchased a drum of prednisolone and a drum of hydrocortisone, ingredients used in separate products. By accident, manufacturing personnel mixed the containers, making the ingredients unusable. QC discovered the mistake and discarded the mixture, resulting in a loss of $45,000. Merrill had to notify Conner; he found him on the golf course, an argument ensued, and Merrill quit. In his "Alcon Story," Merrill asserted, "I got along with Conner just fine from the very first day. But I didn't like him." Thus ended Merrill's twenty years at Alcon. He had been there almost since its inception and deserves credit for forty or so products developed during the critical first years. There is no doubt that he was indispensable to Alcon "fulfilling the founders' vision." To replace him, Conner promoted Fleming to direct QC, a position he held for almost twenty years.[64]

When Merrill joined Alcon, his team developed and tested products and sent a New Drug Application (NDA) to the FDA according to rules implemented in 1938. The 1962 Kefauver-Harris Act expanded these mandates and required clinical studies. This led to the creation of a new department, Regulatory Affairs (RA), which supervised the preparation of every NDA and organized an appropriate team to defend the application to the FDA. An NDA presented every aspect of a new product, from formulation and toxicology to packaging and process development. Clinical studies and statistical reports were key components, but the most important document was the proposed package insert, which included a disease indication and summarized the clinical studies, especially regarding efficacy and safety. At this stage, the situation in RA at Alcon, in the industry, and at the FDA best exemplified Alexander's axiom: we don't know what we are doing but we will figure it out. Conner transferred RA to the Executive Department in 1966, claiming increased regulations justified this. At the time RA consisted of two people, Henry A. Whissen, a former Air Force officer and FDA inspector, and Faye Wheeler.[65]

Alcon's early products used a few well-known active ingredients formulated at different concentrations (fig. 3.19). The second decade of product development created new therapies and products. The company pioneered the organization of ophthalmic products into groups based on a therapeutic or surgical category as a means to differentiate its products from competitors. With few modifications, Alcon's categories continued into the twenty-first century: glaucoma therapies, anti-inflammatory steroids, antibiotics, combination steroids and antibiotics, antivirals, decongestants, mydriatics, cycloplegics, diagnostics, dry eye therapies, contact lens solutions, and surgical products and adjuncts.[66]

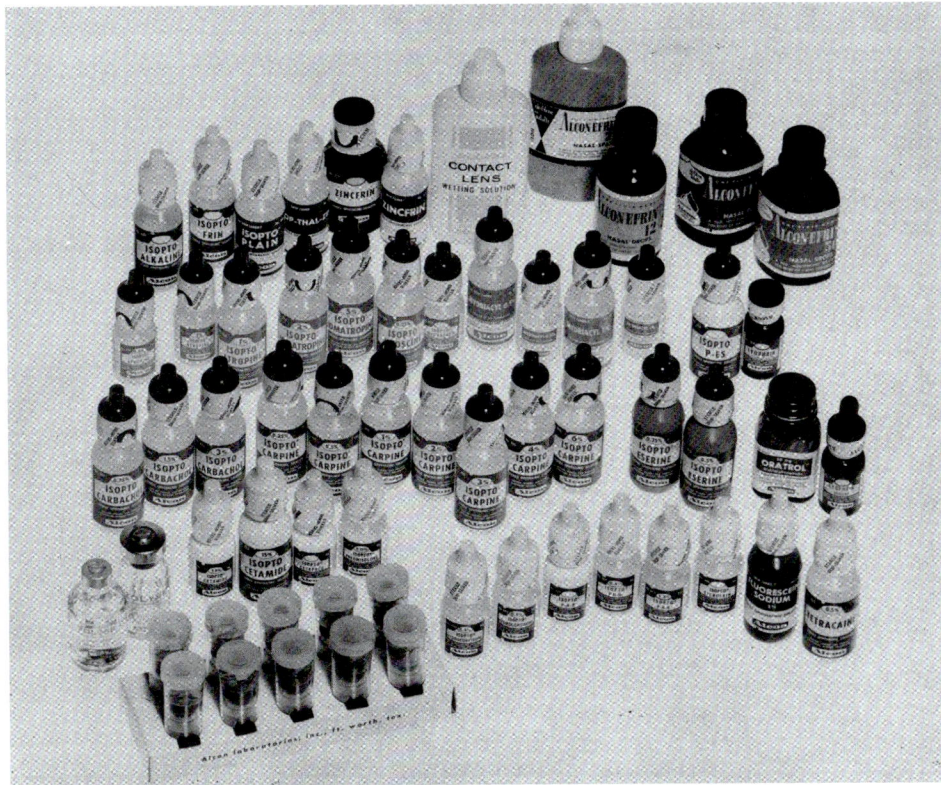

FIG 3.19
Alcon products, 1962 (AHR)

Glaucoma occurs when pressure inside the eye is abnormally high. The treatment is to reduce the pressure, for which pilocarpine is effective because it increases the outflow of liquid in the eye. Isopto Carpine, in various concentrations, was Alcon's primary glaucoma therapy. Pilocarpine had three drawbacks: (1) its duration of action was short, (2) it constricted the pupil and blurred vision, and (3) its effectiveness decreased over time. Thus, some glaucoma patients needed an additional drug to control pressure. Alcon developed Isopto Carbachol, a more potent molecule, for these patients (fig. 3.20). Decreasing the production of fluid in the eye also lowers intraocular pressure. Carbonic anhydrase inhibitors (CAIs), used to prevent altitude sickness and lower blood pressure, also lowers pressure in the eye. CAIs had to be administered as tablets, and had serious systemic effects, affecting the body's electrolytes. Thus, ophthalmologists weighed efficacy against side effects for each

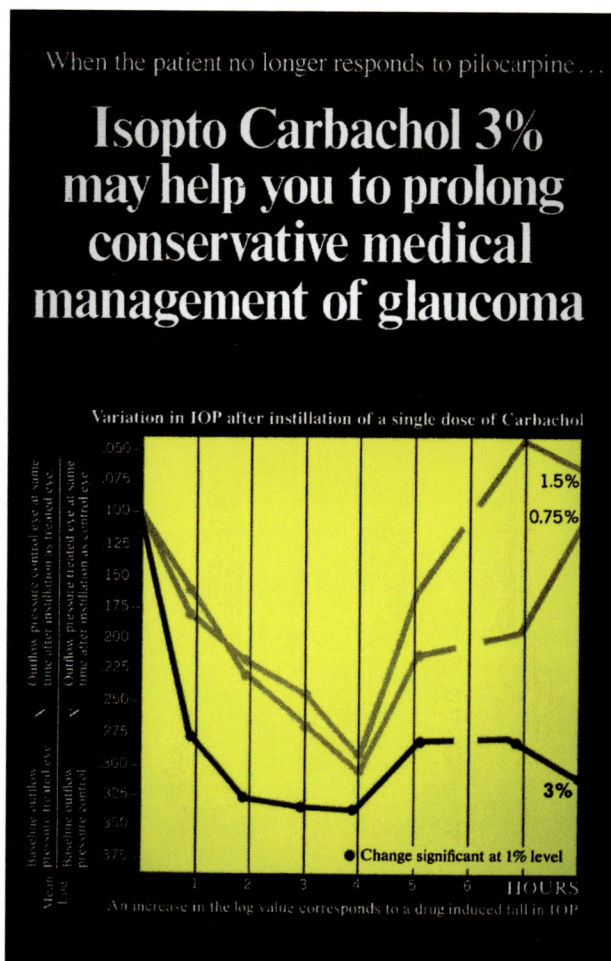

When the patient no longer responds to pilocarpine . . .

Isopto Carbachol 3%
may help you to prolong
conservative medical
management of glaucoma

patient. Dichlorphenamide is an effective oral CAI, and Alcon introduced this medication in 1960 as Oratrol tablets. Alcon purchased the off-patent dichlorphenamide tablets from a contract manufacturer, though later they were manufactured at Conal.[67]

Epinephrine is an adrenergic drug, naturally produced by the adrenal gland, which in the early twentieth century was found to reduce eye pressure in glaucoma patients. Epinephrine quickly degrades in an aqueous solution exposed to air, but the solution can be freeze-dried in a process known as lyophilization, and in this form it remains stable for a few years. Alcon contracted with Ben Venue Laboratories to lyophilize an epinephrine bitartrate solution in a small vial, stable for two years. When a pharmacist reconstituted the lyophilized epinephrine using a diluent made by Alcon, a glaucoma patient had a stable, effective solution for ninety days. Alcon launched Lyophrin in 1961. The medication, instilled at night to minimize blurred vision due to dilated pupils, reduced pressure for up to twenty-four hours (fig. 3.21). Lyophrin was also used as an adjunct therapy when pilocarpine's effects began to wane.[68]

An inflamed eye is swollen and red, and often has excess mucous. Potent steroid ophthalmic drops reduce inflammation, while antibiotics treat bacterial infections. Thus, the combination of a steroid and antibiotic in one product gives ophthalmologists the best option to treat or prevent inflammation and infection at the same time. Cortisol is a natural corticosteroid produced in the adrenal gland, and hydrocortisone and prednisolone are examples of first- and second-generation synthetic corticosteroids. Alcon introduced products containing these steroids, but, while effective, they were difficult to suspend. A more potent steroid, dexamethasone, was synthesized in the mid-1950s and Fleming developed it into a breakthrough product, Maxidex (fig. 3.22). Dexamethasone alcohol is insoluble in water, but the chemical powder can be micronized. Fleming created an isotonic, comfortable formulation of 0.1 percent dexamethasone alcohol (micronized) that easily resuspended. Organon of the Netherlands owned the dexamethasone alcohol patent and Alcon needed exclusivity. Discovering Organon's president Joe Ruvane would attend a seminar at Harvard, Schollmaier arranged to room with him, after which Organon signed an exclusive deal.

At $56,000 a kilogram, dexamethasone alcohol was the most expensive raw material Alcon had ever purchased. Approved by the FDA in June 1962, Maxidex was launched immediately (fig. 3.23). And it was successful. Merck Sharp & Dohme launched its own 0.1 percent dexamethasone sodium phosphate product, NeoDecadron, but Maxidex became the standard treatment for inflammatory conditions of the conjunctiva and the anterior chamber, as well as for postsurgical trauma. Maxidex was one of Schweitzer's first advertising campaigns, and later Buchanan became its product manager. Maxidex and other products using dexamethasone alcohol prevailed in the crowded marketplace of ophthalmic anti-inflammatory pharmaceuticals.[69]

Maxitrol was Alcon's third-generation steroid and antibiotic combination. In the previous decade, Merrill mixed prednisolone and sodium sulfacetamide, which Alcon marketed as Isopto Cetapred drops and ointment. He followed with Isopto P H N a few years later.

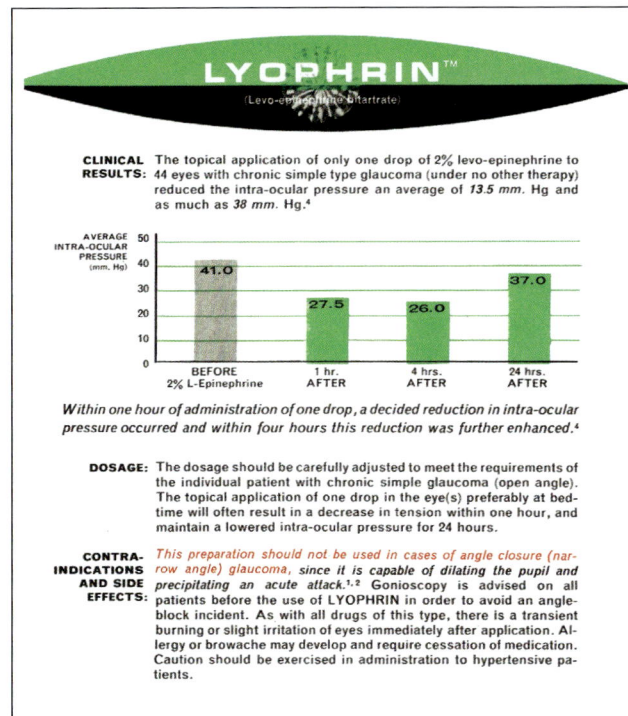

FIG 3.21
Lyophrin reference card mailed to ophthalmologists, 1961 (Courtesy of Founders' Museum, Alcon)

FIG 3.22
Maxidex (TOM, AM)

FIG 3.23
Maxidex highlighted at the 1963 AAOO
meeting. *On the left*, Dick Sisson. (AHR)

Ointments were nighttime treatments, and this became important when treating blepharitis, an inflammation of the eyelids characterized by crusty deposits, often accompanied by staphylococcus bacteria. Daily washing eyelids with soap usually prevents blepharitis, but chronic cases need treatment. When sulfa drugs became an ophthalmology medication, they effectively treated blepharitis. With the introduction of Maxitrol, Alcon marketed Cetapred to treat the condition. At the time, a major competitor, Allergan, had introduced its sulfacetamide product, Blephamide, to treat blepharitis, and it began to dominate that market. However, Allergan's product was available only as drops. Illustrating the genius of collaborating with Kallir, Philips, Ross, Alcon promoted the value of using both Isopto Cetapred drops and ointment for twenty-four-hour control (fig. 3.24).[70]

Maxitrol, which combined a steroid, dexamethasone alcohol, with two antibiotics, polymyxin and neomycin, was the major product Alcon launched in the early 1960s. Still, the company almost failed when it introduced Maxitrol in the United States. The campaign began well but after three months the product was not selling. Leone, as national sales director, and Schollmaier met with district managers in Arlington, Texas. The managers explained why it took longer to get the product off the ground. Leone and Schollmaier left the meeting depressed, but in the parking lot Leone suddenly sprang from the car and ran back. Inside he exclaimed, "*Is this a good product?*" They all agreed it was the first really good product the company had developed. Schollmaier later wrote about the dramatic event: "He [Leone] looked them all in the eye and asked, 'Can each of you sell one doctor?' Of course, they all thought that could be done. George said, 'Good. Go do it.' Call me as soon as you've sold one doctor. Then we'll talk about how to sell another." Leone also told them if they did not call in four days, they would need to look for another job. It worked, and Maxitrol became a profitable product. This episode illustrates the influence of Leone and Schollmaier as a team, as well as Leone's ability to focus people's attention.[71]

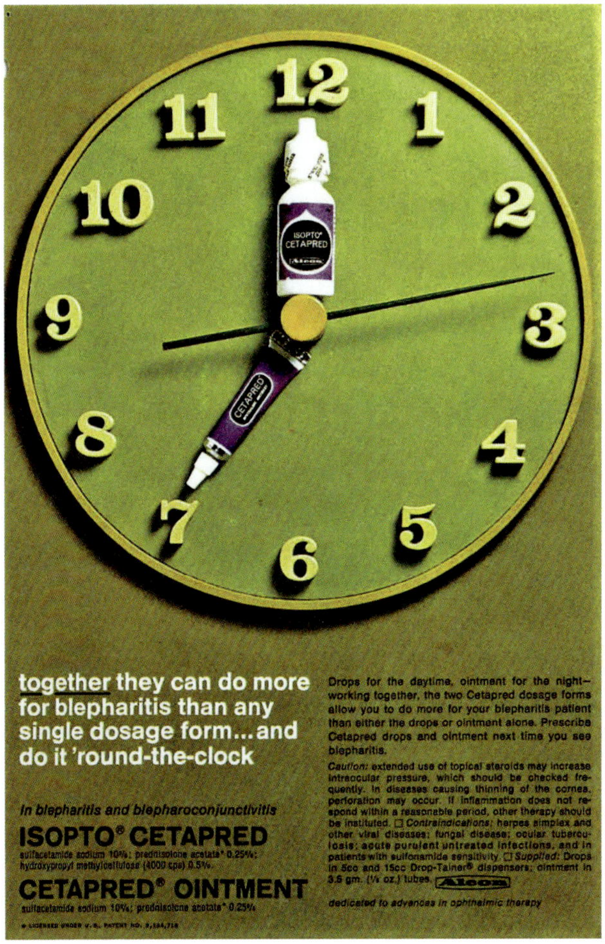

Since 1953 Isopto Cetamide had been Alcon's only single entity anti-infective medication. While sodium sulfacetamide was effective, other antibiotics were discovered, but most killed only a narrow range of bacteria. Then neomycin sulfate and polymyxin B sulfate were combined to kill more bacteria in a skin therapy product known as Neosporin. In 1965 Alcon launched as second-generation antibiotic, Statrol drops and ointment, a blend of 3.5 percent neomycin sulfate and polymyxin B sulfate at 16,250 international units (IU) per milliliter with 0.12 percent phenylephrine HCl. While the latter ingredient was mostly cosmetic, reducing redness in the red eye, the two antibiotics provided the main therapeutic effect by stopping ocular infections. In launching Statrol, another brand name created by Schollmaier, the marketing and sales groups initiated promotion campaigns, usually adding Statrol to a Maxitrol program.[72]

Mydriatics are drugs that dilate the pupil. Cycloplegics also do this, but they also prevent the lens from focusing. These drugs are used for refraction, surgery, and therapies. A dilated pupil allows a thorough examination of the eye. Another use is in cataract and retinal surgery so a surgeon can access the part of the eye beyond the pupil. Certain uncommon diseases respond to cycloplegic therapy. A Swiss company in Basel, Hoffmann-LaRoche, patented tropicamide for systemic diseases and licensed its ophthalmic use to Alcon in the 1950s. Fleming created the ophthalmic formations for 1 percent and 0.5 percent tropicamide and obtained FDA approval. Alcon launched it as Mydriacyl in the spring of 1960. It had both mydriatic and cycloplegic action and produced a quick dilation with a short duration of blurred vision. In a 1967 product emphasis program, Leone and Schweitzer col-

FIG 3.24
Isopto Cetapred drops and ointment for twenty-four-hour treatment of blepharitis, advertisement, 1967 (AHR)

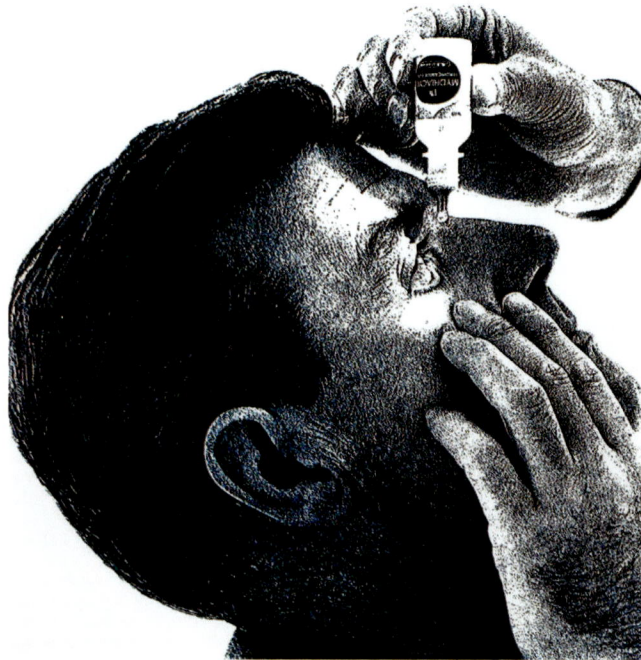

Available again: Mydriacyl 1%

How Mydriacyl® can simplify refractions

1 **The Mydriacyl routine is simple:**
two drops are instilled 5 minutes apart.

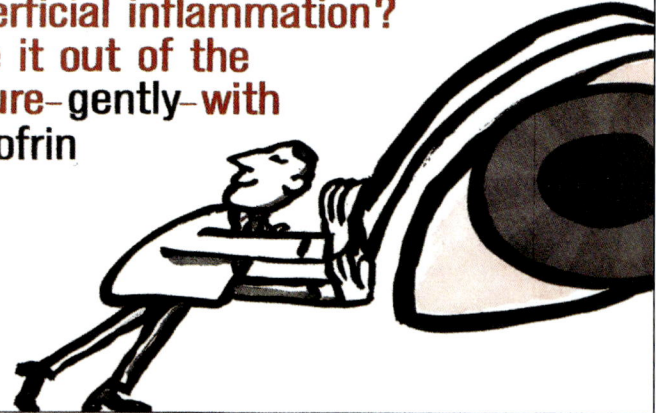

**Superficial inflammation?
Ease it out of the
picture–gently–with
Sterofrin**

Next time you see red, itching,
tearing eyes that need mild, yet effective
steroid/decongestant action prescribe
Sterofrin. It offers your patients...

rapid symptomatic relief
gently subdues the inflammation
and allays the itch
quickly soothes and whitens
the red, irritated eye

a double therapeutic bonus
formulated to resist tear washout
to facilitate complete drug action
6cc per vial; several days' extra therapy
at no extra cost

Alcon
dedicated to advances in ophthalmic therapy

Contraindicated in Herpes simplex and other
viral diseases; fungal disease; tuberculosis
and acute purulent untreated infections.
Precautions: extended use of topical steroids
may increase intraocular pressure, which
should be checked frequently. In diseases
causing thinning of the cornea, perforation
has been known to occur with the use of topical steroids. If the inflammation does not respond within a reasonable period, other forms
of therapy should be instituted. If sensitivity
reaction is observed, discontinue use. Slight
dilation of the pupil may occur in some patients.

Sterofrin®

Active: prednisolone acetate* 0.25%,
phenylephrine hydrochloride 0.12%,
hydroxypropyl methylcellulose
(4000 cps) 0.5%

*LICENSED UNDER U.S. PATENT 3,124,718

FIG 3.26
Rebranded Sterofrin,
advertisement, 1967 (AHR)

FIG 3.25
"How Mydriacyl can simplify refraction,"
advertisement, 1967 (AHR)

laborated with Kallir, Philips, Ross and created a sophisticated advertisement highlighting Mydriacyl's advantages (figs. 3.25). Its functionality makes it a long-standing product still marketed today.[73]

Combining two or more active ingredients in an ophthalmic formulation has two clear rationales, one therapeutic and one monetary. The surface of the eye has a finite volume, so when a drop exceeds that, the excess spills out. If it is an expensive drug, the loss is not only therapeutic but monetary. One way to minimize spillage is to place two or more drugs in the same formula so the patient instills one drop instead of two or three. In the 1950s, R&D and marketing developed several combinations. For example, Isopto Sterofrin had hydrocortisone and phenylephrine to treat "inflammatory and allergic conditions." Schollmaier worked with Kallir, Philips, Ross to rebrand Isopto Sterofrin as simply Sterofrin and relaunch it with a sophisticated advertisement (fig. 3.26). Meanwhile, Fleming combined atropine sulfate and prednisolone to create Isopto Mydrapred, which treated uncommon inflammations of the iris and cornea and assisted in corneal transplants and cataract surgery. Both products were sold for several years.[74]

Contact lens technology has a long history that begins in the early 1800s. In the late 1950s the most common type was a hard corneal lens made of polymethyl methacrylate (PMMA). While PMMA contact lenses corrected vision, they repelled water and collected debris, which required a special wetting solution to lubricate and cushion the lens. Alcon's first contact lens product, Contact Lens Wetting Solution, launched in 1961, was promoted as "a superior wetting and cleansing agent for all types of contact lenses." It also was the first of a series of contact lens wetting, cleaning, and disinfecting solutions and systems sold by Alcon.[75]

By the 1990s Alcon dominated the market for cataract surgery, the most common eye surgery, but the journey began in 1958. The natural lens is clear but often becomes opaque as people age, eventually causing blindness. Early efforts to treat cataracts date as far back as the fifth century BC. By the 1950s, the practice was to wait until the patient was almost blind before performing an intracapsular cataract extraction (ICCE), in which the lens and its capsule were removed. It was a high-risk procedure. Any product that facilitated safer removal would be a major advancement. Alcon introduced three in the 1960s. Professor José Ignacio Barraquer of the Centro de Oftalmología Barraquer in Barcelona, Spain, demonstrated that the enzyme alpha-chymotrypsin dissolved lens muscle fibers, allowing the cataractous lens to be easily removed. The Armour Pharmaceutical Company purified alpha-chymotrypsin from a bovine pancreas. Alcon purchased vials of lyophilized alpha-chymotrypsin from Armour and filed an NDA for Zolyse; it was approved in 1958 (fig. 3.27). This was reconstituted with BSS, Alcon's proprietary isotonic balanced salt solution launched in 1959. Fleming and Louis J. Girard, an ophthalmologist at Baylor College of Medicine in Houston, collaborated on creating BSS, which was safer for eye tissues than similar salt solutions. Alcon originally packaged the sterile compound in a glass vial that could be placed on a surgeon's operating tray. In 1967 the company relaunched BSS in a modified Drop-tainer, to which an irrigating needle could be attached (fig. 3.28).

In 1964 Dr. Richard D. Sudarsky invented a disposable cryoextractor for the cataractous lens in which freon cooled a sheathed copper probe to -5^0C. When touched to the

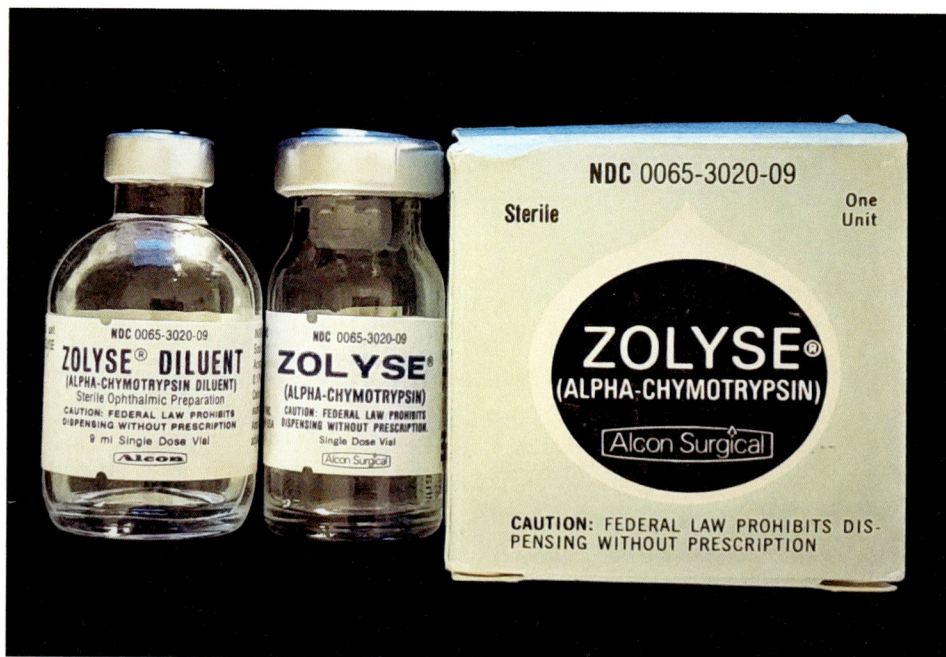

FIG 3.27
Zolyse, 1958 (TOM, AM)

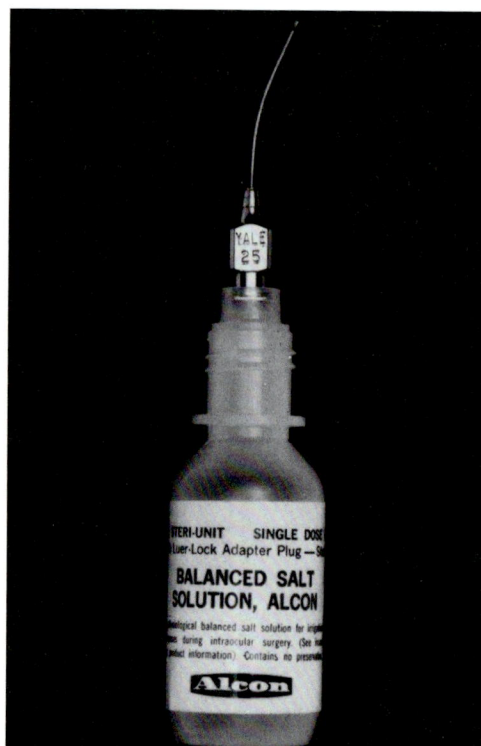

FIG 3.28
BSS with 25-gauge irrigation cannula, 1967
(AHR)

lens, it froze to the surface. Once attached, the cataract lens was safely removed. Alcon licensed the Cryophake and manufactured the sterile disposable units; an improved version, Cryophake II, was launched in 1966 (fig. 3.29). For some parts of the world, Alcon marketed a small portable ethylene oxide sterilizer designed for the Cryophake. A companion product was the sterile disposable Optemp, a cautery for eye surgery. As long as cryo-extraction surgery dominated cataract extraction, these Alcon products dominated ophthalmic surgical suites.[76]

The Kefauver-Harris amendments to the FD&C Act in 1962 made guidelines for NDAs more extensive and complex. A few weeks afterward, Alcon filed the NDA for idoxuridine, an ophthalmic antiviral drug. Created in the 1950s as a cancer treatment, idoxuridine had been abandoned due to its toxicity. Dr. Herbert Kaufman, a resident in the Massachusetts Eye and Ear Infirmary of Harvard Medical School, discovered that idoxuridine effectively treated ocular herpes simplex infections. Alcon obtained the rights to develop idoxuridine and conducted a thirteen-month clinical study in thirty-two hundred patients. The FDA approved the NDA on June 28, 1963, and Alcon soon launched Dendrid (fig. 3.30). Dendrid was the first antiviral drug approved for ocular use.[77]

In May 1962 the Alcon board of directors approved creation of the Alcon Eye Research Foundation to support "progress toward better eye health and preservation of vision." Maxwell was the first chairman, and the trustees were Conner and the Rev. Granville T. Walker, minister of the University Christian Church. The trustees donated $135,000 toward constructing the research building of the Wilmer Eye Institute at Johns Hopkins University. Conner was friends with Dr. A. Edward Maumenee Jr., who had been the director of the Wilmer since 1955. Over the next thirty-five years, the Alcon Eye Research Foundation donated millions of dollars to ophthalmology departments and institutes and expanded its charter to include individuals, civic organizations, and nonprofit institutions not associated with the ophthalmology community.[78]

A large part of Conner's success lay in his innovative thinking, which can be seen in

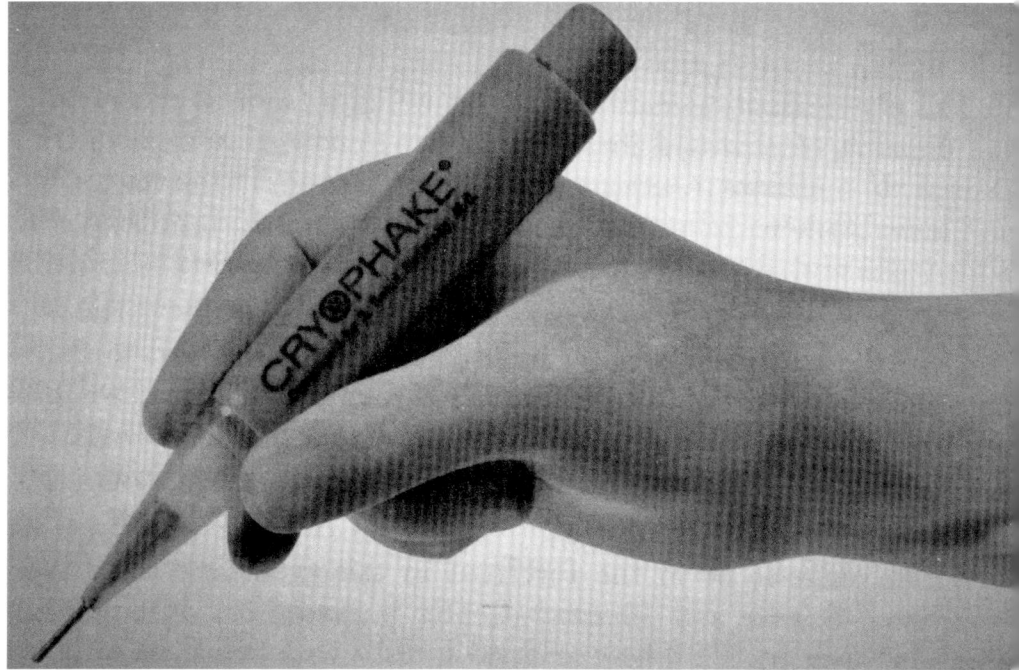

FIG 3.29
Cryophake II, 1966 (AHR)

FIG 3.30
Promoting Dendrid, Alcon's new
antiviral medication, 1963 (AHR)

his concept for Senior Eye Residents Visiting Alcon (SERVA). In 1959 there were approximately two hundred fourth-year ophthalmology residents in the United States. In the proposed SERVA program, all fourth-year residents would spend a weekend at Alcon. They would tour the facilities, meet the executives and R&D scientists, hear lectures about Alcon's projects and products, and be feted at a local restaurant. Schollmaier explained Conner's rationale: "Bill reasoned that our future lay entirely with ophthalmologists. He felt that if we could get to know them early on in their careers, that if we could communicate to them our intense commitment to advancing ophthalmic technology, then we could build on this relationship in the years ahead."

A key element of Conner's concept of the SERVA program was transportation in a company-owned airplane. This was hotly debated. Although the value of having residents visit Alcon was clear, Alcon directors were reluctant to buy a plane. The exchange between Conner and Neighbors during the July 28, 1959, board meeting summarized the dispute: "Dr. Neighbors–I think it could be a luxury right now that we could ill afford. Mr. WCC [Conner]—I don't view it as a luxury. Dr. Neighbors—I would not put it down as a necessity." Expense was the major hurdle: the plane would cost almost $350,000. Alcon's sales that year were $2 million with a profit of $163,000 and the company was borrowing money to build its new campus. In early 1960, the board provisionally approved the SERVA program but delayed leasing a plane by tying it to a minimum volume of $30 million in annual sales.[79]

Conner's interest in the plane did not abate. Alexander never saw the value of Alcon owning a plane but that did not prevent him from taking his son, Denny, for a test flight in a turboprop aircraft at Fort Worth's Meacham Field. When Milton Barley joined the finance group in 1962, he was assigned the task of calculating the cost of air travel for the SERVA program. Every time, he concluded that flying the residents first class on a commercial flight was far less expensive than the cost of Alcon owning a plane. Whenever the topic arose, Schollmaier opposed it, for which both he and Barley expected Conner to fire them. The airplane debate finally ended sometime in the early 1970s. The first SERVA occurred in 1963 (fig. 3.31), with residents arriving on commercial flights, but the costs proved prohibitive and the program was suspended. R&D was still in its infancy, and it was determined that funds were better applied to the expansion of facilities. Alcon never bought a plane, and it even instituted a policy that no employee on company business could fly in a charter or private aircraft. In any case, the SERVA program restarted in the 1980s.[80]

When Alcon bought land for the south campus, it also acquired eighty-four acres belonging to a small private airfield, Russell Field. Wiggins, an Alcon director, and J. Franklin Campbell, a Fort Worth dermatologist, bought the adjacent ninety-one acres. Beginning in 1958, Alcon's board discussed converting the eighty-four acres into an industrial park, much like the Amon G. Carter Industrial Park located to the south. By 1959 deliberations focused on combining Alcon's land with the acreage owned by Wiggins and Campbell and creating the Alcon Park Corporation. There were tax advantages, and Alcon could reassign any outstanding loans as a liability for the Alcon Park Corporation. In 1960 Wiggins and Campbell sold Alcon forty-two acres. Alcon combined its 126 acres with Wiggins and Campbell's remaining acreage to create the South Freeway Corporation, 62 percent of which Alcon thus owned. Later the name was changed to Highland Terrace Park Company. The land remained vacant until the 1980s, allowing then for Alcon's facility expansion, creating the world's largest ophthalmic specialty company campus.[81]

Alcon's new campus administration building opened in 1961. Its main entrance,

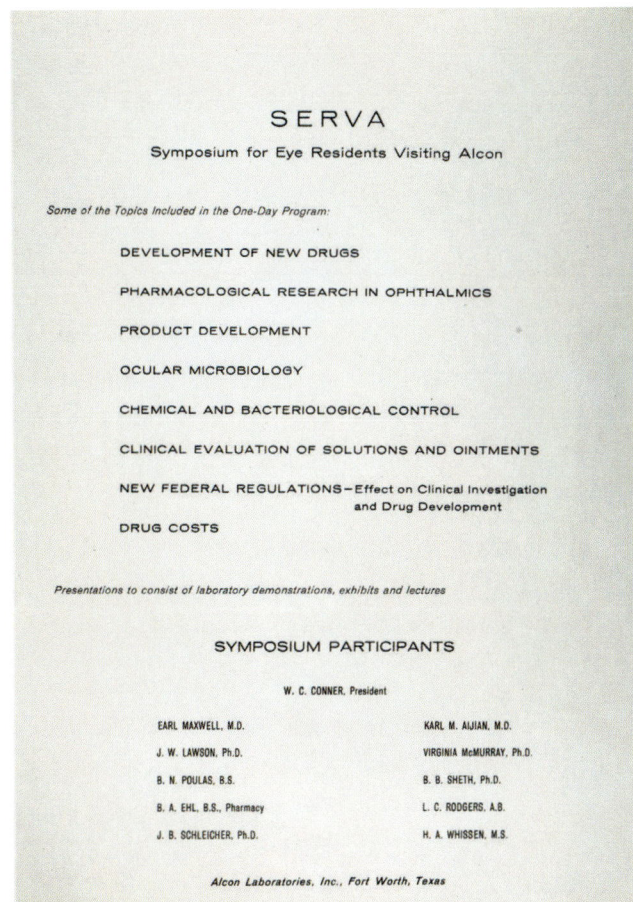

FIG 3.31
SERVA, Senior Eye Residents Visiting Alcon, 1963–1964 (AHR)

through double-glass doors into a spacious glass-lined atrium, was classic mid-century modern architecture. The two-office personnel department could be found in the far corner. Until then, each department had done its own hiring, with most candidates located through existing employees or employment agencies. Alcon only began to advertise jobs in the local newspaper in 1962. While Alcon had an employee handbook before 1961, policies and salary guidelines were mostly informal. The first personnel director was Walter V. Roberson, a taciturn, straitlaced man, who joined the company in 1963. In the 1960s and early 1970s, individuals seeking a job at Alcon often came to the campus and filled out an application. If their experience met an existing opening, they might be interviewed by the hiring department that same day. This happened to Howard Luttrell in October 1969 and Martha Siegel in July 1970. More typically, applications circulated around the departments and promising candidates were invited for interviews.

A job offer started a formal process that included a physical examination and reference checks. On the first day of work, Roberson would discuss Alcon policies with a new employee, introduce the insurance plan, and explain the PST. Often, Roberson displayed a graph showing that with Alcon's PST, a twenty-three-year-old person could expect to retire as a millionaire. He also strongly encouraged everyone to contribute to the United Way Fund. Roberson then escorted the employee to his or her supervisor. Tours of the campus were given monthly to all recent hires, with the manufacturing line being the highlight. Camaraderie was high at Alcon, and the cafeteria was the central meeting point. There was ample time to meet everybody because all employees had an hour for lunch as well as morning and afternoon coffee breaks.[82]

As the number of Alcon employees increased, the personnel and finance departments became more formally structured under Andrews. Payroll issued each person a unique number: Conner was 1; Alexander, 2; Newton, 3; Merrill, 4; and so on. Schollmaier was the sixtieth person hired under this system. When a person left the company, that number was retired and never used again. The number was used for many purposes, and long-term employees remembered theirs forever. Alexander and Conner often credited Alcon's success to its employees and the reward system with programs like PST and an option for medical insurance offered by New York Life, beginning in 1957. Premiums were paid by Alcon with an initial cost to the employee of about $85 per year to insure a family. Insurance paid 80 percent of medical costs, after a $50 deductible. By the end of the decade, prescription coverage was added with a small co-pay. In general, Alcon's medical insurance provided more extensive coverage for less cost than most companies in the area.

Every year Alcon contributed to the PST; for example, the contribution in 1959 was $43,394, in 1960, $57,228, and in 1961, $73,911. The PST was governed by a committee of Alcon employees who invested the assets in a balanced fund, which steadily increased. Just as Roberson told new employees, many retired as millionaires. Alcon made one major change in the vesting period: in the mid-1960s a person became fully vested after ten years. About 1961 Alcon began bestowing service awards—brooches for women and lapel pins for men—based on years of employment. Each was an exquisite piece of jewelry fabricated by local jewelers, Haltom's Jewelers being one. The design centered on Alcon's logo, with rubies, sapphires, or diamonds denoting the number of employment years (fig. 3.32). Awardees in Fort Worth were invited to join Conner in the executive boardroom for a ceremony, plus coffee and cookies.[83]

Known for its innovative marketing strategies, Alcon had success using a series of surrealistic paintings of the human eye, the work of medical illustrator Emil Gustav Bethke. Born in North Dakota in 1906, Bethke became interested in medical illustration while a student in the art department at the University of Iowa, and a part-time job at the University Hospital. Soon he was specializing in drawing the eye and became the medical illustrator at the Institute of Ophthalmology at Presbyterian Medical Center in New York City. In 1957 he combined his knowledge of the eye and its diseases and created a series of twelve abstract, surrealistic oil paintings, entitled *Fantasia Ophthalmologica*. Bethke was struck by how "closely anatomical details within the eye resembled everyday things." He described his *Iris Arrangement* (fig. 3.33) as "a study showing that the human iris calls for recognition of its own inherent beauty."

When Zolyse was launched in 1959, Alcon purchased Bethke's twelve surrealistic paintings of the eye and began displaying them at medical meetings. Hundreds of printed copies were used for promotion. In 1960 a reprint of *Lacus Lacrimalus* was mailed to ophthalmologists with a letter promoting Zincfrin. The executive boardroom in the new administration building had specially designed cupboards for the permanent display of the twelve original paintings. Intrigued by Bethke's abstract interpretations, Conner commissioned him to explore the mission and people of Alcon, resulting in a series of paintings

FIG 3.32
Alcon service awards, two to thirty-five years, 2021 (Author's collection)

FIG 3.33
Emil Bethke,
Iris Arrangement
(AHR)

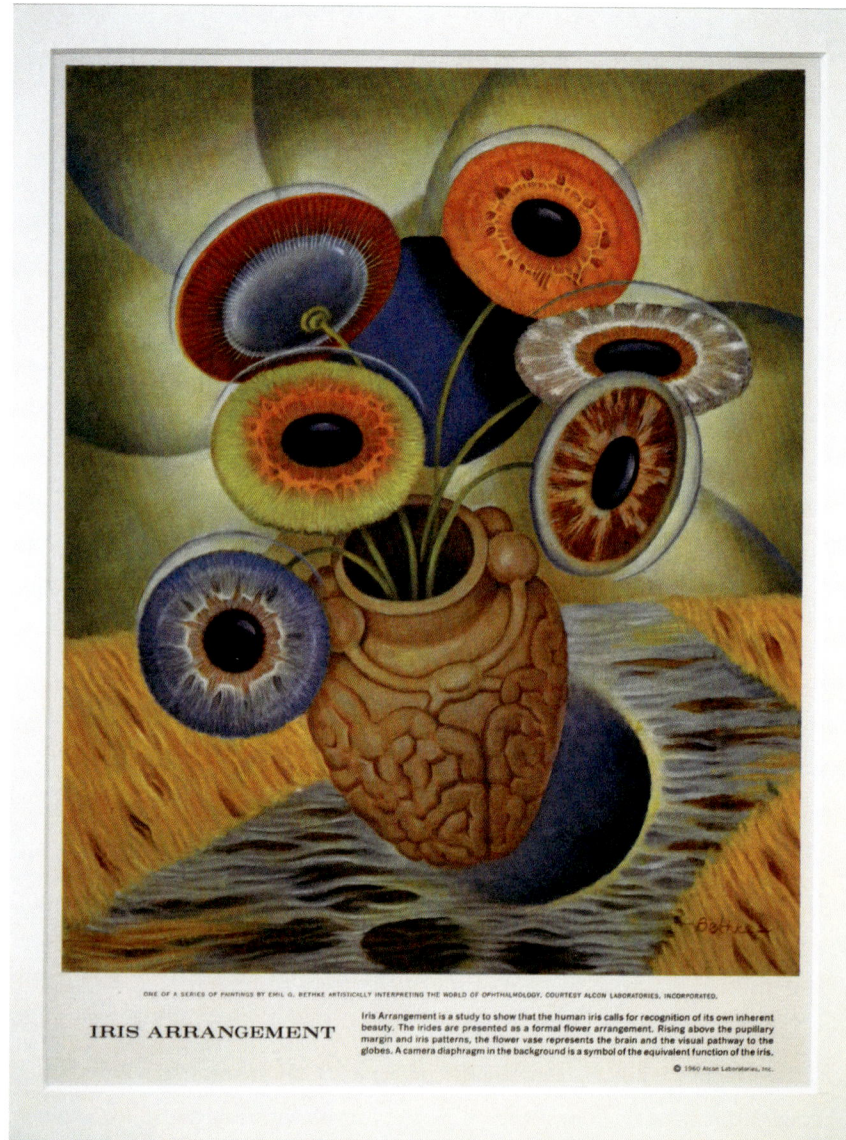

ONE OF A SERIES OF PAINTINGS BY EMIL G. BETHKE ARTISTICALLY INTERPRETING THE WORLD OF OPHTHALMOLOGY. COURTESY ALCON LABORATORIES, INCORPORATED.

IRIS ARRANGEMENT

Iris Arrangement is a study to show that the human iris calls for recognition of its own inherent beauty. The irides are presented as a formal flower arrangement. Rising above the pupillary margin and iris patterns, the flower vase represents the brain and the visual pathway to the globes. A camera diaphragm in the background is a symbol of the equivalent function of the iris.

© 1960 Alcon Laboratories, Inc.

entitled *Executive Appraisal*, one being *The Flame*. For a person unfamiliar with the eye's anatomy, the paintings can be jolting; they appear surrealistic, with unusual colors and images. Nevertheless, Alcon employees came to embrace the value and importance of these rare paintings.[84]

Alexander was deliberative and believed in revisiting critical decisions to see if actions needed to be modified; Conner was less reflective. As the latter's son, Halden, later wrote,

"He was never in doubt." Conner's and Alexander's complementary personalities were well matched but at times Alexander's caution made him apprehensive about Conner's larger-than-life persona. One issue for Alexander was Alcon's international profile, and Buhler often invited him for lunch to explain how the International Division helped Alcon "become a global company listed on the New York Stock Exchange." He showed Alcon's new manufacturing and marketing operation in Canada to Alexander, and in mid-May 1964 they went to Mexico City. It was during this visit that they received a letter from Maxwell with the alarming news that Conner had suffered a heart attack. Maxwell noted that several people had agreed to represent Conner in his upcoming commitments, and he did not think the incident was sufficiently serious for them to return to Fort Worth. It proved to be a key event for Alcon.[85]

In addition to leading Alcon, Conner had an active family life during which, according to Halden, they "did lots of things together." Conner also participated in social, commercial, and civic endeavors, seeking leadership roles in almost every organization he joined and helping to modify their charters and operations. By 1957 Alcon hired an administrative assistant, Wanda Calvert, to manage Conner's non-Alcon responsibilities. He also chose to be visibly active in the PAAO and the Pharmaceutical Manufacturers Association (PMA), attending annual meetings and serving in executive roles for both organizations. In 1959 he was one of three vice presidents for the PMA, and he later led regional chapters and various committees. He also served with government agencies, such as when President Eisenhower asked him to advise the Small Business Administration. Moreover, he participated in local, regional, and national activities of the Republican Party. In Fort Worth, he became a director for banks and other businesses. Socially, Conner served in many capacities at the Colonial Country Club, including several terms as president. Conner was active in the Fort Worth Chamber of Commerce. He led fundraising drives for the local Tuberculosis Society, Texas Boys Choir, Campfire Girls, Fort Worth Community Theater, National Fund for Medical Education, and others. Three organizations in particular took much of his time—Junior Achievement, the Society to Prevent Blindness, and the United Fund. Moreover, he and Alexander were prominent in the University Christian Church. Supporting the Sportworthians, Texas Christian University's football booster club, led to Connor's role in participation in the creation of the TCU Research Foundation, after which he became a trustee of TCU. He spent much of each day at Alcon, but he lunched with business leaders at the Fort Worth Club. On March 20, 1964, the *Fort Worth Star-Telegram* commented that in addition to being a TCU trustee and director of its foundation, Conner was also "a director of 18 other businesses, research and charitable organizations."[86]

At some point, Conner and Alexander accepted that they had exceeded their skill level and that Alcon needed to undergo a transition. This likely started about 1957, when they infused the company with MBA graduates. But there were other signs that they needed help from better equipped, academically trained executives. The company was outgrowing both of them. By 1958 Merrill could no longer rely on formulating known pharmacological compounds. Advances in eye research had to be led by young, innovative ophthalmologists and scientists. Johnson's departure on Black Friday in 1961 was another clear sign; the complexity of his assignments exceeded his skills. Conner's decision to locate a top-notch scientist to lead R&D to the next level was correct, but he lacked the skills, insight, or process to find one, and the hiring of Priddle was an abject failure. Conner and Alexander also discovered that acquisitions brought many unfamiliar problems. Fortunately, Schollmaier's marketing aptitude and Leone's selling expertise kept driving Alcon's sales upward, and by 1964 it was clear international growth was a long-term commitment. Halden Conner recalled the 1960s as "unsettled times." He continued, "Alcon reached a point where, 24 hours a day, seven days a week, [Conner] still couldn't keep hold of it all." Schollmaier was blunter: "It's typical, I think, of a lot of entrepreneurs that they're chasing something in their outside lives as well as in their company. Bill was involved with too many clubs … he really needed to rethink everything."[87]

All came to a head on the afternoon of May 15, 1964. Conner had to be hospitalized, but he was fortunate. DeWitt Neighbors, an Alcon board member and foremost Fort Worth cardiologist, concluded that he had suffered a heart attack. As he was examining Conner, the Alcon executive asked, "Dee, how bad is this?" Neighbors replied, "Bill, what happened, what difference does it make? You're a dead man. You know, why do we worry about the details? … Look at your lifestyle. … This is just inevitable. It's going to happen again and you'll be gone." Conner took several weeks off, stopped smoking, began to walk daily, ate healthier, and, when he returned to work, took an afternoon nap in his office. He bought a yacht, a fifty-foot Hatteras (fig. 3.34), and passed the examination for a captain's license. Unless he was out of town on business, most weekends found him with his family and invited guests sailing on the Texas Gulf Coast. However, some habits remained unchanged. He arrived early to work each day and took his lunch downtown at the Fort Worth Club. He may have withdrawn from some organizations—for example, in subsequent years, his name never appears with the United Fund drives—but he did not slow down. The *Fort Worth Star-Telegram* in November 1965 listed his directorships and the organizations in which he still actively participated, and their number was almost exactly the same as before his cardiovascular episode.[88]

Alcon continued to grow, from one hundred employees to almost four hundred, including thirty overseas. When touting Alcon, Alexander and Conner always credited the company's success to its employees, referred to as the *Alcon Family*. At Alcon, *family* meant camaraderie in pursuit of common goals. The layout and location of the campus fostered solidarity. Monday through Friday, morning to night, everybody worked in collaboration, and friendships developed as employees mingled during lunch and coffee breaks. Camaraderie spilled out beyond working hours into popular bowling leagues and other sports and social activities. The sense of family was expressed by many. Lowell Dix from manufacturing recalled, "What I really liked about it was that we were just one big happy family basically; people really loved their job. ... People would ... pitch in and do whatever was necessary to get the job done." Alma Collins, also from manufacturing, remembered, "Once we did get to know each other, really know each other: we were like family." Barry Schlech from R&D, Schweitzer from marketing, and Alberta Renick from the library all spoke fondly of the Alcon Family. Lorenzo-Daniell recalled, "I remember my first Christmas party with Alcon: it was like a big family having a party." These sentiments were ingrained into memories, especially for those whose employment began in the 1960s and 1970s. They were young—in their twenties and thirties—and many stayed at Alcon until they retired; for some, Alcon was the only employer they ever had. The cumulative years of experience among these employees and the wide array of issues they faced and problems they solved cannot be underestimated. There are various reasons for Alcon's success; this is one. It all goes back to Alexander and Conner's notion of the *Alcon Family*.

At the end of Alcon's first decade, annual sales reached $1 million and profits were just shy of $200,000. Ten years later, in 1967 annual sales reached $11,579,565 and profits

FIG 3.34
Seven Cs, fifty-foot
Hatteras yacht, 1964 (AFP)

FIG 3.35
Alcon Sales and Net Income—
1958–1967 (TOM, AM)

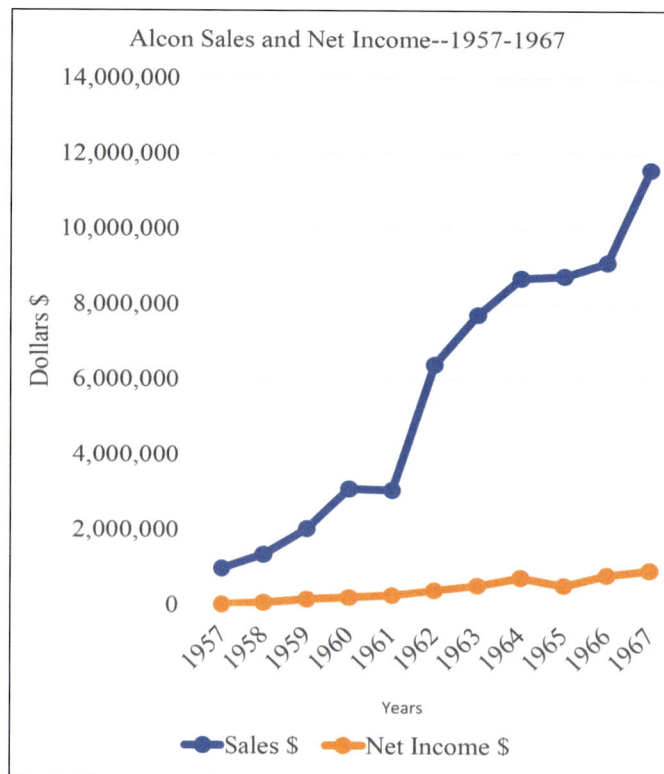

Alcon Sales and Net Income--1957-1967

increased to $951,208 (fig. 3.35). Another way to compare the first two decades is by using cumulative sales and net profits. Cumulative sales in the first ten years were $3.379 million, and for the second decade, $61.781 million. Cumulative net income rose from $64,592 to $4.716 million. While the acquisition of Conal fueled some of the growth after 1961, the bulk of the increase was a result of breakthrough products such as Zolyse, Statrol, Maxidex, Maxitrol, Mydriacyl, Dendrid, BSS, and Cryophake. Henceforth, Alcon's growth relied on the discovery, development, and marketing of entirely new therapies or devices. These future cutting-edge products would require new skills in technology and management across every department. Alcon's goal in the first decade was to reinvest profits. While that remained the focus from 1958 through 1967, the company began to pay modest dividends, the first being five cents per share in April 1966.

* * *

From 1958 through 1967 Conner and Alexander, and the *Alcon Family*, had established their firm as the dominant pharmaceutical force in the ophthalmic world. The two leaders were justifiably gratified by Alcon's accomplishments from 1958 to 1967. To celebrate, they invited citizens of Fort Worth to visit their campus to commemorate Alcon's twentieth anniversary (fig. 3.36).[90']

It had been a dynamic, hectic adventure, yet the journey was not complete. As the 1960s ended, ophthalmology, commerce, and technology were on the verge of remarkable, powerful changes. The next decade would require extraordinary scientists, managers, marketers, salesmen, financial experts, formulators, packing engineers, and others to evaluate and harness the most promising developments. Novel, flexible organizational ideas would be needed from talented leaders. Alcon's future would be decided in the next ten years.

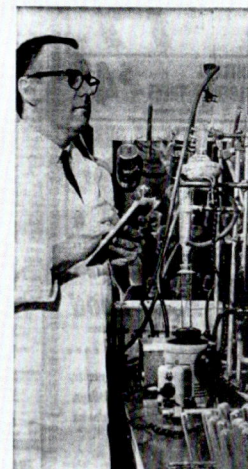

Alcon

We're Number 1

We might have been only Number 2 if we'd started our business anywhere but Fort Worth

It will be twenty years ago Tuesday that we opened the doors of our Business as a corporate body. Now, we're Number 1 in the ophthalmological pharmaceutical specialty and have an international operation active in 63 countries, another pharmaceutical company, and two plastics manufacturing companies in our corporate family. Just like those two battling car-rental companies, we've not gone soft, and we certainly haven't forgotten our friends –those who helped us in the lean years, who contributed to our growth with patience and counsel.

To all our friends, customers and supporters–especially in those early years– we want you to know that you are Number 1 with us.

We sincerely want to say "thanks" to each of you for your help and support. We would appreciate having the opportunity to do this in person – Won't you please come by our business, 6201 South Freeway, ON TUESDAY, MAY 16, BETWEEN 9:00 A.M. and 4:00 P.M. for birthday cake and coffee and visit with us?

　　Bill Conner　　Bob Alexander

Alcon

The Alcon Story

May 16, 1947—Founding of Alcon Laboratories, Inc.
1955—Alcon enters international market.
1958—Groundbreaking for Alcon Complex.
1962—Purchase of subsidiaries—Conal Pharmaceuticals, Inc., Chicago, and Service Engineers, Inc., Fort Worth.
1966—Marketing of first surgical instrument—CRYOPHAKE.
1966—Purchase of Polyco, Inc., Atlanta and New Orleans.
1967—Groundbreaking for Alcon Science and Research Center, Fort Worth.

FIG 3.36
Twentieth-anniversary invitation to public: "We're Number 1" (*FWST*, May 14, 1967)

Chapter 4

"We're Partners. Let's Try to Build a Great Company."

1968–1977

Alcon
LABORATORIES

The history of Alcon cannot be told in a straightforward way with organizational charts based upon a static hierarchy. Alcon's transformation was fluid and organic, and its story is one of people, products, leadership, focus, innovation, and debate. For many, Alcon's trajectory during its third decade was exhilarating—and the reason so many top-notch individuals spent their entire careers there. Bill Conner and Bob Alexander regularly acknowledged that the strength of the company lay in having such people, the *Alcon Family*.

Individuals found Alcon in a variety of ways, especially personal connections. Gerald Hecht and Robert E. Roehrs met in the mid-1960s as doctoral candidates in the Purdue University School of Pharmacy. When Roehrs contacted him in 1969, Hecht was the ophthalmic pharmaceutical director in R&D at Alcon. After two years teaching at the West Virginia University School of Pharmacy, Roehrs had become disillusioned with academia, so he became the head of ophthalmic product development at Alcon. He started in July 1970 and soon met Conner during one of Conner's Friday afternoon strolls. Conner was interested in Roehrs's experience in clinical pharmacy at West Virginia, where he helped start its program. Clinical pharmacists collaborate with physicians in selecting optimal drugs and dosages, and help monitor patients for the therapy's effectiveness and safety. The role of clinical pharmacists and their training intrigued Conner, who always looked for something new to sponsor. Through Alcon's connections at the Wills Eye Hospital, Thomas Jefferson University Hospital, Philadelphia, and the Wilmer Eye Institute, Johns Hopkins School of Medicine, Baltimore, the company began sponsoring clinical pharmacists to join ophthalmology residents on rounds.[1]

The science of pharmacy had moved beyond Alexander and Conner's generation, and so had the management of a technology-based pharmaceutical company. People who thrived at Alcon were those willing to embrace challenges, adapt to changing industry mandates, develop new technologies, and accept constructive criticism. For those individuals, there was no better place in the 1960s and 1970s than Alcon. They became part of three seminal events: Alcon's listing on the New York Stock Exchange (NYSE) in 1971; Ed Schollmaier becoming president in 1972; and Alcon's acquisition by a well-known non-pharmaceutical company in 1977. These and other events transformed Alcon's organization, leadership, technology, facilities, products, and marketing strategies.[2]

Alcon's strength lay in how the two founders complemented each other: Conner was decisive, while Alexander was deliberate. Yet their close relationship had come to a crossroads. Alexander's son, Denny, understood the complexity of the relationship: "Bill Conner and my father were very contrasting personalities, and I think the contrasts were enlarged or broadened as the years went on. Bill was the visionary, more the entrepreneur. Dad was much more practical, more down to earth. That made the two personalities a good blend." Conner's son, Halden, described the situation well: "Bill and Bob ... were trying to figure out how they were going to go forward, how they were going to survive and what they were going to do with each other. ... Operationally, Alcon was Bill Conner's domain. ... But from a stockholding perspective, Bob and Bill were equal. ... This created great natural conflicts for Bob, Bill and the board."[3]

As Alcon became a $10 million company in the mid-1960s, it had outgrown the duo's talents, so they brought Schollmaier and George Leone to Fort Worth and placed them in charge of marketing and sales. Schollmaier and Leone described Alexander's nature as collaborative while noting that Conner often made decisions without consulting others, unless he needed the board's approval. As 1968 began, Conner consolidated his presidential role, while Alexander focused on Conal and managing Schollmaier and Leone. However, their relationship was not typical of American company structures. Conner dominated as the final decision-maker, although he increasingly listened to Schollmaier and Leone. Alexander told Schollmaier and Leone that he was frustrated at being sidelined by Conner. Conner had elevated Alexander to vice chairman of the board, a less operational role. The situation became complicated since, after Conner and Alexander, Leone and Schollmaier owned or had options on the greatest number of Alcon shares.[4]

Whatever transpired between Alexander and Conner never affected their ownership of

Alcon shares. In June 1958 the stockholders authorized amending the firm's charter to issue one million shares and let existing shares be exchanged on a one-to-one basis. The number of shares remained unchanged until April 25, 1969, when stockholders endorsed a split and increased the number from one million to four million. At this point, holders of both stock and stock options owned 1,352,470 of the authorized shares. The remainder could be used for growth.[5]

In March 1971 Alcon proposed selling 250,000 unissued shares, and several stockholders offered an additional seventy-five thousand shares at a share price of $50.25. To justify the price, the prospectus noted that Alcon stock had climbed from $19.25 in 1968 to $52.25. Earle Shields, in the Fort Worth office of Merrill Lynch, Pierce, Fenner & Smith, managed the sale. Alcon anticipated earning almost $12 million from the sale, using about $10.5 million to retire debts, and spending $1.5 million on R&D projects, a joint venture, facility renovation and expansion, and overseas operations. Based on sales and growth data, Alcon projected that its 1971 fiscal year sales would be nearly $30 million, with a profit slightly over $2 million. The sale succeeded, and Shields gave Conner a check for $11,875,000.[6]

The March 1971 prospectus is revealing in other ways. The three highest-paid officers, not including bonuses, were Conner ($57,000), Alexander ($43,250), and Schollmaier ($62,700). The remaining officers (Leone, Buhler, Sam S. Barklis, Glenn Wilkins, Henry P. Kologe, Dale B. Hinson) and directors (Harold Beasley, Gordon Ellis, Gene Engleman, John Glover, DeWitt Neighbors, D. O. Tomlin) received an aggregate compensation of $332,038. The prospectus also provides a good inventory of the major stockholders. Alexander owned 153,254 shares (10.55 percent), Conner had 146,414 (10.08 percent) and the remaining officers and directors held 375,774 (25.86 percent). Just fifteen people owned 46.49 percent of Alcon's shares. However, many sold shares after the 1971 sale, reducing their ownership to 30.86 percent. Alexander kept 93,254 shares (5.48 percent), Conner, 131,414 (7.72 percent), and the other officers and directors, 300,774 (17.66 percent). As trustees, Alexander controlled another 5,650 shares and Conner, 16,736. In any case, the dominant set of shares remained in a few hands. In June 1971 Alcon made another stock split that increased the outstanding shares from 1,730,000 to 2,595,000.[7]

The March 1971 prospectus also provided a good insight into Alcon's recent business. The company had borrowed more than $10 million to finance acquisitions and fund operations. Alcon had acquired Lawton Company, Center Laboratories, Madland Laboratories, Oftalmología, S.A. (renamed Oftasa, located in Mexico), and Établissements A. Couvreur, S.A. (in Belgium). Through a joint venture, Alcon began developing polymer and collagen products for medical and cosmetic applications in 1970. Alcon's consolidated sales had increased from $9.4 million in 1966 to $24.6 million in 1970, while net income had increased from $843,000 to $1.6 million. Alcon paid modest quarterly dividends over this period and retained most of its earnings to finance expansion, which it intended to continue. Since 1967 pharmaceutical products' contribution to sales had been 67 percent, surgical devices 17 percent, and plastic containers 16 percent. Pharmaceuticals dominated income at 87 percent, while surgical devices contributed 10 percent and plastic containers 3 percent.

Alcon itself manufactured and marketed approximately 25 prescription ophthalmic pharmaceuticals. Isopto Carpine for the treatment of glaucoma accounted for approximately 16 percent of sales in 1970, and no other ophthalmic product accounted for over 5 percent. Conal's uriceutical, Urised, contributed approximately 5.5 percent of sales, but no other urological product accounted for more than 0.6 percent.[8]

Alcon owned all plants manufacturing pharmaceuticals sold in the United States. These plants produced about 44 percent of products sold abroad; all overseas production by third parties was closely supervised. In the United States, Alcon's marketing and sales were divided into Domestic Products (ophthalmics, optical, ophthalmic surgical products), Specialty Products (urology, allergy, pediatric products), and the Lawton Company (surgical instruments). Within the United States, 118 MSRs sold Alcon's products. About 95 percent of Alcon's domestic sales were with 490 pharmaceutical wholesalers, 40 optical distributors, 400 surgical supply dealers, and 2,200 hospitals and physicians. Outside the United States, most products were sold through fourteen subsidiary companies in almost seventy-five countries. The International Division maintained its operational headquarters in Fort Worth, with regional offices in selected cities. In its 1971 annual report, Alcon noted its intention to be listed on the NYSE. The NYSE approved Alcon's application in September. On October 4, Alcon joined the NYSE when 2,756,921 shares were listed under the ALC label. It was a great achievement for Alexander and Conner, and a grand occasion for Fort Worth. On the preceding Friday, the Chamber of Commerce honored the two with a luncheon at the Fort Worth Club. The *Fort Worth Star-Telegram* reported that Alcon was the second Tarrant County–founded company listed on the NYSE. Alexander and Conner, their wives, other Alcon officers, and various business leaders journeyed to New York for the first listing (fig. 4.1). The duo appeared on the trading floor with the NYSE president, each received a strip of the ticker tape (fig. 4.2), and ceremoniously bought shares, one hundred apiece. Conner donated his to Research to Prevent Blindness, while Alexander gave his to the Texas Society to Prevent Blindness. Alcon's listing on the NYSE ranked among the company's top historic events.[9]

Leadership changes had preceded the NYSE listing. In 1968 the technical departments of Alcon were consolidated into the Science & Technology Division (S&T), charged with research, product development, quality control, and regulatory affairs. Alcon spent about 10 percent of its sales on this group. Alcon employed about 1,300 people, of whom about 130 worked in S&T, 500 in manufacturing, 350 in marketing and sales, and the remainder in administration and accounting. The company's stock option and profit-sharing plans were meant to attract and retain high-caliber employees in all of these areas, but S&T became especially crucial.[10]

In 1968 Schollmaier and Leone led marketing and sales, Buhler continued building the international business, Bob Carter managed Manufacturing, Harvey Andrews headed the Finance Department, and Earl Maxwell, soon to retire, directed S&T. Unbeknown to all, in June, Conner hired Sam Steven Barklis, a physician, as general manager of S&T. Barklis proposed exploring "biomedical engineering, psycho-pharmacology, dermatology, and other potential new specialty areas." When he presented his vision to Conner's management team, Schollmaier was devastated. He recalled, "My God, we've finally got to a point where we've got a guy who wants to take us off the cliff! We had worked so hard to get focused on ophthalmology and now our R&D director wanted to take us in a completely different direction." The hire also blindsided Alexander. Although Conner never said so, many employees understood Barklis might replace Conner when he retired. Andrews realized his opportunity to lead Alcon had vanished, so he left and started a personalized medical information company. The arrival of Barklis ushered in a tumultuous period at Alcon.[11]

The Newcomen Society in North America through lectures preserved business history in the United States. In October 1969 it honored Alexander and Conner. At the award dinner in Fort Worth, prominent executives heard the two men recount "The Story of Alcon Laboratories, Inc.: Prescription for Success." Alexander attributed Alcon's success to its employees and its deliberate specialization in the needs of ophthalmologists. Conner focused on the word *specialize*, referring to Alcon and ophthalmology, and Conal and urology. Conner declared that the past had shown that "diversified specialization was the right path for continued growth." He noted that Alcon had inaugurated its S&T building, increasing research in ophthalmology but expanding into other medical specialties. Conner proved prophetic: Alcon went on a buying spree, acquiring companies in a variety of specialties—allergy, pediatrics, and dermatology. It also signed a co-development agreement for a hemo-

FIG 4.1
Bill and Mary Frances Conner and
Catherine and Bob Alexander (*center*)
at the NYSE, Oct. 4, 1971 (AHR)

FIG 4.2
Left to right: Robert Haack,
Bill Conner, and Bob Alexander
reading ticker tape listing Alcon's
price (Courtesy of Founders'
Museum, Alcon)

static agent for surgeons and a contract to evaluate a new compound reputed to enhance learning. By early 1972 the fates of most of these ventures, and Barklis, were settled.[12]

Even before Conner's Newcomen Society speech, Alcon had implemented the plan he outlined. Food Machinery and Chemical Corporation (FMC), football based in San Jose, California, announced on October 9, 1969, a licensing agreement with Alcon to develop medical and cosmetic uses of FMC's microcrystalline collagen. One year later, Alcon and FMC formed a joint venture company, Avicon, located on Alcon's Fort Worth campus, to develop microcrystalline collagen. Both companies agreed to finance Avicon on an equal basis with an initial investment of $500,000 each. Barklis believed psychopharmacology was the frontier of new therapies, and he in-licensed an mRNA compound from International Chemical and Nuclear (ICN) that was purported to improve learning. On May 1, 1970, for $4,630,400 plus 3,600 Alcon shares worth $69,600, Alcon acquired Center Laboratories, a supplier to allergists and pediatricians. On June 30, 1971, in exchange for 201,340 of its shares, Alcon acquired the outstanding stock of the William A. Webster Company in Memphis. It manufactured and marketed suppositories for adults and children. On April 28, 1972, Alcon exchanged 707,000 shares and took ownership of Owen Laboratories, a small dermatology specialty company in Dallas.[13]

Alcon management also acquired ophthalmic companies. Borrowing $1,250,000, they bought Madland Laboratories, an ophthalmic pharmaceutical company specializing in glaucoma therapies based in Milwaukee, on June 23, 1969. For approximately $500,000 Alcon bought Fluorescite, a diagnostic solution used to visualize retinal blood, from C. F. Kirk Laboratories and Moore Kirk Laboratories in June 1970. To complement its mydriatic line of ocular medicines, in November 1971 Alcon purchased, for $1,650,000, three products from Schieffelin & Company: two mydriatics-cycloplegics and a soothing astringent for irritated eyes. Two years later, Alcon paid $2,200,000 for the Chicago firm of Mager & Gougelman, the premier manufacturer and distributor of customized prosthetic eyes since 1851. New technology paved the way for soft contact lenses, so Alcon signed a licensing agreement with Israel-American Technology, of New York, for its soft contact lens polymer. This was terminated in March 1971, so in 1974 Alcon signed a second agreement for a soft lens polymer patented by Hydro Optics, of New York, only to cancel the deal soon afterward. Flow Laboratories in Palo Alto, California, a developer of cleaning and sterilizing solutions for soft contact lenses, signed a nonexclusive agreement with Alcon in 1975 to market these products. Alcon acquired Lafayette Pharmacal, a manufacturer of radiopaque diagnostic pharmaceuticals, in 1977. The most significant licensing agreements occurred in 1977, for tobramycin from Eli Lily and for betaxolol from Synthélabo in Paris, France.[14]

Buhler searched for acquisitions outside the United States, and in 1968 Alcon bought Laboratorios Otto, S.A. in Buenos Aires. In March 1970 Alcon spent $548,000 for a majority share in Oftalmología, S.A., an ophthalmic pharmaceutical company in Mexico with robust export sales to Central America. Also in South America, Alcon acquired ophthalmic patents and trademarks from Companhia Industrial Delfos, of Rio de Janeiro, in June 1970, and three years later bought its ophthalmic manufacturing plant; this cost $100,000. In Europe, Alcon in April 1970 acquired Établissements A. Couvreur, S.A., a Belgian firm that manufactured and marketed pharmaceutical products and distributed hospital equipment and products in Belgium with exports to Africa; the cost totaled $1.37 million. In March 1972 Alcon got Quimico Farmacéutico Iberhis, S.A., in Barcelona. While Alcon debated how to enter the contact lens market, it made its first international foray by purchasing Nu-Syte Lab, an English company that developed and sold hard and soft contact lenses. In late 1975 Alcon acquired Farmila Farmaceutici Milano S.P.A., a leading ophthalmological and dermatological company in Milan. Alcon gave Farmila $2 million in cash plus an unspecified note. With these acquisitions, Alcon acquired manufacturing facilities overseas to support and expand its existing markets.[15]

While owning Service Engineers guaranteed Alcon's supply of plastic containers, the subsidiary struggled to expand its product line beyond what Alcon needed. The Polyco acquisition did not fix this. Between 1968 and 1970, plastics comprised 16 percent of Alcon's sales but only 3 percent of profits. Most sales were to Alcon. Moreover, plastic technology had advanced beyond Service Engineers' ability to meet emerging government and industry standards. Alcon manufacturing and R&D pursued other suppliers, and on May 2, 1970, Alcon sold Service Engineers for an undisclosed amount to Dougherty Brothers of New Jersey, one of the larger companies collaborating with Alcon for better Drop-tainers. One year later, Alcon sold Polyco at a loss of $176,000 to the Dorsey Company of Chattanooga. Alcon then divested the Lawton Company's general surgical instrument assets in 1974 but retained its line of ophthalmic surgical instruments. The sale to the Seamless Hospital Products Division of Dart Industries generated $4.2 million, in this strategic retreat Alcon lost $324,000.[16]

Barklis pushed to transform S&T at Alcon. After graduating from the University of Chicago Medical School, he had taught biochemistry at the University of Illinois College of Medicine and was a leading researcher at the Illinois Neuropsychiatric Institute. Before joining Alcon, Barklis served as the director of microbiology research at Ciba Pharmaceutical Company. To increase R&D, Barklis brought with him a synthetic chemist (Robert J. Adamski), two biochemists, a project director, and a recruiter of scientific personnel. Barklis divided S&T into five departments: Research, Development, QC, Medical, and Administration. Ted Fleming continued as QC director, as did Bill Padgett in Administration. Barklis hired a cadre of physicians who became core decision-makers. John D. Mullins directed Development, which included product development, led by Hecht; analytical chemistry, under Richard D. Poe; and packing engineering, led by Michael Helixon. Barklis directed Research himself, appointing Charles M. Kagawa as assistant director. The research groups focused on urology, pharmacology, toxicology, microbiology, biochemistry, and medicinal chemistry.[17]

Barklis was keen to attract a young chemist who had tamed the chaotic and unprofitable clinical laboratories at the University of California, San Francisco. A native of India, Dilip N. Raval obtained his doctoral degree at the University of Oregon and then worked for Varian, which developed instruments for chemical analyses. On several occasions in 1969, Barklis offered Raval a leadership role in R&D. Raval refused each time, so Barklis sweetened the deal, offering Raval a position as a consultant. Conner, also impressed by Raval, offered him Barklis's job if Barklis left. In October 1970, Raval joined Alcon as its research director. Not familiar with ophthalmology, he recruited a leading ophthalmologist, Samuel B. Aronson of the University of California, San Francisco, to be his consultant. The same year he also hired Howard M. Leibowitz, chair of the Department of Ophthalmology at Boston University Medical School and an expert in external diseases, to be another consultant. Two years later, in 1972, Raval recruited Steven Podos, soon to be the chair of the Department of Ophthalmology at Mount Sinai Medical School in New York City, to advise on glaucoma therapies. The use of recognized leaders in the ophthalmology academic world as consultants became common practice in Alcon R&D for the next twenty-five years. An early example of the consultants' value occurred with Aronson's critique of the rudimentary macro-examinations of animal eyes, leading Beasley and two young scientists to develop a quantitative system using the ophthalmologist's slit lamp, a paradigm that federal regulatory agencies began requiring for the chemical and pharmaceutical industries. Raval also implemented performance standards for his scientists to document contributions and focused on projects that mattered. His expectations were exacting, and his critiques pointed.[18]

FIG 4.3

Science & Technology scientists, 1969. Kneeling (*left to right*): Harold Wright (chemistry), unidentified, Danny Roles (QC), John Allen (process development), Ron Williams (urology research), Neal Bigelow (product development). Standing (*left to right*): Lee Heinrichs (chemistry), unidentified, Linda Thom (biochemistry), unidentified, Betty Fortenberry (pharmacology), Roxie Uberman (pharmacology), Elizabeth Taylor (biostatistics), unidentified, Carol Smith (project management), Roxie unknown. (AHR)

FIG 4.4

Alcon Fort Worth campus, 1971 (AHR)

By 1970 S&T employed 130 people, which included four M.D.s, thirty PhDs, ten master's degrees, and sixty-six bachelor's degrees (fig. 4.3). From 1966 to 1970, the number of scientists at Alcon had increased from 73 to 130, while annual S&T expenses had grown from nearly $1 million to $2.5 million. Moreover, after the 1968 expansion, the modern laboratories occupied fifty thousand square feet (fig. 4.4). Conner's vision of Alcon becoming an ophthalmic research center was becoming a reality; Alcon had the staff and facilities but had yet to produce new therapies.[19]

Psychopharmacology had become an area of interest for Conner when he hired Barklis. Shortly after his arrival, he established a program to test drugs for psychotropic properties and signed a testing agreement with ICN. Milan Panić, a Yugoslavian resistance fighter in World War II, biochemist, and 1956 political refugee, started ICN in his garage in 1959. In 1966 ICN developed the mRNA molecule ribaminol, and tests suggested that it enhanced learning. Newspapers throughout the United States reported on the potential applications for ribaminol. However, Alcon's studies in laboratory rats did not reproduce ICN's findings, so the agreement was terminated. Thereafter, this research disappeared from Alcon's annual reports. It was not the start Barklis wanted, and it was not the only time he overpromised and underdelivered.[20]

For Alcon, basic research was left to academic centers and the National Eye Institute. What Alcon did is aptly described as applied research. R&D used in vivo and in vitro models to test chemical compounds for a specific therapeutic activity. Alcon depended upon other pharmaceutical companies allowing it to test their inventories. If a chemical produced a desirable response, it moved from research to development and a Project Plan was created for testing in toxicology, formulation, microbiology, chemistry, packaging, process development, and other scientific functions to demonstrate the product was safe, sterile, stable, and preserved. Clinical studies were conducted to establish that the drug was effective and safe in patients. The scientific reports were organized into an NDA and sent to the appropriate government agency, such as the FDA.

Productive R&Ds have a continuous stream of projects that become the lifeline of any pharmaceutical company. After a product is marketed, issues may arise that require resolution by R&D; at Alcon these efforts were classified as Product Support. Once a new product was launched, marketing usually asked for additional data to use in promotional efforts; Alcon named these studies Market Support. As noted, every older Alcon product had to be reformulated and revisions submitted to the FDA after new regulations appeared. When

FIG 4.5
George Leone (AHR)

Barklis arrived, Product Support endeavors, in place since 1963, continued, consuming almost 75 percent of R&D resources. More scientists were hired, but most of R&D's resources continued to be devoted to Product and Market Support. The situation deteriorated with the acquisition of new companies. It is a good example of how Alcon leaders had to learn from failures and successes. Barklis clearly lacked foresight when he failed to insist that Alcon leaders identify priorities. He committed R&D to an increasing number of projects and, as a result, production of new products stagnated. Marketing and sales complained—Schollmaier and Leone criticized R&D. About the time Barklis arrived, Alcon launched its Contique line of contact lens products, which came from the creative insights of Schollmaier and his product manager, Norman Dewar. Contique succeeded. Barklis promised to deliver the new contact lens products by late 1971; however, when he found himself behind schedule and over budget, his situation became critical.[21]

Barklis's grandiose plans seldom came to fruition, of which the contact lens case was a prime example. Leone had hired thirteen MSRs to sell three new contact lens products, but when R&D failed to deliver these, he was forced to lay them off. The lack of consistency in R&D, and Barklis, became a point of contention between Schollmaier and Conner. However, it was not the only problem Schollmaier faced. Complications surrounding the Lawton Company and Center Laboratories forced Schollmaier to spend much time in New York. At the same, the joint venture with FMC to develop microcrystalline collagen, or Avitene, diverted R&D resources. Conner then made another unilateral decision. On February 4, 1972, he called Schollmaier into his office. What occurred set Alcon's course for the next twenty-five years.[22]

Conner started the conversation: "How long is it going to take you to fire Barklis?" Schollmaier countered, "Barklis is your guy. I thought I was supposed to try to work with him." Conner responded, "Well, my first assessment of you as the future president of the company is to see how long it takes you to get rid of this guy and get on the track we want to get on." Promoted at that instant to president and COO of Alcon, Schollmaier fired Barklis that afternoon and made Leone the vice president of S&T, responsible for R&D, QC, RA, and Manufacturing (fig. 4.5). He told Leone, "We're partners. Let's try to build a great company, one that has the strength of working well together." Schollmaier years later explained his rationale: "I chose George Leone because he had a tremendous insight into what was needed technologically in the business, and he was very good at getting guys to work together."[23]

Leone's intellect and experience fit this new role, and Alcon would benefit from his management style and strategic concepts. Since inception, Alcon had developed a specialized sales force focused on eye care specialists. But by 1971 R&D wanted to move Alcon, according to Leone, "into a broad area of the pharmaceutical industry, and there was no way we were going to survive as a very small company doing that." He believed Alcon's success lay in its "ability to carve out a specialty market in ophthalmology where the broad-based pharmaceutical industry, because of its priorities and structure, could not effectively compete." This became the underlying principle that transformed Alcon into a $2 billion ophthalmic specialty company by 1997. The journey was uneven and eventful, and it began on February 4, 1972. For the next thirteen years, the divisions of S&T—R&D, QC, RA, and Manufacturing—underwent structural and functional changes in response to advances in science and technology, with team members taking on increasingly diverse roles. After solving countless complex challenges, young folks hired in the 1960s and 1970s evolved into experienced managers and leaders.[24]

FIG 4.6
Dilip Raval (AHR)

Leone wanted Raval (fig. 4.6) to head R&D, but Schollmaier discovered resistance elsewhere in top management, particularly from Buhler, who was "absolutely convinced that R&D was totally screwed up" and Raval "was part of the problem." Initially, Schollmaier asked Raval to lead R&D, QC, RA, and Medical, reporting to Leone. Raval and Leone talked many times about how to let R&D focus on the important task of producing new products. Raval insisted that he needed to keep the Medical group in R&D and manage R&D exclusively. So, Fleming, head of QC, and Dale Hinson, head of RA, reported to Leone. Raval understood that for R&D to create products, it had to focus on that sole task. Reflecting Leone's belief that Alcon could only survive as an ophthalmic specialty company, Raval disbanded the urology pharmacology group. The heads of microbiology, pharmacology, and biochemistry resigned, giving Raval the opportunity to re-form R&D.[25]

One major personnel change occurred: with one exception, all medical doctors resigned and were not replaced. John H. Tenery, a retired colonel of the Army Medical Corps, continued to direct the development of Avitene. Alcon's experience with Barklis and his physicians convinced Schollmaier, Leone, and Raval that there must be a better way to handle R&D. As Schollmaier told Raval, "We don't have to have MDs. You just run the medical department as you want." For the next twenty-five years, Alcon never employed a physician in a management role in R&D. At the time, this was unheard of in the pharmaceutical industry. Government regulations require a medical doctor to sign protocols and clinical reports, to assess physicians selected as clinical investigators, and to make medical judgments about reported adverse events. Beasley, who joined Alcon's board of directors in 1951 and had consulted with R&D scientists almost every Wednesday since, offered a solution. He became R&D's first medical monitor. He continued his Wednesday afternoon visits, only now he worked with managers in the clinical science group, doing what the government required. As the number and scope of studies expanded, six more ophthalmologists became weekly medical monitors. This arrangement had an important advantage—medical monitors were not dependent on Alcon for the bulk of their income and could, and often did, give frank advice without concern for their livelihood. The many safe and effective products produced by R&D validated the medical monitor concept. Clinical protocols and final reports designed and written by experienced scientists were not constructed in a vacuum. Several scientists in the clinical group had doctoral or master's degrees, had studied in academic ophthalmic research laboratories, or had worked in another segment of the drug development process, often at Alcon. These scientists used ophthalmic medical specialists to design protocols and interpret the results. Finally, Alcon had a successful clinical studies program.[26]

Raval also revived R&D by staffing it with those deemed most competent. He started with about fifty scientists. He placed Charles A. Robb in charge of Technical Services, consisting of toxicology (McDonald), microbiology (Barry Schlech), analytical chemistry (Poe), and biochemistry (O. J. Lorenzetti). Mullins directed the pharmaceutical department with Hecht managing process development (fig. 4.7) and Roehrs overseeing formulation science. Robert Adamski continued as the head of medicinal chemistry and also managed the pharmacology unit soon to be led by Louis DeSantis. Henry Baldwin, Margaret Drake, and Betty Fortenberry became the nucleus of the clinical science group. Raval made it clear to everyone that their priority was new product development. To that end, he initiated a written annual review to assess each one's contribution to R&D's productivity. He insist-

FIG 4.7
Process Development team, 1975.
Left to right, top row: Carol O'Brien,
Toby Sata, Bob Tavernier, Harvey
Zimmerman, Tom Prado, David Stancil,
Tony Fajkus, Mary Glover; *bottom row*:
Ralph Blum, Gene Park, Bruce Hook, Bob
Beck, Ed Bohm. (AHR)

ed that R&D managers appreciated the critiques from marketing and sales, and he invited Dick Sisson, Alcon's national sales manager, to speak to R&D leaders. He also asked Leone to attend. Raval remarked that it was "the most critical talk of R&D" he ever heard. Sisson bluntly told the scientists that he had recommended that Schollmaier close "R&D and save that money." Schollmaier recalled, "There was a lot of infighting in those days about R&D."

Leone succinctly described the conflict that had emerged between R&D and marketing in an interview with *Pharmaceutical Executive* in 1985: "In the early phases, I think it is a serious mistake to involve the marketing function. I feel it is the responsibility of your R&D people to determine where the future of therapies is going and where the future of technology is going. It is the responsibility of the marketing people at the proper time to make their input into how they want that product profiled and positioned and the type of documentation they need to convince the doctor of its merits." Raval knew he had to educate Leone and Schollmaier on the difficulties of developing a new product. So, he invited them to R&D's Thursday morning project review meetings. These were not superficial show-and-tell sessions but rather in-depth hearings of a project's problems and resolutions. Fainthearted and defensive individuals wilted under the critique; those with the self-confidence to listen and absorb alternative ideas thrived. In retrospect, these meetings were essential for Raval in shaping R&D leaders into a productive team. Schollmaier commented, "[Raval] was a tough guy. I would attend all of his Thursday morning review meetings. I had thought I was tough, but he was much tougher. ... He'd cut guys to the quick and say, 'I'm not listening to this.'" With Raval in control, how R&D operated within Alcon was resolved in a debate moderated by Schollmaier.[27]

Schollmaier well understood that he could not succeed as Alcon's president without a productive R&D. Two occurrences helped him resolve what he called the "R&D problem." For the second time, he decided that Alcon had to stop chasing other medical specialties. He sought the counsel of John Hartman, a well-known investment manager. Hartman focused upon two points: building a successful management team for one medical specialty was hard enough; building multiple teams for multiple specialties was almost impossible. Moreover, to grow each business in each medical specialty, you needed multiple productive R&Ds. About the latter, Hartman bluntly stated, "You won't be able to do that." Taking Hartman's advice, Schollmaier attended an organizational program at Harvard, which he said "helped [me] get straightened out" about R&D.[28]

Back in Fort Worth, Schollmaier presented his thoughts to the Corporate Coordinating Committee (CCC), a regular Friday morning leadership meeting. The board was irritated by R&D: "Where the hell are the products?" They complained R&D was months late with new products. Schollmaier responded, "What do you think? We're not going to make it, are we, with R&D?" Buhler and others said no. Schollmaier continued, "If R&D is a failure, how long can we continue to grow?" Everyone agreed maybe three or four years. Schollmaier retorted, "Why don't we agree that we will run this baby hard for three years and then we'll all quit and go work together someplace else." An indignant Buhler responded, "You're a nut." Schollmaier noted that this had been the same conversation for the past two years. R&D was "screwed up" and "we can't get it unscrewed. We don't want to listen to what Raval tells us about what it would take to get it unscrewed." Buhler, he said, had unrealistic expectations. Schollmaier counseled the group, "Let's listen to [Raval]." Raval then presented his argument: "You have the budget all wrong. You've used variable budgets. If the year isn't going to work out the way you think it's going to, you people in management reduce the budgets 10 per cent. You can't do that in an R&D budget. You have to hire your people, start your projects, run them for a year and leave people in R&D alone."

Schollmaier shifted the focus of the meeting by agreeing with Raval: "Good point. You need ... to have a commitment for two or three years. You've got 27 projects right now.

How many can you handle?" Raval responded, "Maybe five." Schollmaier conceded: "All right. ... I want you to pick the three most important projects and if you can't get those three out, you're gone. You understand? And I'll get the marketing guys off your back. Now, what else?" Raval continued, "What happens is we get a product ready to go and then the marketing guys say they don't like it. They say, 'It doesn't have X, Y, Z characteristics.'" Schollmaier agreed: "All right, you're saying you need a guarantee that whenever you do finish a project, it will be a marketing success. I agree: that's what we need to do." Turning to the management team, he said, "Let's talk about the consequences of each of these decisions. First of all, if a budget cut is required during the year, it comes from you, you, you and you—not from [Raval]. ... Is that understood? Second, the projects that are in R&D are owned by me, ... not any of the divisions. *I* own the projects. That means I can delay them, restructure the priorities, manage the characteristics. They're mine until I turn them over to you. Understood? Now, for any product we introduce, we're not going to come back with excuses six months later that if we had only had the X factor we would have been successful. *Because we need every one to be a winner.*"

For the next twenty-three years, R&D conducted its business following these principles. Leone and Schollmaier, but no marketing people, attended Thursday R&D project reviews. Both heard about the trials and tribulations of developing a drug and were among the first to know about its weaknesses and strengths. There were no surprises when an NDA was filed with the FDA. The CCC became the forum where Schollmaier and Leone took the lead in preparing marketing when a drug was approved. This process ensured that a marketing plan was in place and manufacturing was ready to produce three batches before a drug's approval. Unique in the pharmaceutical industry, Alcon now launched a new product within a few days or weeks after FDA approval.[29]

While Raval restructured R&D, the FDA and government agencies elsewhere in the world continued to revise their regulations. While the 1963 GMPs were primarily directed toward manufacturing, the rules changed how R&D scientists operated. *Process management* became the operative phrase. It required standards to design and maintain facilities, validate processes, write and follow standard operating procedures (SOPs), identify who is responsible for what, train and retrain, maintain documentation, practice proper hygiene, maintain and use the correct equipment, conduct independent audits, and build quality into the product life cycle. Every R&D group that conducted experiments reported in an NDA had to establish SOPs, another resource-intensive activity. A good example of the extent of regulations is the validation process for the analytical department. Factory representatives calibrated analytical equipment annually. Chemists prepared and implemented protocols for validation, which required repeated analyses of the same bulk sample to be replicated. Raw materials, inert ingredients, bulk product, the final product, and stability samples all required validation, while SOPs also applied to QC and Manufacturing in cycles that never seemed to end.

In the early 1970s, the FDA also began proposing Good Laboratory Practices (GLPs). While intended primarily for pharmacology and toxicology studies, GLPs affected R&D and QC. Protocol development became formalized, and likewise record-keeping, data entry, result tabulations, statistical analyses, and report preparations. During the late 1970s, Good Clinical Practices (GCPs) appeared in government regulations, with many of the formalities of the GLPs. Informed consent and Investigational Review Boards represented two unique features of GCPs, which like GMPs and GLPs required paper records. Independent audits resulted in organizational audit functions in R&D, QC, and Manufacturing. The ultimate goal is to ensure that the data used to approve and manufacture medicines for humans are factual and reliable. Alcon's growth coincided with the expansion of governmental regulation. Scientists, manufacturing technicians, federal and state bureaucrats—everybody—learned simultaneously.[30]

GMPs, GLPs, and GCPs resulted in a plethora of written documents. When Raval took over R&D, word processing equipment had already been introduced. S&T during the fall of 1971 created the Word Processing Center (WPC). It provided services for other departments, but R&D dominated its workload. Scientists dialed a special number, connected to the WPC, and dictated reports, protocols, SOPs, and other documents. They also delivered tabular data to the WPC, where specialists entered the material, which they stored on floppy disks. WPC returned hard copies to the originator, who edited the text before WPC produced a final version using high-speed printers. The WPC reduced the reliance on secretaries, resulting in savings used to hire scientists. Initially, Alcon's WPC was a three-person operation—Marjorie Sheets, Beth Hunnicutt, and Louise Graham—but by 1974, Ardella Jackson and Elvera Johnson had joined the team. By then the WPC produced about forty-five thousand pages each month. The Avitene NDA, filed in July 1974, consisted of forty-eight thousand pages, almost all produced by the WPC. The automated features of Alcon's WPC resulted in increased efficiencies at a time when the demand for typed records and documents exploded.[31]

While word processors were simplified computers, the 1970s also saw the advent of increasingly sophisticated computer systems in QC and R&D. Data are often reduced to tables; the increased need for statistical evaluations of tabular data due to GCPs and GLPs created a new reliance on computer systems. R&D created its first biostatistical group, led by Walter Eaton Knowles, which used computer-based data sets. Computers also performed automated data collection required for the increased scope and volume of stability studies. Additionally, analytical equipment used for chemical analysis became the first to include microcomputers to calculate and present data graphically. Once these microcomputers were tied to mainframe computers, not having to manually transfer data resulted in increased efficiency and accuracy.

With a degree in chemistry from Southern Methodist University, Howard Luttrell joined Alcon's QC department on November 2, 1969. When a batch of a product was manufactured, a few hundred samples, set aside for stability studies, were stored at different levels of light, temperature, and humidity. Over the next few years, samples were randomly analyzed. The objective was to determine if the active drug or inactive ingredients degraded during the product's shelf life. Luttrell realized that "many of these analytical procedures could be automated and interfaced with a computer to collect and calculate data and results." He convinced IT to enter the data into the mainframe computers, the first time Alcon used these to automate scientific data for laboratory experiments. Luttrell left in 1972 to get his doctorate in chemistry at SMU. By then, S&T had purchased a computer program from the Upjohn Company that managed stability studies, so Lloyd Hodgkins hired Annabelle Corboy, a programmer, to implement it for QC. Corboy worked with Johnny Hammonds in IT, but the results often took a week or more. To quickly generate tabulated results, Corboy outsourced the task to an independent computer company.[32]

In July 1970 Martha Siegel, a chemist with a bachelor's degree from Tulane University and a master's degree from Tufts University, joined R&D. Assigned to conduct analytical chemistry tests for Edwin Dorsey, Siegel used ultraviolet and atomic absorption spectrometric analysis; both generated data easily amenable to computerization (fig. 4.8). Meanwhile, R&D had purchased a PDP-8 computer, the first successful minicomputer, and Siegel employed the Upjohn stability program. Corboy and Siegel collaborated in this effort. Corboy became the initial member of R&D's first IT unit and helped other scientific units utilize the PDP-8. By 1975 Baldwin, now in charge of R&D's administrative and central services, needed a dedicated team to expand R&D's use of computer systems; he hired Norman R. Stemple, a professor of chemistry at Texas Christian University who had worked at IBM. Stemple established a temporary time-share arrangement with TCU's computers and after two years bought the VAX-11/785, a first-generation superminicomputer. As 1978 began,

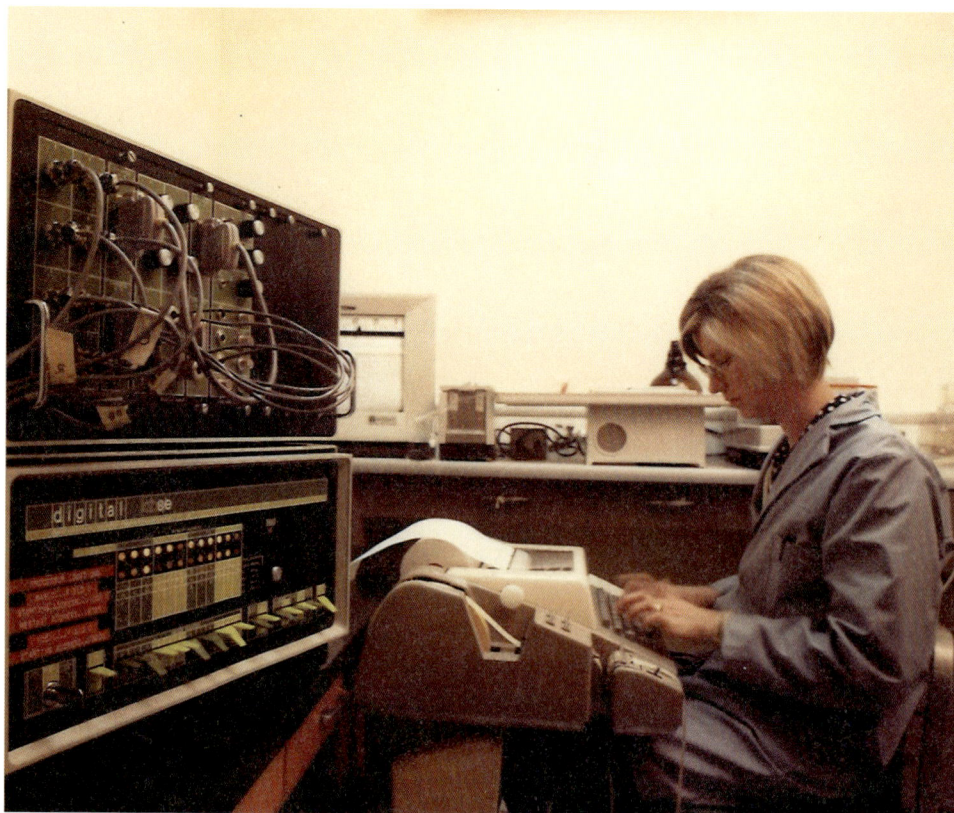

FIG 4.8
Martha Siegel using the Digital PDP-8 microcomputer (BAS, Alcon Materials, TCU)

FIG 4.9
Alcon drug research and development process, 1972–1997 (TOM, AM)

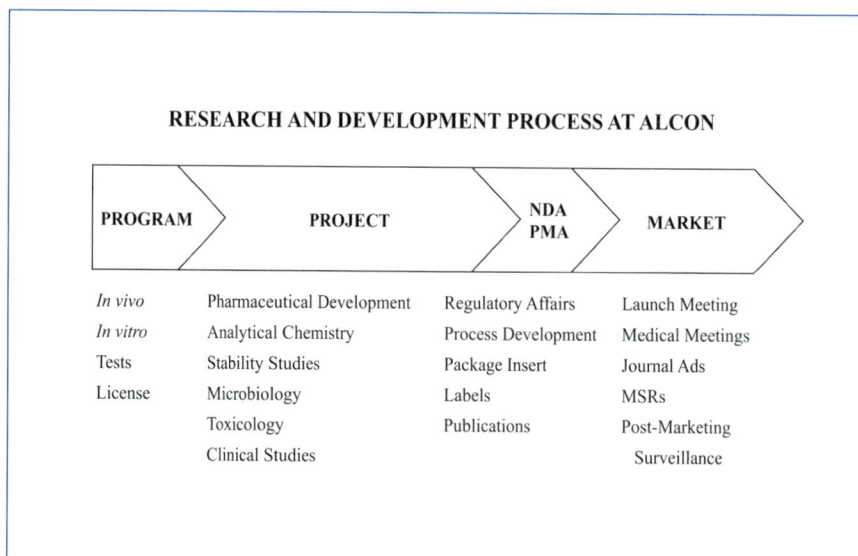

RESEARCH AND DEVELOPMENT PROCESS AT ALCON

PROGRAM	PROJECT	NDA PMA	MARKET
In vivo	Pharmaceutical Development	Regulatory Affairs	Launch Meeting
In vitro	Analytical Chemistry	Process Development	Medical Meetings
Tests	Stability Studies	Package Insert	Journal Ads
License	Microbiology	Labels	MSRs
	Toxicology	Publications	Post-Marketing
	Clinical Studies		Surveillance

Stemple and Corboy set about integrating the VAX into various R&D operations, the first being stability studies of new products and the WPC.[33]

When Raval took charge of R&D, about 75 percent of its resources were devoted to supporting products as they were reformulated to meet new FDA requirements. Raval and Leone prioritized products for reformulation, freeing resources for new product development. By 1974 Product Support and Market Support had reorganized so that about 75 percent of resources were dedicated to Alcon's future products.[34]

The R&D process has two phases: research to discover new therapies and development to transform them into safe, viable products (fig. 4.9). Schollmaier, Leone, and Raval agreed that, while acquisition of companies and products had value, Alcon's future depended on licensing compounds and devices from other companies. Thus, the principal function of the Research Department in R&D became developing in vivo and in vitro testing models to screen other companies' compounds. The group that synthesized new chemicals, medicinal chemistry, focused on one or two classes of compounds. Identifying in-licensing compounds became a responsibility of the pharmacology and microbiology groups. Once they identified a compound or class of compounds, Alcon contacted the company that owned the patent and requested a test sample.

Requesting samples became a refined process, perfected by three men—Leone, Raval, and Adamski, the head of Research and a medicinal chemist who understood chemical molecules and screening assays value. Soft-spoken and deliberate, he honed his skills at soliciting visits to pharmaceutical companies. He, Leone, and Raval would call on the company and convince skeptical scientific and executive managers that letting Alcon test their compound did not jeopardize their projects. This resulted in agreements whereby Alcon committed to a testing profile within a specified timeframe, and the compound-lending company promised to supply a limited quantity and give Alcon the first right to license for development. If Alcon exercised that option, Adamski, Leone, Raval, and sometimes Schollmaier would negotiate a licensing agreement with milestone payments and a royalty on sales.[35]

When a sample arrived, the pharmacology or microbiology group performed in vivo and in vitro tests. If a compound produced the desired response, then the pharmaceutical group explored formulation properties, analytical chemistry created assays, and toxicology studied ocular safety. After several successful reiterations of this cycle, a development plan was prepared. The plan outlined the studies and resources required to file an NDA after clinical, stability, and safety studies met FDA or other governments' guidelines. Studies to support an NDA could involve a few hundred scientists for several years and cost tens of millions of dollars, so implementing and executing a plan was never straightforward. Most issues were complex, and solutions were seldom simple. Successful project leaders were patient, resolute, and confident, with pragmatic problem-solving skills.[36]

When the Kefauver-Harris amendments became part of the FD&C Act in 1962, pharmaceutical companies created RA departments as liaisons with the FDA. There was no precedent, so everybody had much to learn. In early 1963, Alcon hired Henry A. Whissen, an FDA inspector and ex-Air Force officer, to establish and lead RA. Whissen's two-person operation advised R&D, QC, and Manufacturing, coordinated FDA inspections, submitted NDAs, and facilitated communication with the FDA. Despite its critical role, RA was underappreciated until Raval arrived. He accepted that Whissen was effective but lacked strategic skills important to the success of RA. Raval asked Hinson, Alcon's corporate counsel, to take charge of the division. Kagawa then transferred from R&D to RA, becoming the first Alcon scientist to take on a regulatory role. Thus, an expanded RA found a new home under Hinson, reporting to Leone.[37]

Under Hinson, RA began to exert itself. By 1974 the number of personnel increased to eight. Instead of citing the *Federal Register*, the government publication for regulations, RA took an active role in advising R&D on development plans. Three innovative products, Statrol, Maxitrol, and Avitene, benefited from RA's proactive involvement. In 1975 Mary Pencis transferred from R&D to the International Division and became responsible for registering Alcon products overseas. While Pencis was not a member of corporate RA, she sourced documents from it and coordinated her filings with it.[38]

When Schollmaier asked Raval to take over from Barklis, he included the QC department in the assignment. Raval told Leone that QC needed to be a stand-alone group reporting to Leone. Fleming had directed QC for many years, and his staff had worked in QC for nearly fifteen years and thus were qualified. Furthermore, Raval argued, considering QC's oversight of finished products, Alcon was better served with both QC and Manufacturing reporting to Leone. Untangling QC laboratories and personnel from R&D went smoothly until complicated by an inspection of Alcon's manufacturing facility by the United Kingdom's Medicines Commission.[39]

Great Britain had revised regulations for approving new drugs with the 1968 Medicines Act. Products had to meet established standards, and manufacturing facilities and quality controls had to be approved. Intending to ship products from Fort Worth, Alcon submitted registration documents to the Medicines Commission, and in 1973 inspectors spent days examining the Fort Worth plant, procedures, and records. The audit unexpectedly revealed more than 190 deficiencies, most pertaining to sterilization and validation controls. This was a rude awakening for Alcon and resulted in revisions of SOPs, GMPs, and GLPs in Manufacturing, QC, and R&D. Alcon looked to Schlech, head of microbiology, to spearhead the effort. Key members of his team included Walter Barrett and Gene Burson from QC and Gene Estes, Kevin Marks, and John Hansard from R&D. Estes, who was experienced in process controls, had come from Bayer Corporation. He had a plan for improvement but Joe Lutteringer, Alcon's chief compounder, refused to help, saying they knew what they were doing. During this impasse, Fleming and QC began reporting to Leone, and Luttrell, who had returned to Alcon, joined the debate. Sisson, promoted to general manager of Domestic Operations, threw his influence behind improvement. Estes tested for bacteria and fungi, and he discovered a common mold, *Aspergillus niger*. New systems established routines for sanitizing and sterilizing the compounding and filling equipment, raw materials, bulk product, and finished product. Validation studies proved the new systems and processes performed as expected.

FIG 4.10
A product label contains essential medical information. Senior Product Inspector Martha Hall, responsible for ensuring the quality of Alcon product labels, 1974. (AHR)

Regulations prompted other personnel changes. Hansard transferred from R&D to manufacturing as the first Sterile Fill Supervisor, "responsible [for making] sure the products remained sterile during the packing process." The QC section in Manufacturing, led by Danny Roles, became responsible for approving each component used in production and approving a product before shipment. Cecil Kemp's material QC unit checked every lot of cartons, bottles, caps, and other packaging material (figs. 4.10, 4.11). During and after production, the inspectors in the products QC section, under Aubrey Baker, checked all products as they were filled and packaged. Inspectors scrutinized filled and labeled Drop-tainers for accurate volume, properly tightened caps, and the correct lot number and expiration date on labels. Even then, after having passed dozens of inspections, the products were still not ready to go. Instead, they were stored in a locked wire cage in the quarantine area until more analyses in the QC laboratory documented that they conformed to specifications. As the scope of quality measures increased, so did the need for skilled personnel. Changes in responsibilities and organization also resulted in frequent training and retraining programs for QC and Manufacturing personnel. This intrusion of

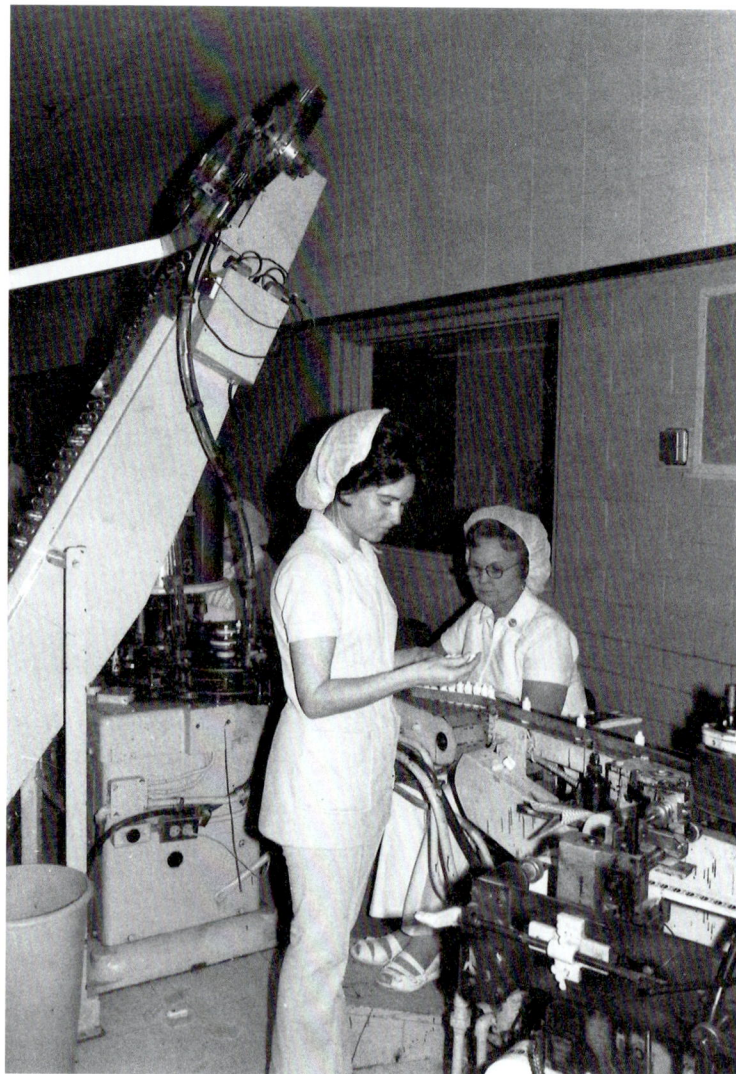

QC into Manufacturing led to the department being renamed Quality Systems (QS) to reflect the emphasis on control systems before and during the manufacture of a product. To emphasize the importance of QS, Leone promoted Fleming to vice president in 1975.[40]

QS responsibilities expanded as Alcon made more acquisitions. Center Laboratories, Owen Laboratories, the William A. Webster Company, and the new plant in Humacao, Puerto Rico—each had its own QS laboratory. To ensure the SOPs and GMPs remained consistent with Alcon's corporate QS standards, a Fort Worth QS person was stationed on-site. Robert "Bob" Garcia went to Puerto Rico, Luttrell to Center Laboratories and later Puerto Rico. By 1974 Alcon manufactured products in sixteen countries. As head of QS,

Fleming toured foreign plants and determined that they needed to revise their SOPs to be consistent with those in the United States. Joe Hart became director of international QS and produced a three-volume technical manual, bringing international production in line with domestic standards.[41]

By 1977 the concept of quality in the pharmaceutical industry had undergone another evolution that came to be known as quality assurance. The University of Dallas, a leader in the field, offered a master's degree, which Fleming and Ernest Litton earned in 1973, as did Roger Poore, inspection manager in QA at Owen Laboratories, in 1974. In the beginning, the QC function at Alcon consisted simply of testing and inspecting raw materials and the finished product. Hodgkins and Fleming championed QS, which created an interactive process between the quality group and Manufacturing that included document control and training. Lastly, Hodgkins and Fleming instituted QA at Alcon. QA included aspects of both QC and QS but focused on manufacturing processes. Feedback on manufacturing processes improved them, ultimately reducing testing and inspections. Teams from QA, R&D, and Manufacturing collaborated to ensure the smooth transition of new products into the marketplace. Alcon QA established vendor interactions and audits, which allowed Alcon to influence vendors' processes and procedures.[42]

Starting in 1977 quality was thus built into Alcon products from beginning to end. While the changes occurred incrementally, they were transformative; the quality function became part of the manufacturing process and facilities standards. As an Alcon ophthalmic product went through various stages of manufacture, several SOPs ensured quality. For example, the QA testing group (fig. 4.12) led by Barrett implemented a four-step protocol. The first step tested and certified raw materials before they combined into a product. In the second, a product batch in large mixing tanks was assayed, ensuring the correct mixture of ingredients. After the product passed through filling, labeling, and packaging, it was tested again. Following these tests, technicians prepared a report and released the product for shipment. But testing continued. QA kept samples for stability tests. In this fourth step, microbiological and chemical assays monitored the product's shelf life. Ramona Puckett coordinated testing and kept track of computer records and samples. Of course, the QA testing group was only part of the total process. An inspection group under Garcia checked packaging materials as they arrived in Manufacturing and a group led by Estes monitored environmental conditions during manufacturing.[43]

By 1970 it became evident that the expansion of the manufacturing facility five years earlier was inadequate. On May 16, 1972, Alexander, Conner, and their grandsons, with

FIG 4.12

QA chemistry testing team, 1977. *Left to right:* back row-Linda Dorie, Kelly Dennis, Hardy Thomas, James Hillis; *middle row*-Beaufort Cash, Ramona Puckett, Tina Mewhinney, Helen Clifton; *front row*-Agnes Reventas, Martia Gotangco, Ruth Ann Henson. (BAS)

FIG 4.13

Ground-breaking, Alcon manufacturing expansion, May 16, 1972 (Courtesy of Taylor Schollmaier)

Schollmaier and his son, broke ground for a forty-thousand-square-foot addition (fig. 4.13). This more than doubled the existing space, allowing for twice as many filling lines and more room for compounding and warehousing. The contractor completed the $800,000 project on schedule in the fall. Lowell Dix, the plant engineer, scoured the country to find equipment and coordinate the manufacture of compounding vats and filling and labeling lines. The following year, when the British inspectors identified deficiencies and QC recommended improvements, changes had to be made. State-of-the-art laminar flow air filtration systems were installed in the compounding and filling rooms. The UV conveyor belt disappeared, and ethylene oxide or gamma irradiation became the mainstays for sterilizing packing components, compounding equipment, and products. Heat sterilization was used for nonplastic packaging, and sterile filtration for heat-sensitive solutions.[44]

By 1972 these manufacturing facilities produced 175 Alcon products, including Drop-tainers, Steri-units, sterile ointment packaging, Contique contact lens solutions, Webcon products, and rhinological preparations. As completed, the manufacturing building held an impressive seventy-five thousand square feet. The new addition was projected to accommodate production needs for the next five years (fig. 4.14). The larger addition on the east expanded warehousing for shipping, receiving, and quarantine. On the south end, the expansion contained a state-of-the-art sterile space and a Class 100 CJ-11 room (pioneered by the aerospace industry for sterile operations) for the production of BSS and other ophthalmic specialty operations (figs. 4.15). The area also had room for a future expansion of conveyor operations and storage.[45]

With the acquisition of Lawton Company and Center Laboratories, Alcon's board promoted Schollmaier to vice president of corporate marketing. These two acquisitions required attention, forcing him to live part-time in New Jersey, close to the facilities. As a result, Leone became general manager for Alcon Domestic Operations, including the Fort Worth manufacturing plant managed by Carter. Leone's role was further emphasized with a promotion to vice president of Alcon Domestic Operations in 1971 and vice president of Science and Technology in 1972, an assignment that included QC and RA. By 1974 Carter's responsibilities had increased to include manufacturing facilities elsewhere in the United States, so he was promoted to vice president of Manufacturing. These changes demonstrated that Alcon manufacturing group was no longer local but national in scope.[46]

Before 1966 Milton Barley, in the finance group, had responsibility for buying raw chemicals and packing materials for manufacturing. He cooperated with Floyd Powell, the plant's production and inventory control manager. When Manufacturing began reporting

FIG 4.14
Drawing of manufacturing plant expansion plan, and photo of six employees with twenty years of service at Alcon, 1972 (BAS)

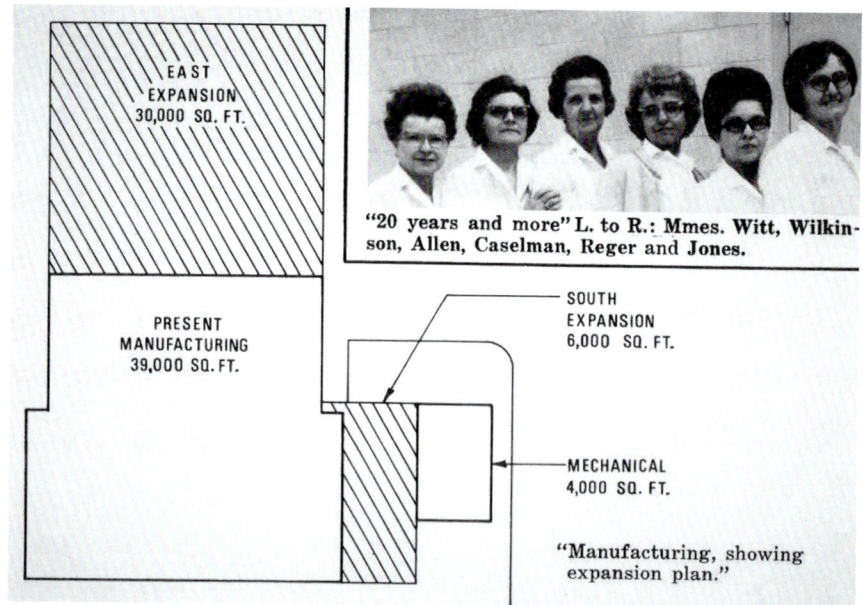

"20 years and more" L. to R.: Mmes. Witt, Wilkinson, Allen, Caselman, Reger and Jones.

"Manufacturing, showing expansion plan."

FIG 4.15
Sterile compounding in the new Class 100 CJ-11 room, 1973 (AHR)

to Leone, Barley transferred and, collaborating with Leone, developed a Materials Department as part of the Manufacturing department. A new organizational concept, it consisted of purchasing, warehouse shipping and receiving, and production planning. Barley hired John Feik as purchasing manager. About this time, Powell left to manage the manufacturing group at Conal. Thus, by 1971 Carter, Lutteringer, Barley, and Feik became the main managers in the Fort Worth plant.[47]

About a year after Alcon acquired Webster Laboratories in 1971, Powell began managing its Memphis plant. Alcon then created Webcon, combining the Conal and Webster product lines, and placed it in the Alcon Specialty Products Division, led by Herbert Kleiman. R&D terminated all non-ophthalmic projects, except for Avitene and a couple of dermatology projects. The few Webcon products that remained, while low in total sales and expense, had high profits. Kleiman's sales force consisted of four district managers and thirty-six salesmen. In the early 1960s the federal government encouraged firms to move their manufacturing plants to Puerto Rico with an inducement of no taxes on profits, providing the profits were not returned to the United States for an extended time period. Alcon could thus use the profits for international expansion. Kologe and Alexander championed construction of a Webcon plant in Puerto Rico; ultimately, Kologe obtained Puerto Rican government approval for a facility at Humacao, about an hour's drive southeast of San Juan.[48]

Construction at Humacao began in May 1973. When completed the plant occupied 39,400 square feet at a cost of $1.4 million (fig. 4.16). Initially, it handled the manufacture of products in the Webcon line, beginning in August 1974. Powell moved from Conal in Chicago to manage the Puerto Rico operation. His team included Garcia; controller Richard Sherman, originally the controller in Webcon's Memphis plant; and Carlos Rodriquez, the production manager from Conal. Powell recalled, "It was probably the most exciting part of my career: there were a lot of sleepless nights. We had six months to get that plant open and running—from scratch!—and as any construction project goes, it never goes as planned. I brought some Puerto Ricans to Chicago and Memphis for training, and they did well. Then when we went to Puerto Rico the same guys couldn't find the door, it seemed like."

Webcon's largest volume product was Urised, a sugarcoated tablet whose manufacture was as much an art form as a formula. The men trained in Chicago could not reproduce the tablet in Puerto Rico. When Schollmaier discovered an elderly man in Chicago had manufactured the tablet for forty years, he told Carter,

FIG 4.16
Alcon Puerto Rico plant, 1973 (AHR)

"You've got to take the old man to Puerto Rico to train the Puerto Ricans." Carter said, "My God, this old guy has never been out of Cook County in his life. He's never been on an airplane. He won't fly; he won't go." Schollmaier responded, "Does he have an adventuresome nephew—somebody who will talk him into it?" Carter came back and said, "Yes, his nephew wants to go with him. But what will we do with his nephew down there?" The ever-practical Schollmaier said, "Put him in a resort hotel, tell him to go to the pool every day." The elderly man solved the problem and retrained the men, and the operation quickly got back on track. Powell's team managed to produce a Urised batch, which the FDA approved and Alcon QA released. The first bottle of Urised came off the production line just nine months after construction began. By the end of 1974, the facility's sixty employees produced seventy-nine thousand tablets daily. As a measure of local loyalty, 30 percent of the original employees celebrated the plant's twentieth anniversary (figs. 4.17).[49]

Alcon's sale of Service Engineers, discussed earlier, involved more than business negotiations. During reformulation studies, fine precipitates sometimes appeared in stability samples packaged in Drop-tainers. Chemical analysis determined they were zinc stearate, a mold release agent used by Service Engineers. Thus, a collaborative program commenced between manufacturing and R&D to find alternative sources for Drop-tainers. Barley and Hecht led the effort. Barley acquired Drop-tainers from various suppliers and Hecht's group conducted stability studies. The analytical chemistry group in R&D and the chemistry group in QC conducted thousands of assays to document that the product's active molecule and key inactive ingredients remained within specifications. They

also looked for minute quantities of plastic resins that might have leached into the product from Drop-tainers. Moreover, the plastics in new Drop-tainers had to undergo toxicology tests as specified by the United States Pharmacopeia (USP) and National Formulary (NF). Both the USP and NF publish standards, tests, and assays for identity, strength, quality, purity, packaging, and labeling for drug substances and excipients. Eventually, the Wheaton Company of New Jersey became the main supplier of Drop-tainers, with Imco of New York as a secondary source. After a supplier was certified, samples of the first three lots of each product using that supplier's containers were retained for microbiological and chemistry assays. Identifying a plastic supplier was a comprehensive, expensive undertaking.[50]

Problems surrounding the sterilization process complicated Alcon's Drop-tainer saga. Alexander's initial Drop-tainer was translucent but this let light penetrate the polyethylene wall, which degraded light-sensitive ingredients, resulting in the product discoloring. Alcon solved the problem by packing light-sensitive products in opaque Drop-tainers. It added titanium dioxide, an inert compound, to the polyethylene slurry during molding. However, opaque Drop-tainers did not let UV sterilization light penetrate, making sterilizing problematic. Using gaseous ethylene oxide (ETO), which had been popular in the 1940s and 1950s, proved effective. When Alcon built its manufacturing plant in 1959, the industrial-size autoclave had both heat and ETO capabilities. As sterilization with UV became problematic, R&D and Manufacturing revisited ETO sterilization, which the pharmaceutical and medical device industry used extensively. When the FDA and the National Institute for Occupational Safety and Health (NIOSH) raised concerns about the safety of the process, the American National Standards Institute (ANSI) created the Z-79 working subcommittee on ETO. McDonald, R&D's head of toxicology, represented Alcon on the committee. At the same time, Schlech joined Task Force no. 6 of the Parenteral Drug Association that established an ETO sterilization standard for medical and pharmaceutical products. Both are examples of Alcon employees representing the company in developing national standards.[51]

Alcon had to sterilize Drop-tainers, surgical devices such as the Cryophake, and products such as solutions, suspensions, ointments, and gels. With ETO, residues may remain on or in a product. ETO degrades to two chemicals, ethylene chlorohydrin and ethylene glycol. Development of ETO sterilization required collaboration. Hecht, head of development in R&D, worked with Manufacturing and analytical chemistry and toxicology in the division. Alcon suspensions, solutions, ointments, and gels were spiked with ascending levels of ETO, ethylene chlorohydrin, and ethylene glycol, then evaluated for ocular safety. Based on the results, Alcon recommended maximum amounts of ETO and its two residues to the Z-79 subcommittee. These were accepted as a regulation by the FDA and NIOSH. In this way, Alcon directly influenced federal regulations and protected a vital means of safely sterilizing its products. The ocular ETO residue regulations remain in effect as of 2024, illustrating how quality science benefited Alcon for fifty years.[52]

Since 1951 Carter's responsibilities had grown as Alcon expanded. He transformed the primitive manufacturing plant on the north side of Fort Worth into a state-of-the-art facility on Alcon's south campus. He managed three expansions and supervised the construction of a Puerto Rico facility. No doubt he relied on others, but as the complexities of manufacture grew under the increasing intrusion of QC, federal agencies, and a host of regulations, Carter took solace on his ranch. He retired in 1976 at age forty-nine, comfortably, in part due to Alcon's generous PST. He later admitted, "I wasn't finding it fun anymore, the way it used to be. I suddenly realized when I got up of a morning that I hated the idea of going to work."

Part of the issue lay with Buhler, who bought firms with manufacturing plants and had recently built a modern facility in Belgium. He operated with little oversight, and to meet Alcon standards he used Charles Dickey from QC, who transferred standards and procedures as the means to implement common practices. When a failure occurred, Buhler held Fort Worth Manufacturing accountable, so he often complained about Carter. In replacing Carter, Leone proposed that Buhler read résumés and interview candidates, and then the two men would agree on who to hire. Schollmaier used the experience to show Buhler that when it came to technology, he did not have the skills to resolve the issues. Decentralizing for sales and marketing had merit, but as Schollmaier noted, "We have to exercise a very high degree of control over our plants, our manufacturing practices, and our limited R&D resources; so, our management of them has to be centralized." In early 1977 Buhler and Leone agreed to hire Bernard "Bernie" Z. Senkowski (fig. 4.18), a US Navy veteran of World War II and chemical engineer with a doctorate from Rutgers University. Employed for twenty-five years at Hoffmann-LaRoche, a pharmaceutical company in New Jersey, he had become responsible for pharmaceutical operations. In experience and education, he was the opposite of Carter, and he was affable, courteous, and engaging. Senkowski commented on the task he faced: "Mr. Schollmaier set conditions that offered me a real challenge and that's exactly what I was looking for. Technologically there were many problems. It was tough at first. But as we began building the Puerto Rican plant and subsequently the Conner Center, the cafeteria, and warehouse, I was at the same time gradually building a first-class team of engineers, architects, and managers." In the decade before he arrived, Alcon had evolved from small groups of young technicians and managers into an organization of experienced scientists and leaders. Leone deserves credit for shaping S&T, but he was fortunate to have Fleming and Raval and then Senkowski as partners. In the following decade, S&T led the way as Alcon increasingly dominated the ophthalmic marketplace.[53]

FIG 4.18
Bernard Senkowski (AHR)

When Schollmaier became Alcon's president, the company owned a hodgepodge of specialty firms. The ophthalmic companies in the United States contributed the bulk of sales and profits. Loosely clustered together were Center Laboratories, Lawton Instruments, Webcon, and Owen Laboratories in the Specialty Products Division, a legacy of Conner's wayward focus on diversification. Schollmaier sold Lawton Instruments and Center Laboratories and consolidated Webcon products to the few that generated profits. Enamored with Owen Laboratories, Schollmaier developed a plan for its growth using minimal R&D resources. How he succeeded is a testament to his strategic patience. It started with the creation of a division, Domestic Operations, which focused on ophthalmic prescriptions, contact lens solutions, and surgical products.

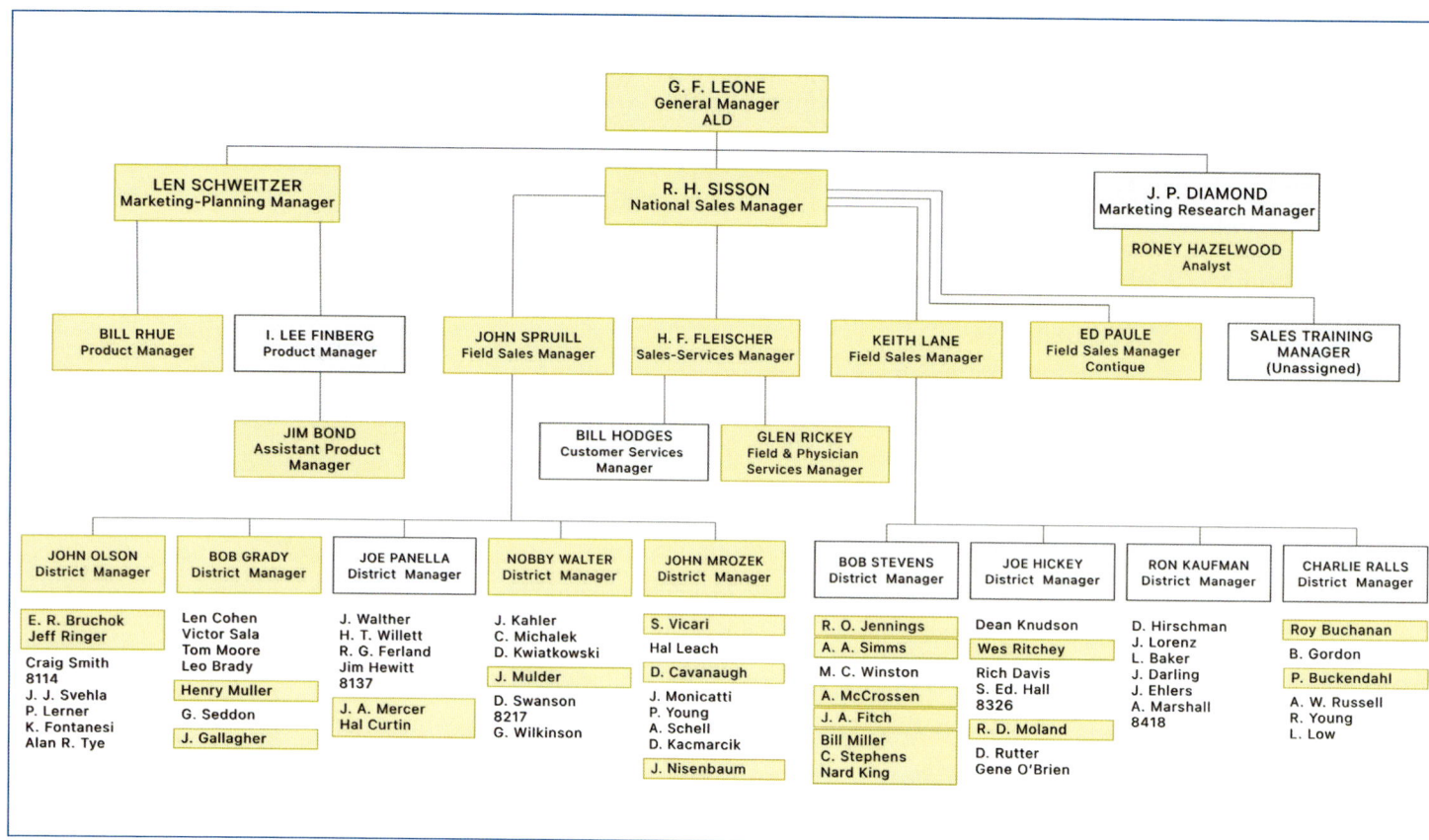

G. F. LEONE
General Manager
ALD

LEN SCHWEITZER
Marketing-Planning Manager

R. H. SISSON
National Sales Manager

J. P. DIAMOND
Marketing Research Manager

RONEY HAZELWOOD
Analyst

BILL RHUE
Product Manager

I. LEE FINBERG
Product Manager

JOHN SPRUILL
Field Sales Manager

H. F. FLEISCHER
Sales-Services Manager

KEITH LANE
Field Sales Manager

ED PAULE
Field Sales Manager
Contique

SALES TRAINING MANAGER
(Unassigned)

JIM BOND
Assistant Product Manager

BILL HODGES
Customer Services Manager

GLEN RICKEY
Field & Physician Services Manager

JOHN OLSON District Manager	BOB GRADY District Manager	JOE PANELLA District Manager	NOBBY WALTER District Manager	JOHN MROZEK District Manager	BOB STEVENS District Manager	JOE HICKEY District Manager	RON KAUFMAN District Manager	CHARLIE RALLS District Manager
E. R. Bruchok Jeff Ringer	Len Cohen Victor Sala Tom Moore Leo Brady	J. Walther H. T. Willett R. G. Ferland Jim Hewitt 8137	J. Kahler C. Michalek D. Kwiatkowski	S. Vicari	R. O. Jennings	Dean Knudson	D. Hirschman J. Lorenz	Roy Buchanan
Craig Smith 8114	Henry Muller		J. Mulder	Hal Leach	A. A. Simms	Wes Ritchey	L. Baker J. Darling	B. Gordon
J. J. Svehla P. Lerner K. Fontanesi Alan R. Tye	G. Seddon	J. A. Mercer Hal Curtin	D. Swanson 8217	D. Cavanaugh	M. C. Winston	Rich Davis S. Ed. Hall 8326	J. Ehlers A. Marshall 8418	P. Buckendahl
	J. Gallagher		G. Wilkinson	J. Monicatti P. Young A. Schell D. Kacmarick	A. McCrossen			A. W. Russell R. Young L. Low
				J. Nisenbaum	J. A. Fitch	R. D. Moland		
					Bill Miller C. Stephens Nard King	D. Rutter Gene O'Brien		

FIG 4.19
Alcon Domestic Operations, organizational chart, 1970 (TOM, AM)

When John Feik interviewed at Alcon in 1970, he was ushered into Conner's office. He later recalled, "I remember asking Mr. Conner what future opportunities in my career might I find that would last for a lifetime? I'll never forget it. Conner replied that Alcon was growing so rapidly that most people have really struggled to maintain the same relative position because their responsibility increased as the company expanded." This turned out to be true for Feik and many others who arrived during these decades. Alcon organizational charts were always in flux.[54]

By 1970 Leone's leadership role incorporated Domestic Operations, which included the domestic sales and marketing groups and manufacturing operations. His organizational chart for sales and marketing showed a vastly experienced team (fig. 4.19). Almost half of the people had been at Alcon for fifteen or more years; importantly, four eventually held leadership positions and eleven were later inducted into Alcon's Hall of Fame. Like R&D, Manufacturing, and QA, Alcon's domestic sales and marketing team became an incubator for effective, productive managers and leaders.[55]

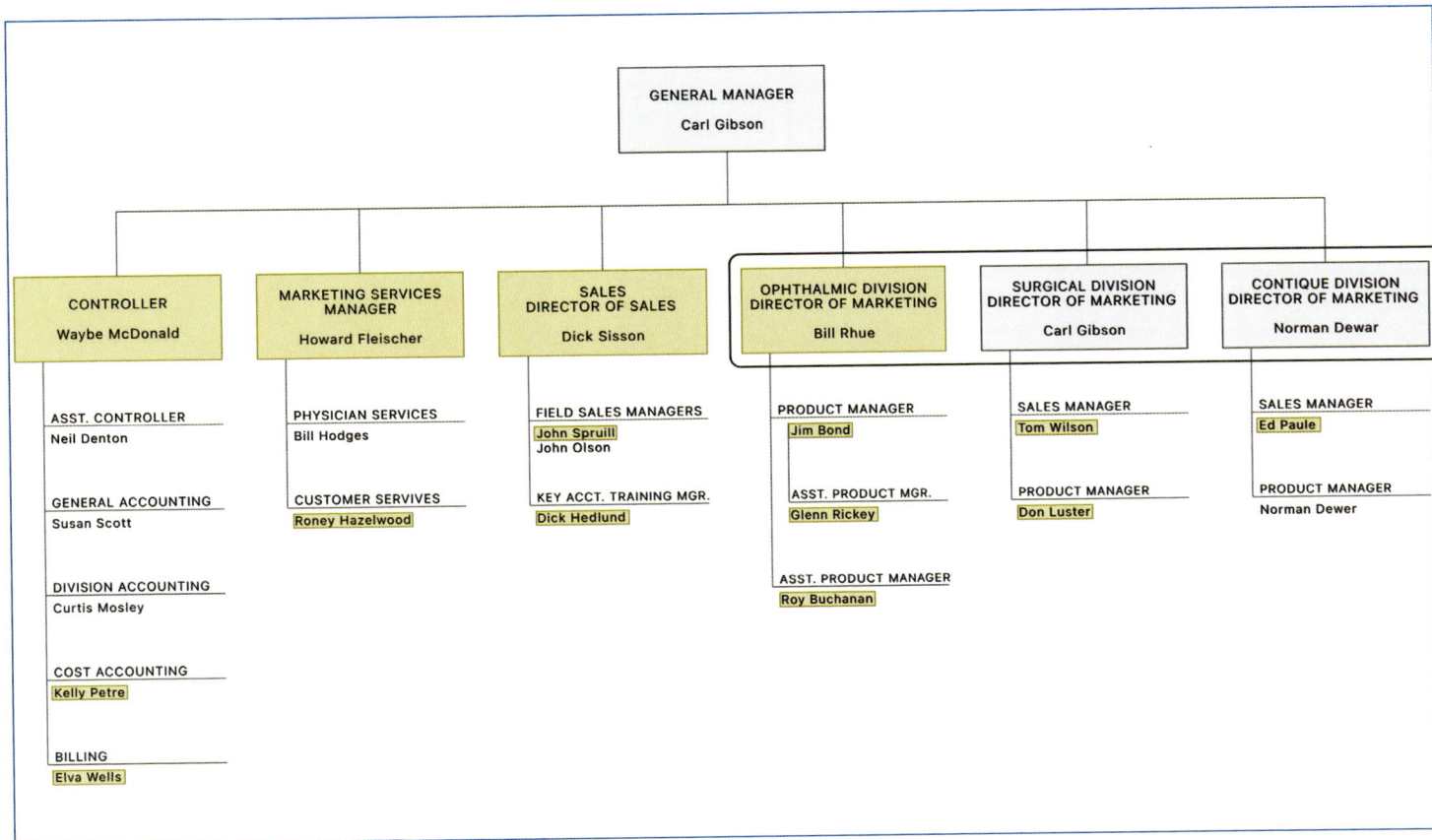

GENERAL MANAGER
Carl Gibson

CONTROLLER	MARKETING SERVICES MANAGER	SALES DIRECTOR OF SALES	OPHTHALMIC DIVISION DIRECTOR OF MARKETING	SURGICAL DIVISION DIRECTOR OF MARKETING	CONTIQUE DIVISION DIRECTOR OF MARKETING
Waybe McDonald	Howard Fleischer	Dick Sisson	Bill Rhue	Carl Gibson	Norman Dewar

CONTROLLER
- ASST. CONTROLLER — Neil Denton
- GENERAL ACCOUNTING — Susan Scott
- DIVISION ACCOUNTING — Curtis Mosley
- COST ACCOUNTING — Kelly Petre
- BILLING — Elva Wells

MARKETING SERVICES MANAGER
- PHYSICIAN SERVICES — Bill Hodges
- CUSTOMER SERVIVES — Roney Hazelwood

SALES DIRECTOR OF SALES
- FIELD SALES MANAGERS — John Spruill / John Olson
- KEY ACCT. TRAINING MGR. — Dick Hedlund

OPHTHALMIC DIVISION
- PRODUCT MANAGER — Jim Bond
- ASST. PRODUCT MGR. — Glenn Rickey
- ASST. PRODUCT MANAGER — Roy Buchanan

SURGICAL DIVISION
- SALES MANAGER — Tom Wilson
- PRODUCT MANAGER — Don Luster

CONTIQUE DIVISION
- SALES MANAGER — Ed Paule
- PRODUCT MANAGER — Norman Dewer

When Leone moved to S&T in 1972, he carried Manufacturing with him, leaving Domestic Operations to focus solely on sales and marketing for ophthalmic prescriptions, surgical products, and contact lens solutions (fig. 4.20). This became the model for Alcon moving forward. In addition to Leone, others had new assignments in 1972: Len Schweitzer moved to Avicon and Keith Lane to Owen Laboratories, while Carl V. Gibson Jr. took over the Domestic Operations Division. Gibson, an SMU graduate and World War II Army veteran, had almost twenty years' experience in sales management at the William S. Merrell Company in Ohio. He joined Alcon's Midwest sales team in 1966, and in 1968, he relocated to Fort Worth as manager of the new ophthalmic surgical group. Under him, Domestic Operations soon included the Specialty Products Division, and Gibson joined Schollmaier, Leone, Buhler, and Kologe in Alcon's Corporate Management Council.[56]

Gibson's Domestic Operations consisted of two marketing groups and the field sales force. The ophthalmic group led by Bill Rhue (fig. 4.21) took responsibility for marketing

FIG 4.20
Alcon Domestic Operations, organizational chart, 1972 (TOM, AM)

FIG 4.21
Bill Rhue (AHR)

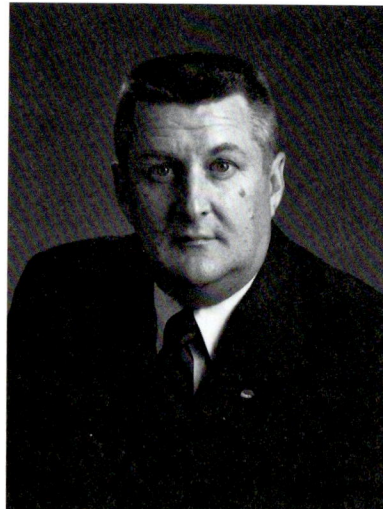

FIG 4.22
Dick Sisson (AHR)

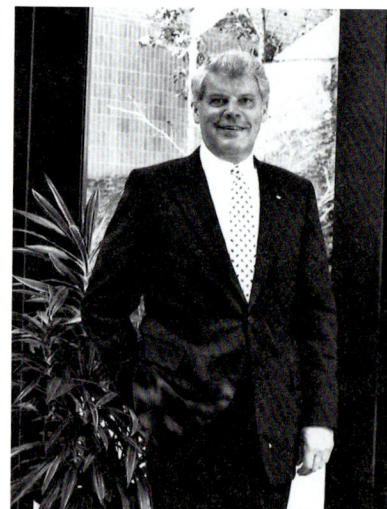

FIG 4.23
John Spruill (AHR)

all pharmaceutical products. A graduate of the University of Virginia, Rhue worked as an MSR and senior product manager for J. B. Roerig, a Pfizer division, before joining Alcon. Dewar directed the optical group in developing plans for the Contique line and OTC products. The field sales force, led by Sisson (fig. 4.22), became a resource for the marketing groups, 65 percent for ophthalmic and 35 percent for contact lens products. The nation was split into two sales regions. John Spruill (fig. 4.23), a graduate of Mississippi State University, took charge of the eastern and midwestern sales region, while John Olson, a University of Florida graduate, was promoted to sales manager for the South and West. Gibson temporarily managed the surgical group, but Tom Wilson oversaw its specialized sales force. Marketing services, supervised by Howard Fleischer, provided support for all three groups. Though almost all were young, all had several years of experience in the ophthalmic pharmaceutical, surgical, or contact lens industries.[57]

Viewing these organizational transformations within the context of the pharmaceutical industry's evolution, it is easy to sense the enthusiasm of Alcon's workforce. The constant opportunity for career growth and development made the company a unique employer in how it approached ocular diseases. A good example is glaucoma, which occurs when the pressure inside the eye, the intraocular pressure (IOP), is too high. A sustained high IOP can cause blindness due to the death of irreplaceable cells in the retina, so controlling it is the first step to preventing glaucoma-induced blindness. In the 1960s and 1970s, pilocarpine eye drops became the mainstay therapy, with options being epinephrine drops and dichlorphenamide tablets. Each medication had side effects, the most common being short-term blurring of vision. Moreover, a treatment often lost effectiveness after a while. In these cases, ophthalmologists increased the drug concentration or added a different drug. The need to control IOP thus offered opportunities for ophthalmic specialty companies.[58]

All glaucoma medications at this time contained well-established chemical compounds; none was novel or had patent protection. In today's vernacular, they were generic drugs. Thus, the entry barrier was low for other companies. In fact, Alcon had several competitors in the glaucoma market: Barnes-Hind; Person & Cov-

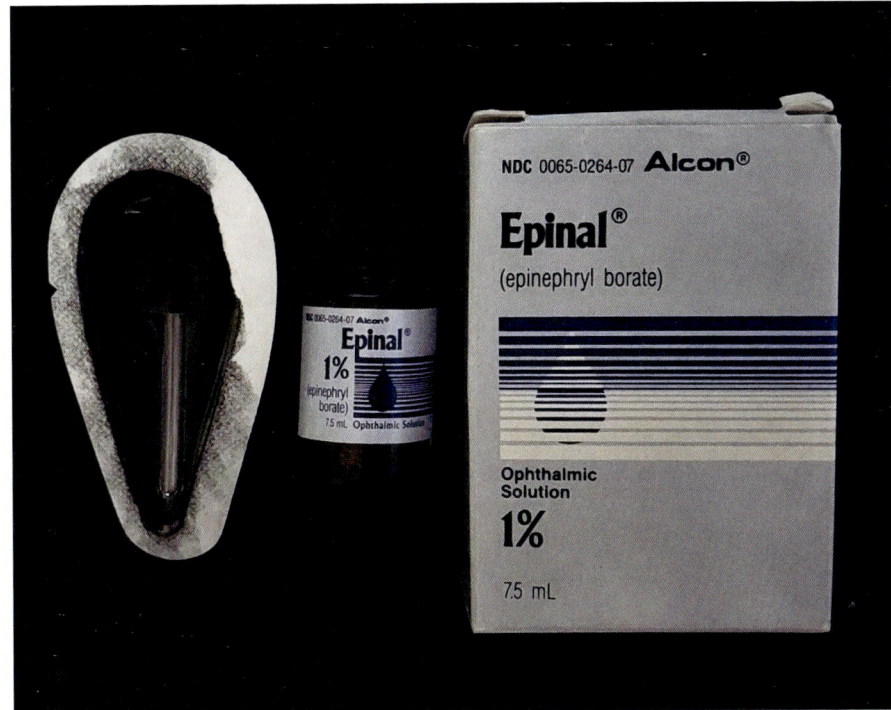

FIG 4.24
Epinal (TOM, AM)

ey; Smith, Miller and Patch; Allergan; Ayerst; Cooke-Barnes; and Professional Pharmacal. However, only Alcon sold all varieties of glaucoma therapies, offering several concentrations of Isopto Carpine and Isopto Carbachol; three epinephrine products (Glaucon, Epinal, and Lyophrin); oral dichlorphenamide (Oratrol); and a combination of pilocarpine and epinephrine (E-Carpine).[59]

Without patent protection, Alcon relied on other technological advantages to sell its glaucoma therapies. The Drop-tainer played a role. Each pilocarpine and carbachol product came with a distinctive green cap so the patient, pharmacist, and ophthalmologist could tell they had the correct product; Alcon was the first company to introduce this safety measure. Every American prescription product has a unique code. Alcon pioneered a process to emboss this on Drop-tainers, which let prescribing physicians and pharmacists know that a patient had received the right medication. Alcon stressed its Isopto products and uniquely stabilized epinephrine formulations (fig. 4.24), which did not degrade. In its promotional literature, Alcon advertised its "Needy Patients Assistance Program," whereby ophthalmologists could request free samples to treat indigent patients. Thus, the marketing group at Alcon had a broad set of strategies.[60]

In 1961 Alcon launched its Glaucoma Tray, a black plastic case containing 2-cc

Drop-tainers of all its glaucoma eye drops and packets of four tablets of Oratrol. The trial sizes allowed the doctor to determine the most effective product at no cost to the patient. The kit also included a convenient reorder card and included twenty-two samples by 1977. The pamphlet "Glaucoma and You" explained the nature and treatment of glaucoma in lay terms, an "emergency card" identified the patient as having glaucoma and named the medication, and there were directions on how to use a Drop-tainer. When an MSR called on a physician, they made sure the Glaucoma Tray was full.[61]

Alcon annually promoted its top seller, Isopto Carpine. During these campaigns, MSRs obtained from each doctor a prescription for Isopto Carpine written on the doctor's personalized prescription pad but minus a signature. A product manager in Fort Worth printed hundreds of copies of each pad, which were given to the ophthalmologist. Preprinted prescriptions not only saved doctors time—all they had to do was sign and hand them to the patient—but also ensured they continued prescribing Isopto Carpine. In the early 1970s, more pilocarpine products emerged, and the federal government explored avenues to cut costs for Medicare patients, as did insurance companies. In this environment, the prescription pad program protected Alcon's products.

The marketing group collaborated with Kallir, Philips, Ross to develop advertising. Product managers bought monthly advertisements in leading journals—the *American Journal of Ophthalmology*, *Archives of Ophthalmology*, *Investigative Ophthalmology*, and others. Alcon highlighted glaucoma products at medical meetings, especially AAOO. Promotional material, brochures, advertisements, and the like passed through an approval process that included marketing and sales, RA, and R&D to ensure that data supported the claims. Product managers presented training and promotion material to MSRs and worked with district managers to maximize the effectiveness of their presentations. The convoluted process involved several divisions, and yet it met the frugal expectations of Conner, Alexander, and Schollmaier. As an illustration, the marketing group had only one calculating machine. This forced product managers to work on weekends, the only time they could access the equipment needed to calculate promotional expenses. Rhue recalled, "Alcon sales continued to grow but marketing budgets were such that product managers had to constantly strive to achieve maximum results with limited funds."[62]

Alcon's streamlined marketing and sales departments led it to the forefront of the glaucoma market during the 1970s, a remarkable outcome for a series of products other companies could copy. It is also an underappreciated component in the company's overall success. Records concerning the ophthalmic market from 1968 through 1978 are sparse, and Alcon seldom cited sales by category. However, beginning in 1973 Alcon data for its ophthalmic prescription products show a revenue of $14.3 million in 1973, increasing annually to $23.8 million in 1977. In 1976 glaucoma drugs were responsible for more than 50 percent of total revenue, and of that three-quarters was from Isopto Carpine. One analyst estimated that in 1976 the total glaucoma market in the United States was approximately $13.5 million, of which Alcon cornered almost two-thirds. Isopto Carpine, the most commonly prescribed pilocarpine formulation, garnered 70 to 80 percent of the market. In any case, by 1977 Isopto Carpine sales totaled about $8 million, approximately 10 percent of Alcon's annual revenue. When additional therapy was needed, ophthalmologists usually chose a carbachol or epinephrine product. In its market, Alcon's Isopto Carbachol owned a 90 percent share by 1976. In the epinephrine area, Glaucon, the product bought from Madland Laboratories, and Epinal, Alcon's proprietary formulation, together earned a 40 percent share. Alcon's dominance of the glaucoma market reflects the effective effort of its sales and marketing organizations and Schollmaier's belief in the "strength of power selling."[63]

Despite this success, technology and science drove the market forward, and Alcon had to respond. In the 1960s the pharmaceutical industry increasingly prioritized drug delivery systems that increased efficacy, reduced side effects, or enhanced patient compliance. By the 1970s pilocarpine had been used to lower IOP for about a century, but it had two limitations: blurred vision and a short duration of action. This changed when Roehrs led Alcon's foray into drug delivery systems, resulting in a pilocarpine gel. His team combined Carbopol 940, a cross-linked polymer of acrylic acid, water, and 4 percent pilocarpine hydrochloride. When instilled in the eye once at night, the gel's higher viscosity controlled IOP for twenty-four hours and virtually eliminated blurred vision. It was a major breakthrough, and Alcon began clinical studies in 1978. This effort faced a strong challenge. A cofounder of the pharmaceutical company Syntex, Alejandro Zaffaroni, created Alza Corporation in 1968. In October 1974 Alza received FDA approval to market Ocusert, a sterile 5-millimeter wafer with a pilocarpine reservoir sandwiched between two permeable membranes. When placed between the lower eyelid and the sclera, the membranes controlled the release of pilocarpine, reducing IOP for one week. But difficulty of insertion and discomfort limited patient compliance, and Alza eventually admitted the product had not been successful. Ocusert never challenged Alcon's pilocarpine products, but an existential threat loomed on the horizon.[64]

One of the dichotomies of eye medications is that chemical compounds with opposite pharmacological actions can produce the same result. Glaucoma is a good example.

During the twentieth century, studies revealed the complexity of the body's nervous system. Of particular interest was the autonomic nervous system, which regulates the brain, heart, lungs, liver, and other vital organs. The autonomic nervous system is divided into parasympathetic and sympathetic systems. In general, the parasympathetic system manages the body in ordinary circumstances; that is, it helps to digest food, slows the heart, and lowers blood pressure. Pilocarpine and carbachol stimulate the parasympathetic system. The sympathetic system organizes the body for action; for example, it speeds up the heart rate and raises blood pressure. Epinephrine, which triggers the fight-or-flight response, is the classic example. Drugs that stimulate the parasympathetic or sympathetic systems are called agonists; ones that block them are antagonists. The sympathetic system has alpha-1, alpha-2, beta-1, and beta-2 receptors, and there can be agonists and antagonists for each of these receptors. Epinephrine is nonselective; it stimulates, or is an agonist for, all four receptors. However, selective alpha and beta agonists and antagonists can also produce the same effect. In the 1960s and 1970s, researchers discovered that beta-blockers lowered IOP. In short, the science behind glaucoma therapies came to be based on human physiology and endocrinology. This challenged MSRs, who were expected to understand the science and to relay that knowledge to ophthalmologists, who themselves were unfamiliar with the new findings.[65]

Evaluating nonselective beta-blockers for reducing blood pressure was in vogue in the medical research community during the 1950s and 1960s. In 1968 researchers at the University of Florida College of Medicine found that timolol lowered IOP in glaucoma patients. It reduced IOP better than pilocarpine, lasted for twelve hours, and did not induce blurred vision—the holy trinity of glaucoma therapy. Timolol blocked both beta-1 and beta-2 receptors; in the physiologist's terminology, it was nonselective. In an interview fifty years later, Herbert E. Kaufman, chair of the Department of Ophthalmology that conducted the research, claimed, "There was reluctance among industry to investigate this drug further in trials because of the absence of a large market." Whether he talked with Alcon is not known; at the time, Barklis managed R&D with a focus on diversifying and Schollmaier was largely absent, dealing with Center Laboratories and Lawton Instruments. Kaufman persuaded a former resident in his department, by then a leading researcher at Merck Sharp & Dohme (MSD), to develop timolol as a glaucoma therapy. As Kaufman explained, "This turned out to be the first good drug to treat glaucoma and a blockbuster product for Merck." MSD filed a patent for timolol and applied to the FDA, getting its approval in 1978. MSD launched the new glaucoma therapeutic product that fall.[66]

By 1974, with Schollmaier in Fort Worth as Alcon's president, Leone in charge of S&T, and Raval managing R&D, Alcon began licensing compounds from other pharmaceutical companies. By then, the ophthalmology community had heard about timolol. Fortunately, Alcon hired a talented pharmacologist, Louis DeSantis, and charged him with finding a beta-blocker to license. As early as the mid-1950s, studies documented that the nonselective beta-blocker propranolol, given orally, intravenously, or topically, lowered IOP, but it also produced corneal anesthesia. DeSantis surveyed the literature on beta-blockers and IOP and identified the ideal characteristics: cardioselective (blocked beta-1 receptors), highly lipophilic (penetrated the cornea into the eye), and lacking a membrane stabilizing effect (did not produce corneal anesthesia). Adamski, R&D's director of research, was responsible for finding compounds to license. He obtained approximately twenty beta-blockers from various companies. DeSantis focused on betaxolol, a beta-1 selective blocker patented by Synthélabo, a subsidiary of the L'Oréal corporation. As a beta-1 selective blocker, betaxolol had safety advantages over timolol. Alcon licensed betaxolol in 1977 and applied to test the molecule to the FDA in 1979.[67]

Treating glaucoma represented a long-term proposition requiring gradually adjusting therapy. In contrast, one of Alcon's banner products, Maxitrol, released in 1965, combined a steroid and an antibiotic, was used in a variety of indications, and produced an immediate response. Maxitrol (dexamethasone alcohol-neomycin sulfate-polymyxin B sulfate) was Alcon's third-generation product of this type after Isopto Cetapred launched in 1953, and Isopto P H N marketed a few years later. A combination product had distinct advantages for the patient: one prescription for less cost and the full effect of the ingredients. Ophthalmologists used the drops and ointments not only in patients with a variety of red eye symptoms but also before and after ocular surgeries to reduce inflammation and prevent infection.[68]

Leone's challenge in 1966 to the field sales force revived Maxitrol; by 1977 it became Alcon's second-leading product, with global sales of $8 million annually and one-fourth of total pharmaceutical sales. Founding the Maxitrol Million Dollar Club in 1966 to incentivize MSRs contributed to this success; Joe Hickey, an MSR in Fort Worth and Houston, became the charter member. Just like it had done for Isopto Carpine, marketing organized promotion campaigns for Maxitrol, and advertisements often appeared in ophthalmologic journals (fig. 4.25). However, selling Maxitrol was different from selling a glaucoma drug. An ophthalmologist saw glaucoma patients infrequently and made decisions about changing therapies gradually. But with a steroid-antibiotic like Maxitrol, the doctor met with pa-

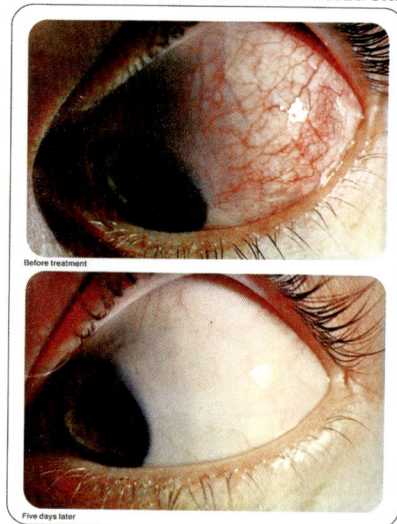

Here's one case treated with Maxitrol...

Before treatment

Five days later

FIG 4.25
Advertisement showing how Maxitrol effectively treated an inflamed eye (AHR)

tients every day and treated them immediately. The MSR knew the next day if the product had satisfied the doctor. In 1977 Maxitrol captured 38 percent of the $10 million domestic steroid-anti-infective market. Schollmaier put it in perspective: "Maxitrol was the product that gave Alcon its growth thrust for the next 10 to 15 years. It was a terrific product. As we grew globally, Maxitrol was the big seller in every market. ... We had a blockbuster and it had a great name."[69]

However, a small group of ophthalmologists and scientists did not endorse antibiotic-steroid combinations, arguing that steroids could mask a fungal or viral infection. Maxitrol's proponents primarily used it because its steroid reduced inflammation and the antibiotic prevented potential infections. To the annoyance of most ophthalmologists, the FDA ordered Alcon to take Maxitrol off the market, expressing concern that general practitioners would use it only for its antibiotic properties. Alcon put "For use by ophthalmologists only" on the label and petitioned to keep it on the market. As the 1970s began, the FDA started using expert advisory committees to consider regulatory positions. In response, Alcon marshaled its experts. Hinson and Kawaga led the defense of Maxitrol. Kagawa organized the scientific rationale supporting the value of a steroid-antibiotic combination, while Hinson lined up medical experts, primarily Jerome Bettman, a professor of ophthalmology at Stanford University. Mathea R. Allansmith, a leading specialist versed in corneal transplants at the Schepens Eye Research Institute of Massachusetts Eye and Ear Infirmary, chaired the FDA committee. In the public meeting, an eminent corneal surgeon declared, "Let me put it this way, gentlemen. I would not do a corneal transplant without Maxitrol, period." The committee recommended that Maxitrol remain on the market, limited to use by ophthalmologists. Alcon had successfully defended its top-tier product.[70]

Ophthalmologists needed a broader-spectrum antibiotic that killed a wide range of bacteria for treating bacterial ocular infections. Most antibiotics killed a narrow range of microorganisms, which, as new antibiotics emerged, developed resistance. There was an exception—Chloromycetin (chloramphenicol) drops sold by Parke-Davis Pharmaceutical Company. However, chloramphenicol, even when used as drops, caused rare fatal blood abnormalities. As the 1970s commenced, a new class of broad-spectrum antibiotics emerged, namely, aminoglycosides. Schlech and his microbiology team in Alcon R&D (fig. 4.26)—which now included Gerald D. "Jerry" Cagle, a doctoral graduate of Ohio State University—screened several aminoglycosides and concluded that tobramycin, patented by Eli Lilly and Company, was highly suited for development into an ophthalmological product. However, to gain access to the compound, Alcon needed a licensing agreement with Lilly, then developing tobramycin

FIG 4.26
Microbiology team, *left to right*:
Gene Estes, Kevin Marks, Jerry Cagle,
Thelma Williams, Barry Schlech,
Jerry Carney, 1976 (BAS)

for a larger market. Lilly was concerned that studies by Alcon would uncover an undesirable aspect of the compound that might jeopardize its development effort. Alcon encountered this concern each time it engaged in licensing discussions. Lilly became an early test case for Alcon's new approach.[71]

Alcon honed its licensing procedure to convince other pharmaceutical companies of their compounds' potential as Alcon products. The process began well before Alcon approached a patent holder. R&D conducted tests to assess a drug's potential. Alcon scientists used validated in vitro and in vivo assays to determine if the drug had a desired safety and efficacy profile. Separate studies assessed initial stability and preservative efficacy. A compound that passed these hurdles became a licensing candidate. After signing an agreement, Alcon scientists ensured that the compound's data, provided by the licensor, met regulatory expectations. Pharmaceutical researchers optimized the formula and toxicologists performed safety studies before testing the drug in humans. Chemical analysis created assays for the raw material compound. The

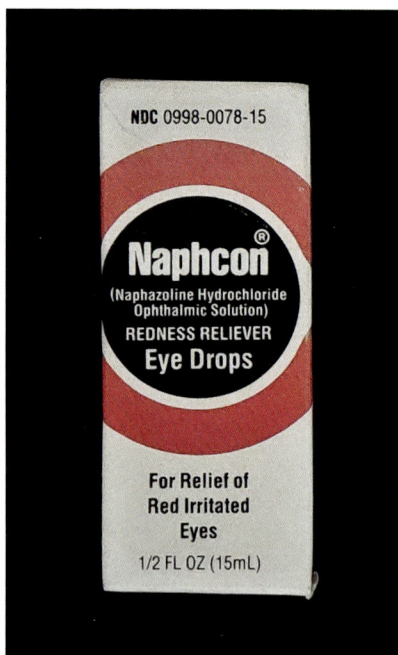

FIG 4.27
Naphcon (TOM, AM)

whole process was, and remains, expensive, complex, and unpredictable, requiring capable, experienced, and tenacious scientists.

After Schlech and Cagle identified tobramycin as their preferred compound, a team led by Raval and Adamski visited Lilly in December 1976 to initiate a licensing request. However, negotiations reached an impasse when Lilly announced it might market it as an eye product. To break the stalemate, Schollmaier met Lilly's president at his headquarters. He showed him a chart and explained, "If you really do a good job you might get a million and a half dollars out of it. ... Here's what we can do on it. ... It's clear that you will make more money licensing it to us than you would marketing it yourself." Lilly gave Alcon a commitment that afternoon. Soon the terms were negotiated, tobramycin was licensed in 1977, and an application went to the FDA in 1978. Thus, as this decade ended, Alcon had begun developing a first-of-a-kind broad-spectrum antibiotic therapy, a new tool for managing ocular infections.[72]

In the ophthalmic world, decongestants contain a vasoconstrictor compound that constricts blood vessels in the eye. Since the 1950s Alcon promoted Zincfrin, Op-Thal-Zin, and Isopto Frin for the treatment of red, itchy eyes. The market changed in the 1960s as competitors, mainly Allergan and Smith, Miller and Patch, introduced new OTC medications. In response, Alcon marketed its products over the counter. Initially, Alcon chose phenylephrine (0.12%) as the vasoconstriction drug, but as physiologists and pharmacologists explored new adrenergic agonists, two compounds, naphazoline and tetrahydrozoline, came into favor for eye decongestant OTC products. In 1971 Alcon introduced Naphcon (0.12% naphazoline), a new formulation of Solutina, the largest-selling decongestant in Mexico, manufactured by Oftasa, a company Alcon bought in 1970. By 1977 Pfizer's Visine (tetrahydrozoline 0.05%) was the dominant ocular decongestant, but Alcon followed at 22 percent of the $7 million US market. Naphcon (fig. 4.27) was the third most profitable product for Alcon after Isopto Carpine and Maxitrol. Rebranding Solutina from Mexico as Naphcon in the United States more than compensated for Alcon's purchasing Oftasa. Alcon differentiated Naphcon as being more comfortable than other ocular decongestants and its marketing group capitalized on this feature.[73]

Alcon did not have an anti-allergy product in its portfolio, the closest being Estivin, a rose petal infusion bought from Schieffelin & Company. Rose water has a long history in the Middle East as a homoeopathic remedy for red, itchy eyes. Founded in 1794, Schieffelin became the largest pharmaceutical company in the United States in the 1800s, and Alcon lore places the launch date of Estivin late in that century. During Prohibition,

Schieffelin found medicinal alcohol to be very lucrative, and it abandoned the pharmaceutical business in 1962 to be a leading producer of champagne. Conner purchased Estivin and two other products, and Feik spent six months arranging the technology transfer so the products could be manufactured in Fort Worth, in a new facility in the basement of the S&T building. Alcon promoted Estivin for the relief of "smog, eye strain from sun and wind, hay fever, and other allergic eye conditions." As Alcon would learn, Estivin had a loyal cadre of users.[74]

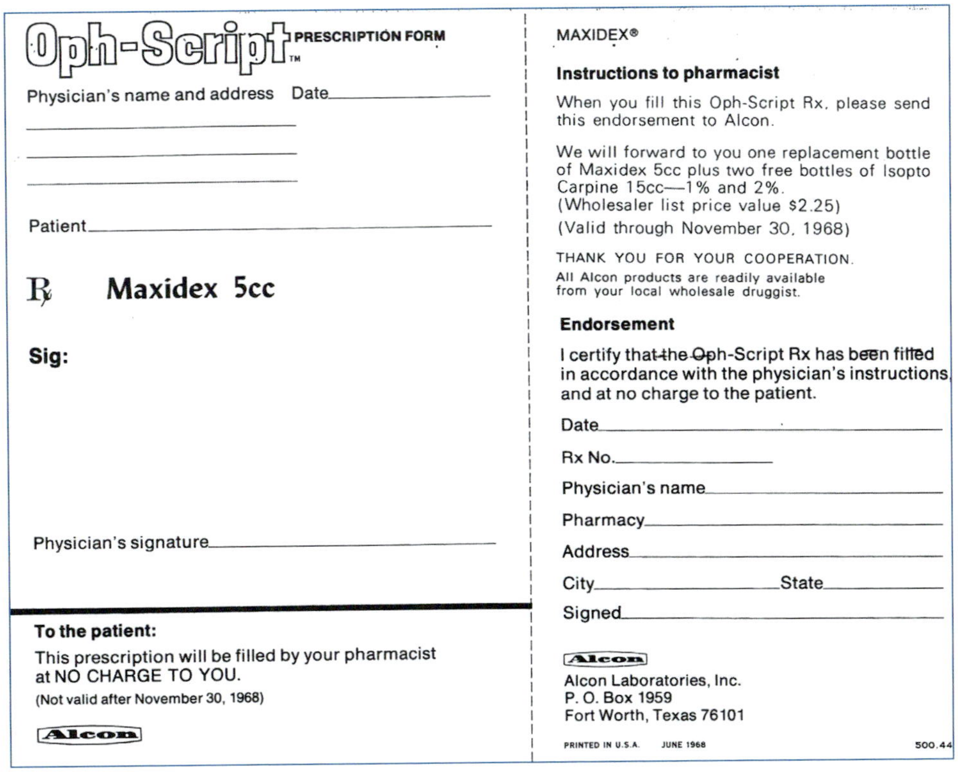

Oph-Script™ PRESCRIPTION FORM

Physician's name and address Date______

Patient______

℞ **Maxidex 5cc**

Sig:

Physician's signature______

To the patient:
This prescription will be filled by your pharmacist at NO CHARGE TO YOU.
(Not valid after November 30, 1968)

Alcon

MAXIDEX®

Instructions to pharmacist

When you fill this Oph-Script Rx, please send this endorsement to Alcon.

We will forward to you one replacement bottle of Maxidex 5cc plus two free bottles of Isopto Carpine 15cc—1% and 2%.
(Wholesaler list price value $2.25)
(Valid through November 30, 1968)

THANK YOU FOR YOUR COOPERATION.
All Alcon products are readily available from your local wholesale druggist.

Endorsement

I certify that the Oph-Script Rx has been filled in accordance with the physician's instructions, and at no charge to the patient.

Date______

Rx No.______

Physician's name______

Pharmacy______

Address______

City______ State______

Signed______

Alcon
Alcon Laboratories, Inc.
P. O. Box 1959
Fort Worth, Texas 76101

PRINTED IN U.S.A. JUNE 1968 500.44

FIG 4.28
Maxidex Oph-Script prescription form (AHR)

The classic prescription anti-inflammatory eye drop was a steroid suspension or ointment formulation. In 1955 Dave Merrill developed two single-entity steroid products—Isopto Cortisone ½%, 2½%, and Isopto Hydrocortisone ½%—and five years later he released the more potent Isopto Prednisolone 0.25%. After Schollmaier licensed dexamethasone alcohol from Organon, Fleming used the Isopto vehicle for the suspension form and developed an ointment product. Schollmaier chose the name Maxidex. Launched in 1964, Maxidex became the first example of Alcon abandoning the Isopto trademark.[75]

Rhue's first assignment at Alcon in December 1970 included marketing campaigns for Maxidex; Glenn Rickey took over in January 1974. Marketing promoted a twenty-four-hour therapy of daytime drops and ointment at night. Maxidex's unique properties extended the time on the eye after instillation of a drop, prolonging efficacy by increasing penetration for dexamethasone into the eye. MSRs liberally distributed reprints and summaries of a radio-labeled dexamethasone study supporting these conclusions. Maxidex Oph-Scripts Rx given to doctors offered free samples to pharmacists (fig. 4.28). In terms of promotion, marketing, and MSR presentations, Alcon managed Maxidex as a flagship therapy and by 1977 had 16 percent of the competitive, single-entity ophthalmic steroid market, worth $5 million.[76]

Several steroids packaged for ophthalmic use appeared in the 1960s and 1970s, giving ophthalmologists a wide range of single-entity products for treating inflammation. Alcon's traditional rival, Allergan, sold three—Prednefrin Forte (1% prednisolone), HMS (1% medrysone), and FML (0.1% fluorometholone alcohol)—and Smith, Miller and Patch marketed Inflamase Forte (1% prednisolone). MSD offered Decadron (0.1% dexamethasone sodium phosphate). Into this crowded market, Alcon launched its own brand of prednisolone acetate (Econopred ⅛% and Econopred Plus 1%). Prednisolone acetate 1%, considered the most potent steroid used in the eye, was marketed for years under regulatory classifications as an "old drug." In the early 1970s, the FDA mandated the submission of an NDA in order to continue selling "old" products, approving Alcon's prednisolone acetate 1% in 1973.

Even research into steroid use in the eye was competitive. Many well-known clinical ophthalmologists published reports on the safety and efficacy of the topical use of ophthalmic steroids. Alcon R&D had its own research program, using models developed by the scientific pharmacology team of Fortenberry and Shirley Hayes. When DeSantis arrived in 1974, he contracted anti-inflammatory studies to various university ophthalmology departments. Alcon ultimately concluded the best compounds were theirs: dexamethasone alcohol and prednisolone acetate. Steroids are potent and the side effects must be managed diligently. Steroid drops treat diseases of the conjunctiva, sclera, cornea, anterior chamber, and the iris-ciliary body (see eye cross section, Appendix 1). Injections of steroids proved effective for maladies in the posterior segment of the eye. Ocular side effects of topical steroid eye drops with long-term use include increased IOP, cataracts, secondary ocular infections, and poor corneal healing. By the 1960s, the use of potent steroids went far beyond the generic formulations that Alexander and Conner had used in starting Alcon. MSRs and marketers, who themselves often had degrees in chemistry, biology, or pharmacy, needed specialized knowledge to converse with ophthalmologists and researchers.[77]

The invention of the slit-lamp biomicroscope and direct ophthalmoscope facilitated the development of drugs that dilate the pupil for in-depth examination of the anterior chamber, lens, vitreous, retina, and optic nerve. Mydriatics dilate the pupil and cycloplegics paralyze the ciliary body, preventing the lens from focusing. Refraction is the process the doctor follows to determine a patient's prescription for eyeglasses or contact lenses, and mydriatics and cycloplegics facilitate this. An ophthalmologist or optometrist instills mydriatic and cycloplegic drugs in almost every patient. The domestic mydriatic-cycloplegic market in 1976 was small, at $2.5 million, of which Alcon had 90 percent. Conner's purchase of two products in 1971 from Schieffelin, Cyclogyl (0.5%, 1% cyclopentolate) and Cyclomydril (0.2% cyclopentolate and 1% phenylephrine), increased Alcon's number of products to five, making it the principal manufacturer of cycloplegics-mydriatics, with 1% Mydriacyl as the primary product. Alcon improved Cyclogyl and Cyclomydril by packaging them in Drop-tainers, enhancing ease of use.[78]

Alcon marketed three artificial tear products. Merrill developed Isopto Tears (0.5% HPMC) and Isopto Alkaline in the 1950s; the latter was rebranded as Ultra Tears when Alcon dropped the Isopto label. To complement the Contique line of contact lens products, the marketing group launched Contique Artificial Tears (2% polyvinyl alcohol). These products were palliative lubricants that did not address the causes of dry eyes. Through a robust sales promotion, Alcon's palliative products garnered about 20 percent of a $5 million market.[79]

The most common results of a dry eye are a small loss of the epithelium on the cornea and a fast breakup of the tear film. This pathology can be seen under magnification after instilling a drop of fluorescein, a diagnostic dye. The chemistry of tears is complex. They are composed of water, proteins (lysozyme being one), electrolytes, carbohydrates, lipids, and mucins. Sometimes production decreases or composition can be deficient in one or more chemicals. Aging and hormones affect the quantity and quality of tears. The FDA asked the National Academy of Sciences to review chemical compounds to define those that were generally recognized as safe and effective (GRAS/E). Although the official results were not released until 1988, it was clear much earlier which ingredients would be granted GRAS/E status. Ophthalmic formulations with these ingredients, sold OTC without making therapeutic claims, could be marketed without an FDA review if proper safety studies had been conducted. Hecht and his team created several formulas, of which one passed in vivo and in vitro experiments. Thus, in 1975 Alcon launched Tears Naturale (fig. 4.29), a combination of dextran 70, glycerin, and HPMC. Patients found Tears Naturale far superior to other products in relieving dry eye symptoms. Under marketing product manager Roy Buchanan, the elegantly packaged Tears Naturale became the first Alcon product to attain annual sales of $1 million in just two years.[80]

After acquiring it in 1970, Alcon's ophthalmic group marketed Fluorescite, a diagnostic solution used to visualize retinal blood vessels. But an impurity in the raw material caused rare anaphylactic reactions, so Adamski and Sam Numijari (fig. 4.30) developed a new synthetic pathway to eliminate the problem. The medicinal chemistry laboratory in R&D became a GMP-qualified facility to manufacture fluorescein, the first time Alcon supplied its own raw material. R&D repackaged 10% Fluorescite in prefilled syringes for intravenous administration and released a 25% option. Rhue handled the marketing of Fluorescite. Dr. Lawrence Yannuzzi, at the Manhattan Eye, Ear and Throat Hospital, pioneered its use to visualize blood flow in the retina (fig. 4.31) and became the leading expert on its clinical use.[81]

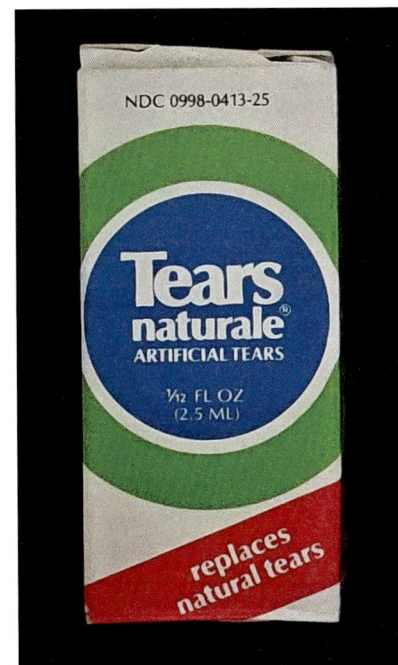

FIG 4.29
Tears Naturale, launched 1975 (TOM, AM)

FIG 4.30
Bob Adamski (*left*) and Sam Numijari
(*right*), synthesizing purified fluorescein
(AHR)

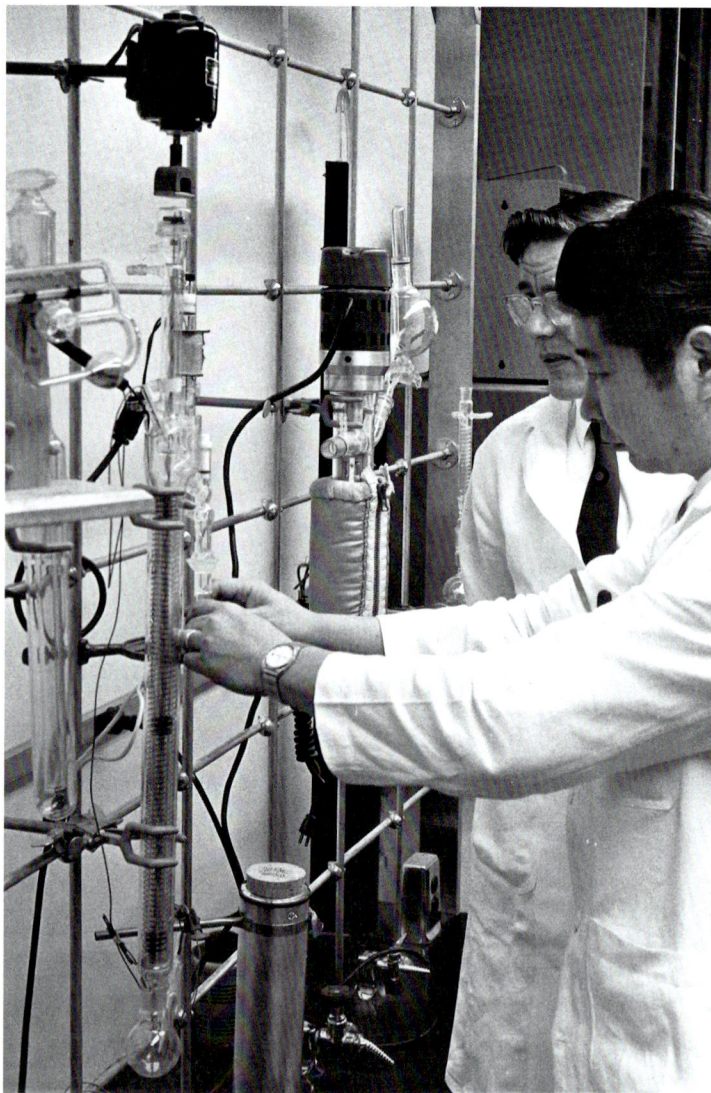

FIG 4.31
Left: Photograph of blood vessels of
the retina; *right*: retinal image three
minutes after intravenous injection
of Fluorescite (BAS)

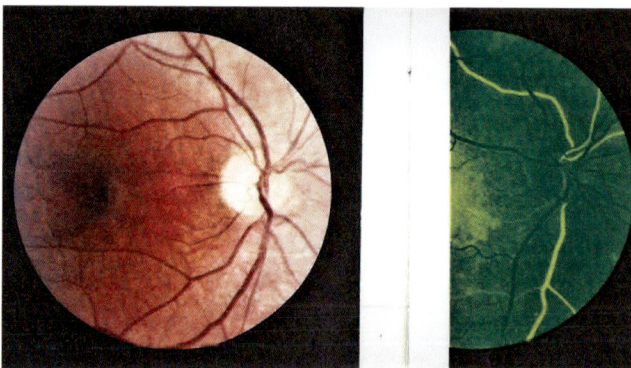

While Leonardo da Vinci receives credit for the theoretical concept of contact lenses, it was only in the 1880s that a German ophthalmologist designed the first contact lens made of blown glass. Plastic contact lenses, made of polymethyl methacrylate, appeared in the 1930s, and by the 1950s small, curved PMMA lenses, commonly known as hard lenses, had been perfected. Though comfortable while floating on the cornea's surface, they could be worn for only part of a day. Hard lenses required conscientious cleaning, storage, and sanitizing regimens, and eye drops to improve comfort. They could also be detrimental to the wearer because they restrict the amount of oxygen to the eye. Rigid gas permeable (RGP) lenses, made of silicone acrylate polymers, emerged as one solution. Another option, known as soft contact lenses, used hydrogel poly-hydroxyethyl methacrylate (HEMA). Both became available on the market in the 1960s and 1970s. Like hard lenses, these needed cleaning, sanitizing, storage, and comfort solutions. In 1971 the FDA approved Bausch & Lomb's (B&L) soft hydrogel contact lens, SofLens, transforming the industry. Soon other companies launched a soft lens, Ciba Vision being a market innovator. By the mid-1980s, soft contact lenses had displaced hard lenses.[82]

During B&L's development of SofLens, many companies producing hard contact lenses, mainly small operations, claimed the new lens materials should be classified as drugs requiring FDA approval. In December 1968 the FDA notified B&L of the need for an NDA for its soft lens. The mandate extended to all non-PMMA lenses and support solutions. Furthermore, the FDA classified the non-PMMA lenses into four categories based on water content and ionic or nonionic composition. When the FDA promulgates new rules, it holds public hearings before an expert panel. The extent to which Alcon participated in the process is difficult to ascertain, but the company spent considerable resources developing and launching its Contique line of products for PMMA contact lenses in 1969 (fig. 4.32).[83]

In late 1965 Schollmaier and Dewar collaborated with Hecht in R&D to patent an electrical cleaning device, which they named Contique Swirl Clean. Hecht and his group produced wetting, soaking, and cleaning solutions for the Swirl Clean. They also formulated a dissolvable cleaning and soaking tablet for use with the Swisher, a device held under running wa-

FIG 4.32
Contique Contact Lens Wetting and Soaking Solutions, Bonus Pak (TOM, AM)

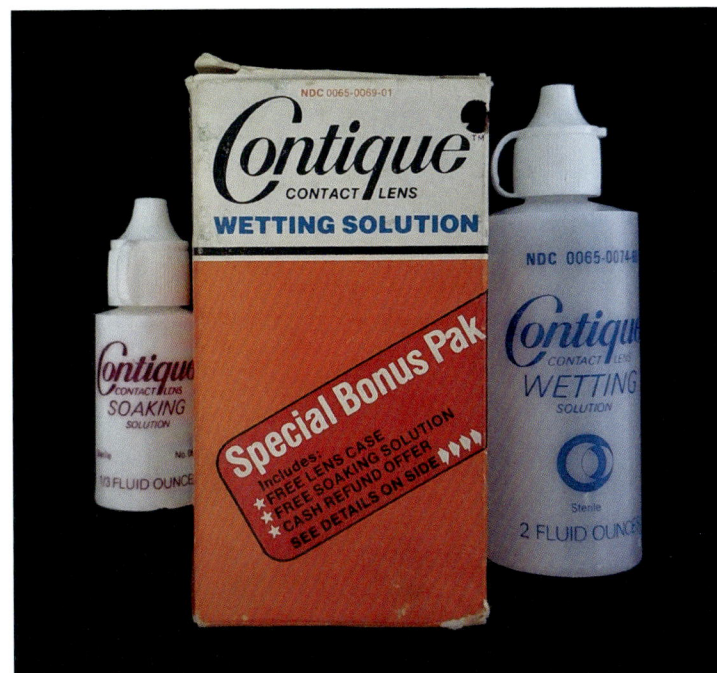

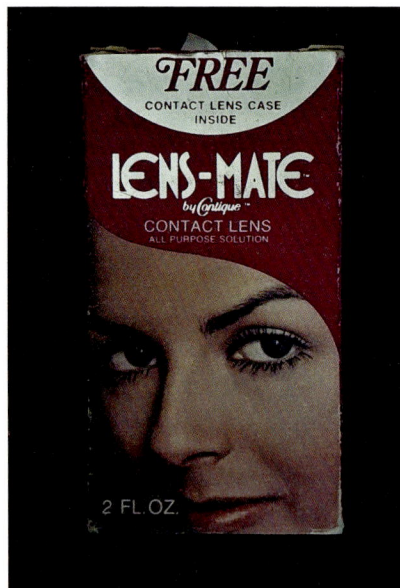

FIG 4.33
Lens-Mate (AHR)

ter. Furthermore, the marketing and R&D teams designed plastic cases for storing lenses. All these products were grouped under the Contique brand and launched in the spring of 1969. R&D also formulated Lens-Mate (fig. 4.33), an all-purpose three-in-one solution that wetted, soaked, and cleaned hard contact lenses. The Contique line had its own artificial tear solution, promoted as a "soothing lubricant for soothing ... dry eyes associated with the wearing of contact lenses." Starter kits contained the Contique solutions, a carrying case, and the "Happy Contacts Booklet" in an attractive package and were sold to ophthalmologists and optometrists. This offered an opportunity for practitioners to earn money distributing Alcon products, and Alcon gained repeat business. In addition to pharmacies, Alcon sold Contique to retail stores, including Wal-Mart, Kmart, Sears, and even Neiman-Marcus. MSRs also gave presentations at optometry schools and organized $50 quarterly drawings at participating stores to generate interest. Sales grew, requiring the 1972 expansion of the manufacturing plant to include a Contique production line (fig. 4.34). Alcon's annual sales of $1.5 million placed it third after Barnes-Hind and Allergan.[84]

In 1972 Alcon faced a strategic choice, though it would be another decade before company leaders agreed on the way forward. After investing $3.5 million—more than Alcon's annual R&D budget—in developing SofLens, B&L overcame technical hurdles in creating soft lenses and emerged as the market leader. PMMA lenses were made on a lathe, which did not work with hydrogel material, so B&L scientists perfected the spin-cast method. While competitors struggled to build scientific teams with polymer chemistry knowledge and experience, Alcon wanted a finished technology. After a faulty start with two companies, Alcon bought the Tresoft contact lens manufacturing plant in November 1977 from the TRE Corporation of California. Alcon intended to distribute Tresoft lenses nationwide and develop a second-generation lens. It changed the TRE name to Alcon Optic Division and placed it in Sisson's group. He assigned James Bond, an experienced marketing executive who transferred from the Owen division, and Peter Hatton, recently a B&L executive, to handle marketing. Alcon Optic Division introduced a unique marketing plan whereby MSRs acted as Tresoft fitting consultants for eye care specialists. Alcon faced a tough climb: by 1978 B&L's SofLens owned a 49 percent share of the domestic contact lens market and by 1982 the worldwide contact lens market had grown to over $350 million. Of this Tresoft had only a trifling share.[85]

Since 1947 Alcon had built its reputation on providing safe, stable, sterile formulations, so it seemed natural that it developed contact lens solutions. However, the four

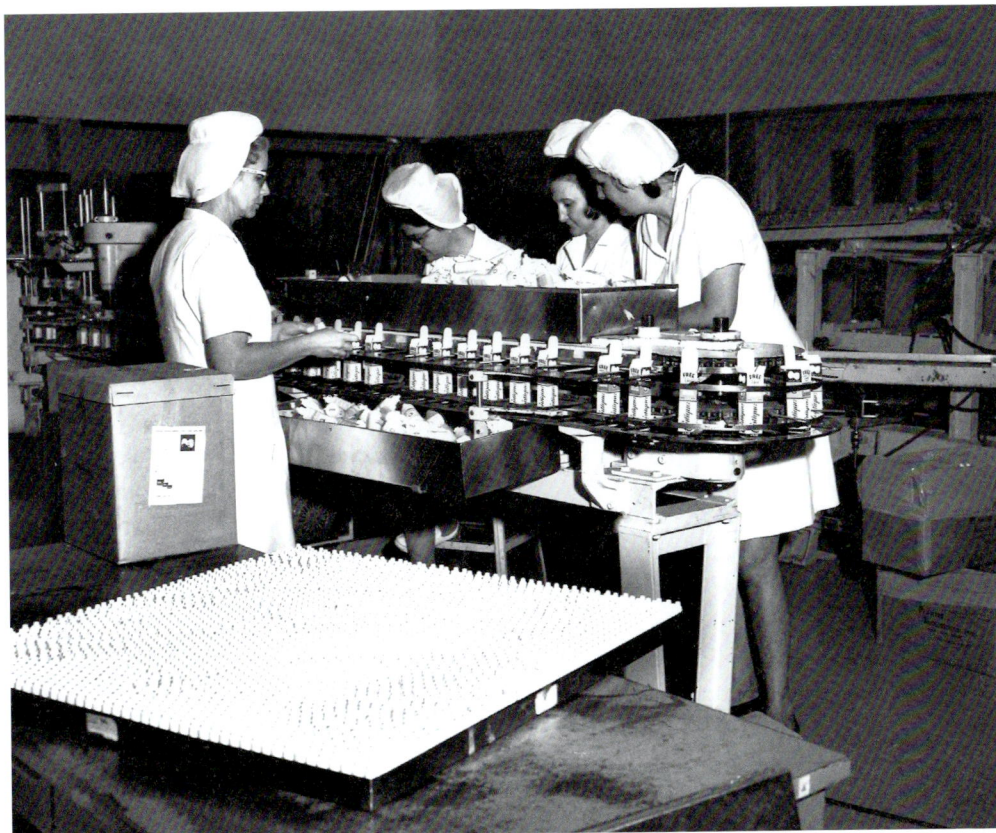

different soft lens polymers all needed unique disinfecting, cleaning, and soaking solutions. In clinical studies, B&L discovered that patients wearing SofLens had a higher incidence of infection by bacteria and the parasite Acanthamoeba, which produced corneal changes that sometimes led to blindness. These observations led the FDA to approve only solutions with a boiling regimen. No chemical disinfectants had been approved by 1977, and certainly Alcon's Contique could not be used with soft contact lenses. By then, Burton, Parsons & Company dominated the market for approved solutions that disinfected and stored soft contact lenses.[86]

Contact lens solutions were not the only challenge for Alcon in the 1970s. After the company bought Lawton in 1967, it operated as a subsidiary with its own home office in New York City. It used Alcon's international market to distribute its stainless-steel surgical instruments, but only about 10 percent of its roughly sixty-seven hundred products were used by ophthalmic surgeons. Distribution occurred through surgical supply houses, though Lawton had salesmen to keep hospitals and surgeons abreast of innovations. The

FIG 4.35
Alcon Surgical, sales and marketing team, 1972 (Bob Grantham, AM)

Alcon Surgical, Sales & Marketing Team, 1972

Lee Humphreys
Tom Weatherby
Bob Grantham
Larry Vines
Walt Dillenback
John Wren
Don Luster Product Manager
Rick Silvey
Daryl Dubbs
Andy Lubrano
Don Jablonski
Jerry Hutcheson
Tom Wilson Sales Manager
Cliff Barth
Wayne Fowler
Steve Quindry

instruments were mostly manufactured in Germany by skilled craftsmen in some 150 independent family-operated plants. Lawton's headquarters moved to Moonachie, New Jersey. Schollmaier hired James D. Alden, who had executive experience in the medical plastics industry, as the vice president in charge of operations for Lawton. Financial and inventory problems led Alcon to send Jerry K. Rutherford, from its finance department, to help resolve them. Schollmaier also devoted months to Lawton, renting an apartment nearby. Nevertheless, chronic problems persisted.

When Alcon bought Lawton, it became totally dependent upon Lawton for ophthalmic surgical instruments. This proved problematic because the subsidiary had high prices and small profit margins and also had too many products in small demand and on back order. Alcon assumed Lawton sold high-quality instruments, but in reality, with so many independent artisans involved, quality control was difficult. Stainless-steel surgical instruments go through passivation, a complex cleaning process that removes impurities from the metal. Any residual impurities show up as rust spots, which proved to be a recurrent problem. Small ophthalmic instruments were particularly affected, and Lawton's product return process annoyed surgeons. By 1973 Conner, Schollmaier, and the board decided to sell Lawton. Schollmaier and Kologe contacted forty-eight potential buyers; only one, Dart Industries, expressed interest. After months of negotiation, Alcon sold Lawton for $4.2 million, losing $150,000. In retrospect, acquiring Lawton was a serious mistake but a lesson well learned for Alcon leaders. Looking back, Rutherford recalled, "I learned more at Lawton than I'd ever learned in college or, even other jobs at Alcon. ... It really broadened me tremendously in my knowledge of business. ... I learned a lot in three years at Lawton." What did Schollmaier learn? In retirement, he taught a business class at TCU, where he highlighted one important point: 90 percent of acquisitions are unsuccessful.[87]

Alcon Surgical, based in Fort Worth under Gibson, focused on selling items needed by ophthalmic surgeons: instruments, devices, and medications. Formed in 1968, the group's dedicated sales force, led by Alcon veteran Tom Wilson, increased to sixteen by 1972 (fig. 4.35). Don Luster, Bob Grantham, Andy Lubrano, and Daryl Dubbs formed the nucleus. In the 1960s the Cryophake, an instrument used to remove cataract lenses, served as the impetus for creating a surgical group focused on ophthalmic surgeons. Alcon also had legacy ophthalmic surgical products—BSS, Steri-units, and Zolyse—and when Cryophake was introduced, the company supported it with a disposable cautery, Optemp (fig. 4.36). Additionally, Alcon sold stainless-steel ophthalmic surgical tools. In 1970, Alcon introduced the EDT-103 tonograph, which measured IOP and outflow of fluid from the anterior chamber. Even at its formation, the surgical group had an array of products for eye surgeons. From the late 1960s into the early 1980s, intracapsular cataract extraction (ICCE) using cryo-instruments was the main technique used in cataract surgery. Cryophake was replaced with Cryophake II and later with Microphake (fig. 4.37). This evolution is a good example of the miniaturization of ophthalmic surgical tools, a trend that accelerated in the 1980s and beyond.[88]

FIG 4.36
Optemp, advertisement (AHR)

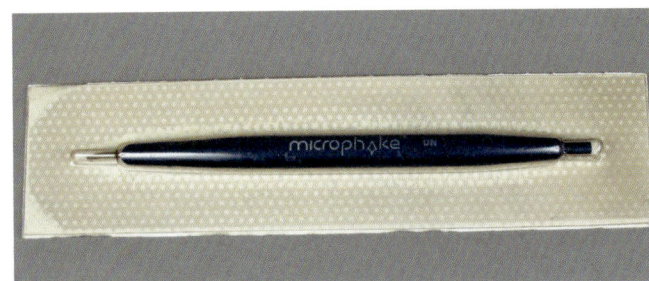

FIG 4.37
Microphake (Used by permission from the National Museum of American History, Smithsonian Institution)

Alcon R&D's expertise resided in creating eye drops, not instruments or devices. Although hired specifically for his experience in developing instruments, Raval advised against getting into electric instruments, given Alcon's limited engineering and service capabilities. Events proved his caution warranted: for example, Alcon Surgical obtained the EDT-103 electronic digital tonograph from a company that developed products for the Defense Department. From the start, problems plagued the EDT-103 until the surgical group hired Maury Rester, an electrical engineer.

Until a major acquisition in 1989, Alcon Surgical obtained and sold instruments without R&D. This reflects a major debate within Alcon—where to use R&D resources. Leone and Schollmaier learned that product development succeeds when a company focuses on a few carefully selected projects, and that ophthalmic prescription products fit their existing infrastructure (QC, sales, manufacturing, and marketing) and had the greatest profits. Nevertheless, Alcon Surgical needed products. Inventors frequently proposed ideas; one was the Alcon Amoils, a cryo-unit using liquid nitrogen, invented by Percy Amoils, a South African ophthalmologist. Another product emerged when Alcon collaborated with Dynatech Corporation of Massachusetts but received an instrument beleaguered with reliability issues. Other products sourced from outside vendors included Eye-Pak (lint-free surgical drapes), Microsponge, Alcon Closure System (needles and sutures for eye surgery), PTG Applanating Pneumotonograph (replacement for the EDT-103), Olympus MTX surgical microscope, Shock Phacofragmentation (fractured cataractous lenses), Grieshaber Hand Instruments (tools for eye surgery), and Grieshaber motorized devices for corneal and vitreous surgery. By 1978 Alcon discontinued all except Eye-Pak drapes and the Alcon Closure System.[89]

On the pharmaceutical side of the surgical business, R&D released BSS, Steri-units, and Zolyse in the late 1950s, and Osmoglyn, an oral osmotic solution to reduce IOP before ocular surgery, in the 1960s. A major risk during ICCE was loss of the vitreous after removal of the cataract, something that can be mitigated by pharmacologically inducing a small pupil. Acetylcholine, the body's natural parasympathetic agonist, constricts the pupil but rapidly degrades when placed in water. Smith, Miller, and Patch sought to avoid this problem by developing a unique vial, in which acetylcholine powder was dissolved. Once administered, the body's enzymes degraded acetylcholine so it had brief action inside the eye. Alcon R&D chose to formulate 0.01% carbachol, a synthetic parasympathetic agonist, in BSS, a solution stable for three years, which produced a small pupil for almost twenty-four hours. After FDA approval, Alcon launched this formulation as Miostat (fig. 4.38) in 1974. At the University of Wisconsin Medical School, Henry E. Edelhauser, an ocular

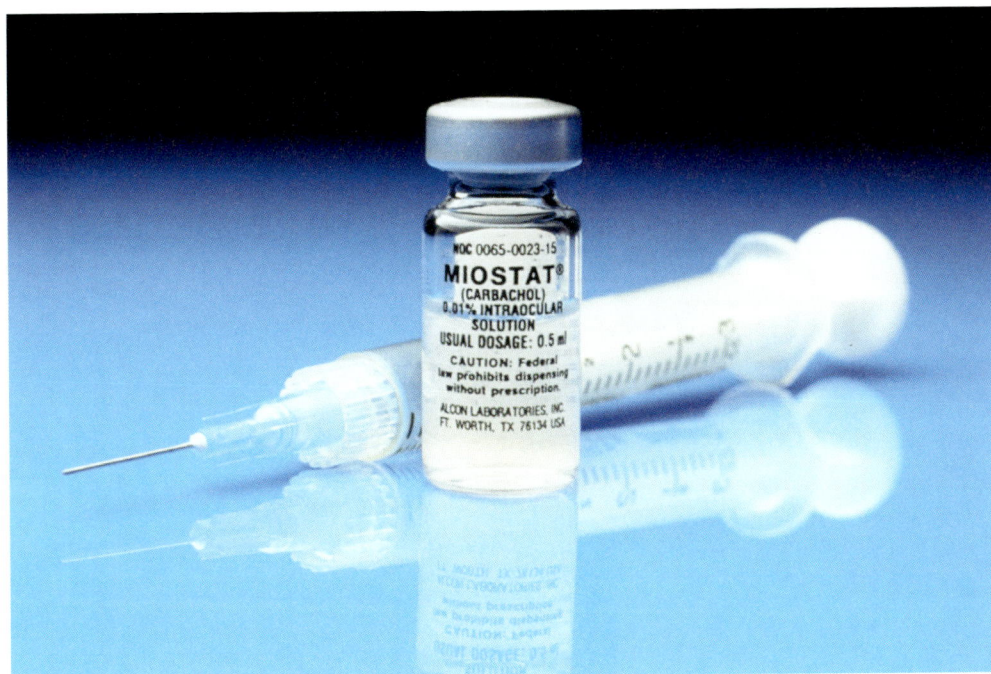

FIG 4.38
Miostat (AHR)

physiologist, found that adding glutathione, a powerful antioxidant, to BSS protected the endothelium. Alcon licensed his invention and filed with the FDA in 1977. R&D resolved glutathione's inherent instability by fashioning a two-part package reconstituted in the surgery room, creating the product known as BSS PLUS (fig. 4.39). By 1977 Alcon Surgical sales totaled $5.8 million, about 7 percent of the company's sales, of which 67 percent came from BSS, Zolyse, Miostat, Steri-units, and Osmoglyn. This led Alcon to discontinue most surgical devices and instruments.[90]

In 1973 Alcon purchased Mager & Gougelman of Chicago, a manufacturer of prosthetic eyes since the 1850s. Ocularistry, the art of creating an artificial eye, extends back to the fifth century BC; by the mid-1850s, glass became the most common material used. With the goal of creating a prosthesis that realistically mimics the remaining eye, the introduction of plastics in the 1940s revolutionized the industry, allowing for a more natural-looking product. Alcon's contact lens products, such as lubricants and hygiene solutions, could also be used by wearers of ocular prosthetics (fig. 4.40), and an antimicrobial artificial tear formulation, Enuclene, was specifically formulated for this market. Thus, Mager & Gougelman seemed a natural fit for Alcon, and it operated as an independent entity, though loosely connected to the Surgical group.[91]

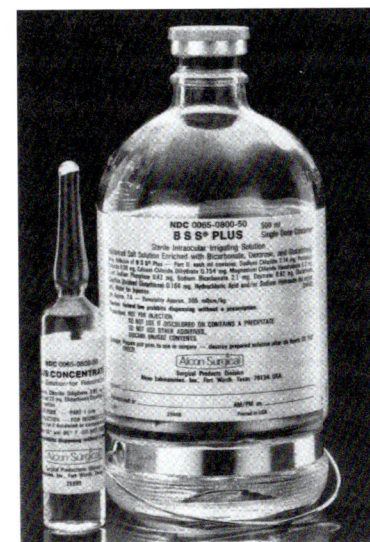

FIG 4.39
First-generation BSS PLUS, two-part solutions (AHR)

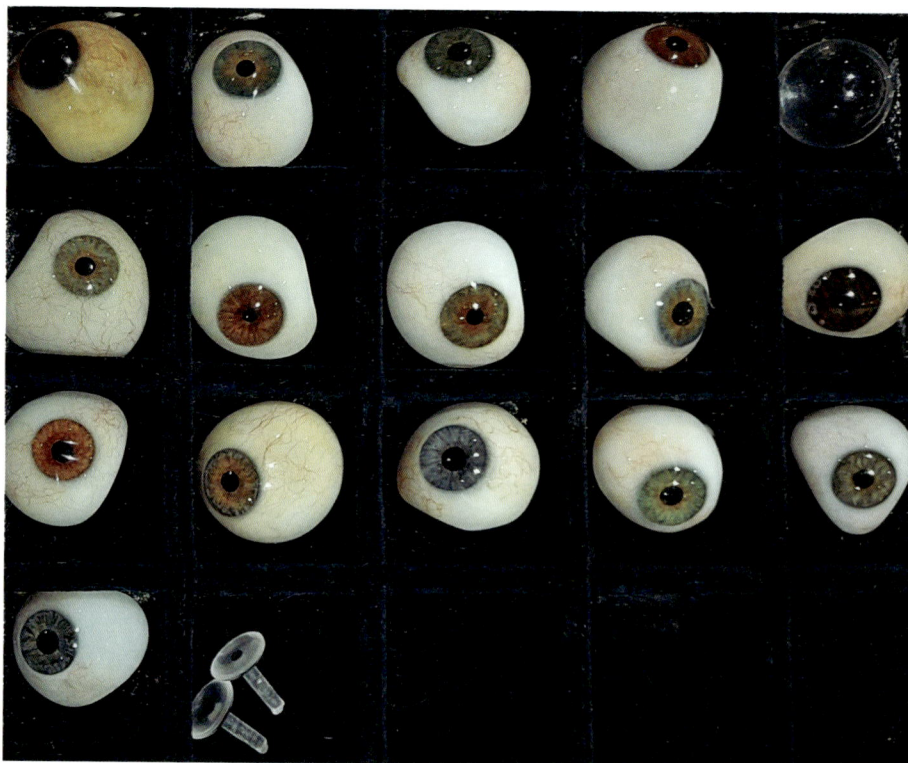

FIG 4.40
Mager & Gougelman prosthetic eyes set (Bob Grantham, AM)

Conner considered Owen Laboratories of Addison, Texas, to be an ideal specialty company for his expansion strategy. Douglas Owen Brown and a small group of investors incorporated Owen Laboratories in 1961. Schollmaier believed the dermatology market bore similarities to the early ophthalmic market since pharmacists still compounded dermatology prescriptions and a handful of companies catered to dermatologists: Schollmaier believed that, following the principles that had worked in ophthalmology, Alcon could succeed in dermatology. He offered Brown a price on several occasions. Late one evening, Brown called Schollmaier at home and said he was ready to sell. Schollmaier drove to Dallas, and they agreed on terms. Alcon paid approximately four times Owen's annual sales of $3 million, a hefty price; Alcon's yearly income at the time was about $30 million. Owen marketed mostly to dermatologists but it also had a line for retailers, beauty salons, and the public. On April 28, 1973, Alcon completed its acquisition of Owen Laboratories and shareholders elected Brown to its board.[92]

Owen Laboratories had a sixty-thousand-square-foot manufacturing facility in Dallas, and Schollmaier appointed Lane (fig. 4.41) as its general manager. In thirteen years with

Alcon, Lane had been an MSR, district manager, regional manager, and field sales manager. Seasoned MSRs and product managers Bond and Bunker also transferred from Alcon Domestic and Alcon International to help with Owen. At the time of acquisition, Owen had fifteen MSRs visiting about thirty-five hundred dermatologists, using similar marketing and sales strategies to those deployed by Alcon. The leading products were Ionil and Ionil T antidandruff shampoos; Nutraderm, a hydrating emollient for dry skin; Pabafilm, a topical sunscreen agent; and Ionax Scrub and Ionax Foam, abrading acne and oily skin cleansers. Its sales went from $3 million in 1972 to nearly $6 million in 1977, fueled in part by the introduction of new products—Nutraplus, a skin moisturizer; Nutracort, a hydrocortisone cream; Ionax Astringent, an acne treatment; Iocon, an antiseborrheic shampoo; PABA Gel, a topical sunscreen; R-Gen-M, a protein shampoo to repair damaged hair; and Losel 250, a prescription therapy for dandruff. During this period, Owen increased its sales force to thirty-three. With the introduction of the aerosol Ionax, Owen invested in an automated line that produced ten thousand cans daily. With larger sales and new products, in November 1977 Owen began a $2.5 million plant modernization.[93]

FIG 4.41
Keith Lane (AHR)

Alcon chose to operate Mahdeen, part of Owen at the acquisition, as a separate division, even though it sourced many products from Owen. Mahdeen marketed skin, hair, and scalp products to wholesalers, barbers, and cosmetologists. In 1974 it created a professional services group that sponsored ear piercing centers in the United States and Canada. Mahdeen had its own sales force of thirty people by 1976. Mahdeen's business plan and marketing and sales strategies were unlike anything Alcon had, so it kept Mahdeen's leadership intact under Jerry Orr. Sales for Medi-Dan dandruff shampoo, marketed as Ionil by Owen, provided one-half of Mahdeen's annual income. Other products included ACV Shampoo, ACV Hair Conditioner, and PHygiene, an astringent cleanser. Although Mahdeen's annual sales doubled to $2.8 million in 1976, they dropped precipitously the following year, triggering a significant restructuring.[94]

To Conner, Center Laboratories of New York, a manufacturer and marketer of diagnostic and therapeutic allergens, seemed to fit the specialty company model. It catered to allergists, although pediatricians and general practitioners also used its products. Alcon bought Center in 1970 and appointed Kleiman as general manager of Alcon Specialty Products, which included Center. Kleiman had quit Alcon ten years earlier, but Schollmaier enticed him back. Jack G. Center and his wife, Thelma, had established the firm in 1945 and continued to manage it under Alcon's direction, though Schollmaier spent months coaching them and learning their business. Center sold a simplified allergy screening set containing the most common allergens. The sets were regionalized with pollen flora and other allergens indigenous to a specific locale, enabling a physician to confirm an allergy with only ten tests. Center also marketed regional and seasonal treatment sets to simplify therapies. It developed Centeral, an alum-precipitated extract for hyposensitization with fewer injections and increased safety, and Cosea, a prescription antihistamine; it also distributed an emergency first aid kit for insect stings. Center also offered personalized extract therapeutic sets, resulting in hundreds of single-use physician products. Allergen extracts had not been standardized, so the FDA formulated standards for specifications, quality control, safety, and efficacy, resulting in plant modernization and effective SOPs. Although following federal mandates had become routine for Alcon, Center and its technical personnel faltered. Despite their best efforts, Center's sales never met Alcon expectations, stagnating at about $1.5 million and generating only meager profit. Thus, in 1977 Kleiman convinced Schollmaier to sell Center, which Alcon did the following year to a German company, making a small profit.[95]

In 1972 Alcon acquired the William A. Webster Company of Memphis, which manufactured and marketed suppositories for adults and children. Alcon combined Conal and Webster into one subsidiary, Webcon, and placed it in the Alcon Specialties Products Division, under Kleiman. When the new Puerto Rico manufacturing plant in Humacao opened in 1974, Alcon moved Webcon production there to benefit from local tax incentives and lower production costs. Simultaneously, Webcon marketing and sales staff in the Memphis office moved to Fort Worth. At the end of 1977, Webcon reorganized to give broader coverage of the domestic market with fewer sales representatives. Alcon no longer invested resources in R&D for Webcon and spent a minimal amount toward marketing. Webcon's sales increased from $5 million in 1974 to $6 million in 1977 as four medications dominated its revenue: Urised, for urinary infections; Cystospaz, for urinary tract spasms; WANS suppositories, for nausea; and Neopap suppositories, for fever. Schollmaier planned to continue producing at low cost, providing profit margins remained substantial or until he sold the franchise.[96]

FMC Corporation began in the late nineteenth century as Food Machinery and Chemical Corporation, which supported the agriculture industry. Like many companies during World War II, it adapted to meet national needs. In 1965 CEO James M. Hait and his son Merritt R. Hait, a recent Cornell Medical College graduate, collaborated with Orlando "Landy" A. Battista, a polymer chemist employed by FMC. Battista had invented Avitene, a microcrystalline collagen derived from cowhides, and Hait realized its potential as a surface

FIG 4.41
Avicon board of directors, 1972.
Back row, left to right: Benjamin C. Cart, H. P. Kologe, P. H. Coyne, Sherman K. Reed; *front row*: Sam Barklis, Raymond Tower, Bill Conner, J. M. Hait, Ed Schollmaier, 1972. (AHR)

anticoagulant to stop bleeding. FMC's Avitene became a target for Conner. Given samples, Alcon R&D, led by Robb, replicated Hait's observations and in October 1969, Alcon and FMC signed a joint venture agreement that created Avicon Inc. (fig. 4.42), whereby mutually funded development studies would be conducted by Alcon R&D. Battista moved to Fort Worth and Hait became a consultant for a team led by Tenery. While Battista continued to promote Avitene as an artificial bone and skin replacement, or for drug delivery, the first project was for a hemostatic indication.[97]

Developing Avitene was an exciting prospect, but the different philosophies of Alcon R&D and Battista hampered the project. Battista had little patience for FDA regulations, and he expected the joint venture to support research into all potential uses for microcrystalline collagen. But Leone and Raval considered Avitene a single-indication product and intended to keep Alcon R&D focused on ophthalmic products. Leone recalled, "I had bad experiences with [FMC] executives. They made me suffer. ... They really did." Raval agreed that "Alcon and FMC had serious differences in management style," but Schollmaier, Conner, and Alcon's board supported the decision to limit R&D's focus to Avitene's hemostatic

FIG 4.43
The Avitene R&D team stands behind all forty-eight thousand pages of the Avitene New Drug Application submitted to the FDA, May 1974. *Left to right*: Al Purser, Willie McNiel, Dorothy Watson, JoAnn Poulos, John H. Tenery, MD, Richard Clemons. (AHR)

FIG 4.44
Combined Ophthalmic and Surgical sales forces training for Avitene launch, June 1976 (AHR)

use. Meanwhile, in vivo and clinical studies demonstrated that it effectively stopped bleeding and was easily absorbed and safe.

Manufacturing microcrystalline collagen on a commercial scale presented unique challenges. The best raw material for Avitene was corium, or the digestible inner layer of beef hide. Schweitzer, the Avicon general manager, located a source at a Texas beef processing plant. Working with Manufacturing, Hecht and the R&D development team designed a process for corium isolation, purification, and microcrystallization, which Alcon successfully scaled up in its Fort Worth plant. Alcon filed the NDA in 1974 (fig. 4.43), and FDA approval followed in 1976. The prime users of Avitene were vascular surgeons, a market in which Alcon had no marketing or sales personnel. Alcon Domestic lent Schweitzer the combined ophthalmic and surgical sales forces (fig. 4.44) for a three-month promotion. Alcon launched Avitene on September 7, 1976, and within eight months sold $2 million, a record for an Alcon product.[98]

Founded in 1906, Lafayette Pharmacal began specializing in radiopaque diagnostic pharmaceuticals in the 1930s. Its oral slurries of barium sulfate were used to examine the stomach and intestines, and its Pantopaque was injected into the spinal cord canal to reveal spinal pathologies. When Alcon acquired Lafayette Pharmacal in 1977, it was well established in the United States and twenty-one countries. However, there is little record of the transaction.[99]

Alcon demanded much from its managerial team. Success was determined by traits such as readiness to do one's job, ability to focus, willingness to accept different job assignments, aptitude, innovativeness, intelligence, pragmatism, energy, and capacity to articulate a viewpoint and then follow the company's decision. While some people thrived, others did not. When Alcon sold Lawton Instruments in 1974, Alden moved to Fort Worth and became the general manager for Alcon Surgical, reporting to Gibson, director of Domestic Operations. With no pharmaceutical experience, Alden was more comfortable selling devices; he faced a steep learning curve selling both pharmaceuticals and devices in the ophthalmic market. Fearing a shift away from instrument sales, Alden opposed Alcon's decision to terminate an agreement with Grieshaber and refused to comply. Alcon sent Bob Grantham to Switzerland to notify Grieshaber, but he discovered Alden had just signed a three-year contract with the instrument supplier. This led to Alden's dismissal, although later Schollmaier admitted to having been aware of his shortcomings before the Grieshaber debacle. Schollmaier similarly hesitated to dismiss Gibson as vice president of Domestic Operations. While being interviewed by a Harvard Business School professor for a case study, Schollmaier recalled, "We were going to have to get more predictable results out of our U.S. [Domestic] operations than we were getting at the time. ... We were having too damn many operating problems." He confessed, "I had known for about two years that [Gibson] wasn't doing the job and that he couldn't do the job, and the performance reviews had clearly recognized that. I also knew that he wasn't going to grow into the job and I had been procrastinating." Schollmaier took over and considered asking Leone to lead Domestic Operations, but by mid-1977, Schollmaier had restructured its leadership. He explained, "One, we just made sure that we had guys in the jobs that were competent and ... brought a lot more commitment and expertise to their jobs. Second, we started ... with a series of meetings, to try to more clearly define what these guys were really accountable for and how they could go about doing their jobs." The next few years would test Schollmaier's hypothesis.[100]

Alcon's 1971 annual report pleased Buhler: "Marketing outside the United States continued to be strengthened significantly during the past year. From 14 percent four years ago, international operations now account for 25 percent of the total revenues of the corporation." Since the beginning, Alcon's strategy had been to provide international ophthalmologists with its products. The initial approach centered on licensing contracts with distributors and shipping medicines from Fort Worth. Buhler continued this but also created subsidiaries in major markets, finding local companies to manufacture Alcon products while maintaining high standards.

In the next phase, Alcon strengthened its international presence by making selective acquisitions. In some cases, it continued the acquired company's brands, but its long-term goal was to own facilities that produced Alcon products. Organizationally, Buhler divided Alcon International into three zones: Europe, the Middle East, and Africa (EURMEA), excluding Eastern Europe; Latin America and the Caribbean islands (LACAR); and Canada, Asia, and the Far East (CAFE), excluding China and Russia. Buhler led International Operations from Fort Worth with regional offices in Antwerp, Mexico City, Bogota, Buenos Aires, São Paulo, Toronto, Sydney, Manila, and Hong Kong. By 1972 Alcon sold products in seventy-seven countries; four years later, it employed almost eight hundred people in nearly one hundred countries. Frank Brophy, International Marketing director, held Alcon's first global marketing meeting in Fort Worth in 1975 with twenty-one representatives from EURMEA, LACAR, and CAFE (fig. 4.45). Nevertheless, frustrated with RA, Buhler set up his own RA operation when he asked Pencis from R&D to join Alcon International. He justified this by the fact that in 1976, International alone made three hundred regulatory submissions for Alcon products to nearly fifty countries. The next year, twenty-two

FIG 4.45
International Marketing meeting, Alcon campus, Fort Worth, 1975. *Pictured left to right*: Ed Schollmaier, Fort Worth; Dave Sculati, Fort Worth; Arthur Delbridge, Australia; Frank Buhler, Fort Worth; Hans Von Hammerstein, Eastern Europe/Austria/Switzerland; Rodolfo Quevedo, Mexico; Mohamed Debakey, Near East; Francisco Fernandez, Venezuela/South Caribbean; Miguel Oller, Dominican Republic; W. C. Conner, Fort Worth; Luis Felipe Serrano, Spain; Harold Cordoves, Caribbean; Carlos Taborda, Brazil; Juan Garcia P., Peru/Ecuador/Bolivia/Colombia; Ron Fawcett, United Kingdom; Marja Kaleva, Scandinavia; Alain Le Cloanec, France; Leon de Chateauvieux, Central America; Tom Grant, Hawaiian Islands/Guam; Charles Dickey, Fort Worth; Thomas Tietze, Germany; Bill Kwan, Canada; Georges Petre, Belgium; Chuck Shively, Fort Worth; Frank Brophy, Fort Worth; Tony Roge, Africa/Middle East; John Fox, United Kingdom; Brian Huntley, Southeast Asia. (BAS)

facilities, half of them owned by Alcon, manufactured Alcon products. In just twenty-five years, Alcon International had become a dominant force in the global market, and a major revenue generator—its 1977 annual sales totaled $35.4 million, 43 percent of Alcon's to-tal. Nevertheless, International needed to address profitability in countries that had price and wage controls and where exchange rates fluctuated.[101]

Frans Van Kets managed EURMEA from its office in Antwerp (fig. 4.46). He had grown the division since he started there in 1965, building it to include sixty representa-tives from twenty-one countries (fig. 4.47). In the early years, Van Kets signed licensing agreements with distributors, but later, under Buhler's guidance, he acquired manufacturing

FIG 4.46
EURMEA office and staff, Brussels, Belgium, 1968. Sitting, *left to right*: Marleen Moris, Jacques Van Damme, Juana Rosa Lorenzo, Etienne Huys, Gilberte Verstrepen. Standing, *left to right*: Robert Rubens, Monique Van Houtven, Francois De Balle, Marie-Christiane Stevens, Frank Brophy, Frans J. M. Van Kets. (AHR)

FIG 4.47
EURMEA meeting, Beirut, Lebanon, 1972 (AHR)

plants in Belgium, France, Italy, and Spain. Alcon also had manufacturing contracts with companies in Iran, South Africa, West Germany, and Portugal. The most strategic acquisition came on April 1, 1970, when Alcon bought Établissements A. Couvreur, S.A. for cash and stock approximating $1.1 million. Couvreur, a leading Belgian marketer and manufacturer of pharmaceutical products, gave Alcon a solid footing in Europe, with significant exports to African and Far Eastern countries. Two years later, Alcon expanded the Couvreur plant to manufacture its ophthalmic products. Alcon also bought out its joint venture partner in Paris, taking control of its manufacturing facility, and acquired a company in Spain for production. In 1973 EURMEA started to import and market Alcon diagnostic products and the Cryophake. With the acquisition of Owen, Van Kets's team reorganized the distribution of its dermatologic line and bought a set of dermatology products from a Spanish company.

The next major strategic acquisition was Quimico Farmacéutico Iberhis, S.A., of Barcelona. Buhler and Schollmaier, convinced Spain would become a top market, toured ophthalmic companies. After several disappointments they found Iberhis, which Schollmaier described as a "well disguised ophthalmological company" since its vitamin supplements were prescribed mostly by ophthalmologists. Alcon renovated its Madrid plant and three years later moved the manufacture of Alcon Iberhis products there. The key expansion started in 1975 with an $8.3 million Couvreur manufacturing, warehousing, and distribution building designed to serve most of Europe. Built in Puurs, Belgium, the 120,000-square-foot ultramodern facility produced 3 million units in 1978. Alcon Germany relocated its headquarters to Freiburg; at this time, it consisted of thirteen employees, six of whom called on ophthalmologists. Aiming to solidify its Italian presence in the ophthalmic and dermatological markets, Alcon acquired Farmila Farmaceutici Milano S.p.A., of Milan, for $4 million in 1977. Buhler sent Allen Baker from Fort Worth to manage its operation. EURMEA's one failed acquisition was Nu-Syte Lab in England, whose contact lens technology was outdated. A major incident disrupted EURMEA in 1976 when the government of Zaire seized $2.4 million of inventory stored in a warehouse. Zaire promised compensation but never delivered.[102]

Buhler's development of LACAR followed Conner's participation in the PAAO. To meet pricing pressures in these Latin American countries, Alcon needed manufacturing plants. Buhler concluded his earliest deal in 1967 with a Mexican pharmaceutical company to manufacture Alcon's ophthalmic line, and two years later he signed a distribution agreement with a firm in Chile. The first significant acquisition occurred in 1969, when Alcon Laboratorios do Brasil Ltda. purchased the CISSA product line from Companhia Industrial Dellos, S.A., the leading ophthalmic pharmaceuticals manufacturer in Brazil. By the next year, Alcon's pharmaceutical line was being sold in South America from plants in Argentina, Brazil, and Colombia. Alcon next bought a majority interest in Oftalmología, S.A., one of the three leading ophthalmic specialty companies in Mexico, giving it a substantial presence in the Mexican and Central American pharmaceutical markets. Twelve months later,

FIG 4.48
Alcon Oftasa, Mexico, 1970 (BAS)

it secured the remaining minority interest in Oftalmología, S.A. At the same time, Alcon expanded operations in Argentina when Carlos de Socio, Alcon's first general manager in Argentina, acquired in 1968 the well-established ophthalmological manufacturer Laboratorios Otto, S.A., in Buenos Aires. A major expansion in productive capacity took place in 1972 when Alcon purchased a new plant in Mexico City. The company relocated its three smaller plants to this facility, renamed the subsidiary Oftasa (fig. 4.48), and hired Dionisio Garcia, an experienced pharmaceutical executive, as the general manager with responsibility for all of Mexico. Three years later, Alcon began manufacturing in Venezuela and introduced Owen dermatological products as the first step for distribution in Latin America. In Alcon's 1976 annual report, Buhler boasted, "Performance in Latin America was exceptional despite the continuing economic problems of inflation and currency devaluations, coupled with mandatory governmental price and wage controls. ... Brazil had the best performance and has become one of our leading international ophthalmic markets. Mexico, Argentina, and Venezuela all ended the year with solid growth." Joining the company in 1971, Leon de Chateauvieux, an expatriate from Cuba, pioneered Alcon's entry into the Caribbean and Central America. Thus, by 1977, Alcon was established as the premier ophthalmic company throughout Latin America.[103]

Led by Geoffrey Crewe, CAFE covered an immense geographical space with diverse ethnicities and a spectrum of government regulations. Japan and Australia were the most lucrative markets. Japanese ophthalmologists had no interest in Maxitrol or Maxidex, but they readily adopted the Cryophake when introduced to the unit sterilizer. Tom Grant, the man Crewe hired as the general manager in Australia, established Alcon's image there as sales grew. When he left to be Alcon's representative in Hawaii, Crewe found Eric Noble, who continued Alcon's expansion in Australia. The Philippines had restrictive import quotas, so Alcon used a Manila-based importer. By 1970 sales had increased to such an

FIG 4.49
Alcon Indonesia staff with products
sold there, 1972 (AHR)

extent that Crewe established Alcon Laboratories Philippines Ltd. and hired the experienced Reynaldo "Ding" de Jesus as general manager. De Jesus contracted with the local
Pfizer plant to produce products and avoid 70 percent duties; he also found a plastics firm
to mold Drop-tainers. From the Philippines, Alcon exported ophthalmic products to Indonesia, Vietnam, Taiwan, Korea, Thailand, Hong Kong, Singapore, Malaysia, and Ceylon
(Sri Lanka). But even with these opportunities, sales in Asia only increased to $600,000 in
six years.[104]

On a trip to Australia in 1971, Buhler met transplanted Englishman Timothy R. G.
Sear, Mead Johnson's regional director. In Buhler's opinion, he was just the man Alcon
needed to boost Asian sales. Sear was invited to Fort Worth, where Buhler, Conner, and
others convinced him to become the region's manager. Alcon's offer proved timely as Sear
had become disenchanted with his prospects since Bristol-Myers had acquired Mead Johnson. Sear inherited Noble in Australia and New Zealand and De Jesus in the Philippines,
and he soon recruited Brian Huntley to oversee Indonesia (fig. 4.49), Singapore, Malaysia, and Ceylon. Altogether, Sear led a team of twenty-two from his office in Hong Kong.
Buhler made it clear that building Alcon's presence in Japan was a top priority, but Sear had
the same problems as Crewe. Japan had a well-developed pharmaceutical industry and dis-

FIG 4.50
Alcon and Teijin sign joint venture agreement, February 1973. *Left:* 2nd, Tim Sear; 4th, Bill Conner; 5th, Frank Buhler; *right*, 1st, Hideya Ono (AHR)

dained foreign products with nothing new to offer. In the early 1970s, under Japanese law, a foreign company could not establish its own wholly owned subsidiary. Alcon needed a joint venture partner if it hoped to expand, and to attract a company it needed proprietary, unique products. Sear felt Avitene was the answer.

Teijin, a diversified artificial fiber company, recognized Avitene's potential. Alcon and Teijin signed a joint venture partnership in February 1973 (fig. 4.50), creating an avenue through which Alcon could access the Japanese market. The leader of this team was English-speaking Hideya Ono, an experienced importer. Ono was streetwise and pragmatic, and he applied himself to the job. The joint venture registered a few Alcon ophthalmic brands, but Avitene never realized its full potential in Japan. When the Japanese government liberalized its policies, Teijin agreed to terminate the relationship. In 1978 Alcon established its own subsidiary company, Alcon Japan Ltd., with Ono as its president.[105]

The Canadian market was a different story. As early as 1968, Buhler had arranged for a third party in Canada to manufacture Alcon products. This fulfilled the needs of Canadian ophthalmologists and supplied the British Commonwealth countries in Asia. Early in 1975 Alcon Canada began construction of its own offices and manufacturing plant

FIG 4.51
Alcon Canada, Mississauga, Ontario
(AHR)

in Mississauga, near Toronto. Completed in 1976, the plant manufactured both Alcon and Owen products (fig. 4.51). Production volume allowed Alcon Canada to begin regular large shipments to Australia and the Far East. Since it was the only non-American source of BSS and the Mahdeen line, some shipments went to Europe. Sear relocated to Fort Worth in 1975 after he was placed in charge of CAFE and LACAR. In 1977 he dismissed his general manager for Canada and hired Bill Kwan, a pharmaceutical executive with an MBA from McGill University.[106]

Thus, by 1978 Alcon International's top executives (fig. 4.52) had diverse pharmaceutical markets, knew their territories, and understood the ophthalmic industry. Buhler directed Alcon's International Division; Van Kets, EURMEA; and Sear, LACAR and CAFE. Moreover, International's second-tier managers were knowledgeable company veterans. Sear's career is illustrative. After his Royal Air Force service, Sear studied economics at Manchester University, became an accountant in New York and Copenhagen, and spent a year

FIG 4.52
Alcon International, *left to right*:
Frank Buhler, Ed Schollmaier,
Tim Sear, Bill Conner,
Frans Van Kets, 1977 (AHR)

at the University of Copenhagen. After graduating, Sear received an MBA scholarship from Indiana University. In 1962 he joined Mead Johnson, responsible for the English-speaking countries of Africa. In 1964, promoted to regional manager for Southeast Asia, Sear moved to Singapore. Three years later he was appointed managing director of Mead Johnson Australia, and he joined Alcon in 1971.[107]

Wilkins, head of the administration department, realized his role at Alcon was redundant, so he left in November 1972 and returned to his former position as director of the United Way of Tarrant County. Wilkins's departure allowed Kologe to consolidate his role as vice president of finance and administration and revamp the division. Hinson transferred to S&T, becoming the director of RA, so Kologe hired George Kremer, whom he had known at Revlon, to become Alcon's legal counsel. Kremer prepared corporate agreements, made SEC and NYSE filings, handled litigations, and served as the corporate secretary. Appointed controller and treasurer, William M. Starz, a graduate of Seton Hall and New York University, transferred from the International Division. His wide-ranging role included developing profit plans and performance reviews, conducting acquisitions, divestiture planning, and managing corporate funds and insurance. Kologe appointed Bobby G. Moore, a University of Texas at Arlington graduate and Korean War veteran, to direct IT with the expectation that he would upgrade computer equipment and support various Alcon divisions. Moore installed state-of-the art IBM 360 mainframe computers.

Kologe moved Carl H. Gottwald, a Navy veteran of World War II, from Owen to be director of personnel and public relations. Kologe told Gottwald that Alcon was committed to providing challenging jobs, a satisfactory working environment, and generous benefits to attract and retain qualified personnel. One was health insurance; for several dollars per month, the policy paid 80 percent of expenses after a fifty-dollar deductible. Everyone got at least two weeks' vacation annually, increasing with length of employment. Alcon offered tuition reimbursement; several people earned master's degrees, and a few PhDs. Started in 1955, Alcon's PST, managed by senior company executives, had over $6.5 million in assets by 1976, with over six hundred US employees participating.[108]

Alcon marketing continually generated new ideas to maintain the company's high profile at industry conventions. By 1969 the number of attendees exceeded the capacity of the Palmer House in Chicago, so in 1970 and 1971, the AAOO met in Las Vegas, and then Dallas the next four years. Alcon began a tradition in 1972 by inviting all AAOO attendees to a barbecue on its campus in Fort Worth. Management expected five hundred people, but thirty-seven hundred arrived, and it took eighty-four buses to bring them from Dallas to Fort Worth. Upon arrival, guests stepped onto a red carpet, where they were welcomed by Alexander, Conner, Schollmaier, and other Alcon officials (fig. 4.53). The visitors toured the S&T facility and manufacturing building. At the inaugural event, which celebrated Alcon's twenty-fifth year, the guests consumed fifteen hundred pounds of ribs, two thousand pounds of brisket, thirty-six hundred ears of corn, and five thousand biscuits. A band played country and western music. The event was a resounding success. Alcon's 1973 barbecue proved equally successful (fig. 4.54). In 1974 the AAOO met in the first week of October,

FIG 4.53
Ed Schollmaier and Bill Conner greet AAOO guests, Alcon's first barbecue, 1972 (Courtesy of Taylor Schollmaier)

FIG 4.54
Four thousand AAOO guests attend
Alcon's 1973 barbecue (BAS)

so Alcon took advantage of the Texas State Fair, inviting doctors and guests to a rodeo and barbecue at the fairgrounds. Ten thousand poster-sized invitations were mailed, and five thousand guests came in 120 buses. Alcon's barbecue returned to its campus in September 1975; this time it included a show by singer-guitarist Jerry Reed. Of these four extravaganzas, Alcon leadership concluded, "Judging from the favorable response, we are confident that our hospitality has created good will toward Alcon and helped create a cordial reception for our salesmen."[109]

On May 16, 1972, Alcon celebrated its twenty-fifth anniversary. Founders' Day recognized the achievements of Alexander and Conner. While the day started with a breakfast sponsored by Fort Worth's business leaders (fig. 4.55), it was largely an *Alcon Family* affair. In his remarks, Alexander said the company had grown because of the "successful, dedicated efforts of the Alcon people," and Conner expressed appreciation to "the Alcon family." The Alexander and Conner families joined three hundred Alcon employees in the courtyard between the campus's three buildings (fig. 4.56). Several employees who had been with the company since the early 1950s received special recognition, and the two founders and Alcon's third employee, Betty Newton, were inducted into the new Alcon twenty-five-year club. No one there ever forgot that day; the photograph in fig. 4.56 provides a glimpse of that special moment. While it is not obvious in the photo, at least two-thirds of the three hundred employees were in their thirties or younger, and many would not retire until twenty to thirty years later. They were a key factor in Alcon's success. Conner and Alexander had planted the seed and nurtured the next generation, but it was Schollmaier, Leone, and a new cadre of leaders, mentored by Conner and Alexander, who led the company into the next twenty-five years. It was unusual to have such continuity of leadership and so many long-term employees in the pharmaceutical industry.[110]

FIG 4.55
Bob Alexander and Bill Conner, Alcon's Twenty-Fifth anniversary, Founders Day, May 16, 1972 (AHR)

Besides working hard, Alcon employees played hard. The 1960s and 1970s are notable for the sports and activities the company offered and in which employees participated. Sports were popular; they included softball, tennis, golf, bowling, bass fishing, bridge, basketball, dune buggy racing, weight lifting, sports car rallies, deep sea fishing, rugby, judo, swimming, and Formula One sports car racing (fig. 4.57). Other activities included acting, butterfly collecting, teaching, Scout mentoring, showing dogs, scuba diving, photography, farming, mineral and gem collecting, and playing music. Alcon and many of its subsidiaries held company picnics. Alexander sponsored Junior Achievement, and each year Alcon organized a walkathon and bowling tournament to raise money. The company sponsored blood drives. Management actively participated in Tarrant County's United Way drive, and most workers contributed. Employees and management created a credit union. Conner, and later Schollmaier, held annual employee meetings and monthly award ceremonies. Conner strolled the campus on Friday afternoons. Schollmaier also made himself available; at lunch he often sat with anyone who was alone. Schollmaier's son, Taylor, occasionally spent time on campus with his father and recalls him talking to many employees. Afterward, his father would tell Taylor who the person was and how they were important to Alcon. Not only

FIG 4.56
Alcon Fort Worth campus employees,
Founders Day celebration, May 16, 1972
(AHR)

FIG 4.57
Sports at Alcon, 1972
(*Spectrum*, Aug. 1972) (BAS)

did Conner and Schollmaier learn what was happening at Alcon, these interactions created a sense of purpose. This was reinforced by the Christmas party, an event everyone anticipated. With several hundred people working on the Fort Worth campus, everyone knew everyone, and the party resembled a family get-together. Kay Harris remembers, "It was just a fun time. It was like a family, it was fun. We enjoyed going to work."[111]

From 1967 Alcon's sales grew sevenfold over a decade to $81.566 million (fig. 4.58). The decade's compounded annual growth rate was 23 percent, which exceeded the goal Alexander and Conner set when they founded the company in 1947. By 1977 sales were ophthalmic products at 61 percent, specialty products at 24 percent, and dermatology at 15 percent. International investment paid off as sales from that division were 43 percent of total revenue in 1977. The largest-selling products were the Isopto Carpine franchise, Maxitrol, Urised, BSS, Tears Naturale, and Cryophake. Alcon paid dividends annually, varying from thirteen to twenty-nine cents per share, and the company continued to spend about 80 percent of its profits on future development. The innovative products in the pipeline prepared Alcon to continue its remarkable growth.[112]

As 1968 began, Alcon's directors were mostly local men: Alexander and Conner; physicians Neighbors and Wiggins Jr.; ophthalmologist Beasley; two prominent Tarrant County business leaders, Tomlin and Engleman; legal counsel Keltner Jr.; Harvard professor Glover; and two Alcon employees, Andrews and Wilkins. Four stayed on the board throughout the next decade—Alexander, Conner, Beasley, and Glover. Andrews resigned in 1968 and Wilkins left in 1972. Gordon Ellis, a Houston, Texas, food executive, served five years (1969–1973). The board's composition significantly changed in 1973 after Alcon joined the NYSE. Denny Alexander and Halden Conner, the cofounders' sons, joined in 1973, as did Schollmaier and Douglas Owen Brown (fig. 4.59). That same year, John B. Rogers, Schollmaier's friend and president of Westchase Corporation and Brooke Enterprises in Dallas, joined for one year. In 1974 Mary Gardiner Jones became a member. A consumer advocate, Jones served on the Federal Trade Commission (FTC) from 1964 to 1973, and during her tenure on Alcon's board she taught at the University of

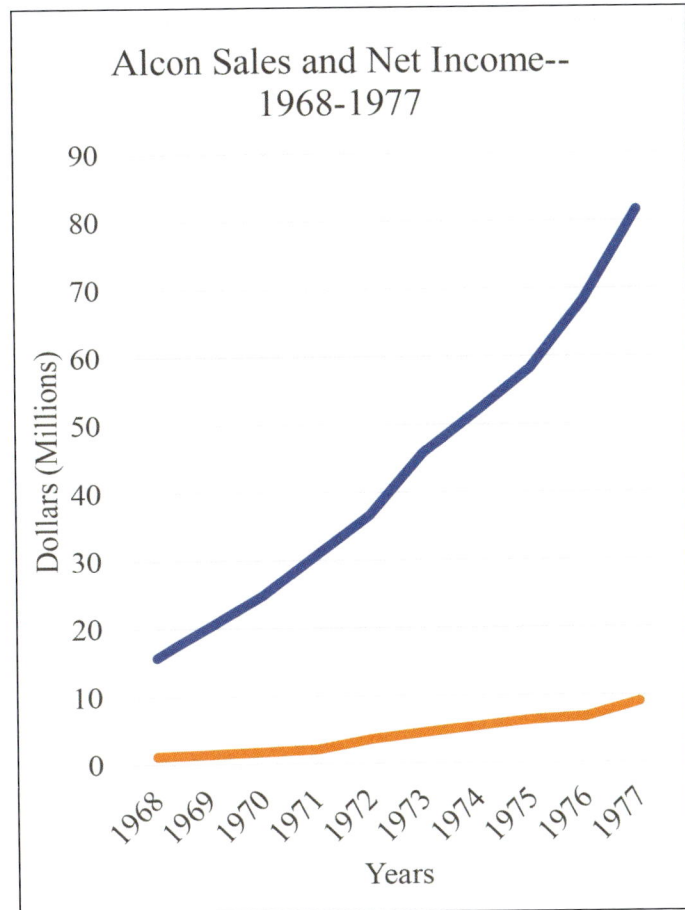

FIG 4.58
Alcon sales and net income, 1968–1977 (TOM, AM)

FIG 4.59
Alcon board of directors, 1973.
Back row, left to right: Ed Schollmaier,
Bob Alexander, John Rogers,
Denny Alexander, Halden Conner,
Doug Brown; *front row*: Gene Engleman,
Harold Beasley, MD, Bill Conner,
Gordon Ellis, John Glover, PhD.
(AHR)

Illinois and was a vice president at Western Union Telegraph Company. Charles D. Tandy, CEO and chairman of Tandy Corporation, joined in 1975. Tandy had grown a leather company into a global leader in consumer electronics. Tandy Corporation became the first Tarrant County–born company listed on the NYSE. Alcon's board was now vastly different from what it was in 1947 when Conner and Alexander presided over convivial monthly dinners. In the 1970s it resembled any other American corporate board, composed of a diverse group of academics, retired bureaucrats, independent executives, and even two young entrepreneurs.[113]

With no extant minutes, it is impossible to ascertain what the board discussed. However, issues spilled out of the boardroom so we do have some idea of the debates that transpired. Given her background as a consumer advocate, Jones had an interest in R&D. She inquired about the safety data the division had on its manufactured products, those marketed overseas, and those licensed from other companies. Summoned to a board meeting, Raval outlined the procedures. Conner's entrepreneurial instincts percolated constantly as he looked for opportunities to replicate Alcon's success. Nearing seventy years old, his hearing diminished, and in his search for the best hearing device, he discovered a hearing aid company. Whereas in the past he might have swayed the board to support this acquisition, the board repeatedly rejected his proposal and became increasingly concerned about him serving as CEO and chairman. Conner's dual role put Schollmaier into a quandary. In his "Alcon Story," he explained, "Bill controlled the board and he was getting advice from some of the directors that it was time to retire but no, he didn't want to. ... There were a few directors who were really against him, who wanted to force the issue, and they were constantly trying to get me to side with them to put some pressure on Bill. I thought they were right, that the time had come for him to retire and move on, but I didn't want to force that so I never did. I didn't want to pressure Conner because he had been like a wonderful father to me." In December 1976, the board brought this matter to a head, and according to Schollmaier, Conner then realized he should cede control.[114]

The SEC restricts insiders, that is, officers and directors, from selling shares without pre-clearance. On April 29, 1975, Alcon published another prospectus for the sale of 239,615 shares at $25⅜. As in 1971, Alexander wanted to continue to diversify his assets, and likely Conner did, too. In Conner's case, he had debts from investments he had made outside of Alcon. It was common knowledge at Alcon that many of these had floundered, so selling Alcon stock let him cover his losses. Alexander sold 60,000 shares, Conner, 119,930, and almost 60,000 were sold by members of Conner's family and a Webster relative. Afterward, Conner retained 236,500 shares (3.76 percent) and Alexander 174,870 (2.78 percent). How this sale affected Conner's debt is not known; nevertheless, in the succeeding months, individuals who owned considerable amounts of stock, such as Leone, worried Conner might have to sell more. In any case, by the summer of 1977, as Conner turned seventy, the board discussed his retirement. During the discussion, Engleman exclaimed, "You know, what we need to do is find out what the true market value of this company is." In the initial period after Alcon listed on the NYSE, its stock price had shot up to $50 a share, but in the past few years, even though the company had grown, it had settled at about $25. Schollmaier realized that selling Alcon would be the means to determine it true value.[115]

Alcon's directors decided to sell Alcon in June 1977; six months later, on December 11, Nestlé took ownership. Over the years, pharmaceutical companies had approached Alcon, but it had rejected all offers. Conner and Schollmaier visited several prospective buyers—

Schering Laboratories, Johnson & Johnson, Merck & Company, American Hospital Supply, and others. Some expressed no interest or offered a price Alcon considered too low. In the meantime, at a PMA meeting Conner met Veikko Reinikainen, a Finnish lawyer working at Synthélabo, a Paris pharmaceutical company owned by L'Oréal. Reinikainen learned about Alcon when Raval and his team visited Synthélabo to license betaxolol. Synthélabo's CEO profiled Alcon to its parent company, L'Oréal, the French cosmetic enterprise. Nestlé owned 25 percent of L'Oréal, whose CEO sat on Nestlé's board of directors, and José Daniel, a Nestlé managing director, served on L'Oréal's board. No longer able to acquire food companies due to FTC concerns, Nestlé sought other opportunities in the United States. Realizing Nestlé's interest in buying a pharmaceutical company, L'Oréal's CEO recommended Alcon and emphasized the value not only to Nestlé but also for Synthélabo and L'Oréal. Reinikainen pestered Conner, but Schollmaier was incredulous when Conner told him about the proposition. 3M, another potential buyer, offered $32 per share, but a share exchange requirement and 3M's ideas for managing Alcon discouraged Schollmaier. Alcon had one condition for the sale—to keep Alexander's and Conner's vision alive by operating Alcon as an independent company, to which 3M would not commit. Finally, Schollmaier visited Nestlé at its headquarters in Switzerland and realized Nestlé was serious.[116]

Nestlé's CEO, Arthur Fürer, had become enamored of Alcon and believed in its potential to be a world-class company. Synthélabo's R&D director's positive analysis of Alcon reinforced Fürer's assessment. On September 21, 1977, Conner, Schollmaier, and unnamed Alcon executives first met with Fürer and Carl L. Angst, Nestlé's second-in-command, in Fort Worth. Schollmaier talked about the future of the ophthalmology market and how Alcon could fulfill the industry's needs. Fürer and Angst summarized the advantages to Alcon of a deal: use of Nestlé's infrastructure, its fiscal resources, and synergy between L'Oréal and Owen. Fürer gave reassurances that Alcon would operate independently under Nestlé, conditioning the offer on Schollmaier remaining in his current position. Conner floated $350 million as a sale price but deferred to Alcon's financial advisor. At a private meeting with Schollmaier, Fürer stood firm at a minimum offer of $41 per share and in a larger group session later that day, Nestlé argued that $43 per share, or $293 million, was an exorbitant sum. This was a productive session as Fürer called Conner that night and they met alone. Conner emphasized Alcon's wish to join Nestlé but only at the right price. Fürer and his team considered their options, completed their analysis, and met with Conner, Schollmaier, and Kologe at the Union League Club, in New York, on October 11. There they offered $42 per share, or $276.5 million. Alcon accepted and a formal agreement followed on October

FIG 4.60
Alcon Fort Worth campus, 1977 (AHR)

FIG 4.61
Alcon ophthalmic, surgical, contact lens,
and dermatologic products, 1977 (BAS)

FIG 4.62
Alcon ophthalmic, surgical, contact lens,
and dermatologic products, 1977 (BAS)

18. In the meantime, having heard rumors of an acquisition, the NYSE halted trading in Alcon stock on October 7. At Kologe's suggestion, to minimize income tax, Nestlé created a Delaware company and assumed ownership of 83 percent of Alcon shares in December and the remainder in January 1978. A few Alcon shareholders split their sale to minimize their own tax consequences.[117]

* * *

It had been a remarkable ten years. Annual revenue increased sevenfold from $18 to $81 million, international sales contributed 40 percent of this, and Alcon's employees numbered nearly two thousand worldwide, working in expanded modern facilities (fig. 4.60). Acquisitions fueled the growth in part, but new technology-based products like Tears Naturale, Naphcon, and Cryophake and an array of ophthalmic, contact lens solutions, surgical, and dermatologic products also drove the expansion (figs. 4.61, 4.62). In the final analysis, Conner's vision of Alcon being a medical specialties company had been tested and failed. Except for Owen, acquisitions had been divested or were for sale, and the board agreed that Alcon should revert to its initial focus: supplying pharmaceuticals and equipment to ophthalmologists.

With Schollmaier at the helm (fig. 4.63), Alcon blazed a more definitive trail toward long-term objectives. He developed a loyal, effective leadership team. Conner described it as "a young team, aggressive in its outlook and dedicated to growth within a growing industry." Conner and Schollmaier had experimented by hiring new people for senior management roles, but they determined that choosing leaders from among the existing employees was far more beneficial to both the workforce and the company. Many of the most effective people in crucial roles were Alcon veterans. As the next decade began, Domestic Operations would be led by Sisson, Lane, and Spruill, with Buhler in charge of International Operations, supported by Sear and Van Kets. Leone strengthened S&T by appointing Raval in charge of R&D and Fleming over QA.

The most important change spearheaded by Schollmaier was strategic: technology was centralized, marketing and sales decentralized. The next decade would determine if that worked. Schollmaier was confident in his choices, writing that "Our real foundation is in our employees' ability to meet and manage the increasingly complex challenges that are part of our multidivisional, multinational Enterprise." Being bought by Nestlé meant more change, and some in the Alcon Family were concerned. The worry was unjustified. Alcon's values were robust, its leaders were pragmatic, and now they had a willing financial backer.[118]

FIG 4.63
Leadership change, Bill Conner
and Ed Schollmaier, 1972 (AHR)

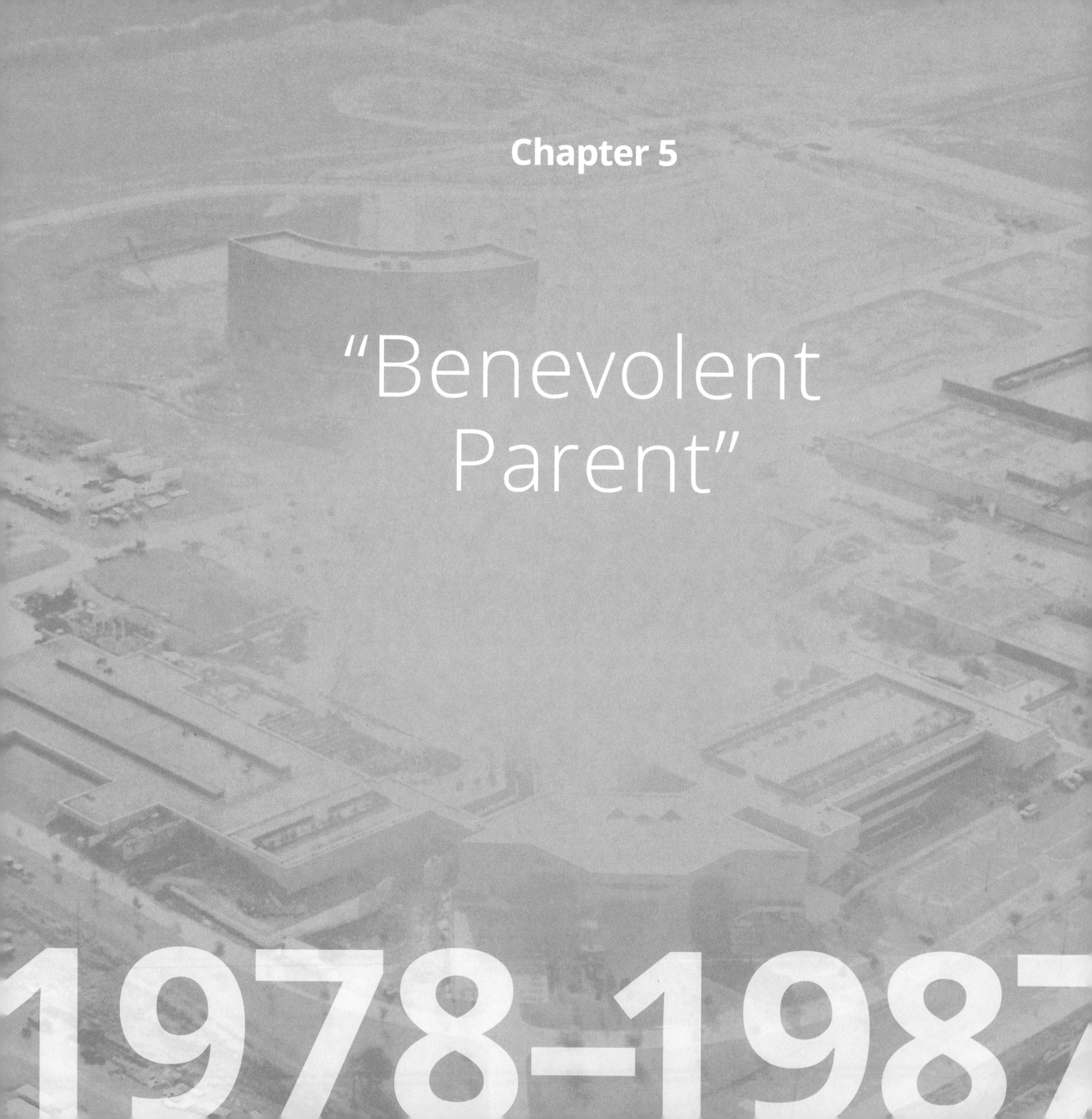

Chapter 5

"Benevolent Parent"

1978–1987

Nestlé took possession of Alcon on January 5, 1978, when 98 percent of Alcon's shares had been tendered. One criterion Bill Conner, Bob Alexander, and the board had in selecting a buyer was that Alcon remain independent. A promising suitor, 3M, irritated Ed Schollmaier when he visited its headquarters in Saint Paul, Minnesota, by pointing out the office he could use during his monthly weeklong visits. Schollmaier had no intention of entering into such an arrangement. Even with Nestlé, Alcon employees had concerns about the relationship.

Beginning in January 1978, Carl Angst visited Fort Worth regularly as Nestlé's representative, meeting with managers and employees to learn their perspectives. During one visit, he spoke frankly with Schollmaier. Angst started: "You have some problems and I've got to get over here often to try to get my arms around these things." Schollmaier responded that Angst could not solve Alcon's problems. Schollmaier outlined his view of their relationship: "What you need to do is, Number one, absolutely satisfy yourself that I understand the problems as you see them. Number two, be assured that I have a good plan for dealing with the problems. And number three, be satisfied that I'm making progress on dealing with them. You can't manage them for me from Switzerland." Schollmaier then pulled out a yellow pad on which he had listed eight problems. An astounded Angst remarked, "I'll be damned! You do know what the problems are and what needs to be done." They talked about plans for each issue until Angst asked, "Now what do we do?" Schollmaier replied, "You ... give me some time to work on these things. "As he left, Angst asked for Schollmaier's list. He folded it and put it in his pocket. Back in Fort Worth months later, Angst unfolded the list, and their dialogue resumed.[1]

FIG 5.1
Carl Angst (AHR)

Angst had a distinguished forty-seven-year career with Nestlé (fig. 5.1). Born in Zurich, he had a doctorate in chemical engineering from Basel University and joined Nestlé in 1946 to manage its North America plants. Returning to company headquarters in Vevey, Switzerland, he became the head of manufacturing in 1958; a decade later, he became the general manager of the Technology Research and Development Division. In 1974 Nestlé's businesses in Canada became his responsibility, and soon afterward he was made responsible for Alcon. Schollmaier first met Angst in August 1977, when he went to Vevey to assess Nestlé's interest in Alcon. Both men were key participants in acquisition negotiations, allowing them to take the measure of each other.[2]

Angst represented an old company. Born in Frankfurt, Germany, pharmacist Henri Nestlé had moved to Vevey in 1830. Disturbed by high infant mortality, in 1847 he set out to discover a substitute for mother's milk and in 1866 marketed a dry formula of sugar and ground grains that had similar nutritional value. In 1875 he sold his firm, which merged with the Anglo-Swiss Condensed Milk Company in 1905. The blend of Swiss and American mentalities contributed to Nestlé's successful acquisition of several companies. In 1929 Nestlé acquired the Swiss chocolate firm Peter, Cailler, Kohler, and six years later it invented Nescafé, the first soluble instant coffee. When Angst joined Nestlé, it was an international corporation with 107 factories on five continents, producing coffee, baby foods, instant beverages, milk products, and chocolate.

The year after Angst arrived, Nestlé merged with Alimentana, another Swiss company, which sold soups, spices, and bouillon cubes. With no acquisitions in the 1950s, Nestlé grew internally and expanded globally. For the 1960s and 1970s, Nestlé focused on diversifying its culinary products, developing new technologies, and searching for growing markets. It acquired companies that sold canned goods, frozen foods, ice creams, chilled foods, wines, mineral waters, and cosmetics, and it even bought restaurants. Its annual turnover increased from $2.5 billion in 1960 to an impressive $9.9 billion in 1974. However, inflation, currency devaluations, and increased prices of commodities muted Nestlé's sales and profits in the 1970s. Restricted by the FTC from acquiring more food businesses in the United States, Nestlé's CEO, Arthur Fürer, sought a nontraditional enterprise in a stable financial sector, which led him to Alcon.[3]

In the 1970s the pharmaceutical industry was one of the fastest-growing sectors of the United States economy. Fürer's interest in Alcon surprised many since it did not seem to be compatible with Nestlé's business strategy. One similarity between the pharmaceutical and food industries is that growth is driven by technological advances. While Alcon did not fit Nestlé's core product strategy, it did fit its core financial strategy. By 1977 Nestlé structured its core businesses along a *functional axis* and a *regional axis*. Nestlé historian Friedhelm Schwarz described the functional axis: "This axis is responsible for planning all important product-related strategies and making all major decisions with respect to products." It consisted of centralized *strategic business units* (SBUs) and a *technology and production/research and development* unit. Nestlé's regional axis was divided into three zones: Europe, the Americas, and Asia/Oceania/Africa. Schwarz explained how the two axes fit together: "Whereas the heads of the geographic zones manage a staff of experts on national and regional markets, the SBUs provide specialists in certain products as well as marketing and technological experts. The interplay of these different dimensions makes for synergies that can far outperform any purely geographical planning."

Schollmaier's vision of decentralized marketing and centralized technology functions almost fit Nestlé's management structure. Alcon had a centralized Science and Technology (S&T) division and, for the United States, separate SBUs for ophthalmic pharmaceuticals, surgical, vision care, and dermatological products. Overseas, its geographical regions bore similarities to Nestlé's, with countries and zones operating with varying degrees of autonomy. The interaction between S&T, the American SBUs, and the International Division became increasingly linked as R&D released new technologically driven products, with centralized management of quality assurance and manufacturing. Like Nestlé's functional axis, Schollmaier centralized Alcon's R&D, QA, RA, and Manufacturing into S&T under Leone. Ophthalmic, surgical, and vision care SBUs had centralized marketing groups and decentralized sales forces. Similar to Nestlé's regional axis, in Alcon's International Division, marketing and sales were decentralized at the country level, though in the 1980s a central marketing group was created to support R&D's new products.[4]

Fürer and Angst were impressed by Schollmaier and came to trust his judgment. Unusual in the Nestlé organization, Alcon operated autonomously. Schollmaier reported to Angst until the latter was replaced a decade later by José Daniel, a fellow member of the initial three-person Nestlé executive committee. Nestlé assigned Pierre Vogel, a long-time employee and experienced financial auditor, as its liaison to Alcon; he had the skills and personality to be effective in this role. In 1981 Helmut O. Maucher became Nestlé's CEO (fig. 5.2). He began his career at his local Nestlé company in West Germany in 1945, becoming the general manager of Nestlé Germany. In 1980 Maucher, Angst, and Daniel comprised Nestlé's executive committee, which managed Nestlé until 1986, when Maucher was also elected chairman of Nestlé's board of directors.

FIG 5.2
Ed Schollmaier, Helmut Maucher,
José Daniel, and Bernie Senkowski tour the
Alcon campus, May 1987 (AHR)

Maucher and Schollmaier displayed similarities in management style and personality. Both shunned ostentatious lifestyles, enjoyed the opera, lived in modest dwellings, and shared a pragmatic outlook. Maucher was reserved and Schollmaier more loquacious, but neither man angered easily. Professionally, they agreed on principles: long-term objectives outweigh short-term; growth depends on technology; strategy must be global; acquisitions must be synergistic; brands must be protected; and customers must be understood. Both men appreciated people at all levels and recognized the importance of training. Most important, they believed that marketing was a job for the boss, and in their commercial spheres, product profiles were global. With full confidence in Schollmaier, Maucher told Nestlé's global companies to take a hands-off approach with Alcon. Alcon took advantage of Nestlé's infrastructure for access to offices, government officials, and purchasing power. As global trade expanded into Eastern Europe, Russia, and China, Alcon made use of Nestlé's presence to set up its own companies and operations. Alcon also benefited from Nestlé's long-term planning, but it was the latter's financial support that was essential. The first example came within months of the acquisition.[5]

Alcon managers planned the construction of an R&D building before the Nestlé acquisition. Charles A. Robb, a senior executive in R&D, was the project manager. Bernard

Senkowski's engineering group collaborated with Robb to design a $13 million R&D building, the most expensive constructed by Alcon. By the time it was ready for approval, Nestlé was involved, so Robb and Schollmaier journeyed to Vevey to sell the project. Angst's frown signaled his opinion of the design, and the Alcon contingent was deflated when it was not approved. Schollmaier recovered quickly: "Karl [*sic*], help me, what can we do differently?" Angst asked, "How long are you going to be doing research?" "Infinitely," came the reply. Angst responded, "This building will be obsolete before you finish it. I'm not doing an obsolete building. Give me a plan that I can support." To cope with the broiling Texas summers, the structure had no windows, which was anathema to the Swiss. Alcon returned with a proposal for a $26 million building overflowing with windows. The plan for what became the William C. Conner Research Center was accepted. Gerald Cagle remembered this as an indication of Nestlé holding Alcon employees in high regard, and it is one reason Jerry Rutherford described the Alcon Family's view of Nestlé as a "benevolent parent."[6]

A $26 million building seemed trivial when Schollmaier next requested financial support. During the 1970s, the contact lens market underwent dynamic transformations. SofLens by B&L led the changes; customers quickly discarded PMMA lenses for more comfortable soft lenses. When the FDA declared that soft lenses and support solutions required premarket approval, firms developing and selling them had to adjust. B&L received approval to market salt tablets dissolved in water and heated as a disinfectant and storage solution, but microbial contamination occurred, so the FDA required saline solutions to be preserved. Burton, Parsons & Co. received early FDA approval to market its product, Boil n Soak. It also sold wetting and storage solutions and by 1977 it held a major share of the market. The firm had begun in 1922 as a family enterprise selling Konsyl, a psyllium fiber laxative. The Burtons and Parsons sold the business to J. S. Tyree in 1949; when he died in 1952, his daughter inherited the firm. Her sons, John A. "Tommy" Manfuso Jr. and Robert "Bobby" Manfuso, concentrated on ophthalmic pharmaceutical and contact lens products. Boil n Soak (fig. 5.3) was their top revenue producer, driving annual sales to $21 million. The company's value was almost $100 million when Schollmaier called Tommy Manfuso and successfully bid $115 million. He flew to Switzerland and pitched the deal to Fürer and Angst, who approved it. This again demonstrated Nestlé's financial role in Alcon's success and of Nestlé's confidence in Schollmaier. In two years, Nestlé had spent $276.5 million to buy Alcon, $26 million to build an R&D facility, and $115 million for Burton, Parsons. Schollmaier noted that the acquisition gave Alcon "an excellent opportunity to enter one of the most rapidly growing health care areas—soft lens care products."[7]

FIG 5.3
Boil n Soak (TOM, AM)

By 1984 the ophthalmic pharmaceutical industry had undergone changes due to mergers and the appearance of new players. Cooper Laboratories acquired Smith, Miller and Patch; Revlon bought Barnes-Hind; and Smith-Kline Corporation purchased Allergan. The launch of a new class of drugs to treat glaucoma, the introduction of intraocular lenses (IOLs), advances in ocular surgery, and the development of soft contact lenses created opportunities. Ophthalmic products were divided into three groups: prescription and OTC pharmaceuticals, contact lenses and support solutions, and surgical devices and instruments. Alcon had a presence in each group. It had an extensive line of ophthalmic prescription and OTC medications; it produced irrigating solutions, stainless-steel hand instruments, and cryoextractors; and, with the purchase of Burton, Parsons, it rounded out its PMMA contact lens solutions with soft lens support products.

To meet the needs of ocular surgeons, Alcon needed more products and technical expertise, so it focused on Cooper Laboratories. Parker Montgomery, a wheeler-dealer, in 1968 had organized a conglomerate that produced pharmaceuticals, biomedical instruments, and dental care, dermatologic, and vision care products. Within Cooper Laboratories, he created CooperVision in the early 1980s. CooperVision marketed Permalens, a soft contact lens; various disinfecting, wetting, cleaning, and storage solutions for them; and a line of ophthalmic pharmaceuticals. Cooper Laboratories bought a Seattle IOL company in 1981 and two years later launched its own IOLs. Angst gave Schollmaier approval to offer $513 million for CooperVision. The deal became complicated. CooperVision management felt marginalized, and one investor sued, claiming the share price of $25 was too low. When the FTC objected, the acquisition seemed doomed. Alcon withdrew its bid, but the episode illustrated Nestlé's willingness to invest on Schollmaier's recommendation.[8]

Neither Schollmaier nor Angst left a copy of their list of Alcon's problems. Nonetheless, Schollmaier resolved each of them during his twenty-year tenure as CEO. At the beginning of 1978, he selected his leaders, all but one a seasoned Alcon executive. He left Leone's organization intact (fig. 5.4), then put Dick Sisson in charge of the Domestic Ophthalmic, Optical, and Surgical Divisions while Keith Lane directed Owen Laboratories. Frank Buhler remained head of the International Division. Under Sisson, Schollmaier installed Herb Kleiman to direct ophthalmic and optical products and John Spruill to lead the surgical group. Optical later became Vision Care, so these remained the SBUs, as Nestle defined them, in the United States operations group through 1997.[9]

Alcon followed a matrix management system that Schollmaier contended worked well. For example, the S&T controller, Rutherford, reported first Leone, the vice president of S&T, and second to the CFO, initially Henry Kologe, later Robert Montgomery. Among many things, the matrix system provided a means of conflict resolution. In an interview with *Pharmaceutical Executive*, Schollmaier claimed, "It forces an awful lot of dialogue and negotiations, and that's what's critical in a company that is rapidly growing—that the people you really depend on talk to each other."[10]

As head of S&T, Leone's responsibilities covered R&D, QA, RA, and Manufacturing. His visits to pharmaceutical companies around the world provided perspectives on organization and problem-solving. As 1977 began, he understood the importance of a strategic vision and saw this in Dilip Raval, Ted Fleming, and a new hire for Manufacturing, Bernard Senkowski. However, he was concerned about RA. A business journal editor characterized Leone as a Renaissance man and down-to-earth manager who believed "in the need to continually search for truths, especially in the laboratories, board rooms, and offices of the high technology industries of corporate America." Leone generated innovative concepts with a pragmatic foundation. His notions of the interaction of R&D and marketing is an example: "I have a very deep conviction that the engine dynamics of the industry is in its research long term—in its ability to bring technical significance to a product line. The marketing is the short-term dynamic delivering that technological significance to the marketplace. The efforts of the two disciplines mesh in a cyclical manner." Another example is the Alcon Research Institute, started in 1982, which provided substantial monetary awards to ophthalmic researchers, which was unique in the pharmaceutical industry. Leone served as a key resource for Alcon's licensing agreements and promoted high standards through technical excellence awards. His recruiting and retaining of senior managers in S&T were unparalleled. RA became a good example.[11]

RA remained the conduit through which Alcon communicated with regulatory agencies. In 1978 it was divided into two groups, the domestic unit headed by Dale Hinson and

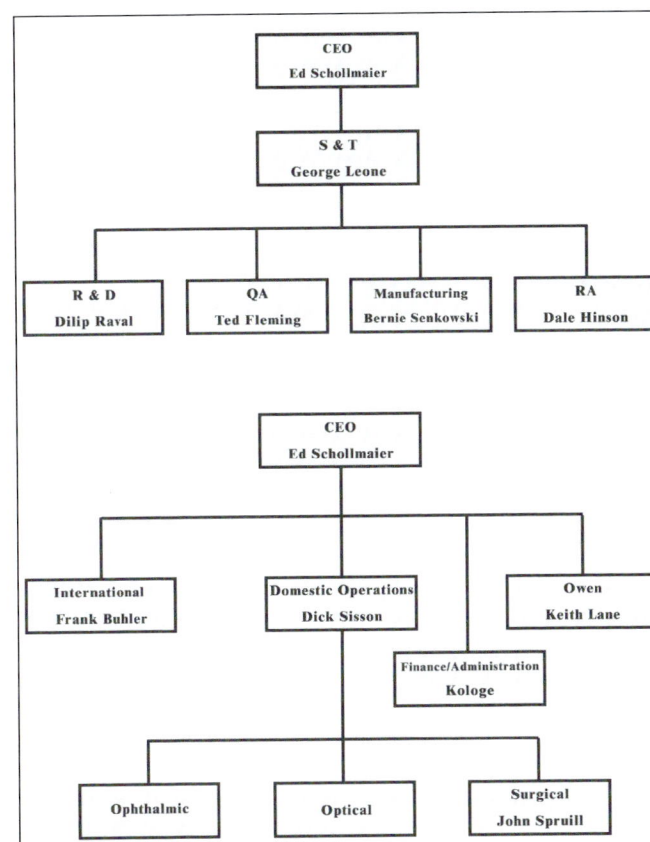

FIG 5.4
Organizational charts for Alcon's key executives, 1978 (TOM, AM)

FIG 5.5
Lewis Horger (AHR)

another in the International Division. Every Alcon medical specialty product was assigned an RA specialist to navigate a maze of regulations. Each specialist collaborated with R&D, Manufacturing, QA, and marketing, as well as the FDA and other agencies. Competent RA specialists were critical for a successful R&D project. For Manufacturing's involvement with the FDA's GMP guidelines, RA focused on escorting federal inspectors during compliance visits, with follow-ups if needed. In 1980 Hinson left Alcon for a legal practice in Washington, DC. His replacement was Lewis M. Horger, a doctoral graduate in pharmacology from Purdue University (fig. 5.5). After working as a bench pharmacologist with Sherman Laboratories, Horger had joined SmithKline & French Laboratories and spent twenty-eight years becoming their vice president of Regulatory Affairs. He came to Alcon in 1983, attracted by its smaller size, fewer layers of management, and the opportunity to shape RA through global registration of innovative products.[12]

Horger envisioned a centralized RA department managing a unified dossier for registering new products. In 1982 an RA specialist's actions in Germany emphasized the need for centralization when she balked at registering a product. She decided that pilocarpine gel would not sell and told Alcon executives on their visit to Germany. Thereafter, RA managers in various countries reported directly to RA in Fort Worth and secondarily to country managers. Mary Pencis and Mike Fenoglio, RA specialists in the International Division, transferred to corporate RA, Horger hired a European RA specialist, and when Henry Whissen retired, Bob Roehrs transferred from R&D and became responsible for ophthalmic pharmaceutical dossiers filed with the FDA. Irish native and RA strategist Michael N. Fitzpatrick joined Horger's team, responsible for the global registration of medical devices, with Dennis McEachern handling the United States and Pencis the overseas filings. With Charles Kagawa's retirement, Fitzpatrick oversaw compliance for manufacturing facilities; he assigned Becky Walker as Alcon's compliance officer. Walker also represented RA in a three-member audit team that assessed Alcon's international manufacturing plants; the other two were from QA and Manufacturing. Leone's success with Horger and the strategy of a centralized RA can be seen with Betoptic, a beta-blocker for treating glaucoma. The product received FDA approval in just sixteen months; within three years, it was registered in fifty countries, a record time frame.[13]

Senkowski (fig. 4.18) implemented a unified global strategic vision: state-of-the-art manufacturing and administrative facilities managed by experienced, skilled leaders, and a top-notch engineering group. Aware of Schollmaier's plan for expansion, knowledgeable about R&D's product pipeline, and cognizant that acquisitions would be made, Senkowski

Process Development Building

and his teams implemented and supervised plans that between 1978 and 1987 transformed Alcon's infrastructure. The year Nestlé acquired Alcon the south campus had three buildings (figs. 3.11, 4.4). The need for a dedicated R&D building was a void Nestlé filled. While the recently constructed Puerto Rico plant eliminated the necessity for more production lines in Fort Worth, this was temporary. Burgeoning sales and marketing teams and the administrative staff had also outgrown their building. The Surgical Division moved three miles north of the campus, the International Division rented the sixth floor of the University Bank building, and part of Domestic Operations relocated to a renovated warehouse south of the campus.

Senkowski transformed the Fort Worth campus into one befitting the headquarters of a global company. Intending to create a first-rate engineering staff, he hired, as director of Engineering, Frank J. Dorsey, an engineer with years of experience, most recently at E. R. Squibb & Sons. Senkowski also hired civil engineer Tran Trong; Trong and his team supervised most of the building projects in the United States. Consistent with Schollmaier's centralization, the Manufacturing Division managed all domestic and international manufacturing processes and construction, focusing on incorporating the latest technology.[14]

FIG 5.6
Alcon campus, 1978 (AHR)

The transition from small-sized lots of a new product in the laboratory to commercial-sized batches in a manufacturing facility is seldom straightforward. In the 1970s R&D's process development group used Manufacturing's lines to scale up from the laboratory. After Leone took over S&T, he and Raval convinced Schollmaier that a modern scale-up facility was essential, and in 1978 the thirteen-thousand-square-foot, $2.3 million Process Development building (fig. 5.6) became operational. It demonstrated its value repeatedly as ophthalmic and contact lens products developed in R&D were commercialized in the 1980s and 1990s.[15]

After Nestlé approved the design of the Conner Center, Fürer attended the groundbreaking ceremony in July 1979 (fig. 5.7). Trong and his team (fig. 5.8) collaborated with architects at Geren Associates/CRS, Fort Worth; engineers Friberg Alexander Maloney Gipson Weir, Fort Worth; and general contractor Robert McKee, Dallas. The center housed several interrelated departments and operations, clustered in three groups: the three-story Administrative and General Laboratory Complex (Group I), the one-story Biological Research Complex (Group II), and the Central Energy Plant (Group III) (fig. 5.9). It contained 227,000 square feet, making it larger than all campus buildings combined, with office and laboratory space for 350 personnel. The total cost was $31.2 million. A natural spring discovered during excavation created a central lagoon, which became a focal point. The modular laboratories, each with its own utilities, had service corridors for maintenance to avoid hampering experiments. The Central Energy Plant housed air-conditioning, heating, and steam equipment.

On September 18, 1982, the Conner Center was formally dedicated (fig. 5.10), and Conner's bronze life-size statue, sculpted by American artist Stanley Bleifeld, was unveiled in the entrance foyer (fig. 5.11). At the dedication, Schollmaier commented, "It is only fitting that this unique center bears the name of the man who through his drive, his strength of commitment, and above all, his vision set in motion an enterprise, Alcon Laboratories." Alcon scientists now staffed laboratories in the world's most modern and largest facility dedicated to ophthalmic research. Occupying twenty-four acres within Alcon's 176-acre campus, it was the largest R&D facility owned by Nestlé. When occupied, the third floor of the Group I wing housed RA, Finance and Administration (F&A), and Corporate Legal until 1987, when most relocated to the Robert D. Alexander Administration Center. Angst proved to be right; even with all the space, the increasing involvement of Alcon in research required more expansion. By 1988 an additional fifty thousand square feet of office and laboratory space was added to the Group II wing, at a cost of nearly $15 million (fig. 5.12).[16]

FIG 5.7
Bill Conner and Arthur Fürer, groundbreaking ceremony, William C. Conner Research Center, 1979 (AHR)

FIG 5.8
Tran Trong, in front of completed Conner Center, 1983 (Courtesy of Special Collections, Central Library, University of Texas at Arlington)

FIG 5.9
Alcon campus, William C. Conner Research Center, 1982 (AHR)

FIG 5.10
William C. Conner Research Center dedication, Bill Conner at the dais, Sept. 18, 1982 (AHR)

FIG 5.11
Bronze statue of William C. Conner.
Left to right: Tran Trong, Stanley Bleifeld, Bill Conner, Charles Robb, 1982 (AHR)

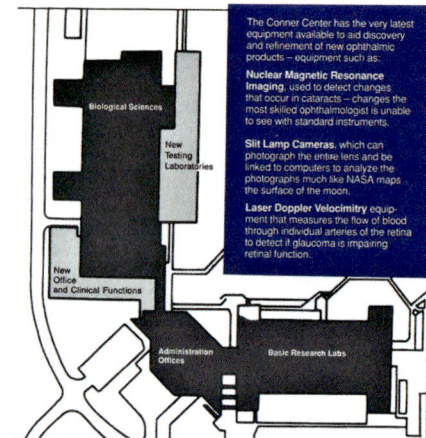

FIG 5.12
Map and description of William C. Conner Research Center expansion, 1987–1988 (AHR)

With administrative offices overflowing, and the Surgical, Vision Care, Ophthalmic, and International Divisions scattered around Fort Worth, Schollmaier proposed constructing a seven-story building, the Alexander Administration Center. Alexander used the original 1959 silver-plated spade in a groundbreaking ceremony on July 16, 1984. Omniplan Architects of Dallas designed the tower, which HCB Contractors, also of Dallas, built. The arch-shaped building featured a glass exterior accented by brick columns and walkways that harmonized with the existing campus (fig. 5.13). Started in 1985, the $25 million edifice was completed on schedule in February 1987, with dedication ceremonies on April 11. The center's 176,000 square feet accommodated six hundred people. The marble wall in the reception area was imported from Carrara, Italy, and framed a seven-and-one-half foot bronze bas-relief of Alexander, also the work of Bleifeld (fig. 5.14). The ground floor contained a visitor reception center, employee training room, health facility, break area, corporate travel agency, and human resources department. On the next five floors, conference rooms and offices along the outer convex and inner concave curves of the building conveyed a feeling of space and light. The building was only seventy-five feet wide, so one was never far from windows overlooking the campus. These floors housed the International, Surgical, Vision Care, Ophthalmic, and F&A Divisions. Senior executives officed on the seventh floor, where a large conference room adjoined the Alcon Hall of Fame, featuring portraits of those who had made significant contributions to the company.[17]

The Alexander Tower necessitated creating a new main entrance to the campus, with the state and city extending Altamesa Boulevard east from Interstate 35W. Near the security facility at the entrance, three fifty-foot flagpoles were erected, flying the United States, Texas, and Swiss flags. When a prominent foreign visitor came, their nation's flag replaced the Swiss flag. The main entrance road terminated in a circular driveway in front of Alexander Tower, with the Landmark Fountain at its center. Schollmaier designed the signature water feature on a restaurant napkin: a fountain in the shape of an eye (fig. 5.13).[18]

With Alcon's campus now accommodating nearly fifteen hundred employees, the need for a large and efficient dining facility became essential. The Crossroads Cafeteria was designed by Geren Associates, Fort Worth, and built by Rogers-O'Brien Construction Company, Dallas. Trong's team managed this $3 million construction project. Consisting of 16,550 square feet, the one-story structure, located between the S&T building and the Process Development plant, looked out on the Conner Center and the lagoon (fig. 5.15). Completed in 1987, the structure had a kitchen and dining area capable of serving five hun-

dred employees, and also a large space, divisible into three rooms, for meetings or special events. The cafeteria prepared and served over seven hundred meals during each breakfast and lunch period. An annex on the south side of the building served as the company store.[19]

With a wider range of products and increased demand for prescription, OTC, and contact lens products, a fourth expansion of the Fort Worth plant began during 1983, and work started on a warehouse the next year. In 1987 a $23 million investment incorporated new technology into lines 8 and 9. Milton Barley had been the Fort Worth plant manager since 1975, but soon after Senkowski took charge, Barley took over the new Corporate Materials and Services department, and Floyd Powell returned from Puerto Rico to resume the role of plant manager. Barley's new responsibilities included corporate purchasing, package engineering, technical services, international manufacturing services, creative services, and later safety engineering. In 1981 Senkowski hired Larry J. Coben, a doctoral graduate of Rutgers University and a pharmaceutical scientist with executive experience in manufacturing technology at Warner Chilcott Laboratories. Coben appreciated the value of GMPs for product quality, so Gene Estes and QA found a kindred soul. Beginning in 1984, manufacturing employees selected an employee of the year—Everette Carpenter, 1984; Jim Green, 1985; and Barry Calicott, 1986. Calicott operated a sophisticated water purification system, a critical job because water was the most common in-

FIG 5.15
Alcon campus, 1987 (AHR)

gredient in Alcon products. Alcon initiated an ambitious Productivity Improvement Program in 1982 with Fort Worth as the trial plant. Soon Alcon facilities all over the world joined the effort, with total savings exceeding $3 million by the end of 1985. The first Silver Plate awarded for this achievement went to the Fort Worth plant in 1985.[20]

Ethylene oxide sterilization of Drop-tainers, plugs, and caps continued to be fraught with residue issues; after studying injection blow molding, Senkowski concluded it was a feasible alternative. In November 198 a new twenty-seven-thousand-square-foot plastic bottle plant began operation, producing approximately fifty million bottles and one hundred million plugs and caps annually. If validation studies confirmed that technology produced

FIG 5.16
Alcon Humacao campus,
Puerto Rico, 1981 (AHR)

sterile units, then Alcon had pioneered a new technique. Until then, the plant produced bottles and caps meeting Alcon's specifications.[21]

Alcon's first manufacturing plant at Humacao, Puerto Rico, was built in 1974; it provided production and distribution facilities for Webcon. It was renovated to meet new GMP requirements and to manufacture Pantopaque, an injectable diagnostic aid produced by the Lafayette plant in Indiana. By 1978 it became clear that ophthalmic pharmaceutical production in Fort Worth would reach maximum capacity. Senkowski and Schollmaier pitched a proposal to Nestlé for a new complex in Puerto Rico. Designed like a campus, Alcon Humacao consisted of six buildings adjacent to the original plant (fig. 5.16). The new complex had three major buildings—a forty-five-thousand-square-foot ophthalmic manufacturing facility, a twenty-thousand-square-foot administration building, and a thirty-thousand-square-foot Avitene production unit, the latter owned by Avicon and managed by Alcon. The remaining three structures served as a cafeteria, energy center, and waste treatment plant. The expansion cost $21.5 million and the annual production of twelve million ophthalmic containers began in mid-1981, as did yearly distribution of almost one million Avitene units. Hurricanes, floods, and strikes delayed the project, but the facility turned out to be one of the most attractive among the pharmaceutical companies in Puerto Rico.[22]

When Powell left the Puerto Rico facility in early 1977, John Feik became the plant manager; Howard Luttrell, the QA head; and George Morey, the controller. It was under them that construction began. During the 1970s several pharmaceutical companies, taking advantage of United States tax regulations and low costs, established manufacturing plants in Puerto Rico, so the FDA opened a branch inspection office. Urised, the most popular Webcon product, contained methylene blue, a diffusible dye visible even when highly diluted; inspectors regularly found blue spots on the walls in the compounding and filling rooms. The FDA considered the splashes a violation, so Alcon painted the walls the same tint as methylene blue. The Drug Enforcement Administration (DEA) also had a Puerto Rico office and conducted inspections whenever a regulated substance was used. One Webcon product, the B&O suppository, was formulated with opium. Luttrell recalled that DEA visits could last days as inspectors reconciled to the milligram the amount of opium that entered the plant to the amount leaving as a B&O suppository.[23]

Feik, Luttrell, and Morey left Puerto Rico about the time validation studies began for the new facility. Senkowksi had hired a person to oversee construction and chose him to replace Feik as general manager, while experienced local people filled the QA and controller positions. Shortly after the plant manufacturing eye drops became operational, sterility failures occurred, and the FDA noted a section of the stainless-steel filling line had not been validated. Senkowski sent Barley to assess the situation in early 1981, resulting in Barley's appointment as general manager. He fixed the validation issue. With the facility back on schedule, Barley needed a competent replacement so he hired Lee Hansen, who managed Cooper Laboratories' manufacturing facilities in Puerto Rico. In 1983 Hansen signed a contract with O'Brien Energy to install and operate a cogeneration electricity plant, resulting in a savings of $1.5 million in electrical costs over five years and allowing independence from the unreliable Puerto Rican electrical grid. It produced up to 2.2 megawatts of electricity and used the heat generated to power a 320-ton chiller providing air conditioning throughout the campus.[24]

At the ten-year anniversary celebrations in 1984, Sisson noted that of the original 65 Puerto Rican employees, 30 remained in the workforce, now 273 in number. The dollar volume of products had grown from $4.6 million to $41.5 million, and the annual volume of production was 15.5 million units with an additional 12 million coming off the line when Opti-Zyme production began. Seven major products were scheduled for production in 1985. The following year the manufacture of Opti-Clean and other contact lens solutions brought the value of production to over $100 million.[25]

FIG 5.17
Allen Baker (AHR)

FIG 5.18
Giorgio Vescovo (AHR)

Alcon's purchase of Burton, Parsons and the development of its own new contact lens products led to an expansion of Alcon Canada's manufacturing, warehouse, and administrative facilities from thirty-four-thousand square feet to fifty-five thousand by 1981. Alcon Canada exported Alcon, Owen, and Burton, Parsons products to Europe and Asia, while the company continued to use contract manufacturers in the Philippines, Singapore, and elsewhere. In 1987 Frances Brotherhood transferred from international marketing in Fort Worth to become Canada's general manager.[26]

As 1978 began, Alcon manufactured products in its new plant in Puurs, Belgium, and in outdated facilities in Paris, Madrid, and Milan. Alcon discontinued Farmila's R&D group in 1977, and one year later, when the owner of Farmila resigned, Buhler sent Allen Baker (fig. 5.17) to Milan to manage the company. Baker hired Giorgio Vescovo (fig. 5.18), a graduate of the University of Bologna who had experience in the chemical industry and in sales and management of the pharmaceutical division of the Italian subsidiary of Dow Chemical. Farmila continued to manufacture its own lines and not Alcon products until the 1980s, when it made Tears Naturale. Alcon did not invest in Farmila's plant and sold the obsolete facility in 1984. Alcon Iberhis leased offices and facilities in Madrid until it purchased eighteen thousand square meters in Alcobendas and built a $12 million manufacturing plant. Dedicated in May 1987, it produced twenty million units of ophthalmic, lens care, and dermatological products annually for EURMEA.

A contact lens manufacturing plant in Munich came with Alcon's 1979 purchase of Burton, Parsons, but after completion of the state-of-the-art facility in Alcobendas, the German plant closed and production shifted to Spain. Alcon's modern administrative and distribution center in Freiburg was completed in 1983. Nestlé transferred a pharmaceutical plant, Laboratoires Etienne in Rumilly, France, to Alcon. Pharmacist Francois Vaucheret moved the Alcon Paris plant to Rumilly; it became a major production facility. The extension of the Rumilly warehouse operation in 1984 doubled its capacity to meet demands in EURMEA. Alcon's 1984 purchase of Produits Ophtalmique Stériles (POS), of Kaysersberg, France, added ophthalmic, contact lens care, and dermatologic products. POS used a new system, form-fill-seal, in which a sterile solution was injected as the container formed. Thus, by the end of 1987, Alcon EURMEA plants had been centralized in four locations: Rumilly, Alcobendas, Kaysersberg, and Puurs.[27]

In March 1986 Alcon Mexico bought Laboratorios Ufarmex, S.A. de C.V., a company with significant ophthalmic and ear, nose, and throat products. Around the same time, Alcon renovated the Oftasa plant in Mexico City. Meanwhile, manufacturing continued in

FIG 5.19
Plant managers meeting, Fort Worth, 1984 (AHR). *Back row (left to right):* Phillipe Lancery, Rumilly, France; Dr. Larry Coben, Fort Worth; François Vaucheret, P.O.S., France; Lee Hansen, Puerto Rico; Wolfgang Saller, Germany; Mike Bordovsky, San Antonio; Dr. Thomas Ottmann, Belgium.
Center row (left to right): Enrique Rueda, Spain; Bob Boa, Canada; Dave Stiles, Canada; John Feik, San Antonio; Dr. Marcelo Schattner, Argentina; Don Brown, Fort Worth; Dr. Garnet Smith, Fort Worth; Michel Roblot, P.O.S., France. *Front row (left to right):* Walter Klein, Fort Worth; Dr. Frank Dastoli, Fort Worth; Benjamin Sarabia, Mexico; George Leone, Fort Worth; Dr. Bernard Senkowski, Fort Worth; Willem Rike, Brazil; Lanette Browder, Fort Worth; Ashok Desai, Fort Worth.

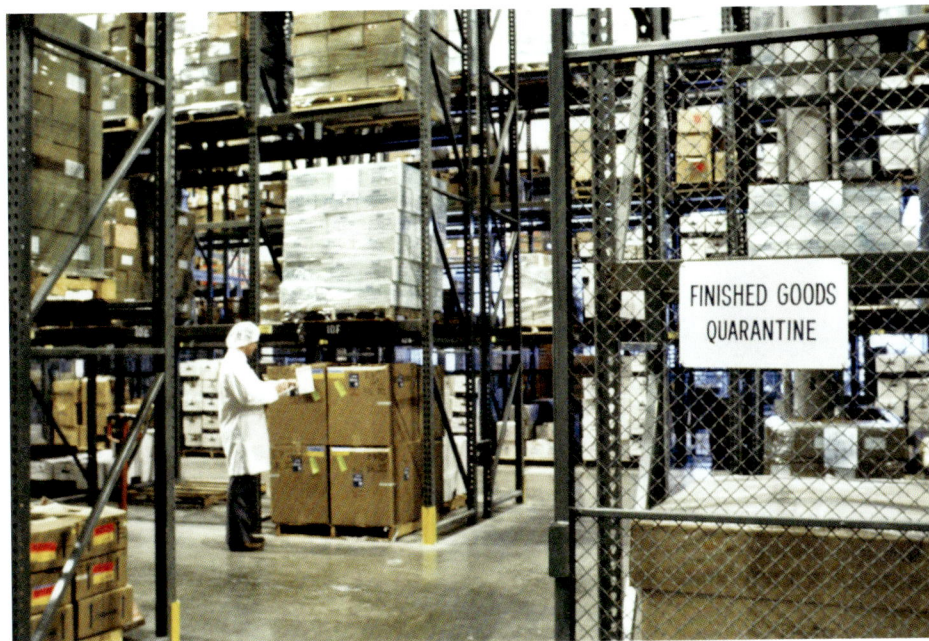

FIG 5.20
Finished goods quarantine warehouse, Fort Worth, 1988 (AHR)

São Paulo, Brazil, and Buenos Aires, Argentina.[28]

Senkowski's Manufacturing Division changed the facilities of Alcon while producing an increasing number of products. The emphasis on training set a tone that contributed to Alcon Manufacturing receiving the World Safety Organization annual award in 1986. Leadership starts at the top, and in 1984 Senkowski began strategizing with managers of Alcon plants worldwide (fig. 5.19) in what became an annual event. By 1988 Alcon's plants were producing an impressive 3 million units weekly (fig. 5.20).[29]

Fleming stayed abreast of trends in QA and earned a master's degree in Quality Systems while working at Alcon. QA's intrusion into the various plants' operations resulted in higher quality, the sterility validation process established by Estes being one of many examples. The Fort Worth plant became the model for overseas facilities. When Buhler began International Operations, he managed Manufacturing and QA by enlisting Charles Dickey to oversee operations and processes, while local managers hired and supervised plant and QA personnel. After a trip to Europe, Fleming told Leone, "We've got to take over international quality control because we have big problems there." Schollmaier had convinced Buhler to give up control of manufacturing facilities overseas, so asking him to also give up QA seemed uncomplicated. Thus, as 1978 began, Fleming embarked toward a centralized QA with global personnel reporting to Fort Worth.[30]

Although Alcon products met high standards, there were consumer complaints. Fleming concluded that a technical background was preferable to administrative experience when evaluating these. He recruited Martha Siegel from R&D to be the Consumer Affairs manager and establish new procedures for handling complaints. Siegel developed a process with three components: if there was a problem, Alcon would fix it; Alcon sought consumer satisfaction with all responses; and Alcon wanted repeat business. Siegel's system funneled all complaints to her group, which explored issues systematically and responded quickly. All sorts of complaints were handled; some were fraudulent, some were false claims made by a competitor, some were humorous. Users of the rose hip infusion Estivin were especially critical. Safety issues warranted extra attention; for that, Siegel initially relied on Harold Beasley. Later a drug surveillance specialist in R&D's Clinical Science department supported Consumer Affairs.

In 1979 Fort Worth employed about 75 in QA and 175 people in Manufacturing. QA involved analytical chemistry testing and microbiological testing. Chemistry activities have been discussed in chapter 4. Microbiological testing evolved with production changes. Many ophthalmic and contact lens products could not be terminally sterilized and were prepared aseptically; thus, all parts of the packaging and the solutions had to be sterilized separately and brought together in a sterile manner. Generally, the bottles, caps, and plugs were sterilized with ethylene oxide or gamma radiation. These components were stored in plastic bags permeable to ethylene oxide and placed in the aseptic filling area, a Class 100 clean room. The bottles were filled with aqueous solutions formulated in stainless-steel vats; the solutions passed through a 0.22 μ filter to remove bacteria. The filling and formulation rooms needed to be free of microorganisms, and Estes established routine monitoring for airborne bacteria and molds. Personnel wore sterile gowns and masks, while entry to the rooms was strictly controlled (fig. 5.21). In the event of contamination, bacteria had to be isolated and identified to find the source of the problem. Anyone who works in a sterile environment can attest to the difficulty of controlling the behavior and migration of bacteria! When he returned from Puerto Rico in 1979, Luttrell (fig. 5.22) was assigned to manage the QA analytical and microbiological testing units. Due to the FDA's evolving guidelines, QA remained involved in the validation of manufacturing processes, an intense learning environment. During this time, Luttrell and his teams continued the automation of and computer interfacing with chemistry methodologies and microbiological procedures. Fleming boasted that Luttrell's automation processes increased assay accuracy and resulted in cost savings of about 50 percent.[31]

Fleming consolidated QA at the Alcon manufacturing facilities in the United States. When sterility and validation issues surfaced at the Puerto Rico plant in 1981, he used the opportunity to have that QA unit report to Luttrell. He also became the direct supervisor of QA at the Burton, Parsons plant in Maryland, and the following year the QA manager at the Owen plant in San Antonio. By then, Alcon employed 192 scientists, technicians, and support personnel in four domestic QA groups. Reflecting on this period, Luttrell recalled, "I have to admit that I really enjoyed the practically non-stop action that operations jobs required. There was always something going wrong, problems to fix, and product that needed to get out the door ASAP." In 1984 Fleming retired after being at Alcon for twenty-nine years. Luttrell's sabbatical to obtain his graduate degree and his tenures at Center Laboratories and Alcon Puerto Rico were valuable, but to be equipped as

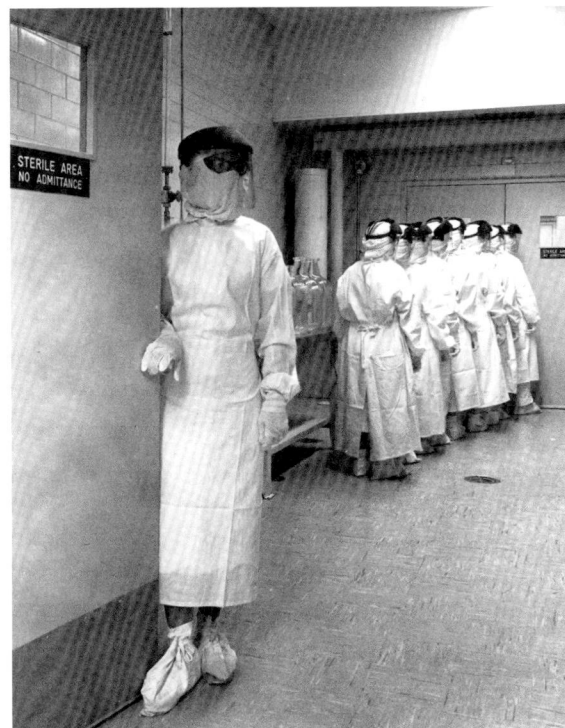

FIG 5.21
Filling room technicians waiting to enter a sterile area, Fort Worth, 1982 (AHR)

FIG 5.22
Howard Luttrell (AHR)

Fleming's replacement, Leone required him to head the Technical Audit Team for a year and attend a management course at Havard. The audits introduced Luttrell to plants overseas and to the domestic surgical product facilities, while attending Havard exposed him to business concepts. During an audit of the Burton, Parsons plant in Munich, Luttrell discovered inadequate steam sterilization of the filling machine; he shut down the plant until a revised, validated process was installed. In January 1985 Leone promoted Luttrell to vice president of QA, in charge of over six hundred employees worldwide.[32]

Luttrell had a similar philosophy to Fleming, a key principle being "*quality* could never be tested or inspected into a product." Quality had to be designed into the product using manufacturing and testing processes, and all had to be validated. He advocated a matrix system in which all plant QA managers reported directly to corporate QA. While they worked with general managers, they remained independent in implementing QA systems and product releases. Corporate QA staffed the plant QA groups and developed policies and procedures for all facilities, emphasizing state-of-the-art technologies. QA's computer program in Fort Worth was installed in the plants, allowing corporate QA to have real-time views of systems, inspections, and testing results.[33]

Between 1972 and 1977, Raval's R&D organization released Tears Naturale, Avitene, Naphcon, Lens-Mate, Duratears, the Fluorescite syringe, Econochlor, and 500 ml BSS. It had several significant projects in the clinical phase, including the broad-spectrum anti-infective Tobrex and a superior ocular surgical irrigating solution, BSS PLUS. Alcon also had a licensing agreement for a new beta-blocker, betaxolol, to treat glaucoma. Thus, up to 1978, Raval exceeded Schollmaier's 1974 dictum of releasing at least three important products, but the existential trial for R&D would occur in the ten years after Nestlé's acquisition. Schollmaier more than kept his commitment to insulate R&D from budget cuts; its annual budget grew almost tenfold, from $5.3 million in 1977 to $56 million in 1987, and its personnel more than doubled. The education level of the scientists grew from 16 percent having a PhD to 24 percent in 1986, and the cohort with a BS or an MS expanded from 37 percent to 45 percent. In 1977 Alcon spent 6.5 percent of its annual sales on R&D; a decade later, yearly expenditures had increased to 11.5 percent. R&D funding in American pharmaceutical firms in 1981 ranged from 8 percent to 17 percent per year. In 1990 Schollmaier claimed that the decade from 1978 to 1987 was preparation for the ten years that followed. Thus, R&D in the 1980s deserves a closer look.[34]

With over a dozen new products released by 1984, Raval concluded that his division had reached a "size and maturity." He appointed Robert Adamski to head research and Ca-

FIG 5.23
R&D leadership, 1984. Gerald Cagle (*left*), Robert Adamski (*center*), Dilip Raval (*right*). (AHR)

gle to direct development (fig. 5.23). In making his announcement, Raval noted the new organization would allow R&D to concentrate on short-, mid-, and long-term programs and projects. He stressed that both groups were equally important and interrelated.[35]

From 1978 through 1987, 80 percent of R&D resources were dedicated to new product development. Of more than a dozen projects, most were ophthalmic pharmaceuticals. When the new building opened, Raval assigned an experienced scientist to manage process development. In the meantime, R&D microbiology became a major advocate of contact lens disinfecting standards with regulatory agencies; it also created a new paradigm for the clinical testing of a novel topical ocular antibiotic. Raval expanded the toxicology department by hiring one experienced scientist and a recent doctorate. Applying newly implemented GCPs, the new Clinical Science group, along with an innovative biostatistical unit, used pioneering protocols to profile the advantages of several drugs studied in humans. The geographic scope of clinical studies expanded to Europe and Japan. As clinical studies evolved, so did the medical monitor staff; Judson Smith, MD, and Cliff Beasley, MD, and Don Brotherman, MD, joined Harold Beasley. To correct R&D's limited expertise in soft contact lenses, Raval recruited an R&D expert from a competitor and transferred a scientist from the laboratory to oversee surgical projects. With R&D operating under guidelines required by GLP, GMP, and GCP regulations, R&D's administrative group centralized records and systematized retention. A Quality Audit Unit monitored compliance. Research expanded with the hiring of scientists having expertise in pharmacology, medicinal chemistry, immunology, inflammation, drug delivery, and nuclear magnetic resonance. Adamski also focused on finding novel compounds from other companies for R&D to develop. Considering that many R&D activities warranted patent protection, Raval recruited a patent attorney, who also prepared licensing agreements. During the 1970s, Alcon filed only three NDAs that were approved by the FDA. One of Raval's goals was to increase the approvals by using project teams that had scientists from various functions led by a member of management. To maintain focus, Raval appointed Richard Poe as the gatekeeper for market support requests from the Ophthalmic, Vision Care, and Surgical Divisions.[36]

In such a multifaceted R&D effort, problems always occur. Pilocarpine gel is a good example. In early 1979 long-term efficacy and safety studies in glaucoma patients had been underway for several months when small, unusual changes were observed at the junction of the cornea and sclera in rabbit eyes. While Pilocarpine gel was Alcon's novel glaucoma therapy, this was the first time animal safety studies had extended beyond one month. The toxicology group, led by Joseph H. Hiddemen, had also started a monkey study, where corneoscleral changes had not appeared. Raval led a team of scientists in discussions with an FDA ophthalmologist. Until then, the pharmaceutical industry and regulatory agencies deemed rabbits to be definitive for ocular safety evaluations. But Alcon's findings prompted a change; in the future, a monkey was considered more reliable for predicting human safety in long-term usage. This changed future ocular in vivo safety protocols and increased costs. Alcon's willingness to discuss research frankly with regulators illustrates its commitment to safe medications. Both clinical and animal studies of Pilocarpine gel were completed in three years, and the FDA received the NDA in May 1982, which it approved on October 1, 1984. The product was released under the trade name Pilopine HS Gel (fig. 5.24). Using an advanced delivery system, it was an important glaucoma therapy that provided twenty-four-hour control of IOP without the visual blurring associated with older treatments.[37]

Ocular fungal infections are rare. Alcon's Natacyn was the first FDA-approved treatment. Before its availability, ophthalmologists used parenteral antifungal medications or pharmacists compounded a prescription of nata-mycin powder acquired from an overseas manufacturer. The FDA was concerned that such prescriptions were not sterile and were of unknown purity and quality, so they approached Alcon to manufacture a topical natamycin product. Alcon agreed. Before approval of the NDA, Alcon provided free samples of Natacyn, and after its approval on October 30, 1978, a unit was shipped to ophthalmologists at a reasonable cost.[38]

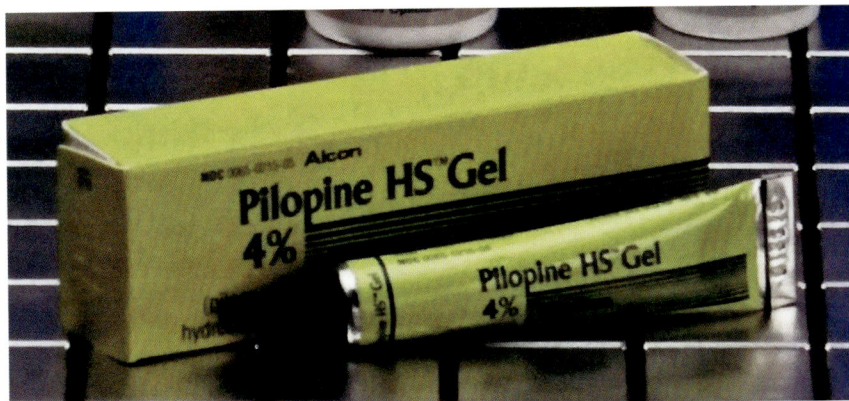

FIG 5.24
Pilopine HS Gel (AHR)

Cagle, an R&D microbiologist, collaborated with two microbiologists from the Cullen Eye Institute at the Baylor College of Medicine in Houston to develop a procedure that quantified the number of bacteria in infected human eyes before and during therapy. At the end of treatment, residual bacteria were measured and the clinical outcome was correlated with the microbiology result. The experimental design became the standard by which the FDA judged ophthalmic antibiotics.[39]

In a multicenter study of over five hundred patients, tobramycin ophthalmic solution was proven more effective, with greater antibacterial efficacy, than the antibiotic gentamicin. During any clinical testing phase, Alcon R&D routinely met with the FDA to review the outcome of clinical and nonclinical studies. This process ensured that all study designs met FDA expectations and mitigated against surprises in the NDA review. After the FDA reviewed an NDA, it sent Alcon an "approvable letter," meaning the NDA was acceptable. In the last step of the approval process, Alcon negotiated the package insert, a significant document since it set the boundaries of what a company could promote about a product. Schollmaier named the solution Tobrex (fig. 5.25) and final approval was granted on December 12, 1980; the next year, the FDA approved the ointment form. The three-and-a-half-year development and approval timeline was extraordinarily short, illustrating the value of the integrated microbiology and clinical-testing paradigms.[40]

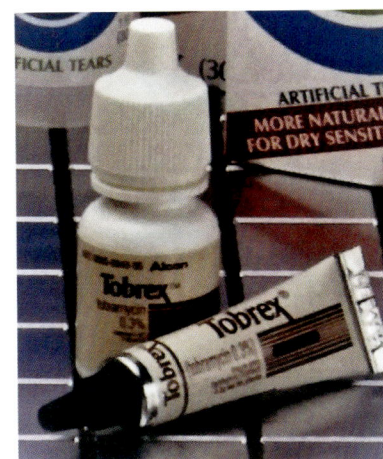

Each project presents unique challenges. BSS PLUS is a good example. The Medical College of Wisconsin's corneal physiologist, Henry Edelhauser, demonstrated that a combination of glutathione and bicarbonate in a standard physiologic solution protected corneal endothelial cells. R&D solved the formula's instability with a two-part glass bottle holding the solutions, which ocular surgeons mixed during surgery (fig. 4.39). Alcon R&D conducted BSS PLUS clinical studies when cataract surgeons were also adopting the use of IOLs

FIG 5.25
Tobrex (AHR)

and phacoemulsification. The human studies conducted on BSS PLUS demonstrated that it protected the endothelium and reduced corneal swelling after cataract surgery and vitrectomy. Alcon also used in vitro human corneal perfusion studies to corroborate the proof of BSS PLUS's efficacy and safety in its NDA, another first for an ophthalmic drug submission to the FDA. BSS PLUS received the FDA's approval on October 28, 1981.[41]

In 1978 Merck Sharp and Dohme of West Point, Pennsylvania, launched Timoptic (0.25% and 0.5% timolol maleate) ophthalmic solution, a nonselective beta-blocker. Instilled on the eyes twice a day, with no visual side effects, it gained acceptance as a first-line therapy for glaucoma, eroding Alcon's share of that market. However, it produced side effects, some life-threatening, for patients with pulmonary and cardiovascular diseases. One year earlier, Alcon had licensed betaxolol from Synthélabo and commenced preclinical studies. Alcon started human studies in 1980. After the 0.5% concentration was chosen, the clinical studies had two objectives: (1) to compare its IOP control to Timoptic 0.5% in glaucoma patients and (2) to demonstrate its safety in patients with pulmonary and cardiovascular diseases. This was the first R&D project where clinical studies were simultaneously conducted overseas. In scale and scope, the studies were the largest Alcon ever sponsored. Clinical supplies were manufactured by R&D's process development group in Fort Worth and, for the first time, in Alcon plants in Canada and Belgium.[42]

Betaxolol 0.5% eye drops reduced glaucoma patients' IOP similar to 0.5% Timoptic, with its incidence of discomfort about twice that of Timoptic. However, Timoptic slowed the heartbeat, most noticeably during cardiovascular stress, and induced lung spasms in asthmatic patients. In 1986 the FDA mandated a box warning in boldface type in Timoptic's package insert to alert patients to "serious or life-threatening risk." This is the most significant FDA warning. Alcon took advantage of the situation, designing a protocol in which glaucoma patients who had a pulmonary reaction to Timoptic switched to 0.5% betaxolol. Working with pulmonologists, Alcon set up controlled studies in which vulnerable patients were required to undergo lung function testing before and after instillation of betaxolol eye drops; no patient had an adverse pulmonary reaction. Moreover, other studies showed that under cardiovascular stress, such as when a patient was jogging, betaxolol did not slow the heart rate. Alcon filed the NDA in mid-1984 and the FDA approved betaxolol on August 30, 1985, with no box warnings. Schollmaier chose the trade name Betoptic (fig. 5.26). Looking to the future, R&D started development of a 0.25% betaxolol delivery suspension, which allowed slow release of betaxolol that created less discomfort. Thus, as this ten-year period came to an end, R&D was ready to release an improved betaxolol product.[43]

When a medication patent expires, pharmaceutical companies can file an Abbreviated New Drug Application (ANDA) and, for antibiotics, an Abbreviated Antibiotic Drug Application (AADA). Prescription medications approved by these routes are known as generics. Requirements for approval are less onerous because preclinical safety studies are few and clinical studies often are not required. From 1978 through 1987, Alcon R&D received approval for nine such products. This led Marketing to promote generics, many of which copied competitors' products. Nonprescription products were also fair game once their patents expired, Naphcon being an example. Naphcon contained an effective vasoconstrictor, naphazoline hydrochloride, which R&D combined with an OTC antihistamine, pheniramine maleate. Once stability, preservative, and safety studies were completed, Alcon registered the formulation in 1979 as a prescription product, Naphcon-A (fig. 5.27), which Marketing promoted for the relief of ocular allergies.[44]

The late 1970s and 1980s produced important technologically advanced contact lenses and, with them, changes in wearing regimens and support solutions. After B&L introduced its HEMA SofLens in 1971, other companies entered the market by acquiring smaller firms that had lens material technologies and scientists. Alcon flirted with this idea, buying Tresoft in 1977, the French company Medicornea in 1981, and Scanlens from a Swedish company in 1982. However, four years later it reversed this strategy on the grounds that lens technology was not its field of expertise and the expense to build polymer technology know-how would cost many times the existing R&D budget. At this time, B&L's R&D budget for soft contact lens and support solutions was four times larger than Alcon's R&D expenditure.

By 1987 the domestic market for contact lenses was HEMA soft lenses, 65 to 75 percent; RGP lenses, 20 to 30 percent; and hard PMMA lenses, 5 percent. Individuals wore lenses during the day, removed them at night for cleaning and disinfecting, then stored them overnight. This regimen created two problems. Protein and other debris in the tear film adhered to the contact lens, providing an ideal environment for bacteria. The contact lens disrupted the normal perfusion of oxygen into the cornea, providing

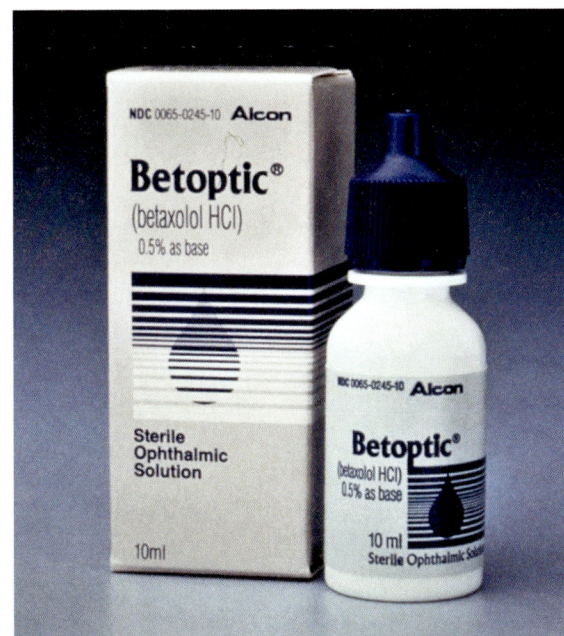

FIG 5.26
Betoptic (AHR)

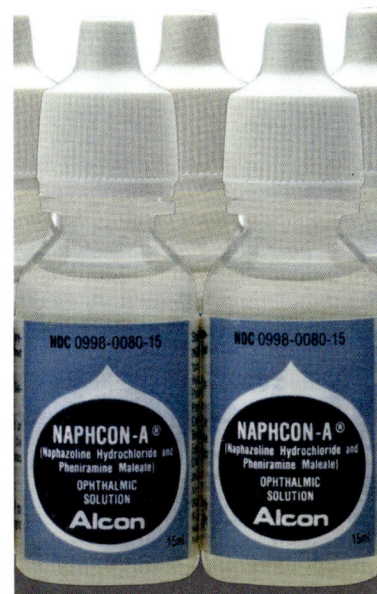

FIG 5.27
Naphcon-A (Richard Rheiner, AM, TCU)

yet another positive situation for infective bacteria and other detrimental microorganisms. Thus, corneal infections were a concern. At first, soft contact lenses were disinfected by heat, Alcon's Boil n Soak being the best-seller. Competitors introduced their own heat-disinfecting solutions, and some produced hydrogen peroxide systems that did not require heat but were difficult to use. The ideal product was a nonirritating, broadly effective chemical disinfectant that also served as a storage solution. In the mid-1980s, when extended-wear contact lenses were introduced, more issues arose. Alcon saw the opportunity for a family of support products, from disinfecting solutions to cleaner, storage, and comfort solutions, so R&D focused on this global market, which grew to $750 million by 1987.[45]

R&D had little expertise in developing contact lens products, so in 1978 Raval hired Kiran J. Randeri, a doctoral chemist from the University of Texas with experience at Allergan. Randeri's team upgraded two products that came with the 1979 Burton, Parsons acquisition: PreFlex, a daily cleaner, and FlexCare, a chemical disinfectant. Both contained effective biocides, thimerosal and chlorhexidine; both irritated the eye and discolored lenses. Competitors marketed products containing sorbic acid, potassium sorbate, and hydrogen peroxide. Alcon's quest led to a novel large molecule biocide, polyquaternium-1 (later branded by Alcon as polyquad), chemically related to the preservative used in Alcon's ophthalmic prescription products. Alcon licensed polyquad from Millmaster Onyx, New York. Biocides often proved deleterious to sensitive ocular tissue, but during in vitro studies polyquad displayed a wide safety margin (fig. 5.28). In clinical and laboratory studies, the formulation, named Opti-Soft (fig. 5.29), met FDA criteria for chemical disinfection of RGP lenses, thermal disinfection of soft lenses, and chemical disinfection for all except group 4 (high water content and ionic) lenses. Alcon filed an application that the FDA approved on August 9, 1985. In the same filing, R&D included Opti-Tears Soothing Drops (fig. 5.29), preserved with polyquad.[46]

Randeri's team also developed complementary lens cleaning products. During normal use, soft contacts and RGP lenses accumulate deposits of proteins, lipids, and carbohydrates. Formulators designed a preserved cleaning product, named Opti-Clean, composed of surfactant and high-molecular-weight polymeric microbeads. When rubbed on the lens, the surfactant removed lipids and the microbeads sheared the protein deposits. Soon, this daily cleaner was reformulated as Opti-Clean II (fig. 5.29), using polyquad as the preservative. Chemists stabilized a combination of enzymes that degraded proteins, lipids, and complex carbohydrates into a dissolvable tablet, labeled Opti-Zyme (fig. 5.29), for weekly use. This multipronged approach resulted in a superior product because competitor solutions con-

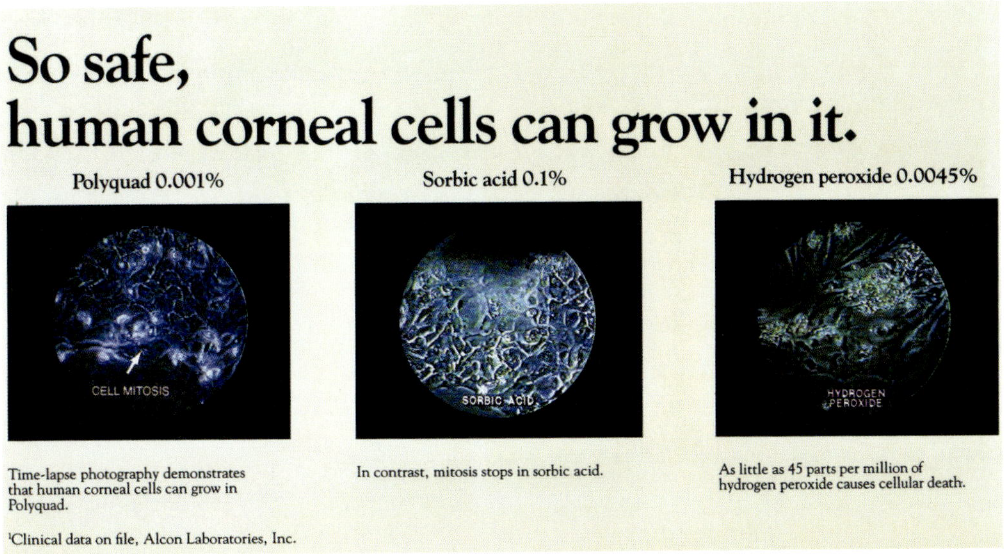

So safe,
human corneal cells can grow in it.
Polyquad 0.001%
Sorbic acid 0.1%
Hydrogen peroxide 0.0045%
CELL MITOSIS
SORBIC ACID
HYDROGEN PEROXIDE
Time-lapse photography demonstrates that human corneal cells can grow in Polyquad.
In contrast, mitosis stops in sorbic acid.
As little as 45 parts per million of hydrogen peroxide causes cellular death.
[1]Clinical data on file, Alcon Laboratories, Inc.

FIG 5.28
"So safe, human corneal cells can grow in it." Polyquad, advertisement P (Sue Faro, AM)

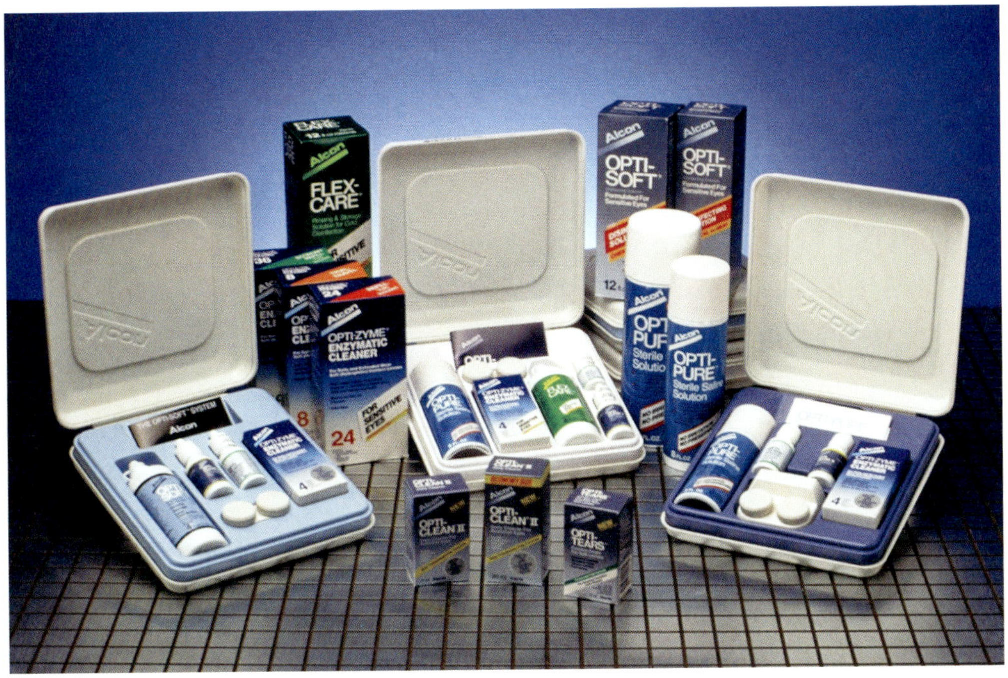

Alcon
FLEX-CARE
OPTI-SOFT
OPTI-PURE
OPTI-ZYME ENZYMATIC CLEANER
OPTI-CLEAN II
OPTI-TEARS

FIG 5.29
Alcon contact lens care products sold in 1987 (AHR)

tained a single enzyme that degraded only protein. The FDA approved Opti-Clean on May 7, 1983, Opti-Clean II on August 9, 1985, and Opti-Zyme on December 22, 1982. By the end of 1985, Marketing had transitioned from the inherited Burton, Parsons formulations to a unique set of products, differentiated from the competition, and established the Opti franchise. After settling a disputed patent claim, Alcon owned polyquad for ophthalmic use and began to establish it as a preservative and disinfectant.[47]

Meanwhile, Adamski's research department scouted for new compounds. Alcon licensed suprofen, a nonsteroid anti-inflammatory, from Janssen Pharmaceuticals, a division of Johnson & Johnson. Nonsteroid compounds are notoriously uncomfortable as eye drops. At the suggestion of a Nestlé scientist working at Alcon, the product development group added caffeine to the formula, enhancing its ocular comfort. Clinical studies demonstrated its value in preventing pupil constriction and reducing inflammation in the anterior and posterior chambers during and after surgery. The need had become important since a wide pupil facilitated IOL inserts during cataract surgery. Ocular allergies are persistent and aggravating. While products such as Naphcon provided temporary relief, patients needed medications that prevented redness and itching. Steroid eye drops were effective, but side effects prevented their prolonged daily use. A mast cell stabilizer, sodium cromoglycate, showed promise, but its efficacy was poor. Mast cells, located in mucosal tissues such as the conjunctiva, play a role in maintaining normal physiological functions and are also implicated in various diseases, including allergies. Thus, one goal of allergy therapy is to prevent mast cells from releasing its noxious contents. A drug that does this is a mast cell stabilizer. DeSantis's group identified lodoxamide as a potent mast cell stabilizer and patented its ophthalmic use, and Alcon licensed the compound from the Upjohn Company of Kalamazoo, Michigan. In a first for Alcon, the Clinical Science group started clinical studies in Europe ahead of the United States. Fort Worth–based Belgium native Annita Verstappen, successfully managed these studies.

Launched in 1981, the antibiotic Tobrex was a success, but Barry Schlech and his microbiology team remained aware of new antibiotics. When Bayer AG of Germany profiled ciprofloxacin, a potent quinolone antibiotic, Alcon licensed it. Preclinical and formulation studies for ciprofloxacin ophthalmic solution and ointment began in 1987. With phacoemulsification and IOLs dominating cataract surgery, protecting the corneal endothelium became paramount, and BSS PLUS was the irrigating solution of choice. In 1983 Pharmacia, of Sweden, launched Healon in the United States. Injected into the eye's anterior chamber before IOL insertion, Healon caused the cornea to vault, thus protecting the endothelium. Healon's active ingredient was hyaluronic acid, isolated from rooster combs. Alcon ask Genzyme, a biotech company in Boston, to use its expertise to synthetize hyaluronic acid. In January 1987 Alcon and Genzyme signed a research development agreement whereby Genzyme gave Alcon exclusive rights to hyaluronic acid ophthalmic products in exchange for financial support. By licensing compounds, R&D ensured it had products for future development.[48]

Adamski came to Alcon as a medicinal chemist; with his expanded duties, he hired Billie Murray York Jr., a recent doctoral graduate from the University of Texas, to head R&D's medicinal chemistry group. Collaborating with DeSantis, York explored chemical derivatives of clonidine, an alpha-2 agonist. One, apraclonidine, reduced IOP in animals and glaucoma patients and produced vasoconstriction, much like Alcon's epinephrine products. However, apraclonidine lost potency after a few weeks of use. Research on glaucoma regarding the relationship between blood flow and vision loss indicated the risk of a vasoconstrictor in any treatment. After intense debate within R&D, the apraclonidine glaucoma project was placed on hold. However, a new indication was proposed—its use after laser surgery of the anterior segment of the eye. Normally the angle between the iris and the cornea is wide (see Appendix 1), but with a narrow or closed angle, the eye cannot adequately drain fluid and IOP increases. A common treatment for closed-angle glaucoma patients involved using a laser to punch a hole at the junction of the cornea and iris, the natural drainage site. This surgery resulted in a dangerous transient increase in IOP that apraclonidine eliminated. Thus, R&D developed 1% apraclonidine, renamed 1% Iopidine, for this use. A small volume (0.25 ml) of 1% Iopidine was packaged as a unit dose. An NDA was filed and approved in the unprecedented time of eighty-seven days, on December 31, 1987. But the debate surrounding the use of apraclonidine to treat glaucoma persisted within Alcon and the glaucoma specialist community.[49]

The outcome with apraclonidine demonstrates the value of creative in-house medicinal chemistry expertise that incorporated algorithms for computer-designed lead compound optimization. Adamski and York also established teams to better understand ocular diseases. Stella M. Robertson formed an immunology-inflammation research unit of eleven scientists (fig. 5.30), and Marjorie F. Lou's group of six biochemists studied cataracts. Pathologies of the retina and cataracts are common with diabetes. In the late 1970s, researchers hypothesized that aldose reductase inhibitors slowed cataracts and retinopathy in diabetics. York convinced management to support a program to design, synthesize, and test aldose reductase inhibitors as oral medications. The best compound was tested in normal human vol-

FIG 5.30
The R&D immunology-inflammation team members. *Left to Right:* Mari Julian, Terry Davis, Martha Jones Bill Howe, Jack Boltralik, Karen Wilson, Stella Robertson, Roger Aoki, Vicki Choate, David Scott. *Seated:* Deborah Lane (TOM, AM; photo a gift from Stella Robertson)

unteers, but this stopped due to undesirable changes in liver enzymes. After debate, R&D decided to confine development projects to topical ocular products, Alcon's expertise. It licensed the non-ophthalmic rights of the aldose reductase inhibitor portfolio to Hoechst, a German pharmaceutical company, for $2 million.[50]

Until 1982 Alcon processed patents using an ad hoc system. Scientists sent ideas to an R&D administrator, who passed them along to Alcon's legal counsel, who gave them to a patent law attorney in Chicago. At this time, patent litigation occurred in federal district and appeals courts, which often resulted in conflicting rulings. In 1982, Congress established the Court of Appeals for the Federal Circuit (CAFC). Two years later, Congress passed the Drug Price Competition and Patent Term Restoration Act, which (1) facilitated development of the American generic drug industry by allowing companies to file ANDAs based on clinical and preclinical data of products previously approved by the FDA and (2) established procedures for generic companies to challenge patent rights of the NDA holder. The CAFC reviewed increased patent litigation since owners gained confidence that they could block infringers. The ANDA legislation elevated the importance of patents for pharmaceutical companies looking to market products for an extended time before generic companies launched their products. Thus, a patent group became part of Leone and Raval's strategy to improve R&D's productivity by capturing ideas in a patent while navigating through patent rights held by others.

In 1982 R&D hired its first in-house patent lawyer, James Arno, who held a doctorate in chemistry from the University of Texas and a law degree from George Washington University. Reporting to Raval, Arno took the lead in preparing license agreements and counseled R&D scientists, resulting in a proliferation of patentable inventions. The volume of work involved in drafting, filing, and prosecuting these patents led to the hiring of additional patent counsel. Gregg Brown, a licensed pharmacist with a law degree from Drake University, came from a patent law firm in Washington, DC, and Sally Steward Yeager, a graduate of Sturm College of Law, University of Denver, soon joined as well. It became apparent that R&D personnel had little understanding of patent law. Under their tutelage, a flood of inventions led to the filing of dozens of patent applications yearly, creating a significant portfolio. The intellectual property department not only protected patents and licenses but also negotiated research agreements with universities and other entities and prepared screening arrangements, consulting contracts, and confidentiality agreements. Successful patent applications during this decade included apraclonidine, BSS PLUS, polyquad, Betoptic, Betoptic S, lodoxamide, and Tobrex. Arno's department resolved disputes amicably and resorted to successful ligation to protect Opti-Zyme, polyquad, and other products obtained in the Surgical Division's acquisition of MID-LABS.[51]

All this work required better computers. By 1982 R&D had replaced its PDP-8 with two PDP-11 and three VAX-11/785 systems, which became the mainstays of R&D digitalization into the early 1990s. Oracle served as the database program through a fourth-generation language, DATATRIEVE, which gave users flexibility to change the program for various needs. After R&D's IT created the WPC and digital databases for product stability studies, new clients sought its expertise. Analytical chemistry became a prime user since its analysis instruments had internal computers that connected to the PDP-11 and VAX systems. A chemist transferred to R&D's IT group and facilitated computerization and storage of the data collected by these analytical machines. The VAX was particularly adaptable to mathematical calculations, allowing Walter Knowles's biostatistical group to efficiently enter data from clinical studies. This led to the Clinical Science group revising its procedures for data collection and verification, and the integration of clinical data and biostatistics resulted in fewer clerical errors and rapid turnaround of reports. Schmidt, of the medicinal chemistry group, used one VAX in designing new drug molecules.

During this time, R&D installed 170 computer terminals to serve three hundred personnel. The VAX system had a word processing capability, so anyone with a terminal could prepare documents on the system. R&D even created an internal email system, the first at Alcon. This resulted in emails replacing memos and scientists composing digital drafts of reports rather than handwritten or oral ones sent to the WPC. At this juncture, the Corporate IT group began to create guidelines harmonizing the hardware and database systems used at Alcon. Nestlé also influenced the choices since it had a contract for low-cost Dell computers and Hewlett-Packard printers.[52]

In the early 1980s, the scope of scientific expertise in R&D's units was such that recognition for outstanding accomplishments could no longer be overlooked. The Technical Excellence Award was initiated by Raval in 1985 when he invited a committee of R&D leaders and a management representative to select recipients based on individual technical excellence. A monetary award and a framed bronze medallion were presented at a celebratory R&D event attended by families and colleagues (fig. 5.31). Speaking at the first annual event, Conner, Schollmaier, and Sisson recognized the accomplishments of the first six recipients.[53]

After visiting dozens of ophthalmic research centers and pharmaceutical companies, Leone concluded that eye research advances required not only the efforts of Alcon scientists but also "basic research by independent investigators associated with universities, medical schools, hospitals and other institutions throughout the world." Hence, the Alcon Research Institute was born in 1981. Unique in the pharmaceutical industry, it recognized and encouraged excellence in vision research. Independent of Alcon, an advisory committee of distinguished leaders in ophthalmology awarded unrestricted grants to researchers with significant achievements. Recipients used the awards at their discretion, their only obligations being to summarize how they applied the funds and to present their work at the Alcon Research Institute Symposium. The symposium fostered cross-fertilization of ideas and provided opportunities for Alcon to develop long-term relationships with preeminent research scientists. The initial grants were $15,000, increasing to $50,000 by 1987, making Leone's program one of the most prestigious in vision research. Leone and Raval asked Steven Podos of the Department of Ophthalmology at Mount Sinai Medical School in New York to serve as the Institute's first chairman. The initial advisory board members included Howard Leibowitz of Boston University Medical Center, Henry Edelhauser of the Medical College of Wisconsin, Bert Glaser of the Wilmer Eye Institute in Baltimore, Anders Bill of

FIG 5.31
Alcon Technical Excellence
program, July 22, 1986 (AHR)

FIG 5.32
Recipients of the 1987 Alcon Research Institute award. *Top to bottom, left column*: Gordon Klintworth, PhD, Duke University; Sohan S. Hayreh, MD, PhD, University of Iowa; Michael Wiederholt, Dr. Med., Freie Universität Berlin; Brenda Tripathi, PhD, University of Chicago; *middle column:* Ramesh Tripathi, MD, PhD, University of Chicago; Joe Hollyfield, PhD, Cullen Eye Institute, Baylor College of Medicine; George Benedek, PhD, Massachusetts Institute of Technology; Michael V. Riley, PhD, Eye Research Institute, Oakland University; *right column:* Morton F. Goldberg, MD, Illinois Eye and Ear Infirmary; Larry Takemoto, PhD, Kansas State University; Henry Kaplan, MD, Washington University; Thaddeus Dryja, MD, Massachusetts Eye and Ear Infirmary. (AHR)

Biomedicum in Sweden, and Abraham Spector of the College of Physicians and Surgeons at Columbia University. At the first symposium in April 1984, fourteen researchers received awards. Seventeen individuals got awards in 1985, fourteen in 1986, and thirteen in 1987 (fig. 5.32). By 1987 the institute had distributed $1,535,000.[54]

In 1978 Schollmaier streamlined the commercial sector into International, Domestic Operations, Owen, and F&A Divisions (fig. 5.4). The key product areas across all divisions were Ophthalmic, Vision Care, Surgical, and Dermatology. Of all Alcon's acquisitions in the past ten years, Owen Laboratories most resembled Alcon, and in six short years, Keith Lane had placed it on a path to success. Beginning in 1980, the Surgical Division was led by John Spruill, while Sisson headed Ophthalmic and Vision Care. Schollmaier thus had a team with whom he had worked for almost twenty years.[55]

Lane's towering height matched his gregarious personality, yet he listened attentively and made choices thoughtfully. His Alcon career blossomed when he revitalized business in the Los Angeles area after Schollmaier fired the sales crew in 1961. By 1978 he was an Alcon vice president and the general manager for Owen, which that year had $8 million in sales. Owen's total revenues grew to $14 million in 1982, $30 million in 1986, and $43 million in 1987. Owen's sales of prescription dermatologic products and skin, hair, and scalp formulations (fig. 5.33) justified a presence in Alcon R&D, which supported one or two dermatology projects. Its Dallas plant had reached its production capacity by 1978, so Lane bought a facility in San Antonio—Texas Pharmacal owned by Warner-Lambert. The purchase agreement included products such as the Allercreme hypoallergenic skin care line and DuBarry cosmetics. Owen agreed to make products for Warner-Lambert and became a contract manufacturer for other companies. During this time, Lane sought the advice of John Feik, who had returned from managing Alcon's Puerto Rico plant. Feik participated in the Warner-Lambert negotiations and convinced Lane to close the Dallas plant, moving all production to the San Antonio facility, now named Dermatologic Products of Texas (DPT). Several Owen products were also reformulated, but the major addition was the in-licensing of Locoid cream, a topical steroid preparation. In 1981 Lane promoted John Cannon to manage the Beauty Care group, a merger of Allercreme, Mahdeen, and DuBarry. Cannon reorganized the unit, recruited new sales and marketing personnel, and embarked on a marketing effort that included a coupon program.[56]

When Lane took charge of Owen in 1972, he relied on the sales and management skills of Steve Clark (fig. 5.34), a native of West Virginia with extensive experience with Westwood, a prominent dermatology company. Lane appointed Clark as a district sales manager and promoted him to assistant national sales manager in 1974. In 1976 he was elevated to national sales manager and in 1981 he became director of sales and marketing. By then, Lane and his staff had moved to Fort Worth, and in 1982 the Owen/Allercreme group was consolidated with the Ophthalmic and Vision Care Divisions, for which Clark became the vice president of sales and marketing.

Concerned about inventories, Sisson visited the DPT warehouse in San Antonio and concluded the problem was not Owen products but the Allercreme, DuBarry, and Mahdeen lines. He reported to Schollmaier, "That's the biggest mess I've ever seen in my life. ... The problem was we were trying to be a Max Factor or a Revlon when we had no idea about the makeup market. Everything was out of date." Buying a company with a cosmetic line was similar to Alcon's purchases of companies outside of ophthalmology. After negotiations, Cannon bought the Mahdeen and DuBarry franchises in July 1983.[57]

FIG 5.33
Owen products, 1981 (AHR)

Lane now managed the Owen and Allercreme franchises, all manufactured at DPT in San Antonio. The skin cleanser Cetaphil, a product that came with the Allercreme purchase, became a top seller. The Owen/Allercreme division returned to its roots, selling to dermatologists. However, fate intervened in December 1985 when Lane died suddenly. Schollmaier recalled that Lane "would do whatever needed doing; no job was too tough to tackle." Clark took over as vice president and general manager. Clark emphasized marketing to dermatologists and pediatricians through direct calls, telemarketing, and TV. In 1985 R&D released DesOwen, a low-potency steroid cream, which helped boost sales to $43 million by the end of 1987. Drawing Owen/Allercreme closer to L'Oréal, the R&D director of dermatology projects transferred to Nestlé and L'Oréal's Centre International de Recherches Dermatologiques in Valbonne, France, to utilize their expertise for future products.[58]

When Dave Alden left Alcon in 1977 and Schollmaier reorganized Domestic Operations, Spruill lobbied to head the Surgical Division, at the time reporting to Sisson (fig. 5.4). Having worked for Alcon since 1957, served as a district and regional manager, and

FIG 5.34
Steve Clark (AHR)

FIG 5.35
Alcon Closure System, 1982 (AHR)

FIG 5.36
Dual-cutting edge needle (Used by permission from the National Museum of American History, Smithsonian Institution)

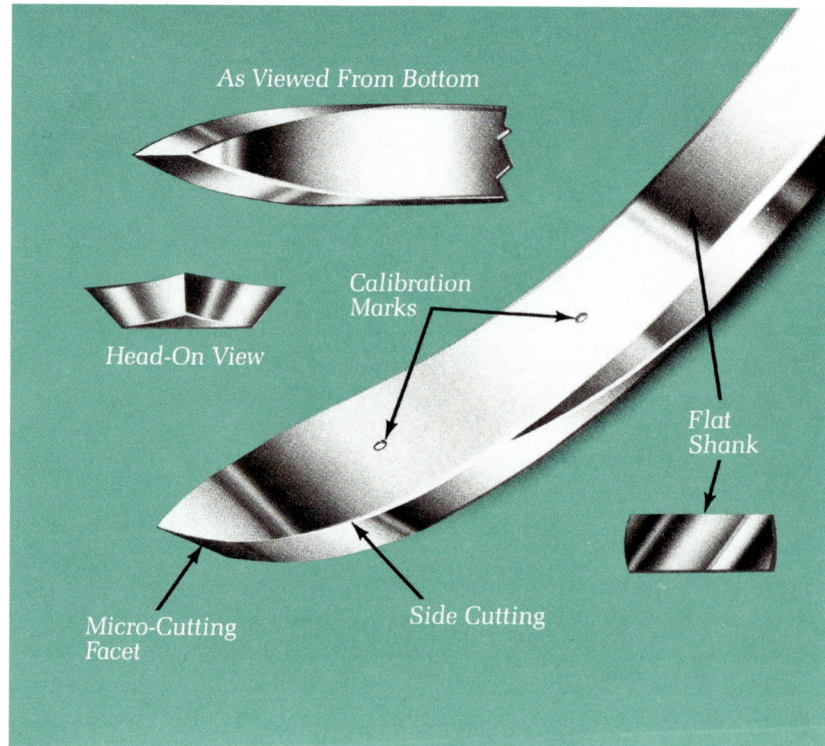

As Viewed From Bottom

Head-On View

Calibration Marks

Flat Shank

Micro-Cutting Facet

Side Cutting

attended every meeting of the AAO, Spruill knew most American ophthalmologists and understood their business. He recognized that ocular surgery was on the verge of a technical revolution. With his tall stature and booming voice, Spruill was an imposing personality who engendered loyalty. He was an effective cheerleader and team player, encouraging people to expand their horizons. Because office space on the Alcon campus was scarce, Spruill's Surgical unit settled about three miles away in a nondescript building on Bryan Avenue. Twenty-one people worked in the group, generating $7 million in sales, 10 percent of Alcon's annual revenue. BSS (15cc, 250cc, and 500cc sizes) and the Alcon Closure System (fig. 5.35), ophthalmic sutures with a dual cutting-edge needle (fig. 5.36), were the best-selling products, but Miostat, an irrigation solution to constrict the pupil, and sponges for wicking the surgery area were also popular. All were single-use products. Nondisposable items included stainless-steel eye surgical instruments, scopes for examining eyes, and devices for measuring the IOP and curvature of the cornea.[59]

Cataract removal had become the most common eye surgery, followed by surgery of the retina. Cataract surgery underwent a remarkable revolution in the 1970s and 1980s. Instead of extracting the entire lens, surgeons began removing just the cloudy protein center, leaving the capsule in place. Charles Kelman, MD, developed this simple, safe process, known as phacoemulsification. It involved inserting a steel probe into the lens capsule, and when the probe vibrated at a high frequency, the lens fractured and the fragments were aspirated using an irrigation solution. Now empty, the capsule was ready to accommodate an IOL, the second major advancement. This new technique opened the door for other developments. Physiologists discovered irrigating solutions that protected the iris and the corneal endothelium. Then viscous materials, injected into the anterior chamber at the time of surgery, vaulted the cornea, keeping it out of contact with the sonicating probe and IOL. During this time, Spruill guided Alcon in acquiring companies with technologies to build a better phacoemulsification machine and create improved IOLs. Alcon R&D also worked with physiologists, chemists, and formulators to design the safest irrigation solution and injectable viscous material.[60]

Alcon's Surgical Division joined the phacoemulsification trend. The first phacoemulsification device, the Cavitron/Kelman, had been introduced in the 1970s by the Cavitron Corporation (fig. 5.37). Initially, phacoemulsification was controversial, but by 1979 it was standard practice. The technique requires a large amount of irrigation solution and Cavitron's president, Bill Freeman, approached Spruill to provide BSS in large-volume bottles.

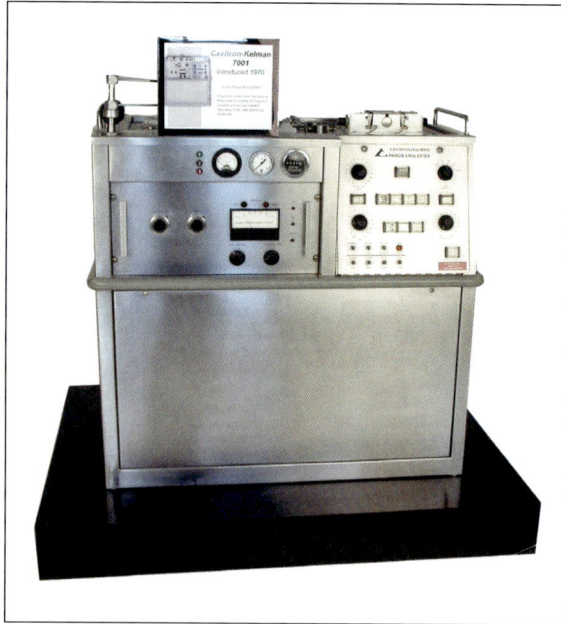

FIG 5.37
Cavitron-Kelman phacoemulsification machine, ca. 1970 (Alcon Museum, Irvine, CA)

In response, Alcon R&D released two sizes, 250 cc and 500 cc. At the time, BSS PLUS was still in clinical trials, but with its approval in October 1981, it became the primary irrigation solution used in cataract and other ocular surgeries. Sensing an opportunity to tie BSS and BSS PLUS to the Cavitron/Kelman device, Maury Rester, the QA manager in the Surgical Division, collaborated with a supplier and created a surgical set with disposable tubing and tips for aspiration, irrigation, and sonicating that worked only with Alcon products; it was sold as the Alcon Surgical System. To ensure that it was a one-use product, Alcon packaging engineers designed the rubber closure to be punctured only once. CooperVision acquired Cavitron, and Freeman continued to improve the phacoemulsification machine and develop other devices for eye surgeons. Though CooperVision and other companies launched products, BSS prevailed in the ophthalmic irrigation solution market until Alcon's BSS PLUS dominated sales, thanks to pioneering in vitro studies by corneal physiologist Edelhauser, unique clinical studies, and superb marketing.[61]

Long-term strategy and resource management is a feature of every industry. Alcon R&D used a prioritization process that was tested in 1974 when Schollmaier asked Raval to narrow his ongoing key projects to three from twelve. Ophthalmology and contact lens projects had priority over surgical and dermatology projects. O. J. Lorenzetti, PhD, directed R&D's surgical projects and had limited resources available. Schollmaier met annually off-site with his top managers to discuss strategic issues. When Spruill requested more support of surgical projects, Schollmaier argued that larger profits came from ophthalmic prescription products. Thus, Spruill faced a conundrum. He intended to use the purchase of CooperVision in 1984 to break through this R&D resource logjam; when the FTC vetoed the sale, Spruill changed tack.[62]

Advances in the design of IOLs occurred in response to the introduction of phacoemulsification. Up to 1984, IOLs had a diameter of six or seven millimeters, thus requiring a large incision in the cornea for insertion. This changed in 1984 when Tom Mazzocco designed and inserted a foldable silicone IOL through a three-millimeter incision. When the CooperVision deal fell through, Spruill focused on buying four ophthalmic surgical enterprises. In the second week of 1985, he signed an agreement to purchase Eye Care, a manufacturer of IOLs. That spring Alcon acquired VXTRA, which produced surgical packs, knives, blades, and disposable and reusable micro-instruments for ophthalmology (fig. 5.38). For years, Spruill's group had sourced the Alcon Surgical System and knives and other surgical kits from VXTRA. To showcase these acquisitions, Spruill hosted Schollmaier's annual conference in Nashville, where the executives toured the new facilities and met the employees (fig. 5.39). In September 1985, Alcon acquired MID-LABS, which manufactured a cataract lens irrigation and aspiration device and a cutting and aspiration machine for vitreous and retinal surgery. Both used disposable tubing and handpieces and BSS or BSS PLUS. Next, Spruill acquired Sharpoint, the supplier of Alcon's Closure System components (fig. 5.35). Along with BSS PLUS, the Closure System franchise had been a mainstay of the Surgical Division's revenue growth since the 1960s. Each of these acquisitions brought a range of products, manufacturing facilities, technical expertise, sales forces, and patent portfolios. Exploring beyond ophthalmic surgical instruments, in October 1987, Alcon acquired Ivy Technologies, which marketed a computer-based office management system; Alcon renamed it the Alcon System.[63]

FIG 5.39
Schollmaier's executive conference, Nashville, 1985. *Left to right*: George Leone, Robert Montgomery, Ed Schollmaier, Tim Sear, John McIntyre, Dick Sisson, John Spruill. (AHR)

Acquisitions are team efforts, and although Spruill was the chief negotiator, he recognized the importance of advice from marketing, R&D, manufacturing, legal counsel, tax experts, patent attorneys, and human resources. Negotiations could be long and arduous. Elaine Whitbeck, an associate general counsel, recalled that "during the Sharpoint deal, we didn't even go to bed." She worked most of her Christmas holiday that year. On a trip to Sharpoint in rural Pennsylvania, the plane slid off the runway in a storm. Kay Miles told the other team members, "You can fly back but I am not getting on that plane." The negotiations also revealed insight into Spruill's values. He told Whitbeck, "While I respect all the hard work that goes into all of the documents that you write, if I cannot end my negotiations with all parties feeling good, because I have to have a long working relationship with them going forward, then I haven't done my job right." This represents an example of concern for other people, a factor that engendered loyalty.[64]

The variety of companies Alcon acquired illustrates how rapidly technology changed ocular surgery. When Spruill took charge of the Surgical group, it sold stainless-steel hand instruments, sutures, and irrigation solutions. It also marketed examination scopes and instruments to measure the eye. The new companies gave Alcon access to new materials and

FIG 5.38
Alcon's sterile, disposable I-Knife
(Used by permission from the
National Museum of American
History, Smithsonian Institution)

technologies for example, lasers. Such technologies required electrical engineers, polymer chemists, mathematicians, physicists, light technologists, computer programmers, and a host of others.

The earliest ocular applications of lasers were for retinal abnormalities such as tears, detachments, and increased blood vessel growth, often seen in diabetic patients. Being transparent, the vitreous humor of the posterior eye lends itself to laser therapies, and by the 1980s the argon laser emerged as the common tool to treat retinal abnormalities. Several manufacturers sold an ophthalmic argon laser. For the general public, lasers also became synonymous with LASIK in the 1980s, a technique used to sculpt the cornea and eliminate the need to wear glasses. Several individuals had patents for LASIK procedures, including pioneers like Francis A. L'Esperance and Steven Trokel. Improving vision in such a way was an exciting development, and in 1985 Cagle in Alcon R&D organized a symposium in Fort Worth with L'Esperance as the main participant. In 1986 L'Esperance cofounded Taunton Technologies, which, in conjunction with L'Esperance Research Institute, intended to commercialize the excimer laser for the eye. Alcon Surgical signed a joint venture with both enterprises.[65]

The efforts of an ophthalmologist in the Department of Ophthalmology at the University of Western Australia in Perth attracted the attention of Alcon's general manager there, who notified Tim Sear. Even by the early 1980s, smaller incisions and a low-profile IOL coupled with phacoemulsification represented a quantum leap for cataract surgery. The search of Graham Barrett for a biocompatible material led to hydrogel, a chemical relative of PMMA used for hard IOLs and contact lenses. Hydrogel absorbed water and became soft and pliable. Locating a supplier of purified hydrogel, Barrett designed a single-piece IOL and implanted the first in 1983. The following year Sear and Lorenzetti proposed to Barrett that Alcon develop his IOL. Barrett moved to Fort Worth and participated in finalizing a single-piece 6 mm concave optic, while R&D conducted safety evaluations on the material and the Nashville IOL facility developed a sterile manufacturing process and conducted stability studies. Lorenzetti and Barrett led training sessions and Alcon began clinical studies in the United States, Europe, and Japan. Modifications led to a foldable model of Barrett's hydrogel IOL, trademarked as IOGEL. In late 1987, IOGEL was launched in Europe and surgical demonstrations were made at the AAO and the recently organized American Society of Cataract and Refractive Surgery. In an industry milestone, Alcon marketed a truly commercial foldable IOL.[66]

Before 1987, 80 percent of ocular surgery was performed by 20 percent of ophthalmologists. Four years after Spruill took charge, he hired Vern Feltner, the former president of Searle Medical Specialties. As director of surgical sales and marketing, Feltner made several recommendations, one being to create prepackaged kits and surgical trays for specific procedures, particularly cataract surgery. Alcon acquiring Sharpoint and VXTRA provided the impetus to create customized surgeon packs. These included BSS, BSS PLUS, Miostat, the Alcon Closure System, and other disposable products. When the contracting company could not meet demand, it became a learning experience for Alcon. After Spruill bought VXTRA, it began to assemble the packs and by 1987 the Surgical Division produced and sold them regularly to about four hundred ocular surgeons.[67]

The Surgical Division's staff and Alcon surgical representatives (ASRs) totaled twenty-one when Spruill became director in 1977. Six years later, there were forty-five ASRs and forty staff in Fort Worth (fig. 5.40); another two hundred fifty employees came with acquisitions in 1985 and 1986. Spruill integrated the new companies, placing all marketing and sales personnel under Feltner's direction and relying on experienced staff as product managers. Henry Meadows, the Surgical Division's controller, recalled that integration went smoothly. Spruill left plant managers in place, and they merged their operations into

FIG 5.40
Alcon Surgical personnel, Fort Worth, June 25, 1985 (AHR)

FIG 5.41
Alcon sales by product group, 1987 (TOM, AM)

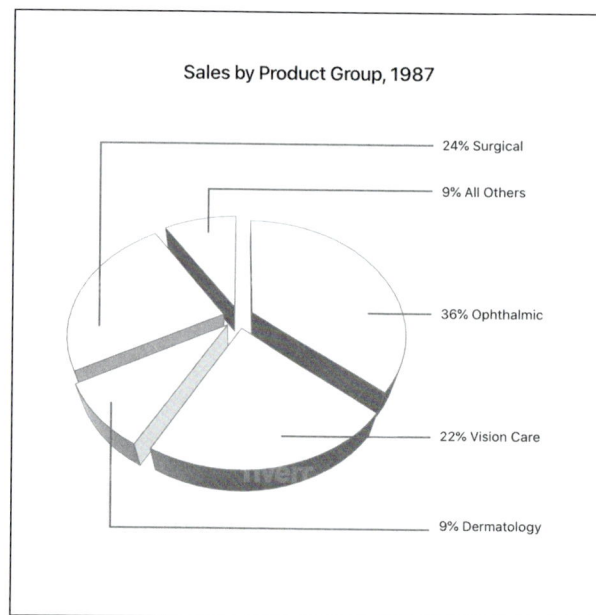

Sales by Product Group, 1987

24% Surgical

9% All Others

36% Ophthalmic

22% Vision Care

9% Dermatology

Alcon's culture, including the matrix concept. In general, their contributions were the products they brought with them; their R&D activities were minimal. By 1987 acquisitions had boosted the profile of the Surgical group, with its sales making up almost 24 percent of total Alcon sales, laying the groundwork for Alcon's largest acquisition in 1989 (fig. 5.41).[68]

The Surgical Division chronicled its growth in the 1980s and 1990s. It had monthly magazines with articles about projects, products, and personnel, while Surgical scrapbooks provided a pictorial history of people and events. The first female ASR, Laura Ziegler, joined in 1981, and by the end of 1983, women were 10 percent of the ASRs. Hired in 1985, Joy Miller became a leading ASR. Each year, the top salesperson for each product category was recognized at the division's annual sales conference in Hawaii, Mexico, or the Caribbean (fig. 5.42). By 1987 Russia had become an innovator of a surgical procedure, keratomileusis, that eliminated the need to wear glasses. In December 1987, Spruill, joined by Baker of International, led a team of development experts to Russia to explore opportunities there.[69]

The Surgical group's anticipated growth prompted Schollmaier to make significant organizational changes in June 1982. He consolidated the dermatology division under Sisson and separated the Surgical Division as a stand-alone group reporting to him. He further focused Alcon resources on ophthalmology and minimized them on specialty products—Avicon, Webcon, and Lafayette. Spruill's group occasionally promoted Avitene, but Schollmaier disbanded the Webcon and Lafayette sales force and marketed their products via direct mail and journal advertising. Schollmaier also explored opportunities to divest Alcon of these assets acquired by Conner in the 1960s and 1970s.[70]

Under Sisson (fig. 5.4), the Ophthalmic and Optical groups expanded their range of products and markets. During this time, Optical became Vision Care in 1985. The Ophthalmic group marketed prescription eye drops, while Vision Care marketed contact lens products, OTC decongestants, and artificial tears. In 1983 Sisson began publishing *Scope*, which chronicled the people, products, and activities of his two dynamic groups.

FIG 5.42
Surgical division national sales meeting, 1981, Puerto Vallarta, Mexico (AHR). A handsome group *(left to right)*: Bob Grantham, John Van Dyke, Daryl Dubbs, Dave Chappel, Barry Gladys, John Spruill. Seated: Greg Booher, Jack Marshall.

FIG 5.44
Jack Weightman and
Diane Smith (AHR)

FIG 5.43
Blaise McGoey (AHR)

Next to Schollmaier, Sisson most influenced the direction of Alcon's Ophthalmic and Vision Care sales and marketing organizations. The 1979 Burton, Parsons acquisition proved to be a watershed event, not only for its successful contact lens products but also for its failures. Burton, Parsons lacked scientific expertise and had a lackluster sales and marketing organization. Sisson needed new, talented leadership and in 1980 he hired Blaise Landry McGoey (fig. 5.43) as the national sales manager, soon promoting him to director of sales and marketing. Before joining Alcon, McGoey had twenty-one years of experience in sales and marketing at Dorsey Laboratories and Winthrop Laboratories. Clifford Jack Weightman (fig. 5.44), a colleague of McGoey at Winthrop, also joined Alcon in 1980 as the national key accounts sales manager. In 1982 Weightman became the director of sales in the Optical group and, when Vision Care formed in 1985, Sisson promoted Weightman to vice president to manage it.[71]

For seventeen years, Sisson, McGoey, and Weightman propelled Alcon to record sales in the American ophthalmic pharmaceutic, OTC, and contact lens solutions markets. R&D contributed new products, as Rick Rheiner, an MSR, district manager, and product manager recalled: "At Alcon ... we always had one new product to launch every 2 years. And boy, I've got to tell you, that made a difference. A new product launch was a big thing." McGoey and Weightman deserve credit for revamping and energizing Ophthalmic and Vision Care sales and marketing. At first, Sisson used a blended sales force, as MSR Dave Sakamoto later characterized it. Rheiner described his typical day as a rookie MSR in 1981: "The first year we had call standards of about 10 sales calls per day. It was five ophthalmologists a day to talk about the prescription pharma. Then we had to see three optometrists, where we would talk about the contact lens care. And then we were also to make two retail or wholesaler calls." Product managers handled multiple products; for example, Roy Buchanan was responsible for OTC artificial tears and prescription mydriatics. By 1985 this approach proved unworkable, especially after R&D released Opti-Soft and Betoptic, new products for different users. Sisson divided his group, Ophthalmic led by McGoey and Vision Care by Weightman, each with its own sales and marketing organizations.

Weightman had the more complex challenge: how to effectively market to optometrists and contact lens–prescribing ophthalmologists while building consumer demand and filling shelves in groceries, pharmacies, and other merchandisers. He put Norb Walter in charge of sales to eye doctors, and Ed Paule got the optical accounts. For the consumer business, Mike Hemric became sales director and Sue Faro headed the marketing research group. In effect, Weightman built his team of nearly two hundred almost from scratch (fig. 5.45). Initially he took twelve MSRs from the Ophthalmic Division and hired the remainder. Dave Sattler, an MSR, district manager, and national accounts manager, characterized Weightman as follows: "Jack was bold, had a customer-focused mentality, and was extremely driven. The culture he created helped us to get through some of the more difficult times and be prepared for when we had good products to really excel in the marketplace." Weightman's loyalty to the people in his division motivated them to excel.[72]

Equally important in the formation of the Vision Care Division was the proliferation of low-cost optometry chains in the late 1970s and 1980s, which shifted customers away from ophthalmologists. In 1978 the FTC removed restraints on advertising prices by eye care dispensers, leading to the increase in optical chains providing affordable optometric services. By 1982 there were almost two thousand optical chain stores in the United States that dispensed about 50 percent of contact lenses. In 1984, of 12,500 licensed ophthalmologists in the country, only about 20 percent fitted contact lenses or glasses. By comparison, there were 22,000 licensed optometrists, of whom 80 percent owned their own practices, and about 20 percent worked for optical chains. The challenge for Vision Care was to serve the needs of both independent and chain store optometrists. At the same time, ophthalmologists remained a significant customer base as some specialized in dispensing contact lens, even forming the Contact Lens Association of Ophthalmologists. Thus, Vision Care MSRs had a diverse group of eye care specialists to service. To attract new

New Product Introduction Meeting

Patrice Joyce, Chicago Area Mgr.; Sal Coco, Washington Regional Mgr.; Kenny Moore, St. Louis Area Mgr.; Dan Webster, Cleveland Regional Mgr.; Donna Heggart, San Francisco Area Mgr. Three new area managers seek advice from the pro's, Dan and Sal.

Jack Weightman, Vice President & General Manager/Vision Care Group discusses the creation of Vision Care Group and reorganization of Alcon's Lens Care business.

(L to R) Sue Faro, Marketing Mgr.; Les Lewis, Eastern Field Mgr.; Fran Kostuk, Lavey/Wolff/Swift Agency; George Neal, Western Field Mgr.; John McIntire, Lavey/Wolff/Swift Agency.

(L to R) Stan Sussan, Boston Area Mgr.; Sal Coco, Washington Regional Mgr.; Mike Sabella, New York Area Mgr.; Chris Gensemer, Cincinnati Area Mgr. at beach party.

Janet Campbell, Sales Promotion Manager, presenting the selling material to Consumer Division for Opti-Soft.

(L to R) Frank Corbett, Corbett Inc.; Ron McGhay, Director of Market Planning/Lens Care; Jack Weightman, Vice President and General Manager/Vision Care.

The National Sales Meeting brings together Advertising, Sales and Marketing with John McIntire, Lavey/Wolff/Swift; Janet Campbell, Sales Promotion Mgr.; Ron McGhay, Director of Marketing; Linda Carlson, San Francisco Regional Mgr.

Director of National Accounts, Jerry Davidson and Tampa Regional Mgr., Ray Peal, discuss sales strategies for Alcon's new products.

FIG 5.45
Members of the 1985
Vision Care team (AHR)

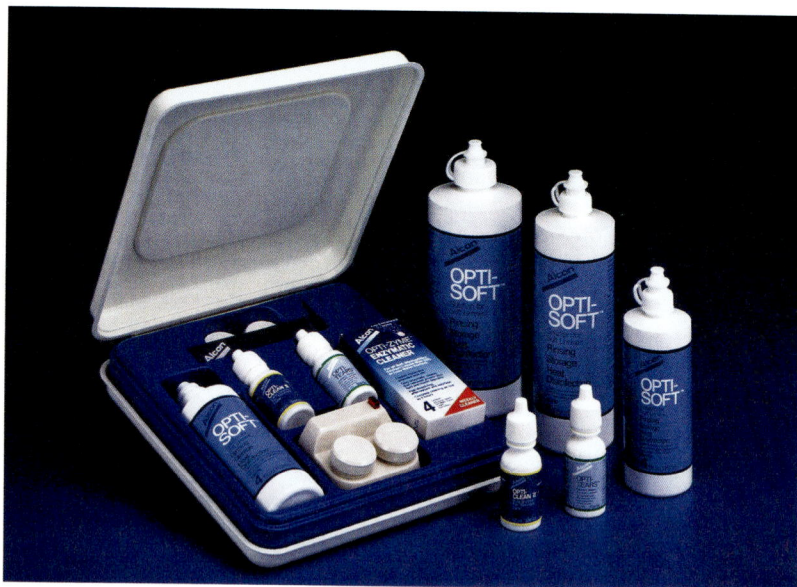

FIG 5.46
Starter kit for the Opti-Soft System,
product launch, 1986 (AHR)

contact lens users, Alcon MSRs dispensed starter kits (fig. 5.46) to optometrists and ophthalmologists, who gave them to new users as a free item or sold them as part of the lens package. The starter kits of course held Alcon disinfecting, storage, and wetting solutions.[73]

Changes in the laws concerning contact lens dispensers created a daunting distribution problem for Vision Care's MSRs. During the 1980s, drug wholesalers and independent drugstores decreased while chain pharmacies grew. Moreover, chain grocery stores established pharmacies, and mass merchandisers, such as Wal-Mart, began selling OTC products and contact lens solutions. Using their strong purchasing power, they bought directly from pharmaceutical and contact lens care product manufactures. Whatever the venue, Alcon's Vision Care competed for shelf space, and as the number of products increased, so did the competition.[74]

Having a relationship with optometry schools became important. After the Ophthalmic Division restarted the Senior Eye Residents Visiting Alcon program for fourth-year residents in ophthalmology, the Vision Care group clamored for an equivalent outreach to future optometrists. In March 1986 Bill Rhue, in charge of professional relations, organized a pilot conference of New Optometrists Visiting Alcon (NOVA). Graduating optometrists and their professors from the University of Houston College of Optometry were invited for a three-day visit, initiating a monthly program of introducing new optometrists from across the United States to Alcon products. The NOVA program also affected the Ophthalmic Division. Optometrists throughout the nation lobbied state legislatures to allow them to write prescriptions for topical eye medications, a right heretofore reserved to ophthalmologists. By 1987 most American optometrists could write prescriptions for many Alcon medications.[75]

Despite there being a dozen competing products for soft lens care, none ensured adequate disinfection without heat. Alcon R&D changed that. In 1975, the company had launched Tears Naturale, an artificial tears therapy that earned $1 million within two years. Ten years later, R&D released an improved version, Tears Naturale II (fig. 5.47), using Alcon's proprietary new preservative and disinfectant, polyquad. Alcon's successful Opti franchise Opti-Zyme and Opti-Clean were enhanced by polyquad. The FDA also approved

R&D's contact lens disinfectant solution containing polyquad, Opti-Soft, but with limitations. An extensive advertising campaign on television and in publications boosted the sales of Opti-Soft, Opti-Clean II, and Opti-Tears products (fig. 5.48) by 60 percent over the previous year. One television advertisement featured the then-unknown actor, Sharon Stone.[76]

The Vision Care group faced a formidable obstacle: Alcon was the only company selling contact lens care products without offering a line of lenses. Alcon converted this into a position of strength by establishing relations with the soft lens companies, making its Opti-franchise the standard for soft lenses. The launch of Opti-Soft in 1986 did not do well because labeling limits tempered the product's acceptance by eye care specialists. The FDA initially approved Opti-Soft's use only in conjunction with heat. Moreover, the FDA did not approve its use with high-water content lenses, an increasingly popular group. As Dave Sattler recalled, "1986 was not a good year." The launch of Opti-Soft was Janet Campbell's first as a product manager; many years later, she recounted how painful it was. But Opti-Soft, while a disappointment, brought changes, as R&D increased efforts to overcome its limitations, finally succeeding in 1988. Meanwhile, Weightman's team capitalized on Opti-Clean II's reputation, switching cleaning products in competitors' starter kits. Weightman's MSRs excelled and by the end of 1987 Alcon controlled 10 percent of the domestic market; it had sold one million starter kits and overtook Allergan as the number two vendor of contact lens care products (fig. 5.49). Sales of Vision Care products totaled 22 percent of Alcon's annual revenue, which by 1987 increased to $107 million, up from $28 million in 1981 (fig. 5.41). Vision Care initiated an annual program of recognizing top sales performers. Meeting in Maui, the first thirteen members were initiated into the Ring of Honor.[77]

The ultimate success of products resulted from key management changes. Schollmaier's vision for Alcon resembled a three-legged stool, held up by Ophthalmic, Surgical, and Vision Care products (fig. 5.4). At first the three domestic groups reported to Sisson, who took charge in 1977. He and Schollmaier intended for Kleiman to lead the Ophthalmic Division. Kleiman's health deteriorated, so Sisson directed the Ophthalmic group, along with other responsibilities. Then in 1985 McGoey took charge as Ophthalmic's general manager and Vision Care went to Weightman. Management then divided the sales force into two parts (Ophthalmic and Vision Care), with two different missions under different leaders. These changes had to have been daunting; that they were implemented with ease reveals McGoey's and Weightman's management skills, communication, and determination. Their close relationship at the same previous employer for fourteen years surely helped. A dozen other experienced personalities also played central roles in the Ophthalmic Division during this decade.[78]

FIG 5.47
Tears Naturale II (AHR)

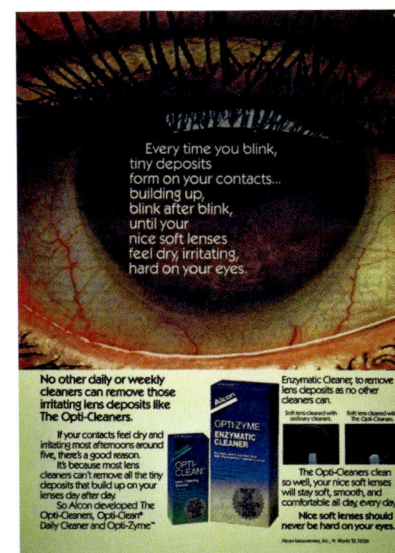

FIG 5.48
Opti-Zyme and Opti-Clean, advertisement (Faro, AM)

FIG 5.49
OptiFair Trade Show, Anaheim, CA, 1987.
Left to right: Bob Burchik,
Eric DeWert, Dave Sakamoto,
Barbara Brennan, Paul Kerstein,
Dave Sattler. (AHR)

In 1980 Kleiman hired Bill Burns, a Slippery Rock University graduate with ten years' experience selling and marketing Norwich Eaton Pharmaceuticals' oral antibiotics to urologists. With FDA approval of Tobrex imminent, Kleiman tasked Burns with developing a marketing plan. Tobrex, a broad-spectrum antibiotic, was a breakthrough, though it was the second aminoglycoside marketed for ophthalmic infections. Schering-Plough, of Kenilworth, New Jersey, had also discovered a potent aminoglycoside, gentamicin, and developed an ophthalmic formulation, Garamycin. Alcon R&D's clinical studies compared Tobrex to Garamycin and found Tobrex to be superior in eradicating ocular infective bacteria, with fewer side effects. Excited about Tobrex, Burns collaborated with Cagle, who led the clinical studies. It was the first time an R&D scientist played an integral part in launching a product. As a breakthrough therapy, Tobrex was the ideal candidate to foster this type of relationship.[79]

Burns produced an eye-catching brochure profiling Tobrex, highlighting its groundbreaking qualities (fig. 5.50): 95 percent effectiveness against a variety of ocular infections and a low incidence of side effects. Once the FDA granted approval, the manufacture of Tobrex proceeded, and early in 1981 the Ophthalmic sales force organized distribution to retail pharmacies in the United States. Cooperation between the sales force and drug wholesalers enabled Tobrex to reach retailers quickly. MSRs learned about the new product in July at regional sales meetings. Sales and marketing embarked on a wide campaign, using journals, direct mailings, and sales promotions. Tobrex was highlighted in the 1981 and 1982 AAO meetings. The December 1981 issue of Alcon's employee publication, *Alcon World News*, discussed the cooperation between R&D, RA, QA, Manufacturing, sales, and marketing. Schollmaier noted at the time, "It is this teamwork which has achieved the present excellent results and which has established a basis for success of future products." It also justified Schollmaier's and Raval's efforts to keep R&D isolated from marketing during product development. The quality of Tobrex and the intense marketing and sales campaign made it the first choice among ophthalmologists for treating common eye infections.[80]

The next product manager, Rick Johnson, took charge of promoting Tobrex in 1983, and for the next several years Tobrex took center stage at AAO annual meetings. Johnson developed promotional strategies beginning in February 1983 with a feature on Eyesat, a dedicated satellite channel offering ophthalmic continuing education. A year later, a video setup in the Conner Center featured Schlech and Cagle profiling Tobrex. For the first time, Alcon sent to ophthalmologists Drop-tainers labeled "Physician's Sample," which contained a small amount of Tobrex. By now, Tobrex sales had accelerated. District manager Bob Nelson recalled, "That product had a lot of advantages over the competition, and once we started getting physicians writing pre-op instructions for it, I mean the product just took off." In addition to ophthalmic surgeons, a new campaign in 1986 promoted Tobrex in the pediatric and family practice specialty markets. Every year through 1987, Tobrex had double-digit sales increases, becoming the Ophthalmic Division's best-selling product in 1986. Such was the demand that it had to be manufactured in Alcon's Puerto Rico plant.[81]

Selling pharmaceuticals is difficult since the result is not immediate; convincing an ophthalmologist is only successful if at some later date they prescribe the product. MSRs had to be tenacious, seldom taking no as the final answer. For example, Joe Barranco, Alcon's Chicago MSR in 1983, tried to see a female ophthalmologist in her office regarding Tobrex. Told to return later, Barranco encountered the doctor in the elevator and for the next two-and-a-half minutes, as the elevator descended, extolled the virtues of pre-operative Tobrex to her along with a dozen other people on the elevator; his pitch was successful. The launch of Tobrex coincided with the introduction of cost-based formularies in hospitals and insurance plans; a prescription product had to be listed in a formulary to be prescribed. It was imperative that Alcon's products were listed, and this responsibility fell to MSRs and district managers. The University of California formulary was one of the largest and most influential in the country, so it was a seminal achievement when Oakland MSR Winford Horsley succeeded in having Tobrex replace Garamycin on the list. Four years after its launch, Tobrex overtook Garamycin as the most prescribed ophthalmic anti-infective ther-

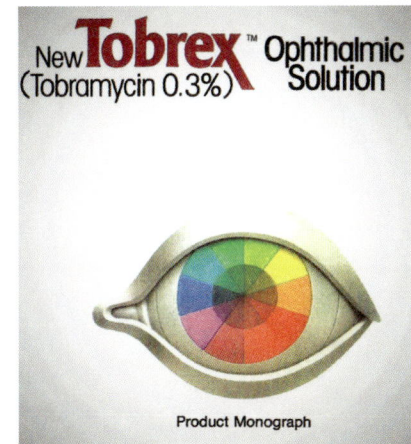

FIG 5.50
Tobrex, product monograph, 1981 (AHR)

apy in retail pharmacies. Tobrex sales and marketing efforts paid off when it became one of the top 200 prescribed medications in the United States; in 1985, Tobrex was number 166 and Maxitrol 176.[82]

Tobrex's great success was a result of Alcon scientists and managers thinking and acting creatively. Any new medication introduced second in the market faces a challenge to overtake the leader. Using innovative clinical designs, the Tobrex product profile gave the MSRs and marketing staff a competitive edge. The safety of a new therapy can be just as important as its efficacy. Tobrex had fewer ocular side effects than Garamycin, and it was not as toxic as the recently released chloramphenicol eye drops by another competitor. Alcon learned the critical importance of timing the product launch; the first shipments of Tobrex came about three months after the FDA's final approval. The experience with Tobrex supported Schollmaier's contention that a medical specialty company had advantages over a broad-based pharmaceutical company: Alcon MSRs interacted with eye care specialists more often and more intensely than Schering-Plough could with Garamycin; Alcon knew the ophthalmic market better; and Alcon was an expert in its specialty, not a generalist like Schering-Plough. Lessons learned with Tobrex prepared Alcon's management for the next breakthrough therapy.[83]

As discussed in chapter 4, Pilocarpine eye drops had been the mainstay of glaucoma treatment since the late nineteenth century. Instilled four times per day, they controlled IOP, but blurred vision was an unfavorable side effect. In the mid-1970s, Alcon R&D made a breakthrough: twenty-four-hour IOP control with its patent-protected 4% pilocarpine gel formulation. The FDA approved Pilopine HS Gel on October 1, 1984. Anticipating approval, the marketing team highlighted the new therapy at the 1983 AAO, which summarized the multicenter clinical study conducted by eighteen recognized glaucoma specialists. The principal investigator, Alan Mandell, and five other investigators attended the exhibit, which fifteen hundred ophthalmologists visited. Shortly after Pilopine HS Gel's approval, Mandell and other glaucoma specialists took part in a videotaped roundtable discussion at a Fort Worth television station, noting that Pilopine HS Gel in a single nighttime dose controlled IOP for twenty-four hours with almost no daytime visual disturbances.

Pilopine HS Gel was Alcon's first unique glaucoma therapy, and McGoey's marketing team planned novel ways to introduce it (fig. 5.51). In March 1985 the national sales meeting heavily emphasized the product. Eighty-five MSRs and twelve district managers attended the five-day program. They reviewed the promotion material, developed a sales narrative, and heard presentations from ophthalmologists and R&D researchers. The at-

FIG 5.51
McGoey's marketing and sales team planning the Pilopine HS launch, 1984. *Left to right*: Blaise McGoey, Len Schweitzer, James Bond, Steve Clark, Rick Johnson, Bob Grantham. (AHR)

tendees toured the Conner Center and manufacturing facility and were feted that night at a formal dinner, where Schollmaier emphasized the "importance of top performance with each new product and how top performers further fuel sales growth and profit growth." Joe Theismann, an All-Pro quarterback for the Washington Redskins, delivered a motivational speech.

The scope and format of this Pilopine HS Gel national launch meeting evolved from the experience gained by selling and marketing Tobrex. Timing the introduction of a new product is fraught with uncertainty, and selling Pilopine HS Gel turned out to be difficult. Like Tobrex with Garamycin, Pilopine had a competitor, Timoptic, an effective glaucoma therapy administered in twice-daily drops without causing any blurring of vision. Creating more problems for the sales team was the delivery system of pilocarpine: a gel. Administering a quarter-inch strip of the gel onto the eye was different than applying drops; as district manager Rheiner recalled, "It was a unique and different delivery concept that the ophthalmologist was unfamiliar with." Moreover, Alcon's next breakthrough glaucoma therapy was in the final stages of FDA approval. Steve Clark, national sales director, declared at the meeting that "a sense of urgency must drive each representative's activities now. Pilopine HS Gel must be established quickly because Betoptic is just around the corner."[84]

In 1977, with sales of $8 million, Isopto Carpine had become Alcon's top product and held two-thirds of the American pilocarpine market. At its inception, R&D developed Pilopine HS Gel to replace Isopto Carpine. However, as already discussed earlier in this chapter, the nonselective beta-blocker Timoptic transformed the dynamics of the glaucoma market. Due to pilocarpine's side effect—blurred vision—until 1978 only patients with high IOP and vision loss were candidates for eye drops. The large patient population labeled as ocular hypertensive without vision loss waited until their vision deteriorated before being treated. With no ocular side effects, ophthalmologists began to prescribe Timoptic eye drops for ocular hypertensive patients. Thus, the size of the United States glaucoma market increased from about $16 million in 1978 to over $100 million by 1987, a trend seen worldwide.

Shortly after Timoptic's introduction, ophthalmologists reported serious pulmonary and cardiovascular reactions, including several deaths. In addition, Timoptic often caused a decrease in heart rate, raising concerns about its use in patients with cardiovascular diseases. This is where Betoptic had an advantage. Betoptic did not affect respiration or heart rate. Beginning in 1979, R&D's Clinical Science department conducted exhaustive studies and trials on Betoptic, the scope and complexity of which had not been seen to date. Physicians and scientists published in journals and presented their results at conferences, so the stage was set for Alcon sales and marketing to capitalize on the attributes of their breakthrough therapy, Betoptic (fig. 5.26).[85]

After filing the NDA in April 1984, Horger, head of RA, requested an expedited review of Betoptic due to its safety profile and the problems associated with Timoptic. The FDA granted Horger's request, triggering a plan to ship the first production lot of Betoptic days after approval. Led by Len Schweitzer, the Betoptic Coordinating Committee, representing R&D, Manufacturing, QA, RA, and Marketing, met weekly to secure approved labeling, packaging components, and raw materials in time for the launch. Instead of a national sales conference, Schweitzer chose to profile Betoptic in two regional sales meetings, one for the eastern territory, one for the western, both in late July. He understood that to sell Betoptic effectively, the MSRs had to understand beta-blocker pharmacology and pulmonary and cardiovascular physiology. Two clinical investigators joined Alcon scientists to present and discuss Betoptic's pharmacology and clinical data. The public relations program reached a broad array of media—television, radio, newspapers, magazines, and trade publications— the centerpiece being a media tour by four Betoptic clinical investigators. A press conference was held in New York at which Betoptic press kits were distributed. Television stations reported the news and ran patient interviews, as did newspapers across the country. For the media tour, fifteen markets were selected, based upon population and presence of glaucoma. In television, radio, and newspaper interviews, Betoptic investigators discussed glaucoma and the need for regular pressure checks. They highlighted the advantages and safety of Betoptic to potential patients. Alcon's preparation succeeded. Approved on August 30, 1985, Betoptic was shipped to distributors days later amid much fanfare (fig. 5.52).[86]

Sisson was fully involved in the Betoptic launch since McGoey was attending the AMP at Harvard. Speaking to MSRs, Sisson exclaimed that Betoptic was the "most exciting event in his 26 years at Alcon." The Alcon booth at that fall's AAO prominently displayed Betoptic's clinical results (fig. 5.53). Besides sales and marketing personnel, R&D members attended to respond to scientific inquiries, and Cagle presented a keynote address to Alcon's Advisory Council. Primed with their recent launch of Pilopine HS Gel, MSRs left the sales meetings determined to make Betoptic succeed. For example, Long Beach MSR Cristina Lea and her district manager teamed up to reverse the policy of a large chain pharmacy, Thrifty Drug, against automatically distributing new products. Learning of Betoptic's safety advantages and Alcon's pricing, Thrifty Drug's vice president of operations ordered shipments to all 147 pharmacies. Success stories abounded; Giles Williams in Kansas City convinced one ophthalmologist to immediately switch four hundred patients to Betoptic. By April 1986, forty-five states had added it to their pharmacies' welfare formularies, as had most hospitals in major population centers. When the Professional Health Plan added it to its formulary, MSRs Liz Leighton in Saint Paul and Stephen Wigg in Minneapolis notified hundreds of ophthalmologists. By the end of 1986, Betoptic owned 20 percent of the ophthalmic beta-blocker prescription market in the United States.[87]

While a 20 percent market share in eighteen months was impressive, growth leveled off toward the end of 1986. Sales and marketing promoted Betoptic for its safety and low price. The increase in pulmonary safety was easily recognized, but anecdotal comments from patients about cardiac benefits were harder to quantify. With sales plateauing, Schollmaier wanted to vividly illustrate Betoptic's cardio-sparing effect, which led to the Brick Campaign. He recalled his fraternity initiation ritual in which each pledge was required to carry a brick for one week, which was physically and mentally fatiguing. He recounted the

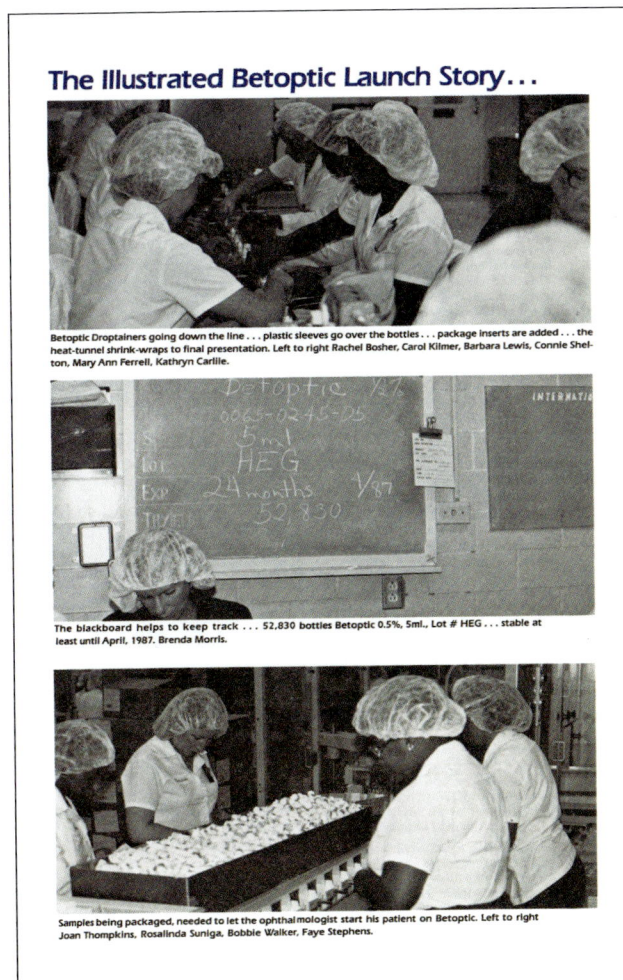

The Illustrated Betoptic Launch Story...

Betoptic Droptainers going down the line . . . plastic sleeves go over the bottles . . . package inserts are added . . . the heat-tunnel shrink-wraps to final presentation. Left to right Rachel Bosher, Carol Kilmer, Barbara Lewis, Connie Shelton, Mary Ann Ferrell, Kathryn Carlile.

The blackboard helps to keep track . . . 52,830 bottles Betoptic 0.5%, 5ml., Lot # HEG . . . stable at least until April, 1987. Brenda Morris.

Samples being packaged, needed to let the ophthalmologist start his patient on Betoptic. Left to right Joan Thompkins, Rosalinda Suniga, Bobbie Walker, Faye Stephens.

FIG 5.52
Betoptic launch in Manufacturing, September 1985 (AHR)

FIG 5.53
Betoptic launch, AAO San Francisco, Sept. 29–Oct. 3, 1985 (AHR)

FIG 5.54
Betoptic brick campaign materials, 1987 (AHR)

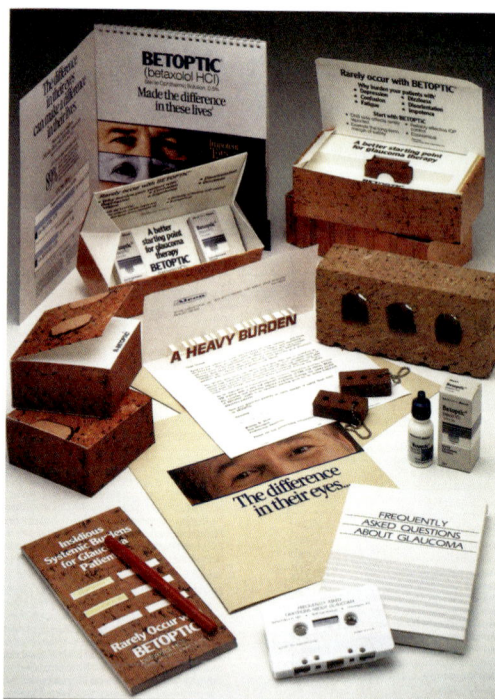

moment he explained his plan to Sisson and McGoey. He put a brick on his desk, at which point "[McGoey] said, 'What's the brick?' That was the idea. I said, 'I want you to carry this brick everywhere you go for a week. When I see you, I want to see that brick. At the end of the week, we're going to talk about the brick.' Blaise said, 'I'll do it.'" Back in Schollmaier's office a week later, McGoey complained about the brick and wanted to get rid of it. Schollmaier's brilliant idea led to MSRs carrying around a brick to plop on each doctor's desk; the doctor would inevitably inquire about it. The brick represented the cardiac burden carried by Timoptic users that was relieved by Betoptic (fig. 5.54). The campaign garnered lots of attention and, by the end of 1987, Betoptic sales had grown to 25 percent of all glaucoma prescriptions in the United States. The sales approach did not appeal to all MSRs, so Schollmaier reluctantly discontinued it in 1988, though he regretted doing so. In any case, by the end of 1987, Betoptic generated $25 million in revenue and marketing was poised to launch the next generation, Betoptic S.[88]

Total revenue for 1987 for the Ophthalmic Division grew 20 percent over the previous year to almost $100 million. Betoptic, Tobrex, Maxitrol, Pilopine HS Gel, Tears Naturale II, and older products such as the Isopto Carpine franchise drove these record sales. Alcon had a 20 percent share of this therapeutic market in the United States, ranking first in unit share and second in total dollar share. The product mix illustrated an emphasis on innovation and resolve from R&D and sales and marketing. The experiences of launching Pilopine HS Gel and Betoptic laid the groundwork for the next decade, when R&D released a new product every year.[89]

Continuing the tradition begun by Conner and Alexander, McGoey recognized top-performing MSRs and district managers. Top performers joined the prestigious President's Club (fig. 5.55) during a weeklong celebration set in Acapulco or Ixtapa, Mexico; Bermuda; Maui; and Barbados. The pinnacle of the week was the presentation of the impressive President's Club ring.[90]

To expand Alcon internationally, Buhler bought local companies in different countries. He also contracted the manufacture of Alcon's products with reputable pharmaceutical companies and dispersed them through overseas distributors. Limitations to his approach emerged when R&D began developing unique therapies and consumer products for eye care. More plants stretched Alcon's QA system, leading to centralization from Fort Worth for Manufacturing and QA. Early in his Alcon career, Buhler had hired Van Kets to manage EURMEA, and he created a nucleus of competent country managers. Buhler's hiring in 1970 of Sear, who took charge of CAFE and LACAR regions, proved to be wise. As

FIG 5.55
President's Club, 1987 (AHR). *Back row (left to right):* Kent Andiorio, Paul Day, Tom Dooley, Ruben Carrillo, Tom Skiff, John Gregoire, Melissa Bruchmann, Gordon Lazarus, O.J. Hart, Jim Niewarowski. *Front row (left to right):* Bob Nelson, Gene Bruchok, Ron Pepe, Rick Rheiner.

1978 began, Sear, Van Kets, and Buhler managed International Operations (fig. 4.52). That year Nestlé moved its Alcon-Nestlé legal corporation to Cham, Switzerland, where it occupied the old offices of the Anglo-Swiss Condensed Milk Company. Baker, whom Buhler assigned to integrate Farmila, relocated to Cham to manage Alcon Pharmaceutical Limited, a subsidiary of Nestlé.[91]

During this time, more individuals who would have crucial responsibilities joined Alcon. The 1982 retirement of Kologe, Alcon's CFO and head of the F&A Division, was one of many changes. Buhler became a senior vice president and led F&A. Schollmaier appointed Sear as vice president of International. Van Kets had left Alcon in 1980; Baker succeeded him and divided EURMEA into two parts, with Xavier Yon managing the northern half and Giorgio Vescovo the south. Sear appointed Bill Kwan to direct CAFE and LACAR to Carlos Taborda. Sear also convinced Helmut Horchler to leave his country-manager role in Germany to direct marketing in Fort Worth. Thus, by 1982, Sear had established his own management team for the International Division (fig. 5.56). In 1985, when Baker returned to the United States, EURMEA consolidated under Vescovo. Juana Rosa Lorenzo came back from Belgium to lead International's human resources department, with Gilberto Cardenas directing the International legal group and Gene Estes, QA.[92]

Horchler and his family landed in Texas in December 1983, and he jumped into his role as director of international marketing. Born in Germany, raised and educated in Los Angeles, Horchler had returned to his homeland and worked in pharmaceutical sales until hired in 1976 by Van Kets to be the country manager of Alcon Germany. In Fort Worth, Horchler had grand ideas for three new products in the pipeline and envisioned marketing campaigns for established products. As a country manager, he had operated somewhat independently, so it came as a shock when he realized his proposed $200,000 budget and staff additions were unrealistic. He encountered Alcon's frugal environment and lengthy approval process for advertisement materials, which included RA, R&D, legal, and other entities. Nevertheless, he and his small staff began to develop promotional materials, giving marketing personnel options to use in their regions. He made his first trip to Mexico and South America and came to respect LACAR's diligent work ethic and the rapport MSRs had with physicians. He surprised Alcon employees in Asia when he asked to join them in the field rather than going on sightseeing tours. Horchler realized the importance of having a local person as the country's general manager, a practice he found uncommon with Nestlé subsidiaries. The scope and quality of booths at national and international meetings improved by importing materials and ideas from Fort Worth and overseas countries. In October 1984 Horchler organized the first worldwide Vision Care marketing managers meeting in Fort Worth and established regular area-wide marketing managers conferences. He promoted competition by helping to launch the first European Cup contest in 1986 for outstanding sales by a country.[93]

FIG 5.56
International management team, Cancun, Mexico, 1982. *Standing, left to right*: Giorgio Vescovo, Allen Baker, Tim Sear, Helmut Horchler, Xavier Yon; *sitting, left to right*: Bill Kwan, J. C. Martin, Carlos Taborda. (AHR)

Horchler and his department assisted Alcon Italy in organizing the XXV International Congress of Ophthalmology of 1986 in Rome. The conference was attended by five thousand eye specialists. Alcon's three-thousand-square-foot booth emphasized the size of the company, its leading role in ophthalmology, its research orientation, and its focus on ethical ophthalmic products. Alcon featured Pilopine HS Gel, Betoptic, and Tobrex, and presented information on Suprofen, BSS PLUS, and IOGEL. Seven R&D scientists made presentations and nine clinical investigators reviewed their studies at two Alcon-sponsored symposiums. Every registrant received a Betoptic brochure. Alcon's presence continued at two satellite meetings, one on glaucoma in Turin, and the second on contact lens care in Taormina. Flying home, Horchler wrote, "Our whole layout focused on service to ophthalmology and was easily the best and most impressive at the congress. Alcon's presence there was an historic one for the company, and Rome was an appropriately historic venue for the presentation of Alcon's position in the world of ophthalmology." Taking advantage of the AAO fall meeting, which many international ophthalmologists attended, international marketing held its first SERVA-style program, Senior Ophthalmologists Visiting Alcon (SOVA) in November 1986, which included a contingent of Dutch glaucoma specialists.[94]

Alcon's presence in EUMEA continued to evolve as leadership changed. Shortly after hiring Horchler in 1976, Van Kets had expanded his area to include Eastern Europe and the Soviet Union. Sales to Eastern European pharmacies and physicians were hampered by byzantine bureaucracies and a lack of currency, so Horchler focused on OTC products. When Horchler joined Alcon, its German division employed just four managers, two secretaries, and six salesmen. He had to clean up the inventory when Alcon sold Lawton Instruments, and he inherited a Munich manufacturing plant with logistical problems when Alcon purchased Burton, Parsons. Melding the two sales and marketing groups presented an extra challenge. To complicate matters, sales of Isopto Carpine tumbled when Timoptic entered the market. When Horchler went to Fort Worth, Marja Kaleva, a long-term Alcon employee and originally an MSR in Scandinavia, then the general manager in the UK, replaced him. She dealt with the unenviable task of laying off personnel at the Munich plant when Alcon moved the manufacture of contact lens care products to Spain in 1987. By then, however, West Germany had grown to the third largest pharmaceutical market in the world, and Alcon sales there approached $20 million.[95]

In 1977 Van Kets hired the energetic Xavier Yon as general manager of Alcon France; Yon became the vice president of Alcon Northern Europe in 1982. His area became particularly effective in selling Alcon's dermatologic products. After Germany, France was the most important ophthalmic market in Europe, and Alcon owned a key manufacturing plant in Rumilly. Then in 1984 Alcon purchased Produits Ophtalmique Stériles (POS), Kaysersberg, France, which manufactured ophthalmic, contact lens care, and dermatologic products (fig. 5.57). The acquisition increased Alcon's market share, giving it the number two position in France. But, as in Germany, integrating two sales and marketing organizations presented challenges. And questions arose about the plant in Rumilly, which produced redundant product lines. The Kaysersberg facility also used a manufacturing process that formed, filled, and sealed a container simultaneously. Francois Vaucheret, Alcon's most experienced plant manager in France, oversaw the expansion of this technology to other lines. Spain's role in Alcon's future centered on Alcon Iberhis's relocation to Alcobendas, a Madrid suburb, in 1984. Thierry Clidiere was hired in 1983 to manage the relocation and grow

Alcon's presence in Spain. Enrique Chico, an experienced pharmaceutical engineer, oversaw the plant, which shipped contact lens care solutions worldwide. In 1979 Van Kets hired Sten-Åke Källmarker, a Lederle executive, as general manager for Alcon in Scandinavia. For the growing Netherlands market, Van Kets hired Georges Laffineur in 1972, and by 1983 he was the general manager there.[96]

In 1978 Baker hired Giorgio Vescovo, a chemist with extensive experience selling in the Soviet Union, Eastern Europe, and the United States. Introverted and intelligent, Vescovo had a sly sense of humor. When Baker left Cham in 1982, Vescovo set up his regional office there. With Horchler's departure from West Germany, Eastern Europe was added to Vescovo's territory, which already encompassed Italy, Greece, Austria, Switzerland, Egypt, and the region of North Africa, Middle East, and Central Asia (fig. 5.58). During this decade, Alcon Italy had two general managers, but the most dynamic was Giuseppe LaMacchia, who had been responsible for marketing, product registration, and the Farmila plant, which Alcon sold in 1984. LaMacchia launched Tobrex in Italy and organized Alcon's presence at the XXV International Congress of Ophthalmology held in Rome in 1986.[97]

Van Kets and Baker deserve full credit for recruiting high-caliber teams that moved Alcon from being reliant on European distributors to dominating European ophthalmic markets with its own companies within each country. Each built local organizations that launched new products, sold existing products, and even established a presence in the dermatologic market. In launching Tobrex, Betoptic, and the IOGEL lens, Alcon transitioned from a company with offices in different countries to being a European company. RA and R&D took part in this transformation. Horger's RA group organized a registration dossier that fit most countries' requirements and prepared RA managers to understand the importance of a global product profile. R&D's Clinical Science group set up studies in Europe with ophthalmologists, cardiovascular and pulmonary physicians, and opinion leaders. Patricia Zilliox, a scientist from the POS acquisition, built the R&D Clinical Science unit in Europe.

FIG 5.57
Produits Ophtalmique Stériles, Kaysersberg, France, 1980 (Courtesy of Joseph Spittler, Obernai, France)

FIG 5.58
Vescovo's team in Cham, Switzerland
Back row; left to right: E. Hoedt,
G. Vescovo, D. Binzegger, E. Galliker,
I. Matt, D. Marbach, R. Staub, B. Grünig,
K. Diethelm; *Middle row, left to right:*
J. Vicki, E. Meyer, U. Knobel, E. Steinmann,
A. Huber, B. Bürgi, R. Schildknecht, W.
Simonsen, V. Cajthaml, R. Lüönd, B. Bark;
Front row, left to right:
S. Betschart, D. Colonnelli, W. Hölzle,
H. Steidel, C. Henchoz, M. Spirig,
R. Morgen, Y. Oguz. (Vescovo
correspondence, TOM, AM)

Each country required separate registration for each product, necessitating visits to each government's regulatory agencies. Collaboration with Fort Worth RA and R&D facilitated Betoptic's approvals in over fifty countries in just three years. In fact, West Germany, Switzerland, and Belgium launched Betoptic in 1985, at the same time as the United States (fig. 5.59). Most other European countries approved Betoptic the following year, leading to simultaneous launches across EURMEA. Horchler assigned Frances Brotherhood to spearhead this effort. She collaborated with marketing managers all over Europe and arranged dozens of roundtable discussions, press interviews, and seminars at ophthalmology society meetings where two leading glaucoma experts, two well-known pulmonologists, an ocular physiologist, and the vice president of Clinical Science (fig. 5.60) profiled Betoptic. The effort demonstrated the maturity and expertise of the EURMEA organization built by Van Kets, Baker, Vescovo, Yon, and the country managers. Driven by Maxitrol, Tobrex, Betoptic, contact lens care products, and dermatologic products in 1987, Alcon Spain's sales reached almost $10 million, West Germany's $20 million, and the UK's $7 million, while EURMEA's annual revenues totaled $117 million (fig. 5.61).[98]

Having no experience in Latin America when he took charge of LACAR in 1975, Sear visited the area frequently to familiarize himself with business in the region and to understand Alcon's position. Brazil, Argentina, and Mexico, where Alcon had manufacturing plants, contributed the most to sales. Sear respected Dionisio Garcia (fig. 5.62), Mexico's manager, and Carlos de Socio (fig. 5.63) in Argentina. Concerned about the Brazil country manager, Sear replaced him with the marketing manager, Carlos Taborda, in 1981. This triumvirate formed the core leadership in LACAR. In Argentina, Sear met Carlos Alejandro Coscia (fig. 5.64), who began as an MSR and became the country's marketing manager. In 1978 Coscia transferred to Uruguay when Alcon acquired Laboratorios Micron, a small, influential ophthalmic company. When Sear became vice president of the International Division in 1981, he appointed Taborda to lead LACAR with Coscia, now in Venezuela, covering Ecuador, Colombia, and Peru, Alejandro Edwards in Chile, and Leon de Chateauvieux covering Central America and the Caribbean. Taborda relocated to Fort Worth, and when Alcon Venezuela closed due to government interference in pricing products, Coscia joined him there. In the meantime, Coscia hired country managers with pharmaceutical experience: Javier Martínez in Ecuador; José Vega, Colombia; and Rodrigo Echeverry, Peru. When de Socio retired in 1985, Sear employed Roberto Quiróz, another experienced pharmaceutical executive, to manage Argentina.[99]

Coscia's experience in Uruguay represents an example of the talent his generation brought to LACAR. By Alcon's standards, Laboratorios Micron's manufacturing facilities were primitive and its annual sales were low, about $150,000. Moreover, the Uruguayan government did not allow the importation of finished products. Like Conal, Laboratorios Micron also made one-off products for about 150 Uruguayan ophthalmologists. Coscia found a local plastic company to fabricate Alcon's Drop-tainer and contracted with Roussel Uclaf, a French pharmaceutical company, to manufacture Alcon products in Uruguay. Over time he converted the 150 ophthalmologists from their unique products to Alcon's line, mainly Isopto Carpine, Maxitrol, Maxidex, Tears Naturale, Naphcon, and Statrol. Within one year, sales had

Launching Betoptic Internationally

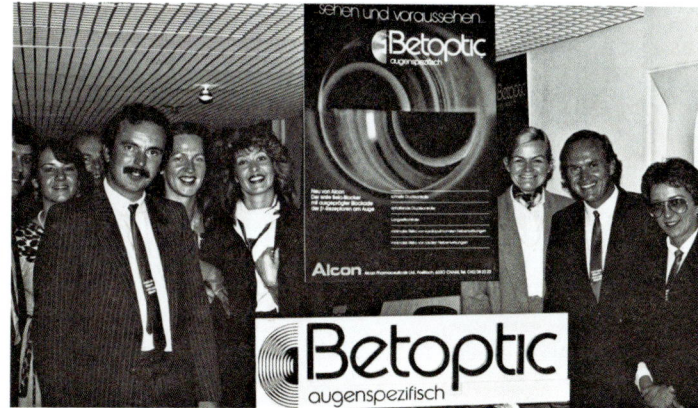

FIG 5.59
Betoptic launch, EURMEA, 1985 (AHR)

FIG 5.60
Betoptic launch, Belgium, 1986 (AHR). Professor Schoene *(far right)*, making his presentation at the Belgium Betoptic seminar, is shown here with fellow panelists *(left to right)*: T.O. McDonald, Alcon R&D; Dr. De Vos, Belgian pulmonologist; and Professors Polanski, USA; Weinreb, USA; and Demailly, France.

Geographic Distribution of Sales, 1987

24% EURMEA

6% LACAR

6% CAFE

62% Total U.S.

2% Japan

KEY:
CAFE - Canada, Far East
LACAR - Latin America, Caribbean
EURMEA - Europe, Middle East, Africa

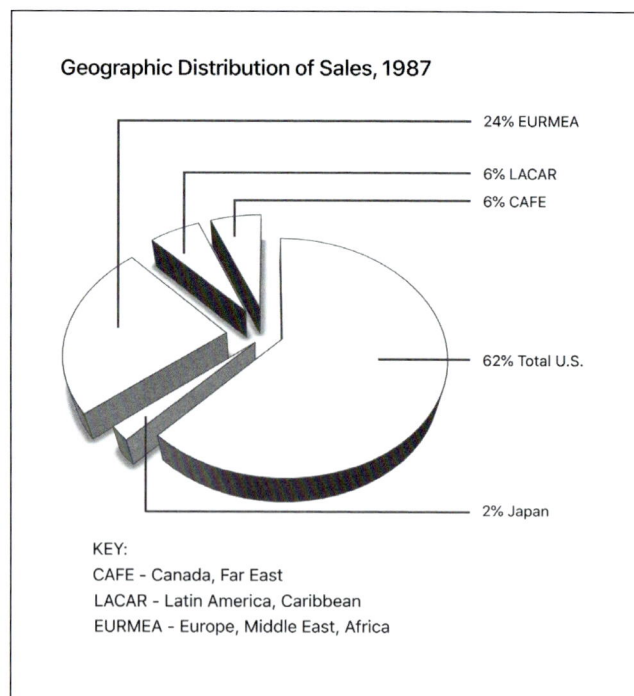

FIG 5.61
Geographic Distribution of Sales, 1987
(TOM, AM)

grown to $1 million and Alcon became the premier ophthalmic company in Uruguay.[100]

Buhler used Alcon's manufacturing competence in Mexico, Argentina, and Brazil, and strong marketing and sales teams, to develop distribution systems throughout LACAR. Needing a larger plant in Brazil, Alcon in 1981 acquired Biosintética, a pharmaceutical company with modern manufacturing facilities in São Paulo. Taborda moved the country's office there and divested the non-ophthalmic products in 1984. In March 1986 Alcon Mexico bought Laboratorios Ufarmex, a company selling ophthalmic and ENT products. Thus, throughout LACAR, Alcon developed a strong infrastructure and attained a dominant market share through acquisition.

While each country in the region had unique challenges, all were affected by fluctuating currencies. The advantage of Alcon doing its own manufacturing meant that its costs and revenues were tied to the local currency. But imported products from the United States had costs set in American dollars, which meant selling in the local currency was not always profitable. Alcon's established products up to the 1980s used common, low-cost ingredients, with Maxitrol, Naphcon, Tears Naturale, and the Isopto franchise making up the bulk of sales. For example, Isopto Carpine sold for about two dollars in Mexico. Once breakthrough products that required expensive raw materials, like Tobrex and Betoptic, came on the market, LACAR faced the dilemma of whether to manufacture locally or import. Fortunately, by this time most of the LACAR region had simplified registration for new ophthalmic pharmaceuticals. With proof of FDA approval, LACAR countries' regulatory agencies allowed new products to be marketed in their countries. Tobrex, Betoptic, Opti-Zyme, and Opti-Clean were launched with strong promotions in each country. In Colombia, Alcon flew a hot air balloon with the Betoptic logo (fig. 5.65) while Brazil boasted that Betoptic was the beta-blocker for the future.[101]

Most LACAR countries had active ophthalmology societies, which Alcon attended with its booths and products. Alcon LACAR considered itself the house for ophthalmologists, figuratively and literally. The company provided a full range of products for eye care specialists. In this decade, most LACAR countries transitioned from distributors to Alcon subsidiaries with their own offices and marketing capabilities. Alcon's LACAR offices were always open for any ophthalmologist to visit, and they often served as venues for associa-

FIG 5.62
Dionisio Garcia, inducted
into Alcon Hall of Fame,
1996 (Courtesy of Alcon)

FIG 5.63
Carlos de Socio, inducted
into Alcon Hall of Fame,
1989 (Courtesy of Alcon)

FIG 5.64
Carlos Coscia (AHR)

tion meetings. These gatherings became training opportunities, further embedding Alcon's products. Following Conner's lead, Buhler and Sear maintained a presence in the PAAO. Like Conner, Sear was a board member of its foundation. Even with currency insecurities and other issues, LACAR contributed 6 percent, $29 million, of Alcon's 1987 annual revenues.[102]

In 1978 offices in Canada, Taiwan, South Korea, Philippines, Singapore, New Zealand, and Australia formed the core of CAFE, with significant sales of Alcon's products. However, Alcon also had a presence in Malaysia, Thailand, Indonesia, Burma, and Hong Kong. Ding de Jesus managed Alcon Philippines and arranged for products to be shipped to nearby countries from a local manufacturer. Eric Noble managed Australia and New Zealand. Sear hired Jeanne Lim Kah-Cheng, known as "Jeanne Chen," to manage Singapore, T. J. Chen in Taiwan, and Y. K. Lee in South Korea. By 1987 T. J. Chen made Alcon the dominant ophthalmic company in Taiwan. Each of these individuals had a unique background, but Jeanne Chen's is the most inspiring. As the only daughter among four sons, Chen insisted on a high school education but failed to convince her father to allow her to attend a university. Hired by a local pharmacy in Singapore, she retailed cosmetics and OTC drugs. Selling

FIG 5.65
Betoptic launch, Colombia,
1987 (TCA; AHR)

more Alcon contact lens solutions than any of her peers at any pharmacy, she came to Sear's attention, and he hired her in 1978. Her sales and managerial successes became legendary.[103]

Like in other international regions, Maxitrol, Naphcon, and the Isopto franchises constituted the bulk of the ophthalmic pharmaceuticals sold in CAFE. Most countries launched Tobrex soon after its approval in the United States. South Korea, Taiwan, Hong Kong, and the Philippines approved Betoptic in mid-1986, so Brotherhood organized another promotional tour by two United States physicians and an R&D scientist. Most countries had streamlined the regulatory process for approval of medical devices, facilitating the launching of IOGEL throughout most of CAFE. By the 1980s contact lenses had become widely used, and thus Alcon's contact lens care solutions found receptive markets. For the most part, a local manufacturer and Alcon's Canadian plant supplied the products sold in Asia, though Alcon's American plants shipped surgical products—needles, BSS, BSS PLUS, and others. In 1985 Canada fielded surgical sales and marketing teams, a concept that others mimicked. Alcon's CAFE subsidiaries also sold Owen's dermatological products, shipped from Texas and Canadian plants. In 1987 the International Division sold eleven million dermatological units.[104]

International diplomacy during the 1970s led to the opening of China for business enterprises. Alcon saw China's one billion inhabitants as a potential market. In December 1984 an Alcon team visited Beijing and Shanghai and met with major optical manufacturers, government officials, and health professionals. In November 1986, at the International Ophthalmology Conference in Guangzhou, Canton, Alcon displayed Betoptic, Alcon Closure System Sutures, BSS PLUS, and intraocular lenses. Invited by the president of the Beijing Union Medical Center College Hospital in 1986, Leone and Raval toured seven medical centers, exploring the scope of their ophthalmic research. These ventures became the first footholds for Alcon in China.[105]

Alcon initially entered Japan in 1973 with its joint venture with Teijin, so in 1978 when the Japanese government relaxed its foreign investment regulations, the joint venture became a wholly owned subsidiary of Alcon. Schollmaier and Sear journeyed to Tokyo to celebrate this milestone and convinced Hideya Ono to lead Alcon Japan as its general manager (fig. 5.66). By 1983 Japan had become a large pharmaceutical market of $96 billion, second only to the United States at $143 billion. By then, Ono's organization had grown to twenty-eight people, with offices in Tokyo and Osaka. Japan had an elaborate process for the registration and approval of pharmaceutical products, but less involved procedures for devices and OTC products. Thus, Alcon Closure Sutures, ophthalmoscopes and pneumatonographs, and OTC products, such as Tears Naturale, drove Alcon's sales into the 1990s. Japanese authorities also set prices for prescription medications, traditionally rewarding innovation. Until Betoptic, Alcon's line of ophthalmic pharmaceuticals was mostly low-priced generic drugs that competed with local products, so importation was unprofitable. In the case of BSS PLUS, Alcon licensed its development to Santen Pharmaceutical Company, Japan's leading ophthalmic enterprise. Alcon chose to develop and register Betoptic and Opti-Free as its initial proprietary entries into the Japanese ophthalmic market. In 1986 Alcon R&D hired Hiro Matsuda, an experienced pharmaceutical researcher at Rohto Laboratories, to head the clinical studies group in Osaka. Lou Horger, head of Alcon RA, also hired a regulatory expert. Registering Betoptic and Opti-Free for sale in Japan proved to be a multiyear learning process for Alcon.[106]

FIG 5.66
Alcon Japan, 1978. *Seated, left to right*: Hideya Ono, Ed Schollmaier, Kabuki actor, Rae Schollmaier, Kabuki actor, Frank Buhler, waiter; *standing,* unknown Alcon Japan employees and waiters, *fourth from left*, Tim Sear. (Courtesy of Taylor Schollmaier)

By 1987 twenty-four hundred people worked in the International Division, up from thirteen hundred seven years earlier (fig. 5.67), an increase reflecting the growth of Alcon globally. In 1977 International sales totaled $77 million, which grew to $125 million eight years later and to $185 million, 38 percent of Alcon's total revenue, by 1987 (fig. 5.61). EURMEA led with 63 percent of International's revenues, followed by CAFE, then LACAR. By 1987 Betoptic was the second biggest selling ophthalmic product in the division and the sale of surgical products was the fastest-growing product line, though contact lens care solutions had increased by 22 percent in the previous year. Clearly, International was integral to Alcon's future prosperity.[107]

Beginning in 1970, Kologe led Alcon's F&A. His financial and legal teams negotiated acquisitions and divestures, and at his instigation the incorporation of Nestlé in Delaware resulted in tax savings for both Alcon and Nestlé. He spent four years integrating Alcon's global entities into Nestlé's corporate structure, then in 1981 announced his retirement. Schollmaier appointed Buhler as his replacement; Montgomery came with him as a vice president and CFO. Buhler had hired the Australian in 1976 and put him in charge of EURMEA's finance department. For more than a decade before joining Alcon, Montgomery worked for KPMG, a global accounting firm, in Papua New Guinea, Australia,

FIG 5.67
International division personnel
in Fort Worth, 1987 (AHR)

Europe, and the United States. Shortly after Nestlé bought Alcon, Montgomery moved to Fort Worth, becoming director of F&A in the International Division before following Buhler to his new job.

Schollmaier tasked Buhler with locating buyers for Alcon's Lafayette group and Konsyl, a daily psyllium fiber that came with the Burton, Parsons acquisition. Buhler found a few buyers, who made meager offers, so he proposed buying the two businesses. With Schollmaier's endorsement, he worked out an agreement with Nestlé and in 1983, at the age of fifty-eight, retired from Alcon. With Buhler's deal, only two of Conner's non-ophthalmic 1960s acquisitions remained—Avicon and Webcon.[108]

Schollmaier appointed Montgomery as senior vice president and put him in charge of F&A; he continued as Alcon's CFO. He had definite ideas on organization, staffing, and functions in his division with Schollmaier's matrix management system affecting him the most (fig. 5.68). In 1982 Alcon had one in-house legal counsel for litigation and general matters and used a patent attorney in Chicago. Montgomery hired John F. McIntyre, an experienced pharmaceutical attorney, as corporate legal counsel, and McIntyre recruited Elaine Whitbeck and Kathleen Knight as associate legal counsels (fig. 5.69). Whitbeck and Knight handled a diverse caseload that included acquisitions, divestitures, contracts, and litigation. Gilberto Cardenas became the chief lawyer in the International Division, while James Arno joined to establish a patent group in R&D. Consistent with the matrix management system, Raval interviewed patent attorney candidates and sought Montgomery's consent in his decisions. Rick Fleck, head of the Human Resources department, placed a representative in each division to harmonize policies and procedures. Montgomery revamped the finance department with Scott Arena, treasurer; John Goodman, tax; Dan Schneiderman, controller; and George Morey, audits. Illustrating the complexity of the matrix organizational structure, each of these departments had representatives in the countries where Alcon had a plant or large presence. Each division also had a controller: Henry Meadows, Surgical; Charles Miller, International; and Jerry Rutherford, S&T. To manage costs, Montgomery overhauled the travel department by contracting with an outside firm that stationed agents in-house to handle airline and hotel reservations.[109]

Montgomery decided the corporate IT department, which mainly supported sales, marketing, and administrative functions, "was in total disarray, bordering on collapse." To rebuild IT, he recruited Dennis Beikman, a graduate of the Illinois Institute of Technology and the University of Chicago's School of Business, with twenty-two years of experience administering information services with G. D. Searle, Baxter Laboratories, and Hyland Laboratories. Beikman discovered Alcon had the classic IT function: systems development, data center operations, and data entry. As he described the situation, "Our receivables were nine months in arrears. We couldn't get sales figures to the field sales force to pay commissions. Errors here, errors there. .... We had programmers leaving left and right. It was a total mess." Fortunately, two current employees, Nick Tsumpis and Tom Caraway, understood the problems. Beikman installed a program with online interactive capabilities allowing decentralized data entry by users, for which he implemented training sessions. He used leaders of dispersed IT units as business system managers for each client group, and they collaborated to determine needs throughout Alcon. RAMIS, a fourth-generation programming language that allowed a user to build a database for a specific need, was crucial to the plan. Alcon participated in the time-sharing Order Net system, used by pharmaceutical distributors and wholesalers to

FIG 5.68
Finance and Administration organization, Las Vegas, 1986.
Left to right: Robert Montgomery, John McIntyre, Scott Arena, Dennis Beikman, Rick Fleck, Dan Schneiderman, George Morey, John Goodman. (AHR)

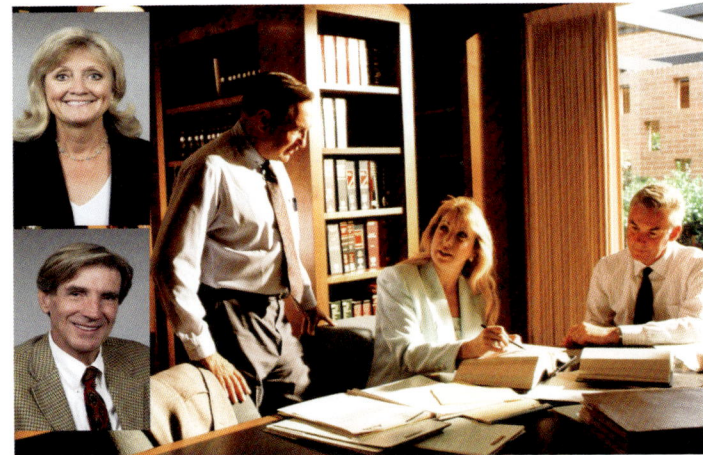

FIG 5.69
Alcon legal team. *Left to right*: Gil Cardenas, Elaine Whitbeck, John McIntyre; *insets*: Kathleen Knight, James Arno. (AHR)

FIG 5.70
Alcon Jamboree for
the AAO, 1987 (AHR)

place orders with manufacturers. Soon, about 40 percent of Alcon's orders went through OrderNet. After assessing Manufacturing's systems requirements, IT selected a program that enhanced "just in time" ordering of materials and components. Beikman installed the ROLM telephone switch to automatically direct calls to extensions, making the PBX obsolete. Realizing the necessity of interconnectivity between buildings on the Fort Worth campus, IT laid fiber-optic cables in time for the opening of the Alexander Tower. By 1985, when Beikman attended Harvard's AMP course, IT had improved so much that it became a case study for Harvard.[110]

Alcon invited attendees of the 1987 AAO conference in Dallas to the Lazy-A Ranch for what was billed as "The Greatest Western Jamboree Ever Held on the Chisholm Trail." For its fortieth anniversary, Alcon pulled out all the stops. That Sunday morning started with thunderstorms, but by noon the sky cleared and two hundred buses brought nine thousand guests to Alcon's campus (fig. 5.70). Welcomed by five hundred Alcon employees, every guest got a cowboy hat and saw a rodeo. Many had their photographs taken sitting on tame longhorns, roping mechanical calves, or riding in a stagecoach. Wild West shootouts, country and western music, mariachi bands, and square dancing entertained everyone. Guests enjoyed the Cantina Mexicana, Big Texas BBQ (fig. 5.71), and Saloon. There were guided tours of the state-of-the-art manufacturing facility, S&T laboratory, Conner Center, and Alexander Tower. As the last bus left, visitors saw a spectacular orange sunset. Schollmaier boasted, "The Jamboree was a huge success. As a result, our friends have a much better understanding of what Alcon is all about. Equally important, our employees had a unique opportunity to come into direct contact, many for the first time, with those whom our company is dedicated to serve. This is a big plus. It cannot help but make us even more unified in our commitment to excellence."[111]

Talking with Schollmaier at the 1983 AAO meeting, an ophthalmologist recalled visiting Alcon in 1964 for SERVA. Schollmaier subsequently had Rhue reactivate the program in 1984. The Ophthalmic and Surgical Divisions hosted SERVA symposiums for about one hundred senior eye residents several times each year. Over two days, R&D scientists highlighted the complexities and costs of developing drugs, from basic research through development. On the last day, Alcon treated the residents to an evening in the Fort Worth Stockyards. In 1986 Vision Care began to sponsor a similar set of meetings, called NOVA, for fourth-year optometry students. In 1987 the International Division launched SOVA for eye specialists from other countries. The largest SOVA followed the annual AAO meeting, with about two hundred doctors attending. Addressing a SERVA group, Schollmaier summed up the purpose of the seminars: "We want you to know that if you use and prescribe our products, we'll be there for you when you have questions or research ideas. ... Our aim is to offer better products for you to use with your patients, and by beginning a long-term dialogue, we can work with you to ensure you can offer the best treatments in the world."[112]

In its fourth decade, Alcon extended its charitable outreach. Dora Moody expanded its medical missions, which she started in 1962, and Roberto Obregon joined her. In addition to collecting surplus Alcon medications for her missions, Moody managed the assignment of those interested in participating in the missions (fig. 5.72). Several humanitarian agencies received donated products: AmeriCares, MAP International, Medical Ministry International, Mercy Ships, Orbis International, and Surgical Eye Expeditions. Conner had been the leader in the 1962 establishment of the Alcon Foundation. After he retired in 1977, Schollmaier created a team to expand the program. The foundation funded medical and sci-

FIG 5.71
Barbecue house, Alcon Jamboree, AAO, 1987 (AHR)

FIG 5.72
Dora Moody on a medical mission, ca. 1985 (AHR)

entific fellowships, purchased equipment, supported symposiums and seminars attended by physicians and scientists, and contributed to United Way, local and national associations for the blind, and hospital expansion programs. Illustrative of Schollmaier's frugal ideas, Marva Clynch, besides being Sisson's administrative assistant, managed the Alcon Foundation all on her own. Records are sparse, but funding during this decade probably averaged $100,000 each year. As an example, in 1983 the foundation awarded $86,000 in 122 contributions to organizations as close as Fort Worth and as far away as the International Congress of Ophthalmology in Rome, Italy.[113]

Alcon employees continued to support United Way. During the 1986 annual fall campaign, 96 percent of the Fort Worth–based employees contributed almost $300,000. Over this decade, the employees and Alcon itself donated several million dollars, which ranked the company among the top two or three among Tarrant County corporations to support the United Way. Moreover, executives and employees served as leaders for annual United Way drives.

Alexander had led Alcon's participation in Junior Achievement. When he retired in 1977, Schollmaier became its major proponent. His role extended to the national level where, in 1979, he joined the board of directors. During his board chairmanship in 1985 and 1986, contributions from Tarrant County increased, with several donations of more than $1 million. Spruill was also active in Junior Achievement. Each year a few hundred Alcon employees played in the Bowl-A-Thon, raising $30,000 to $70,000. Moreover, Alcon employees served as mentors to scholarship winners and consultants to student-run Junior Achievement companies; others taught basic economics in various programs. In 1986 Alcon launched the Adopt-A-School program, whereby employees became mentors for students at Rosemont Middle School.[114]

The company continued to host its annual Christmas party, while divisions began their own traditions. A collective giving spirit thrived at Alcon. R&D filled Christmas stockings for the Salvation Army's Angel Tree project. Proceeds from Manufacturing and QA's annual bake sale bought food and clothes for needy families. Throughout the Fort Worth area, twelve Alcon employees competed in local marathon and 5K races. In 1987 Alcon started its own annual 5K race for runners and walkers; 129 employees participated. When Alexander Tower opened in early 1987, it was equipped with an employee exercise facility. Managed by a professional trainer, the workout equipment was well used; martial arts classes and aerobic instruction were also offered. Alcon subsidiaries had their own activities. A four-woman firefighter team from Alcon France in Rumilly participated in the 1983 French national finals. Beginning in 1978, Alcon Brazil organized an exercise club and constructed tennis and volleyball courts and an indoor soccer arena. Alcon Colombia fielded a competitive bicycle team. In Puerto Rico, the pharmaceutical manufacturing facilities formed a basketball league, with the Alcon team winning the championship in 1984. The women in Alcon Puerto Rico held an annual pool tournament.[115]

Alcon's total revenue grew from $111 million in 1978 to $486 million in 1987, a remarkable increase of $375 million (fig. 5.73). Each year International Division sales constituted about one-third of this revenue; in 1987 it contributed 38 percent. Thus, overseas income kept pace with domestic sales. Acquisitions contributed in part to this remarkable

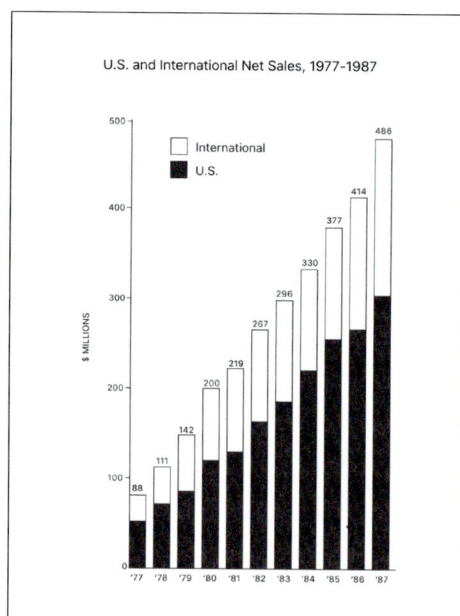

U.S. and International Net Sales, 1977-1987

FIG 5.73
US and International annual sales,
1977–1987 (TOM, AM)

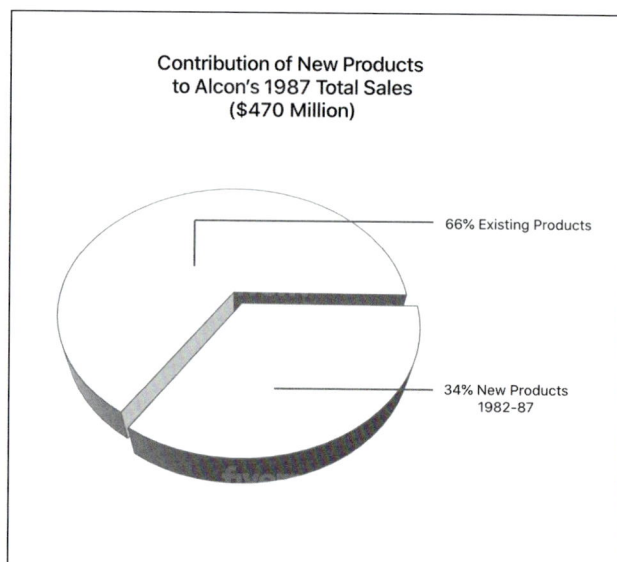

Contribution of New Products
to Alcon's 1987 Total Sales
($470 Million)

66% Existing Products

34% New Products
1982-87

FIG 5.74
Contribution of new products to
Alcon's 1987 total sales (TOM, AM)

increase in revenue, but the impact of new products grew in significance as the decade progressed. Products released by R&D since 1982, such as Betoptic, Tobrex, Opti-Clean, Opti-Zyme, and BSS PLUS, produced 34 percent of the annual income by 1987 (fig. 5.74). Ophthalmic products provided over one-third of the revenue, 24 percent came from Surgical, and 22 percent from Vision Care. The Dermatology Division and non-ophthalmic lines (Webcon, Avicon) each produced 9 percent of the total. After Nestlé acquired Alcon in 1977, Alcon no longer filed an annual report, and Nestlé folded Alcon profits into its own. With one exception, Alcon never publicly revealed its net profit from 1978 to 1987. In 1986 Alcon published *Alcon Today and Tomorrow*, a report describing the company, in which it reported a net profit of 11 percent, or $41.5 million, for the previous year. Commenting in the company magazine, *Alcon World News*, Schollmaier noted that "1987 was a banner year for Alcon. In many ways it was the most outstanding performance period in the company's 40-year history. Impressive gains were made in all product lines—Ophthalmic, Surgical, Vision Care, and Dermatology—both in the US and internationally. Sales increased overall by 17% over 1986 to a record $486.2 million. Both sales and profits achieved the budget plan objectives for the year."[116]

The years 1978 through 1987 represent the first full decade of Nestlé ownership. During this period, Alcon revenues totaled $2.842 billion. Assuming a yearly profit of 10 percent, Alcon contributed $284 million to Nestlé, or slightly more than what Nestlé paid when it acquired Alcon. Moreover, for the year 1985, for which there is a complete set of data, Alcon's annual sales equaled 2 percent of Nestlé's revenue and a remarkable 5 percent of its profits. Nestlé had made a prudent investment! Alcon also benefited from the relationship. Nestlé invested about $150 million in acquisitions and over $100 million in new construction and renovation of Alcon facilities.[117]

To commemorate the first decade of their relationship, Nestlé gave the Alcon campus a massive granite boulder from the Swiss Alps (fig. 5.75). Beyond financial success, Nestlé's ownership brought fundamental changes to Alcon. Alexander and Conner stepped away

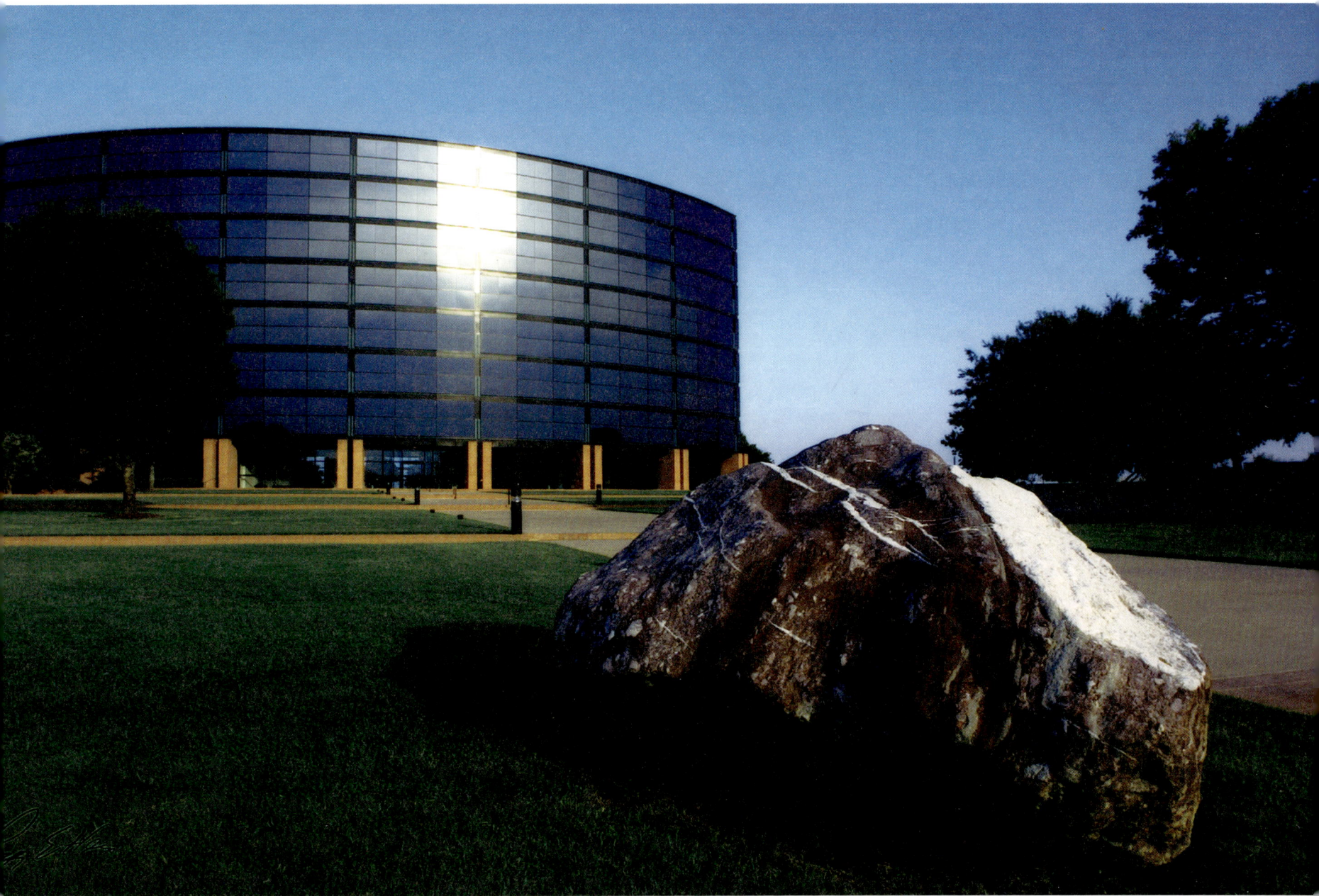

FIG 5.75
Alexander Tower and granite boulder from
the Swiss Alps, gift of Nestlé (AHR)

from the company, but their legacy endured in two imposing architectural structures on Alcon's campus—the Conner Research Center and the Alexander Administrative Center. Other parts of the campus also reflected Nestlé's investment. Manufacturing now had nine production lines, an innovative facility produced Drop-tainers, employees ate at a new cafeteria, and the Conner Center was expanded. Plans were underway for an auditorium, increased production capacity, an Alexander Center annex, and a power co-generation plant. In Puerto Rico, Alcon constructed a manufacturing plant to handle increased demand for its eye care products. Overseas, Alcon modernized other manufacturing facilities, consolidating the number to seven—Spain, France, Belgium, Canada, Mexico, Brazil, and Argentina. The company also divested its non–eye care products, except for Webcon and Avicon, and it planned to expand the dermatology line.

Schollmaier's centralization of S&T was successful, with QA systems achieving uniform-quality products in multiple manufacturing locations. The global network of plants followed standard GMPs. New RA processes and procedures resulted in quality submissions to the FDA and rapid approvals, not only in the United States but also overseas. Investment in R&D paid off in the development of flagship brands—Tobrex, BSS PLUS, Betoptic, and the Opti franchise. Moreover, R&D had a full pipeline of future products. In 1987 Schollmaier noted that R&D's 1987 budget of $50 million equaled the cumulative profits of Alcon's first thirty years (1947–1977).[118]

While acquisitions help to gain market share, Alcon learned the pitfalls of buying the wrong type of company. Acquisitions to the Surgical Division were mostly successful, bringing new products, capable managers, and useful facilities. The Ophthalmic and Vision Care Divisions grew organically, with new products and everyone learning what worked in launching, marketing, and selling such products. The International Division moved away from using distributors or acquiring companies to marketing and selling products in a centralized fashion, expanding its market, and growing its global team.

Schollmaier often said the previous ten years had prepared Alcon for this decade. Of Alcon's first-generation leaders, only Leone remained; the second generation (Schollmaier, Lane, Sisson, Spruill, and Buhler) led Alcon into the 1980s. Across all divisions, third- and fourth-generation leaders matured into competent managers, having absorbed a variety of learning experiences. Those joining Alcon in the 1960s and 1970s worked in a dynamic environment that required adaptability and an element of risk-taking as they transferred across divisions and assignments. Not only did this develop their professional skills, it also built an integrated workforce. Everyone knew everyone. Growing from a small company to a larger one facilitated this process, and likely contributed to Schollmaier's matrix system functioning as well as it did. Nevertheless, transformations in the industry, eye care science, and government regulations made it imperative that Alcon find new external talent. And it did. Across all functions, new people contributed to the decade's growth and success.

This chapter began by equating Nestlé to a benevolent parent, and Nestlé certainly supported Alcon financially. However, taking the parenting analogy one step further, Nestlé allowed Alcon to retain its own identity. Nestlé left Alcon as a stand-alone subsidiary, with its own management, its own policies and procedures, its own retirement and PST. Even though Alcon did not fill a Nestlé *core product strategy*, it significantly contributed to Nestlé's *core corporate financial strategy*, increasing profits substantially. Alcon lore focuses on the grand vision of Conner and Alexander, but Fürer had a similar vision, for both Nestlé and Alcon.

Chapter 6

"We've Attracted the Best People"

1988–1997

Alcon *LABORATORIES*

Bill Conner and Bob Alexander prided themselves on employing "good people." Ed Schollmaier upped the tribute, claiming that Alcon "attracted the best people." All were correct. By 1988 Alcon's global workforce had extensive experience, many employees having been with the company for twenty years or more, happy to be in an environment that rewarded performance and encouraged initiative at all levels. The years from 1988 to 1997 became a golden era after decades of organization and planning and learning by trial and error. It was an integrated team; one part of which consisted of homegrown Alcon employees, and another made up of developing leaders handpicked during the acquisition of CooperVision. By 1997 Alcon had fulfilled the vision of its founders, fifty years after it began in a small shop on Main Street in Fort Worth. It was a global ophthalmic firm, with 10,500 employees, 14 plants, and hundreds of products sold in 125 countries. Annual revenues had reached $2 billion, and future prospects were boundless.

Strategic acquisitions and investments boosted Alcon's presence in the world ophthalmic market, making the International Division a major contributor in sales. As vice president of CAFE, Helmut Horchler restarted Alcon's presence in Vietnam. His accomplishments are illustrative of ability and initiative merging with Alcon's philosophy of developing people. At the end of the Vietnam War, Alcon had a dominant presence in South Vietnam, but US laws prevented American enterprises from conducting business there. However, embargo rules exempted medicines, so in 1993 Horchler explored Vietnam's potential as an ophthalmic market. Travel to Vietnam was difficult; acquiring a visa came with challenges, and in-country immigration and customs procedures were drawn-out affairs. Meeting with ophthalmologists in Ho Chi Minh City, previously Saigon, Horchler concluded Vietnam had potential, but he had to go to Hanoi to conduct business. There, with the assistance of the country manager of the Sanofi Pharmaceutical Company he met Lê Thị Minh Hoa, who organized Horchler's visits to eye hospitals and the Ministry of Health. During these visits he obtained a $3,500 order from a distributor and product registration forms from the government.

Confident of Vietnam's potential, Horchler returned a few months later, intent on hiring Minh Hoa and opening an office in Ho Chi Minh City. She agreed to become Alcon's chief representative in Vietnam at $200 per month, four times her previous salary. There were obstacles to her employment by an American company. He recalled, "Vietnamese could not deal in US $s and could not have an account in a foreign bank. The solution we came up with was for me to open a bank account in my name with an Australian bank and give [Minh Hoa] signatory right over my account." Horchler noted also that Minh Hoa was fiercely independent, which contributed to Alcon's success in Vietnam. When he retired in 2004, twenty-five people worked for Alcon Vietnam and annual sales were $10 million.[1]

Horchler represents one example of leadership development at Alcon. He served as a country manager, international marketing director, and general manager of CAFE. In any organization, leadership change is inevitable. Conner was prescient when he told John Feik during his job interview that everyone would have opportunities for career growth. Almost every manager filled multiple roles. The International Division rotated employees from various countries to the home office to broaden their views and enhance their skills. Employees in Domestic Operations transferred from one group to another. Having multiple jobs became the hallmark of a successful employee. Sandy Howell started as a secretary and became a director in Commercial Customer Service. Conner and Alexander promoted employee development. Their experience at Harvard led them to create a program wherein upper management attended Havard, MIT, Stanford University, or the International Institute for Management Development in Lausanne, Switzerland. Employees had opportunities for on-site training courses and classes at nearby universities. In 1988 the International Division established the mid-level executive development program managed by A. J. Hiltenbrand, which Domestic Operations used. By any measure, Alcon prepared employees for expanded responsibility.[2]

A significant test of Alcon's development programs occurred in 1988, when several senior executives retired. Carl Angst, Schollmaier's Nestlé supervisor, was replaced by José Daniel, but Alcon's relationship with Nestlé did not change. George Leone and Schollmaier had been partners since the early 1960s, and the organization they built had been the bedrock for excellence in S&T. Leone retired in 1988, as did Bernard Senkowski, who transformed manufacturing and left his legacy in the construction of numerous first-class facilities worldwide. Then Lewis Horger, the head of RA, retired after fashioning a strategically productive unit that registered numerous products released by R&D. Ted Fleming retired a few years earlier after directing QA since the 1950s. All occupied major roles in S&T and were difficult to replace, but Schollmaier had individuals working at Alcon who extended their legacies.[3]

Leone promoted Howard Luttrell as Fleming's replacement to lead QA. Luttrell had begun as an analytical chemist in QA at Alcon in 1969. He left to obtain a doctorate in chemistry from SMU. Returning to Alcon, Luttrell had QA assignments at Center Laboratories, the company's plant in Puerto Rico, the facility in Fort Worth, and then all plants in the United States. He joined the technical audit team, giving him exposure to the International and Surgical Divisions. He also attended the AMD at Harvard. Promoted to vice president in January 1985, Luttrell was responsible for QA for the next eleven years. During Senkowski's tenure, he placed Bruce C. Rudy, a doctoral graduate in chemistry from the University of Georgia, in charge of the plant in Fort Worth. Rudy had an MBA from Columbia University and, after he attended Havard, became vice president of Manufacturing/Engineering.[4]

Horger's departure prompted speculation about where RA would report. One possibility was Manufacturing. Dilip Raval, in charge of R&D, knew this would not work. Jerry Cagle, vice president for development, proposed that he fill the role, with RA becoming a department in R&D. Cagle spent one year over RA until Alcon hired William Hubregs, a doctoral graduate of the University of Arizona with several years of experience at Bristol-Myers/Mead Johnson and Smith, Kline, & French Laboratories. Schollmaier placed Dick Sisson, who also led Domestic Operations, in charge of QA and Manufacturing/Engineering. Thus, by 1990, Leone's S&T organization had been redistributed.[5]

There were five members of Alcon's senior leadership team (fig. 6.1). Tim Sear, supported by Allen Baker, led the International Division, with Giorgio Vescovo in charge of EURMEA, Horchler for CAFE, and first Carlos Taborda, then Carlos Coscia, for LACAR. In addition to QA and Manufacturing, Sisson also managed United States operations for Ophthalmic and Vision Care products, which were directed by Blaise McGoey and Jack Weightman. John Spruill led the expanding Surgical Division. Between them, this leadership team had 152 years of experience at Alcon. Quite often, when employees got together, they would compare the years they had worked at

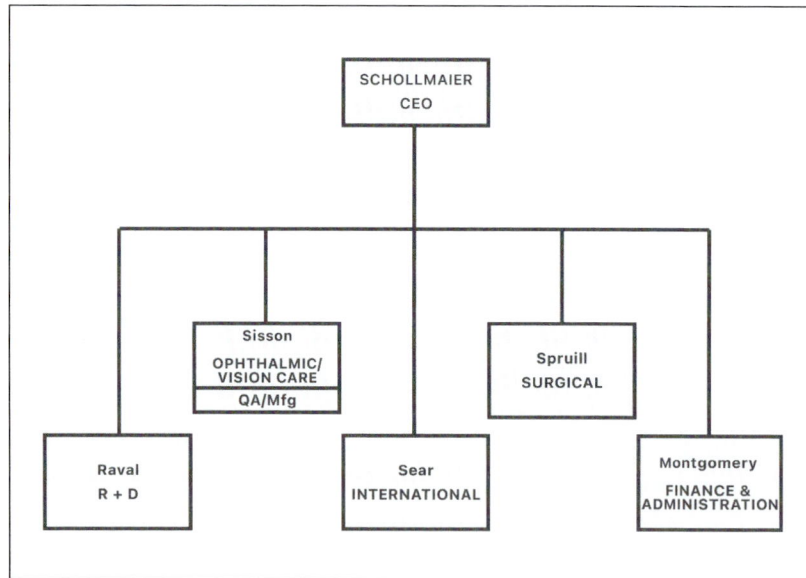

FIG 6.1
Organizational chart, senior executives, 1988 (TOM, AM)

Alcon. It was an illustration of the experience found in and across divisions. It also shows two of Alcon's strengths—continuity of management practices, and employees who had solved a broad array of problems, individually and collectively. Few other pharmaceutical companies had such a legacy in the twentieth century.

In the evolving ophthalmic market, Alcon made strategic acquisitions to maintain its presence. The Boil n Soak disinfectant that came with the Burton, Parsons acquisition initially dominated the competitive soft contact lens solutions market, but Alcon's Opti-Soft made marginal inroads. BSS PLUS and the Alcon Closure System dominated the irrigation and suture arena, and IOGEL became Alcon's initial entry into the foldable IOL sector in the expanding cataract surgery market. However, there was a void in R&D's product development in cataract and retinal surgical instruments and leading-edge IOL technology. Alcon made a major acquisition in 1988 to rectify the issue.

Alcon's failed acquisition of CooperVision in 1984 had been a setback. In the years after, Cooper Laboratories sold most of its ophthalmic products and soft contact lens lines to Johnson & Johnson. It rebranded itself as CooperVision and focused on ophthalmic surgical instruments in an Irvine, California, facility and an IOL group in Bellevue, Washington. CooperVision's board sought opportunities to reduce its debt. At the same time, they acquired Cavitron and blended it into the Irvine organization, where Bill Freeman and his staff improved its phacoemulsification device, which had become the standard for cataract surgeons. CooperVision also bought California Intraocular Lens Company (CILCO), based in Huntington, West Virginia. CILCO sold IOL products preferred by many cataract surgeons. With this merger, CooperVision had the leading market share for IOLs. In addition to CooperVision having market-leading instruments and IOLs, Alcon believed by 1989 that it had top-notch managers and scientists. So, it made an offer. As in 1984, the proposal instigated an FTC review, but this time Schollmaier made it clear that Alcon's position did not constitute a restraint of trade. The FTC voted nine to one to approve the purchase. Nestlé paid the $300 million purchase price, and Alcon boasted that it was "now able to supply ophthalmic surgeons with virtually every product used in their endeavors to restore or preserve vision."[6]

Alcon had never before acquired a company the size of CooperVision—sixteen hundred employees, several facilities, and annual sales of $200 million (fig. 6.2). Alcon management decided to keep the surgical instrument manufacturing and R&D organization in Irvine and authorized the construction of the Irvine Technology Center (ITC). Alcon's San Leandro facility closed, and its projects and selected personnel moved to Irvine or Houston. Alcon's Custom Pak plant in Nashville consolidated with a similar CooperVision facility in Houston. Alcon kept CooperVision's IOL plant in Huntington and moved equipment and personnel from its facility in Nashville. CooperVision's R&D organization in Bellevue was downsized and the technicians and managers, plus their IOL fabrication equipment, moved to a building near the main campus in Fort Worth. The sales and marketing groups in Irvine and Bellevue transferred to Fort Worth, and the field sales force joined Alcon's Surgical Division. CooperVision's branches had operated independently, so the transition to a more structured environment came with a measure of angst. Spruill focused on the individuals thought to have leadership skills Alcon could harness and assigned Baker to manage the integration. Baker had a unique ability to implement decisions in a firm but diplomatic manner. CooperVision's head of Human Resources in IOL, Ardis Kvare, assisted Baker and Spruill with the integration, and an on-site visit to Fort Worth by CooperVision executives solidified the process (fig. 6.3). An important factor that convinced many to relocate was the housing market in Fort Worth, where prices were about one-third what they were in California.[7]

CooperVision was not the only acquisition in this period. In August 1989 Alcon bought Biophysic Medical, Inc., in California and Biophysic Medical, S.A., in Clermont-Ferrand, France. This company developed, assembled, and marketed ophthalmic lasers and imaging devices. On June 9, 1992, Alcon acquired the IOL business of the 3M Company, gaining a manufacturing facility in Santa Barbara, California, and IOL technology that included a multifocal lens. On March 3, 1989, Alcon bought Dr. Thilo & Company, GmbH, an ophthalmic company based in Sauerlach, West Germany, that manufactured eye medications and contact lens care products. This acquisition increased Alcon's presence in the German market. For $20 million, Alcon purchased Laboratorios Plos, a high-quality local ophthalmic manufacturer, extending Alcon's market share in Argentina. In June 1995 Spanish authorities approved Alcon's purchase of Laboratorios Cusí, S.A. (fig. 6.4), an ophthalmic pharmaceutical company founded in 1902 at El Masnou near Barcelona. The acquisition

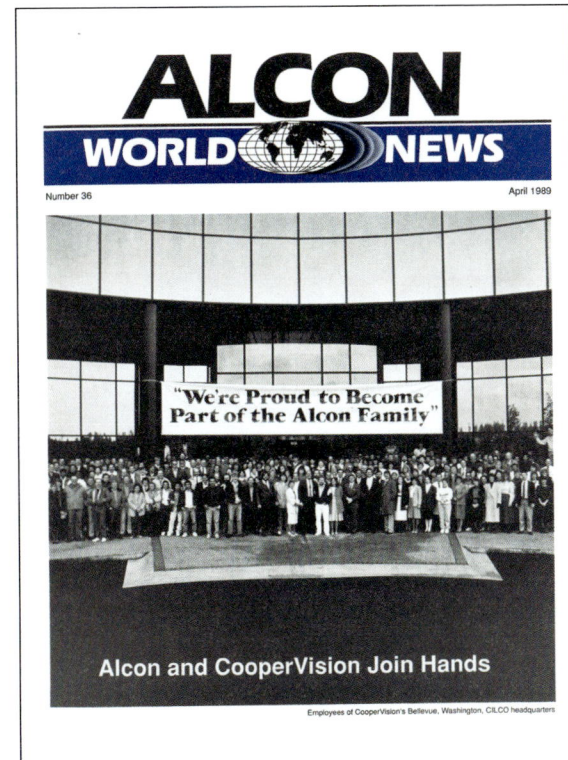

FIG 6.2
CooperVision joins the Alcon Family
(*AWN*, April 1989) (AHR)

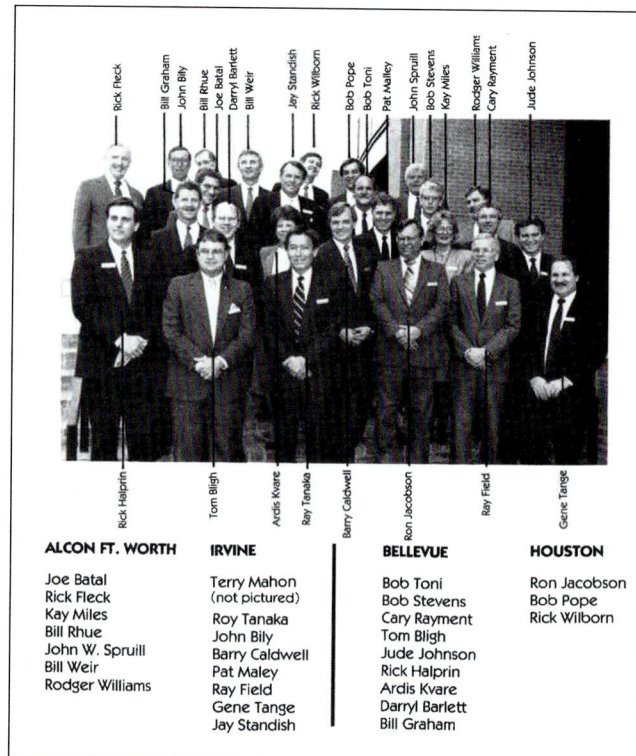

Photo labels (top row, left to right): Rick Fleck, Bill Graham, John Bily, Bill Rhue, Joe Batal, Darryl Barlett, Bill Weir, Jay Standish, Rick Wilborn, Bob Pope, Bob Toni, Pat Malley, John Spruill, Bob Stevens, Kay Miles, Rodger Williams, Cary Rayment, Jude Johnson

Photo labels (bottom, left to right): Rick Halprin, Tom Bligh, Ardis Kvare, Ray Tanaka, Barry Caldwell, Ron Jacobson, Ray Field, Gene Tange

ALCON FT. WORTH	IRVINE	BELLEVUE	HOUSTON
Joe Batal	Terry Mahon	Bob Toni	Ron Jacobson
Rick Fleck	(not pictured)	Bob Stevens	Bob Pope
Kay Miles	Roy Tanaka	Cary Rayment	Rick Wilborn
Bill Rhue	John Bily	Tom Bligh	
John W. Spruill	Barry Caldwell	Jude Johnson	
Bill Weir	Pat Maley	Rick Halprin	
Rodger Williams	Ray Field	Ardis Kvare	
	Gene Tange	Darryl Barlett	
	Jay Standish	Bill Graham	

FIG 6.3
Alcon Surgical and CooperVision executives from Fort Worth, Houston, Irvine, CA, and Bellevue, WA, meeting in Fort Worth, 1989 (*AWN*, April 1989) (AHR)

brought four hundred employees into the Alcon Family and a facility capable of producing fifty thousand units per day. Cusí had a 44 percent share of the Spanish market and a significant export market in Alcon's EURMEA territory. Its acquisition allowed Alcon to move the production of its own pharmaceutical products from the plant in Alcobendas, Spain, leaving the latter the prime manufacturing facility of contact lens solutions for EURMEA. Alcon R&D in Fort Worth began integrating seventy scientists from Cusí and their projects into its organization. Dwight Horton, EURMEA area controller, commented, "With Alcon's strength in the surgical side and Cusí's in the ophthalmic area, we have created a strong, full-service ophthalmic company in Spain." Alcon also inherited a museum focused on the rich history of ophthalmology. In 1993 Alcon purchased an IOL and ophthalmic suture company in Beijing.[8]

The remaining non-ophthalmic acquisitions made in the 1960s and 1970s were sold, making Alcon truly an "ophthalmic house." For $31 million in late 1987, Alcon divested the Avitene product line and its plant in Puerto Rico to MedChem Products of Woburn, Massachusetts. On July 31, 1988, Alcon sold its Mager & Gougelman subsidiary to three ocularists who were branch managers. In December 1992 PolyMedica Industries of Woburn bought the Webcon franchise and its Puerto Rico plant for $45 million. Alcon sold the Couvreur non-ophthalmic products to Synthélabo, the pharmaceutical division of L'Oréal.[9]

The relationship between Galderma, Nestlé, Owen Laboratories, and Alcon was complex. In 1977 L'Oréal recommended that Nestlé acquire Alcon. Daniel, a senior managing director for Nestlé, served on L'Oréal's board, and the CEO for L'Oréal, François Dalle, sat on Nestlé's board. Nestlé owned 25 percent of L'Oréal and Liliane Bettencourt, the major shareholder of L'Oréal, owned 3 percent of Nestlé. Obviously, Nestlé and L'Oréal had intertwining interests. When Daniel became Schollmaier's boss, a plan emerged for Alcon's dermatology subsidiary, Owen Laboratories. By then, annual sales of Owen products had grown to $50 million, almost all in the United States. In 1987 the director of dermatology projects in Alcon R&D transferred to L'Oréal's Centre International de Recherches Dermatologiques, located in Valbonne, France. The following year Daniel proposed a joint venture between L'Oréal and Nestlé, called Galderma (fig. 6.5), to market Owen products in France. It was to be the first step toward increasing sales of Owen products outside the

United States. Schollmaier agreed that Owen had potential for international success but felt it could do it under Alcon. Negotiations were friendly and intense. Nestlé and L'Oréal prevailed.

Galderma was created in France, and Sear convinced Xavier Yon, Alcon's general manager there, to head the venture. Yon, a perfect choice, reported to L'Oréal's CEO, Lindsey O. Jones. Yon's scope became worldwide and in 1991 Steve Clark, Galderma's general manager in the United States, began reporting to him. Soon, Yon created Galderma subsidiaries and built a first-rate management team composed of former Alcon country managers. Owen/Galderma products continued to be manufactured in San Antonio, while Alcon donated its ophthalmic facility in Rumilly to Galderma. As predicted, Galderma's annual sales reached nearly $300 million in 1997. Schollmaier reluctantly gave up Owen to Galderma. Although its products lay outside of Alcon's core strategy, he had bought Owen in 1972 and nurtured its development. In any case, he emotionally considered Galderma's sales to be part of Alcon's revenues.[10]

In 1988 Alcon's fourteen manufacturing plants produced 255 million units per year at a cost of about $170 million. Sales quadrupled during the next decade, until approximately 1.5 billion units were being produced annually by 1997 (fig. 6.6). Plants spread across seven countries, employing thousands of people who produced a broad spectrum of products. Everything was manufactured under stringent, often aseptic, conditions and tested often before shipping. By then, Alcon had operated under a centralized Manufacturing/Engineering organization for almost twenty years led by three corporate vice presidents: Senkowski (1977–1988), Rudy (1989–1992), and André Bens (1993–2008). Bens, a doctoral graduate in industrial pharmacy from the University of Ghent, joined Alcon Belgium as a QA manager in 1982 and moved to Fort Worth in 1985 to direct the overseas QA.[11]

By the end of 1997, Alcon had consolidated its production facilities and regional distribution warehouses. In the United States, needles, sutures, and knives were made in Sinking Springs, Pennsylvania; IOLs in Huntington; Custom Paks in Houston; and cataract and vitreous surgical devices and other ophthalmic instruments in Irvine. Ophthalmic prescription solutions, ointments, and suspensions; Vision Care products; and surgical solutions (BSS PLUS and others) were manufactured in Fort Worth and Humacao, Puerto Rico. In LACAR, plants in Mexico City and São Paulo made ophthalmic therapeutics and Vision Care products. Alcon Belgium was the foremost plant outside the United States, producing ophthalmic therapeutics, surgical products, and Custom Paks. Alcon Cusí supplemented the ophthalmic therapeutics, and Alcon Kaysersberg provided the unique form-fill-seal

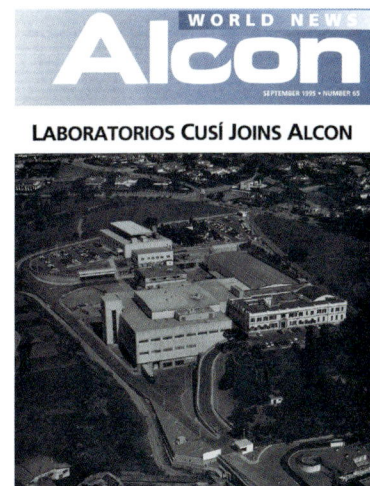

FIG 6.4
Laboratorios Cusí joins Alcon
(*AWN*, September 1995) (AHR)

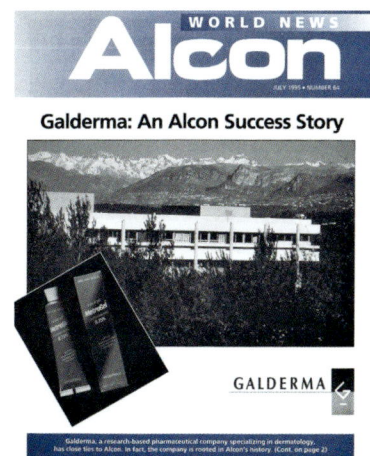

FIG 6.5
Galderma: An Alcon success story
(*AWN*, July 1995) (AHR)

FIG 6.6
Product-labeling machine (AHR)

products, which were unpreserved, small-sized, and single-use. Alcobendas was the prime source for Vision Care products sold outside the United States. From its start in a converted garage in Fort Worth to a complex of globally integrated modern plants, Alcon's growth in fifty years was unparalleled.

By the late 1980s, demand led to a major expansion of the Fort Worth plant, where four hundred people worked (fig. 6.7). Dubbed "Project 10-14," the $31 million reconstruction added five lines (fig. 6.8), increasing capacity to 70 million units annually. Line 10 was dedicated to filling Drop-tainers, with line 11 for large-volume contact lens solutions. Line 12 operated two small-volume filling operations, one for glass and one for plastic containers. The glass line included Miostat and BSS PLUS Part II, while the plastic line produced the Steri-units. Line 13, dedicated to 15 ml and 30 ml BSS products, represented an improvement in productivity with filling, particulate inspection, and blister packaging occurring in a continuous batch operation instead of separately. A larger mixing tank increased batch size as well. Line 14 became Alcon's first large-volume (250 ml and 500 ml) parental solutions producer for BSS and BSS PLUS, eliminating the need for contracted manufacturers. The massive construction effort converted the existing seventy-thousand-square-foot ware-

FIG 6.7
Fort Worth plant employees, 1989 (AHR)

house into a production facility, expanded the building for a larger warehouse, and added new utility and equipment areas. The project involved the installation of new high-efficiency particulate air (HEPA) filters and ten-thousand-liter compounding tanks, and construction of a new water treatment facility, multiple offices, and a computer control center that managed the manufacturing processes. A new sterilizer increased capacity by 50 percent. The production area was on the first floor and the compounding room and computer monitoring station were on the second. The validation team from Manufacturing, R&D, QA, RA, Corporate Engineering, and Plant Engineering wrote procedures for each product and piece of equipment. For line 10 alone, this required twenty protocols and fifty-five new operating procedures. The facility became operational in the spring of 1991; capacity increased again when another stainless-steel tank was installed in late 1996. Plant manager Keith Bell boasted, "By 1999, we plan to produce all BSS/BSS Plus sold and used globally—right here in the Fort Worth Plant ... to reduce the cost of goods by 30 to 40 percent."[12]

Corporate Engineering proposed a co-generation energy plant to increase the power efficiency of the Alcon campus. Completed in 1988, the ten-thousand-square-foot, $7 million facility (fig. 6.8) provided 40 percent of the electrical needs during peak use and 100 percent for off-peak hours. Industrial jet turbines, powered by natural gas, generated electricity and recycled exhaust heat provided air-conditioning and heat throughout the campus. Alcon's cogeneration plant was the first of its kind in the Fort Worth area.[13]

Meanwhile in Puerto Rico, renovation allowed the manufacture of additional products and created a new thirty-thousand-square-foot warehouse. By 1992 the facility operated

FIG 6.8
Fort Worth plant, lines 10 to 14
expansion (AHR)

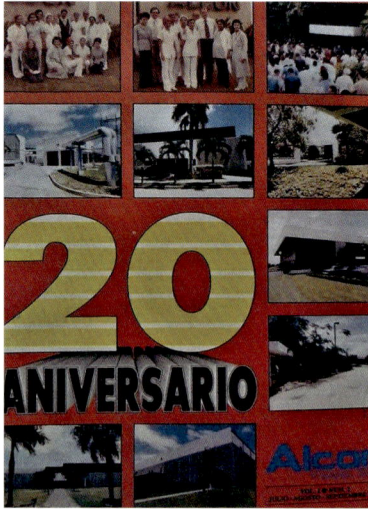

Co-Generation Plant

Line 10 - 14 Expansion

FIG 6.9
Alcon (Puerto Rico), twentieth
anniversary, July–September, 1994 (AHR)

FIG 6.10
Alcon campus, 2000 (AHR)

ASPEN

DISTRIBUTION
CENTER

TOWER C

SURGICAL
TOWER

SCHOLTMAIER
AUDITORIUM

PD EXP

CONNER
CENTER
EXP. 2

CROSSROADS

CONNER CNTR EXP. 1

S&T EXP

two shifts (fig. 6.9) and sent products to all parts of the globe. Most went by ocean freight, but some temperature-sensitive products, such as Viscoat, left by air or refrigerated freight. Although the facility produced less than 25 percent of Alcon's worldwide output, it generated a significant portion of overall profits.[14]

After years of planning, Alcon Sterile Product Expansion, better known as ASPEX, became the firm's most extensive and expensive construction project. At a cost of $125 million, ASPEX (fig. 6.10) resulted in the erection at Fort Worth of a 333,000-square-foot, state-of-the-art manufacturing facility, renovation of a 200,000-square-foot distribution center (fig. 6.10), and the conversion of the obsolete plastic bottle facility into the second co-generation plant. Started in 1993 and fully operational in 1997, after being validated by a Fort Worth team of experts and approved by the FDA, the plant operated four Drop-tainer lines and one large-volume line for contact lens solutions, producing approximately 50 million units annually. The whole process of design, construction, equipment selection, and validation complied with current and anticipated regulatory requirements. Alcon management invited the FDA to be a partner in all phases. Managers organized the products into seven families based on similar processes and procedures, thereby reducing the number of validation studies required. After convincing the FDA of the value of this approach, the Manufacturing, QA, and RA validation team completed its studies, resulting in new processes and training programs. The Dallas office of the FDA inspected the new plant for two weeks and found no deficiencies. Alcon estimated the FDA collaboration reduced the time from design to operation by fourteen months.[15]

In addition to the new manufacturing facilities, the building footprint on the Fort Worth campus grew extensively from 1988 through 1997. Started in 1986, a $10 million, fifty-thousand-square-foot addition to the Conner Research Center was completed in early 1988 (fig. 6.10). This addition housed analytical chemistry, pharmaceutical science, medicinal chemistry, and pharmacology laboratories; it also had offices for the global Clinical Science and RA personnel. Started in 1996 and finished in 1998, the next expansion of the Conner Center added 125,000 square feet of laboratories, a new vivarium, and facilities for long-term stability sample storage (fig. 6.10). The expanded center occupied almost four hundred thousand square feet. Construction in 1993 enlarged the Process Development building, erected in 1978, by ten thousand square feet (fig. 6.10). R&D's emphasis on global clinical studies resulted in this addition being dedicated to preparing and shipping clinical study supplies worldwide. The CooperVision acquisition resulted in two technical groups joining R&D: IOL and surgical instrument development. Several IOL scientists transferred

FIG 6.11
R&D's IOL fabricator, 1991 (AHR)

FIG 6.12
Alcon Irvine Technology Center,
Irvine, CA, 1992 (AHR)

to Fort Worth and settled into an off-campus facility, the Will Rogers Annex. The building was modified to accommodate the technical personnel and unique equipment used to design, construct, test, and manufacture next-generation IOLs (fig. 6.11). By 1998 approximately 750 scientists and support personnel worked in the Conner Center, Process Development building, and Will Rogers Annex; another 150 at the Irvine Technology Center; and 100 Clinical Science and RA personnel served overseas.[16]

At the time Alcon acquired CooperVision, the latter's surgical instrument innovation and manufacturing took place in an obsolete building. A new facility had already been designed, so a decision had to be made as to its location. Since the specific skills required were more commonly found in California, Alcon chose to build in Irvine. The ITC filled four buildings: manufacturing, warehouse, R&D, and an auditorium with a training surgical laboratory. With a total of two hundred thousand square feet, the ITC was in use by late 1990 (fig. 6.12).[17]

Back in Fort Worth, twelve thousand square feet were added to the S&T building (fig. 6.10). The August 1990 addition provided more office and laboratory space for QA. The R&D patent group moved into a section, as did the international legal department and the corporate audit group. The addition also provided a venue for training sales representatives.[18]

When the S&T building was constructed in 1968, it contained the largest meeting facility on the Fort Worth campus, capable of seating ninety people. In June 1988 Alcon began a seven-thousand-square-foot amphitheater, later named Schollmaier Auditorium. Tran Trong, manager of engineering projects, led the project (fig. 6.10). This facility, designed to accommodate medical and scientific symposia, seated two hundred people in an arrangement patterned after Harvard lecture halls. A motion sensor automatically activated the audiovisual system. Presenters had access to multiple slide projectors, television monitors, videotape units, a 16mm projector, a stereo sound system, and a nine-by-eighteen-foot screen suitable for single or multiple projection programs—all controlled from the speaker's lectern.[19]

Following the CooperVision acquisition, Alexander Tower was overfull, forcing groups off campus. Corporate Engineering designed a four-story building, with approximately 120,000 square feet of space, that matched the external appearance of Alexander Tower (fig. 6.10). A skybridge connected the top floor to the fourth floor of the tower. Three surgical training rooms were located on the first floor, along with the company's fitness center. Office space on the other three floors, occupied in late 1992, held four hundred people. By the end of 1997, Alcon had the largest, most modern ophthalmic specialty company facilities in the world.[20]

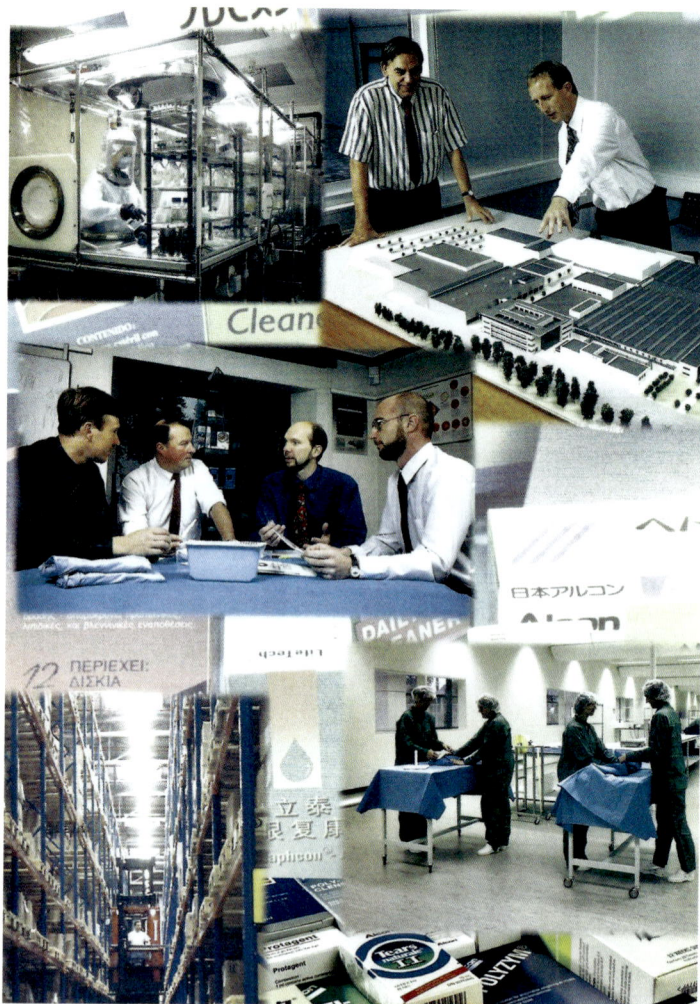

FIG 6.13
Alcon Belgium (Alcon EuroVision #2, 1997) (TOM, AM)

The CooperVision acquisition led to the consolidation of other plants in the United States. ITC became the sole facility for developing and manufacturing cataract and vitreous surgical instruments, lasers, and other sophisticated surgical devices. Alcon's cutting-edge ophthalmic needles, sutures, and knives continued to be produced at the plant in Sinking Springs. In 1997 a fifteen-thousand-square-foot addition to that facility was completed, adding a microbiology laboratory, cafeteria, and other amenities. CooperVision also owned a Houston facility for custom packages for ophthalmic surgeons, so Alcon combined its Custom Pak surgical kits and consumable products and relocated from Nashville to Texas. A major expansion of fifty-two thousand square feet was completed there in 1996. In addition to upgrading plants, Alcon established new distribution centers, with the first in Fort Worth. The second, a 110,000-square-foot warehouse staffed by forty-three personnel, opened in Elkridge, Maryland. Next came a center in Reno, Nevada; it opened in 2000.[21]

Alcon Couvreur in Puurs, Belgium, became the major manufacturing and distribution center overseas, supplying products for EURMEA and other parts of the world (fig. 6.13). By 1997 it shipped products to eighty countries. The company's Belgian plant expanded to handle the increased volume from the acquisitions of CooperVision and Dr. Thilo. In addition to modernizing production lines, a 1992 project created a new two-story office building and company cafeteria and added ninety thousand square feet to the warehouse. Six years later, new construction doubled the warehouse space, while upgrades to the production line included compounding facilities for solution and ointment preparations. By then, international Custom Pak surgical kit sales had grown to justify a dedicated line.[22]

R&D's release of unpreserved and other products resulted in a $25 million expansion of sixty thousand square feet and renovation of the facility at Kaysersberg in 1995. Two new high-speed, form-fill-seal lines doubled the plant's capacity. The project also included a new warehouse, shipping docks, material handling areas, cafeteria, locker rooms, offices, and an upgrade to the QA laboratories. Upon completion, the plant produced 167 million units annually, including 10 ml to 15 ml containers of Opti-Free and other contact lens solutions, and 0.4 ml to 0.8 ml unit-doses of Betoptic S and Bion Tears, a dry eye therapy.[23]

The 1995 acquisition of Laboratorios Cusí resulted in a realignment of the plant in Alcobendas, which had been modernized in 1990. Alcobendas became the major production site for Vision Care products sold internationally. The Cusí campus converted to manufacturing Alcon products and underwent renovation and upgrades of production, packaging, warehousing, and offices. By 1997 manufacturing had consolidated into four European plants (Puurs, Belgium; Kaysersberg, France; Alcobendas and El Masnou, Spain), with a distribution center in Freiburg, Germany, and a second fifty-two-thousand-square-foot distribution center and country headquarters in England at Hemel Hempsted.[24]

Mexico and Brazil manufacturing sites remained the mainstays in the LACAR zone. The Mexico City production line, warehouse, and administrative facilities underwent makeovers in 1989 and again two years later. With the scope of ophthalmic therapeutics increasing, especially ointments, and new Vision Care products in demand, by 1998 Alcon's plant in São Paulo underwent significant renovations. By 1997 a modern auditorium and surgical wet lab opened in São Paulo, which facilitated the introduction of Alcon surgical devices and IOLs to ophthalmic surgeons from South America. That same year, Argentina's Buenos Aires plant closed, but a distribution center began construction.[25]

Following the modernization projects, Alcon began shipping products to the CAFE region and closed its Canada manufacturing plant in 1989. By 1997 an increased presence in Japan justified construction of a sixty-eight-thousand-square-foot distribution center in that country. Upon the 1993 acquisition of the IOL and suture manufacturing facility in Beijing, plant modernization began and personnel from ITC installed new technology and trained production crews.[26]

By the early 1990s, Alcon had transformed its manufacturing processes, much of which became automated and computerized. Alexander and Conner could not have anticipated such sophistication, but they would be proud that their promise of reliability and quality lived on. As in 1947, Alcon customers could still depend on a quality product that was sterile with known, measured ingredients.

When Senkowski retired in 1988, Schollmaier turned to Sisson to handle Manufacturing and QA, while Rudy, Senkowski's understudy, took over global manufacturing. In 1992, when Rudy left, Sisson selected André Bens to replace him (fig. 6.14). Senkowski left in place a seasoned set of managers. Harold Camp came with VXTRA, took over the IOL facility in Nashville, and moved to Huntington when Alcon consolidated IOL production there. Free-

FIG 6.14
André Bens (AHR)

man directed ITC; upon his retirement, Kenneth E. Lickel took charge, while Bill Richardson led domestic surgical manufacturing operations from Fort Worth. When Larry Coben joined R&D in 1991 to direct the renovated process development center, Jack Panoyan, Alcon Canada's plant manager, replaced him as the manager of the Fort Worth manufacturing plant. The close relationship between QA and Manufacturing allowed QA to become a source of manufacturing managers. In the United States, these included Kevin Marks, Keith Bell, and Gene Estes. Sisson also used other experienced executives for emergencies. In 1993 the general manager of the Puerto Rico plant became seriously ill, so Sisson sent Milton Barley to fill this role. Beginning in 1993, Bens concentrated on consolidating QA and Manufacturing for better economies of scale, automation of production, expansion of facilities, construction of new plants, continuous improvement of quality and manufacturing costs, and preparation of future management. A hallmark of Alcon's success is continuity of leadership. In the Manufacturing Group, it is worthwhile to note that there were just five top managers over Alcon's first fifty years—Dave Merrill (three years), Bob Carter (twenty-seven years), Senkowski (eleven years), Rudy (four years), and Bens (fourteen years).[27]

By January 1987 Luttrell had been the Alcon QA vice president for two years. An Alcon QA veteran since 1969, he had a broad knowledge of products and familiarity with personalities in the laboratories and manufacturing plants. Moreover, his views of the role of QA at Alcon had matured under the tutelage of his predecessor, Fleming. Luttrell explained, "Quality, in all its aspects, had to be designed into the product, its processes in manufacturing and testing, and those aspects formally validated." During his tenure, about six hundred scientists and managers worked in QA.[28]

The integration and relationship of QA personnel with plant managers is the epitome of Schollmaier's matrix concept. All plant QA directors and staff reported to Corporate QA while maintaining a relationship with general management. When it came to compensation and evaluations, Corporate QA worked with International's human resource director and the country managers. Corporate QA ensured that QA laboratories worldwide were staffed with competent and professional managers. It developed SOPs for use in all facilities with an emphasis on state-of-the-art technologies. One example was a computer program that centralized databases and allowed Corporate QA in Fort Worth to keep track of real-time test results from all the plants. Implementing this global computer system coincided with the IT Division's increasing dominance, and Corporate QA responded by assigning a person to facilitate QA's IT needs. Another extension was the consolidation of global and domestic product complaints into one group.[29]

During Luttrell's tenure, three significant operational improvements were implemented. First, robotic analytical equipment was placed in QA laboratories. Robotic technology had matured, and Alcon installed Zymark Corporation's PyTechnology system, which automated testing of several lots of a product at once (fig. 6.15). Robotic automation meant faster start-up times, greater flexibility, standardized laboratory technique, higher precision, improved productivity, and high sensitivity and specificity. Thus, assays productivity increased. Second, the validation of SOPs was transferred from Manufacturing to QA. This was the culmination of the proposals Estes had initiated after the 1973 British inspection. Third, a Quality Engineering Function was developed for most plants to improve manufacturing processes. One outcome was an audit system to assure supplier quality. Instead of testing every lot of materials that Alcon purchased, QA established audit paradigms and certified a supplier. QA thus accepted suppliers' certificates of analysis and did not test and inspect every lot shipped to Alcon, saving time and money.[30]

Founded in 1947, the International Standards Organization (ISO) established benchmarks for technology and manufacturing. In the 1990s the European Union (EU) began requiring ISO certification for devices and manufacturing plants prior to product marketing. EU governments approved for-profit companies, called Notified Bodies, to act as certification agents. Alcon chose TÜV Rheinland, in Cologne, as its ISO certification agent. In its simplest form, ISO certification of manufacturing plants focused on QA and management based on documentation of appropriate design, construction, maintenance, validated SOPs, and personnel training. Alcon had developed a similar system over the preceding two decades, and so processes and systems that Alcon QA had implemented facilitated its ISO certification. Led by QA, by 1998 Alcon completed ISO certification of its plants (fig. 6.16).[31]

QA personnel increasingly migrated to Manufacturing. In 1988 about 40 percent of the supervisory personnel involved in the planning and production of Alcon products had been QA managers. Estes held various positions in QA before becoming the manager of the Custom Pak facility in Houston and later transforming the form-fill-seal facility in Kaysersberg. Bell held various assignments for QA, became production manager in the Fort Worth plant, then served as acting plant manager in Puerto Rico and manufacturing manager for the Fort Worth plant, and finally returned to QA as corporate vice president.

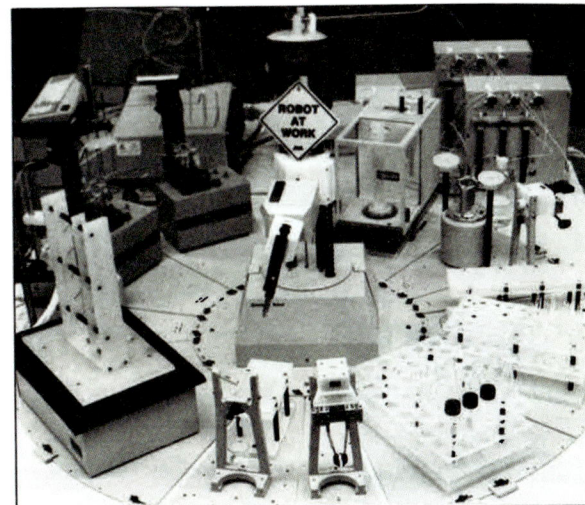

This photo depicts the robot which is the device in the center of the circle. It is actually an arm that moves around a 360° circumference with various pieces of instrumentation that do each part of the assay. The arm can attach itself to three different types of hands each of which is designed to perform a specific function such as dispensing fluids into testing vials, shaking solutions, injecting sample into spectrophotometer. All operations are being controlled by a computer and a hard copy printout of each step is provided as back-up documentation.

FIG 6.15
QA robotics (AHR)

ISO 9000: Just Another Audit?
by Stephen P. Carder, General Manager Alcon Spain

Alcon Spain's ISO 9000 implementation and internal audit teams hosted a formal dinner to celebrate being the first Alcon International facility to earn "CE" accreditation.

FIG 6.16
Alcon Spain, ISO 9000 certification (AHR)

Philippe Van Aerde went from QA director to plant manager in Belgium. QA chemist Irma Vicente became RA manager in Puerto Rico. Gilberto Dalesio served as QA director in Argentina and Spain, then moved to manufacturing in Europe. Maria Teresa Rodriguez, a QA microbiologist in Puerto Rico, became production manager of the plant. Erwin Vanhaecke went from QA director in Belgium to director of QA for International, to vice president of Corporate QA, and finally head of QA for Novartis, which acquired Alcon in 2010. Ed McGough started as QA manager of the surgical plant in Sinking Spring, moved to QA in Puerto Rico, transferred to Corporate QA in Fort Worth, then became the Fort Worth plant manufacturing manager; he recently retired as senior vice president in charge of Global Manufacturing and Technical Operations. Bens became the director of Corporate QA for international operations, migrated to Manufacturing as director of international operations, then in 1993 became vice president of Manufacturing and Engineering, and in 2001 was promoted to senior vice president of Global Manufacturing, QA, Engineering, and Supply Chain. Significantly, only three people led QA during Alcon's first fifty years—Merrill (ten years), Fleming (thirty years), and Luttrell (ten years). This is yet another example of the continuity of leadership that made Alcon successful.[32]

In 1974 Schollmaier told Raval that R&D productivity would be evaluated in three years and any deficiency would be grounds for dismissal. The fact that Raval remained until 1997 indicates his success. Raval's R&D by 1988 had experienced scientists and managers in every position. Many had participated in the development of new, innovative products, the most recent being Betoptic S and Opti-Free. When Leone retired in 1987, Raval reported to Schollmaier, another indication that R&D productivity was crucial for Alcon. Raval focused on educating management about the scientific uncertainties in developing therapeutics and devices, and in prioritizing the projects that minimized uncertainties but delivered innovative products. He assembled a crack team and made vital organizational changes. The many products released from 1988 to 1997 that propelled Alcon's global annual sales to $2 billion is a testament to Raval's success.[33]

As 1988 began, R&D employed about 550 scientists with an annual budget of $56 million. Over the following decade R&D spent a cumulative $1.185 billion, doubled its personnel, and grew its annual budget to over $200 million. Raval divided R&D into four operational groups: Cagle, Development; York, Research; Adamski, Licensing; and Hubregs, RA. Development, which took the bulk of the resources (people and dollars), included Toxicology, Microbiology, Analytical Chemistry, Pharmaceutical Science, Process Development, and Clinical Science. One significant change centralized the Pharmaceutical and Clinical Science departments, which left the project managers, called Medical Specialty Directors (MSDs), to concentrate on coordinating scientific tasks for each project in their portfolios; the three MSDs corresponded to Alcon's three product areas—Ophthalmic, Vision Care, and Surgical. At this time, Clinical Science and RA were rapidly expanding in the EU and Japan (figs. 6.17, 6.18). SOPs set parameters for the collection of data so that preclinical and clinical study results met the quality standards needed for global registration. The global, centralized RA included personnel from countries with large markets and was also divided into specialty groups corresponding to the three product areas. In total, about a dozen leaders managed all of R&D.[34]

FIG 6.17
Bill Hubregs and Alcon Japan RA, 1993. *Left to right*: Akiko Kikuchi, (first name unknown) Ohmura, Yoshi Fukazawa, Takao Sudo, and Bill Hubregs. (TOM, AM) (Photo gift from Bill Hubregs)

When Alcon acquired CooperVision, Raval rationalized the personnel and resources in Irvine and Bellevue. R&D at ITC reported to Fort Worth, and it took one failed candidate before Raval hired Donn Lobdell, who had thirty years of experience in developing medical devices. Freeman introduced Lobdell to Raval, who made an ingenious proposal. He asked Lobdell to interview the ITC staff in manufacturing and R&D and present a report. After doing so, Lobdell joined the ITC staff in late 1991. Raval faced a different challenge with Robert Stevens and CooperVision's IOL R&D group in Bellevue. Convincing people to leave the Pacific Northwest for Texas was not easy. Raval and Spruill organized an open house in Fort Worth attended by staff from Bellevue. Scientists presented the Alcon story and outlined R&D projects. Ultimately, ten people, including Stevens, who became the head of the R&D Surgical Department, relocated to Fort Worth. Two crucial-scientists were Bill Graham, who had technical and institutional IOL knowledge with a clinical perspective, and Anil Patel, whose research IOL conceptions were among the best in the industry (fig. 6.19). Several other personnel also proved to be outstanding assets.[35]

FIG 6.18

Clinical Research Associate training, Fort Worth, 1991. Back row, *Left to right, back row*: Lieve Convents, Belgium; Hirochika Nakajo, Japan; Masaaki Asazuma, Japan; Unknown; Anne Marie Amend, Germany; Claudia Leah, France; Cassandra Burroughs, USA; David Parson, UK. *Left to right, front row*: Toshio Ikemoto, Japan; Koichi Yoshikawa, Japan; Junko Ueda, Japan; Ceri Jones, UK; Angela Gheorghiu, Italy; Monica Wagner, Germany; Tim Brewer, USA; Denise Zanecchia, USA; Inez Carels, Belgium; Satoru Numajiri, Japan/USA. Inset, *Left to right*: Valerie Parkman, Marie Eggleston, Novelly Turner. (TOM, AM)

Hubregs took charge of RA in late 1988 and found that he "had an outstanding staff." He had more than two decades of regulatory experience with two major pharmaceutical companies. The late 1980s was a period of transition in regulations. In 1987 the FDA hired ophthalmologist Wiley A. Chambers to head the group that approved new ophthalmic medications. He reformatted the INDs and NDAs, requiring submissions to be digital databases with integrated biostatistical and clinical reports. Chambers encouraged discussions of development plans and clinical protocols as new compounds moved from one clinical phase to the next. Although his criteria for approval were strict, he was open to innovative clinical designs. Alcon took advantage of these changes, which were facilitated by Bob Roehrs, Alcon's RA contact with the FDA, who established a productive rapport with Chambers.[36]

Alcon's contacts with the FDA during the development phase of a new drug or device were structured, formal, and conducted by experienced scientists. The FDA also inspected manufacturing plants. While inspectors were trained, their expertise and experience varied, and there was high turnover. In Alcon's experience, at times FDA guidelines were applied arbitrarily. RA's compliance officer, Rebecca Walker, recalled that FDA inspectors' preliminary decisions were often reversed after a dialogue, and sometimes it seemed that decisions were subjective. The Puerto Rico plant went through a spate of disagreements on a sterilization process with a new inspector, and the dispute turned personal. Sisson and Schollmaier went to the FDA regional office, where discussions with the chief inspector finally resolved the issue and the inspector in question was barred from future inspections of Alcon's plant. Schollmaier decided Alcon needed a more collaborative relationship with FDA inspectors, so when he took the revalidation results back to the FDA, he asked them for advice on the construction of Alcon's ASPEX plant, which the agency gave.[37]

In the mid-1980s, Alcon had to register each new product with every country in Europe, but in the 1990s the EU created the European Medicines Evaluations Agency (EMEA). Under the new regulations, registration in one member country meant approval in all. This unified process reinforced the necessity for Alcon RA to centralize product registrations from Fort Worth. Hubregs hired an ex-member of the UK Medicines Commission to manage the RA group for the EU. Both the RA and Clinical Science groups in the EU had regional directors with plans approved by Fort Worth R&D. The situation in Japan was different. When Alcon decided to register R&D's new products there, development plans were approved in Fort Worth, a practice uncommon in Japan. Registration processes in Japan were archaic and presented challenges for Alcon R&D personnel in Japan and Fort Worth. Thus, Hubregs's dealings with Japan had unique issues.[38]

The acquisition of CooperVision added a different product category for RA. David Krapf came to Fort Worth with the CooperVision staff, joining Michael Fitzpatrick's RA group. In the United States, contact lens solutions, IOLs, and ophthalmic surgical devices required a PMA dossier for registration, though some surgical products were classified as drugs requiring an NDA. In the EU, contact lens solutions followed the centralized EMEA process, while surgical devices fell under the CE mark registration process. In Japan, drugs, contact lens solutions, and surgical devices were registered under the jurisdiction of Koseisho in the Ministry of Health and Welfare.[39]

The licensing of new compounds acquired from pharmaceutical companies to serve as foundations for new Alcon products had been a major objective since S&T organized in 1972. Under Leone and Raval, several successful products evolved. As noted in the previous chapter, this resulted from the licensing push from 1978 to 1987. In the following decade, Adamski's effort secured more licensing agreements: broad-spectrum antibiotic, ciprofloxacin (Bayer AG, Leverkusen, Germany); an anti-allergy drug, emedastine (Kanebo Ltd.,

FIG 6.19
Tres amigos: Three key R&D IOL leaders. *Left to right:* Bill Graham, Anil Patel, Robert Stevens, 1991 (TOM, AM) (Photo gift from Robert Stevens)

Tokyo); another anti-allergy drug, olopatadine (Kyowa Hakko Kogyo, Ltd., Tokyo); and a viscoelastic, hyaluronic acid (Genzyme, Boston). Leone and Raval's new licensing plan, led by Adamski, became one of the most significant strategic decisions made during Alcon's first fifty years.[40]

York's Research department focused on the discovery of new compounds. He divided the Pharmacology Group into two units and hired several scientists with pharmaceutical experience. He also set up groups to perform basic research on glaucoma, cataracts, and ocular inflammation, much like what was conducted at academic institutions. His department added scanning and transmission electron microscopy and nuclear magnetic resonance imaging technologies to study these diseases. Nevertheless, the strength of the Research Department was its in vivo and in vitro screening models that evaluated new compounds. The drugs Adamski licensed from other companies are examples that emerged from this milieu.[41]

York enhanced the capability to synthesize new compounds. The previous chapter discussed the incorporation of algorithm models for computer-designed lead compound optimization. York hired Evan Kyba, a first-rate synthetic chemist from the University of Texas, to lead the Medicinal Chemistry Group. By the early 1990s, Alcon medicinal chemists and pharmacologists had narrowed a long list of carbonic anhydrase inhibitor (CAI) molecules synthesized in R&D to one that showed promise as a glaucoma therapy. Brinzolamide, a highly specific, noncompetitive CAI, was sent to the Development Department. At the same time, research by László Z. Bitó at Columbia University demonstrated that prostaglandin F2-alpha (PGF-2α) molecules lowered IOP. Kyba's chemists designed PG-F2α compounds and identified a patentable molecule, which they named "travoprost." It also became a project for Development.[42]

A major impediment to the production of these new projects involved the availability of raw materials, both for R&D and Manufacturing. Alcon had no external source for the raw materials of apraclonidine, the active ingredient in Iopidine, brinzolamide, or travoprost. Raw materials for lodoxamide, used in the new anti-allergy product Alomide, and emedastine, used for Emadine, failed to materialize from licensing companies. The supplies for polyquad, the disinfectant molecule used in Opti-Free, were limited. Thus, Alcon needed either to manufacture these compounds or locate a reliable external source. As a first step, R&D constructed a chemical synthesis laboratory in the Conner Center. In the meantime, York and Kyba searched for a viable commercial company and settled on Chemisches Institut Schäfer in Bubendorf, Switzerland. Alcon and Chemisches Institut Schäfer formed a joint venture, AMCIS (a contraction of America and Chemisches Institut Schäfer), with equal ownership. A thirty-two-thousand-square-foot structure was built in 1996 and, after being approved by Alcon's Technical Audit team, passed FDA inspection. Alcon now had a reliable, high-quality source for several molecules used in its products.[43]

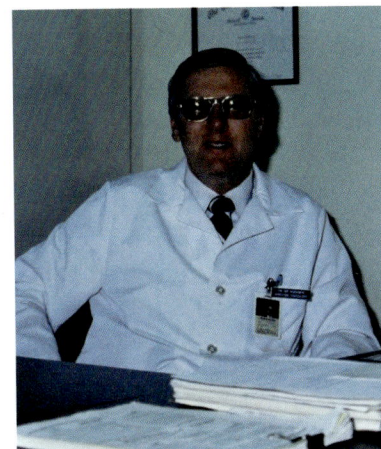

FIG 6.20
Joe Hiddemen (AHR)

Every R&D project used resources located in Joseph Hiddemen's technical service group, PreClinical Development (fig. 6.20). Hiddemen had overseen Toxicology since 1977, and later when Charles Robb retired in 1989, he replaced him as head of PreClinical Development. Hiddemen and his group leaders had almost eighty years of experience between them. They and their staff performed toxicology, microbiology, and analytical chemistry support for all R&D. They had state-of-the-art instruments and dozens of scientists and technicians who had worked at Alcon many years, and they were well versed in applying functional expertise to studies required for registering any new Alcon product. Their competence is illustrated by the number of Technical Excellence awards earned; Microbiology and Analytical Chemistry each won six. In 1994, Tom Wernet, an Alcon microbiologist since 1967, managed the newly created Technical Documentation Department, responsible for preparing the multidisciplinary, interdivisional sections of regulatory documents. After Alcon acquired Cusí, R&D retained about three dozen scientists; directed by Josep Guasch. Alcon R&D in Spain developed new formulations for the EURMEA and LACAR markets and was responsible for reregistering marketed products required by EMEA regulations.[44]

Projects always encounter issues during development, some of which threaten individual projects' viability. For example, after its launch in the early 1980s, Tobrex had become the most prescribed ophthalmic antibiotic worldwide. In the meantime, new broad-spectrum antibiotics, quinolones, emerged. In 1985 Alcon licensed ciprofloxacin from Bayer AG. An advantage in licensing a compound developed by another company is access to their scientific data, especially chemical and safety data in the Drug Master File (DMF). While Bayer management saw the advantage to licensing ciprofloxacin to Alcon, some in their R&D and marketing teams had reservations, resulting in incomplete access to their DMF and limited quantities of raw material during the first two years. An IND was filed in the summer of 1987 after Alcon management resolved both issues, but by then R&D was two years behind two competitors also developing a quinolone ophthalmic antibiotic. Given priority, the seventy-three-member ciprofloxacin team, led by Roehrs, Barry Schlech, and Robert Abshire, expedited the process. First to approval meant first to launch and first in market share.[45]

FIG 6.21

R&D antibiotic, anti-allergy,
and anti-inflammatory products
(TOM, AM; AHR)

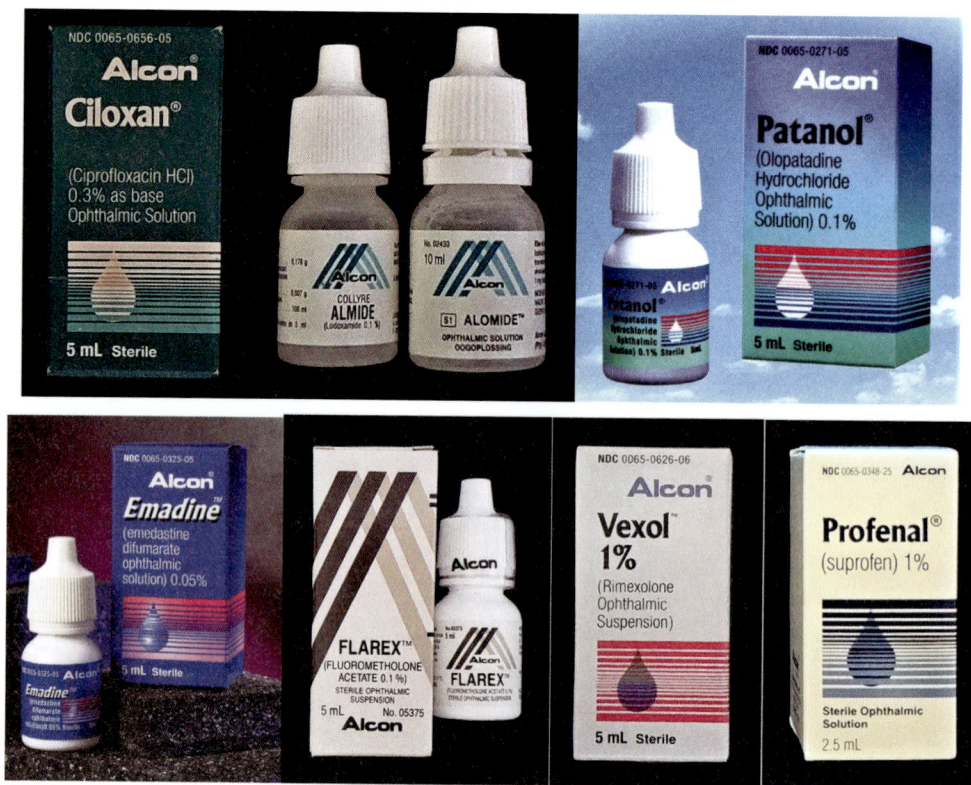

Alcon had one advantage over competitors—it had established the regulatory standard for clinical study design tied to bacteria profiles in patients with its Tobrex studies. The value of the centralized Clinical Science Department became apparent. This cadre of specialists, known as Clinical Research Associates (CRAs), were experienced in overcoming logistical hurdles, finding investigators with the appropriate patients, and retrieving data. The centralized group was designed to insert a qualified scientist to manage the clinical studies. Since these studies required collaboration with microbiologists, Abshire transferred from the Microbiology Group to lead the effort. Alcon had one other advantage—in addition to a product to treat bacterial conjunctivitis, it pursued the treatment of corneal ulcers, a devastating infection that no ocular antibiotic product was labeled to treat. This was the second project for which clinical studies were conducted overseas and in the United States at the same time; Abshire even had investigators in India for the corneal ulcer protocol. Alcon's Microbiology unit supervised over seventy contracted laboratories to test bacterial cultures within hours of arrival; fifteen thousand swabs were processed from more than three thousand patients. Three years after filing the IND, and twenty-three days after the last patient visit, thirty volumes of the digitally formatted NDA, a first for Alcon R&D, went to the FDA. The ciprofloxacin team and RA quickly responded to FDA inquiries, the last on December 30, 1991. At 6 p.m. on New Year's Eve, the FDA faxed an approval letter. Process Development made the first three batches in Manufacturing, and the Ophthalmic Division launched Ciloxan Ophthalmic Solution on February 27, 1992 (fig. 6.21). From filing the IND to market launch, it had been a remarkably short thirty-six months. Alcon was the first to market an ophthalmic quinolone product and, even better, it had a new treatment indication that competitors were not pursuing.[46]

In another example of project challenges, in the 1980s Naphcon-A became Alcon's top-selling anti-allergy product. In a review of older products, the FDA requested clinical data to support combining its two active ingredients. Demonstrating the contributions of specific ingredients in a combination product is a formidable hurdle in ophthalmic clinical studies, and more so in patients with ocular allergies. Ocular allergies are seasonal, and patients exhibit variable symptoms depending on environmental allergens that change every day. Patients also have varying degrees of allergic ocular disease. Clinical Science encountered these problems when it studied Alomide in the mid-1980s, which delayed FDA approval until 1993 (fig. 6.21). In the late 1980s, Mark B. Abelson, a professor at Harvard and Schepens Eye Research Institute in Andover, Massachusetts, developed the Provocative Conjunctival Allery Challenge Model (PCACM). Known allergens were intentionally instilled onto patients' eyes, with the goal of making them exhibit ocular allergy symptoms. Variables could be controlled since this provocation was performed outside the normal allergy season, and patients' allergy status was measured on the day of each test. Moreover, a medication could be tested for preventive (instilled before the allergen provocation) or therapeutic (instilled after the allergen provocation) purposes. Chambers of the FDA collaborated with Abelson in developing the PCACM. Clinical Science performed in Abelson's laboratory a preliminary study that documented how each ingredient in Naphcon-A contributed to its efficacy. A larger study in Austin confirmed the results, and the FDA renewed its approval of Naphcon-A, allowing Alcon to continue marketing it.[47]

With this model accepted by the FDA and the EMEA, Clinical Science evaluated emedastine and olopatadine, compounds licensed from Japanese pharmaceutical companies. Stella Robertson transferred from the Research Department in 1993 and inherited a team of experienced CRAs who had organized PCACM studies for Naphcon-A. Both emedastine and olopatadine were proven to be preventive and therapeutic, unique label claims not heretofore approved by regulatory agencies. Patanol (olopatadine) and Emadine (emedastine) were launched domestically and overseas in 1996 and 1997 (fig. 6.21). Raw material supply issues limited Emadine's distribution, but over time Patanol dominated the global ocular allergy market. By the end of 2000, Patanol's global annual sales reached $100 million.[48]

Ophthalmic steroid products have been used since the 1950s. Maxidex had been Alcon's premier anti-inflammatory therapy since the 1960s. Flarex (0.1% fluoromethalone acetate) was launched in 1991 (fig. 6.21) and proved to be safer but not as effective as Maxidex or Pred Forte. In 1988 Alcon licensed rimexolone from N.V. Organon in Holland. About one hundred R&D scientists worked on the rimexolone team. Rimexolone is insoluble in water, but pharmaceutical formulators used their knowledge and experience to create a new suspendible formulation, which Alcon patented. Clinical studies for conjunctival and iris inflammation demonstrated superior efficacy compared to the market and clinical standard, prednisolone acetate, and rimexolone had a lower potential to raise IOP in patients. After completing eleven studies involving eleven hundred patients, R&D filed an NDA in May 1994. The FDA approved it seven months later. The package insert included an additional therapeutic indication for treating inflammation of the anterior chamber, particularly after ocular surgery, which no other ophthalmic steroid could claim. Vexol was launched in May 1995 (fig. 6.21). Cataract surgery results in the release of prostaglandins that constrict the pupil and induce inflammation in the anterior chamber. Clinical studies demonstrated Profenal, a nonsteroid anti-inflammatory, inhibited pupil constriction. The FDA approved the NDA on December 23, 1988, and the Surgical Division launched Profenal in May 1989 (fig. 6.21).[49]

Alcon had dominated the steroid-antibiotic combination market since the 1950s, its premier product being Maxitrol, introduced in the mid-1960s. During the 1980s, R&D patented the combination of dexamethasone alcohol and tobramycin, named TobraDex. When Maxitrol was approved, the FDA also established class labeling for steroid-antibiotic combinations—steroid-responsive ocular inflammations where risk of infection exists. RA convinced the FDA that a clinical study in cataract patients was sufficient to evaluate safety and efficacy. The NDA for TobraDex, filed in 1986, was approved on August 1, 1988. Ninety hours later, Manufacturing placed in quarantine the first lot of TobraDex (fig. 6.22).[50]

As discussed earlier, released in 1985, Betoptic had two weaknesses in comparison to the market leader, Timoptic: higher incidence of discomfort and slightly less IOP reduction. Rajni Jani's formulation team in Pharmaceutical Science discovered the addition of Carbopol 940 polymer resin beads (fig. 6.22) bound the active molecule, betaxolol, result-

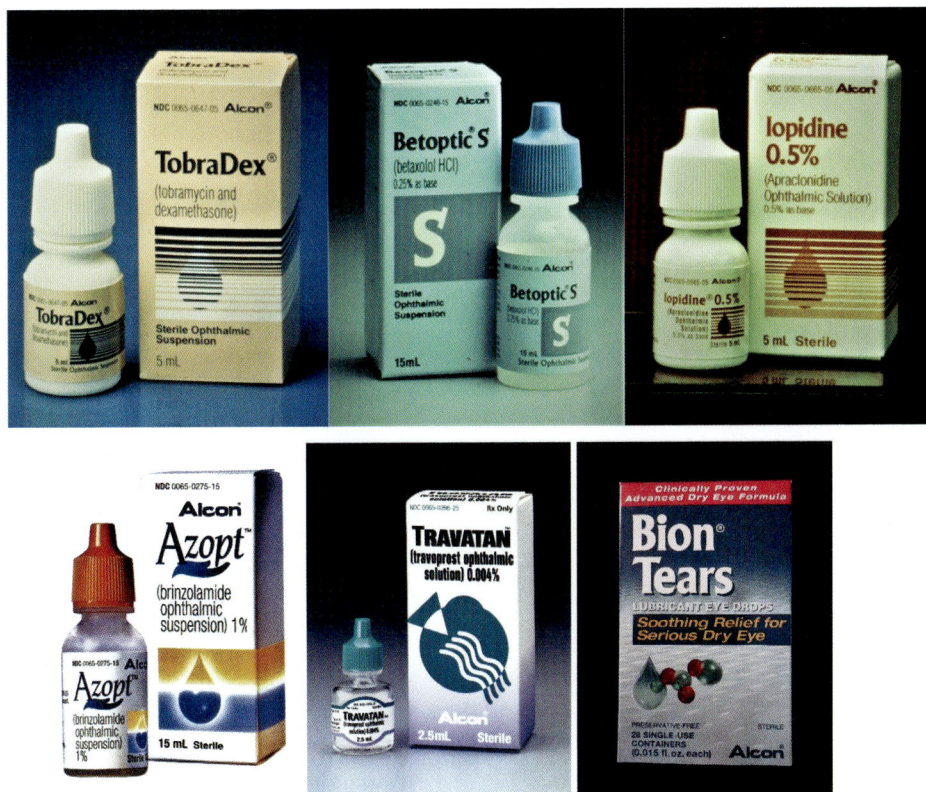

FIG 6.22
R&D antibiotic combo,
anti-glaucoma, and dry
eye therapies (TOM, AM;
AHR)

ing in a suspension that slowly released betaxolol after instillation. Countless experiments determined the right cationic resin, particle size, concentration, and combination with the polymer to create the elegant betaxolol micro-suspension. This unique, patented drug delivery vehicle reduced the concentration of betaxolol from 0.5% to 0.25%, eliminating most of the discomfort while improving IOP reduction. Clinical Science conducted studies over eighteen months with thirty investigators in the United States and Europe, enrolling over one thousand patients. The FDA approved Betoptic S on December 29, 1989, and the first shipments coincided with a national sale launch on February 12, 1990.[51]

Many glaucoma patients require more than one drug to control IOP, and since the introduction of beta-blockers in the 1970s, pilocarpine had become the adjunctive therapeutic drug of choice. The Pharmaceutical Group successfully combined 0.25% betaxolol and 1.75% pilocarpine HCl using the patented Carbopol 940 polymer resin beads formulation. After completing the necessary preclinical and clinical studies, an NDA was approved on April 17, 1997.[52]

In the meantime, the debate about developing Iopidine 0.5%, an α-2 agonist, as a glaucoma therapy continued. There were significant challenges: when dosed regularly it produced allergic reactions in a small number of patients; its efficacy slightly decreased over time; and it was a potent vasoconstrictor with uncertain side effects in the long term. Still, its value within the glaucoma specialist community was heightened during presentations at a 1992 FDA advisory committee hearing. Many had been investigators in clinical studies, and matters came to a head at Alcon when a competitor started its own α-2 agonist glaucoma project. On July 30, 1993, the FDA approved Alcon's NDA with a label indication for short-term adjunctive therapy in glaucoma patients requiring additional reduction in IOP. This labeling placed Iopidine 0.5% in a new category for glaucoma medications (fig. 6.22).[53]

R&D's Research Department patented a CAI molecule, brinzolamide, for treating glaucoma. Another pharmaceutical company was exploring a similar compound, dorzolamide. Alcon had to create its own DMF for the raw material, which required extensive safety and chemical experiments, in addition to formulation, sterility, stability, and clinical studies. The eye-drop formulation presented a challenge since brinzolamide was not water-soluble, but a comfortable suspension product was developed, unlike the competitor's product. Alcon filed its NDA on January 28, 1997. The FDA approved Azopt, the trade name for brinzolamide, on April 1, 1998; Alcon launched it a month later.[54]

Pharmacia, a Swedish pharmaceutical company, began developing László Bitó's PGF-2α as a glaucoma primary therapy. When R&D's medicinal chemists synthesized travoprost, its own PGF-2α patented molecule, it became an expedited project with the most expensive drug development budget in Alcon's first fifty years. The raw material alone cost almost $1 million per kilogram, and the PreClinical department had to perform extensive safety and raw material characterizations. The NDA went to the FDA on July 7, 2000, and was approved on March 26, 2001. Weeks later, Marketing launched the product, Travatan (fig. 6.22).[55]

By 1988 Alcon R&D had released over a dozen generic drugs. The Hatch-Waxman Act of 1984 encouraged companies to develop and market generic products, and the FDA codified the approval process. A proprietary product became a potential generic drug when it lost patent protection, but the generic formulation had to identically match the registered product. Several Alcon products were approaching expiration of their patents in 1988, and so at the behest of the Patent Department, R&D explored new formulations as a way to extend coverage. Betoptic S is a good example. At the same time, competitors were a rich source of generic products. R&D created a five-scientist team, directed by Haresh Bhagat, to reverse engineer competitor formulations whose patents were expiring. Bhagat's group staged its work so that an application was ready for the FDA the day a patent expired. The Generic unit submitted sixteen ANDAs. All were approved by the FDA and sold under Alcon's generic label, Falcon. The most prominent products were antibiotics or glaucoma medications (fig. 6.23).[56]

Schollmaier created the Falcon entity. That Merck, Sharp & Dohme's Timoptic was the market leader for glaucoma always rankled him, and he hoped the Patent Department would find flaws in its patent, though it was due to expire soon. He visited Merck's CEO in the early 1990s and proposed licensing Timoptic to Alcon to be developed as a generic product. Merck agreed to the proposal, which included a substantial royalty. Falcon launched its generic Timolol 0.25% and 0.5% in January 1996, one week after the FDA approved it.[57]

FIG 6.23
Falcon generic products
(TOM, AM; AHR)

Alcon planned to include polyquad as the prime ingredient for Opti- brand contact lens products. Opti-Soft, launched in 1985, had been a disappointment but a learning experience—only cold disinfectants used for all soft contact lenses could be commercially successful. R&D scientists began exploring remedies even before Opti-Soft was released to Marketing as Alcon had opted out of the lens market and committed to developing and selling support solutions. In Alcon's favor, products could be promoted for all contact lenses, but the disadvantage was that it had to wait until new lenses were marketed before it could create solutions for the new product. There were almost ninety brands of contacts by 1998. Up to 1987 several major lens fabricators developed and sold support solutions. However, from 1988 to 1997 the trend moved from wearers buying new lenses annually to more frequent replacement. The standard interval rapidly changed from monthly to biweekly to daily. Wearers also had other choices, with RGP lenses and, by the 1990s, lenses fabricated from silicon hydrogel. As a result, consumers increasingly chose to wear soft contact lenses, and thus the demand for support solutions expanded. Alcon capitalized on more wearers needing to disinfect, clean, and store contacts.[58]

During this decade, R&D developed and released eight contact lens products, an enviable record. This was in no small part due to a major discovery by Masood A. Chowhan. He

FIG 6.24

Opti-Free evaluated by R&D's Clinical Science, Vision Care unit, 1993. *Left to right, front row*: Dana Sager, Marion Tudor, Janey McGrath, Linda Gower; *back row*: Peter Conroy, Jerry Stein, Mike Christensen, Jacqueline Barry. (AHR)

FIG 6.25

Opti-Free daily cleaner, disinfectant, enzymatic cleaner, and rewetting drops (AHR)

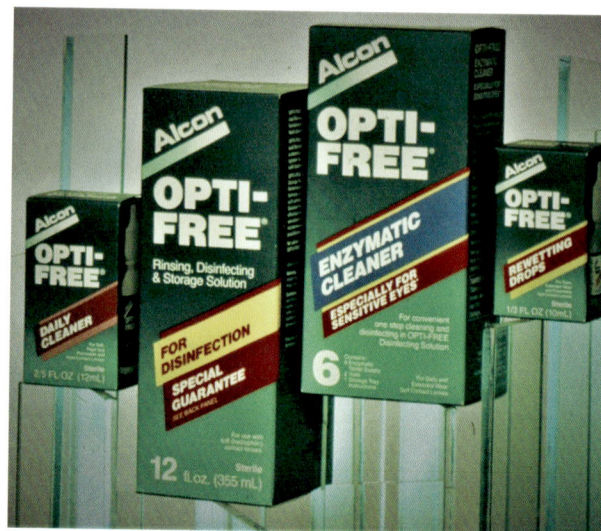

found that by adding citrate, an anionic complexing agent, polyquad was prevented from binding to soft lens materials, thus improving its disinfecting effectiveness. This significant change in Opti-Soft's formulation resulted in a series of new products, and Alcon leaped to the lead market position in contact lens solutions. R&D's Vision Care team conducted the necessary preclinical and clinical studies (fig. 6.24) and filed with the FDA on June 23, 1987, receiving approval on July 21, 1988. Marketing launched Opti-Free Rinsing, Disinfecting, and Storage Solution on September 18, 1988 (fig. 6.25). The product's nomenclature was shortened to Opti-Free, which became the flagship Vision Care product. Having found the secret of formulating polyquad as a disinfectant and preservative, R&D's Vision Care team set about modifying and testing existing products, resulting in a series of contact lens support products built around the Opti-Free brand. Released in 1990 were Opti-Free Daily Cleaner, Opti-Free Enzymatic Cleaner, and Opti-Free Rewetting Drops (fig. 6.25). RGP lenses received their own polyquad product when Opti-Soak was released by R&D in 1995. For their Opti-Free contributions, five members of the R&D Vision Care group received Technical Excellence Awards. Leading the group in the early 1990s was Ralph Stone, a veteran development scientist from Bausch & Lomb who joined Alcon when Randeri transferred to Pharmaceutical Sciences.[59]

In response to the changing market, the R&D team made further formulation modifications, developing Opti-One disinfectant and storage solution for frequent replacement lenses. Marketing introduced this product in the spring of 1994. Until then, contact lens wearers using the Opti-Free system used at least three products to clean, disinfect, and store lenses. Laboratory and clinical studies with Opti-One demonstrated that it cleaned frequently replaced lenses. Scientists then modified the citrate component, resulting in a single product that, in addition to disinfecting and storing, also cleaned the lens when rubbed between the fingers. This formulation had no surfactant ingredient like competitor products (surfactants are the foaming, cleansing component in soaps). The FDA reviewer balked at approving this multipurpose solution, claiming surfactants were necessary. Schollmaier joined the R&D and RA team that visited the FDA. Hubregs recalled, "In spite of overwhelming evidence on cleaning effectiveness for the new 'rub and rinse' cleaning claim for Opti-Free, the FDA reviewing chemist refused to accept that—without a surfactant, the product could not be labeled for cleaning." Even a well-known, non-surfactant chemist failed to convince the FDA official. At an impasse, Schollmaier pulled two tubes from his coat pocket, shook both; one was frothy and cloudy and the other clear. He asked the chemist which he would rather put in his eye and then identified the frothy tube as a com-

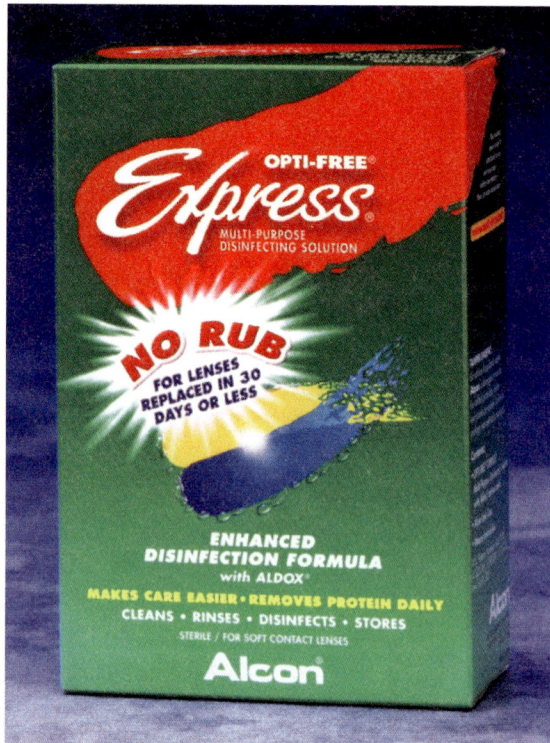

FIG 6.26
Opti-Free Express, 1995 (AHR)

petitor's cleaning solution with a surfactant and the clear tube as Alcon's new formulation. The FDA approved the product in November 1996, which Alcon sold as Opti-Free Express (fig. 6.26).[60]

Around the same time, formulation chemists solved a decades-long problem by stabilizing a liquid pancreatic enzyme to be dissolved in the Opti-Free solution. This project had started in the mid-1980s when Rolf Schäfer, who later formed the AMSIS joint venture with Alcon, collaborated with R&D contact lens scientists. Laboratory and clinical studies demonstrated the new product's effectiveness for use as a daily cleaner for protein deposits on contact lenses. Vison Care marketed it as Opti-Free Supra Clens; its main advantage was the convenience, safety, and efficacy of a liquid product. Thus, the Opti-Free brand soon dominated the global market.[61]

The 1980s were transformative for ocular surgery. Several procedures became noninvasive when surgeons began using diode dye and neodymium-yttrium aluminum garnet (YAG) lasers. Miniaturized specialty probes and cutting devices enhanced vitreous surgery, making it safer and more effective. Implantation of IOLs improved patients' vision and allowed them to enjoy an unencumbered lifestyle. While BSS PLUS made ocular surgery safer, so did the introduction of a viscoelastic solution, the first being Healon, for cataract surgery. Phacoemulsification technology also boosted the safety and outcomes of cataract surgery. When foldable IOLs were introduced, which allowed incisions of three millimeters (⅛ inch) that needed only one or two sutures, phacoemulsification became the prevailing surgical technique. As a result, cataract surgery changed from a complicated procedure requiring hospitalization to day surgery at out-patient centers. These innovative procedures were made safer by single-use, sterile surgical products. All these transformations challenged Alcon and its competitors to provide better devices that further improved surgical outcomes for ophthalmic patients.

Alcon's acquisitions of CooperVision and Biophysic in 1989 brought a raft of marketed products to the Surgical Division. These included a market-leading phacoemulsification device; noninvasive, diagnostic ultrasound tools; surgical and diagnostic lasers; imaging devices, keratometers, and specular microscopes that measured corneal properties; a series of non-foldable IOLs; a viscoelastic for cataract surgery; patient-ready sterile, single-use kits and trays; surgical microscopes; and probes, irrigation cannulas, and vitreous cutting tools among several single-use instruments. These were complemented by existing vitreous surgical systems, IOLs, ocular needle and sutures, handheld stainless-steel ophthalmic surgical instruments, and custom packs obtained when Alcon made other acquisitions. Alcon also had legacy products used by surgeons: BSS PLUS, Miostat, Steri-units, eye drapes, surgical wicks, and several pharmaceutical therapeutics. The new surgical R&D groups—instruments at ITC and IOL in Fort Worth—developed new tools and therapeutics as single-use products, along with surgeon-friendly microscopes and digitized devices that automated the collection of biometrics.[62]

By 1990 cataract surgery had become routine with standardized tools, devices, and medications. This transition led to better outcomes and an increase in cataract procedures worldwide. With the new technology, almost every ophthalmologist could perform the procedure, as opposed to surgeons who specialized in the earlier difficult surgery. Alcon's contribution in instruments and IOL technologies, therapeutics, and training for surgeons and nurses accelerated this democratization of cataract surgery. Cataract surgery became a significant income generator for ophthalmologists. In the United States, it was Medicare-eligible and regimented from start to finish. Alcon provided products for every step, and one way to do so effectively was to market a surgical kit. Custom Paks eliminated the need for surgical centers to clean, organize, and sterilize components. Instead, the surgical team could simply depend upon Alcon to provide organized sets that assured sterility. Surgery on the retina and vitreous required different tools but offered a similar opportunity for consolidation into a procedure-specific set. Thus, Alcon had opportunities for several product niches.[63]

When Lobdell took charge of the Instrument R&D Group at the ITC in 1991, the Cavitron/Kelman phacoemulsification device, the instrument used to break up a lens before extraction, had been around for several years, but it had drawbacks. Lobdell discovered a two-year-old project that had languished under unrealistic performance expectations set by Marketing. Raval's directive to Lobdell gave his team the responsibility for determining performance features. This harkened back to Schollmaier's promise to Raval in 1974 and the way R&D had operated since then. Electronics, fluidics, digitized formats, and instrument miniaturization technologies had evolved. The development team included mathematicians, computer programmers, nano-electricians, hydrologic engineers, plastic and metal fabricators, and a host of others with mechanical, engineering, computer, materials science, and additional skills. After four years and $20 million, the cataract instrument team released the Series 20000 Legacy (fig. 6.27), which Surgical Marketing introduced at the 1993 meeting of the American Society of Cataract and Refractive Surgery. The Legacy's most strik-

FIG 6.27
Legacy 20000 phacoemulsification machine (AHR)

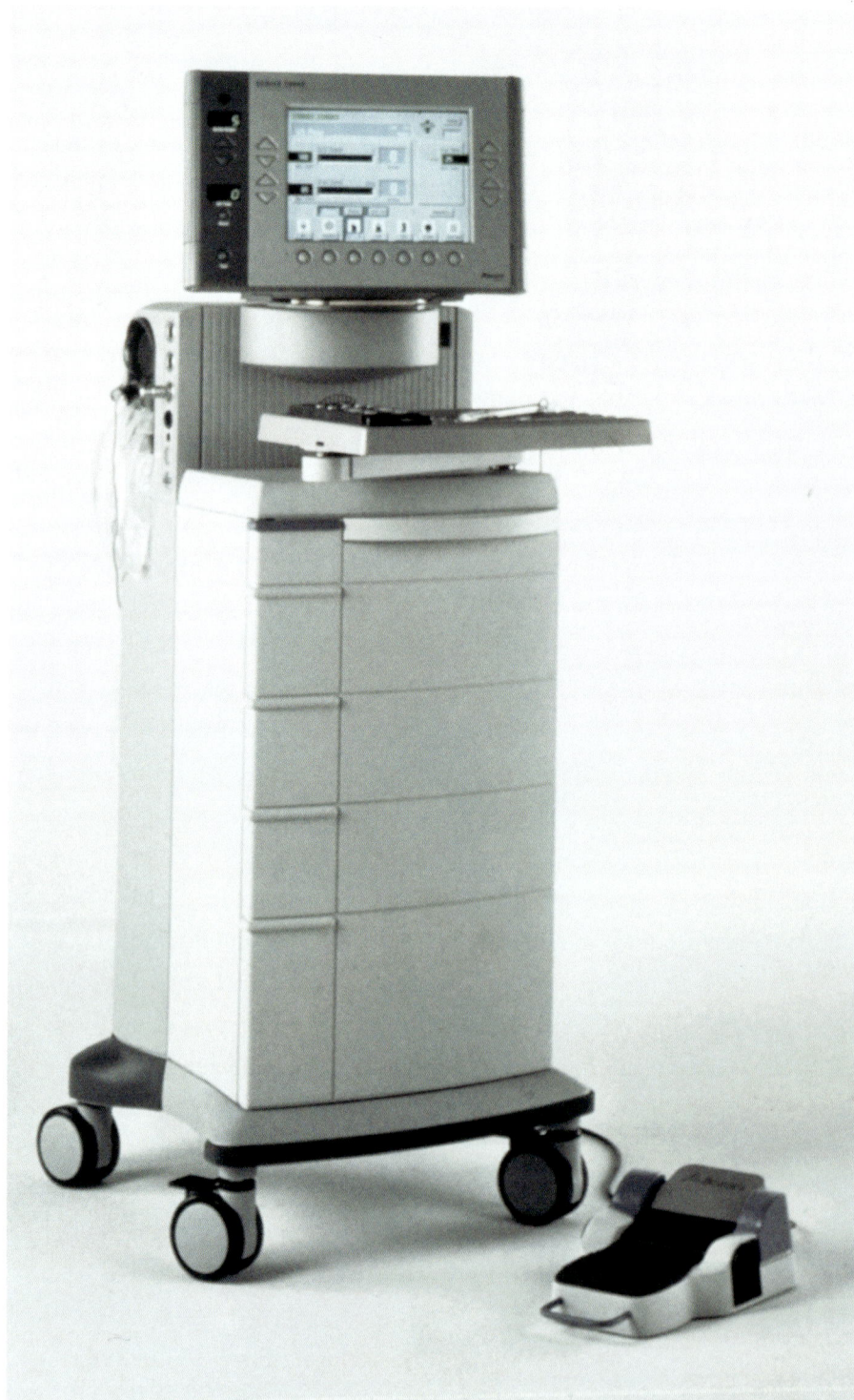

ing innovations were its touch-activated color screen and a hard drive, which permitted the operator to download software. One attractive enhancement was modular construction, allowing surgeons to upgrade the system as new features became available. The patented, bent Turbo-Sonic (fig. 6.28) needle tip decreased the average phacoemulsification time by 40 percent and made more precise incisions. Legacy's automatic voice confirmation, a safety feature for each phase of the surgery, impressed surgeons. Legacy was designed for Alcon's single-use products: BSS PLUS, tubing, connectors, and others. Subsequent improvements involved software, handpieces, micro tips, video overlay, and others. Alcon dominated the phacoemulsification market and by 1997 sold over four thousand Series 20000 Legacy instruments.[64]

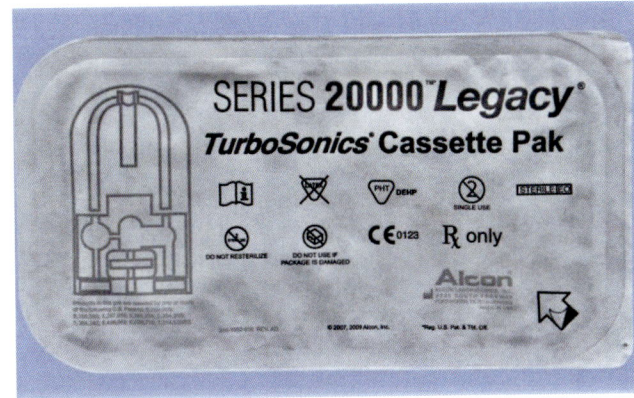

FIG 6.28
TurboSonics Cassette Pak (AHR)

Cataract procedures are performed in the anterior chamber of the eye. Going beyond the lens, surgeries involving the retina or vitreous humor require specific tools and technologies. Alcon expanded into this field in 1985 with the acquisition of MID-LABs and its MicroVit device. Vitreous surgery involves removing foreign bodies or unhealthy tissue from the back of the eye. Such devices need capabilities for cutting, aspiration, irrigation, and illumination (fig. 6.29). In 1990 the R&D Group at ITC launched its own device, the Series 10000 Ocutome, which included an advanced foot switch that provided minute control of these functions. It was Alcon's premier vitreous surgical device until 1996, when R&D released the Accurus, which combined five complex surgical computers in one integrated console (fig. 6.30). Its icon-driven touch screen simplified complex vitreous surgeries while enhancing safety. A seventeen-member Retinal Advisory Council and several ophthalmic nurses worked with the Instrument R&D Group on the design for Accurus.[65]

By 1994 R&D had consolidated its teams from San Leandro and the Biophysic acquisition in France and California into the ITC, which employed scientists and engineers supporting diverse technologies including lasers, ultrasound, ultrasonics, optics, electromechanics, electronics, and disposables. One project from Biophysic resulted in Ophthalas 532 YAG, a solid-state frequency double YAG laser for secondary IOL capsular cataracts. A companion product, the Ophthalas SP Argon Laser, a portable argon laser for repairing a torn or bleeding retina, had been released by the France Biophysic group. In 1997 R&D at ITC redesigned the photocoagulating argon laser and released it as the Ophthalas 532 EyeLite. In the same year, it released the reconfigured UltraScan B/A echograph (fig. 6.31). R&D at ITC also collaborated with external companies. Working with Metaphase, Inc.,

FIG 6.29
Vitreous surgical single-use kit (AHR)

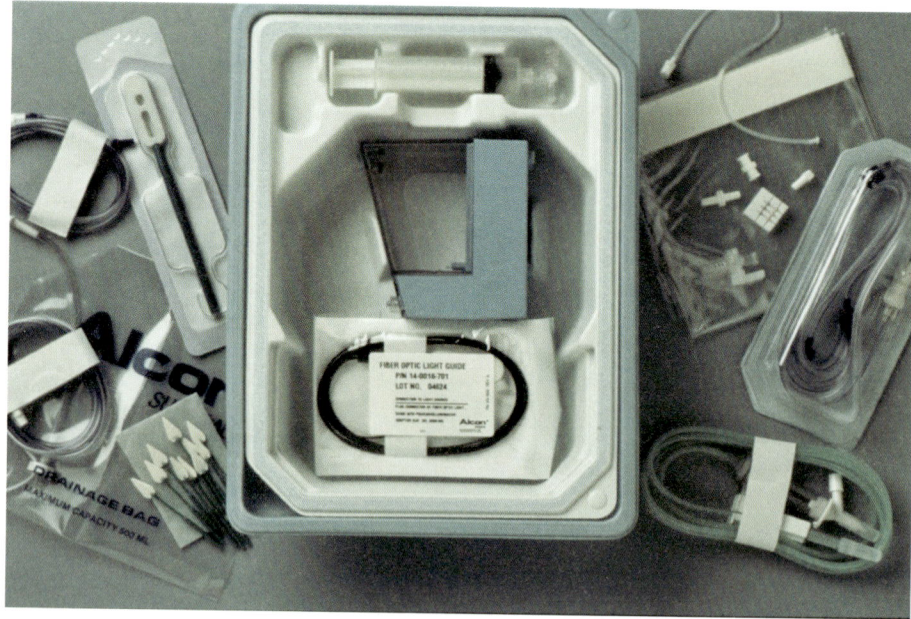

FIG 6.30
Accurus manufacturing and R&D
teams at ITC, 1998. Manufacturing:
Doug Downing, Bob Stuart, Steve Peran,
Majid Aslam, Susan Barajas, Kevin Khong,
Gina Bui, Ron Wright, Ben Juarez; R&D:
Bill Fraser, Sandra Keh, John Huculak,
Nelson Guzman, Josef Rosenthal,
Quang Ngo, Roaslie Grossman,
Kirk Todd, Rick Zaleski, Roger Thomas
(Courtesy of Cathy Jensen)

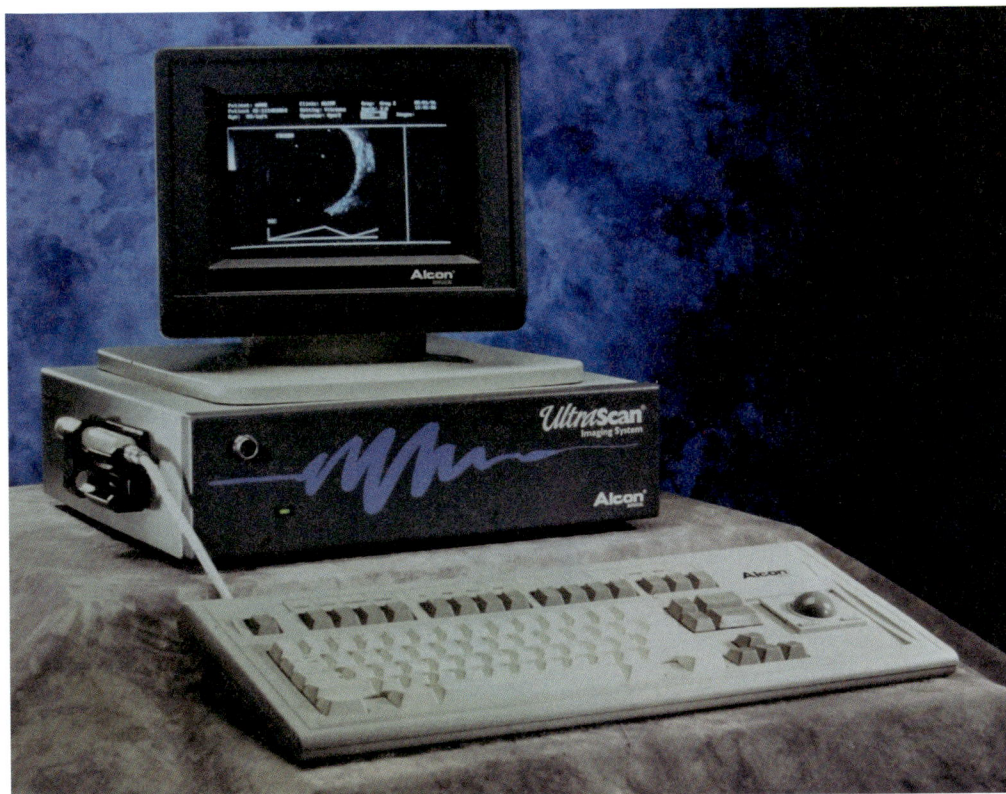

FIG 6.31
UltraScan Imaging System (AHR)

ITC introduced automated, portable, handheld keratometers, the Renaissance TM Series. Speaking of their accomplishments in 1997, Lobdell said, "We have a very structured approach to product development. We focus on products that support Alcon's Surgical systems and that impact the outcomes of surgical intervention. We design platform equipment with proprietary consumables." The strategy proved successful. By the end of 1997, instrument products developed by R&D since 1992 accounted for more than 45 percent of Alcon's worldwide instrument sales.[66]

The inner surface of the cornea is lined by the endothelium, a single cell layer (Appendix 1). Endothelial cells do not divide; the maximum number exists at birth. Significant loss of endothelial cells leads to an irreversibly cloudy cornea and decreased vision. Protection of the endothelium during ocular surgery is paramount. When an incision of the cornea is made, aqueous leaks and the anterior chamber collapses. When injected into the anterior chamber, a viscoelastic vaults the cornea from the zone of cataract surgery. At the time of the CooperVision acquisition, R&D's viscoelastic project, a fermented source of hyaluronic acid, was almost complete. CooperVision brought Viscoat (fig. 6.32), a combination of hy-

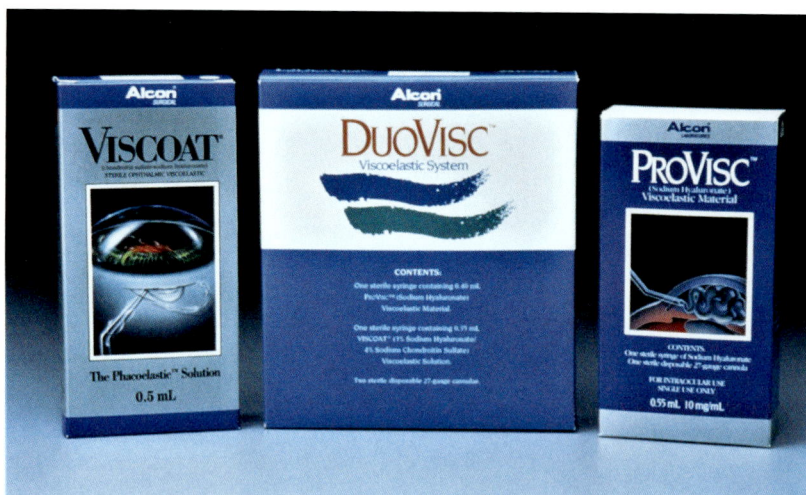

FIG 6.32
Viscoat, DuoVisc, ProVisc (AHR)

aluronic acid and chondroitin sulfate, to Alcon. Hyaluronic acid arches the cornea but is difficult to aspirate following IOL insertion. Viscoat also vaults the cornea but is easier to aspirate, and chondroitin sulfate adds a protective layer on the endothelium. Nevertheless, in the 1990s cataract surgeons disagreed on which one was the best. Surgical Marketing promoted Viscoat and when ProVisc, Alcon's Healon-like product, was approved by the FDA in 1994, Alcon launched DuoVisc (fig. 6.32), providing cataract surgeons with options.[67]

Stevens and a small team of polymer scientists came to Fort Worth from CooperVision. Stevens supplemented his team by hiring scientists with technology expertise. With Alcon, he had access to chemists, formulators, toxicologists, microbiologists, and other scientific groups. Before the move, Raval and Stevens examined the ongoing projects at CooperVision. By the time his group moved to Fort Worth, Stevens had reduced the number to four: a foldable IOL, a UV blocker IOL, a multifocal IOL, and a smaller-incision IOL. At Schollmaier's insistence, CooperVision was fully integrated into Alcon during a period of rapid adjustment. Stevens recalled, "It was a huge shift in corporate culture." A significant difference was in R&D's relationship to marketing. At Alcon, marketing was peripheral to the implementation and conduct of R&D projects, whereas at CooperVision it led the development process.[68]

Stevens, Patel, and Graham had perceptive insights into developments in IOL surgery. They had contacts with opinion leaders and exposure to cataract surgery theaters worldwide. Their polymer science experience and understanding of its potential resulted in the IOLs they developed. The team also brought core IOL-fabrication equipment (figs. 6.11). Of the two dozen or so team members, nine were acknowledged for their contributions and recognized with R&D Technical Excellence Awards. But their talents were put to the test when the number one priority project, AcrySof, encountered problems.[69]

CooperVision had filed a PMA for the Jaffe one-piece, biconvex IOL, which the FDA approved in time for a 1990 launch. Stevens's team completed development and clinical testing of the diffractive, multifocal IOL, trademarked as ReSTOR. It was launched in 1992. A fourth IOL, SLimplant, designed for smaller incisions, appeared in 1993. These IOLs were made of PMMA and used thin extruded haptics for fixation within the posterior capsule. Haptics are the appendages of the circular IOL and are compressible, enabling fixation of an IOL. In the early 1990s, Alcon and its competitors marketed IOLs composed of PMMA with two extruded haptics. However, Stevens's technologists developed a hydratable, foldable PMMA polymer.[70]

At end of the 1980s, foldable IOLs inserted through small incisions had become the future for cataract surgery. Silicone IOLs and Alcon's IOGEL started this trend. But these had two disadvantages: they unfolded quickly, potentially damaging the endothelium, and they often decentered, resulting in blurred vision. Trademarked as AcrySof, the hydratable PMMA unfolded gradually and could be affixed with small, extruded haptics. This polymer could be molded into variable thicknesses for different focal lengths, providing a series of IOLs for a cataract surgeon to fit the specific needs of patients. Moreover, its surface properties allowed the incision of minute, diffractive rings that resulted in a multifocal IOL. Thus, Alcon's IOL R&D group developed two AcrySof IOLs—fixed focus and multifocal.[71]

AcrySof was transformative because it was foldable. The folded 5.5 mm diameter IOL with its two haptics (fig. 6.33) could be inserted through a 1.5 mm incision. A single suture or in some cases no suture was required, resulting in minimal incision-induced astigmatism. But IOL scientists faced significant challenges. The AcrySof polymer produced a tacky surface, which hindered unfolding and made insertion difficult. Albert R. LeBoeuf found a patentable process that eliminated stickiness by coating the surface of AcrySof. In most clinical studies, the AcrySof IOL was folded by forceps and inserted. Another team, led by Steven L. Van Noy, explored alternative delivery systems. One version, the AcryPak, used a preloaded AcrySof ready to be folded on the surgical table. The second system placed an unfolded AcrySof in a device called the "wagon wheel," allowing the surgeon to fold it at insertion. Clinical studies initiated in 1990 enrolled more than twelve hundred cataract patients, with almost one-half from Japan and the EU. Graham and his crew trained dozens of investigators on using AcrySof. After a year, overall vision was corrected to 20/40 or better in 97 percent of cases. Moreover, the incidence of posterior capsular cataracts was fewer than that for PMMA IOLs, an outcome ultimately attributed to a ridge on the edge of the AcrySof IOL. Government approvals by Japan and the EU of AcrySof came in 1994, and the FDA followed in 1995.[72]

Pharmaceutical and device development projects sometimes have problems once the products are in widespread use, though most do not present a risk to efficacy or safety. Since AcrySof was marketed overseas first, International launched with the wagon wheel packaging, and several months later the AcryPak appeared in the United States. Within weeks, domestic cataract surgeons observed minute "glistenings" at the IOL's periphery, though

FIG 6.33
AcrySof folded by forceps
and ready to be inserted (AHR)

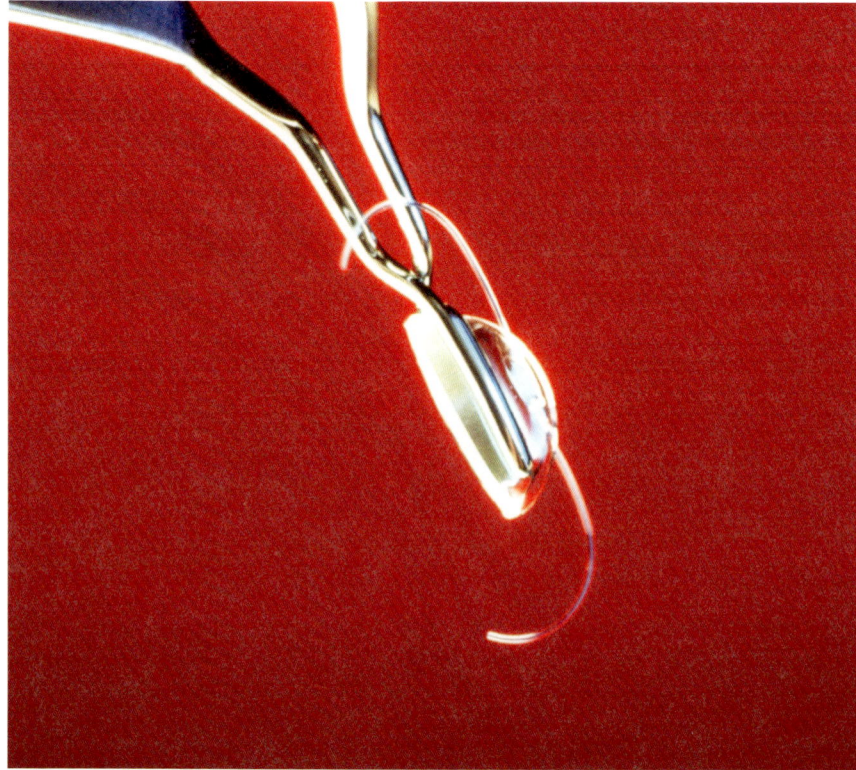

these microvacuoles did not interfere with patients' vision. Alcon Surgical halted the domestic distribution of AcrySof while the R&D IOL team determined the cause. They found that microvacuoles did not occur in patients outside the United States, so the Surgical Division began distributing the wagon wheel package domestically. The IOL Surgical team also designed a single-piece AcrySof, which replaced the extruded haptics, and finished a multifocal AcrySof product. The polymer itself could also be impregnated with a UV-filtering chemical, which filtered out most harmful UV rays to the retina; it was named AcrySof Natural. All three were successfully launched shortly after 1997.[73]

In Alcon's lexicon, *technology transfer* referred to R&D's transfer of a product's manufacturing steps to Manufacturing. Initially, technology transfers for IOLs were straightforward since the manufacture of all IOLs used the common step of lathing, but the technology, polymer, and tools required to produce AcrySof were complex. Moreover, R&D equipment and personnel were in Fort Worth and the manufacturing facility in Huntington, which lathe-cut IOLs. Making the process more difficult still, the AcrySof polymer had to be made and molded into an IOL in one day. A new production line was built, designed specifically for AcrySof, at Huntington. Often technology transfers do not proceed smoothly, and AcrySof was no exception. Nonetheless, after several attempts, Camp, head of the Huntington facility, and his crew perfected the process in time for AcrySof's market launch.[74]

The integration of an acquired company into a new parent company can be fraught with uncertainty and risk. One of Raval's strengths was his ability to select the right person for a job. His selection of Lobdell was arguably the reason his group yielded successful, innovative products. Likewise, Raval recognized the expertise and institutional IOL knowledge of Stevens's unit when he relocated it to Fort Worth as part of the integration of CooperVision. The products developed by these groups amounted to 70 percent of Surgical's global sales by the end of 1997.

The CooperVision acquisition had a major impact on the operations of the Intellectual Property (IP) team led by James Arno. Their assets included patents and patent applications for surgical operating systems and associated products. There were also IP disputes. IOL companies encouraged cataract surgeons to customize lenses, and some filed patent applications, even though the "new" designs were frequently indistinguishable from originals. Such patents led to IOL companies being sued. Alcon inherited several disputes with the CooperVision acquisition, creating the need for more IP staff. During this time, the company hired Barry Copeland, Jeff Schira, Patrick Ryan, and Michael Mayo. In addition to their law degrees, Schira's and Ryan's undergraduate studies were in engineering; at Alcon both concentrated on surgical IPs. Copeland and Mayo had BS degrees in chemistry and biochemistry, respectively, and their experience added depth for Ophthalmic and Vision Care IPs.[75]

The IP group filed patents for IOLs, surgical devices, and single-use surgical products and, working with R&D, they applied for patents to protect a large array of new Ophthalmic and Vision Care products. These included the viscoelastic ProVisc, anti-infective Ciloxan, antiglaucoma medications Azopt and Travatan, and the various polyquad disinfectant, artificial tear, and cleaner products. The ProVisc patent was unsuccessfully challenged by Pharmacia. The IP group also contributed to the growth of Alcon generic products under the Falcon brand. Their discovery of weaknesses in Ciba Vision's Voltaren and Merck's Timoptic patents permitted Alcon to introduce competitive generic products. The IP group negotiated research agreements with universities, screening and consulting contracts with pharmaceutical firms, and confidentiality agreements. The activities of the IP group from 1988 through 1997 were remarkable in terms of what they accomplished and its impact on Alcon.[76]

FIG 6.34
Technical Excellence Awardees, 1989
(AHR)

Latest recipients of R&D's Technical Excellence Award (left to right): Dan Kuzmich, Phil Cash, Darell Turner, Ruth Ann Rosenthal, Abe Clark and David Rauls.

From 1988 through 1997, forty-eight R&D scientists received Technical Excellence Awards (fig. 6.34). The awardees came from every discipline and were recognized for contributions to specific products. The annual Alcon Research Institute award increased from $50,000 in 1988 to $60,000 in 1992 and again to $100,000 in 1993. By 1997, 186 awards had been granted to researchers in fourteen countries, totaling almost $11 million. Speaking of the institute in 1997, Schollmaier commented, "This meeting is turning into one of the premier research meetings in the US. Other meetings have become overcrowded and somewhat fragmented; the ARI Symposium has held its focus on advanced research into ocular disorders."[77]

Although Alcon's reputation with eye specialists focused on pharmaceutical preparations, it sold surgical devices (sutures, Cryophake), solutions (BSS, BSS PLUS), and medications (Steri-Units, topical antibiotics) for surgeons. With the acquisition of CooperVision, Alcon took the lead in developing and marketing state-of-the-art cataract and retinal surgical devices, foldable IOLs, and viscoelastics. At the time of the CooperVision acquisition, Spruill's division consolidated the nucleus of a sales and marketing organization. When Baker joined Spruill in 1989, the Surgical Division had first-rate leadership. Spruill was in his element, directing his four hundred employees with plants in Fort Worth,

Nashville, Sinking Spring, and San Leandro, and annual sales of slightly more than $100 million. Alcon's Closure System (sutures and needles) and its BSS PLUS irrigation solution led their markets. In the chaotic market for IOLs and cataract and retinal surgical devices in the 1980s, Alcon was just one of several competitors. The 1989 CooperVision and Biophysic purchases secured Alcon's Surgical Division as worthy of a leading ophthalmic device company. These acquisitions added almost sixteen hundred personnel, sales of about $200 million, and facilities in Clermont-Ferrand, Irvine, Huntington, and Houston.[78]

Since CooperVision had been cobbled together via acquisitions and was not totally integrated, Alcon intended to immediately and fully merge its new addition. The company wanted to take advantage of the rapidly changing competitive environment since hospitals and surgical centers wanted multiproduct suppliers. Alcon managers expected CooperVision's operations to present significant cultural and procedural differences, making integration challenging. In addition to acquiring new products, technology, and facilities, Alcon was attracted to the quality of the employees at CooperVision and Biophysic and their second-tier managers (fig. 6.3), many of whom it hoped to keep. Alcon leaders knew Barry Caldwell, the head of sales and marketing for surgical instruments; he worked for Webcon in the 1970s. Spruill and Baker spent much time convincing people to move to Fort Worth; Cary Rayment (fig. 6.35) was one. Native to the Northwest, Rayment and his wife were reluctant to relocate. Spruill convinced Rayment to come to Fort Worth and commute back and forth to Seattle. Rayment thrived at Alcon and within a year he and his wife moved, as did other families in a similar situation. Rayment later became Alcon's fourth CEO in 2004.[79]

Compensation became an issue for those relocating. Alcon had competitive wages for a company in North Texas. But many CooperVision folks lived in California, where salaries were larger due to a higher cost of living. This resulted in a challenging situation, as one long-term Alcon employee recalled. Most CooperVision employees recruited by Alcon accepted the move to Fort Worth and the Surgical Division's new organization was in place by early 1990, but integrating the two entities from a business perspective proved more complex than expected. CooperVision, like Alcon, had an entrenched culture. An Alcon employee involved in the process concluded that while the newcomers were "very smart people, very good people, very committed," they were also "accustomed to free wheeling and dealing, and not a tremendous amount of structure." In contrast, Alcon was very structured and had a deeply engrained procedural mentality due to the high retention rate of the workforce.[80]

Spruill divided marketing and sales into two groups based on products. For Surgical Products, he merged elements from Alcon and CooperVision. Rayment took charge of Sur-

FIG 6.35
Cary Rayment (AHR)

gical Products: IOLs, Alcon Closure Systems, solutions and drugs, viscoelastic, and Custom Paks. The Surgical Products group understood that ocular surgeons, operating room nurses, hospitals, and surgicenters had specific needs. On the marketing team, product managers for these five areas were a mixture of experienced Alcon employees and former CooperVision personnel. Bill Weir headed the sales organization. In addition to the Fort Worth staff, there were fourteen division sales managers and over one hundred territory managers based throughout the United States.[81]

Without an existing instrument marketing or sales organization, Spruill adopted CooperVision's organization. Caldwell directed the Instrument Products group with Scott Manning in charge of marketing, supported by product managers. Don Fagen was the national sales manager supervising seven divisional managers, twelve sales specialists, and forty-two territory managers. Caldwell intended Alcon to "be the undisputed market leader in developing, manufacturing, marketing, and distributing cataract and vitreoretinal instrumentation and accessory products for use in all surgical sites."[82]

Support groups for marketing and sales were extensive. Andy Lubrano, the longest-serving member in the Surgical Division, led a unit of eleven in Sales Service, which made sure sales representatives had tools and supplies to complete a sale. In a matrix relationship to both the Ophthalmic and Surgical Divisions, Bob Nelson led the Managed Care Group, which provided a team approach in the development of bundling and pricing programs to segments of the multi-hospital market, including alliances, ambulatory surgical centers, and health management organizations. Each Alcon division had a finance team. The Surgical Finance unit under Henry Meadow had thirty-four people, mostly Alcon veterans, in three parts: controller (Rick Halprin); business systems (Charles King); and planning/reporting (Brad Kling). The centralized Surgical Materials Management team, led by Ron Hensell, expanded to ten people. The Business Support unit combined the efforts of sixty-five employees in customer support, sales, records management, business support training, project administration, and administrative support. Most were in four Customer Support groups, providing telephone coverage from 7 a.m. EST to 5 p.m. PST and handling about one thousand calls per day. Alcon veteran Daryl Dubbs led Training and Education Services, overseeing a cadre of thirteen. Dave Blunt and A. J. Hiltenbrand handled international training, while Greg Booher and John Copeland worked with the United States staff. In 1990, Dubbs's department conducted nearly ninety courses with over two thousand physicians attending. These courses, often at medical meetings such as the AAO, included didactic and wet labs, giving surgeons practical experience with Alcon products. When Spruill took charge of the Surgical Division in 1977, there were twenty-one employees. Illustrative of his division's growing role at Alcon and the expansion of ophthalmic surgical procedures, by 1990 he led a team of two thousand, including Manufacturing, QA, and R&D.[83]

An excellent salesman, Spruill set about selling the concept of an integrated surgical division to existing Alcon personnel and the CooperVision newcomers. He achieved this through personal interaction and by writing articles for *Surgical Insights*, the division's magazine. Frequent themes were teamwork and customer satisfaction, both highlighted in the division's mission statement (fig. 6.36). The first step in building a premier sales team took place in July 1989, when both the former CooperVision and Alcon surgical sales forces came to Fort Worth for cross-training. "United for Success" was the theme at the second joint sales meeting in 1990. Spruill and Baker also used Alcon's Junior Achievement bowling tournament in Fort Worth to enhance Alcon Family ties to remote groups (fig. 6.37). The most sustained effort at ensuring a first-class, integrated sales force was Alcon Consumer Focus. Spruill entrusted Maury Rester, who had worked with him since 1977, to lead the program. Rester's lectures and editorials focused on providing full customer satisfaction, solving problems, and anticipating product and service requirements. Commenting in 1991 on the progress of integrating CooperVision, Schollmaier said, "We've carefully built the two organizations into one while at the same time enhancing the quality of the products and the services we offer to our valued customers."[84]

When Rayment took charge of Surgical Products in 1989, his department managed a wide array of products. The solutions and drugs included BSS, BSS PLUS, Miostat, TobraDex, Profenal, and Iopidine 1%, as well as mydriatics and local anesthetics. Approval of Ciloxan in 1992 added a valuable antibiotic option. Alcon Closure Systems (knives, needles, sutures, etc.) had been

Vision Statement

We are partners with our customers now and forever more in improving and preserving sight; together, our contribution to mankind's quality of life will far exceed what can be accomplished separately.

We delight our customers by far exceeding their expectations. We listen to our customers and continually seek their ideas. We view customers as family, as they do us, and together we share common dreams and values. Our customers eagerly seek all of our products because the entire Alcon Surgical team is committed to providing the very best quality and services. Our customers recognize that we are uniquely devoted to the field of ophthalmology, and never doubt our sincerity and long-term commitment to excellence.

We have a work environment where everyone can have fun, is empowered, valued, trusted, feels secure, and is encouraged to share any news, good or bad. We treat each individual with dignity and respect. We encourage creativity and personal development and reward performance and honest effort. We find a better way of doing things each day and constantly challenge the status quo. Alcon is the kind of company where we would want our family or closest friends to work. We realize we have a choice, and we choose to work for Alcon.

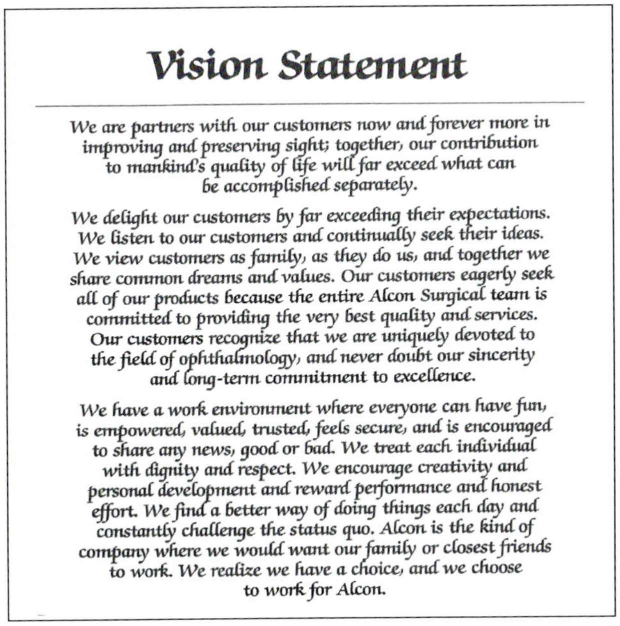

FIG 6.36
Surgical's vision statement

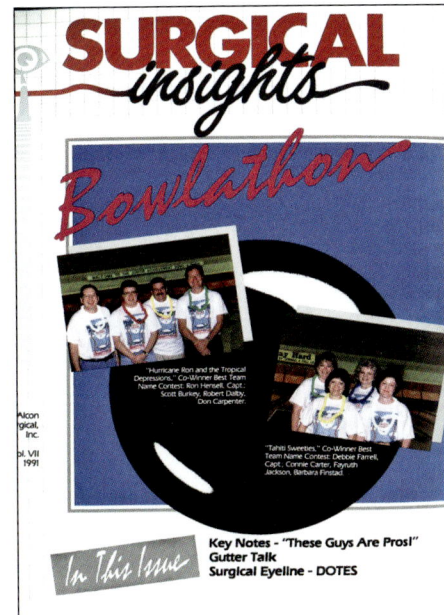

FIG 6.37
Surgical Division's Bowlathon teams, 1991 (*Surgical Insights*, 1991) (AHR)

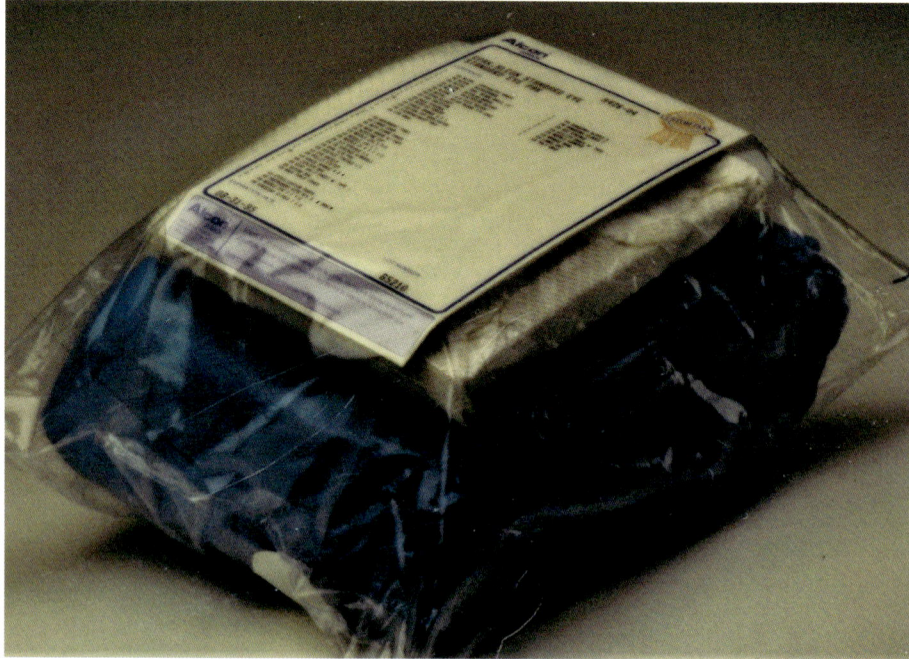

FIG 6.38
Surgical Division's Custom Pak (AHR)

around for two decades, as had drapes and absorbing wicks. Two innovative products, Excalibur S needle and Pair Pak II, were released in 1989. Viscoat came with CooperVision, and ProVisc was launched in 1994. Alcon packaged both together as DuoVisc (fig. 6.32). The initial range of Alcon IOLs was limited compared to CooperVision. All were nonfoldable PMMA IOLs. Thus, when R&D released AcrySof in 1994, and then subsequent models, Alcon had its own brand that became the number one choice of cataract surgeons worldwide. Alcon had a Custom Pak facility, but CooperVision in Houston had a larger customer base, so all Custom Pak (fig. 6.38) preparations and distribution moved there. With Alcon's range of viscoelastics, needles, sutures, knives, and drugs, Rayment's Surgical Products team had a powerful set of options to satisfy its customer base.[85]

The choice of ophthalmic instruments for Caldwell's group to market and sell was robust; most came from CooperVision, Biophysic, or earlier acquisitions. For the surgeon, the principal products were phacoemulsification and vitreous surgery devices, each with its own set of accessories. At the time of the CooperVision acquisition, the Cavitron/Kelman Phaco-Emulsifier Aspirator was a premier product. With the launch of the Legacy 20000 (fig. 6.27) in 1993, Alcon Surgical had a product that made a quantum leap in functionality. Major improvements allowed Alcon to continue to dominate this segment of the cataract market. Vitreous surgery devices were intricate and constructed around single-use components such as the multifunctional cutting-irrigating-aspiration-illumination tips. Through the MID-LABs acquisition in the 1980s, Alcon sold MicroVit, and in 1990 the R&D group at ITC released its own improved vitreous surgical device, the Series 10000 Ocutome. Six years later the Instrument Group launched Alcon's premier vitreous surgical device, the Accurus (fig. 6.30).[86]

During the 1980s Alcon acquired marketing rights to an ocular surgical microscope. CooperVision brought the UltraScan Digital B ultrasound, the Model 2500 Nd:YAG Laser, and the PRO-CEM 4 endothelial microscope. Biophysic Medical had its own Mini

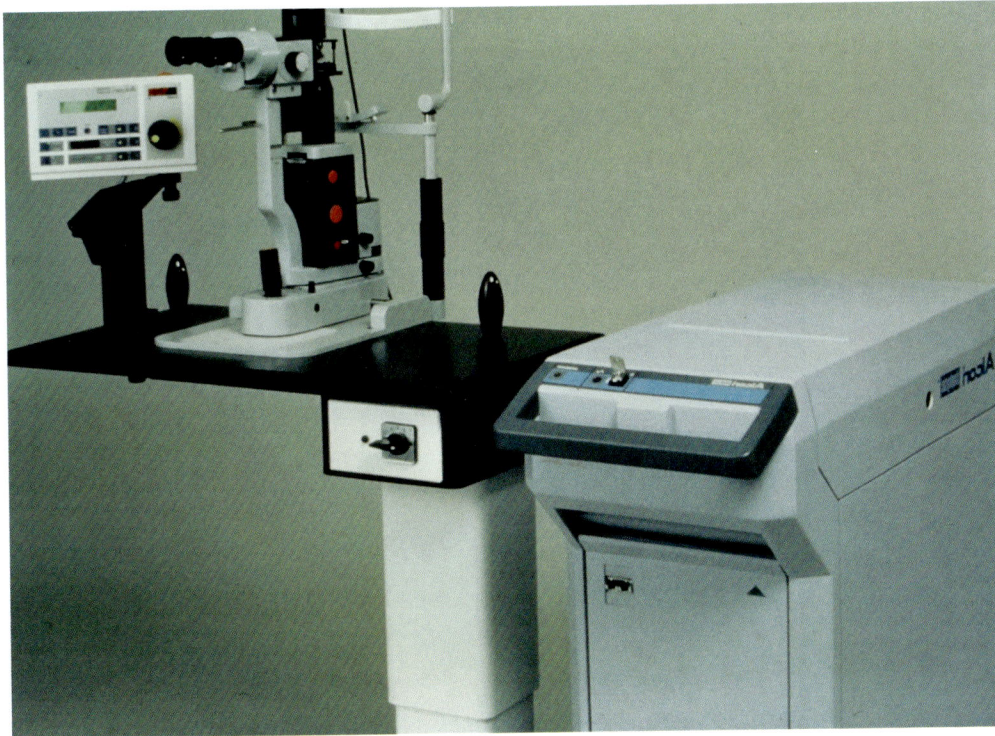

FIG 6.39
Ophthalas 532 YAG laser (AHR)

B-Scan ultrasound, the solid-state Ophthalas 532 YAG laser (fig. 6.39), and the portable Ophthalas SP Argon laser. Improvements led to the 1997 launch of Ophthalas 532 Eye-Lite and a redesigned ultrasound, the UltraScan B/A echograph. In 1992 Alcon launched automated, portable, handheld keratometers, the Renaissance TM series. EyeMap EH-290 Corneal Topography System (fig. 6.40), a diagnostic tool for astigmatic cataract surgery, appeared in 1995. By 1997 Caldwell's team had a full array of tools and devices in their arsenal.[87]

Surgical Division sales grew from 35 percent of Alcon's total in 1988 to 47 percent in 1997. Full credit must be given to the marketing and sales teams, whose enthusiasm, skill, and rapport with physicians led to sales that eclipsed Alcon's other market segments (fig. 6.41). Two new products, AcrySof and Legacy 20000, both became number one products in their areas. In virtually every surgical product category, Alcon dominated domestically and overseas. In term of dollars, the Surgical Division contributed $138 million in 1988, then $980 million in 1997, proving the importance of R&D-developed superior products and experienced, enthusiastic marketing and sales teams. This extraordinary growth reflects

FIG 6.40
EyeMap EH-290 Corneal
Topography System (AHR)

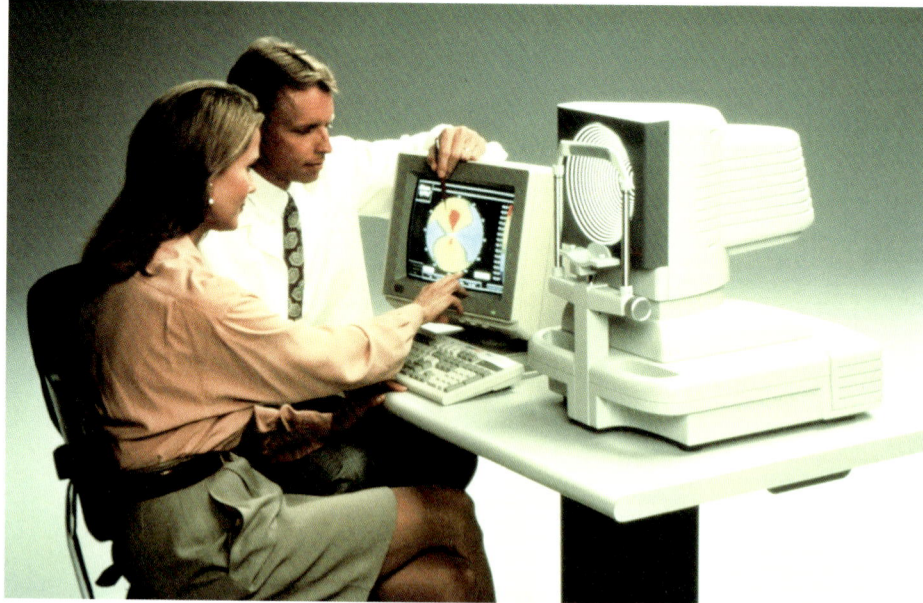

FIG 6.41
Surgical Division sales meeting, 1993
(AHR)

the leadership of Schollmaier, Spruill, Baker, and Raval, especially in integrating CooperVision's talent and technology. It reflects the value of Schollmaier's choice in 1977 in selecting Spruill to lead the Surgical Division. Without question, Spruill's personality, vision, and leadership drove the successes achieved after 1977.[88]

Spruill did not live to celebrate his division's accomplishments on Alcon's fiftieth anniversary in 1997. He died on July 6, 1994, after a three-year illness. The Society for the Prevention of Blindness had recently given him its 1993 People of Vision Award. Speaking of this, Spruill said, "Of course I am very honored. But you know, it's something you really enjoy, it's not really work. We all grew up together, turned gray together, and built the company together." Speaking at Spruill's induction into Alcon's Hall of Fame, Schollmaier said, "John is a natural fit in the Hall of Fame. His efforts helped bring Alcon to the forefront of the ophthalmic industry. He has a real passion for work—and for people. He's just a rare individual." Baker added, "John has a way of putting something on the table that might scare the daylights out of us all, but then make it sound so beautifully simple that we couldn't resist trying it. And the funny thing is, nine times out of ten, it worked." Imposing in stature, Spruill left a giant legacy, which the Surgical Division, recognized with the annual John W. Spruill Leadership Award.[89]

In addition to overseeing QA and Manufacturing/Engineering, Sisson led the Vision Care and Ophthalmic Divisions. Opti-Soft's launch in 1985 did not meet expectations, but in the process Weightman's Vision Care team learned to innovate in marketing, selling, and product positioning. They became familiar with optometrists and ophthalmologists who prescribed contact lenses and retailers who sold contact lens products to consumers. Weightman focused on hiring and developing superior people with the skills required for the tough contact lens market. Alcon faced obstacles as a company selling contact lens products without a line of contact lenses. Eye care professionals challenged Alcon on this point, but it helped hone Vision Care's selling and marketing skills, resulting in a determined and successful team. By 1987 the problems with contact lenses created by two preservatives, thimerosal and sorbic acid, were acknowledged; meanwhile, hydrogen peroxide lens disinfectants were inconvenient for the wearer and, when used improperly, caused eye irritation. There was a need for a safe and simple-to-use disinfectant and storage solution. Thus, the market and Weightman's group were ready when in 1988 Alcon R&D released its Opti-Free Rinsing, Disinfecting, and Storage Solution with polyquad. The FDA authorized its use without heat and for all soft lenses. When the FDA approved Opti-Free Daily Cleaner and Opti-Free Rewetting Drops, both with polyquad, along with Opti-Free Enzymatic Clean-

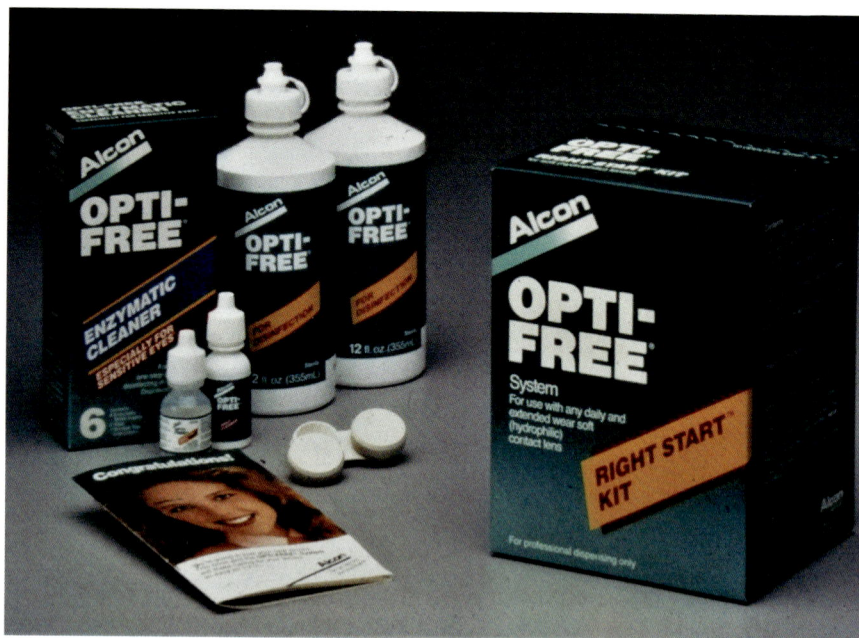

FIG 6.42
Opti-Free starter kit (AHR)

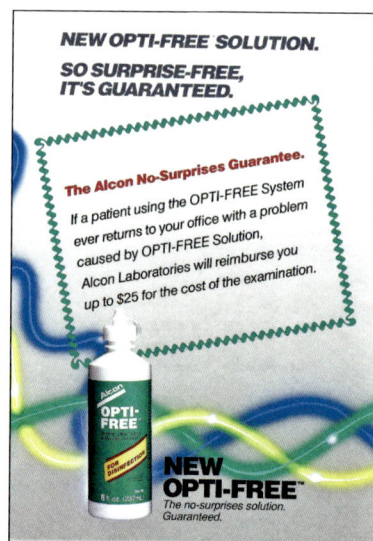

FIG 6.43
Opti-Free guarantee (Sue Faro, AM)

er tablets, Alcon had in the Opti-Free franchise a total disinfectant and cleaner system. It packaged these as starter kits dispensed by practitioners and system kits purchased by patients (6.42).[90]

Though the Opti-Free formulation incorporated a minor change—the addition of citrate—it was different from Opti-Soft, so Weightman's division launched Opti-Free as a new product. They settled on the name Opti-Free, since it was free of thimerosal and sorbic acid. Unlike hydrogen peroxide it was hassle-free for wearers and did not sting. Opti-Free was simple to use with an easy-to-remember regimen. In charge of the marketing effort, Sue Faro created the launch campaign called "free of surprises." Alcon offered prescribers the Opti-Free guarantee: If a patient had any problem caused by Opti-Free, Alcon would pay $25 for lost office time (fig. 6.43). Faro tapped into Martha Siegel's Consumer Complaint group in QA to handle patient or prescriber calls for Opti-Free. Faro recalled, "We put several thousand dollars in the marketing budget aside to cover these claims. Yes, we had claims, but they were less than 1% of the kits we dispensed. So, the no surprises guarantee really was a good marketing tool to get doctors over their reluctance to try the product."[91]

Faro's marketing materials and product profile focused on polyquad. Based upon microbiological data, even at a 0.001% concentration, polyquad was an effective disinfectant with broad-spectrum antimicrobial activity, and as a storage solution it provided continuous antimicrobial activity for safer lens storage. In a visually appealing two-page brochure, Faro noted that polyquad was too large a molecule to penetrate the matrix of contact lenses (fig. 6.44). It did not irritate the eye and did not require rinsing or a neutralizer. Opti-Free with polyquad caused no hypersensitivity reactions. One patient commented, "I almost felt like giving up wearing lenses until I tried *Opti-Free* and now I feel wonderfully free from that burning, uncomfortable feeling in my eyes."[92]

Weightman divided his sales force into two groups. One called on prescribers—optometrists, ophthalmologists, and optical chains—and the other on national retailers, such as Wal-Mart, Target, Walgreens, CVS, etc. Alcon packaged Opti-Free with its companion cleaning and rewetting products in starter kits and distributed these to prescribers, who

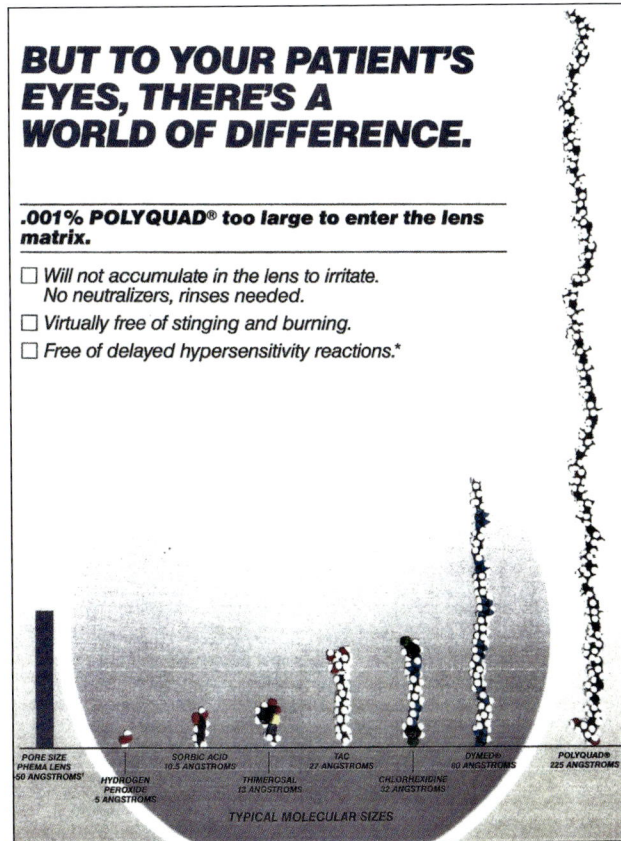

FIG 6.44
Polyquad in Opti-Free, advertisement (Faro, AM)

in turn passed them on to patients. Satisfied wearers could buy Opti-Free solutions from retail stores. Marketing director Bill Burns and product manager Janet Campbell introduced Opti-Free on September 14, 1988, in Alcon's new state-of-the art auditorium (fig. 6.45). According to Weightman, both sales forces left the presentation determined to make Opti-Free the top-selling contact lens solution. Within ninety days, the national accounts group had sold $1 million worth of Opti-Free starter kits, and by the end of 1989 they captured the number one position in the market. This success caused Sisson to believe the Opti-Free line could reach $100 million in sales within five years. In celebrating the most successful product launch in Alcon lens care history, the Vision Care Group rewarded the top producers with a trip to London.[93]

Each year through 1994 became a banner year for the Opti-Free line, with Vision Care's annual sales growth averaging 20 percent. Its total sales were $215 and $237 million in 1993 and 1994. Launching Opti-Free Daily Cleaner, Opti-Free Rewetting Drops, and Op-

ti-Free Enzymatic Cleaner tablets—in 1990 and 1991—gave the sales force new ways to promote the Opti-Free franchise. Vision Care placed Opti-Free advertisements on several prime-time shows and on *Good Morning America* and the *Today Show* in 1990; more television advertisements followed two years later. In a 1993 media blitz, full-page advertisements appeared in *People*, *Cosmopolitan*, *Glamour*, and other magazines "comparing the ease and comfort of wearing an old pair of jeans to the contact lens comfort provided by Opti-Free."

In addition, the sales force promoted Opti-Free products to professionals at conferences such as the American Academy of Optometry, American Optometric Association (AOA), and Contact Lens Association of Ophthalmologists. During the June 1991 AOA meeting in Dallas, over two thousand eye-care professionals were invited to Alcon's Lazy-A Ranch, where they enjoyed barbecue; toured the Conner Center, QA, Manufacturing, and the Alexander Tower; heard country and western music; and applauded rodeo riders (figs. 6.46, 6.47). By 1991 twenty sales representatives focused on retailers. Vision Care had an Optical Chain Advisory Board since this market segment, in which Alcon held a leadership position, made the majority of lens care purchases. In 1991 Vision Care convinced Wal-Mart to boost its lens care sales by offering customized programs encouraging wearers to buy multiple Alcon products. Impressed, Wal-Mart placed a $1 million order. Starting in 1992, Vision Care presented educational programs to all American schools of optometry. By 1993 more than twenty-five hundred students had participated in the

NOVA program. Weightman also formed Vision Care's Blitz Team, which in 1992 and 1993 targeted optometric accounts that used competitors' products; the team converted over two thousand practitioners to Opti-Free and other Alcon products. These programs plus thousands of routine calls contributed to Opti-Free maintaining its market leader position.[94]

Even though the contact lens solution market was flat in 1993, sales for Opti-Free reached $101 million (fig. 6.48), a celebrated milestone that eclipsed Sisson's prediction by two years. Weightman boasted, "To achieve our goal, we had to take share from our competitors. And take share we did." At the January national sales meeting in 1994, Weightman saluted the MSRs: "You are the finest trained, most enthusiastic, most skilled sales force in the profession." Vision Care continued to increase its market share in 1994, closing the year with sales of $220 million. However, by 1994 disposable contact lenses had become the future wave, threatening Opti-Free's dominance. Everyone's fears were realized in 1995; it was a tough year. The combined impact of disposable lenses and consumer preference for one-bottle disinfectant systems made the lens care market more competitive. The Vision Care group ended 1995 at 87 percent of planned revenue. Daily cleaners and enzyme cleaners also faced declining sales due to the shift to low-maintenance lenses, although weekly disposable lenses still needed daily disinfecting and cleaning. R&D modified the citrate ingredient in Opti-Free again and, following the dramatic meeting with the FDA where Schollmaier convinced authorities to approve a rub and rinse claim, Vision Care launched Opti-Free Express, a single-bottle disinfectant and cleaner (fig. 6.49). Some lens wearers produce an unusual amount of protein in their tears, which accumulates even after short-term wearing. R&D developed a daily liquid formulation, marketed as Supra Clens (fig. 6.50), one drop of which was added to Opti-Free Express in the overnight lens storage case.[95]

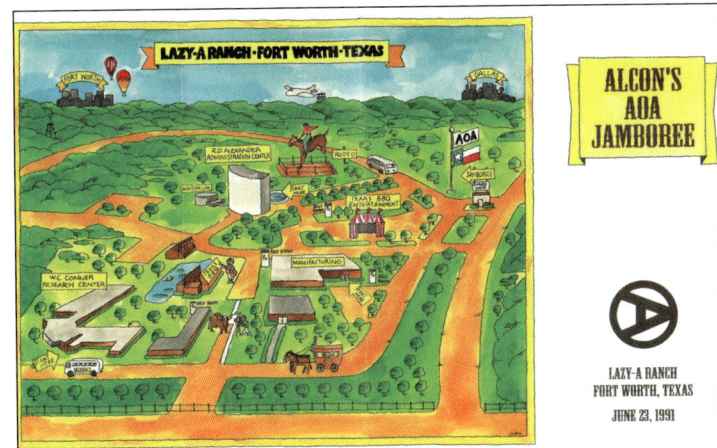

FIG 6.46
Lazy-A Ranch, Alcon's AOA Jamboree, brochure, 1991 (AHR)

FIG 6.47
Alcon's AOA Jamboree, 1991 (AHR)

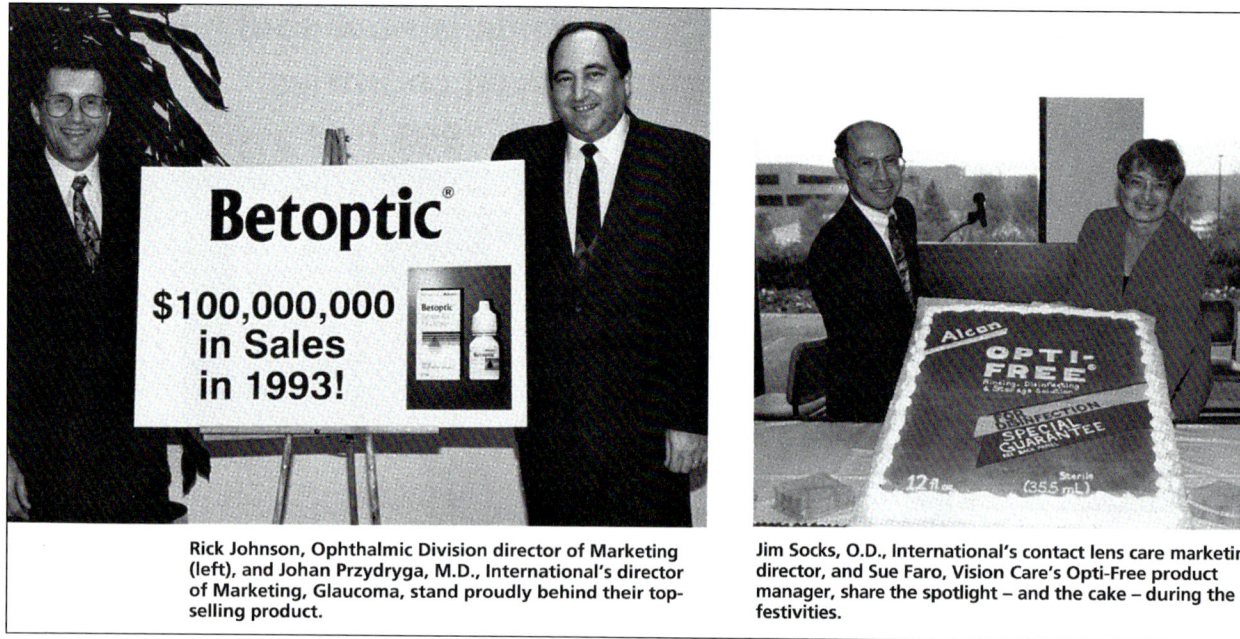

Rick Johnson, Ophthalmic Division director of Marketing (left), and Johan Przydryga, M.D., International's director of Marketing, Glaucoma, stand proudly behind their top-selling product.

Jim Socks, O.D., International's contact lens care marketing director, and Sue Faro, Vision Care's Opti-Free product manager, share the spotlight – and the cake – during the festivities.

FIG 6.48
Betoptic and Opti-Free, Alcon's first
$100 million products (AHR)

FIG 6.49
Opti-Free Express, advertisement (AHR)

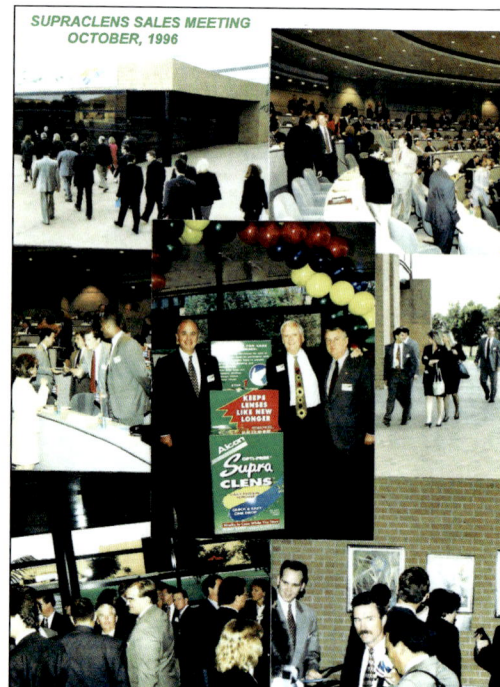

FIG 6.50
Supra Clens introduction, 1996 (AHR)

Vision Care was also responsible for Alcon's OTC eye products. The FDA approved Naphcon-A as an OTC product; its sales continued to be strong. The other major OTC product area was artificial tears. By changing the preservative to polyquad, Alcon created Tears Naturale II, which the FDA made an OTC product. Both Vision Care and Ophthalmic sales forces gave samples of Tears Naturale II to optometrists and ophthalmologists, which they liberally distributed to dry eye patients. The artificial tear market grew to $17 million annually, attracting other companies to market their own brands. Unpreserved artificial tear products packaged in unit doses offered Alcon a new sales opportunity. Alcon launched Tears Naturale Free in 1990, and 145 MSRs from the Vision Care and Ophthalmic sales groups introduced the product (fig. 6.51).[96]

Opti-Free Express, Supra Clens, Tears Naturale II, Tears Naturale Free, and Naphcon-A recharged Alcon in the contact lens solutions and OTC markets and helped drive the 1996 global sales for Vison Care products past $300 million. The 1996 launch of Opti-Free in Japan contributed to this turnaround. Beginning with a core of veteran sales personnel, Vision Care management hired and trained a cadre of young, enthusiastic people, who learned the subtleties of the contact lens market. Vision Care global sales grew from $107 million in 1987 to $380 million in 1997, an impressive, nearly fourfold increase. Seventy percent of Vision Care sales by 1999 were due to Opti-Free, Opti-Free Express, and Supra Clens. Moreover, the Opti-Free and Opti-Free Express brand became Alcon's first $150 million product. Vision Care contributed from 13 percent to 22 percent of Alcon's annual worldwide sales from 1987 through 1997, a consistent performance on which the company depended on the last decade of its first fifty years.[97]

Of course, top sales representatives continued to receive Ring of Honor award trips (fig. 6.52). In 1989 the Vision Care sales force was the first to use laptop computers, replacing handwritten call reports and creating a database on customer information, profiles, and orders. The sales personnel shared their daily appointments and communicated with each other via an internal email system. In 1992 the Vision Care and Ophthalmic Divisions combined their Customer Service departments. Sandra Howell, an Alcon administrator since the mid-1960s (fig. 6.53), led the Ophthalmic group. By then, Alcon had married its telecommunications and computer systems, allowing customer service representatives to immediately see customer account details. Howell noted, "They're impressed with our speed and efficiency. ... It gives a very favorable impression of Alcon, and

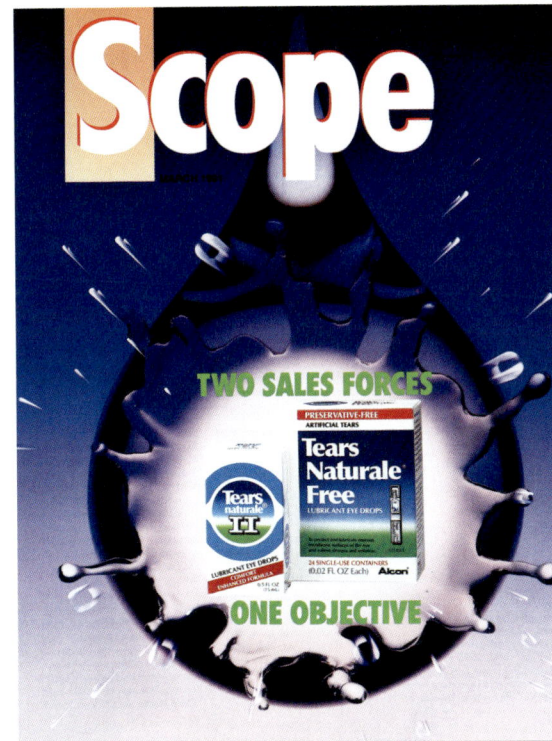

FIG 6.51
Tears Naturale Free (*Scope*) (AHR)

FIG 6.52
Ring of Honor Winners and
top performers, 1993 (AHR)

Jack Weightman, Vision Care Group vice president and
general manager (center), honored 1993 Ring of Honor
winners, including (l-r): Mike Ross, Mike Mason, Tracy
Moody, Karen Siesing, Jeff Mech and Julian Byfield.

Marv Morrison and Kevin Buehler (back row left and right
congratulate Vision Care Group's Consumer Division top
'93 performers (l-r): Linda Crandall, Mark Mischik, Fran
Farber, and Kerrie Kiernan with Food Enterprises.

makes our customers feel more comfortable doing business with us." Weightman retired
at the end of 1996. Mike Hemric, who had served in the Vision Care sales force and as
national sales and marketing director, replaced him. Other organizational changes occurred, including placing Kevin Buehler in a leadership role; he would later become an
Alcon CEO.[98]

Schollmaier's assertion that investments in R&D, QA, Manufacturing, and the Ophthalmic Division would pay off was correct. R&D released a new prescription product every
year between 1988 and 1997, QA and Manufacturing shipped them within days of approval, and marketing and sales used innovative concepts in their launches. More than one
hundred MSRs called on over twelve thousand ophthalmologists, hundreds of hospitals
and ambulatory surgical centers, and thousands of local and chain pharmacies. Most of the

Ophthalmic MSRs had been with Alcon for several years, and some, like R. O. Jennings and John Fitch, for thirty years. Sales and marketing directors and staff had experience in the field, as did several product managers. Sisson, executive vice president of Domestic Operations, had joined Alcon in 1959, and McGoey, the general manager and vice president of the Ophthalmic Division, started in 1980. The collective experience of the division meant it was primed for the flood of launches from 1988 through 1997.[99]

In the 1990s large-scale changes in American health care forced a response from Alcon. To control costs, health care providers turned to managed care, generics, and pharmacy formularies. Physicians looked for economies of scale and increased bargaining power by consolidating their practices. Hospitals merged with physician groups, laboratories, diagnostic centers, and pharmacies. Insurance companies started negotiating with physicians for discounts. The most common physician groups came to be known as Preferred Provider Options (PPOs) and Health Maintenance Organizations (HMOs). As PPOs and HMOs gained power, they leveraged the cost of drugs and devices. Even Alcon used managed care organizations to control its employee health care costs. To support its role in this new environment, Alcon created a managed care division that placed products with PPOs and HMOs. It began in 1988 with Bob Yates and a small staff that negotiated with groups. Bob Nelson took charge in 1992, when the Managed Care Division was formally established. His team increased marketing expertise, hiring a registered pharmacist with an extensive background in the managed care market.[100]

Within this organizational milieu, the Ophthalmic Division launched fourteen prescription and twelve generic products. During this time, no one in the United States pharmaceutical industry was more productive. By January 1989, four years after it was first marketed, Betoptic 0.5% had achieved annual sales of $50 million. After FDA approved Betoptic S 0.25% on December 29, 1989 (fig. 6.22), Manufacturing shipped the first batch on February 12, 1990 (fig. 6.54), the same day marketers introduced it to ninety MSRs at a national sales meeting on the Fort Worth campus (fig. 6.55). The patented delivery system slowly released betaxolol to the eye, resulting in greater patient comfort and a reduction in the amount necessary to lower IOP. Graphic designer Lee Wright described his brochure's eye-catching Betoptic S theme: "I settled on a motif that incorporated a stylized shield shape that also has the appearance of a tear drop. Then I added my interpretation of the way the new delivery system worked ... the activity between the carbopolymer, the resin beads, the sodium ions and the betaxolol molecules" (fig. 6.56).[101]

FIG 6.53
Sandra Howell (AHR)

FIG 6.54
Betoptic S packaging line (AHR)

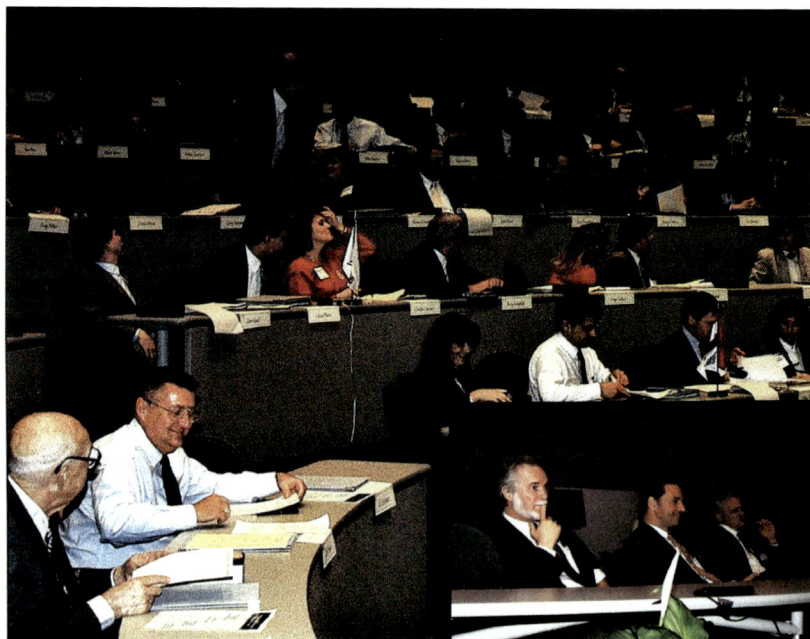

FIG 6.55
Betoptic S launch, 1990 (AHR)

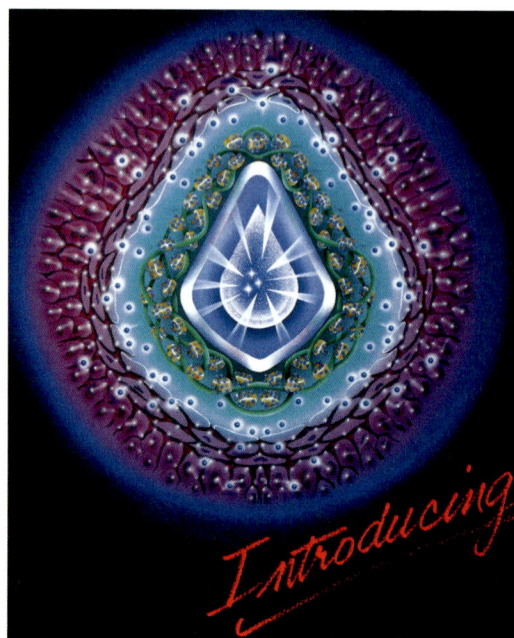

FIG 6.56
Illustration by Lee Wright introducing Betoptic S shows how betaxolol binds to carbapol 940 microbeads (AHR)

The year before Betoptic S's launch, Schollmaier chaired meetings every six weeks to explore innovative ways to introduce this ground-breaking therapy. At the February 1990 launch (fig. 6.57), McGoey told the MSRs, "What we have now is new, significant technology in the form of a delivery system that is far more advanced than that of any other ophthalmic product. This new delivery system provides comfort ... equivalent effectiveness ... within the context of the superior safety of betaxolol." Ophthalmic marketers held conferences, in the United States and overseas, led by glaucoma specialists highlighting the safety, ocular comfort, and efficacy of Betoptic S. One conference theme encouraged physicians to think about the whole patient before prescribing a beta-blocker (fig. 6.58). Marketing director Rick Johnson explained that the discussions were "designed to keep the lines of communication open between Alcon and those ophthalmologists who are having the greatest impact on the way glaucoma is approached."[102]

To keep the MSRs focused on Betoptic S, they were encouraged to participate in sales contests for annual trips to Paris in 1990, 1991, and 1992. There they attended working sessions at Synthélabo. Runners-up received domestic travel vouchers and cash awards. All the efforts paid off. Betoptic S helped sustain growth each year, with sales hitting $103 million in 1993 (fig. 6.48). By 1997 Betoptic S had a 30 percent market share, almost $150 million, of the $500 million worldwide beta-blocker glaucoma market.[103]

Glaucoma management begins with a single drug; when necessary, other medications are added. If the IOP remains uncontrolled, the patient may require laser surgery or, as a final step, invasive surgery to create a new drainage route to reduce the pressure. Glaucoma specialists, led by Alan Robin of Johns Hopkins University and Allan Kolker, the president of the American Glaucoma Society, promoted the use of Iopidine in patients with uncontrolled IOP. Alcon filed an NDA for Iopidine 0.5% (fig. 6.22). Approved in July 1993, Ophthalmic marketers, led by Rick Rheiner, profiled its value to MSRs for glaucoma patients on maximum tolerated medical therapy (fig. 6.59). A few weeks later, Rheiner debuted Iopidine 0.5% to ophthalmologists at the AAO.[104]

FIG 6.57
National sales meeting, Betoptic S, 1990 (AHR)

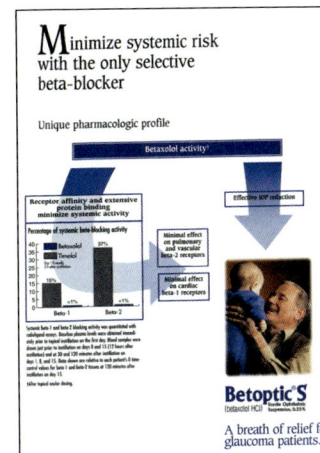

FIG 6.58
Betoptic advertisement
(Rheiner Papers, AM, TCU)

FIG 6.59
Iopidine 0.5% ready to ship (AHR)

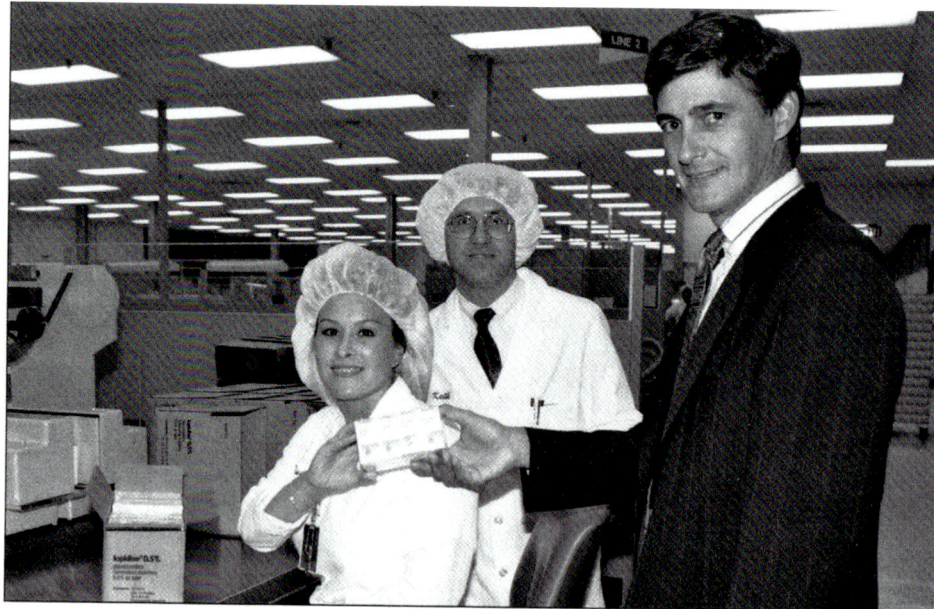

Manufacturing's Gina Livingston, packaging operator, and Keith Bell, senior production manager, hand Ophthalmic's Rick Rheiner a package of Iopidine 0.5%, all shrink-wrapped and ready to go.

FIG 6.60
Azopt and Emadine (AHR)

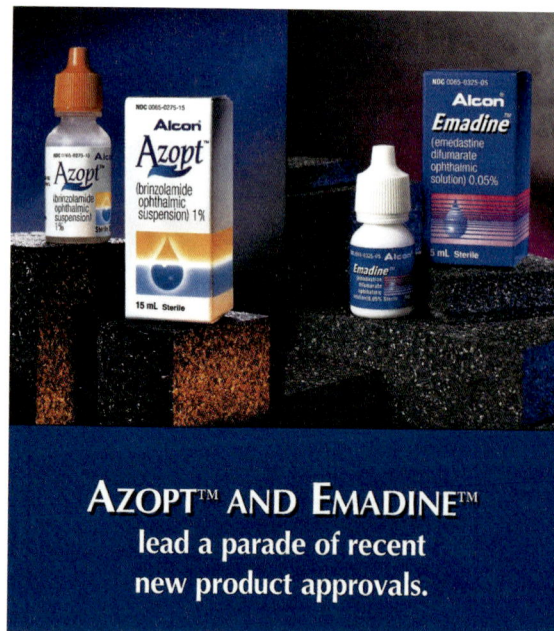

AZOPT™ AND EMADINE™
lead a parade of recent
new product approvals.

By the mid-1990s, glaucoma therapies were in flux. For twenty years, beta-blockers had been the mainstay remedy, but now Alpha-2 adrenergics, such as Iopidine 0.5%, were growing in popularity as alternatives. In 1994 topical CAIs became another option when the FDA approved Merck's Trusopt. Alcon had its own proprietary topical CAI, Azopt, which the FDA approved in early 1998 (figs. 6.22, 6.60). Both Azopt and Trusopt lowered IOPs equally, but Alcon's pharmaceutical scientists had created a comfortable formulation, superior to Merck's product. Alcon launched Azopt in May 1998. But Xalatan, a prostaglandin F-2-alpha (PGF-2α), emerged as the new major new glaucoma therapy, which Pharmacia began to market in late 1996. Alcon had its own PGF-2α, Travatan (fig. 6.22), in clinical studies; it received approval in 2000. Thus, moving into the next decade, Alcon had several therapies for this market.[105]

With Naphcon and Naphcon-A, Alcon dominated the allergy prescription market for two decades. When the FDA declared Naphcon-A an OTC product, Alcon needed a new prescription therapy. Allergic reactions in humans are a mix of variables, the two most relevant being mast cells and histamine. Mast cells are intracellular bags that when ruptured release histamine, well known for causing the itchy red eyes, and other noxious chemicals. In the late 1970s, Fisons, in Ipswich, England, and Rochester, New York, marketed Opticrom eye drops, a low-potency mast cell stabilizer, which the FDA recalled from the market. Alcon licensed lodoxamide, a potent mast cell stabilizer, from the Upjohn Corporation and R&D completed clinical studies, mainly in Europe; it was marketed by International as Alomide in March 1990. Alomide (fig. 6.21) was introduced to Alcon's domestic MSRs in the same meeting as Iopidine 0.5% and presented to ophthalmologists at that fall's AAO meeting, where "it drew a great deal of attention." Commenting on its introduction, Mike Hemric, national sales director, noted the fortuitous timing: "We have a three-month window to obtain physicians trial of Alomide before the allergy season." Considering Alomide's success in Europe, Alcon expected to fill the void left by Opticrom's withdrawal.[106]

Planning for the introduction of Patanol began well before FDA approval on December 18, 1996. Marketing noted that "every so often, a new product enters the market with such compelling therapeutic advantages that you can barely contain your enthusiasm for it." Patanol was the first therapy to merge antihistamine and mast cell stabilizing action (fig. 6.21). This unique dual action enabled it to be effective in minutes and last up to eight hours, longer than other ocular allergy therapies. In February 1997 Alcon introduced Patanol to a select group of ophthalmologists, allergists, and optometrists at a conference in Fort Worth. Mark Abelson, whose provocative model R&D had used, was the expert speaker. In

FIG 6.61
Patanol's "Patty" *Left to right:*
Ed Schollmaier, Blaise McGoey,
Dr. Mark Abelson, Ashish Pal,
Tim Sear, Dr. Marino Discepola
(AHR)

March, Alcon distributed one thousand kits containing product samples and evaluation forms to doctors across the country. They reported favorable outcomes for both onset and duration of action, and many requested more samples. That same month, the Ophthalmic sales force attended a national launch meeting with an emphasis on extensive training on Patanol, competitive products, market knowledge, and sales execution. Abelson gave educational and motivational presentations. A new face exploded onto the Alcon scene, "Patty," an eye icon and mascot for Patanol (fig. 6.61). Within six months, Patanol claimed a 20 percent share of the ocular allergy market, making it the fastest-growing product in Alcon's history. By 1999 it had annual sales of $50 million and later became Alcon's fourth $100 million product.[107]

The powerful ocular antihistamine product, Emadine, was approved by the FDA on December 29, 1997 (fig. 6.60). Launched in early 1998, Emadine completed Alcon's extensive anti-allergy product line (fig. 6.21). What set it apart was its safety and efficacy in patients as young as three years old. With Alomide, Patanol, and Emadine, Alcon led the anti-allergy market.[108]

Alcon dominated the ocular anti-infective market with Isopto Cetamide (1950s), Statrol (1960s), and Tobrex (1970s). Clinical studies for Ciloxan resulted in therapeutic claims for bacterial conjunctivitis and corneal bacterial ulcers, a sight-threatening condition. The FDA approved Ciloxan 0.3% on December 31, 1990, months before two competitors' broad-spectrum fluoroquinolone antibiotics (figs. 6.21, 6.62). Alcon veteran and Ciloxan product manager Glenn Rickey organized the debut at the February 1991 sales meeting (fig. 6.63) by exhibiting two thoroughbred horses, named Ciloxan and Tobrex, on the Alcon campus. He stressed that "the two drugs now in combination give us a lock on the market." Every year through 1997, the market share growth of Ciloxan averaged 15 percent to 20 percent. The FDA approved the ointment dosage form in March 1998, even for patients as young as two years of age. Thus, throughout its first fifty years, Alcon developed, manufactured, and marketed the number one ophthalmic antibiotic, an enviable record.[109]

Ocular inflammation can be a serious and potentially sight-threatening condition. It is a risk after surgery or trauma, or results from diseases such as keratitis, uveitis, or retinitis.

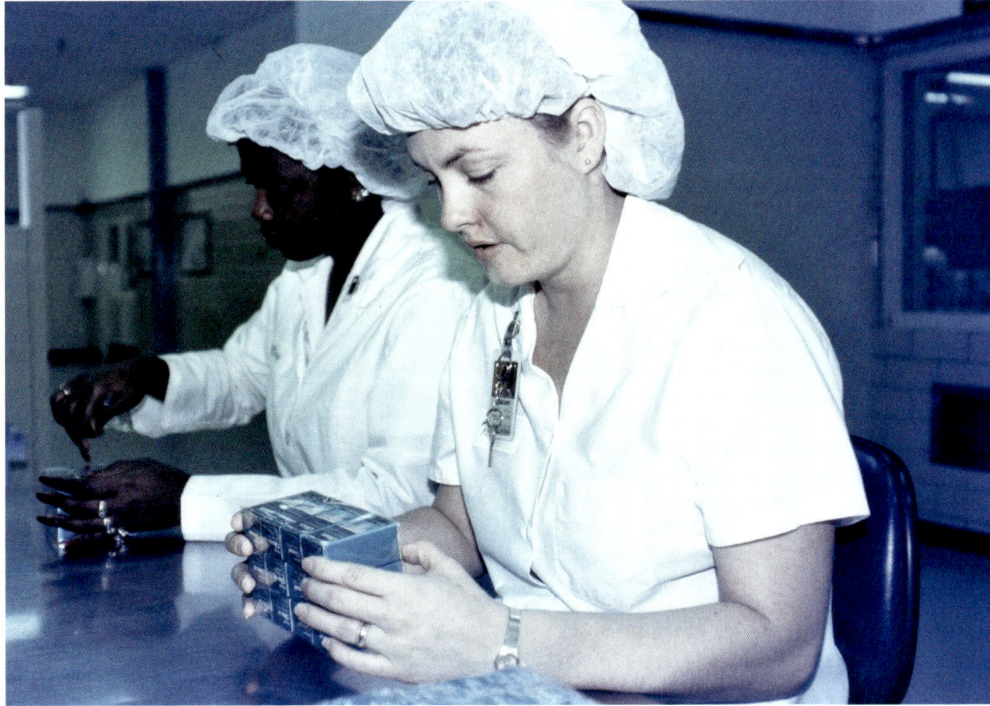

FIG 6.62
Packaging Ciloxan (AHR)

Steroids are the most effective therapeutic. In a highly competitive market, Alcon's steroid products claimed about a one-third market share, while Allergan, Alcon's archrival, had dominated this segment since the 1960s. The main drawback to instilling potent steroids for more than several days is their propensity to increase IOP. Marketing promoted Flarex in 1991, a compound like one introduced by a competitor (fig. 6.21), but, although it had low potential to raise IOP, it was perceived as less effective.[110]

Alcon licensed a new steroid, rimexalone, and the FDA approved it under the brand name Vexol (fig. 6.21) on December 30, 1994. Vexol had a chemical structure that differed from other ophthalmic steroids, was the first to be approved in twenty years, and was the first to have a post-surgical indication. Marketing's introduction for Vexol was comprehensive. At the May 1995 Association for Research in Vision and Ophthalmology (ARVO) meeting, Abelson presented a clinical overview to thirty ophthalmic clinical researchers. At the October AAO meeting, C. Stephen Foster of the Massachusetts Eye and Ear Infirmary, a leading authority on uveitis, ocular inflammation, and steroid use, discussed Vexol's clinical findings. Alcon initiated a pre-launch release of newspaper articles quoting cornea specialists. Marketing conducted a trial with eight hundred cataract surgeons and corne-

▲ *District competitions during the meeting kept everyone on their toes. All contestants had a "racing form" for use in recording answers to key questions.*

▲ *Dr. Harold Neu, (l) one of the foremost experts on antimicrobials, with Mike Hemric, Ophthalmic Division Vice President, Sales.*

▲ *These 10 members of the Ciloxan Task Force conducted field tests of promotional materials to help in refining the selling message: (l-r) – Gordon Lazarus, Mike Miller, Dave Hill, Mike Mueller, Ginger Thompson, Chris Coleman, Marian Perich, Frank Flaherty, Dale Seibt and Joel Ellis.*

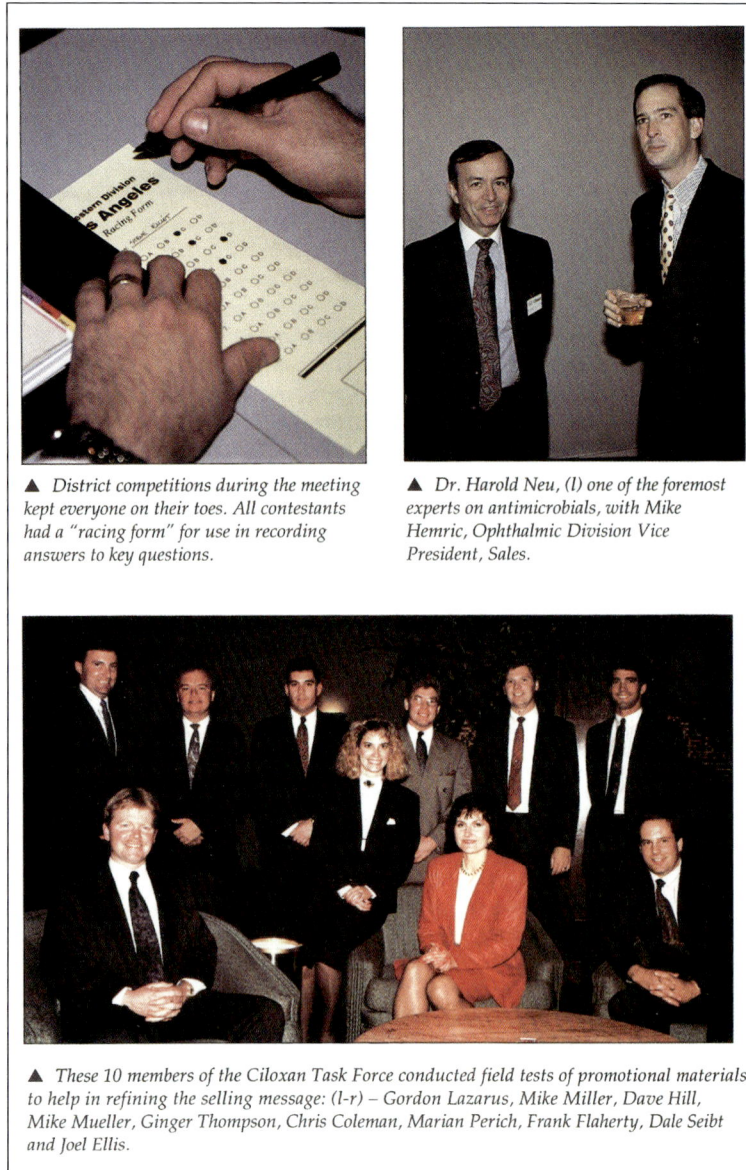

FIG 6.63
Ciloxan launch (AHR)

al specialists. Lastly, it held a three-day orientation meeting with the sales force. To provide additional motivation, Alcon instituted a new incentive plan. MSRs were compensated based on the number of Vexol prescriptions written by ophthalmologists; this commission program was a first for Alcon. By September 1996 Vexol owned 10 percent of the ophthalmic steroid prescription market, and its share continued to increase.[111]

Steroids and antibiotics are used in combination to reduce inflammation and prevent postoperative infections. Since its introduction in 1965, Maxitrol was the drug of choice until the arrival of TobraDex twenty years later. FDA approval of TobraDex (tobramycin and dexamethasone) ophthalmic suspension and ointment in August and September 1988 (fig. 6.22) initiated the final stage of a marketing campaign that had begun months earlier. Before its approval, the name TobraDex was found to have high acceptability among ophthalmologists. Sales aids and a direct mailing campaign had been developed and tested, and a special test kit for large practices was organized. A distribution plan for wholesalers was designed, as well as a training program for MSRs. Barley organized Manufacturing for rapidly preparing a batch (fig. 6.64). FDA approval occurred on a Thursday; by Monday a lot was compounded, filled, labeled, and stored in quarantine. It shipped two weeks later. Within a few months, 25 percent of high-volume surgeons used it postoperatively; seven hundred surgeons made post-surgery changes in their operating theater; seventeen leading hospitals placed TobraDex on their formularies; over three hundred hospitals and ambulatory surgicenters stocked it; almost every retail pharmacy agreed to carry it; and physicians had been notified where their patients could get this new product.[112]

The combined 1989 sales of TobraDex and Maxitrol were 50 percent more than for Maxitrol the previous year. Rickey praised the Ophthalmic MSRs: "This rapid success is all the more remarkable since it was achieved when Allergan was also introducing their new combination product Pred-G." By June 1989 TobraDex had its first $1 million in monthly sales; next to Betoptic, the TobraDex launch was the most successful by the Ophthalmic Division. In that month, TobraDex and Maxitrol held the number one position, a 40 percent share, in the steroid-antibiotic segment. By the end of 1989, TobraDex surpassed all other steroid-antibiotic preparations to become the number one ophthalmic combination product. By 1997 ear specialists and pediatricians prescribed TobraDex drops for external ear infections. That year, TobraDex annual sales totaled $60 million as Alcon continued to dominate the market, as it had since steroid-antibiotic combinations were introduced in the 1950s.[113]

Alcon strengthened its position in the competitive artificial tears category when the Ophthalmic Division launched its newest product, Bion Tears, in April 1993 (fig. 6.22). Bion Tears resembled the composition of natural tears and represented a valuable therapy in the dry eye specialist's toolkit. "This product is not for everyone," said artificial tears product manager Dave Hinchey. "We are positioning it for the moderate to severe dry eye patient. It fills a gap in the unpreserved tear market, and we expect it to be a winner." Patients suffering from Sjogren's syndrome, a devastating disease that robs moisture from the body, were prime candidates for the therapy. The product contained a bicarbonate buffering agent, which evaporated through plastic vials, so Bion Tears was packaged in four single-dose units within a foil pouch.[114]

Beginning in the late 1970s, Alcon started selling generics. It began to copy and sell competitor products whose patents had expired and even sold some of its older leading products as generics (fig. 6.23). For example, a few years after the launch of Ciloxan, Alcon marketed Tobrex and later Maxitrol as generics. Alcon generic sales mostly focused on glaucoma medications, and in the mid-1990s the company created its own generic company, naming it Falcon. After Schollmaier negotiated a licensing agreement with Merck, Falcon started marketing 0.25% and 0.5% Timolol. Next, generics for DPE (an epinephrine solution) and Betagan (a nonselective beta-blocker), both sold by Allergan, were introduced. In

HOT OFF THE LINE!
Part of Manufacturing's team celebrate the first batch of TobraDex®. Front row (left to right): Bobby Howard, Robert Bonner, Lois Wallace, June Ristan, Maria Taylor, Tham Do, Betty Cabness, Maria Garcia, Rosetta Francis. Back Row: Leon Harper, Hildegard Larabell, Shannon Mellor, Jeff Stone, Rosemary McClure.

PASSING THE TOBRADEX!
(Left to right) Len Schweitzer, Dr. Larry Coben, Director of Fort Worth Manufacturing, Blaise McGoey, and Bob Nelson.

FIG 6.64
The ninety-hour launch of TobraDex (AHR)

A Toast to 1988 and 1989

(l-r at table from front center) Ed Hicks, DM-Los Angeles; Don Vincent, DM-Dallas; Bob Reising, DM-Chicago; Ed Mosman, DM-San Francisco; Lee Hansen, President and General Manager (Alcon-Puerto Rico); Bob Grantham, Director of Sales Training; and Steve Richardson, DM-St. Louis.

(l-r) Jaime Soler, Engineering Director (Alcon-Puerto Rico) and Jorge Alfonso, Director of Operations (Alcon-Puerto Rico)

Left to Right Front Row: Lee Hansen, Rick Rheiner, Glenn Rickey, Doug Hilton, Nard King, Maria Santiago, Len Schweitzer, Fred Garber, Hank Muller, Jorge Alifonso
Left to Right Back Row: Bill Burns, Ed Mosman, Bob Nelson, Blaise McGoey, Glenn Moro, Ron Pepe, Bob Reising, Fred Novasak, Don Vincent, Bob Yates, Norb Walter, Steve Richardson, Bob Grantham, Tom Skiff, Rick Johnson, Ed Hicks

Maria Santiago, Quality Assurance Director (Alcon-Puerto Rico) and Fred Garber, Senior Products Mgr.

Production line at Alcon-Puerto Rico.

Puerto Rico's beauty varies from mountains (upper left) to coastline (lower right).

FIG 6.65
President's Club, Puerto Rico, 1989
(AHR)

January 1996 the Falcon sales force and the Managed Care team conducted a two-week blitz, visiting accounts that generated 80 percent of glaucoma drug sales. Falcon delivered mailings via *PharmAlert*, a newsletter sent to retail pharmacies, health maintenance associations, purchasing organizations, and hospitals. Falcon offered patient information materials to sixteen thousand ophthalmologists. Although Alcon never reported the magnitude of its generic sales, it noted that in six months Falcon's Timolol gained a 29 percent share of the Timoptic market in the United States.[115]

Launching fourteen new prescription therapies and twelve generic products kept the marketing and sales teams in the Ophthalmic Division busy. Rheiner, who had been an MSR, district manager, and product manager, placed introducing new products into perspective: "Customers are resistant to a sales rep coming in and asking for time to discuss the same product they've been hearing about for years. ... That makes it hard to get customers' attention and keep a sales force enthusiastic and motivated. But we always had something new. Some were better than others, but there were always new products. New product launches were, for me, the most exciting times at Alcon." The Ophthalmic team had effective leadership in McGoey, experienced directors of marketing, and veteran sales and production managers. When veterans retired, their positions were filled from within the field sales force, while everyone in the home office rotated through a variety of roles. Schollmaier and Sisson shepherded these processes, their talent at selecting the right person for the right position at the right time proving invaluable. Consistent with Nestlé philosophy, Schollmaier was, in effect, Alcon's chief marketing officer. Continuation of the President's Club, started by Alexander and Conner, emphasized the role of top-performing sales representatives (fig. 6.65).[116]

New products—Betoptic S, TobraDex, Ciloxan, Vexol, Alomide, Patanol, Iopidine 0.5%, and Falcon generics—propelled Ophthalmic annual sales increases of 20 percent or more. The Betoptic franchise became Alcon's first $100 million product, and global sales for the division grew from $146 million in 1987 to $680 million in 1997. These sales amounted

FIG 6.66
Tim Sear's International division management team, 1993. *Left to right*: Keith Bell, Bill Kwan, Gene Estes, Fred Pettinato, Frances Brotherhood, Martin Vogt, Giorgio Vescovo, Peter Connelly, Carlos Coscia, Tim Sear, Charles Miller, Nick Tsumpis, Gilberto Cardenas, Lou Liguori, Carlos Taborda, Helmut Horchler. (AHR)

to 30 percent and 43 percent of Alcon's revenue as the ophthalmic marketing and sales organizations capitalized on R&D's productivity. By the end of fifty years, Alcon's Ophthalmic Division had outpaced all competitors, becoming number one in its category with about 30 percent of the total market.[117]

By 1988 Sear had overseen Alcon's International Division for six years (fig. 6.66). Nearly twenty-six hundred people worked for Alcon overseas (fig. 6.67). That year, International contributed 36 percent of Alcon's revenue by selling products in nearly one hundred countries. Sear's tenure coincided with the boom in R&D productivity, with most products being launched in the United States before being sold overseas. Three exceptions were Betoptic, Alomide, and AcrySof.[118]

Sear worked to replicate Alcon's culture across the International Division. One way was to invite upper and middle managers to Fort Worth. Some accepted jobs there; others came for intensive training and instruction. Eric Noble left his general manager role in Australia to become International's marketing director in Fort Worth. Yasuhide Fukushima, Alcon Japan's ophthalmic marketing director, spent one year in Fort Worth to prepare for Betop-

FIG 6.67
Various International facilities (AHR)

FIG 6.68
Mid-level management course,
International, 1994. *Left to right*:
Pedro Coloma (Spain), Beatrice
Champeix (France), A. J. Hiltenbrand
(Fort Worth), Raffaela Pelli (Italy),
John Crellin (UK), Shikoku Tanaka
(Japan), Hans Barcheski (Germany), Sergio
Levy (Brazil), and
Adrian Cooke (Australia).
(AHR)

tic's launch in Japan. To extend Fort Worth's influence to overseas personnel, Sear tapped into training programs led by Dubbs, creating a cadre of trainers in nine countries with large ophthalmic markets. Realizing the value of senior management attending Havard, Sear asked Hiltenbrand for a mid-level executive development program (fig. 6.68). International created a Marketing Associate Program in Fort Worth, where product managers attended a two-month-long course; Toril Vadset, of Alcon Norway, and Francoise Guthux, of Alcon France, graduated from the program in 1992. Emulating other divisional leaders, Sear rotated people through different roles. The CooperVision acquisition and Galderma divestment presented opportunities for such personnel transfers. Several country managers joined Galderma, and Sear filled the vacancy in Britain with CooperVision executive Fred Pettinato. Pettinato later headed International Marketing when Noble transferred to Galderma, Australia, in 1993. By 1988 Sear had his operational vice presidents. He kept Giorgio Vescovo in charge of EURMEA and, when Taborda transferred to Galderma in 1995, Alcon veteran Carlos Coscia, vice president of North LACAR, took over the entire LACAR territory. Sear assigned Horchler to manage CAFE in 1987.[119]

By 1992 Germany, France, Italy, the UK, Spain, and Portugal generated about 70 percent of EURMEA's $227 million revenue, and sales from that area were about half of all international sales each year. Betoptic and Betoptic S were major factors in boosting sales, as were Alomide, Ciloxan, BSS PLUS, Opti-Free, sutures, Viscoat, and AcrySof. There was not an area-wide manager for many products, so the marketers in each country depended upon International Marketing in Fort Worth for guidance and product brochures. This centralized marketing was possible because ophthalmologists had melded into a global community, taking guidance from a handful of experts. R&D's strategy of conducting clinical studies internationally created a network of physicians whom International Marketing could utilize. The division sponsored symposia where local ophthalmologists were introduced to new therapies and products in presentations given by invited leaders in the field. With Betoptic and Betoptic S registrations completed in most EURMEA countries, they were ideal products to promote through meetings. Betoptic conferences attended by a few hundred EURMEA physicians were held in destinations such as Madeira, Portugal; Luxor, Egypt; and Athens, Greece. Jon Somp, marketing manager for Sweden, organized one in Umeå for Nordic ophthalmologists. Alcon Italy's annual sales of Betoptic increased by 42 percent a year after the Luxor symposium! When Betoptic became a $100 million product in 1993, International sales contributed $20 million.[120]

In 1991 Alcon launched Alomide in France, Britain, Belgium, Greece, and Canada. Assigned to Fort Worth for a fifteen-month training period, Somp wrote the Alomide product monograph that EURMEA used. In 1992 a marketing campaign coordinated by the Alcon France general manager, Thierry Clidiere, was implemented. A televised conference, with an audience of eleven hundred ophthalmologists in eleven cities, was held, while follow-up roundtable events coincided with allergy season. It was an effective strategy, with Alomide taking a 9 percent share of the ocular allergy market within seven months. Equally successful marketing campaigns followed for Ciloxan, Patanol, and TobraDex, while Italy also set the standard for sales in Opti-Free and Opti-Free Enzymatic Cleaner.[121]

After the CooperVision acquisition, surgical product sales in EURMEA grew quickly. Until the early 1990s, phacoemulsification for cataract surgery was uncommon in Europe, but the inclusion of European surgeons in AcrySof clinical studies brought a change. When Legacy 20000 was introduced, surgical laboratory demonstrations were held at medical conventions and at Alcon facilities around the world in the first globally coordinated product rollout, in this case for AcrySof. Leading the Fort Worth–based team was Mike Southard, who remarked in 1996, "Global introduction of AcrySof has been relatively gradual. We introduced it as markets become more involved with phacoemulsification techniques." Beginning in 1990 Southard paved the way by organizing IMPACT (International Medical Panel for the Advancement of Cataract Treatment), where experts discussed trends in cataract surgery. In little more than a year, AcrySof was the best-selling single product in the international market, which helped it become Alcon's first $200 million product. By 1997 Alcon held a 50 to 60 percent market share in every country where AcrySof was sold. The demand for BSS PLUS, Viscoat, and single-use items for cataract surgery increased in tandem with AcrySof and Legacy 20000 sales, and Alcon obliged by selling Custom Paks. In 1995 Vescovo assigned Beatrice Champeix as EURMEA's product manager for Custom Paks (fig. 6.69). She studied the concept and processes in Houston, then trained EURMEA's surgical product managers. Demand justified a Custom Pak line in Alcon's plant in Belgium (figs. 6.13).[122]

After the collapse of the Soviet Union in 1989, Eastern Europe and the Baltics offered expansion opportunities. By the mid-1990s, Alcon established subsidiaries in most former Soviet-bloc nations, creating marketing and sales teams in each. In 1994 Vescovo asked Françoise Ganet, who came with the Biophysic Medical acquisition and spoke Russian, to set up an office in Russia. She faced multiple challenges with a culture unfamiliar with market dynamics, used to centralized planning, and spread across eleven time zones. By 1994 Alcon sold about thirty products across the region, Betoptic being the most popular. In 1996 Giuseppe Luigi LaMacchia, general manager of the Middle East and Greece, absorbed Russian and Eastern Europe into his region. LaMacchia was an example of experienced leadership found in every region of Vescovo's EURMEA.[123]

When Taborda requested a return to Brazil, Sear split LACAR into southern and northern zones, assigning Coscia to the latter, based in Fort Worth. Coscia took charge of all of LACAR when Taborda transferred to Galderma. Coscia's philosophy was that Alcon facilities were always accessible to the ophthalmologist community. He prioritized modernization of the plant in Mexico City. During this decade Mexico and Brazil became the dominant countries for manufacturing. With the CooperVision acquisition came its problematic Latin American office in Miami, and Coscia had to integrate it into Alcon. Of primary concern were its financial failings; for example, it sold $1.1 million but had returns

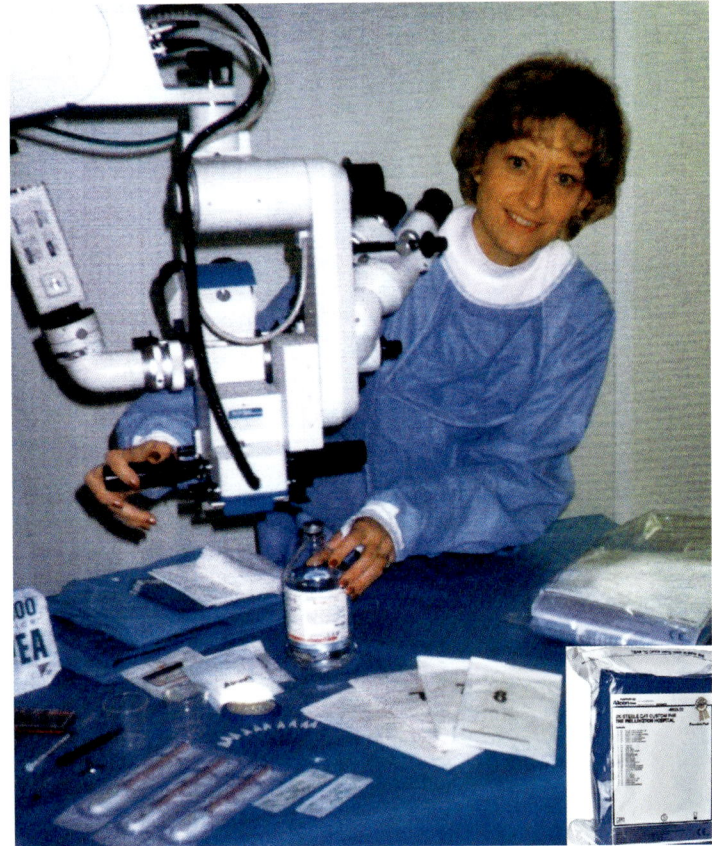

FIG 6.69
Beatrice Champeix and Custom Pak
(Alcon EuroVision #1, 1996)
(TOM, AM)

of $1 million. Moreover, CooperVision had not effectively introduced phacoemulsification into Latin America. Coscia called on William De La Peña, an experienced cataract surgeon in Los Angeles, to teach the procedure throughout LACAR, paving the way for the Legacy 20000. Then the launch of AcrySof became the focus for LACAR in 1996. Alcon locations throughout South America hosted training programs, while Alcon Brazil constructed a surgical laboratory containing Alcon's full line of products and made it available to ophthalmologists and ophthalmology residents. The facility included a fifty-seat auditorium with audiovisual capabilities linked with the surgical suite. AcrySof rapidly became the most popular foldable IOL in the region.[124]

Surgical Division products developed into a major source of revenue for LACAR, as did pharmaceutical and Vision Care products. Betoptic S enhanced Alcon's share in the beta-blocker market and so did other ophthalmic therapies—Vexol, Alomide, Ciloxan, TobraDex, Iopidine 0.5%, and Patanol, along with the old standbys Maxitrol and Tobrex. Opti-Free and its related products established a strong presence. This proliferation of pharmaceutical and contact lens products, coupled with the introduction of AcrySof, surgical devices, and single-use products, presented a new conundrum for LACAR marketing and sales. Now a LACAR ophthalmologist often had visits by multiple Alcon MSRs, who themselves did not know when other sales personnel had visited that doctor or what were their promotion messages. Coscia explained, "The point is that there was a lot of misunderstanding because one rep didn't know what the other was doing." Coscia sought advice from Alcon IT and Nestlé managers in the LACAR region and settled on using laptops as a communication tool. He appointed Néstor Álvarez, then marketing manager for Alcon Argentina, as head of LACAR business development in Fort Worth, and hired Eduardo Blas as his IT business manager. This team created a unique computer program, the first outside the United States, that allowed MSRs to share details of their calls on ophthalmologists.[125]

Inflation and currency exchange rate fluctuations complicated conducting business in most LACAR countries. Coscia explained, "You have to have the right managerial tools to handle this. You need to be convinced that you can handle it, and ... you need to be flexible, willing to change plans from day to day." LACAR country managers became experts and continued to increase sales and profits. Monetary considerations were not the only hurdles in the LACAR region. Geographic diversity was huge—from idyllic islands in the Caribbean to vast Argentinian pampas, Amazonian jungles, and Andean mountains and highlands. Politics were often turbulent and at times explosive. On one occasion, an Alcon Colombian MSR was wounded in a firefight between guer-

FIG 6.70

LACAR meeting, Santiago, Chile, April 1992. *Back row, left to right*: José Vega, Colombia; Danilo Salazar, Colombia; León Zapata, Mexico; Enrique Freire, Uruguay; Alejandro Edwards, Chile; Gabriel Díaz, Fort Worth; Tim Sear, Fort Worth; Rodrigo Echeverry, Venezuela; José Siluán, Colombia; Artemio Avila, Central America; unidentified; Máximo Andrieu, Argentina; John Fonvielle, Fort Worth; Rafael Martínez, Mexico; Alejandro Hip, Chile; Lourdes Corrales, Mexico; unknown, Colombia; Juan Carpena, Peru; unidentified; Lou Liguori, LACAR/CAFE, Fort Worth; Laurent Attias, Fort Worth. *Lower row, left to right*: Fernando Alonso, Puerto Rico/Central America; Daniel Rivera, Argentina; Víctor Castrillejo, Uruguay; Javier Martínez, Ecuador; Roberto Quirós, Argentina; Andrés Cánepa, Uruguay; Carlos Coscia, Fort Worth; Néstor Álvarez, Argentina; rest of row unidentified. (TOM, AM) (Photo gift from Carlos Coscia)

rillas and local authorities; Alcon supported his recovery until he returned to his duties a year later. Outside the capital cities, distances were often immense, complicating travel. Earthquakes occurred; one partially destroyed Alcon Chile's new office the day before its inauguration. Everyone pitched in to make repairs so the ceremony was delayed only one week. Coscia noted, "Our sales people are very dedicated. In Latin countries where a doctor's office is routinely open until late at night, it is not uncommon to find one of our MSRs calling on a physician at 10 o'clock in the evening, not because the *company* expects it, but because the MSR believes that this is what the market requires."[126]

Coscia groomed the next generation of leaders (fig. 6.70), but Alcon's presence in LACAR began when Conner introduced products in Colombia and took a leadership role in PAAO, an organization he supported until his death. Continuing the tradition, Sear took the lead role in the Pan-American Ophthalmological Foundation, the PAAO's fund-

FIG 6.71

6.71 CAFE executives, 1997. *Left to right, top row*: George Briscoe (Australia), Tony Rico (Fort Worth), Tim Sear (Fort Worth), David Baldwin (New Zealand), Raymond Ip (Hong Kong); *middle row*: Michael Goh (Malaysia), Normand Boudreault (Canada), Glen Burgess (Australia), James Lai (Taiwan), Y. K. Lee (South Korea), Ed Gonzales (Hawaii), Jimmy Castro (Philippines), Shrinivasan (India), Nick Gorshenin (Australia), unidentified ophthalmologist; *front row*: Nasir Khan Nasri (Pakistan), Jeanne Chen (Singapore), Renea Keish (Fort Worth), Chepa Wang (China), Helmut Horchler (Fort Worth), Khun Theeraporn (Thailand), Lê Thị Minh Hoa (Vietnam), Indawati Santoso (Indonesia), David Rath (Australia). (TOM, AM) (Photo gift from Helmut Horchler)

ing auxiliary, and other LACAR executives have followed suit. Between 1988 and 1997, annual sales from LACAR increased from $28 million to $120 million.[127]

CAFE encompassed twenty-three countries, ranging from Canada, the North and South Pacific Ocean, islands in the western Pacific, and inland from China through Pakistan—one-fourth of the earth's surface and two-thirds of its people. The region had a spectrum of economies, from impoverished to well developed, with pharmaceutical industries ranging from almost nonexistent to sophisticated and productive. Japan was the second-largest ophthalmic market in the world. Horchler was the fourth general manager of CAFE and the most successful, overseeing sales growth from $17 million to almost $320 between 1988 and 1997. Over the years, he developed a set of superb managers and executives (fig. 6.71). Imbued with Alcon's culture and unafraid of new experiences, Horchler had energy, pragmatism, and ethics, making him an ideal area manager.[128]

In several CAFE countries, the ophthalmic market was insignificant, and Alcon often used local distributors to manage its small presence. These markets included Nepal, Pakistan, Myanmar, Maldives, Sri Lanka, Laos, Cambodia, Bangladesh, Indonesia, and India. Although Alcon initially entered Indonesia in the 1960s, its presence had faded, but Horchler's interest focused on the potential of a populace of 200 million. In the corrupt business culture, he found a distributor and hired a country manager, Indahwati Santoso, who had a background in pharmaceutical sales. Santoso's relationship with Alcon and Nestlé was erratic, sales were inconsistent, and the distributor re-exported contact lens solutions to the United States, intending to resell them for profit. Santoso and Horchler refocused on a single practice of fourteen ophthalmologists who controlled eye surgical procedures in Indonesia. Horchler sold them the phacoemulsification device by crediting $5 for each IOL they bought. But business remained "unpredictable and fluctuated wildly," in part because of political instability. Until the CooperVision acquisition, Alcon had no business in India. CooperVision's distributor insisted that Horchler attend India's largest ophthalmology congress, held under tents outside Ahmedabad. Alcon had superior products, but its prices were ten times that of local companies, making them unappealing. So, Alcon began offering superior, swift, dependable service, which eventually paid off in improving sales figures.[129]

With annual sales at about $50,000, Sri Lanka was a backwater for Alcon, but Horchler explored opportunities. Alcon donated a Legacy 20000 to the largest eye hospital there, forcing sales of its single-use products and IOLs. He found a distributor and hired Diljaran Jacob as the country manager, and sales exploded to $1 million a year. Jacob, ever pragmatic, installed an UltraScan device in Alcon's office, and ocular surgeons sent their patients to be measured for the correct IOL prior to surgery. Alcon sold the lens directly to the patients, who took them to the surgeon. Horchler inherited Pakistan's country manager, Nasir Khan Nasri, but he had poor sales. Alcon's distributor, Ali Gohar, who imported unlabeled, finished products, did little better. The first batch of Opti-Free products had to be destroyed when the glue on the Pakistan-produced labels contaminated each container. Alcon Belgium subsequently sent labels, cartons, and glue. The CooperVision acquisition marginally increased Alcon's business in Pakistan. Alcon had no presence in Cambodia until Horchler negotiated an agreement with the largest ear, eye, nose, and throat hospital in that country. Alcon donated a phacoemulsification device and trained surgeons for cataract surgery. It

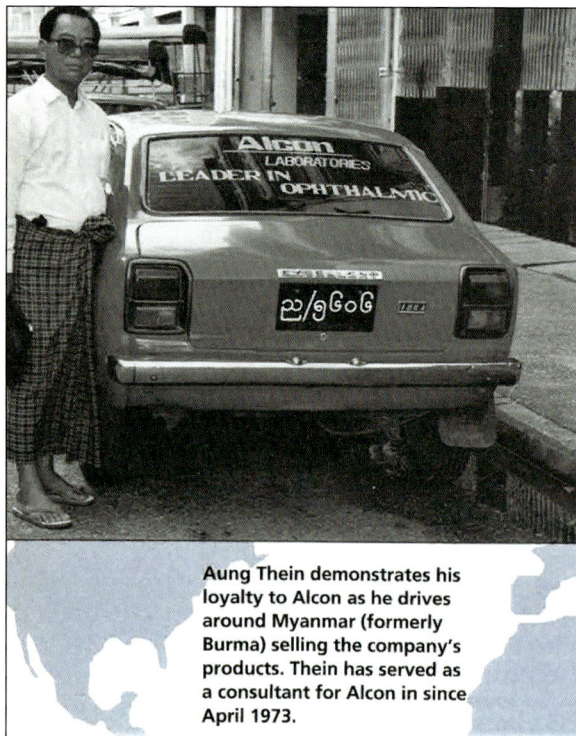

Aung Thein demonstrates his loyalty to Alcon as he drives around Myanmar (formerly Burma) selling the company's products. Thein has served as a consultant for Alcon in since April 1973.

FIG 6.72
Aung Thein, Myanmar (AHR)

staffed a pharmacy where patients could buy its products, including IOLs. Horchler recalled, "Eventually our investments paid off and a viable business was established." Sales in Myanmar were minuscule, but Alcon had a representative there since 1973, Aung Thein (fig. 6.72). Horchler met the leading eye doctor and offered the same deal he had in Indonesia—that they pay Alcon $5 for each procedure, implant Alcon IOLs, and use its single-use surgical products. In general sales grew, although Alcon had to compete against illegal importation of its own and competitor products, sold in optical shops and even barbershops; Horchler never found a way of controlling the black market. In Nepal, a used excimer laser that Alcon had earlier donated distracted the main surgeon in the country to such an extent that his cataract surgeries decreased and Alcon sales plummeted. Alcon posted modest sales in Laos, Bangladesh, and Maldives, and none in Bhutan.[130]

Five Asian countries represented viable growth opportunities—China, Malaysia, Singapore, Thailand, and Vietnam. Following a visit to China, Horchler encountered Chepa Wang, whom he hired as the country manager, and she employed Peter Huang (fig. 6.73). Wang and Huang contracted with a half dozen distributors, and over six years Alcon's business grew to several million dollars. Alcon faced a dilemma when the Beijing IntraOcular Company (BIC) offered to assemble needles and sutures locally to lower costs. Alcon was reluctant to allow access to its proprietary technology, but a deal was struck by which the companies distributed each other's products. BIC could not compete with Alcon's high standards, so it approached Alcon with a purchase offer and was integrated into Alcon China. In the meantime, Alcon China worked with the Ministry of Health to register its pharmaceutical products. By the time Horchler retired in 2004, Alcon China's annual sales were $37 million.

Singapore, CAFE's most profitable area, was led by Jeanne Chen. CooperVision's Asian headquarters was in Singapore, but its business was in shambles. After Alcon acquired CooperVision, Chen admirably consolidated the two companies and organized Alcon's participation at the XXVI International Congress of Ophthalmology, held in Singapore in March 1990 (fig. 6.74). Under Chen, Alcon dominated the ophthalmic and surgical markets in Singapore. When Horchler took over CAFE, Malaysia's country manager had just resigned. Horchler hired Michael Goh and credited him for Malaysia's success. In Thailand, not satisfied with stagnant sales of $200,000 per year through distributors, Horchler hired Khun Theeraporn as Alcon's country manager. During the next fifteen years, she grew Alcon Thailand to one hundred people and $20 million in annual sales. Her first hire was Siriwan Charoenvitvorakul, who assembled an all-female sales team of thirteen. In 1993 Horchler turned to reviving Alcon's presence in Vietnam. As discussed earlier, Minh Hoa, an employee of Roussel Uclaf, a French pharmaceutical company, guided Horchler during his first Hanoi visit. Returning a few months later, Minh Hoa and Horchler went to Ho Chi Minh City where, after an extended interview, with most of the questions directed by Minh Hoa toward Horchler, he hired her (fig. 6.73). Sales had to adapt to the local culture. In Vietnam, ophthalmologists worked for the government until the afternoon, then saw private patients, to whom they sold medications. Horchler credited Minh Hoa's hard work and creativity for increasing sales and earning a profit in the second year. Ten years later the annual sales exceeded $8 million and in 2018, with Minh Hoa still in charge, Alcon was one of the largest American firms in Vietnam, with sixty employees.[131]

When Horchler arrived in 1987, Alcon had established businesses through distributors or its own subsidiaries in Hong Kong, Taiwan, Philippines, Australia, New Zealand, South Korea, Japan, and Canada. Each of these countries had a well-known process for registering new products. Except for in Japan, dossiers with data collected in the United States were acceptable. With an emphasis on launching Alcon's ophthalmic medications and Opti-Free franchise, registrations soon followed after the FDA approved each NDA. As with the other CAFE countries, the CooperVision acquisition influenced the products sold, and Alcon registered and began marketing AcrySof, Legacy 20000, and a myriad of single-use products. Surgical laboratories at medical conferences and in hospitals provided training, and Horchler

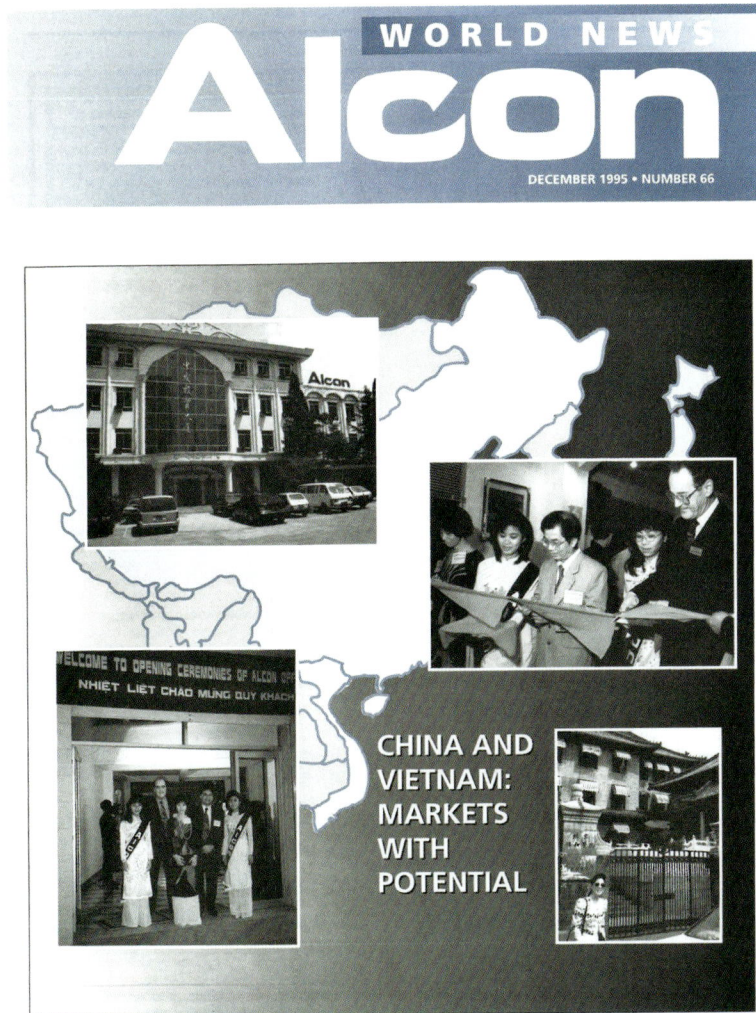

FIG 6.73

Alcon in China and Vietnam. *Clockwise from top left*: Alcon's Beijing office; Nguyen Trong Nham, *center*, Vietnam's Ministry of Health, joins Lê Thi Minh Hoa, *far left*, country manager, and Helmut Horcher, *far right*, to cut the ribbon opening Alcon Vietnam's office; Chepa Wang, Alcon China's country manager, visits Peking Medical College; representatives from Alcon Australia and Alcon Hong Kong join the Alcon Vietnam staff at the grand opening ceremonies. (*Alcon World News*, December 1995) (AHR)

FIG 6.74
Alcon booth, XXVI International Congress of Ophthalmology, Singapore, March 18–24, 1990 (AHR)

was fortunate that one Alcon phacoemulsification expert, George Briscoe, located in Australia, attended sessions. Southard, surgical marketing manager and IOL specialist in International, promoted AcrySof.[132]

Alcon had established its presence in CAFE beginning with Geoffrey Crewe in the 1960s and Sear in the 1970s. Thus, when Horchler took charge in 1987, he inherited a cadre of experienced country managers and representatives. But he made changes. Alcon's office in Hong Kong was the regional base at an annual cost of $500,000. Horchler determined that hiring country managers was more economical. With the regional office disbanded, he relied on James Lai to be Taiwan's country manager. Although sales grew, managing Taiwan was complicated. Sales of contact lens products were somewhat stable, but sales of surgical products occurred at the whim of the distributor, a friend of Lai. Taiwan sales did reach $20 million. The Philippines was one of the first countries to sell Alcon products and for a while a contract manufacturer exported them to other CAFE countries. In 1987 Alcon Philippines annual sales were $1.5 million, but Nestlé's audit identified problems. Alcon needed a competent manager before the next Nestlé audit. To that end, the company hired Jimmy Castro, an experienced Johnson & Johnson executive in the Philippines. Horchler later wrote, "Jimmy turned out to be a good hire and a good manager," though sales never flourished as anticipated. Alcon in New Zealand and Australia were affiliated. The New Zealand staff was small and its sales modest, mostly pharmaceuticals, though eye surgeons embraced AcrySof and Custom Paks.[133]

Alcon's presence in Australia had been strong from the time Frank Buhler went there in the early 1960s (fig. 6.75). The country manager, Noble, had moved to Fort Worth, replacing Horchler as head of International Marketing. David Rath, a former Alcon employee then working for CooperVision, replaced Noble. Rath, an effervescent product of the Australian Outback and an ex-rugby player, knew all of Australia's one thousand ophthalmologists. He built an organization that kept Alcon sales at or near the top in all categories.

FIG 6.75
Alcon Australia, Sydney
headquarters (AHR)

Betoptic had a 15 percent share of the glaucoma market fifteen months after its introduction, and Opti-Free earned a 19 percent share thirty months after its launch. Integrating the CooperVision organization was problematic, and capable people from both companies resigned. Nevertheless, Alcon dominated Australia's ocular surgical market. Rath generated loyalty from his team, and they usually exceeded annual sales goals. Sear delayed Horchler's supervision of Canada until 1989, when it accounted for 60 percent of CAFE revenues. By then, Sear had promoted Canadian native Frances Brotherhood to general manager. She oversaw the closure of the plant and the construction of a new distribution facility, completed on time and on budget, and Betoptic rolled out smoothly. Schollmaier was impressed and when a joint venture with VISX ran into major problems, Brotherhood became Alcon's representative and Normand Boudreault replaced her in Canada. Alcon Canada's sales were consistently among the highest in CAFE.[134]

As the second largest ophthalmic market in the world, Japan attracted the attention of every Alcon upper manager. Seventeen years after joining Alcon, Hideya Ono, Alcon Japan's general manager, retired in 1989. His understudy for several years, Kuni Iwata, replaced him. Alcon Japan had few proprietary products and registering new ones meant repeating preclinical and clinical studies according to Japanese guidelines. Clinical studies were performed under the direction of a committee of prominent ophthalmologists. These R&D activities took years, seven and a half in the case of Betoptic. Like elsewhere, as Schollmaier and Raval intended, R&D in Fort Worth managed RA and Clinical Science in Japan. By 1997 Betoptic (fig. 6.76), BSS PLUS, Opti-Free, Viscoat, AcrySof, Legacy 20000, and a host of single-use items were all registered in Japan. Alcon Japan sales increased: $28

Professor Tano lectured on Vitrectomy during one of three concurrent Alcon-sponsored luncheon seminars at the Congress.

A large and appreciative crowd attended the Betoptic launch seminar.

Professor Kitazawa, a well-respected glaucoma specialist, made a presentation during the launch seminar.

But Iwata noted that the Betoptic launch is just the beginning. Anticipated new product launches in 1995 include Opti-Free®, Provisc® and Iopidine® 1% for laser surgery. Now that Betoptic has opened the door for Alcon pharmaceutical products in Japan, the company plans to take advantage of the opportunity and grow the business.

The Alcon booth at the Japan Clinical Ophthalmology Congress was a highlight of the meeting. Ed Schollmaier, left, joined Professor Hida and Alcon's Lou Liguori, Mr. Iwata and Mr. Satoh, Japan's surgical sales manager, for a tour.

FIG 6.76
Betoptic launch in Japan (AHR)

million in 1990, $129 million in 1995, $180 million in 1997. Horchler managed Japan for five years before his supervisor, Lou Liguori, took over. At Liguori's insistence, R&D moved from Osaka to Tokyo, causing several projects—Ciloxan, Azopt, and Travatan—to be delayed. Iwata left Alcon Japan at the end of 1996, about the time Liguori died, and was replaced by Kenichi Kodama, a retired executive of Marion Merrell Dow in Japan.[135]

International Division's annual sales quadrupled between 1988 and 1997. New surgical, ophthalmic, and vision care products allowed International to grow its percentage of total Alcon revenue. Sear should be credited for his foresight in appointing Vescovo, Coscia, and Horchler. On the world stage, like in Fort Worth, Alcon's success can be attributed to its sound management.[136]

LASIK, visual acuity correction by a laser, attracted entrepreneurs who saw its potential for millions of people. However, ownership of the proprietary rights was complicated by competing patents, and Alcon's brief experience with LASIK was fraught with legal issues. VISX, founded in 1986 by two New York ophthalmologists, manufactured a LASIK device and began to register it with regulatory agencies worldwide. VISX resolved a patent dispute in 1990 by merging with Taunton, a competitor, and signed an agreement giving Alcon distribution rights. Immediately, problems arose as both parties had unrealistic expectations. Schollmaier put Sear in charge. He moved Alcon Canada's country manager, Brotherhood, to Fort Worth to work with VISX in selling the devices. Registration efforts needed technical support, so Raval asked Charles Robb, a retired R&D executive, to handle this. However, chaos ensued, relationships suffered, and registrations faltered. Devices shipped overseas arrived without notice, yet Alcon was expected to set up the instruments. VISX frequently changed marketing strategies and modified pricing without consulting Alcon. In 1996, with everyone's emotions frayed and a legal dispute raging, Schollmaier negotiated a separation and the venture was terminated. Thus, LASIK was a popular segment of the market in which Alcon, at the pinnacle of ophthalmology, did not participate.[137]

By 1994 Robert Montgomery had been CFO and head of F&A for twelve years, with around one thousand employees worldwide. F&A also handled Human Resources, the Legal Department, and IT (fig. 6.77). Of all the divisions at Alcon, Schollmaier's matrix concept was most evident in F&A, with financial controllers, HR representatives, and IT managers scattered throughout all divisions around the world (fig. 6.78). However, part of the team was centralized, with finance auditors, legal counsels, and tax and treasury personnel located in Fort Worth. F&A was responsible for Alcon's three-year strategic plan, sent to Nestlé annually, and the yearly budget and profit plan. Commenting on F&A's broad role, Montgomery noted, "Alcon's decentralized, entrepreneurial nature makes it essential to have consistent policies consistently applied. ... We foster an environment that encourages creativity and innovation, but we also provide a safety net of limits." When Montgomery retired in June 1996, Charles Miller, a sixteen-year F&A veteran, replaced him.[138]

HR fulfilled an important role at Alcon, going well beyond merely hiring staff. HR Vice President Jack Walter explained, "Today ... we're also responsible on a global basis for developing attractive and affordable compensation plans, enhancing benefits packages without substantially increasing costs, training and coaching managers and supervisors, and devising personnel policies that are fair to all." In addition, HR was responsible for campus security, health services, and travel. Alcon offered improved medical insurance without substantially increasing employee contributions. One means of doing so was a Wellness Program that rewarded those who participated. Additional employee benefits included dental and vision coverage; more earned vacation and sick leave days; short-term and long-term disability insurance; and life insurance. If Alcon wanted to attract and retain the best people, it had to provide an environment superior to all competitors. Alcon was committed to its employees, so it did just that.[139]

The Legal Department consisted of a corporate lawyer group (fig. 5.69) that served Domestic Opera-

FIG 6.77

Finance and Administration meeting, Scottsdale, AZ, 1994 *(Back row – left to right)* Dennis Beikman, John McIntrye, John Goodman, Charles Miller, Jack Walters, Scott Arena, Robert Montgomery; *(Front row – left to right)* George Morey, Tom Mitchell, Brad Kling, Dan Schneiderman, Jerry Rutherford (TOM, AM) (Photo gift from Charles Miller)

FIG 6.78

Alcon International Financial Meeting, Nestlé, Vevey, Switzerland, October 1992 (TOM, AM) (Photo gift from Charles Miller)

FIG 6.79
Dennis Beikman (AHR)

tions; an international team; a patent law group; and a trademarks unit. John McIntyre, Alcon's chief legal counsel, directed an efficient department that managed the company's general needs and hired outside counsel for niche issues that arose. From 1982 through 1997, Alcon's Legal Department resolved about three hundred lawsuits without a major loss.[140]

By 1988 Dennis Beikman had been in charge of IT for six years (fig. 6.79). He had embarked upon establishing uniformity in the hardware and software all over the Fort Worth campus and globally. He had created a team of business system managers to coordinate these efforts so that IT operations functioned normally while new systems were implemented. An example occurred when the company migrated to Dell computers and Hewlett-Packard printers, leveraging Nestlé's agreements with both companies. IT chose to install and use the Microsoft operating system and its Office components. Alcon was an early adopter of new technology, so by 1988 IT installed a fiber optic network, creating a sophisticated communication architecture. The IT infrastructure was upgraded using RAMIS, a fourth-generation programming language. IT implemented a suite of financial and accounting software, which included graphics, developed by J. D. Edwards to operate in every language. Vescovo, EURMEA vice president, claimed the results were outstanding. One example was Customer Service, where telecommunications systems were integrated into the computers, allowing representatives to identify doctors calling and their history of using Alcon products. IT also installed the first laptops for the MSRs in Vision Care and Ophthalmic, as well as in R&D's Clinical Science Department. These early laptops were large, bulky machines, but by 1997 more compact Dell laptops were being introduced.[141]

By 1990 Alcon held several SERVA and NOVA sessions each year, inviting eye specialists to Fort Worth for an introduction to R&D activities. After the CooperVision acquisition, Dubbs modified his training arena to include a full-size replica of a typical ophthalmic surgical room, complete with Alcon surgical devices and ophthalmic products. For SERVA in 1991, Dubbs adapted his phacoemulsification course into a day of lecture and hands-on wet-lab experience. Bill Rhue, the SERVA director, recalled, "In every respect, it was one of the most successful programs we have ever conducted." Thereafter all SERVA sessions in Fort Worth included an extra day for the phacoemulsification course. Taking advantage of the annual AAO and ARVO conferences, Alcon also scheduled SERVA programs at these meetings. By 1992 eighteen hundred American ophthalmology residents had attended a SERVA session, and each year five hundred American optometrists attended the NOVA program. International ophthalmologists participating in the Senior Ophthalmologists Visiting Alcon (SOVA) sessions held in tandem with the AAO meeting typically numbered two hundred. Talking to the attendees at one session, Schollmaier remarked, "Our aim is to offer better products for you to use with your patients, and by beginning a long-term dialogue, we can work with you to ensure you can offer the best treatments in the world." When Rhue and Roy Buchanan retired in 1992, Dubbs and Diane Smith took charge of SERVA, NOVA, and SOVA responsibilities.[142]

As already discussed, Alcon's support for medical missions was the brainchild of Dora Moody in the 1960s. When she retired, Andy Lubrano took charge; in 1993 he turned the assignment over to Winona Mueller, Sear's administrative assistant. The program evolved from providing products at the request of a doctor to a formal process of assessing need. Individual doctors or charities provided documentation of an invitation from a country, association with a nonprofit charitable organization, and collaboration with a local doctor. In 1996 the Medical Missions group worked with more than eleven hundred physicians, sent donations to more than 80 countries, and supported about five hundred ophthalmic humanitarian efforts by contributing virtually every product that Alcon made. Each year, Alcon donated products valued between $10 to $15 million. In one project, a team collected over five thousand pairs of eyeglasses; all were sent overseas.[143]

The Alcon Foundation continued to support local nonprofits and institutions. The Fort Worth Opera, Fort Worth Symphony, Casa Mañana Theater, Annual Thanksgiving Fund, Goodfellows, Fort Worth Jaycees, and many others received donations. The Warm Place, which provided grief support for children and their families, received an annual contribution; it had been founded by Alcon retiree Bill Starz. Each year assistance was provided to state and national chapters of the Society to Prevent Blindness. The foundation partially funded several ophthalmic conferences, one being the International Congress of Ophthalmology in Singapore in 1990. The Alcon Foundation continued to support Orbis's Flying Eye Hospital. As another example of how senior personnel handled more than one responsibility, Marva Clynch (fig. 6.80) managed the Alcon Foundation while also serving as the administrative assistant for both Schollmaier and Sisson. Employed since 1966, Clynch represented the ultimate professional administrative assistant

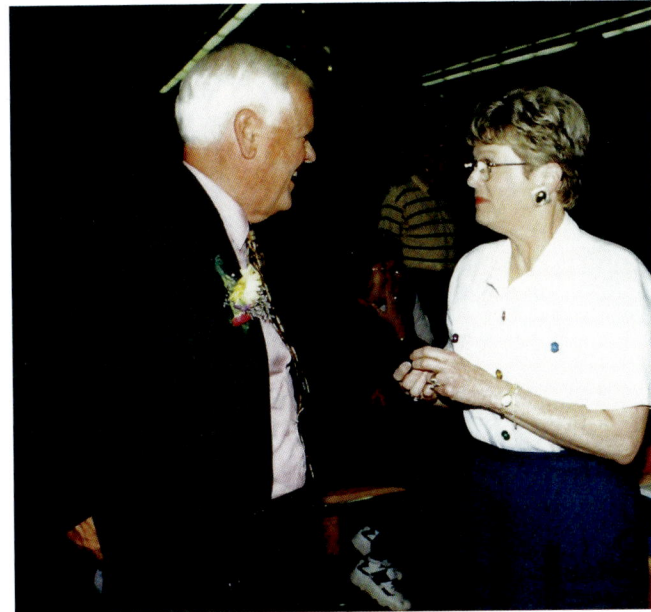

FIG 6.80
Ed Schollmaier (*left*),
Marva Clynch (*right*), 1998
(AHR)

FIG 6.81
A division Christmas Party, Fort Worth, 1990 (AHR)

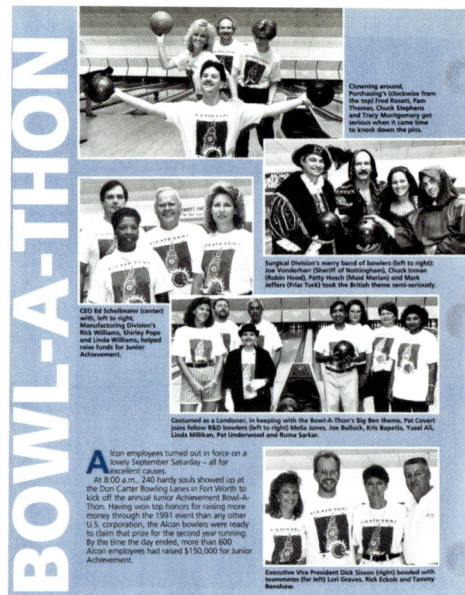

FIG 6.82
Bowl-A-Thon, 1992 (AHR)

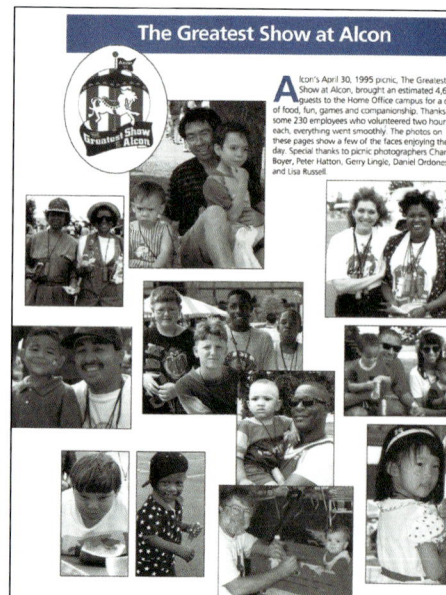

FIG 6.83
Company picnic, 1995 (AHR)

at Alcon.[144]

The expanded capacity of the Alexander Tower in 1987 brought everyone in Fort Worth back on campus; most employees ate lunch in the Crossroads Cafeteria. A new sense of community emerged as personnel mingled during their breaks. With twenty-five hundred people on campus, social spaces were lively and friendly. Divisional Christmas parties remained the pinnacle of the social calendar (fig. 6.81). Christmas was celebrated across the campus with an employee choir, a Salvation Army "Forgotten Angel" project, and other adopt-a-family and Angel Tree donation programs. Manufacturing mechanic Jeri Rimel constructed life-sized Christmas-themed papier-mâché images displayed in Alexander Tower. To allow employees more time to celebrate holidays, Alcon began the practice of closing from Christmas Eve until January 2. Alcon recognized countries' different religious celebrations and national holidays by granting employees an opportunity to participate in them.[145]

As mentioned previously, Alcon's tradition of contributing a fair share to Tarrant County's United Way began with Conner and Alexander, and as Alcon acquired companies the custom expanded. Contributions were considerable—$850,000 in 1993, $1 million in 1993. In total for this decade, Alcon employees contributed over $10 million. Not only did Alcon employees donate money, many served as leaders at the county level; Miller was the county chairman in 1994.[146]

One of Alexander's legacies was Alcon's support of Junior Achievement, an international program that exposed scholars from pre-K through high school to the importance and scope of business practices. In the 1980s, Alcon employees began Bowl-A-Thons to raise funds. Schollmaier volunteered for Junior Achievement both locally and nationally, and he passed this leadership role to Spruill. A few hundred employees in Fort Worth and in Alcon subsidiaries eagerly participated in Bowl-A-Thons (fig. 6.82) that raised between $150,000 and $250,000 annually. To increase donations and extend involvement, Spruill corralled those not interested in bowling into participating in bingo, fashion shows, auctions, jeans days, and even an executive car wash to raise funds. These extra events added another $100,000 to Alcon's yearly contribution.[147]

The on-campus Junior Achievement activities evolved into a company picnic, held each spring (fig. 6.83). Annual picnics became common at overseas facilities, too. To celebrate $1 billion in annual sales, three thousand employees and their families enjoyed carnival games, a petting zoo, a western band, a miniature train, and tables of hamburgers, hot dogs, ice cream, and cold drinks. The Alcon Family was large enough to support

FIG 6.84
Alcon athletes (AHR)

▲ In only its second year of competition in a regional benefit Corporate Sports Battle, the **Alcon Corporate Sports Battle team** placed second to win the Silver Medal. The athletes competed with 11 teams in Dallas, Texas, on August 2, 1996. Individual honors went to **Greg House**, Top Male Finisher in the 5K race and **Cindy Steenbergen**, Outstanding Female Athlete.

◄ **Cindy Steenbergen**, Alcon Labeling Services administrator, poses with medals won as a top ranked masters (over 40 years old) sprinter. She began seriously running track only one year ago, after placing second in the Corporate Sports Battle. Steenbergen captured the 1996 U.S. Masters Indoor 200 meter championship in March at the National Indoor Championship in Greensboro, North Carolina. Recent wins for Steenbergen include first place in the 100-meter dash (in 12.6 seconds) at the Texas Masters Championship, August 10 in Arlington, Texas, and first place in both the 100-meter and 200-meter dash at the U.S. Outdoors Masters Championship August 15-18 in Spokane, Washington.

sports teams and competitions, including barrel racing, rodeos, scuba diving, marathons, triathlons, table tennis, cycling, motorcycling, and skydiving to name a few. An eighteen-member team competed in regional Corporate Challenges and Cindy Steenbergen, from Manufacturing, won national sprint titles for her age group (fig. 6.84). Overseas, Alcon employees also engaged in a variety of athletic events, such as baseball, squash, windsurfing, swimming, tennis, and others. Brigitte Fuhr, at Alcon Germany, won several triathlons. Alcon even had a three-member triathlon team named Opti-Free![148]

In 1988, the beginning of its fifth decade, Alcon's global annual sales totaled $551 million, which increased to $1 billion in 1991 and $2 billion in 1997, a remarkable four-fold increase (fig. 6.85). CooperVision's revenues added to this growth; acquired in 1988, it contributed $221 million increase for 1989 revenues. However, the main driver was the list of new products developed, manufactured, and marketed during this period. In 1993 Betoptic and Opti-Free became Alcon's first $100 million products, and AcrySof reached $100 million by mid-1996; it would become Alcon's first $200 million product by 1998. These three alone accounted for 25 percent of Alcon's $2 billion global sales in 1997.[149]

fig. 6.98 Annual Sales

2500
2000
1500
1000
500
0

Millions

1988 1989 1990 1991 1992 1993 1994 1995 1996 1997

Sales by Division

Surgical 35%   Ophthalmic 43%   Vision Care 21%

1988

Surgical 47%   Ophthalmic 34%   Vision Care 19%

1997

Sales by Geographical Region

US 64%   Int'l 36%

1988

Int'l 44%   US 56%

1997

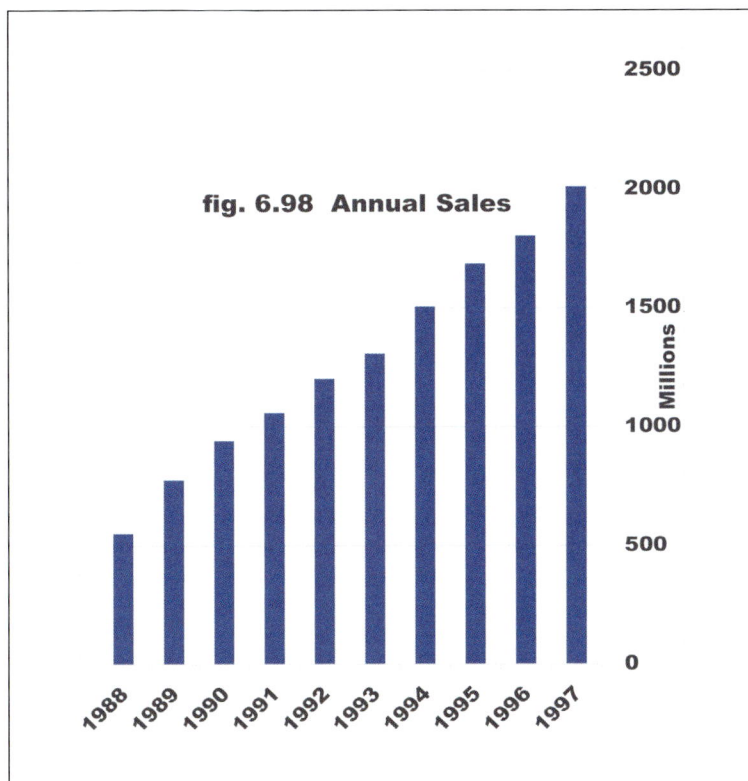

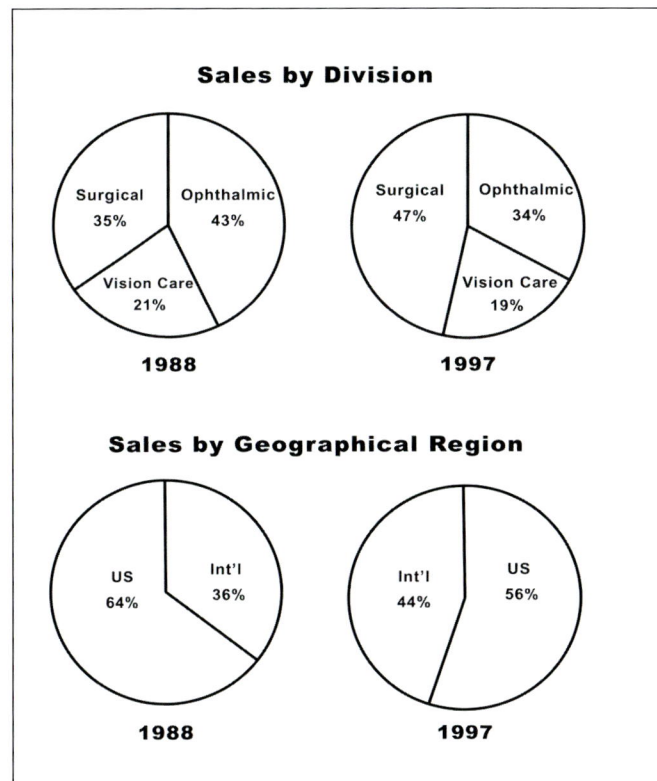

The Surgical Division's portion of total revenue grew from 35 percent in 1988 to 47 percent in 1997 (fig. 6.86). Surgical's dominance affected the share for Ophthalmic and Vision Care. The Ophthalmic Division's share changed from 43 percent in 1988 to 34 percent in 1997 (fig. 6.86). Meanwhile, Vision Care's dynamics remained constant at 21 percent in 1988 and 19 percent in 1997 (fig. 6.86). Revenue evolution included geographic changes. In 1988, US sales dominated at 64 percent with the International Division contributing 36 percent of total sales (fig. 6.86). The dynamic changed by 1997, when International's share increased to 44 percent. Alcon's cumulative sales from 1988 through 1997 equaled $12.843 billion, a record befitting the top ophthalmic specialty company in the world. Its products were sold in 125 countries and, with rare exceptions, Alcon dominated every ophthalmic, vision care, and surgical market segment.[150]

On May 12, 1997, Alcon employees around the world celebrated the company's fiftieth anniversary (fig. 6.87). Alcon had reached the pinnacle—$2 billion in revenue and recognition as the premier ophthalmic specialty company in the world. Alexander and Conner always claimed that Alcon hired *good* people. Schollmaier elevated the

FIG 6.85
Annual sales, 1988–1997 (TOM, AM)

FIG 6.86
Sales by product area; Sales by geographic region across the globe, 1988 and 1997 (TOM, AM)

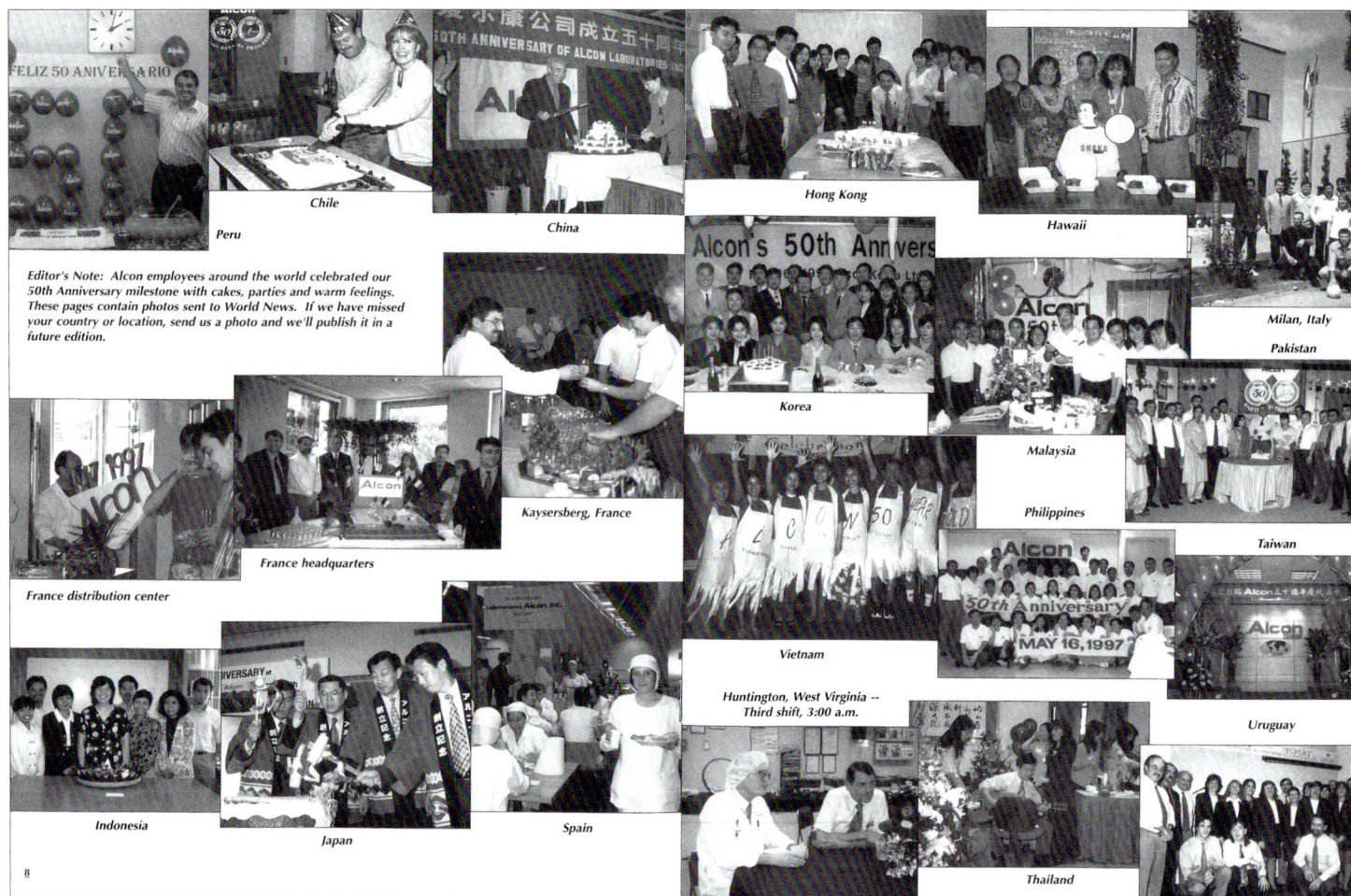

FIG 6.87
Alcon's fiftieth anniversary
worldwide celebrations (AHR)

statement by declaring the company hired the *best* people and retained them. He asserted that the prior four decades were a preparation for 1988 through 1997, a banner decade that was the apex of his Alcon career. By this stage, about 10,500 people worked for Alcon, many of whom had been with the company for more than twenty years, an illustration of the mutual commitment between employees and company.

* * *

The transformation of Alcon during this decade was extraordinary. The company sold its non-ophthalmology assets, Avicon and Webcon, and spun off its dermatology business to Nestlé and L'Oréal, focusing entirely on ophthalmology. Alcon's physical appearance in Fort Worth evolved, creating a huge capacity for production increases. Distribution centers were added in Fort Worth and Maryland, and overseas in Argentina, Japan, Germany, and Britain. With the completion of the ITC, Alcon had the finest ophthalmic device manufacturing and R&D center in the world. Globally, Alcon rationalized its manufacturing facilities, modernizing plants in Mexico, Brazil, and Puerto Rico, and updated the newly acquired Cusí laboratory and factory in Spain. Elsewhere in Europe, the Kaysersberg plant was renovated, as was the facility in Belgium. By the end of 1997, Alcon had fourteen manufacturing plants—six in the United States, two in Spain, and one each in Puerto Rico, Mexico, Brazil, France, Brussels, and Beijing.

Corporate Manufacturing/Engineering directed these renovations, operating under Schollmaier's matrix concept. When Senkowski retired, his replacement left after a short period and then Bens took charge, the fourth manufacturing director in Alcon's first fifty years. Fleming, vice president of QA, retired at the same time, replaced by Luttrell, the third QA leader in this fifty-year period. This decade saw the climax of QA's integration into Manufacturing, in which quality was built into a product before and during the production process. QA became the cradle for plant managers. The people who enforced in-process controls and validation became the directors of plants or production lines. Corporate QA continued its evolution, in direct control of QA laboratories in the various plants. Luttrell led the IOS certification of Alcon's plants. By any standard, QA and Manufacturing had become integrated state-of-the-art organizations that assured quality in procedures and processes, producing a trusted and reliable product.

By 1996 Raval, R&D's executive vice president, directed several hundred scientists and regulatory specialists in Fort Worth, Irvine, and overseas. He had served in this capacity for twenty-six years, an unusually long tenure in the pharmaceutical and medical device industries. By the same year projects were conducted globally, meeting universal standards, and except for in Japan a single file was used to register products worldwide, reducing costs while ensuring a uniform brand. When Alcon acquired CooperVision, Raval appointed a well-qualified person to lead R&D at ITC. He also ensured the best IOL technologists from CooperVison went to Fort Worth and reduced their projects to the few most likely to succeed. Experienced development specialists produced an NDA or PMA annually, a productivity uncommon in the pharmaceutical and device industries. R&D licensed compounds from other companies and discovered three proprietary molecules for treating glaucoma. During this ten-year period, R&D released more than two dozen new products, of which three accounted for one-fourth of Alcon's global sales in 1997.

Acquiring CooperVision was strategic. Along with surgical products, it came with the technology and technologists to create the premier phacoemulsification device, Legacy 20000, and the foldable AcrySof. The acquisition included a cadre of management, marketing, and sales personnel that was knowledgeable, discerning, and well connected to the global trends of ocular surgery. Thanks to them, AcrySof was Alcon's first $200 million product. By 1997 the Surgical Division accounted for 47 percent of global revenues for Alcon. Integrating the corporate culture of CooperVision into Alcon's matrix came with complications. However, Spruill and Baker made it work, protecting tenured employees and finding leadership roles for recent arrivals; one former CooperVision employee became Alcon's CEO fifteen years later.

The Ophthalmic and Vision Care Divisions under Sisson had the enviable task of launching new products every year. Opti-Free allowed Vision Care's marketing and sales to recover from the discouraging Opti-Soft experience. As the contact lens market evolved, R&D modified the Opti-Free franchise to fit consumer needs, and innovative marketing concepts helped produce Alcon's first $150 million product. In the Ophthalmic Division, the new and more comfortable Betoptic S became the first $100 million therapy; the division also launched two glaucoma medications—Iopidine 0.5% and Azopt. Equally important, with TobraDex and Ciloxan, Alcon continued its domination in the steroid-antibiotic and ocular antibiotic markets. Moreover, of the three novel anti-allergy therapies introduced, Patanol set record sales, becoming Alcon's fourth $100 million product.

Internationally, a steady stream of new eye therapeutics shored up Alcon's presence in the ophthalmic prescription and OTC markets. Foreign Betoptic sales contributed significantly to it becoming a $100 million item. Moreover, Alomide became the first product introduced overseas ahead of the United States, expanding the anti-allergy market. With Opti-Free's introduction, Alcon made significant inroads into the contact lens disinfectant market, and Opti-Free Express expanded its position. As phacoemulsification cataract surgery grew in popularity, Legacy 20000 and AcrySof gained acceptance, especially in developed countries. Moreover, the introduction of Custom Paks put Alcon in a favored role among foreign ocular surgeons. Product introductions helped increase the International Division's share of Alcon's sales, but equally important were sales gains in Japan and other countries, particularly Singapore, Thailand, China, and Vietnam, where women led the sales teams. Meanwhile, Alcon's expansion into Eastern Europe and Russia added opportunities. By 1997 all these together led to the International Division contributing 44 percent of Alcon's global revenues.

Alcon's annual revenue climbed from $551 million to $2 billion between 1988 and 1997, the decade that caps its fifty-year history. The foundational vision of two pharmacists in 1947 had come to fulfillment by 1997, when Alcon truly became the most prestigious ophthalmic house in the world. On the cusp of a new era, with a new generation of leadership, the future looked bright.

Chapter 7

A Vision's Legacies

Three key factors propelled Alcon to global success—the Alcon Family, creative leadership, and innovative products. Without the entrepreneurial leadership and vision of Bill Conner and Bob Alexander (frontispiece), their pharmacy would not have expanded out of its small premises in downtown Fort Worth. It was the skillful direction of Ed Schollmaier and George Leone that led Alcon into its golden era and beyond as the world's foremost ophthalmic house. The impact of Alcon innovation cannot be understated. Dave Merrill and Ted Fleming created the first sterile products conceived around common ophthalmic medications packaged in the revolutionary Drop-tainer. Dilip Raval later implemented management concepts that enabled Alcon R&D to focus its resources strategically, resulting in countless breakthrough products.

A growing pharmaceutical business requires responsive production capability, and Fleming and Luttrell and their teams established quality assurance processes. Adequate facilities are essential, and Bob Carter deserves credit for creating Alcon's first modern manufacturing facility that Bernie Senkowski modernized in response to growing demands. Marketing and sales teams led by Dick Sisson and John Spruill used innovative strategies to drive Alcon's products to dominance in the crowded ophthalmic pharmaceutical, vision care, and surgical markets. Beginning in the early 1960s, Frank Buhler set in motion Alcon's international penetration and by 1982 created the nucleus of an organization with great potential. Tim Sear reorganized the International Division to be one of Alcon's highest revenue producers. Allen Baker led domestic and international operations, building organizations composed of personnel with wide-ranging experiences. Robert Montgomery reformed Alcon's support infrastructure of information technology, human resources, financial, and legal counsel.

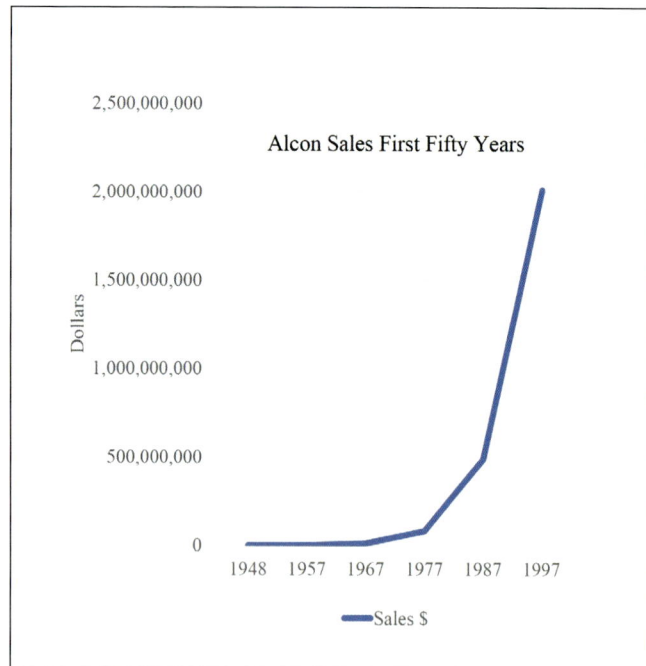

FIG 7.1
Alcon sales first fifty years, 1948–1997
(TOM, AM)

Leadership, facilities, and products are tangibles recorded in extant files that prove their role in Alcon's success. Harder to define, but essential to success, is the Alcon Family, the sum of many individual efforts. Alcon would not exist without its people. Conner asserted that Alcon hired good people. Schollmaier boasted they hired the best and worked to retain them. Most of this cadre had multiple jobs within the company, creating institutional knowledge unique in an industry notorious for high turnover. Everyone at Alcon knew each other, if not personally, then by reputation, and collectively they knew every eye care specialist in the world. This shared knowledge afforded valuable insight into ophthalmic science and product development, supported by pioneering marketing and selling skills. The Alcon Family became an industrial juggernaut that generated $2 billion in annual sales by 1997 (fig. 7.1).

Alcon was committed to recruiting and retaining capable and motivated staff globally. It offered competitive pay and liberal benefits, including generous retirement plans. The work environment was satisfying, and career advancement was attainable for anyone who proved worthy. Alcon, as the international leader in preserving or restoring eyesight, was a noble enterprise that was family-oriented and a fun place to work. When a position became available, Alcon's leaders first promoted from within a department or, with cross-training, from within the company. If an external search was required, the first consideration went to candidates with in-company references. Longevity was revered. Monthly coffees with senior management celebrated service anniversaries, for which employees received commemorative pins and had their work highlighted by supervisors. *Alcon World News* praised the high percentage of long-serving employees.

Alcon offered generous health insurance, college tuition reimbursement, and other benefits, such as on-campus fitness centers, to attract and retain employees. Nonetheless, performance was regularly assessed. When action plans to remedy deficiencies failed, nonperformers were dismissed. When a person with a history of success faltered in a new assignment, they were not fired but instead assigned another position more suited to them. If a high-performing employee chose to explore opportunities elsewhere, human resources kept in contact, offering reemployment; in almost every case when that person returned, they contributed to Alcon's success.[1]

Those who spent most of their working life at Alcon have their own sense of the characteristics shared by long-term employees. For the most part, Alcon people were tenacious, self-confident, pragmatic, dedicated, outspoken, congenial, and hardworking. Discussions about issues, problems, strategies, plans, and just about any subject were boisterous, yet mostly devoid of personal rancor. Once a decision was made, everyone implemented it, even if they had not endorsed it. The Alcon Family was composed of team players who respected the roles and responsibilities of all members, and successes were shared in lively celebrations. Alcon employees participated in company-wide events, such as picnics and team games, often in support of worthy civic goals. At the end of their careers, retirees left with the sense that their accomplishments had contributed to the company's collective achievements; there was, and still is, enormous pride in having worked at Alcon. These are the values of the Alcon Family.

The seeds for Alcon's success began before its incorporation in 1947, when Conner and Alexander became licensed Texas pharmacists in Fort Worth. With the economy retooling after World War II, they established a pharmacy that morphed into a pharmaceutical company. There were numerous seminal events over the next fifty years, one being the creation of the name Alcon, which Catherine Alexander created by combining the first letters of both men's last names. But there was also Conner's penchant for civic involvement. A modest $200 travel budget from the Kiwanis Club supported a promotional road trip to Los Angeles with Alexander. They found an unmet niche market—eye care, a market that was further revealed the next year at the annual conference of the AAOO.[2]

Alcon's product concept was built on the premise that a prescriber could trust its quality—known, measured ingredients in a sterile, preserved, safe solution. In 1953 Alexander invented the Drop-tainer, a pivotal discovery that revolutionized the dispensing of eye drops from a sterile plastic, squeezable bottle. Encouraged by a Fort Worth business leader, Conner and Alexander attended a Harvard Business School management course. What they learned proved essential as they collaborated to build a management structure that endured through five decades.[3]

By 1957 Alcon was well established in the United States. Merrill and Fleming had developed nearly three dozen products around the Isopto brand. Alexander had assembled an exceptional sales team centered on veteran Leone and newcomers Schollmaier, Sisson, Spruill, and Keith Lane. Meanwhile, Conner promoted Alcon and its products overseas, and later Buhler created Alcon's International Division. Another key step was the expansion of manufacturing, laboratory, and administrative facilities on a 180-acre site south of Fort Worth. A misguided marketing campaign in 1961 nearly bankrupted Alcon, but Schollmaier devised and implemented a rescue plan. As a harbinger of their future leadership roles, Schollmaier and Leone were relocated to Fort Worth and put in charge of marketing and sales. In the meantime, Conner decided to diversify, and Alcon acquired other pharmaceutical companies that focused on urology, allergy, dermatology, surgical instruments, and even vascular surgery. However, advances in ocular pharmacology, pharmaceutical sciences, and ocular surgery led Alcon to refocus on ophthalmic products.[4]

The decade from 1968 through 1977 was transformative. Alcon was listed on the New York Stock Exchange in 1971. Schollmaier became president in 1972 with Leone as executive vice president, and between them they set an attitude of leadership that persisted well beyond their tenures. Alcon was bought by Nestlé in 1977, which provided financial support to continue innovative growth. Leone centralized R&D, QA, Manufacturing/Engineering and RA into S&T, a new concept in the pharmaceutical industry. Raval was appointed to take charge of R&D. Leone kept Fleming in QA and hired Senkowski to manage Manufacturing/Engineering and Horger for RA. QA embarked on a long-term effort to improve manufacturing processes, while R&D's comprehensive licensing effort produced three lucrative products—BSS PLUS, betaxolol, and tobramycin. In total, in this decade R&D released six novel ophthalmic products, six generics, and a surgical hemostat. After removing two failed operational leaders, Schollmaier assigned Sisson to lead the Ophthalmic and Vision Care Divisions, Spruill the Surgical Division, and Lane the Dermatology Division. Alcon also acquired new companies overseas, launching an increased presence in South America and Europe. Major manufacturing facilities were established in Puerto Rico and Belgium.[5]

Relying on Nestlé's support, Schollmaier led Alcon into its fourth decade. The firm embarked upon the construction of modern R&D, manufacturing, and administrative facilities worldwide. The pivotal acquisition of Burton, Parsons gave Alcon the leading contact lens disinfectant solution product. The polyquad license resulted in the Opti-Free franchise. The introduction of Betoptic placed Alcon in second position in the growing glaucoma therapy market based on novel marketing and global launches. Spruill acquired intraocular lens, sutures and needles, cataract, and vitreous surgical device companies, and created a custom pack for ophthalmic surgeons. In these ten years, R&D released six novel and six generic ophthalmic therapies, six innovative vision care solutions, and three new surgical products. Fleming's QA integration continued into manufacturing processes as Senkowski consolidated and renovated plants worldwide. Sear took over the International Division; by the end of the decade, it was a high-revenue producer. By 1987 Alcon was the global leader in most ophthalmic products markets, except for IOLs and cataract-vitreous surgical devices. Schollmaier's team then evolved as first-generation managers Fleming, Buhler, and Leone retired, followed by Senkowski and Horger. The new leaders, including Sisson, Spruill, Raval, Montgomery, Howard Luttrell, and André Bens, brought a wealth of Alcon institutional knowledge.[6]

The final decade in this history, 1987–1997, began when Carl Angst retired and José Daniel at Nestlé became Schollmaier's supervisor. Daniel convinced Schollmaier to transfer Alcon's dermatology business to Galderma, owned by Nestlé and L'Oréal. Several Alcon leaders joined the France-based venture, which increased global sales to $300 million by 1997. Meanwhile, Alcon R&D produced fourteen novel therapeutic and twelve generic ophthalmic therapies and seven new Opti-Free franchise products. It also released seven new IOLs, a series of surgical-suite devices, including market leaders for cataract and vitreous surgeries, and many single-use products. Domestic and international marketing and sales teams launched new products every year. Betoptic became Alcon's first $100 million product, Opti-Free its first $150 million product, and the revolutionary foldable IOL, AcrySof, the first $200 million product. Of Alcon's $2 billion total sales in 1997, these three contributed 25 percent.

Alcon's footprint in Fort Worth continued to expand with the completion of the Alexander Tower, enlargement of the S&T and R&D buildings, construction of Schollmaier Auditorium, installation of several production lines, and the opening of the modern ASPEX manufacturing facility. Overseas and in Puerto Rico, every plant was modernized, and production capacity increased with the acquisition of Cusí Laboratories in Spain. The acquisition of CooperVision brought new IOL and surgical device facilities and technologists, as well as a leadership team that broadened Alcon's existing executive expertise.[7]

At the end of 1997, Schollmaier retired as CEO at the age of sixty-four. He had led Alcon for twenty-five years, a remarkable tenure in the pharmaceutical and surgical device industry. Schollmaier staged his retirement over three years, putting in place executives he wanted to replace his team. Sisson left his Domestic Operations role in 1996 and was replaced by Sear, who became Alcon's CEO in 1998. Baker became Alcon's COO and also took charge of the International Division. Raval retired as head of R&D in 1996, and twenty-three-year Alcon R&D veteran Jerry Cagle took charge. Commenting on Raval's contribution to Alcon, Schollmaier boasted that in 1996 products released by R&D in the past

FIG 7.2
R&D's contribution to Alcon's domestic sales in 1996 (*AWN*, April 1997) (AHR)

ten years accounted for 70 percent of annual revenues (fig. 7.2). Montgomery also departed in 1996, replaced by Charles Miller, a sixteen-year Alcon veteran. Schollmaier thus cultivated the most experienced set of leaders in the global ophthalmic pharmaceutical and surgical device industry. By the end of Sear's tenure as CEO in 2004, Alcon's annual sales grew to $4 billion. The company dominated almost every market segment in the global ophthalmic pharmaceutical and surgical device industry.[8]

In the 1950s Conner showed a remarkable projected sales growth chart to Alcon visitors. His vision became a prophecy as Alcon's sales increased to $2 billion by 1997 (fig. 7.1). A strong, innovative sales and marketing ethos and technologically driven products played pivotal roles in leading Alcon to this dominant position in the global ophthalmic market. Beginning about 1977 the trajectory reflects, in part, Nestlé's investments and arm's-length management. After World War II, American industry grew exponentially due to veterans' educational programs and federal investment in science, medicine, and technology. A cross section of the people who emerged during these times were found in the Alcon Family and the company's leadership. Undeniably, implementation of Medicare in 1962 was important; elderly folks endure a substantial portion of ocular diseases. Moreover, ophthalmology science rapidly evolved, creating product opportunities for Alcon.

Alcon, however, could not have risen to global dominance without having been acquired by Nestlé. By 1977 Alcon had a leadership, organizational, and managerial philosophy that almost mirrored that of Nestlé, making integration seamless. Nestlé leaders Arthur Fürer, Helmut Maucher, Angst, and Daniel had confidence in Schollmaier. As Nestlé's largest noncore acquisition, Alcon was given autonomy to manage its own future, on the condition that financial goals were met, which they were. By 1997 Alcon contributed 4.6 percent of Nestlé's annual sales and a remarkable 12 percent of its profits. No other Nestlé product group was as lucrative as Alcon. In fact, Alcon's cumulative profits from 1977 to 1997 were at least twice that of Nestlé's total investments in Alcon.[9]

On March 23, 2002, Nestlé tendered 25 percent of Alcon stock in a public offering on the New York Stock Exchange at $33 per share; Nestlé earned $2.3 billion. In 2008 Nestlé sold another minority interest in Alcon of 74 million shares at $143 per share to Novartis, a Swiss pharmaceutical enterprise based in Basel; Nestlé earned $10.5 billion. At this point, Nestlé still owned 52 percent of Alcon shares. In August 2010, Novartis exercised its option, paid $28.3 billion, and acquired Alcon's outstanding shares from Nestlé. From 2002 to 2010, Nestlé earned $41.1 billion from the sales of its stake in Alcon, a company it bought for $269 million in 1977. Novartis had a substantial portion of the contact lens market and transferred that segment to Alcon. In June 2018 Novartis announced that it intended to keep Alcon's pharmaceutical business and spin off the contact lens and ophthalmic device segment into an IPO. On April 9, 2019, Alcon was listed on the New York Stock Exchange for the third time. In its annual report that year, Alcon reported annual sales of $7.4 billion ($4.2 surgical and $3.2 vision care sales); by this time, employed 22,142 people. Michael Ball, the chairman of the board of directors, and David Endicott, CEO, both experienced in the industry, lead Alcon today.[10]

The legacy of Alcon's first fifty years is historic. It was the principal enterprise that created and shaped the global ophthalmic pharmaceutical, vision care, and surgical markets. Undoubtedly Conner, Alexander, Schollmaier, and Leone were the main drivers. Alcon was a fertile training arena that prepared managers for executive positions. Three became Alcon CEOs—Sear, Cary Rayment, and Kevin Buehler. Alcon alumni also took leadership positions in other pharmaceutical companies. Fred W. Lyons Jr. worked for Alcon for over a decade in the 1950s and 1960s before becoming the CEO of Marion Merrell Dow, a company whose growth mirrored that of Alcon. In 1982 Buhler purchased Alcon's Lafayette group and Konsyl, a psyllium fiber. He sold the enterprise for several million dollars in May 2003, when he retired. John Cannon, manager of the Mahdeen and DuBarry franchises, bought these from Alcon in July 1983; he operated the successful company as Mediceutical until his death in June 2002. In 1989 John Feik and his partner, H. Paul Dorman, bought Dermatological Products of Texas, an Alcon facility in San Antonio, and created DFB, headquartered in Fort Worth. DFB and related companies developed and marketed dermatological and wound-healing products. They sold most of it for several hundred million dollars to Smith & Nephew, a UK pharmaceutical company, in 2012. When Alcon disbanded its R&D group at Produits Ophtalmique Stériles at Kaysersberg, France, in 1989, Nicole Martin-Spittler founded Laboratoires Pharmaster, a contract ophthalmic manufacturing facility in Erstein, near Strasbourg. It became the largest plant in the European Union that manufactured unpreserved ophthalmic solutions. Martin-Spittler sold the facility to the Synerlab Group in 2010. When he retired from Alcon in 2006, William "Bill" Burns founded Encore Vision to develop therapies for presbyopia, an age-related decrease of near vision. Encore Vision investors sold their invention to Novartis in December 2016 for a few hundred million dollars.

Alcon alumni also became senior executives in related industries. Marketing executive Stuart Raetzman became a Galderma CEO; Jacqualyn Fouse, ex-Nestlé treasurer and Alcon CFO, became the COO of Celgene and then CEO for Agios Pharmaceuticals, whose

FIG 7.3
Dick Sisson with Caballero, champion of champions Peruvian horse, 2014 (Photo gift of Molly Sisson Carter) (TOM, AM)

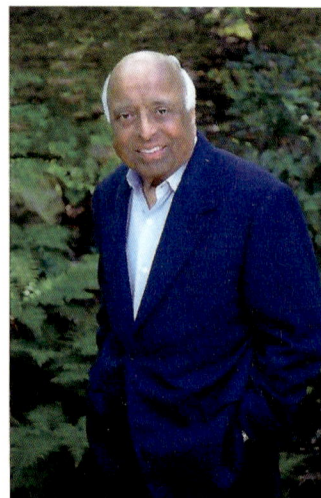

FIG 7.4
Dilip N. Raval, fine arts photographer, 2017 (Courtesy of Dilip N. Raval)

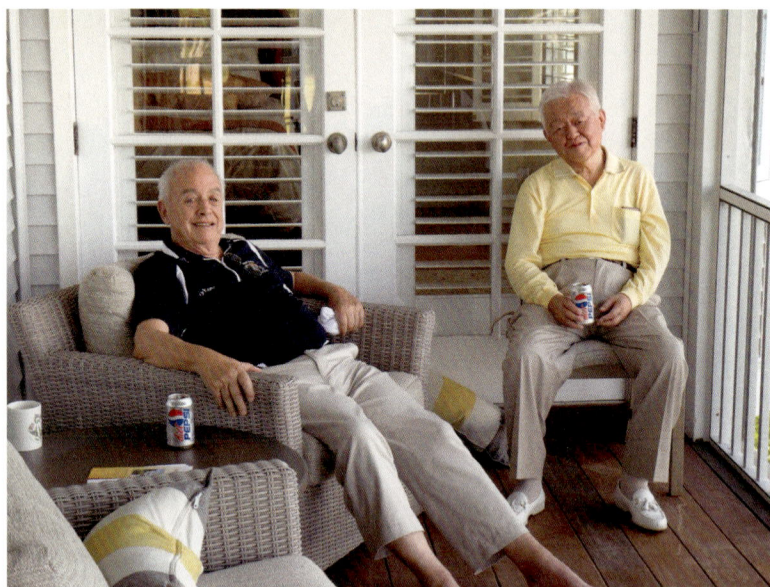

FIG 7.5
Tim Sear and Sachiake Ibe, Useppa Island, Florida (Photo gift of Judith Sear) (TOM, AM)

board she currently chairs. Ex-Alcon R&D scientist Adrienne Graves was CEO of Santen's United States division; Patricia Zilliox, retired senior Alcon R&D executive, is currently CEO of Eyevensys, a Paris biotech company; Stella Robertson, an ex-Alcon R&D executive, helped to found Fort Worth–based Bios Partners, an enterprise that invests in biotech companies. Many former Alcon employees started small development or consulting companies in retirement, or served on boards of directors for pharmaceutical enterprises of all types. Even Bill Conner's son, Halden, continued the Conner family habit of entrepreneurship by creating his own ophthalmic biotech company, Nacuity.[11]

Other Alcon retirees took different paths. Sisson bought a small ranch near Fort Worth and raised champion Peruvian horses noted for their smooth gait, *paso llano* (fig. 7.3). Raval's photographs have appeared in exhibits in the United States and India (fig. 7.4). Sear served as Alcon chairman emeritus until 2009. He then was a director on several boards of public companies, invested in real estate, bought a small farm, and bought and sold antique banknotes. One of Sear's most treasured friendships was with Sachiake Ibe, president of Zeria Pharmaceutical, a Japanese pharmaceutical company (fig. 7.5). Montgomery (fig. 7.6) returned to Australia's Gold Coast, served on the boards of various Australian and American companies, and managed major asset sales and divestitures for public companies. Baker continues to operate a farm and ranch west of Fort Worth (fig. 7.7).

Leone joined Alcon in 1950 as the company's second salesman. Later, he became the national sales director and general manager for Domestic Operations before leading S&T. Speaking of appointing Leone to manage S&T, Schollmaier said, "There was no road map. I had confidence that George would provide outstanding leadership in focusing on what could be done and would get full commitment. I knew that he wouldn't get distracted or discouraged. I knew that he was totally trustworthy and that problems would be addressed, not swept under the carpet." Raval explained Leone's attitude toward new product development: "He saw what it would take to put R&D in the big picture. He then set priorities and emphasized the excellence and integrity of the R&D effort. His great contribution to R&D was teaching scientists how to be successful in a commercial setting." Leone regarded the Alcon Research Institute, a major legacy, as a prime example of his belief in excellence. It was said that without Leone there would be no Alcon, such was his impact on the company.[12]

After his retirement in 1988, Leone remained active in civic, educational, and commercial endeavors. He continued as an executive committee trustee of the Alcon Research Institute until 1998. For several years, he served on the board of governors of the Harris Methodist Health Foundation in Fort Worth. He continued his active participation in the

FIG 7.6
Robert Montgomery, ca. 2021
(Photo gift of Robert Montgomery)
(TOM, AM)

FIG 7.7
Allen Baker, 2023 (Photo gift
of Allen Baker) (TOM, AM)

Yoga Society of New York as a member of the board of directors and for the San Francisco Yoga Society. A graduate of Texas Wesleyan University, Leone served on its board of trustees. The university honored him as a distinguished alumnus in 1979 and 2009, and with an honorary degree in 1990. The George F. and Mary L. Leone Foundation supported scholarships at universities and charitable organizations. Leone was remarkably active until his death at the age of ninety-four on June 26, 2021.[13]

Schollmaier's career at Alcon spanned thirty-nine years; fittingly, his retirement coincided with the company's fiftieth anniversary. A superb salesman, Schollmaier covered his Pennsylvania territory in a company Volkswagen. Having gained practical experience in the field and academic training at Harvard, he was the first to create a strategic plan that saved Alcon from bankruptcy in 1961. The concept was simple. The early-stage me-too ophthalmic products were sold by the strength of power sales and the Alcon name. Over time new products featured technical advantages until finally there were significant breakthroughs. This required real capability in R&D and the skill to source, test, and license products from pharmaceutical companies outside the ophthalmic industry, talents he nurtured. Schollmaier wrote that this "was a realistic conceptualization of our R&D." He later explained, "It became apparent that we had to develop a unique, innovative, technically-competent enterprise. We had to develop a continual flow of new products, get them rapidly approved by the FDA and be able to produce them in an economical, timely fashion with absolutely no compromise in quality." Recognizing R&D's importance to the company's future growth, Schollmaier assured its budgetary resources, kept it focused on appropriate priorities, and made the commitment that marketing would launch all new products successfully. He remained the chief marketer and salesman, and reinforced Alcon's brand by naming each new product.[14]

Developing and manufacturing technology-driven products meant little without innovative marketing strategies and a well-trained, enthusiastic sales force. The 1960s through 1970s was an era of team building, which ensured Alcon's long-term prosperity. Under Schollmaier's tutelage, Buhler, Lane, Sear, Sisson, and Spruill became outstanding leaders. Alcon's globalization resulted in selling products throughout the world and sharing learning experiences across markets. During this time, Schollmaier narrowed Alcon's focus by shedding non-ophthalmic products. Having the broadest ophthalmic product line allowed Alcon to achieve market penetration unlike that of any competitor. The CooperVision acquisition was a critical part of this strategy and installed Alcon as the leader in ophthalmic devices. Falcon generics, another Schollmaier idea, added more strength. By 1997 Alcon was a formidable global force, selling products in three areas—ophthalmic, vision care, and surgical—for eye care specialists.[15]

Schollmaier emphasized keeping the best people growing in their jobs and working well together. His cadre of experienced individuals, at all levels and in all departments, created a body of institutional knowledge unlike any competitor and gave Alcon another unmatched advantage. Schollmaier and his management team were instinctively frugal, a practice instituted by Alexander and Conner. Costs were ruthlessly cut; as a result, efficiency increased, profits grew, and investments expanded. This approach allowed Alcon to pay good salaries, build top-notch facilities, buy the best technology, and make appropriate acquisitions at the right time. After his retirement, Schollmaier explained, "What has made Alcon great? Well, Alcon has great people, who work effectively together to achieve ambitious common objectives. If a company can make this come alive and stay focused, greatness is possible." Schollmaier's legacies are unparalleled. In recognition of his service, the Schollmaier Auditorium was dedicated in 1998, in the presence of retired Nestlé executives Fürer, Angst, and Daniel (figs. 7.8, 7.9). By letting Schollmaier do his job, they had secured Alcon's continued success.[16]

Schollmaier was popular on campus. When he expressed anger, he did so privately. He offered encouragement while emphasizing priorities, but his humble demeanor concealed a determination for success. He took great pleasure in getting to know the Alcon Family. He seldom scheduled lunches with his staff, preferring instead to meander to the company cafeteria, where he would find someone sitting alone or someone he did not know and join them for lunch. Most of the human-interest stories in the *Alcon World News* resulted from these encounters. He understood the value of every member of the workforce, and he was no less inquisitive when he met

FIG 7.8
Ed Schollmaier at Schollmaier
Auditorium dedication, June 1998
(AHR)

FIG 7.9
Schollmaier Auditorium dedication, June 1998.
Left to right: Arthur Fürer, Tim Sear, Carl Angst,
Ed Schollmaier, José Daniel. (AHR)

FIG 7.10
Ed and Rae Schollmaier Arena, TCU, 2015
(Courtesy of TCU)

employees overseas. In their private life, Schollmaier and his wife, Rae, were unpretentious, even while immersed in Fort Worth's vibrant society. They lived in the same modest house from 1966 until 2011, only enlarging it in the mid-1990s to accommodate visiting grandchildren. They did, however, travel extensively and collect art.[17]

Away from Alcon, Schollmaier had two passions, supporting serious music (the opera and symphony in Fort Worth) and TCU basketball. He and his wife were avid philanthropists and founded the Schollmaier Foundation to support a variety of charities. They were active members of the boards of local opera and symphony organizations, and in the 1990s they spearheaded the Fort Worth Opera's endowment drive. As a reflection of their love for classical music, the Schollmaier Foundation donated $500,000 to the TCU School of Music to buy fifty-two Steinway pianos, making it the tenth all-Steinway school in the United States. Beginning in 1996 Schollmaier became a TCU trustee. He chaired the building and grounds committee and played a key role in the $320 million renovation of the TCU Commons and student center. As lovers of TCU basketball, the Schollmaiers donated the initial gift of $10 million for the $72 million renovation of the basketball arena, later renamed in their honor (fig. 7.10). He was also a member of the TCU Neeley School of Business International Board of Visitors, a recipient of Neeley's Ike Harrison Award, and taught in the Neeley School. The Schollmaier Foundation also funded the Science and Technology Building at Texas Wesleyan University and created the Elmer Kizer Community Scholars Program at the University of Cincinnati. Named after the high school principal who gave Schollmaier a home after his mother died, the scholarship goes to a first-generation college student from Cincinnati. Among his many awards was the 2015 Golden Deeds Award from the Exchange Club in Fort Worth for his exceptional service. Rae died in October 2015, and Ed six years later, ending five decades, 1970 to 2021, during which a member of the Alcon Family served as a TCU trustee (the others were Conner and Denny Alexander).[18]

Schollmaier joined a fledgling company that had already established traits for success. For that, thanks are due to Conner and Alexander. Some might argue that the Drop-tainer was the most transformative element not only of Alcon's history but of the entire ophthalmic industry. Alexander invented the plastic, squeezable container in 1953 as a vehicle for safely administering eye drops. Despite being soft-spoken, Alexander was a skilled salesman. His ability to build meaningful relationships with ophthalmologists solidified Alcon's early presence and created a foundation for growth. Applying ideas from Harvard, he restructured the sales department; the company's steep increase in sales over the next decades is a testament to his skill in training and managing the domestic sales force. Five men sig-

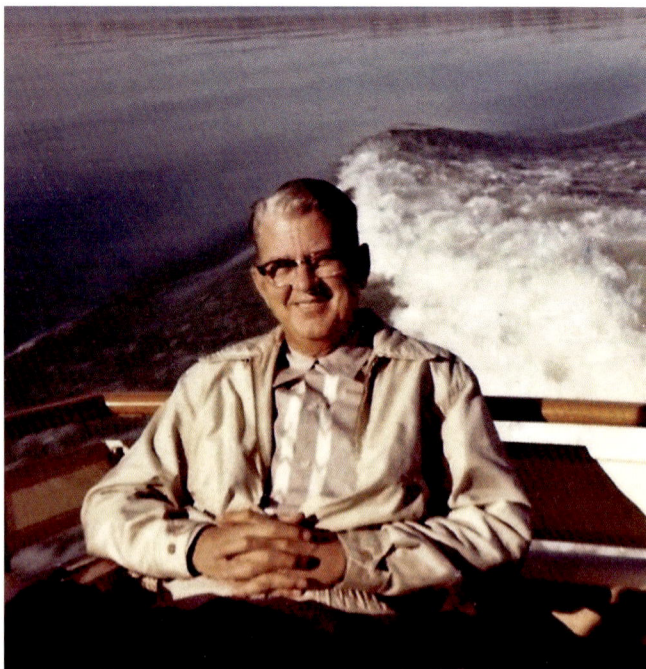

FIG 7.11
Bob Alexander boating on
a local lake, ca. 1980 (AFP)

nificant in Alcon's development—Schollmaier, Leone, Sisson, Spruill, and Lane—evolved from this milieu. It was Alexander's speech to the New Enterprise Club during his time at Harvard that drew Schollmaier to Alcon. That legacy alone is noteworthy. His work ethic, humility, willingness to learn, and ability to forge lasting relationships were fundamental in establishing the Alcon Family and its work culture. As this narrative has demonstrated, the Alcon Family was a prime reason that the company became so dominant in the ophthalmic industry. An imposing seven-floor building, the R. D. Alexander Administration Center located on the Alcon campus in south Fort Worth, is a monument to its namesake. Speaking at the dedication, Schollmaier asserted that "without Bob Alexander, Alcon Laboratories would not have begun, survived, or succeeded."[19]

When Nestlé took possession of Alcon at the end of 1977, Alexander's management role ceased. At nearly sixty-five years of age, he retired and embarked on a leisurely tour of the United States in a recreational vehicle with his wife, Catherine. An important part of those travels was Bob's casual visits with people he met all over the country, finding out about them and listening to their stories. And they would probably not know they were talking to a successful entrepreneur—another example of his interest in all kinds of people and building new relationships, making them feel valuable, akin to how he fostered the Alcon Family. Bob also spent time in his boats on the local lakes, a habit he began early in his married life (fig. 7.11). He continued his association with Junior Achievement, another of his legacies to the Alcon Family. Both he and Catherine sustained their philanthropy, particularly for the Society to Prevent Blindness, for which they received the People of Vision award in 1982. Bob was appointed to the board of the Tarrant County Regional Water District and later was reelected to this agency. He maintained a leadership role in the YMCA of Metropolitan Fort Worth, the Tarrant County Mental Health and Mental Retardation Board, the Child Study Center at Harris Hospital, the Fort Worth Chamber of Commerce, and University Christian Church. The Alexanders established the Robert D. and Catherine R. Alexander Foundation, which continues to support the arts, charitable societies, universities, and various organizations supporting eye research and preservation. He passed away on October 11, 1985.[20]

Catherine survived Bob by eighteen years. Her principal legacy to the ophthalmic industry is the name Alcon, but she joined her husband at Alcon's booth at the AAOO annual

FIG 7.12
Catherine Alexander at the
Vision and Resource Center (AFP)

meetings, where for thirty years she was as well-known as her husband. Even after his death, she often attended, accompanied by an Alcon representative. Catherine was active in organizations that worked to preserve vision, particularly in children. In 1984 she received the Shield Award from Delta Gamma for "25 years of distinguished achievement in the field of sight conservation." She led the transformation of the Child Study Center into the Cook Children's Eye Clinic. Today the Alexander Vision and Resource Center offers free vision exams and reading glasses to those unable to pay, free medical care for more serious ocular diseases, and support for parents of vision-impaired children (fig. 7.12). Catherine was a patron of the Texas Ballet and a member of the University Christian Church. A minister there recalled, "Catherine was deeply engaged in life. When there was a cause, she felt connected to, she supported it."[21]

Conner died in January 1992 at the age of eighty-three. Always the consummate entrepreneur, he was, according to Schollmaier, a force to be reckoned with, and for Alcon he was a "tremendous optimist and visionary." While Alexander sold Alcon products, Conner sold

Alcon, the vision and its potential to the ophthalmic community, the pharmaceutical industry, investors, and the general public. Conner became the public face of Alcon in all his endeavors. In his opinion, he had three main legacies—Alcon, the Alcon Foundation, and the William C. Conner Educational Investment Fund at TCU. In 1962, while Alcon struggled financially, Conner established the foundation to support the expansion of the Wilmer Eye Institute in Baltimore. Over the next fifty years, the foundation donated millions of dollars to local, state, national, and international charities. For its part, the investment fund illustrated Conner's unique entrepreneurial focus. In 1972 he donated sixteen thousand shares of Alcon stock to TCU, creating the fund. He intended to provide students with the opportunity to make real-world investments. Every year about a dozen senior and graduate students manage the fund, and the profits are divided between TCU and the Department of Ophthalmology for the Baylor College of Medicine at Dallas. By 2021 about one thousand TCU alumni had participated and the fund held almost $3.5 million. By its fiftieth anniversary in 2023, it had dispersed several million dollars. At least one hundred schools in the United States copied Conner's idea. Few people leave such a varied legacy as Conner, one that incorporates commercial, charitable, and educational realms.[22]

Conner participated, often in a leadership role, in dozens of ophthalmic and business organizations. Among these were the PMA, PAAO, the Advisory Council of the Wilmer Institute, Project Orbis, the National Advisory Eye Council of the National Institutes of Health, the Texas State Commission for the Blind, the National Medical Foundation for Eye Care, and the Society to Prevent Blindness. To support ophthalmic medicines in the PMA, he formed the ophthalmic pharmaceuticals subcommittee, which he chaired. At the PAAO, he discovered no involvement by ophthalmic pharmaceutical companies; he formed a committee for that purpose and invited Alcon's competitors to join. He helped create the Pan-American Association in Ophthalmology Foundation, which funds scholarships, travel, and educational activities. He remained involved in this foundation until his death (fig. 7.13). Conner also participated in the non-ophthalmic arena, becoming involved in numerous organizations. Some of these included the board of the University Christian Church in Fort Worth, the President's Council of Texas Wesleyan College, the President's Council of the University of North Texas, the TCU Research Foundation, the TCU Board of Trustees, the National Fund for Graduate Nursing Education, United Way, and the Fort Worth Chamber of Commerce. Additionally, he served on the board of directors of several corporations. Conner also received dozens of awards. By any measure, his impact was far-reaching.[23]

FIG 7.13
Pan-American Day proclamation,
Bill Conner and Tim Sear, 1985
(Courtesy of Pan-American Association of
Ophthalmology)

Conner was seventy years of age when Nestlé bought Alcon, but the windfall reignited his entrepreneurial nature. Now with time for other ventures, he settled on three investments in particular. As his hearing diminished, Conner invested in a hearing aid manufacturer, Prescriptor, and presented a purchase opportunity to the Alcon board. When they turned him down, he bought the company and created Freedom Hearing Health Group (fig. 7.14). Next, he invested in Tarrant Health Protection Plan, a private health maintenance organization created by Alcon's first CFO, Harvey Andrews. In 1984 Conner and partners opened Capital National Bank in Fort Worth. All three enterprises were struggling by 1987 but Conner, now eighty, optimistically argued that "it's really a question of determining which is the correct path, finding ways to measure success and then committing to it." Freedom Hearing Health Group was the only one in business thriving when Conner died in 1992. Ever the optimist, he believed his investments would eventually turn a profit and talked openly about the risks inherent in the free enterprise system. For Conner, risk was a small price to pay for the thrill of being an entrepreneur. Alcon was the pinnacle of his entrepreneurial spirit and his greatest legacy.[24]

* * *

Alexander and Connor's influence upon Alcon did not end when they retired in 1977. Conner's vision of Alcon becoming a grand ophthalmic house had been infused into the Alcon Family. Alexander ingrained his ethos into the Alcon Family, patiently collaborating and solving many challenges. The most direct effect was the leaders they hired, trained, and placed in key management roles. What Leone, Schollmaier, Fleming, Sisson, Lane, Buhler, and Spruill learned under Alexander and Connor led them to develop successful strategies and hire the best people, creating an organization that made Alcon the premier ophthalmic specialty company by 1997. It is unusual for two founders of a company in United States commerce to have such a pronounced influence for fifty years, but they did. Alcon remains their unparalleled legacy.

In the history of United States business, Alexander and Conner represent the archetypal entrepreneurs of the early twentieth century. Focusing on eye specialists, they created a firm that within fifty years became the dominant enterprise in its market. Just as the first letters of the last names of the founders smoothly combined for their new company's name, the different but complementary personal skills they had made them very effective partners for the early success of the business. Their common appreciation for the value of good, dedicated people, rewarded fairly for performance in a family-like environment, built a solid foundation for their business, a successful organization still thriving today, over seventy-five years after its founding in 1947.

William C. Conner, Chairman of the Board, Hearing Health Group, Inc.

My hearing loss led me to FASAR ... a group of radar engineers ... and a concept called "selective amplification"

FIG 7.14
Bill Connor, ever the entrepreneur, 1986
(WCCP, TCU)

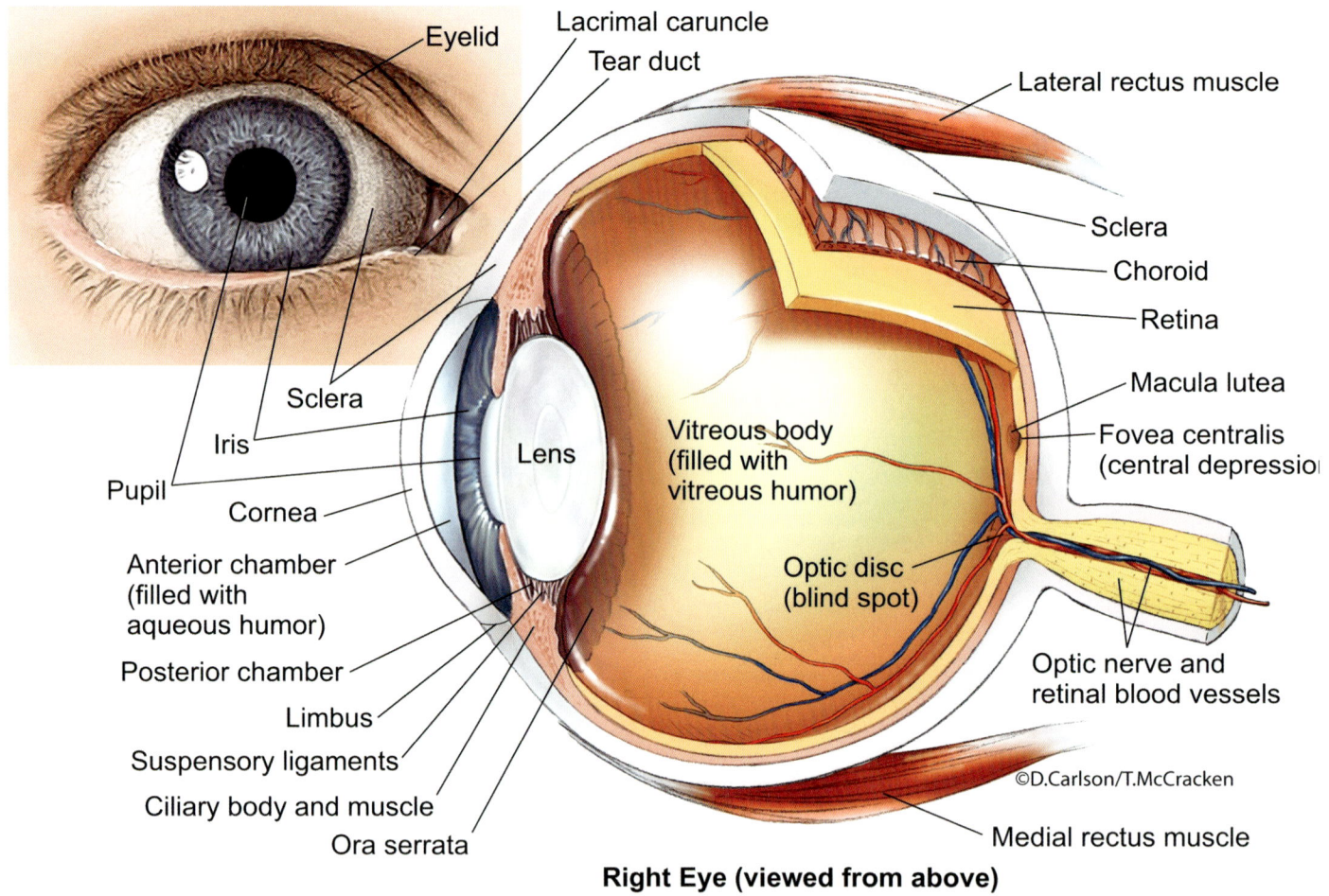

Eyelid

Lacrimal caruncle

Tear duct

Lateral rectus muscle

Sclera

Choroid

Retina

Macula lutea

Fovea centralis
(central depression

Vitreous body
(filled with
vitreous humor)

Optic disc
(blind spot)

Optic nerve and
retinal blood vessels

Sclera

Iris

Pupil

Cornea

Anterior chamber
(filled with
aqueous humor)

Posterior chamber

Limbus

Suspensory ligaments

Ciliary body and muscle

Ora serrata

Lens

©D.Carlson/T.McCracken

Medial rectus muscle

Right Eye (viewed from above)

Cross section of the eye
(Used by permission from
Carlson Stock)

Bibliography

Archival Material and Collections

Alcon Historical Records (AHR). Records Management. Alcon, Inc., Fort Worth, Texas.

Alcon Laboratories, Inc., Collection (ALC). Tarrant County Archives, Fort Worth, Texas.

Alcon Materials (AM). (Search by name.) Special Collections. Mary Couts Burnett Library. Texas Christian University (TCU), Fort Worth.

Alcon Oral History (AOH). (Search by name.) McDonald, Thomas O. (TOM). AM.

"Alcon Story." (Search by name.) Cobb, Dean, and Loral Cobb. AM.

Alexander, Bob, Family Papers (AFP). In possession of Denny Alexander, Fort Worth, Texas.

Alexander, Catherine, Oral History (CAOH). Video recording. Alexander Family Papers (AFP). In possession of Denny Alexander, Fort Worth, TX.

Alexander Family Interview. Apr. 5, 2021. TOM. AM.

Cobb, Dean, and Loral Cobb. AM.

Conner Family Interview. May 2, 24, 2021. TOM. AM.

Conner, William Clarence. Alcon Collection. Special Collections. Mary Couts Burnett Library. TCU. [WCCP]

Dallas County Clerk, Dallas, TX.

HBS Faculty Biographical Information. Special Collections. Baker Library, Bloomberg Center, Harvard Business School.

HBS Retired Case Collection. Special Collections. Baker Library, Bloomberg Center, Harvard Business School.

Luttrell, Howard, Papers (HLP). TOM. AM.

Marriage Records, 51:332. Dallas County Clerk, Dallas, TX.

McDonald, Thomas O. (TOM). Alcon Materials (AM). pecial Collections. Mary Couts Burnett Library, TCU.

Nestlé Historical Archives. Vevey, Switzerland.

Schlech, Barry A. (BAS). Alcon Records. Special Collections. Mary Couts Burnett Library, TCU.

Schollmaier, Edgar (EHS). AM. Special Collections. Mary Couts Burnett Library, TCU.

Schollmaier, Edgar (EHS). Papers. In possession of Taylor Schollmaier, Boulder, CO.

Schollmaier, Edgar. (EHS) Records. AHR.

Stanford University Biographical Files Collection (SC1136). Biography/Organization History. Special Collections & University Archives. Stanford Libraries, Stanford, CA, Online Archive of California.

Tarrant County Clerk, Fort Worth, TX.

Texas Department of State Health Services, Austin.

Texas Secretary of State, Austin.

Texas State Board of Pharmacy, Austin.

Texas State Securities Board, Austin

Books and Articles

Abelson, M. B., W. A. Chambers, and L. M. Smith. "Conjunctival Allergen Challenge: A Clinical Approach to Studying Allergic Conjunctivitis." *Archives of Ophthalmology* 108 (1990): 84–88.

Adamczyk, Diane T., and Siret D. Jaanus. "Antiallergy Drugs and Decongestants." In Bartlett and Jaanus, *Clinical Ocular Pharmacology*, 245–61.

Alcon Annual Report, 2019. Alcon.

https://s1.q4cdn.com/963204942/files/doc_financials/2019/ar/ALC-Annual-Report-2019.pdf.

"Alcon Debuts as Independent, Publicly Traded Company." Alcon Media Release, Apr. 29, 2019. https://www.alcon.com/media-release/alcon-debuts-independent-publicly-traded-company.

"Alcon/Genzyme Agreement." *Pink Sheet: Pharma Intelligence*, Jan. 5, 1987.

"Alcon Hits the Big Board." *Fort Worth* (Chamber of Commerce magazine), Oct. 1971, 28.

"The Alcon Story." *Alcon Today and Tomorrow*, 1989. ALC.

Alexander, Robert D., and William C. Conner. "The Story of Alcon Laboratories, Inc.: Prescription for Success." Newcomen Society in North America, Fort Worth, TX, Oct. 21, 1969. EHS. AM.

Allen, R. C. "Betaxolol in the Treatment of Glaucoma: Multiclinic Trials."

Ophthalmology 91, supp. (1984): 142.

"Alumnus of the Year Award; Dr. George F. Leone, BS '49, HON '90." *Wesleyan Magazine* (Texas Wesleyan University), Fall 2009, 22.

Amoils, S. P. "The Joule Thomson Cryoprobe." *Archives of Ophthalmology* 78 (1967): 201–7.

Anderson, H. Allen. "Amarillo, TX." *Handbook of Texas Online* (hereafter *HBTO*). Texas State   Historical Association (hereafter TSHA). Accessed May 9, 2021. https://www.tshaonline. org/handbook/entries/amarillo-tx.

Atkins, J. M., B. R. Pugh, and R. M. Timewell. "Cardiovascular Effects of Topical Beta-blockers during Exercise." *American Journal of Ophthalmology* 99 (1985): 173–75.

Attar, Roya. "About Red Caps: Mydriatics and Cycloplegics." *Optometry Times*, June 9, 2019. https://www.optometrytimes.com/view/all-about-red-caps-mydriatics-and-cycloplegics.

Autian, John. "Development of Standards for Plastics to Be Used in Pharmacy and Medicines." *Journal of Dental Research* 45, no. 6 (1966): 1668–74.

Axelrod, Peter. *Big Thoughts Are Free: The Authorized Biography of Milan Panić*. New York: Peter Lang, 2015.

Baldwin, H. A., T. O. McDonald, and C. H. Beasley. "Slit-Lamp Examination of Experimental Animal Eyes, II: Grading Scales and Photographic Evaluation of Induced Pathological Conditions." *Journal of the Society of Cosmetic Chemists* 24 (1973): 181–95.

Barkman, R., M. Germanis, G. Karpe, and S. Malmborg. "Preservatives in Eye Drops." *Acta Ophthalmologica* 47 (1969): 461–75.

Barr, J. T., and N. J. Bailey. "History and Development of Contact Lenses." In *Clinical Contact Lens Practice*, edited by Edward S. Bennett and Barry A. Weissman, 1–8. Philadelphia: J. B. Lippincott, 1993.

Barr, Joseph T. "Twenty Years of Contact Lenses." *Contact Lens Spectrum*, June 2006. https://www.clspectrum.com/issues/2006/june-2006/20-years-of-contact-lenses.

Barrett, Graham D. "A New Hydrogel Intraocular Lens Design." *Journal of Cataract & Refractive Surgery* 20 (1994): 18–25.

Bartlett, Jimmy D., Richard G. Fiscella, Siret D. Jaanus, and Howard Barnebey. "Ocular Hypotensive Drugs." In Bartlett and Jaanus, *Clinical Ocular Pharmacology*, 139–74.

Bartlett, Jimmy D., and Siret Jaanus. *Clinical Ocular Pharmacology*. 5th ed. St. Louis: Butterworth-Heinemann, 2008.

Baum, Jules, and Michael Bazara. "The Evolution of Antibiotic Therapy for Bacterial Conjunctivitis and Keratitis: 1970–2000." *Cornea* 19 (2000): 659–72.

Because All Skin Can Be Sensitive. Brochure. Allercreme. AHR.

Berry, D. P., E. M. Van Buskirk, and M. B. Shields. "Betaxolol and Timolol: A Comparison of Efficacy and Side Effects." *Archives of Ophthalmology* 102 (1984): 42–45.

Blumenkranz, Mark S. "The Evolution of Laser Therapy in Ophthalmology: A Perspective on the Interactions between Photons, Patients, Physicians, and Physicists: The LXX Edward Jackson Memorial Lecture." *American Journal of Ophthalmology* 158, no. 1 (July 2014): 12–25.

Boskabady, Mohammad Hossein, Mohammad Naser Shafei, Zahra Saberi, and Somayeh Amini. "Pharmacological Effects of *Rosa Damascena*." *Iranian Journal of Basic Medical Sciences* 14 (2011): 295–307.

Boyle, Erin L. "Foldable IOLs Ushered In New Cataract and Refractive Paradigm." *Ocular Surgery News*, June 1, 2007. https://www.healio.com/news/ophthalmology/20120331/foldable-iols-ushered-in-new-cataract-and-refractive-paradigm.

Brown, Gregg. "History of Alcon's Intellectual Property Operations, 1983–1987." TOM. AM.

Bruch, Carl W. "Factors Determining Choice of Sterilization Procedure." In *Industrial Sterilization: International Symposium, Amsterdam, 1972*, edited by G. Briggs Phillips and William S. Miller, 119–24. Durham, NC: Duke University Press, 1973.

Bruch, Mary K. "Regulatory Review of Sterilization Control of Drugs in the United States." In *Sterilization of Medical Products*, edited by Eugene R. L. Gaughran and Karl Kereluk, n.p. New Brunswick, NJ: Johnson & Johnson, 1977.

Bucci, M. G., A. Missiroli, J. Pecori-Giraldi, and M. Virno. "The Local Administration of Propranolol in the Therapy of Glaucoma." *Bollettino d'oculistica* 47 (1968): 51–60.

Buenger, Walter L. "Leonard Brothers." *HBTO*. Accessed Apr. 23, 2021. https://www.tshaonline.org/handbook/entries/leonard-brothers. TSHA.

Buratto, Lucio. "History and Evolution of Nuclear Expression and Cortex Aspiration." In Buratto and Packard, *History and Evolution of Modern Cataract Surgery*, 75–92.

Buratto, Lucio, and Richard Packard. *History and Evolution of Modern Cataract Surgery*. Fabiano: Milan, Italy, 2019.

Buratto, Lucio, and Mike Southard. "The Impact of IMPACT." In Buratto and Packard, *History and Evolution of Modern Cataract Surgery*, 253–64.

"But Can She Type?" *Alcon World News*, Apr. 1988. ALC; AHR.

Cagle, Gerald, Scott Davis, Allan Rosenthal, and Judson Smith. "Topical Tobramycin and Gentamicin Sulfate in the Treatment of Ocular Infections: Multicenter Study." *Current Eye Research* 9 (1981): 523–34.

Calimbahin, Samantha. "Ed Schollmaier, Former Alcon CEO and TCU Donor, Dies at 87." *Fort Worth: The City's Magazine,* Sept. 17, 2021.

Candia, Oscar A. "Remembering Steven M. Podos, M.D., 1937–2009." *Investigative Ophthalmology & Visual Science* 21 (2010): 1262.

Carden, Art. *Retail Innovations in American Economic History: The Rise of Mass-Market Merchandisers.* Independent Institute. Revised Mar. 29, 2012. https://www.independent.org/pdf/working_ papers/79_retail_innovations.pdf.

Charters, Lynda. "Confessions of an Innovator." *Ophthalmology Times,* Mar. 1, 2018. https://www.ophthalmologytimes.com/view/confessions-innovator.

Coben, Larry Joel. "Modern Suppository Manufacturing." *Drug Development & Industrial Pharmacy* 3 (1977): 523–46.

Coben, Larry J., and Nicholas G. Lordi. "Physical Stability of Semisynthetic Suppository Bases." *Journal of Pharmaceutical Sciences* 69, no. 8 (1980): 955–60.

Conner, Bill. Interview by Rose Tulecke. *Fort Worth* (Chamber of Commerce magazine), Nov. 1976, 33.

Cooper, R. L., and I. J. Constable. "Infective Keratitis in Soft Contact Lens Wearers." *British Journal of Ophthalmology* 61 (1977): 250–54.

Cooper, Sherry L. "1971–2011: Forty-Year History of Scope Expansion into Medical Eye Care." *Optometry* 83 (2012): 64–73.

Davis, Geetha. "The Evolution of Cataract Surgery." *Missouri Medicine* 113, no. 1 (2016): 58–62.

Dell, S. J., J. M. Rubin, G. M. Lowry, K. Campbell, V. Springer, R. Dobbs, and M. B. Abelson. "Evaluation of Naphcon-A and Individual Constituents by Provocative Antigen Challenge." *Investigative Ophthalmology & Visual Science* 35, suppl. (1994): 183.

Dunn, T. L., M. I. Gerber, E. Fernandez, M. D. Iseman, and R. M. Cherniak. "Timolol-induced Bronchospasm: Utility of Betaxolol as an Alternative Ocular Hypotensive Agent in Patients with Asthma." *Clinical Research* 33 (1985): 20A.

Dusseau, Jean-Yves, Patrick Duroselle, and Jean Freney. "Gaseous Sterilization." In *Russell, Hugo & Ayliffe's Principles and Practice of Disinfection, Preservation and Sterilization,* edited by Adam P. Fraise, Peter A. Lambert, and Jean-Yves Maillard. 4th ed. Oxford,: Blackwell, 2004.

Edelhauser, Henry F. "The Balance between Corneal Transparency and Edema." *Investigative Ophthalmology & Visual Science* 47 (2006): 1755–67.

Edelhauser, Henry F., Diane L. Van Horn, Patricia Miller, and Harlan J. Pederson. "Effect of Thiol-oxidation of Glutathione with Diamide on Corneal Endothelial Function, Junctional Complexes, and Microfilaments." *Journal of Cell Biology* 68 (1976): 567–78.

Estes, G. K., and G. H. Luttrell. "Approach to Process Validation." *Pharmaceutical Technology* 7, no. 4 (1983): 74–84.

FDA. Department of Health, Education, and Welfare. 21, *Code of Federal Regulations*, sections 211 and 821. "Ethylene Oxide, Ethylene Chlorohydrin, and Ethylene Glycol: Proposed Maximum Residue Limits and Proposed Maximum Exposure Limits." *Federal Register* 43, no. 122 (Fri., June 23, 1978): 27474–85.

Fraunfelder, F. T., G. C. Bagby Jr., and D. J. Kelly. "Fatal Aplastic Anemia following Topical Administration of Ophthalmic Chloramphenicol." *American Journal of Ophthalmology* 93, no. 3 (1982): 356–60.

Freeman, David M. "Obituaries: Richard Gordon Scobee, M.D., 1914–1952." *Archives of Ophthalmology* 48 (1952): 663–65.

Friedman, Alan H. "In Memoriam: Stephen M. Podos, M.D. (1937–2009)." *Archives of Ophthalmology* 128 (2010): 189–90.

Gad, Shane Cox. *Pharmaceutical Manufacturing Handbook: Regulations and Quality.* Hoboken, NJ: Wiley-Interscience, 2008.

Gammel, H. P. N. *The Laws of Texas.* Vol. 1. *Supplement Volume to the Original Ten Volumes, 1822–1897.* Austin: Gammel's Book Store, 1929.

"George Leone Named Marketing Manager." *EyeLites* (Alcon), Apr. 13, 1967. Vol. 3, AHR.

Glazer, Zorach R. *Special Occupational Hazard Review with Control Recommendation for the Use of Ethylene Oxide as a Sterilant in Medical Facilities.* US Department of Health, Education, and Welfare, Public Health Service, Center for Disease Control, National Institute for Occupational Safety and Health, no. 77–200. Washington, DC: US Government Printing Office, 1977.

Goldberg, Ivan, Frank S. Ashburn Jr., Michael A. Kass, and Bernard Becker. "Efficacy and Patient Acceptance of Pilocarpine Gel." *American Journal of Ophthalmology* 88 (1979): 843–46.

Goldin, Claudia, and Lawrence F. Katz. "A Most Egalitarian Profession: Pharmacy and the Evolution of a Family-Friendly Occupation." *Journal of Labor Economics* 34, no. 3 (2016): 705–45.

Grasela, T. H., Jr., and J. J. Schentag. "A Clinical Pharmacy-Oriented Drug Surveillance Network: I. Program Description." *Drug Intelligence &*

Clinical Pharmacy 21 (1987): 902–8.

Haas, J. S., and D. L. Merrill. "The Effect of Methylcellulose on Responses to Solutions of Pilocarpine." *American Journal of Ophthalmology* 54: 21–24.

Handbook: Good Laboratory Practice (GLP): Quality Practices for Regulated Non-clinical Research and Development. 2nd ed. Geneva: World Health Organization and Tropical Disease Research, 2009.

Handbook for Good Clinical Research Practice (GCP): Guidance for Implementation. Geneva: World Health Organization, 2002.

Harbin, T. "Recurrence of a Corneal Pseudomonas Infection after Topical Steroid Therapy: Report of a Case." *American Journal of Ophthalmology* 58 (1964): 670–74.

"Harold C. Johnson." *Alcon World News*, Aug. 1997. ALC; AHR.

Harvey, Suzanne. "Ed Schollmaier Eyes New Horizons." *Pharmaceutical Executive* 2, no. 1 (1985): 20–24.

Havener, William H. *Ocular Pharmacology*. 2nd ed. St. Louis: C. V. Mosby, 1970.

———. *Havener's Ocular Pharmacology*, edited by Thomas F. Mauger and Elson L. Craig. 6th ed. St. Louis: Mosby: 1994.

Heer, Jean. *Nestlé: 125 Years, 1866–1991*. Vevey, Switzerland: Nestlé, 1992.

Hernandez, H., R. Cervantes, A. Frati, R. Hurtado, and T. O. McDonald. "Cardiovascular Effects of Topical Glaucoma Therapies in Normal Subjects." *Cutaneous & Ocular Toxicology* 2 (1983): 99–106.

Herring, Tom. "Harold Johnson." *Alcon World News*, Dec. 1993. ALC; AHR.

Holly, F. J., and M. A. Lemp. "Tear Physiology and Dry Eyes." *Survey of Ophthalmology* 22 (1977): 69–87.

Horchler, Helmut. *A Journey Well Traveled*. N.p.: Self-published. Helmut W. Horchler. AM.

Hunt, William R. "Mineral Wells, TX." *HBTO*. Accessed June 26, 2021. https://www.tshaonline.org/handbook/entries/mineral-wells-tx. TSHA.

Immel, Barbara. "A Brief History of the GMPs: The Power of Storytelling." Compliance Leadership Series. Immel Resources LLC. Accessed July 13, 2021. http://biomanufacturing.org/uploads/files/305429596362804820-brief-history-of-gmps.pdf.

Jampel, Henry D., Alan L. Robin, Harry A. Quigley, and Irvin P. Pollack. "Apraclonidine: A One-Week Dose-Response Study." *Archives of Ophthalmology* 106, no. 8 (1988): 1069–73.

Jani, R., O. Gan, Y. Ali, R. Rodstrom, and S. Hancock. "Ion Exchange Resins for Ophthalmic Delivery." *Journal of Ocular Pharmacology and Therapeutics* 10 (1994): 57–67.

Kador, P. F., J. H. Kinoshita, and N. E. Sharpless. "Aldose Reductase Inhibitors: A Potential New Class of Agents for the Pharmacological Control of Certain Diabetic Complications." *Journal of Medicinal Chemistry* 28 (1985): 841–49.

Kass, Rudolph. "Business School's Advanced Management Program Provides 13-Week Training Course for Already-Successful Executives." *Harvard Crimson*, Nov. 10, 1950. https://www.thecrimson.com/article/1950/11/10/business-schools-advanced-management-program-provides/.

Kaufman, H., E. L. Martola, and C. Dohlman. "Use of 5-iodo-2'-deoxyuridine (IDU) in Treatment of Herpes Simplex Keratitis." *Archives of Ophthalmology* 68 (1962): 235–39.

"Kefauver-Harris Amendments Revolutionized Drug Development." *FDA Consumer Health Information*, Oct. 2012. https://www.fda.gov/consumers/consumer-updates/kefauver-harris-amendments-revolutionized-drug-development.

Kelman, Charles D. "The Genesis of Phacoemulsification." *CRSTEurope*, Sept. 2006. https://crstodayeurope.com/articles/2006-sep/0906_14-php/.

Kirschenbaum, Matthew G. *Track Changes: A Literary History of Word Processing*. Cambridge, MA: Belknap Press, 2016.

Kline, Oram R., Douglas J. Symes, Ole J. Lorenzetti, and Joseph M. deFaller. "Effect of BSS Plus on the Corneal Endothelium with Intraocular Lens Implantation." *Cutaneous & Ocular Toxicology* 2 (1983): 243–47.

Kock, Paul. "The Evolution of Phacoemulsification." In Buratto and Packard, *History and Evolution of Modern Cataract Surgery*, 51–74.

Koetting, James F., and Jule Griebrok Jose. "Contact Lens Products." In *Ocular Therapeutics and Pharmacology*, edited by Philip P. Ellis, 249–58. 7th ed. St. Louis: C. V. Mosby, 1985.

Kowalski, Wladyslaw. *Ultraviolet Germicidal Irradiation Handbook: UVGI for Air and Surface Disinfection*. Heidelberg: Springer, 2009.

Krachmer, Jay H., and John J. Purcell. "Bacterial Corneal Ulcers in Cosmetic Soft Contact Lens Wearers." *Archives of Ophthalmology* 96 (1978): 57–61.

Krantz, John C., Jr. "New Drugs and the Kefauver-Harris Amendment." *Journal of New Drugs* 6, no. 2 (1966): 77–79.

Krystel-Whittemore, Melissa, Kottarappat N. Dileepan, and John G. Wood. "Mast Cell: A Multi-Functional Master Cell." *Frontiers in Immunology*, Jan. 6, 2016. https://www.frontiersin.org/articles/10.3389/fimmu.2015.00620/full.

Lale, Cissy Stewart. "Catherine Alexander." *Legacy of Love* (Cook

Children's Hospital), Fall 1990, p. 20.

Lamb, Jacqueline, and Tim Bowden. "The History of Contact Lenses." Accessed July 18, 2021. http://eu-ireland-custom-media-prod. s3.amazonaws.com/UKMEAEU/eSample/9780702071683-sample-chapter.pdf.

Lee, P., Y. Shen, and M. Eberle. "The Long-Acting Ocusert-Pilocarpine System in the Management of Glaucoma." *Investigative Ophthalmology* 14 (1975): 43–46.

Leibowitz, Howard M. "The Alcon Research Institute: A Model for Interaction between the Pharmaceutical Industry and Academic Medicine." *Archives of Ophthalmology* 111 (1993): 1039–40.

Leibowitz, Howard M., Robert A. Hyndiuk, Gilbert R. Smolin, Robert A. Nozik, Gerard J. Hunter, Gerald D. Cagle, and D. Scott Davis. "Tobramycin in External Eye Disease: A Double-Masked Study vs. Gentamicin." *Current Eye Research* 1, no. 5 (1981): 259–66.

Leibowitz, Howard M., and Allan Kupferman. "Concurrent Corticosteroid-Antibiotic Therapy for Inflammatory Keratitis." *Archives of Ophthalmology* 95 (1977): 682–85.

Levy, J. "Myocardial and Local Anesthetic Actions of β-adrenergic Receptor Blocking Drugs: Relationship to Physicochemical Properties." *European Journal of Pharmacology* 2 (1968): 250–57.

Lewis, P. R., T. G. Phillips, and J. W. Sassani. "Topical Therapies for Glaucoma: What Family Physicians Need To Know." *American Family Physician* 59, no. 7 (1999): 1871–79.

Lightman, Susan. "Does Aldose Reductase Have a Role in the Development of the Ocular Complications of Diabetes?" *Eye* (Journal of the Royal College of Ophthalmologists) 7, pt. 2 (1993) 238–41.

Lippman, Richard, William Gleason, and Paul White. "Contact Lens and Solution Regulation." *Contact Lens Spectrum*, Feb. 1, 1997.

Long, Christopher. "Tanglewood, TX." *HBTO*. Accessed Apr. 18, 2021. https://www.tshaonline.org/handbook/entries/tanglewood-tx. TSHA.

Luttrell, Howard. Interview. "Dr. Howard Luttrell Reviews Alcon History." *Alcon QA International* 3, no. 5, Sept.–Oct. 1995. HLP.

_____. "My Journey from Bench Chemist to Vice-President at Alcon Labs." HLP.

Maloney, William F. "The Remarkable Evolution of Cataract Surgery Makes the Past 20 Years a 'Golden Age.'" *Ocular Surgery News*, June 1, 2002. https://www.healio.com/news/ophthalmology/20120331/the-remarkable-evolution-of-cataract-surgery-makes-the-past-20-years-a-golden-age.

March, W. F., R. M. Stewart, A. I. Mandell, and L. A. Bruce. "Duration of

Effect of Pilocarpine Gel." *Archives of Ophthalmology* 100, no. 8 (1982): 1270–71.

"Marking a Milestone in Contact Lenses." *Contact Lens Spectrum*, Mar. 1, 1996. https://www.clspectrum.com/issues/1996/march-1996/marking-a-milestone-25-years-of-soft-contact-lens.

Maucher, Helmut. *Leadership in Action: Tough-Minded Strategies from the Global Giant*. New York: McGraw-Hill, 1994.

McCarey, Bernard E., Henry F. Edelhauser, and Diane L. Van Horn. "Functional and Structural Changes in the Corneal Endothelium During In Vitro Perfusion." *Investigative Ophthalmology & Visual Science* 12 (1973): 410–17.

McDonald, T. O., C. Beasley, A. Borgmann, and D. Roberts. "Intraocular Administration of Carbomylcholine Chloride." *Annals of Ophthalmology* 1 (1969): 232–39.

McDonald, T. O., K. Kasten, R. Hervey, S. Gregg, A. R. Borgmann, and T. Murchison. "Acute Ocular Toxicity of Ethylene Oxide, Ethylene Glycol, and Ethylene Chlorohydrin." *Bulletin of the Parenteral Drug Association* 27 (1973): 153–64.

McMahon, Timothy T., and Karla Zadnik. "Twenty-Five Years of Contact Lenses: The Impact on the Cornea and Ophthalmic Practice." *Cornea* 19 (2000): 730–40.

Merrill, D. L., T. C. Fleming, and Louis J. Girard. "The Effects of Physiologic Balanced Salt Solutions and Normal Saline on Intraocular and Extraocular Tissues." *American Journal of Ophthalmology* 49, no. 5 (1960): 895–98.

Moore, M. B., J. P. McCulley. M. Luckenbach, H. Gelender, C. Newton, M. B. McDonald, and G. S. Visvesvara. "*Acanthamoeba* Keratitis Associated with Soft Contact Lenses." *American Journal of Ophthalmology* 100 (1985): 396–403.

Moreddu, Rosalia, Daniele Vigolo, and Ali K. Yetisen. "Contact Lens Technology: From Fundamentals to Applications." *Advanced Healthcare Materials* 8, no. 15 (2019). https://doi.org/10.1002/adhm.201900368.

Morrison & Fourmy's Fort Worth City Directory, 1918, 1920, 1922, 1923, 1924, 1925, 1927. Dallas: R. L. Polk, 1918, 1920, 1922, 1923, 1924, 1925, 1927.

Morrison & Fourmy's Fort Worth City Directory, 1929, 1930, 1932, 1941, 1946, 1949. Dallas: Morrison & Fourmy, 1929, 1930, 1932, 1941, 1946, 1949.

Murphy, Victoria S. "Hamilton, TX (Hamilton County)." *HBTO*. Accessed Apr. 22, 2021. https://www.tshaonline.org/handbook/entries/hamilton-tx-hamilton-county. TSHA.

Nalley, Catlin. "Material Gains: 50 Years of the Soft Contact Lens; A Closer

Look at the Evolution of Lens Materials and What Comes Next." *Review of Cornea and Contact Lenses*, Apr. 15, 2001. https://www.reviewofcontactlenses.com/article/material-gains 50-years-of-the-soft-contact-lens.

Nelson, W. L., F. T. Fraunfelder, J. M. Sills, J. B. Arrowsmith, and J. N. Kuritsky. "Adverse Respiratory and Cardiovascular Events Attributed to Timolol Ophthalmic Solution, 1978–1985." *American Journal of Ophthalmology* 102, no. 5 (1986): 606–11.

New England Historic Genealogical Society. *Massachusetts Vital Records, 1911–1915*. Vol. 613. Boston: New England Historic Genealogical Society.

New Tobrex (Tobramycin 0.3%) Ophthalmic Solution. Product monograph. Alcon. Miscellaneous promotional material, vol. 9.1. AHR.

News-Makers. *Chemical and Engineering News* 29, no. 41 (1951): 4206.

Nicolaou, Kyriacos C., and Stephan Rigol. "A Brief History of Antibiotics and Select Advances in Their Synthesis." *Journal of Antibiotics* 71 (2018):153–84.

The 1932 Panther. Yearbook. Central High School, Fort Worth, TX, 1932.

"Novartis Announces Intention to Seek Shareholder Approval for 100% Spinoff of Alcon Eye Care Devices Business." Novartis Media Release, June 29, 2018. https://www.novartis.com/news/media-releases/novartis-announces-intention-seek-shareholder-approval-100-spinoff-alcon-eye-care-devices-business-initiates-share-buy-back-usd-5-bn.

Ofner, S., and T. J. Smith. "Betaxolol in Chronic Obstructive Pulmonary Disease." *Journal of Ocular Pharmacology and Therapeutics* 3 (1987): 171–76.

Passmore, Jack W., and Robert P. Hughes. "A Sterile Disposable Cryoextractor (Cryophake)." *British Journal of Ophthalmology* 51, no. 6 (1967): 423–31.

Pate, J'Nell. *North of the River: A Brief History of North Fort Worth*. Fort Worth: TCU Press, 1994.

"Pfizer Buys Globe." *Cattleman* 48, no. 5 (1961): 131.

"Pharmaceutical Formulations Completes Acquisition of Konsyl Pharmaceuticals." *Pharmabiz.com*, May 19, 2003. http://test.pharmabiz.com/news/pharmaceutical-formulations-completes-acquisition-of-konsyl-pharmaceuticals-15620.

Phillips, Charles R., and Saul R. Kaye. "The Sterilizing Action of Gaseous Ethylene Oxide, I: Review." *American Journal of Hygiene* 50 (1949): 270–79.

Physician's Desk Reference for Ophthalmology. 11th ed. Oradell, NJ: Medical Economics, 1982.

Physician's Desk Reference for Ophthalmology. 14th ed. Timoptic package insert, 127. Oradell, NJ: Medical Economics, 1986.

Physician's Desk Reference for Ophthalmology. 26th ed. Betoptic package insert, 206–9. Montvale, NJ: Medical Economics, 1986.

Piascik, M. T. "The Pharmacology of Adrenergic Receptors." Lecture, University of Kentucky, Lexington, Aug. 27, 2012. http://www.uky.edu/~mtp/OBI836ADR_Lecture1_2012_final.pdf.

Pink Sheet. "Alcon Focusing on Its Ophthalmic Drug Business with Sale." *Generics Bulletin: Pharma Intelligence*, Apr. 21, 1986.

Pitts, R. Edwin, and Jay H. Krachmer. "Evaluation of Soft Contact Lens Disinfection in the Home Environment." *Archives of Ophthalmology* 97 (1979): 470–72.

Polansky, J. R. "Comparison of Plasma Beta Blocking Activity of Betaxolol and Timolol." *International Ophthalmology Clinics* 29 (1989): S17–S18.

Portello, Joan K., and David M. Krumholz. "Dilation of the Pupil." In Bartlett and Jaanus, *Clinical Ocular Pharmacology*, 329–42.

Proposed New Facilities, Alcon. 1957. Brochure. Alcon Laboratories. AFP.

Rathjen, Fred. "Panhandle." *HBTO*. Accessed May 9, 2021. https://www.tshaonline.org/handbook/entries/panhandle. TSHA.

Reed, Kimberly K. "Diseases of the Lacrimal System." In Bartlett and Jaanus, *Clinical Ocular Pharmacology*, 415–36.

Reilly, Gregory W. "The FDA and Plan B: The Legislative History of the Durham-Humphrey Amendments and the Consideration of Social Harms in the Rx-OTC Switch." Harvard Law School Student Papers (2006 Third Year Paper). https://dash.harvard.edu/handle/1/8965550.

Rizzuti, A. Benedict. "Alpha-Chymotrypsin (Quimotrase) in Cataract Surgery." *Archives of Ophthalmology* 61, no. 1 (1959): 135–40.

Robitaille, Denise. "Why ISO 9001 Still Matters." *Quality Magazine*, Nov. 17, 2022. https://www.qualitymag.com/articles/97222-why-iso-9001-still-matters.

Rubin, Ronald P. "A Brief History of Great Discoveries in Pharmacology: In Celebration of the Centennial Anniversary of the Founding of the American Society of Pharmacology and Experimental Therapeutics." *Pharmacological Reviews* 59 (2007): 289–359.

Ryan, Stephen J. "Obituary: A. Edward Maumenee (1913–1998)." *American Journal of Ophthalmology* 125, no. 4 (1998): 582–84.

Sariri, R. "Protein Interaction with Hydrogel Contact Lenses." *Journal of Applied Biomaterials & Biomechanics* 2 (2004): 1–19.

"Schieffelin & Somerset and Co." In *International Directory of Company Histories*, edited by Thomas Derdak and Jay P. Pederson, 323–25.

Detroit: St. James Press, 2004.

Schifrin, Leonard G., with William J. Rich. *The Contact Lens Industry: Structure, Competition, and Public Policy*. Health Technology Case Study 31. OTA-HCS-31. Washington, DC: U.S. Congress, Office of Technology Assessment, Dec. 1984.

Schoene, R. B., T. Abulan, R. L. Ward, and C. H. Beasley. "Effects of Topical Betaxolol, Timolol, and Placebo on Pulmonary Function in Asthmatic Bronchitis. *American Journal of Ophthalmology* 97 (1984): 86–92.

Schollmaier, Ed. *EHS Says*: *A Collection of* Alcon World News *Editorials*. Sept. 1981–Dec. 1997. ALC.

Scholtz, Sibylle. "History of Ophthalmic Viscosurgical Devices." *CRSTEurope*, Jan. 2007. https://crstodayeurope.com/articles/2007-jan/0107_06-php/.

Schwarz, Friedhelm. *Nestlé: The Secrets of Food, Trust and Globalization*. Translated by Maya Anyas. Toronto: Key Porter Books, 2002.

Scott, Mollie Ashe, Jeffrey E. Heck, and Courtenay Gilmore Wilson. "The Integral Role of the Clinical Pharmacist Practitioner in Primary Care." *North Carolina Medical Journal* 78 (2017): 18–85.

Sendrowski, David P., Siret D. Jaanus, Leo Paul Semes, and Michael E. Stern. "Anti-inflammatory Drugs." In Bartlett and Jaanus, *Clinical Ocular Pharmacology*, 221–44.

Senkowski, Bernard Z. Interview by Sandra Stewart Holyoak, Secaucus, NJ, Mar. 25, 1997. Rutgers Oral History Archives, Rutgers University, New Brunswick, NJ. https://oralhistory.rutgers.edu/images/PDFs/senkowski_bernard.pdf.

Shields, M. Bruce, and Elizabeth A. Hodapp. "Glaucoma 25 Years Ago." *Glaucoma Today*, Feb. 2011. https://glaucomatoday.com/articles/2011-feb/glaucoma-25-years-ago.

Short, C., R. H. Keates, E. F. Donovan, M. Wyman, and P. W. Murdick. "Ocular Penetration Studies, I: Topical Administration of Dexamethasone." *Archives of Ophthalmology* 75 (1966): 689–92.

Shuler, Judee. "Executive Profile: George Leone." *Pharmaceutical Executive* 5, no. 7 (1985): 22–30.

Sidhu, P. "Endangered Jaborandi." *British Dental Journal* 217 (2014): 2–3.

Sinskey, Robert M. "Phacoemulsification and IOLs." *CRSTEurope*, Sept. 2006. https://crstodayeurope.com/articles/2006-sep/0906_14-php/u.

Smick, Kirk L. "The Evolution of Dual Disinfection: Where We Are Today." *Review of Cornea & Contact Lenses*, Jan. 24, 2011. https://www.reviewofcontactlenses.com/article/the-evolution-of-dual-disinfection-where-we-are-today.

Smith, Ronald E. "In Memoriam: A. Edward Maumenee, Jr., MD, 1913–1998." *Ophthalmology* 105 (1998): 1131–33.

Southard, Mike. "History from an Ophthalmic Surgical Company Viewpoint." In Buratto and Packard, *History and Evolution of Modern Cataract Surgery*, 231–51.

Spiegel, Joy C. "Alcon: Keeping Its Vision Global." *Fort Worth* (Chamber of Commerce magazine), June 1989, 29–33.

Stark, Walter J., Warren R. Fagadau, Robert H. Stewart, Alan S. Crandall, Joseph M. deFaller, Troy A. Reaves Jr., and Pamela Edwards Klein. "Reduction of Pupillary Constriction." *Archives of Ophthalmology* 104, no. 3 (1986): 364–66.

Stein, J., R. Stark, and K. Randeri. "Comparison of Chemical and Thermal Disinfectant Regimens: A Retrospective Data Analysis." *International Eyecare* 2 (1986): 570–78.

Stine, G. T. "Clinical Investigation of a New Mydriatic and Cycloplegic Drug." *E.E.N.T. Digest* 22 (1960): 11–15.

"Stuart Raetzman Appointed CEO of Nestlé Skin Health." Galderma Media Release, May 22, 2017. https://www.galderma.com/us/news/stuart-raetzman-appointed-ceo-nestle-skin-health.

Surgical Instrument Catalog. New York: Lawton, 1957.

Swan, Kenneth C. "Use of Methylcellulose in Ophthalmology." *Archives of Ophthalmology* 33 (1945): 378–80.

Szczotka-Flynn, Loretta, Donald G. Ahearn, Joseph Barr, William Joe Benjamin, Tina Kiang, Jason J. Nichols, Oliver D. Schein, Ralph P. Stone, and Lynn Winterton. "History, Evolution, and Evolving Standards of Contact Lens Care." *Contact Lens and Anterior Eye* 31, suppl. 1 (2013): S4–S8.

Turner, J. E., W. H. Lawrence, and J. Autian. "Subacute Toxicity Testing of Biomaterials Using Histopathologic Evaluation of Rabbit Muscle Tissue." *Journal of Biomedical Materials Research* 7, no. 1 (1973): 39–58.

Vilas-Boas, Ines M., and C. Patrick Tharp. "The Drug Approval Process in the U.S., Europe, and Japan: Some Marketing and Cost Implications." *Journal of Managed Care & Specialty Pharmacy* 3, no. 4 (1997): 459–65.

Wheeler, J. R. "History of Ophthalmology through the Ages." *British Journal of Ophthalmology* 30 (May 1946): 264–75.

Wickum, Suzanne M., and John F. Amos. "Cycloplegic Refraction." In Bartlett and Jaanus, *Clinical Ocular Pharmacology*, 343–47.

William C. Conner Foundation: Educational Investment Fund, 2021 Annual Report. Neely School of Business, TCU, Apr. 27, 2022. https://

neeley.tcu.edu/Premier-Programs/Educational-Investment-Fund/Annual-Report-2021.

Worley's Dallas City Directory, 1931–1936, 1942–1943, 1944. Dallas: John F. Worley, 1931–1936, 1943, 1944.

Yannuzzi, L. A. *Fluorescein Ophthalmoscopy and Photography of the Ocular Fundus.* Dallas: Alcon Laboratories, 1972.

_____. "Interpretation of Fluorescein Angiography." *Proceedings of the Second International Symposium on Fluorescein Angiography.* Tokyo, n.p.: 1972.

Yolton, Diane P., and Susan P. Haesaert. "Anti-Infective Drugs." In Bartlett and Jaanus, *Clinical Ocular Pharmacology*, 175–220.

Zeff, Stephen A. "The Contribution of the Harvard School of Business to Management Control, 1908–1980." *Journal of Management Accounting Research* 20 (2008): 175–208.

Zimmerman, T. J., R. Harbin, M. Pett, and H. E. Kaufman. "Timolol and Facility of Outflow." *Investigative Ophthalmology & Visual Science* 16 (1977): 623–24.

Zimmerman, T. J., and H. E. Kaufman. "Timolol: A B-adrenergic Blocking Agent for the Treatment of Glaucoma." *Archives of Ophthalmology* 95 (1977): 601–4.

_____. "Timolol: Dose Response and Duration of Action." *Archives of Ophthalmology* 95 (1977): 605–7.

Government Documents

Aoki, K. Roger, and Louis M. DeSantis. "Use of Lodoxamide to Treat Ophthalmic Allergic Conditions." Assignee: Alcon Laboratories. US Patent 6,457,126. *Official Gazette of the United States Patent Office* 1179, no. 2 (Oct. 10, 1995): 1083.

"Certain Antibiotic-Steroid Combination Drugs for Ophthalmic Use." *Federal Register* 36, no. 127, pt. 1 (June 21, 1971): 13282.

Charter–Alcon Laboratories, Inc., May 16, 1947. Texas Secretary of State, Austin.

Dabrowska, Agata, and Susan Thaul. *How FDA Approves Drugs and Regulates Their Safety and Effectiveness.* CRS Report (Congressional Research Service, May 8, 2018). https://sgp.fas.org/crs/misc/R41983.pdf.

Hecht, Gerald, and Neal H. Bigelow. "Stabilized Aqueous Borate Complexes of Biologically Active Catecholamines." Assignee: Alcon Laboratories. US Patent 3,808,317. *Official Gazette of the United States Patent Office* 921, no. 3 (Apr. 16, 1974): 2079.

Hecht, Gerald, and Charles D. Shively. "Ophthalmic Solution." Assignee: Alcon Laboratories. US Patent 4,039,662. *Official Gazette of the*

United States Patent Office 931, no. 1 (Aug. 2, 1977): 315.

National Center for Biotechnology Information. "PubChem Compound Summary for CID 2200, Antazoline." *PubChem.* Accessed Dec. 18, 2021. https://pubchem.ncbi.nlm.nih.gov/compound/Antazoline.

_____. "PubChem Compound Summary for CID 5419, Tetrahydrozoline." *PubChem.* Accessed Dec. 18, 2021. https://pubchem.ncbi.nlm.nih.gov/compound/Tetrahydrozoline.

_____. "PubChem Compound Summary for CID 11079, Naphazoline Hydrochloride." *PubChem.* Accessed Dec. 18, 2021. https://pubchem.ncbi.nlm.nih.gov/compound/Naphazoline-hydrochloride.

"Ophthalmic Drug Products for Over-the-Counter Human Use." *Federal Register* 53, no. 43, pt. 2 (Mar. 4, 1988): 7075–93.

Schoenwald, Ronald D., and Robert E. Roehrs. "Sustained Release Ophthalmic Drug Dosage." Assignee: Alcon Laboratories. US Patent 4,407,792. *Official Gazette of the United States Patent Office* 1035, no. 1 (Oct. 4, 1983): 267.

Schollmaier, Edgar H., Norman R. Dewar, and Gerald Hecht. "Means for Cleaning Contact Lenses or the Like." Assignee: Alcon Laboratories. US Patent 3,614,959. *Official Gazette of the United States Patent Office* 891, no. 3 (Oct. 19, 1971): 1381.

US Census, AR, Pulaski County, 1920, 1930.

US Census, MA, Suffolk County, 1910.

US Census, OH, Jefferson County, 1940.

US Census, TX, Coryell County, 1910; Dallas County, 1920, 1930; Hamilton County, 1910, 1920, 1930; McClellan County, 1920; Parker County, 1920, 1930; San Saba County, 1910, 1920, 1930; Tarrant County, 1930, 1940.

World War II Draft Registration Cards for Texas. Oct. 16, 1940–Mar. 31, 1947.

Records of the Selective Service System. RG 147. Box 306. National Archives, St. Louis, MO.

Periodicals

Abilene (TX) Reporter-News

Alcon-o-gram (AOG). Vol. 1, AHR.

Alcon QA International. HLP.

Alcon Today and Tomorrow. ALC.

Alcon World News. ALC; AHR.

Arkansas Gazette (Little Rock)

Baltimore Evening Sun

Baton Rouge State Times Advocate

Beaumont (TX) Journal

Binghamton (NY) Sunday Press

Boston Globe

Brattleboro (VT) Reformer

Bryan Street Journal (Alcon). AHR.

Cambridge (OH) Daily Jeffersonian

Cincinnati Enquirer

Clifton (TX) Record

Commercial and Financial Chronicle (New York City)

Corpus Christi (TX) Caller-Times

Dallas Morning News

Danville (VA) Bee

Denton (TX) Record-Chronicle

Denver Post

Detroit Free Press

Eye on Tomorrow (Alcon). ALC.

EyeLites (Alcon). Vol. 3, AHR.

Fort Worth News-Tribune

Fort Worth Press

Fort Worth Star-Telegram

A Gazeta da Farmácia (Rio de Janeiro)

Grand Junction (CO) Daily Sentinel

Greensboro (NC) Record

Harvard Crimson (Harvard University)

Helsingin Sanomat (Helsinki)

Honolulu Star Advertiser

Indianapolis News

Investor's Reader (Merrill Lynch)

Jornal do Commercio (Rio de Janeiro)

Kansas City Business Journal

Lafayette (IN) Journal & Courier

Lakeville (CN) Journal / Millerton (NY) News

Las Vegas Review-Journal

Lexington Herald-Sun

Longview (TX) News-Journal

Los Angeles Times

Memphis Commercial Appeal

Miami News

Milwaukee Sentinel

Modesto (CA) Bee

New York Sunday News

New York Times

Newark Star-Ledger

News Summary (Federal Trade Commission)

Nocona (TX) News

Northwest (Tarrant County) Sun (North Richland Hills, TX)

Oakland Tribune

Panhandle (TX) Herald

Pasadena (CA) Independent Star-News

Pittsburgh Post-Gazette

Quincy (MA) Patriot Ledger

Racine (WI) Journal Times

Rambler, The (Texas Wesleyan University)

Richmond Times-Dispatch

Rochester (NY) Democrat and Chronicle

San Antonio Light

San Bernardino County Sun (San Bernardino, CA)

San Diego Union

San Francisco Chronicle

San Francisco Examiner

San Jose Mercury News

San Mateo (CA) Times

Scope (Alcon). AHR.

Seattle Times

Seguin (TX) Gazette-Enterprise

Spectrum (Alcon). BAS, AM; Vol. 2, AHR.

St. Louis Post-Dispatch

Surgical Insights (Alcon). AHR.

Surgical Journal (Alcon). AHR.

Tampa Tribune

Texas Jewish Post (Fort Worth)

Tyler (TX) Morning Telegraph

Update 1987: Alcon Today and Tomorrow. ALC.

Van Nuys (CA) Valley News

Venice (CA) Evening Vanguard

Vision & Commitment (Alcon). AHR.

Waco (TX) Tribune-Herald

Wall Street Journal

Wall Street Transcript

Washington Evening Star

Waxahachie (TX) Light

Websites and Blogs

Alumni Directory. Harvard Business School.
https://www.alumni.hbs.edu/community/Pages/directory-search.aspx.

"Alza Corporation." Company-Histories. Accessed Dec. 12, 2021. https://www.company-histories.com/ALZA-Corporation-Company-History.html.

"ARI Research Grant Recipients." Alcon Research Institute. Accessed November 11, 2024. https://www.alcon.com/alcon-research-institute.

Behrens, Ashley. "Cataract Surgery." Johns Hopkins Medicine. Accessed Feb. 19, 2022. https://www.hopkinsmedicine.org/health/treatment-tests-and-therapies/cataract-surgery.

"Biography: Jackie Fouse, Ph.D." Agios Pharmaceuticals. Accessed May 14, 2023. https://investor.agios.com/board-member/jacqualyn-fouse.

"Board of Regents: Regent Emeritus William De La Peña, M.D." University of California. Accessed Jan. 13, 2023. https://regents.universityofcalifornia.edu/about/members-and-advisors/bios/william-de-la-pena.html.

"A Brief Overview of Our History." FMC. Accessed Dec. 27, 2021. https://www.fmc.com/en/company/our-history.

"Bruce Coleman Rudy." Obituary. Died Feb. 6, 2016. Tribute Archive. https://www.tributearchive.com/obituaries/4088535/Bruce-Coleman-Rudy.

Chudler, Eric. "Neuroscience for Kids." University of Washington. Accessed Dec. 12, 2021. https://faculty.washington.edu/chudler/auto.html.

Cole, Jason. "Dexamethasone Briefing—Its Chemistry and History." Cambridge Crystallographic Data Centre. June 17, 2020. https://www.ccdc.cam.ac.uk/Community/blog/dexamethasone/.

"Dr. Adrienne Graves." Glaucoma Research Foundation. Accessed May 14, 2023. https://glaucoma.org/team/adrienne-graves-phd/.

"Ed and Rae Schollmaier Arena." TCU Men's Basketball. Accessed May 16, 2023. https://gofrogs.com/sports/2018/7/13/facilities-tcu-facilities-basketball-html.aspx.

"Estivin, Sterile Ophthamalic [*sic*] Solution." National Museum of American History. Accessed Dec. 18, 2021. https://americanhistory.si.edu/collections/search/object/nmah_328378.

"Excmo. Sr. D. José Daniel Gubert." Real Academia de Ciencias Económicas y Financieras. Accessed May 14, 2023. https://racef.es/es/academicoscorrespondiente-extranjero/jdaniel.

FDA. "A Brief History of the Center for Drug Evaluation and Research." FDA. As of Jan. 31, 2018. https://www.fda.gov/about-fda/fda-history-exhibits/brief-history-center-drug-evaluation-and-research.

_____. "A Guide to Drug Safety Terms at FDA." Consumer Health Information. FDA. Accessed Feb 10, 2022. https://www.fda.gov/media/74382/download.

"The History and Evolution of Prosthetic Eyes." Industries for the Blind and Visually Impaired. Accessed Dec. 25, 2021. https://ibvi.org/blog/the-history-and-evolution-of-prosthetic-eyes/.

"Howard M. Leibowitz, MD, FACS." Boston University School of Medicine. Accessed Nov. 17, 2021. https://www.bumc.bu.edu/ophthalmology/faculty-directory/howard-m-leibowitz-md-facs/.

Karim, Amin H. "Jinnah Hospital Karachi." Good Old Karachi. Posted June 30, 2018. https://goodoldkarachi.com/2018/06/30/jinnah-hospital-karachi/.

"Leader in Innovative Treatments for Oxidative Stress." Nacuity Pharmaceuticals. Accessed May 15, 2023. https://www.nacuity.com/.

"Medicines Act, 1968." Chap. 67. Legislation.gov.uk. Accessed Aug. 23, 2021. https://www.legislation.gov.uk/ukpga/1968/67/contents.

National Registry of Drug-Induced Ocular Side Effects. Accessed Mar. 25, 2022. http://www.eyedrugregistry.com/.

"Our Family History." Mager & Gougelman. Accessed Dec. 25, 2021. https://www.magerandgougelman.com/history.

Pan-American Association of Ophthalmology. Accessed May 21, 2023. https://paao.org/.

"PAOF Board of Directors." Pan-American Association of Ophthalmology.

Accessed Apr. 7, 2022. https://paao.org/paof/paof_governance/.

"Patricia Zilliox, PhD, President and CEO." Eyevensys. Accessed May 14, 2023. https://eyevensys.com/management-team/patricia-zilliox/u.

"Poison Control Pharmacist: Education and Career Information." Medical and Healthcare. Accessed Aug. 9, 2021. https://medicalandhealthcare.com/professions/pharmacology/poison-control-pharmacist-education-and-career-information.html.

"Purchase USP–NF." USP.org. Accessed Nov. 25, 2021. https://www.usp.org/usp-nf-purchase.

"Quality Management Systems—Guidelines for the Application of ISO 9001:2015." International Standards Organization. Accessed Nov. 27, 2022. https://www.iso.org/standard/66204.html.

Roberts, John. "Fort Worth Public Market Building." Accessed May 28, 2021. Architecture in Fort Worth. http://www.fortwortharchitecture.com/publicmarket.htm.

Rogers, Tony. "Everything You Need to Know about Polyethylene (PE)." *Creative Mechanisms* (blog). Sept. 14, 2015. https://www.creative-mechanisms.com/blog/polyethylene-pe-for-prototypes-3d-printing-and-cnc.

"Stella M. Robertson, PhD, Co-founder and Partner." Bios Partners. Accessed May 14, 2023. https://biospartners.com/team/.

"Urised (Oral)." Drugs.com. Accessed July 6, 2021. https://www.drugs.com/cons/urised.html.

"Veikko Reinikainen." Wikipedia. Last modified Mar. 28, 2020. https://fi.wikipedia.org/wiki/Veikko_Reinikainen.

Walker, David N. "My Uncle Willy." June 13, 2011. https://davidnwalker.com/2011/06/13/my-uncle-willy/u.

"We Are a Custom Injection Molding and Tool Building Company." Imco, Inc. Accessed Nov. 25, 2021. http://www.imcoinc.org/.

"We Facilitate Standardization Solutions." ANSI. Accessed Nov. 26, 2021. https://www.ansi.org/.

"Wheaton Science Products." Company-Histories.com. Accessed Nov. 25, 2021. https://www.company-histories.com/Wheaton-Science-Products-Company-History.html.

"Why Retinal Ganglion Cells Are Important in Glaucoma." Glaucoma Research Foundation. Accessed Dec. 12, 2021. https://www.glaucoma.org/glaucoma/why-retinal-ganglion-cells-are-important-in-glaucoma.php.

"Wiley Chambers, MD." Ophthalmology Innovation Source. Accessed Nov. 30, 2022. https://ois.net/wiley-chambers/.

"WMA Declaration of Helsinki–Ethical Principles for Medical Research Involving Human Subjects." World Medical Association. Accessed Feb. 7, 2022. https://www.wma.net/policies-post/wma-declaration-of-helsinki-ethical-principles-for-medical-research-involving-human-subjects/.

Endnotes

Preface

1. *Grand Junction (CO) Daily Sentinel*, Dec. 13, 1990.

2. *FWST*, Jan. 13, 1999.

3. *FWST*, Sept. 18, Oct. 3, 2021.

Chapter 1

1. *Worley's Dallas City Directory, 1944*; Jim Socks, Feb. 16, 2021, AOH.

2. *Morrison & Fourmy's Fort Worth City Directory*, *1946*; *FWST*, June 16, 1944; *Northwest (Tarrant County) Sun* (North Richland Hills, TX), Dec. 1, 2020.

3. US Census, TX, Coryell County, 1910, Hamilton County, 1910, 1920, 1930; *FWST*, Jan. 14, 1992; Death Records, 1960, 1966, Vital Statistics Section, Texas Dept. of State Health Services; Walker, "My Uncle Willy" (website); Halden Conner and Debbie Conner Norris, interview (hereafter Conner Family Interview), May 2, 24, 2021, TOM, AM.

4. *FWST*, Dec. 27, 1963, Feb. 23, 1972, June 3, 1979, Mar. 18, 1988; *Texas Jewish Post* (Fort Worth), May 22, 1986; Conner family interview; *Clifton (TX) Record*, Oct. 24, 1924.

5. Long, "Tanglewood, TX"; *Morrison & Fourmy's Fort Worth City Directory, 1918, 1920, 1922–25, 1927, 1929–30, 1932*; US Census, TX, Tarrant County, 1930, 1940.

6. Pate, *North of the River*, 22–29, 54–55, 58–68, 99–103, 137–46; Robert Denny Alexander, Lane Anne Alexander Kimzey, and Anita Alexander Taylor, interview, transcript (hereafter Alexander Family Interview), Apr. 5, 2021, TOM, AM.

7. Bob at Leonard's and Everybody's, CAOH.

8. *FWST*, Nov. 18, 1924, Feb. 27, 1925, Oct. 31, 1975; *Arkansas Gazette* (Little Rock), Mar. 11, 1920, Aug. 8, 1921; New England Historic Genealogical Society, *Massachusetts Vital Records*, 613:225; US Census, MA, Suffolk County, 1910; US Census, AR, Pulaski County, 1920.

9. *FWST*, Feb. 27, 1925, Jan. 31, 1926, Mar. 10, 1955, May 7, 1966, Oct. 31, 1975; *Waxahachie (TX) Light*, Oct. 2, 1929; *Denton (TX) Record-Chronicle*, Sept. 17, 1930; *Fort Worth Press*, Feb. 18, 1927.

10. *Arkansas Gazette*, Aug. 8, 1921; *Abilene (TX) Reporter News*, Sept. 10, 1931; *Waco (TX) Tribune-Herald*, May 23, 1929.

11. Murphy, "Hamilton, TX (Hamilton County)"; Conner family interview; Meeting Minutes, May 15, 1928, Texas State Board of Pharmacy; Megan G. Holloway, Asst. General Counsel, Texas State Board of Pharmacy to Tom McDonald, letter, May 19, 2019, TOM, AM; *FWST*, June 3, 1979.

12. Meeting minutes, May 15, 1928, Texas State Board of Pharmacy; Holloway to McDonald, letter, May 19, 2019.

13. *FWST*, Sept. 3, 1952, June 3, 1979; US Census, TX, Dallas County, 1930, San Saba County, 1910, 1920, 1930; Birth Records, Vital Statistics Section, Texas Department of State Health Services; Marriage Records, 51:332, Dallas County Clerk, Dallas, TX; *Denver Post*, June 6, 20, 23, 1929; Conner family interview.

14. *Worley's Dallas City Directory, 1931–36*; US Census, TX, Dallas County, 1930; *FWST*, June 3, 1979; *Longview (TX) News-Journal*, May 31, 1936.

15. Buenger, "Leonard Brothers"; Leonard's and Everybody's and pharmacy school, CAOH; Pate, *North of the River*, 40–42; Robert D. Alexander grades, New Mexico Board of Pharmacy, AFP; Robert D. Alexander, Registered Pharmacist, June 1, 1944, New Mexico Board of Pharmacy, Albuquerque, NM, AFP; Gammel, *Laws of Texas: Supplement Volume to the Original Ten Volumes*, 1:242–47; Meeting Minutes, May 15, 1928, Nov. 10, 1929, Oct. 17, 1933, Mar. 19, May 14, Nov. 12, 1934, Texas State Board of Pharmacy; Robert Denzil Alexander, Pharmacist, Registration by Reciprocity, Jan. 22, 1935, Texas State Board of Pharmacy, Austin, AFP; *FWST*, June 6, 1946. In June 1946, Lt. Cody H. Wheeler died in a crash of a US Army transport plane near Naples, Italy.

16. Meeting Bob, CAOH; *Northwest Sun*, Mar. 21, 2001. In her 2001 oral history, Catherine Alexander described the dance scene in Tarrant County.

17. US Census, TX, McClellan County, 1920, Tarrant County, 1930; *The 1932 Panther;* Marriage, CAOH.

18. Working for Ben Weeks, Meeting the Conners, CAOH.

19. US Census, TX, Tarrant County, 1940; *Morrison & Fourmy's Fort Worth City Directory, 1941*; Working for Ben Weeks, the Conners, pregnant, Wyeth training, CAOH; Alexander and Conner, "Story of Alcon Laboratories"; *Fort Worth News-Tribune*, Oct. 18, 1985.

20. Denny Alexander, Lane Anne Kimzey to author, emails, May 2, 2021, TOM, AM; *Worley's Dallas City Directory, 1942–44; Morrison & Fourmy's Fort Worth City Directory, 1946*; Visiting, CAOH; Bill and Bob on *Bob Kat*, Jim Socks, AOH; Bill and Bob fishing, Jackie Barry to author, email, Apr. 16, 2021, TOM, AM; Wyeth photo, AFP; *Dallas Morning News*, Feb. 12, 1956; W. H. Westphal to R. D. Alexander, July 28, 1945, AFP.

21. World War II Draft Registration Cards for Texas; *FWST*, June 3, 1979; Westphal to Alexander, July 28, 1945; Alexander and Conner, "Story of Alcon Laboratories"; Agreement between W. C. Conner and R. D. Alexander, AFP.

22. *Fort Worth Press*, Sept. 19, 1945; *FWST*, June 3, 1979, June 28, 1987, Mar. 18, 1988; *Texas Jewish Post*, May 22, 1986; Alexander and Conner, "Story of Alcon Laboratories; "Alcon Story," *Alcon Today and Tomorrow*, 1989, pp. 6–7.

23. Alcon Prescription Laboratory checks, AFP; Alexander and Conner, "Story of Alcon Laboratories"; *Texas Jewish Post*, May 22, 1986; *Fort Worth Press*, Sept. 19, 1945; *FWST*, June 3, 1979, June 28, 1987, Mar. 18, 1988. The expenditures to equip the pharmacy are revealing: Internal Revenue, 80 cents; Ayerst, McKinna, and Harrison, $5.88; Retail Druggist Selling System, $293.92 and $440.70; Pepsi-Cola, $10; Carton, Glass and Harrison, $12.54; The Upjohn Company, $258.68; Wyeth, Inc., $740.73; W. J. Gutherie (rubber floor mats), $48.75; and Marvin D. Evans and Co. (printing), $15.28.

24. Herring, "Harold Johnson"; "Harold C. Johnson," *AWN*; *FWST*, June 8, 1997; Dave Merrill, "Alcon Story," Feb. 19, 2004.

25. Alexander and Conner, "Story of Alcon Laboratories"; Balance Sheet, and Profit and Loss Statement, 1947, Alcon Prescription Laboratory, AFP; *Texas Jewish Post*, May 22, 1986; *FWST*, Sept. 2, 1946

26. Alcon Arlington Heights Prescription Laboratory, Profit and Loss and Balance Sheet, Mar. 31, 1947, AFP; Alcon Laboratories, Incorporation Papers, County Clerk, Tarrant County, box H 142, ALC; Charter–Alcon Laboratories, Inc., May 16, 1947, Texas Secretary of State.

27. Alcon Laboratories, Incorporation Papers; Alexander and Conner, "Story of Alcon Laboratories"; "But Can She Type?"

28. Bill Conner's Formula Book, Wanda Calvert, AM; Merrill, "Alcon Story"; Annual Financial Statements, 1947–49, AFP. Miraculously, Bill Conner's notebook filled with various medicinal formulations survives. Some of the additional ACL products were Alco-Mi-Cos Ear Drops, Alcon Pro-Pen Ear Drops, and Alcon Anti-Yeast Suppositories.

29. Merrill, "Alcon Story"; Walker, "My Uncle Willy."

30. Robert Roehrs, Aug. 28, 2019, AOH.

31. Alexander and Conner, "Story of Alcon Laboratories"; *Fort Worth News-Tribune*, Oct. 18, 1985; Statement of Income and Expenses, Eight Months ended Dec. 31, 1947, ALC.

Chapter 2

1. *AWN*, Oct. 1988; Rathjen, "Panhandle"; Anderson, "Amarillo, TX"; *Fort Worth News-Tribune*, Oct. 18, 1985; *Dallas Morning News*, May 9, 1982.

2. Balance Sheet, and Profit and Loss Statement, 1948–50, Alcon Prescription Laboratory, AFP; Alexander and Conner, "Story of Alcon Laboratories"; *FWST*, Nov. 12, 1948, Jan. 10, 1949.

3. *FWST*, June 9, 1949, Nov. 2, 1952, June 26, Nov. 4, 1953; *Morrison & Fourmy's Fort Worth City Directory, 1949*; Mike Gibson, Jay Gibson (sons of John R. Gibson), telephone conversations with author, May 12, 13, 2021, TOM, AM; US Census, TX, Parker County, 1920, 1930, Tarrant County, 1930, 1940; *Texas Jewish Post*, Oct. 4, 1951; Meeting Minutes, Sept. 19, 1928, Texas State Board of Pharmacy; Charter, Alcon Prescription Laboratories, May 24, 1949, Texas Secretary of State.

4. Financial Statements, Apr. 1950, 1951–54, Alcon Prescription Laboratory, AFP; Memorandum Agreement, AFP; Mike Gibson, Jay Gibson, telephone conversations with author, May 12, 13, 2021; *FWST*, Oct. 30, 2016.

5. Sales and Net Profit Summary, Index, 4:1, AHR; Annual Financial Statements, 1947–49, AFP; "But Can She Type?" Walker Vitamin Products, Inc., Mount Vernon, NY, produced a range of vitamins, which they licensed to distributors.

6. Alexander and Conner, "Story of Alcon Laboratories"; *FWST*, June 3, 1979, June 18, 1987, July 18, 1988; Annual Financial Statements, 1948–49; Photographs, AFP.

7. Wheeler, "History of Ophthalmology," 264–75; Nicolaou and Rigol, "Brief History of Antibiotics," 153–84; Rubin, "Brief History of Great Discoveries in Pharmacology," 289–359.

7. Annual Financial Statements, 1948–49; Sales and Net Profit Sum-

mary, Index, 4:1; Merrill, "Alcon Story."

8. Alexander and Conner, "Story of Alcon Laboratories"; *FWST*, Oct. 4, 1949, June 3, 1979, June 28, 1987; *Texas Jewish Post*, Oct. 4, 1951; Bill Conner, interview by Rose Tulecke, *Fort Worth*, 33; *Panhandle (TX) Herald*, Oct. 14, 1949.

9. Edgar H. Keltner Jr. (1919–2011), "Alcon Story," Feb. 19, 2004.

10. Annual Financial Statements, 1949–50, AFP; George Frank Leone (1926–2021), "Alcon Story," Mar. 15, 2004; George Leone, May 6, 2019, AOH.

11. EHS, *EHS Says*; Leone, "Alcon Story."

12. Leone, "Alcon Story"; *Rambler* (Texas Wesleyan University), Feb. 23, 1948; Leone, AOH; "George Leone Named Marketing Manager," *EyeLites*, Apr. 13, 1967.

13. Merrill, "Alcon Story"; Roberts, "Fort Worth Public Market Building" (website). The building at 1400 Henderson Street, opened in 1930, was added to the National Register of Historic Places in 1984.

14. Annual Financial Statements, 1950–51, AFP; *AOG*, Oct. 15, 1957; Robert "Bob" Willis Carter (1927–2015), "Alcon Story," Feb. 17, 2004; *Spectrum*, June 1977; *FWST*, Jan. 28, 2015.

15. Monthly Remuneration for Salesmen, Alcon Sales by Territory, 1950–51, AFP.

16. Harold Beasley, MD, Alcon Hall of Fame Inductees, AHR; *AWN*, Aug. 1992; author's recollections. Dr. Beasley was the author's key mentor from 1965 until 1999.

17. *FWST*, Feb. 10, 1952; Annual Financial Statement, 1952, AFP; *Wall Street Journal*, Dec. 7, 1993; *Wall Street Transcript*, Mar. 22, 1973; *San Jose Mercury News*, May 6, 2012; Reilly, "FDA and Plan B."

18. *FWST*, Sept. 3, 1952; Conner family interview, May 2, 24, 2021, TOM, AM.

19. *FWST*, Sept. 3, 1952; Conner family interview

20. Monthly Sales by Territory, 1951–53, AFP; Alexander family interview, Apr. 5, 2021, TOM, AM; Conner Family Interview; Amy Erisman (daughter of Charles Rohrer), phone conversation and email, June 17, 2021, TOM, AM.

21. Stockholders Meeting, June 9, 1953, AFP; Notice of Special Meet-ing of Stockholders, July 7, 1953, box H 142, ALC.

22. Kenneth C. Swan (1912–2007), "Use of Methylcellulose in Ophthalmology," 378–80; Havener, *Ocular Pharmacology*, 2nd ed., 172–80, 188–89, 192–95, 206–7, 214–17, 276, 338, 420, 476–77.

23. Alberta Renick Glassford (1913–2004), "Alcon Story," Jan. 5, 2004; Merrill, "Alcon Story." William "Bill" A. Padgett (1925–2009).

24. Stockholders Meeting, June 9, 1953; Charles Evans Dickey (1925–2010), "Alcon Story," Feb. 16, 2004; Merrill, "Alcon Story"; Kowalski, *Ultraviolet Germicidal Irradiation Handbook*, 1–13; Dusseau, Duroselle, and Freney, "Gaseous Sterilization," 401–35; Barkman, Germanis, Karpe, and Malmborg. "Preservatives in Eye Drops," 461–75.

25. Conner Family Interview; US Census, TX, Dallas County, 1920, 1930, Tarrant County, 1940; *St. Louis Post-Dispatch*, June 23, 1952; Freeman, "Obituaries: Richard Gordon Scobee, M.D.," 663–65; *FWST*, Aug. 18, 1987.

26. Dickey, "Alcon Story"; *AOG*, Sept. 18, 1956, Mar. 1, Oct. 15, 1957, Jan. 15, July 1, Aug. 1, 1958, Aug. 1, 1958, Sept. 1960, Nov. 1960. The employees, departments, and dates of hire: production, Fern Bearden (Jan. 1951), Pauline Allen (Mar. 27, 1952), Georgia Castleman (Sept. 29, 1952), Mayne Dodd (Oct. 1952), Lula Thomas (Aug. 6, 1953), Ola Reger (Nov. 7, 1953); shipping, Lottie Mae Wilkerson (Apr. 20, 1951); advertising, Clara Ledbetter (Aug. 13, 1952), Rachel Ramirez (Oct. 1952); accounting, Charlie Richardson (Jan. 15, 1950); Zincfrin and Isopto Cetamide, advertisements, promotional material, vol. 9, AHR.

27. Sales Documents, 1954–55, AFP; Annual Financial Statement, 1949, AFP.

28. Notice of Special Stockholders Meeting, Dec. 2, 1954, box H 142, ALC; Alcon Laboratories, Incorporation Papers, County Clerk, Tarrant County, box H 142, ALC; Alcon Laboratories Charter Amendment, Jan. 1955, Texas Secretary of State.

29. Earle Shields to Tom McDonald, conversation, fall 2007; Conner family interview.

30. Condensed Financial Statement, 1955–56, box H 142, ALC; Alcon to Dr. John W. Garrett Jr., MD, letter, Mar. 9, 1955, box H 142, ALC; *FWST*, June 9, 1955.

31. Condensed Financial Statement, 1955–56; Monthly Statement of Operations, 1955–56, AFP.

32. Monthly Statement of Operations, 1955–56.

33. Havener, *Ocular Pharmacology*, 2nd ed., 47–50, 223–32, 276–78, 336, 473–74.

34. Leone, "Alcon Story"; *AOG*, Mar. 1, 1957; Vincent Juliano, Aug. 4, 2019, AOH; George Leone's remuneration, memo from R. D. Alexander, Feb. 23, 1955, Sales Documents, 1954–55, AFP.

35. Stockholders Attending, Stockholder Proxies, Alexander Document, June 1955, AFP.

36. Kass, "Business School's Advanced Management Program."

37. *FWST*, Dec. 22, 1952, Oct. 3, 4, 10, 1955, Sept. 24, 1958, Oct. 19, 1959, Sept. 5, 1961, June 8, 1997; *AOG*, Oct. 1, 1957.

38. Minutes, Board of Directors, 1956–58, AFP; *AOG*, Dec. 15, 1956; AMP 29, AMP 30, Carton 1, Executive Education, Baker Library, Harvard Business School; *Investor's Reader*, Nov. 17, 1965, p. 12.

39. Condensed Financial Statement, 1955–56; Monthly Statement of Operations, 1955–56, AFP; ALFW, "Profile and Prognosis," prepared by Market Research and Financial Section, Jan. 15, 1958, AFP; Minutes, Board, 1956–58; *EyeLites*, Apr. 13, 1967; *Spectrum*, June 1977; *AOG*, Apr. 6, 19, May 4, June 29, Oct. 15, Nov. 1, 15, 1956.

40. "Proposed New Facilities, Alcon," brochure, 1957, AFP.

41. Theodore Carl "Ted" Fleming (1924–2016), "Alcon Story," Jan. 8, 2004; *FWST*, Mar. 13, 2016.

42. Minutes, Board, 1956–58; *AOG*, Aug. 2, 1956.

43. Fleming, "Alcon Story"; Condensed Financial Statement, 1955–56.

44. Alexander family interview; EHS, *EHS Says*.

45. Conner family interview.

46. *AOG*, Apr. 6, July 13, 1956, June 15, 1957.

47. *AOG*, Mar. 1, June 1, Oct. 15, Nov. 1, Dec. 15, 1957; Minutes, Board, 1956–58; ALFW, "Profile and Prognosis"; AFP; *Spectrum*, Apr., 1972.

48. *AOG*, May 1, Nov. 1, 1957; *FWST*, July 8, 1994; Minutes, Board, 1956–58; Material pertaining to Robert D. Alexander and William C. Conner, 8:1, AHR; Notes on Division Conferences, R. D. Alexander, AFP. John Woodruff Spruill (1932–1994).

49. "Proposed New Facilities." Joseph Parker Floyd (1926–1994).

50. *FWST*, July 17, 1957; Minutes, Board, 1956–58.

51. *AOG*, Mar. 15, May 15, Sept. 15, Oct. 1, 15, Nov. 1, 1957.

52. Minutes, Board, 1956–58; *Tyler (TX) Morning Telegraph*, Sept. 19, 1960; Alumni Directory, Harvard Business School (website), accessed June 9, 2021.

53. Minutes, Board, 1956–58.

54. *AOG*, Oct. 1, Dec. 15, 1957; *AWN*, Dec. 1993.

Chapter 3

1. EHS, "25 Years of Friendship," *EHS Says*, 28–30; EHS, "Alcon Story," Feb. 17, Mar. 16, 17, 2004.

2. *Proposed New Facilities*, Alcon, brochure, 1957, AFP; *AOG*, Oct. 15, 1958.

3. ALFW, "Profile and Prognosis," prepared by Market Research and Financial Section, Jan. 15, 1958, AFP.

4. *FWST*, Sept. 6, 1982, Aug. 2, 1993; Alumni Directory, HBS (website) (searched: Harvey Andrews), accessed June 21, 2021; Minutes, Board, 1958; Zeff, "Contribution of the Harvard School of Business to Management Control," 187–90.

5. Alumni Directory, HBS (website) (searched: Herbert Kleiman, Frederick Lyons, William Glover, Robert Rapp, George Leone, David Merrill, and Robert Carter), accessed June 21, 2021; EHS, "Alcon Story"; EHS, *EHS Says*, 28–30; *AOG*, Feb. 15, 1958.

6. EHS, "Alcon Story."

7. EHS, "Alcon Story."

8. EHS, "Alcon Story"; *Cincinnati Enquirer*, Jan. 9, 1955; US Census, OH, Jefferson County, 1940.

9. EHS, "Alcon Story."

10. EHS, "Alcon Story."

11. *AOG*, June 1, 1957, July 1959; *FWST*, June 9, 1955, June 15, 1958, June 22, 1959; Minutes, Board of Directors, 1958–59, AFP; ALFW, Statement of Operations, 1958–59, AFP; Annual Report, 1959, ALC.

12. Annual Report, 1959; Minutes, Board, 1958–59; *AOG*, Aug.

15, Nov. 1, 1958, Sept. 1959, Mar. 1960; *FWST*, Oct. 21, 1962; *Spectrum*, Apr. 1972; the author's recollection of his tour as a new employee, Jan. 1966.

13. Annual Reports, 1959–62, ALC; Minutes, Board, 1959; *AOG*, Sept. 1959, Mar. 1960; Carter, "Alcon Story"; Lowell Dix, "Alcon Story," Jan. 7, 2004; *FWST*, June 22, 1959; *Spectrum*, Apr. 1972.

14. Annual Reports, 1963, 1965–67, ALC; *Spectrum*, Apr. 1972.

15. *FWST*, Feb. 3, 1959, Apr. 16, 1961, May 17, 1967; *AOG*, Feb., May, June, Aug., Sept., Oct., Nov., Dec. 1960, Jan. 1961; Annual Reports, 1960–62, 1964, 1967–68, ALC; Fleming, "Alcon Story"; Minutes, Board of Directors, 1959–60, AFP.

16. *AOG*, Feb., May, June, Aug., Sept., Oct., Nov., Dec., 1960, Jan. 1961; *Spectrum*, June 1976; Telephone conversation with John Roberts, Fort Worth architect, June 25, 2021, TOM, AM

17. Annual Reports, 1961–62; EHS, "Alcon Story."

18. EHS, "Alcon Story"; *AOG*, June 1960; Annual Reports, 1959–60. Searches of newspaper advertisements at www.newspapers.com reveal Alconefrin was sold mostly in Texas, the Midwest, and parts of the South. Joseph "Joe" Parker Floyd (1926–1994) was Alcon's director of advertising.

19. EHS, "Alcon Story."

20. EHS, "Alcon Story"; Hunt, "Mineral Wells, TX"; *FWST*, June 28, 1987; Annual Reports, 1959–60.

21. EHS, "Alcon Story"; Leone, "Alcon Story", TCU; Dick Sisson, "Alcon Story," Feb. 20, 2004.

22. Annual Reports, 1960–62; Andy Lubrano, "Alcon Story," Feb. 20, 2004.

23. *AOG*, May 15, 1958; *Texas Jewish Post*, Apr. 5, 1962; *Commercial and Financial Chronicle* (New York City), Apr. 16, 1959; Minutes, Board, 1958–59; Stockholders Attending, Stockholder Proxies, Alexander Document, June 1955, AFP.

24. Minutes, Board, 1958–59; *FWST*, Sept. 19, 1958; Articles of Amendment to Articles of Incorporation of Alcon Laboratories, Inc., June 13, 1958, Texas State Securities Board, Austin; *FWST*, Aug. 17, Sept. 17, Oct. 15, Nov. 11, 1958, Mar. 24, May 14, Aug. 20, Oct. 1, Nov. 18, Dec. 24, 1959, Feb. 16, Apr. 13, July 20, Sept. 14, Nov. 13, Dec. 24, 1960, Feb. 25, May 7, Aug. 13, Nov. 26, Dec. 29, 1961, Mar. 6, June 10, Aug. 28, Nov. 17, 1962, June 14, Sept.

15, Dec. 18, 1963, Mar. 12, June 18, Sept. 20, Dec. 20, 1964, Mar. 19, July 15, 1965, Mar. 18, June 20, Sept. 19, Dec. 21, 1967; *Abilene (TX) Reporter-News*, Sept. 19, Dec. 18, 1965, Mar. 19, June 11, Sept. 20, 1966, Dec. 18, 1965. I have cited periodic stock prices as representative samples.

25. Stockholders Attending, Stockholder Proxies, Alexander Document, June 1955, AFP; George Leone's Remuneration, memo from R. D. Alexander, Feb. 23, 1955, Sales Documents, 1954–55, AFP; Annual Reports, 1960–67; Minutes, Board, 1958–60; Alcon Laboratories Employee Stock Option Plan, Board of Directors Meeting, Mar. 2, 1959, AFP.

26. William C. Conner to Alcon Shareholders, Sept. 18, 1961, ALC; Alexander and Conner, "Story of Alcon Laboratories."

27. *AOG*, Aug. 1959, June, May, Sept. 1960; *FWST*, Sept. 19, 1961, article copy at AFP, and Vol. 1, AHR; "Pfizer Buys Globe," 131; *Boston Globe*, Sept. 27, 1961; Dora Moody, "Alcon Story," Feb. 18, 2004.

28. Annual Report, 1962; *FWST*, Jan. 26, Feb. 27, 1962, Jan. 20, Nov. 6, 1966; *Dallas Morning News*, Jan. 28, Feb. 25, June 28, 1962; Alcon Laboratories, Inc., Prospectus, Mar. 31, 1971, Merrill, Lynch, Pierce, Fenner & Smith, AFP.

29. Krantz, "New Drugs and the Kefauver–Harris Amendment," 77–79; "Kefauver–Harris Amendments Revolutionized Drug Development," *FDA Consumer Health Information*; Annual Reports, 1962–65; *FWST*, July 1, 1962: Richard Poe, telephone conversation, May 14, 2019, TOM, AM; Milton Barley, email to author, July 6, 2021, TOM, AM.

30. *FWST*, Dec. 4, 1966; Annual Reports, 1965–68. Alcon consolidated sales and profits and never revealed how Service Engineers performed. Nevertheless, several Alcon employees recalled that Service Engineers contributed little to Alcon's yearly balance sheets.

31. *Dallas Morning News*, Jan. 28, 1962; *FWST*, Feb. 27, 1962; Annual Reports, 1962–65; Fleming, "Alcon Story."

32. Annual Reports, 1965–68; Floyd Powell, "Alcon Story," Jan. 8, 2004; Fleming, "Alcon Story"; Fred Lyons, telephone conversation with author, Sept. 2019, TOM, AM; "Urised (Oral)," Drugs.com (website).

33. Jerry Rutherford, May 29, 2019, AOH; *FWST*, Dec. 20, 1967; *Dallas Morning News*, Dec. 22, 1967; Annual Report, 1968; EHS, "Alcon Story"; *Surgical Instrument Catalog*, 240–323.

34. Minutes, Board of Directors, 1952–53, 1956–58, AFP; Keltner, "Alcon Story"; *Tyler (TX) Morning Telegraph*, Sept. 19, 1960; *FWST*, Jan. 3, 1958.

35. Minutes, Board, 1958–60; Annual Reports 1959–67; *Texas Jewish Post*, Nov. 16, 1978; *Seguin (TX) Gazette-Enterprise*, Aug. 29, 1968; *Nocona (TX) News*, Nov. 28, 1968; *FWST*, June 23, 1961, Oct. 23, 1992; *Dallas Morning News*, July 18, 1972; John Desmond Glover, HBS Faculty Biographical Information, Special Collections, Baker Library, HBS.

36. *AOG*, Jan., Apr., July 1958, Aug., Sept., Nov. 1959; Lubrano, "Alcon Story."

37. EHS, "Alcon Story."

38. EHS, "Alcon Story"; Sisson, "Alcon Story."

39. *AOG*, Mar., Apr., May, Oct., Nov., Dec. 1957, Jan., Mar., Apr., May, July, Aug., Sept., Oct. 1958, Apr., May, Aug., Sept., Oct., Nov. 1959, Jan., Feb., Mar., Apr., May, June, Oct., Nov., Dec. 1960, Jan. 1961; *FWST*, Dec. 11, 16, 1959; Sisson, "Alcon Story."

40. EHS, "Alcon Story"; Annual Reports, 1961–62; Leone, AOH; Leone, "Alcon Story.

41. Leone, "Alcon Story"; Alcon Laboratories, Inc. (Condensed), HBS Retired Case Collection, box 47, folder 115, Special Collections, Baker Library, HBS.

42. Leone, "Alcon Story"; Alcon Laboratories, Inc. (Condensed), HBS Retired Case Collection.

43. Employee List, 1966, Sandy Howell, AM; *AWN*, Apr., June, Nov. 1985, Jan., July 1986, Dec. 1990, Jan., June, Aug., Dec. 1992, July, Dec. 1993, Sept. 1995, Mar. 1996, Apr. 1997, May 1998, Sept. 1999; *Spectrum*, July 1974, Aug. 1994, Mar. 1996; *AOG*, Oct. 1960.

44. Annual Report, 1962; *Product Reference Guide*, 1962, AFP; *Product Reference Guide*, 1964, vol. 05.06.048, AHR; EHS, "Alcon Story."

45. EHS, "Alcon Story"; *AWN*, Apr., Aug. 1988; Warren Ross, Alcon Hall of Fame Inductees, AHR.

46. Annual Reports, 1963–66; Len Schweitzer, May 17, 2019, AOH; *FWST*, June 9, 1965, Apr. 16, 2006; *Dallas Morning News*, Nov. 29, 2006; Alcon Laboratories, Inc. (Condensed), HBS Retired Case Collection; Maxitrol Program Book, 1966, AHR; *AWN*, Dec. 1997, Aug. 1998.

47. *AOG*, Jan. 15, 1958; *EyeLites*, Apr. 13, May 31, June 29, Oct. 6, 1967.

48. *FWST*, Mar. 24, 1963, Apr. 19, July 19, 1964, Apr. 30, 1967, Apr. 18, 2007; Employee List, 1966, Sandy Howell, AM; *EyeLites*, Apr. 13, 1967. The most complete data set for an Alcon organizational chart remains the December 1966 Employee Address List, which was circulated to all employees.

49. *AOG*, Jan. 15, 1958; Minutes, Board, 1958–59; Annual Report, 1964; *AWN*, Feb. 1990, June 1992; Employee List, 1966, Sandy Howell, AM; *FWST*, May 11, 2012.

50. *AOG*, Sept. 1, Nov. 1, 15, 1957, Jan. 1, 15, 1958, Sept. 1959, Apr., June 1960; Employee List, 1966, Sandy Howell, AM; Fred Lyons and Tom McDonald, telephone conversation, June 2019, TOM, AM; Dennis Beikman, Prakash Rao, and Nick Tsumpis, June 22, 2019, AOH; *FWST*, Jan. 24, 1965.

51. *FWST*, Feb. 20, 1966, Oct. 23, 1992; EHS, "Alcon Story"; Annual Reports, 1966–67; Employee List, 1966, Sandy Howell, AM; *Spectrum*, Jan. 1987.

52. Juliano, AOH; Minutes, Board, 1958–59; *AOG*, May 15, 1958.

53. *AOG*, May 15, 1958, June 1960; Annual Reports, 1960–61; *FWST*, Aug. 16, 1964

54. Annual Reports, 1962–67; *FWST*, Dec. 7, 1961, Feb. 23, Aug. 16, 1964, June 2, 1965.

55. Frank Buhler, "Alcon Story," Feb. 20, 2004; Juana Rosa Lorenzo-Daniell, "Alcon Story," Jan. 7, 2004; *AWN*, Apr. 1993.

56. Lorenzo-Daniell, "Alcon Story"; *AWN*, Aug. 1989; *Spectrum*, Dec. 1971.

57. *AWN*, Dec. 1988, Mar. 1992, Aug. 1989, Apr. 1993, July 1995, Nov. 1999; *Spectrum*, Dec. 1971; Jacques Van Damme, "Alcon Story," Oct. 23, 2004; Lorenzo-Daniell, "Alcon Story."

58. Geoffrey Crewe, "Alcon Story," Mar. 18, 2004; *AWN*, Dec. 1981, Jan. 1986, Apr. 1993, Apr. 1997.

59. Employee List, 1966, Sandy Howell, AM.

60. *AOG*, Oct. 1958, May, Dec., 1960, Jan. 1961; *FWST*, Oct. 8, 1958, June 21, 1959, Dec. 14, 1961, May 25, Sept. 2, 6, 1962, June 30, Apr. 7, Sept. 5, 1963, Feb. 9, 1964, Jan. 28, 1966, Apr. 26, May 16,

1967, Dec. 12, 1971; Annual Reports, 1959, 1961–63, 1966–67; Moody, "Alcon Story"; *AWN*, Dec. 1981, Mar. 1984, Sept. 1985, Oct., Dec. 1987, Dec. 1990, July 1993.

61. *FWST*, July 7, 1963, Jan. 5, May 9, 1964, Feb. 10, Mar. 12, 1965, July 14, 2004; *AWN*, Nov. 1986; News-Makers, *Chemical & Engineering News*, 4206; *Pittsburgh Post-Gazette*, Apr. 22, 1957; *Tampa Tribune*, Sept. 15, 1976; *Rochester (NY) Democrat and Chronicle*, Oct. 2, 1974; Karim, "Jinnah Hospital Karachi," Good Old Karachi (website); Richard Poe, "Alcon Story," Jan. 9, 2004; Fleming, "Alcon Story"; EHS, "Alcon Story." The author remembers the vivid stories told to him by Ruby Zellers and George Riddle, both employees at the time. The author started at Alcon on December 13, 1965, and Priddle was fired the following Monday. Priddle became vice president for Bausch & Lomb's contact lens development.

62. Anita Tippett, "Alcon Story," Jan. 9, 2004; Edward Dorsey to Tom McDonald, chemical assays, telephone conversation, May 19, 2019, TOM, AM; Employee List, 1966, Sandy Howell, AM; Sidhu, "Endangered Jaborandi," 2–3. Core R&D members who made a career at Alcon include Dr. Mullins, Gerald D. Hecht, PhD, Richard Poe, PhD, Edwin D. Dorsey, PhD, Betty Fortenberry, John A. Allen, Jose Molina, Henry Baldwin, Ramona Puckett, Anita Tippett, Ann Duncan, Eldred Keys, Russell Borgmann, PhD, DVM, Charles M. Kagawa, PhD, Numajiri, and the author.

63. Employee List, 1966, Sandy Howell, AM; Immel, "Brief History of the GMPs"; Howard Luttrell, "My Journey from Bench Chemist to Vice-President at Alcon Labs," Howard Luttrell Papers (hereafter HLP), TOM, AM.

64. Merrill, "Alcon Story"; Fleming, "Alcon Story"; Poe, "Alcon Story"; Annual Report, 1967; Carter, "Alcon Story."

65. FDA, "Brief History of the Center for Drug Evaluation and Research," FDA (website); Employee List, 1966, Sandy Howell, AM; Annual Report, 1967; *Spectrum*, July 1988; *AWN*, June 1984.

66. Annual Report, 1962; *Product Reference Guide*, 1962.

67. Annual Report, 1962; *Product Reference Guide*, 1962; Havener, *Ocular Pharmacology*, 375, 385–89; Milton Barley, email to author, July 18, 2021, TOM, AM.

68. Annual Report, 1962*; Product Reference Guide*, 1962; Havener, *Ocular Pharmacology*, 172–80, 383; *FWST*, Dec. 14, 1961; Barley, email to author, July 18, 2021

69. Cole, "Dexamethasone Briefing," Cambridge Crystallographic Data Centre (website); Annual Report, 1962; *Product Reference Guide*, 1962; EHS, "Alcon Story"; Fleming, "Alcon Story"; Havener, *Ocular Pharmacology*, 277–78; Schweitzer, AOH; Roy Buchanan, July 23, 2019, AOH; Bob Nelson, Aug. 23, 2019, AOH.

70. Havener, *Ocular Pharmacology*, 133

71. *AWN*, Oct. 1988; EHS, "Alcon Story."

72. *Product Reference Guide*, 1974, Regulatory Affairs copy, AHR; Annual Report, 1965; *EyeLites*, Feb., Mar. 6, Apr. 13, 1967.

73. Attar, "About Red Caps"; *Product Reference Guide*, 1962; *EyeLites*, Apr. 13, 1967; Fleming, "Alcon Story"; Havener, *Ocular Pharmacology*, 198–201; *AOG*, Apr. 1960; Stine, "Clinical Investigation of a New Mydriatic and Cycloplegic Drug," 11–15.

74. *Product Reference Guide*, 1962

75. Lamb and Bowden, "History of Contact Lenses"; Szczotka-Flynn et al., "History, Evolution, and Evolving Standards of Contact Lens Care," S4–S8; *Product Reference Guide*, 1962.

76. Davis, "Evolution of Cataract Surgery," 58–62; Rizzuti, "Alpha-Chymotrypsin (Quimotrase) in Cataract Surgery," 135–40; Merrill, Fleming, and Girard, "Effects of Physiologic Balanced Salt Solutions and Normal Saline on Intraocular and Extraocular Tissues," 895–98; *AOG*, Oct. 1959, Feb. 1960; *AWN*, Feb. 1991; Alexander and Conner, "Story of Alcon Laboratories"; Annual Report, 1966; Passmore and Hughes, "Sterile Disposable Cryoextractor (Cryophake)," 423–31; *Product Reference Guide*, 1962.

77. Kaufman, Martola, and Dohlman, "Use of 5-iodo-2'-deoxyuridine (IDU) in Treatment of Herpes Simplex Keratitis," 235–39; *FWST*, June 30, 1963.

78. Annual Report, 1962; *FWST*, May 25, June 24, 1962; Conner family interview; Smith, "In Memoriam: A. Edward Maumenee, Jr., MD," 1131–33; Ryan, "Obituary: A. Edward Maumenee," 582–84.

79. Minutes, Board, 1958–60; *AWN*, Mar. 1986; Annual Report, 1959.

80. Alexander Family Interview; *AWN*, Mar. 1986; Conner Family Interview; Milton Barley, June 20, 2019, AOH; Minutes, Board, 1960.

81. Minutes, Board, 1958–60; Annual Reports, 1962, 1971–1973, ALC; Deeds, 2716:227–28; 2854:501–3, 3295:208–10, 3490:51–57, 4272:541–46, 6262:751–53, Tarrant County Clerk,

Fort Worth

82. Luttrell, "My Journey"; Martha Siegel, July 26, 2019, AOH; Henry Baldwin, July 15, 2019, AOH; Sandy Howell and Marva Clynch, July 2, 2019, AOH; *FWST*, Nov. 25, 1962, Mar. 25, 2016; Author's recollections.

83. "Your Group Benefits featuring Major Medical Expense Insurance," 1957, Miscellaneous Records, AHR; *AOG*, Jan. 20, Aug. 1960; Dix, "Alcon Story"; Ed Schollmaier's retiree card, in possession of Taylor Schollmaier, Boulder, CO.

84. *Spectrum*, June 1976; Annual Report, 1960; *Lakeville (CN) Journal / Millerton (NY) News*, Sept. 27, 1984, Oct. 16, 1986, Oct. 2, 1988, Feb. 16, 1995

85. Buhler, "Alcon Story"; Halden Conner, "Alcon Story," Jan. 6, 2004; Earl Maxwell, MD, to R. D. Alexander, May 19, 1964, File: R. D. Alexander, AFP; *FWST*, Feb. 23, 1964.

86. *OG*, Dec. 1957, May 1958, May 1960; *FWST*, Feb. 20, 1955, Feb. 9, 1958, Feb. 11, Apr. 10, 29, Oct. 8, 1959, Jan. 7, Apr. 6, 22, May 20, June 5, 16, 26, 1960, Jan. 26, Feb. 5, Apr. 19, 22, Sept. 3, Nov. 3, 16, 1961, Apr. 19, May 3, July 9, Sept. 14, 19, Nov. 2, 1962, Apr. 17, 30, June 27, Dec. 13, 18, 25, 27, 1963, Jan. 15, Jul. 1, Aug. 30, 1964; Wanda Calvert, July 22, 2021, AOH; Conner, "Alcon Story."

87. Conner, "Alcon Story"; Conner family interview; EHS, "Alcon Story."

88. Conner family interview; Calvert, AOH; *FWST*, Sept. 14, Nov. 20, 24, 1965, Oct. 2, 1966, Oct. 8, Nov. 10, 1967, Mar. 20, Dec. 17, 1968; Wanda Calvert, Conner's administrative assistant, conversation, July 24, 2021, TOM, AM.

89. *AOG*, Oct. 1957, Dec. 1957, Jan. 1958, July 1958, Sept. 1958, Jan. 1961; Annual Report, 1967, 1970, ALC; Lubrano, "Alcon Story"; Dix, "Alcon Story"; Lorenzo-Daniell, "Alcon Story"; Glassford, "Alcon Story"; Alma Collins, "Alcon Story," Feb. 16, 2004; Barry Schlech, July 19, 2019, AOH; Schweitzer, AOH; *AWN*, Dec. 1981, Mar. 1984, Aug. 1987, July 1988, Apr., Aug. 1989, Apr. 1990, June, Aug. 1992, Dec. 1995, Jan. 1996, Apr. 1997.

90. Annual Reports, 1958–67.

Chapter 4

1. Robert Roehrs to author, email, Jan. 20, 2020, TOM, AM;

Roehrs, AOH

2. Scott, Heck, and Wilson, "Integral Role," 18–85; "Poison Control Pharmacist," Medical Health and Care (website); Grasela and Schentag, "Clinical Pharmacy-Oriented Drug Surveillance Network," 902–8.

3. Denny Alexander, "Alcon Story," Jan. 5, 2004; Halden Conner, "Alcon Story."

4. EHS, "Alcon Story"; Leone, "Alcon Story."

5. Minutes, Board of Directors, 1958–59, AFP; *FWST*, Sept. 19, 1958; Articles of Amendment to Articles of Incorporation of Alcon Laboratories Inc., June 13, 1958, Texas State Securities Board; Annual Report, 1959–69, ALC; *AOG*, May 15, 1958; Minutes, Board, 1958–59; Buhler, "Alcon Story"; *FWST*, Jan. 18, 1969; *Dallas Morning News*, Apr. 29, 1969.

6. Annual Report, 1971, ALC; ALFW, "325,000 Shares, Alcon Laboratories Inc., Common Stock, Prospectus," Mar. 31, 1971, Merrill Lynch, Pierce, Fenner & Smith, AFP; *FWST*, Mar. 31, Apr. 8, 1971.

7. ALFW, "325,000 Shares"; Denny Alexander, conversation with author, summer 2021, TOM, AM; *FWST*, June 5, 1971; *Spectrum*, Dec. 1971, Oct. 1986.

8. ALFW, "325,000 Shares"; Annual Report, 1966–71, ALC.

9. ALFW, "325,000 Shares"; *FWST*, June 5, Oct. 2, 4, 1971; *Spectrum*, Dec. 1971; "Alcon Hits the Big Board," *Fort Worth*, 28; ALFW, Listing Application to New York Stock Exchange, Aug. 4, 1971, AFP.

10. ALFW, "325,000 Shares"; *FWST*, Oct. 4, 1971.

11. *AWN*, Oct. 1987; Annual Report, 1969; EHS, "Alcon Story"; *FWST*, May 2, Nov. 14, 1968, Feb. 26, 28, 1969, Feb. 8, 2009.

12. Annual Report, 1968–72, ALC; Alexander and Conner, "Story of Alcon Laboratories"; *FWST*, Oct. 1, 22, 1969.

13. *Pasadena (CA) Independent Star-News*, Oct. 13, 1968; *Oakland Tribune*, June 5, 1970; *FWST*, Nov. 19, 1967, Sept. 16, 1969; *Venice (CA) Evening Vanguard*, Dec. 31, 1966; ALFW, "325,000 Shares"; ALFW, "239,615 Shares, Alcon Laboratories, Inc., Common Stock, Prospectus," Apr. 29, 1975, Merrill

Lynch, Pierce, Fenner & Smith, AFP; *FWST*, Aug. 8, Oct. 9, 1969, Mar. 4, 18, Sept. 9, 1971, Apr. 28, May 3, July 3, 1972, May 4, Dec. 17, 1974; *Dallas Morning News*, Aug. 8, 1969; *Memphis Commercial Appeal*, July 1, 1972; Annual Report, 1969–70, 1972–75, ALC; *AWN*, Dec. 1972, July 1973, Jan. 1974; *Alcon Today and Tomorrow*, 1986; *San Francisco Chronicle*, Oct. 9, 1969.

14. ALFW, "325,000 Shares"; ALFW, "239,615 Shares"; *FWST*, June 24, Oct. 9, 1969, Oct. 20, 1970, Mar.14, 1972 Nov. 9, 1973, Mar. 9, 1983; Annual Report, 1969–72, 1974–76, ALC; Alexander and Conner, "Story of Alcon Laboratories"; *Spectrum*, Dec. 1971; *FWST*, Nov. 17, 1971, Nov. 1973; *AWN*, Apr. 1987; *Spectrum*, Dec. 1971, Oct. 1974; *Binghamton (NY) Sunday Press*, May 30, 1971; *New York Sunday News*, Dec. 5, 1971; *San Francisco Chronicle*, Oct. 9, 1969; Stock analyst report, Apr. 30, 1976, F. Eberstadt & Co., AFP.

15. *AWN*, Jan., Aug. 1992, Apr. 1993, July 1995; *FWST*, Jan. 24, Mar. 21, 29, 1970, Feb. 27, Jun. 19, Sept. 28, 29, 1973; Annual Report, 1970–77, ALC; ALFW, "325,000 Shares"; *Jornal do Commercio* (Rio de Janeiro), June 25, 1970; *A Gazeta da Farmácia* (Rio de Janeiro), Dec. 1974, 16.

16. ALFW, "325,000 Shares"; ALFW, "239,615 Shares"; Annual Report, 1970–74; *FWST*, Mar. 19, May 8, 1970, June 1, 24, 1971, Oct. 25, Dec. 21, 1973.

17. Annual Report, 1969–70; *FWST*, Mar. 5, 2006, Sept. 28, 2007, Feb. 8, 2009, Oct. 13, Dec. 29, 2013; *New York Times*, July 21, 1996; *Honolulu Star Advertiser*, June 21, 2015.

18. Dilip Raval, "Alcon Story," Oct. 29, 2004; Dilip Raval, May 27, 2019, AOH; Annual Report, 1970; *San Francisco Chronicle*, July 14, 2013; "Howard M. Leibowitz," Boston University School of Medicine (website); Howard M. Leibowitz to author, email, Aug. 30, 2021, TOM, AM; *AWN*, Jan. 1995; Friedman, "In Memoriam: Stephen M. Podos," 189–90; Candia, "Remembering Steven M. Podos," 1262; *New York Times*, Oct. 12, 2009; Baldwin, McDonald, and Beasley, "Slit-Lamp Examination of Experimental Animal Eyes, II," 181–95. Henry A. Baldwin and Thomas O. McDonald were the two toxicologists.

19. Annual Report, 1966–70.

20. Baldwin, AOH; Axelrod, *Big Thoughts Are Free*; *Pasadena Independent Star-News*, Oct. 13, 1968; *Oakland Tribune*, June 5, 1970; *FWST*, Nov. 19, 1967, Sept. 16, 1969; *Venice Evening Vanguard*, Dec. 31, 1966. Ruby Zeller and the author, Thomas O. McDonald, performed the tests at Alcon.

21. Baldwin, AOH; Schlech, AOH; Raval, "Alcon Story"; Tom Mc-Donald, "Alcon Story," Oct. 28, 2004.

22. Raval, "Alcon Story"; Raval, AOH; Annual Report, 1963, 1969, 1971–72; Leone, "Alcon Story"; EHS, "Alcon Story"; *FWST*, Aug. 8, Oct. 9, 1969, Jan. 8, 1970, Oct. 14, 1970, Oct. 4, 1971; Jerry Rutherford, telephone conversation with author, Aug. 17, 2021, TOM, AM.

23. Leone, "Alcon Story"; EHS, "Alcon Story"; Shuler, "Executive Profile: George Leone," 22–30.

24. Leone, "Alcon Story"; EHS, "Alcon Story"; Raval, AOH; Shuler, "Executive Profile: George Leone," 22–30; Barry Schlech to author, email, Aug. 17, 2021, TOM, AM.

25. EHS, "Alcon Story"; Leone, "Alcon Story"; Raval, "Alcon Story"; Raval, AOH; Shuler, "Executive Profile: George Leone."

26. EHS, "Alcon Story"; Leone, "Alcon Story"; Raval, "Alcon Story"; Raval, AOH; Shuler, "Executive Profile: George Leone"; Baldwin, AOH

27. EHS, "Alcon Story"; Leone, "Alcon Story"; Raval, "Alcon Story"; Raval, AOH; Shuler, "Executive Profile: George Leone."

28. EHS, "Alcon Story"; Leone, "Alcon Story"; Raval, "Alcon Story"; Raval, AOH; Shuler, "Executive Profile: George Leone."

29. EHS, "Alcon Story"; Leone, "Alcon Story"; Raval, "Alcon Story"; Raval, AOH; Shuler, "Executive Profile: George Leone."

30. Dabrowska and Thaul, "How FDA Approves Drugs," Congressional Research Service; Gad, *Pharmaceutical Manufacturing Handbook*; *Handbook: Good Laboratory Practice*; *Handbook for Good Clinical Research Practice*.

31. *Spectrum*, Aug. 1972, July 1974; Kirschenbaum, *Track Changes*.

32. Luttrell, "My Journey," HLP; Annabelle Corboy, July 19, 2019, AOH; *AWN*, June 1987.

33. Corboy, AOH; Siegel, AOH; *Spectrum*, Oct. 1986.

34. Autian, "Development of Standards for Plastics," 1668–74; Turner, Lawrence, and Autian, "Subacute Toxicity Testing of Biomaterials," 39–58;

35. Harvey, "Ed Schollmaier Eyes New Horizons," 20–24; Shuler, "Executive Profile: George Leone"; EHS, "Alcon Story"; Leone, "Alcon Story"; *AWN*, Apr. 1997. This paragraph is also based on

the author's career observations and experiences at Alcon.

36. This paragraph is based on the author's career experiences at Alcon in collaboration with his R&D colleagues in preparing and executing several dozen project plans.

37. *Spectrum*, Feb. 1973, Aug. 1974, July 1998; Employee List, 1966, Sandy Howell, AM; Annual Report, 1967, 1969, 1971–77; *AWN*, June 1984, Oct. 1987, Apr. 1988, Aug. 1994, Apr. 1997; *FWST*, Mar. 20, 2005.

38. *Spectrum*, Aug. 1974, Dec. 1988; Mary Pencis, May 23, 2019, AOH.

39. EHS, "Alcon Story"; Leone, "Alcon Story"; Raval, "Alcon Story"; Raval, AOH; Fleming, "Alcon Story"; Leone, AOH; *Spectrum*, Nov. 1972, Dec. 1974.

40. "Medicines Act 1968," Legislation.gov.uk (website); *Spectrum*, July 1974, Feb., Nov. 1975; Luttrell, "My Journey," HLP; Aubrey Baker, Nov. 23, 2021, AOH.

41. *Spectrum*, Dec. 1972, June, Oct. 1974; Luttrell, "My Journey," HLP.

42. *Spectrum*, July 1973, Aug., Nov. 1977; Definitions of QC, QS, and QA, Howard Luttrell, Nov. 20, 2021, HLP; Luttrell, "Howard Luttrell Reviews Alcon History"; *Alcon Today and Tomorrow*, 1986.

43. *Spectrum*, July 1973, Aug., Nov. 1977.

44. Alcon Press Release, May 16, 1972, vol. 6, AHR; *Spectrum*, Apr. 1972.

45. *Spectrum*, July 1972, Mar. 1976.

46. *EyeLites*, May 19, 1969; Annual Report, 1969, 1971, 1973; Alcon Press Release, Oct. 1970, vol. 6, AHR; *Spectrum*, Feb. 1972, Feb. 1975.

47. Barley, AOH; John Feik, May 19, 2019, AOH.

48. *Spectrum*, Sept. 1974, Feb. 1975; Barley, AOH; Feik, AOH; Powell, "Alcon Story"; Henry Kologe, "Alcon Story," Oct. 29, 2004; EHS, "Alcon Story"; Taylor Schollmaier, Nov. 13, 2021, AOH.

49. *Spectrum*, Nov. 1973, Sept., Oct. 1974; Barley, AOH; Powell, "Alcon Story"; EHS, "Alcon Story"; *AWN*, Sept. 1981, Jan. 1995; Annual Report, 1973–75.

50. Rogers, "Everything You Need to Know," *Creative Mechanisms* (blog); "Wheaton Science Products," Company-Histories.com (website); "We Are a Custom Injection Molding and Tool Building Company," Imco, Inc. (website); plastic bottles, Milton Barley to author, email, July 6, 2021, TOM, AM; Aubrey Baker, AOH.

51. Milton Barley to author, email, Nov. 26, 2021, TOM, AM; Phillips and Kaye, "Sterilizing Action of Gaseous Ethylene Oxide, I," 270–79; "We Facilitate Standardization Solutions," ANSI (website); McDonald, "Alcon Story"; Carl W. Bruch, "Factors Determining Choice of Sterilization Procedure," 119–24; ethylene oxide, Schlech to author, email, Jan. 4, 2022, TOM, AM.

52. Mary K. Bruch, "Regulatory Review of Sterilization Control"; Glazer, *Special Occupational Hazard Review*, US Dept. of HEW, National Institute for Occupational Safety and Health, 5, 15, 23, 26, 31, 49; McDonald, Kasten, Hervey, Gregg, Borgmann, and Murchison, "Acute Ocular Toxicity," 153–64; FDA, Dept. of HEW, "Ethylene Oxide, Ethylene Chlorohydrin, and Ethylene Glycol," *Federal Register*, 27482; Howard Luttrell to author, email, Nov. 26, 2021, Howard Luttrell correspondence, TOM, AM.

53. Leonard Schlesinger, "A Chief Executive Looks at Change: Ed Schollmaier of Alcon Laboratories," Managing Organizational Effectiveness (MOE) Follow-up, HBS, May 1977, EHS, AM; *AWN*, June 1987, Apr. 1989; *Spectrum*, Apr. 1972; Aubrey Baker, AOH; LaDelle Brearly, July 17, 2019, AOH; Barley, AOH; Carter, "Alcon Story"; Senkowski, interview by Holyoak; Lanette Browder, Senkowski's administrative assistant, telephone conversation with author, July 18, 2019, TOM, AM; Annual Report, 1977.

54. Feik, AOH.

55. *EyeLites*, Dec. 15, 1970; year of hire for individuals was discovered by searching for their anniversary dates in *Alcon World News*, *Spectrum*, and *EyeLites*; Alcon Hall of Fame Inductees, AHR.

56. EHS, "Alcon Story," Feb.17, 2004; *FWST*, Aug. 12, 1982; *Cincinnati Enquirer*, Feb. 6, 1952, Jan. 2, 1961, Apr. 20, 1963; *EyeLites*, Feb. 19, 1971; *Spectrum*, Feb. 1972, June 1973.

57. Bill Rhue's recollections, TOM, AM; *EyeLites*, Dec. 15, 1970; *AOG*, Jan., Dec. 1960; *Spectrum*, Aug. 1972; Annual Report, 1972.

58. "Why Retinal Ganglion Cells Are Important," Glaucoma Research Foundation (website); Havener, *Ocular Pharmacology*, 127, 174, 375, 447–48, 450, 455, 458–62.

59. Havener, *Ocular Pharmacology*, 127, 174, 375, 447–48, 450, 455, 458–62; *Product Reference Guide*, 1974, Regulatory Affairs copy, AHR; *Los Angeles Times*, Mar. 1, 1972. In the 1970s Smith, Miller

and Patch was acquired by Cooper Laboratories.

60. *Product Reference Guide*, 1974; Haas and Merrill, "Effect of Methylcellulose," 21–24; Hecht and Bigelow, "Stabilized Aqueous Borate Complexes," US Patent, 2079; *EyeLites*, Feb., May 18, Aug. 13, 1967.

61. *Product Reference Guide*, 1974; *AOG*, Jan. 1, 1961; *EyeLites*, Feb. 1967.

62. Bill Hodges, product manager, Aug. 25, 2021, AOH; Joe Diamond, Aug. 23, 2021, market research, AOH; Len Schweitzer, product and marketing manager, AOH; Bill Rhue, marketing manager, Apr. 27, 2019, AOH; Roy Buchanan, product manager, AOH.

63. Annual Report, 1975–77; Stock analyst report, Apr. 30, 1976; Stock analyst report, Feb. 1974, Merrill Lynch, Pierce, Fenner & Smith, AFP; Stock analyst report, Feb. 17, 1977, Merrill Lynch, Pierce, Fenner & Smith, EHS, AM.

64. *Modesto (CA) Bee*, Feb. 21, 1986; *San Francisco Examiner*, Sept. 26, 1971, Aug. 26, 1974, July 9, 1987; *San Mateo (CA) Times*, Dec. 26, 1974; "Alza Corporation," Company-Histories (website); Lee, Shen, and Eberle, "Long-Acting Ocusert-Pilocarpine System," 43–46; Goldberg et al., "Efficacy and Patient Acceptance," 843–46; Schoenwald and Roehrs, "Sustained Release Ophthalmic Drug Dosage," US Patent, 267.

65. Chudler, "Neuroscience for Kids," University of Washington (website); Piascik, "Pharmacology of Adrenergic Receptors"; Bartlett et al., "Ocular Hypotensive Drugs," 139–74.

66. Charters, "Confessions of an Innovator"; Zimmerman and Kaufman's key publications were Zimmerman, Harbin, Pett, and Kaufman, "Timolol and Facility of Outflow," 623–24; Zimmerman and Kaufman, "Timolol: Dose Response and Duration of Action," (1977): 605–7; Zimmerman and Kaufman, "Timolol: A B-adrenergic Blocking Agent," 601–4. The premier US ophthalmic research organization in 1969 was the Association for Research in Ophthalmology (now the Association for Research in Vision and Ophthalmology). It met in Sarasota, Florida, in May 1969. The author presented a paper there, the first for an Alcon R&D scientist since 1960. Barklis and the author were the only Alcon attendees. Barklis met with Kaufman but the subject is unknown.

67. Bucci et al., "Local Administration of Propranolol," 51–60; Levy, "Myocardial and Local Anesthetic Actions," 250–57; Ruffat, *175 ans d'industrie pharmaceutique française*; Raval, AOH; *Spectrum*, May–June 1985; McDonald, "Alcon Story"; Louis DeSantis, Dec. 18, 2021, AOH; Raval, AOH.

68. Havener, *Ocular Pharmacology*, 278–79, 293–97; Stock analyst report, Feb. 17, 1977.

69. *AWN*, Oct. 1988, Feb. 1989; Annual Report, 1965, 1973, 1975; *EyeLites*, Dec. 1968; EHS, "Alcon Story"; Stock analyst report, Feb. 17, 1977.

70. EHS, "Alcon Story"; *AWN*, Oct. 1987; Mathea Reuter Allansmith, box 1, folder 80, and Jerome W. Bettman, box 3, folder 106, Biography/Organization History, Stanford University Biographical Files Collection (SC1136), Special Collections & University Archives, Stanford Libraries; Leibowitz and Kupferman, "Concurrent Corticosteroid-Antibiotic Therapy," 682–85; Harbin, "Recurrence of a Corneal Pseudomonas Infection," 670–74; "Certain Antibiotic-Steroid Combination Drugs," *Federal Register*, 13282.

71. *FWST*, Aug. 18, 1967; *Product Reference Guide*, 1974; Stock analyst report, Apr. 30, 1976; Baum and Bazara, "Evolution of Antibiotic Therapy," 659–72 (2000); *AWN*, Dec. 1981; Shuler, "Executive Profile: George Leone"; Harvey, "Ed Schollmaier Eyes New Horizons"; *Spectrum*, May–Aug. 2004; Yolton and Haesaert, "Anti-Infective Drugs," 175–96, 217–19.

72. Gerald "Jerry" Cagle, "Alcon Story," Apr. 24, 26, 2006; McDonald, "Alcon Story"; Schlech, AOH; Raval, AOH; EHS, "Alcon Story."

73. *Product Reference Guide*, 1974; Stock analyst report, Feb. 17, 1977; *EyeLites*, Oct. 1973; *AWN*, July 1983; National Center for Biotechnology Information, "Naphazoline Hydrochloride," "Tetrahydrozoline," and "Antazoline," PubChem (website).

74. Boskabady et al., "Pharmacological Effects of *Rosa Damascena*," 295–307; Derdak and Pederson, "Schieffelin & Somerset and Co.," 323–25; "Estivin, Sterile Ophthalmalic [*sic*] Solution," National Museum of American History (website); *Product Reference Guide*, 1974; Annual Report, 1972–73, 1975; *Spectrum*, May–Aug. 2004; ALFW, "239,615 Shares"; Siegel, AOH; Schlech, AOH; Rick Rheiner, Oct. 12, 2019, AOH; Rick Johnson, Aug. 9, 2019, AOH; Bill Rhue, telephone conversation, July 22, 2019, TOM, AM.

75. *EyeLites*, Jan. 1967, Sept. 22, 1967, Dec. 15, 1970; Howard Fleischer, "Dear Doctor" letter, Sept. 1968, Promotional Material, vol. 9, AHR.

76. *AWN*, Nov. 1984, July 1996, Aug. 1998; Annual Report, 1974;

EyeLites, Dec. 15, 1970, Apr. 19, 1971; *Spectrum*, Jan. 1974; William M. Buchanan, "Dear Doctor," letter, Sept. 26, 1973, Promotional Material, vol. 9, AHR; Stock analyst report, Feb. 17, 1977; Short, Keates, Donovan, Wyman, and Murdick, "Ocular Penetration Studies, I," 689–92.

77. *Product Reference Guide*, 1974; *Physician's Desk Reference for Ophthalmology*; Sendrowski et al., "Anti-inflammatory Drugs," 221–44 (note: the endnotes on p. 242 list the major ophthalmic steroid researchers); McDonald, "Alcon Story"; DeSantis, AOH; Roehrs to author, email, Jan. 20, 2020.

78. Portello and Krumholz, "Dilation of the Pupil," 329–42; Wickum and Amos, "Cycloplegic Refraction," 343–47; *Product Reference Guide*, 1974; Stock analyst report, Apr. 30, 1976; Roehrs to author, email, Jan. 20, 2020; *EyeLites*, Feb. 19, 1971.

79. *Product Reference Guide*, 1974; Stock analyst report, Apr. 30, 1976; McDonald, "Alcon Story"; Reed, "Diseases of the Lacrimal System," 426, 429; *AWN*, Apr. 1989; Annual Report, 1971.

80. Holly and Lemp, "Tear Physiology and Dry Eyes," 69–87; Reed, "Diseases of the Lacrimal System," 414–35; *Spectrum*, June, Nov. 1977; Annual Report, 1975–77; Stock analyst report, Feb. 17, 1977; Stock analyst report, Apr. 30, 1976; Raval, AOH; Buchanan, AOH; Lee Wright, Sept. 2, 2019, AOH; Hecht and Shively, "Ophthalmic Solution," US Patent, 315; "Ophthalmic Drug Products," *Federal Register*, 7075–93.

81. Baldwin, AOH; Rhue, telephone conversation, July 22, 2019; *Product Reference Guide*, 1974; *EyeLites*, Dec. 15, 1970; *Spectrum*, Dec. 1971; Yannuzzi, *Fluorescein Ophthalmoscopy and Photography*; Yannuzzi, "Interpretation of Fluorescein Angiography."

82. McMahon and Zadnik, "Twenty-Five Years of Contact Lenses," 730–40; Barr and Bailey, "History and Development of Contact Lenses," 1–8; "Marking a Milestone in Contact Lenses."

83. McMahon and Zadnik, "Twenty-Five Years of Contact Lenses"; Barr and Bailey, "History and Development of Contact Lenses," 1–8; Moreddu, Vigolo, and Yetisen, "Contact Lens Technology."

84. Annual Report, 1969–76; *EyeLites*, Jan. 26, 1970, Oct. 1973; *Spectrum*, Apr. 1972, Jan. 1974; Alcon Care Booklet, Product Guide, 1974, AHR; Schollmaier, Dewar, and Hecht, "Means for Cleaning Contact Lenses," US Patent, 1381; *FWST*, May 21, 1969; Stock analyst report, Feb. 17, 1977; Stock analyst report, Apr. 30, 1976.

85. *Spectrum*, Nov. 1977; McMahon and Zadnik, "Twenty-Five Years of Contact Lenses"; Moreddu, Vigolo, and Yetisen, "Contact Lens Technology"; Schifrin and Rich, *Contact Lens Industry*, US Congress, Office of Technology Assessment, 1–61.

86. Moreddu, Vigolo, and Yetisen, "Contact Lens Technology"; Krachmer and Purcell, "Bacterial Corneal Ulcers," 57–61; Cooper and Constable, "Infective Keratitis," 250–54; Moore et al., "*Acanthamoeba* Keratitis," 396–403.

87. Annual Report, 1968–75; Rutherford, AOH; Bob Grantham, telephone conversation, Aug. 20, 2021, TOM, AM; EHS, "Alcon Story"; TCU course notes, spring 2003, EHS Papers, in possession of Taylor Schollmaier, Boulder, CO; *Spectrum*, Feb. 1972.

88. *Spectrum*, Sept. 1974; Annual Report, 1971; Bob Grantham, Aug. 1, 2019, AOH; Grantham, telephone conversation, Aug. 20, 2021; *Product Reference Guide*, 1974.

89. Raval, AOH; Grantham, AOH; Grantham, telephone conversation, Aug. 20, 2021; Amoils, "Joule Thomson Cryoprobe," 201–7; Annual Report, 1971; *Product Reference Guide*, 1974; *Spectrum*, July 1972; ALFW, "239,615 Shares"; "Surgical Related Events," Jack Marshall to Roy Buchanan, July 13, 1989, memo, AHR; *Surgical Products Division History, 1973 to 1984*, book 1 (scrapbook), AHR; Olympus MTX surgical microscope, photograph, Misc. Promotional Material, vol. 9, AHR; Shuler, "Executive Profile: George Leone"; Harvey, "Ed Schollmaier Eyes New Horizons."

90. *Product Reference Guide*, 1974; Edelhauser et al., "Effect of Thiol-Oxidation of Glutathione with Diamide," 567–78; McCarey, Edelhauser, and Van Horn, "Functional and Structural Changes," 410–17; Henry F. Edelhauser, Alcon Hall of Fame Inductees, AHR; McDonald et al., "Intraocular Administration of Carbomylcholine Chloride," 232–39; "Surgical Related Events," Marshall to Buchanan, July 13, 1989, AHR; *Surgical Products Division History, 1973 to 1984*, book 1.

91. *FWST*, Nov. 9, 1973; "Our Family History," Mager and Gougelman (website); "History and Evolution of Prosthetic Eyes," Industries for the Blind and Visually Impaired (website); *AWN*, Apr., Aug., Oct. 1987; *Spectrum*, Jan., Oct. 1974; *Product Reference Guide*, 1974; Grantham, AOH; Grantham, telephone conversation, Aug. 20, 2021.

92. *AWN*, July 1988, July 1995; Annual Report, 1972–75; EHS, "Alcon Story."

93. Annual Report, 1972–77; *Spectrum*, Jan. 1972, July, Nov. 1973, Apr. 1974, Nov. 1975, Aug. 1977; *AWN*, Jan. 1986; *Alcon Today*

and Tomorrow, 1986; Harvey, "Ed Schollmaier Eyes New Horizons"; Keith Lane, Alcon Hall of Fame Inductees, AHR.

94. *Spectrum*, Feb. 1972, Sept., Oct., Nov. 1974; Annual Report, 1974–77; Stock analyst report, Feb. 17, 1977; Stock analyst report, Aug. 12, 1975, Rotan Mosele, AFP; Stock analyst report, Aug. 5, 1977, Rauscher Pierce Research, AFP; *FWST*, Oct. 27, 1976.

95. Annual Report, 1970–77; Luttrell, "My Journey," HLP; EHS, "Alcon Story"; *Spectrum*, Nov. 1974; Stock analyst report, Feb. 17, 1977; Stock analyst report, Apr. 30, 1976.

96. EHS, "Alcon Story"; Annual Report, 1971–77; *AWN*, Dec. 1982; Herbert Kleiman, Alcon Hall of Fame Inductees, AHR; Stock analyst report, Feb. 17, 1977; *Spectrum*, Oct., Nov. 1974; Rebecca G. "Becky" Walker Papers, AM.

97. "Brief Overview," FMC (website); Annual Report, 1970–72; *FWST*, Oct. 9, 1969, Dec. 2, 1991; *San Francisco Examiner*, Oct. 9, 1969; *Spectrum*, Dec. 1971, Dec. 1972, Apr. 1974, June 1976; John H. Tenery, Charles A. Robb, Tom McDonald, Alcon Hall of Fame Inductees, AHR.

98. *Spectrum*, June, Oct. 1976, Aug., Nov. 1977; Leone, "Alcon Story"; Raval, "Alcon Story"; Annual Report, 1972, 1974, 1976; Schweitzer, AOH; *Texas Jewish Post*, Dec. 11, 1980; *FWST*, May 22, 1974, Apr. 27, 1976.

99. *Lafayette (IN) Journal & Courier*, Dec. 29, 1962, Jan. 26, 1971, Jan. 25, 1972, Jan. 25, 1977, July 7, 1978, Feb. 26, 1979; *FWST*, Mar. 9, 1983.

100. Grantham, telephone conversation, Aug. 20, 2021; *FWST*, Aug. 19, 1976, Apr. 24, 1977; Schlesinger, "Chief Executive Looks at Change"; Annual Report, 1977.

101. Annual Report, 1970–71, 1976–77; *Spectrum*, Sept. 1974; Pencis, AOH.

102. *AWN*, Jan. 1986, Aug. 1987, Mar. 1992, Apr. 1993, July 1995, Jan. 1992, Nov. 1999; Annual Report, 1968–77; *Spectrum*, Nov. 1977; *Van Nuys (CA) Valley News*, Jan. 5, 1977.

103. Annual Report, 1968–77; *AWN*, Jan. 1986, Sept. 1989; Dionisio Garcia, Leon de Chateauvieux, Carlos de Socio, Carlos Taborda, Alcon Hall of Fame Inductees, AHR.

104. Annual Report, 1971–72; Crewe, "Alcon Story"; Buhler, "Alcon Story."

105. Annual Report, 1973–77; Buhler, "Alcon Story"; Tim Sear, "Alcon Story," Mar. 17, 2004; *FWST*, Feb. 27, 1973; *AWN*, Oct. 1983, Feb. 1990, Apr. 1993, June 1996, Dec. 1997; *Alcon Today and Tomorrow*, 1986.

106. Annual Report, 1971–77; Buhler, "Alcon Story"; Sear, "Alcon Story"; *AWN*, Dec. 1981, Apr. 1993, Dec. 1997, Mar. 1999; *Alcon Today and Tomorrow*, 1986.

107. Sear, "Alcon Story"; *FWST*, Aug. 19. 1976.

108. *FWST*, Nov. 21, 27, 28, 1972, June 13, 1973, Aug. 15, Dec. 17, 1974, Aug. 19, 1976, Oct. 6, 2015, Mar. 3, 2020; Annual Report, 1972–77; *AWN*, Sept. 1981, July 1983, June 1987, Sept. 1989; Henry P. Kologe, William M. Starz, Alcon Hall of Fame Inductees, AHR; *Spectrum*, Feb. 1972, Nov. 1973, Aug. 1974, Nov. 1975, Mar. 1976; *Brattleboro (VT) Reformer*, July 30, 1945.

109. *FWST*, Sept. 26, 1972, Sept. 18, 1973; *Spectrum*, Nov. 1972, Nov. 1973, Oct. 1974, Nov. 1975; Buchanan, AM.

110. *Spectrum*, June 1972; *FWST*, May 17, 1972.

111. Luttrell, "My Journey," HLP; Kay Harris and Gregg Harris, Aug. 16, 2019, AOH; Siegel, AOH; Schlech, AOH; Baldwin, AOH; Rebecca G. "Becky" Walker, July 25, 2019, AOH; Buchanan, AOH; Howell and Clynch, AOH; Grantham, AOH; Taylor Schollmaier, AOH; *Spectrum*, Dec. 1972, Oct. 1974.

112. Annual Report, 1968–77.

113. Annual Report, 1968–77; *New York Times*, Jan. 7, 2010; *FWST*, Aug. 16, 1972, Nov. 5, 1978.

114. Halden Conner, "Alcon Story"; Denny Alexander, "Alcon Story"; EHS, "Alcon Story"; Raval, "Alcon Story"; Raval, AOH; Howell and Clynch, AOH; Sandy Howell, "Alcon Story," Mar. 19, 2004; Schlesinger, "Chief Executive Looks at Change"; Calvert, AOH.

115. ALFW, "239,615 Shares"; Howell, "Alcon Story"; EHS, "Alcon Story"; Leone, "Alcon Story."

116. Ruffat, *175 ans d'industrie pharmaceutique française*; DeSantis, AOH; Raval, AOH; *Helsingin Sanomat* (Helsinki), May 8, 1998; "Veikko Reinikainen," Wikipedia (website); *New York Times*, Jan. 22, May 28, 1975; Heer, *Nestlé: 125 Years*, 263–373; *News Summary*, Federal Trade Commission, Jan. 24, 1975, Apr. 27, 1979; José Daniel, Dec. 9, 2021, AOH; Pierre Vogel, April 22, 2021, AOH; EHS, "Alcon Story."

117. EHS, "Alcon Story"; "Projet d'Acquisition Pharmaceutique aux USA," Dr. Bartolini, Directeur Recherche de Synthélabo, Alcon Files, 100000-A, Nestlé Historical Archives; "Alcon—Visite á Fort Worth," Sept. 21, 1977, M. A. Fürer (MF), Alcon Files, 100000-A, Nestlé Historical Archives; "Alcon—Interet de l'acquisition," Oct. 3, 1977, MF, Alcon Files, 100000-A, Nestlé Historical Archives; Arthur Fürer, Carl Angst, and José Daniel, Biographies, Nestlé Historical Archives; *FWST*, Oct. 18, Nov. 2, Dec. 11, 1977; Nestlé Annual Report, 1978, Nestlé Historical Archives; Arthur Fürer, "Ed Schollmaier, In Commemoration of Your Outstanding Leadership of Alcon Laboratories," June 9, 1998, EHS Papers, in possession of Taylor Schollmaier, Boulder, CO.

118. Alexander and Conner, "Story of Alcon Laboratories"; *Spectrum*, Nov. 1977.

Chapter 5

1. EHS, "Alcon Story"; Taylor Schollmaier, AOH.

2. Carl Angst, Biography, Nestlé Historical Archives; Arthur Fürer, "Ed Schollmaier, In Commemoration of Your Outstanding Leadership of Alcon Laboratories," June 9, 1998, EHS Papers, in possession of Taylor Schollmaier, Boulder, CO; EHS, "Alcon Story."

3. Schwarz, *Nestlé*, 16–24; Heer, *Nestlé*, see chaps. 1–8

4. Schwarz, *Nestlé*, 24–34; Sear, "Alcon Story"; Vogel, AOH; EHS, "Alcon Story"; Leone, "Alcon Story"; Carl Angst, José Daniel, Arthur Fürer, Biographies, Nestlé Historical Archives. The author had firsthand experience in observing how a Nestlé SBU operated. When he retired in 2004, he served as a consultant for five years to the R&D of the Nestlé Nutrition SBU.

5. Schweitzer, AOH; Cagle, "Alcon Story"; Wright, AOH; Nelson, AOH; Sear, "Alcon Story"; Vogel, AOH; Schwarz, *Nestlé*, 24–29; Maucher, *Leadership in Action*, ix–xii. Maucher's management beliefs are found throughout his book, and Schollmaier's are found in his "Alcon Story" and in dozens of interviews with people who worked at Alcon.

6. EHS, "Alcon Story"; Cagle, "Alcon Story"; Sear, "Alcon Story"; Baldwin, AOH; Schlech, AOH; Raval, "Alcon Story"; *AWN*, Feb. 1989; Vogel, AOH; Rutherford, AOH.

7. *Washington Evening Star*, Feb. 19, 1956, Feb. 10, 1955, May 29, 1981, Feb. 17, 1984; *Richmond Times-Dispatch*, Feb. 11, 1981; *Danville (VA) Bee*, Mar. 24, 1955; *Lexington Herald-Sun*, Sept. 29, 1963; *Indianapolis News*, May 8, 1978; *Detroit Free Press*, Dec. 12, 1975; *Miami News*, Dec. 2, 1979; *FWST*, May 17, Aug. 10, 1979; *Dallas Morning News*, Aug. 10, 1979; *Greensboro (NC) Record*, June 10, 1981; Burton, Parsons & Co. v. Parsons, 146 F. Supp. 114 (D.D.C. 1956) (Nov. 21, 1956), *Justia*, https://law.justia.com/cases/federal/district-courts/FSupp/146/114/2183141/.

8. *FWST*, Apr. 28, May 22, July 7, 28, 1984; *Dallas Morning News*, July 28, 1984; *San Francisco Chronicle*, Apr. 14, May 18, 1976, Jan. 28, 1979, Mar. 8, June 2, Nov. 26, 1983, May 18, June 1, 29, Dec. 13, 1984; *Seattle Times*, July 18, 1979, Feb. 2, 1983; *San Diego Union*, Feb. 18, 1977; *Newark Star-Ledger*, Jan. 25, 1976, Nov. 30, 1978, Jan. 28, 1979; *Richmond Times-Dispatch*, Oct. 17, 1974, May 13, 1977; *Cambridge (OH) Daily Jeffersonian*, Dec. 9, 1982; *San Antonio Light*, June 14, 1979; *Quincy (MA) Patriot Ledger*, Apr. 5, 1984; *Las Vegas Review-Journal*, Oct. 22, 1981; *Baton Rouge State Times Advocate*, Oct. 17, 1974; *Milwaukee Sentinel*, June 12, 1984; *Beaumont (TX) Journal*, Jan. 13, 1978; *Racine (WI) Journal Times*, July 30, 1984; *Miami News*, Dec. 3, 1979; *Corpus Christi (TX) Caller-Times*, Jan. 1, 1980; *San Bernardino County Sun* (CA), Mar. 29, 1980; *Wall Street Journal*, Dec. 7, 1979; *Los Angeles Times*, July 27, 1989; EHS, "Alcon Story"; Robert Stevens, "Alcon Story," Mar. 19, 2004; *Physician's Desk Reference for Ophthalmology*, 11th ed., 52–156.

9. *AWN*, Dec. 1982, Feb. 1989.

10. Harvey, "Ed Schollmaier Eyes New Horizons," 20–24; *Spectrum*, Dec. 1988; Robert Montgomery, May 18, 2021, AOH.

11. Shuler, "Executive Profile: George Leone," 22–30; Leibowitz, "Alcon Research Institute,"1039–40.

12. *AWN*, Feb. 1989; Walker, AOH; Roehrs, AOH; Pencis, AOH.

13. Cagle, "Alcon Story"; Walker, AOH; Roehrs, AOH; Pencis, AOH; *AWN*, June 1984, Sept.–Oct. 2000; *Spectrum*, Sept. 1985, Dec. 1988.

14. *AWN*, Dec. 1981; *Alcon Today and Tomorrow*, 1986; *AWN*, Feb. 1989; *Update 1987: Alcon Today and Tomorrow*, 1986.

15. *Spectrum*, June, Nov. 1977; Annual Report, 1977, ALC; Tran Trong, Mar. 8, 2022, AOH.

16. *AWN*, Sept. 1981, Mar. 1986, Feb. 1989; *Update 1987: Alcon Today and Tomorrow*, 1986; *Dallas Morning News*, Sept. 26, 1982; *Alcon Today and Tomorrow*, 1990; *Spectrum*, Nov. 1986; *FWST*, July 17, 1979, Sept. 18, 1982, July 27, 1984; Trong, AOH.

17. *AWN*, Sept. 1984, Mar. 1986, Feb., 1989; *Update 1987: Alcon To-*

day and Tomorrow, 1986; *Alcon Today and Tomorrow*, 1990; Robert D. Alexander Administration Center Dedication (brochure), ALC; *FWST*, July 27, 1984; Trong, AOH; *Scope*, Dec. 1984.

18. *AWN*, Aug. 1989; Elaine Whitbeck and Kurt Grimm, Jan. 12, 2022, AOH; Trong, AOH.

19. *AWN*, July 1983, Feb. 1989; *FWST*, May 24, 1983; Trong, AOH.

20. Barley, AOH; *AWN*, Mar., July 1986, Apr. 1988, Feb. 1989; *Spectrum*, Aug. 1977; *Update 1987: Alcon Today and Tomorrow*, 1986, ALC; Luttrell, "My Journey," HLP; Howard Luttrell to author, telephone conversation, Jan. 29, 2022, TOM, AM; Coben, "Modern Suppository Manufacturing," 523–46; Coben and Lordi, "Physical Stability of Semisynthetic Suppository Bases," 955–60.

21. *Update 1987: Alcon Today and Tomorrow*, 1986; *AWN*, Oct. 1988.

22. *AWN*, Sept. 1981.

23. Luttrell, "My Journey," HLP; Feik, AOH; Luttrell to author, telephone conversation, Jan. 29, 2022.

24. Luttrell, "My Journey," HLP; Howard Luttrell to author, telephone conversations, Jan. 29, 30, 2022; Barley, AOH; Alcon Hall of Fame Inductees, AHR; *AWN*, July, Oct. 1983, Sept. 1985, Dec. 1988.

25. *AWN*, Nov. 1984.

26. *AWN*, Dec. 1981, Apr. 1988.

27. *AWN*, Sept. 1984, Sept. 1985, May 1986, Apr. 1989; *Alcon Today and Tomorrow*, 1986; *Update 1987: Alcon Today and Tomorrow*, 1986; Francois Vaucheret, "Alcon Story," Oct. 23, 2004; Giuseppe Luigi LaMacchia, "Alcon Story," Oct. 24, 2004; Giuseppe Luigi LaMacchia, Apr. 16, 2021, AOH; Jacques Van Damme, Apr. 20, 2021, AOH; Giorgio Vescovo to author, emails, Mar. 27, Apr. 3, May 25, 2021, Feb. 1, 2022, TOM, AM; Spiegel, "Alcon," 29–33.

28. *AWN*, June 1984, Apr. 1987; *Update 1987: Alcon Today and Tomorrow*.

29. *AWN*, Feb., Apr. 1987; *Alcon Today and Tomorrow*, 1986; *Update 1987: Alcon Today and Tomorrow*, 1986.

30. *AWN*, Oct. 1983, Sept. 1985; *Spectrum*, June 1974; Luttrell, "My Journey," HLP; Fleming, "Alcon Story."

31. Luttrell, "My Journey," HLP; "Dr. Howard Luttrell Reviews Alcon History," *Alcon QA International*, Sept.–Oct. 1995, HLP; Estes and Luttrell, "Approach to Process Validation," 74–84; *Alcon Today and Tomorrow*, 1986; Fleming, "Alcon Story."

32. Luttrell, "My Journey," HLP; Luttrell, "Dr. Howard Luttrell Reviews Alcon History"; Fleming, "Alcon Story."

33. Luttrell, "My Journey," HLP; Luttrell, "Dr. Howard Luttrell Reviews Alcon History"; Siegel, AOH; Ed Schollmaier to Howard Luttrell, handwritten note, Jan. 21, 1997, HLP; Dick Sisson to Howard Luttrell, handwritten note, Jan. 21, 1997, HLP.

34. EHS, presentations to Nestlé management, AHR; William "Roy" Buchanan, "Alcon History, Year by Year," William "Roy" Buchanan, AM; "Alcon Sales Soar," EHS Records, AHR.

35. *Spectrum*, Aug. 1985; *Alcon Today and Tomorrow*, 1986.

36. *AWN*, Apr. 1988; EHS, presentations to Nestlé management; Buchanan, "Alcon History, Year by Year," Buchanan, AM; "WMA Declaration of Helsinki–Ethical Principles for Medical Research Involving Human Subjects," World Medical Association (website). Adrienne Johnston and Glenn Riddle formed the nucleus of R&D's quality audit unit.

37. March et al., "Duration of Effect of Pilocarpine Gel," 1270–71; Havener, *Havener's Ocular Pharmacology*, 6th ed., 123; "Products with Approved NDAs and AADA/ANDAs (US)," Rebecca G. "Becky" Walker, AM; *AWN*, Apr. 1985. The author was one of four Alcon R&D scientists at this spring 1979 FDA meeting.

38. Roehrs, AOH; Pencis, AOH; Havener, *Havener's Ocular Pharmacology*, 6th ed., 314, 319–20; "Products with Approved NDAs and AADA/ANDAs (US)," Walker, AM.

39. Cagle, "Alcon Story"; *Houston Chronicle*, Jan.19, 2022; Roehrs, AOH.

40. "Products with Approved NDAs and AADA/ANDAs (US)," Walker, AM; Cagle et al., "Topical Tobramycin and Gentamicin Sulfate," 523–34; Leibowitz et al., "Tobramycin in External Eye Disease," 259–66; Cagle, "Alcon Story"; Roehrs, AOH.

41. Kline et al., "Effect of BSS Plus on the Corneal Endothelium," 243–47; Edelhauser, "Balance between Corneal Transparency and Edema," 1755–67; "Products with Approved NDAs and AADA/ANDAs (US)," Walker, AM; Roehrs, AOH; Pencis, AOH.

42. Roehrs, AOH; McDonald, "Alcon Story." The clinical glaucoma unit in Alcon R&D included Margaret Drake, Richard Ward, Larry Bruce, PhD, and Tom McDonald, PhD.

43. Hernandez et al., "Cardiovascular Effects of Topical Glaucoma Therapies," 99–106; Berry, Van Buskirk, and Shields, "Betaxolol and Timolol," 42–45; Ofner and T. J. Smith, "Betaxolol in Chronic Obstructive Pulmonary Disease," 171–76; Atkins, Pugh, and Timewell, "Cardiovascular Effects of Topical Beta-Blockers," 173–75; Dunn et al., "Timolol-Induced Bronchospasm," 20A; Schoene et al., "Effects of Topical Betaxolol, Timolol, and Placebo," 86–92; Allen, "Betaxolol in the Treatment of Glaucoma, 142; "Guide to Drug Safety Terms at FDA," Consumer Health Information, FDA (website); Timoptic package insert, *Physician's Desk Reference for Ophthalmology*, 14th ed., 127; Betoptic package insert, *Physician's Desk Reference for Ophthalmology*, 26th ed., 206–9; Jani et al., "Ion Exchange Resins for Ophthalmic Delivery," 57–67.

44. "Products with Approved NDAs and AADA/ANDANDAs (US)," Walker, AM; *AWN*, July 1983.

45. *Baton Rouge State Times Advocate*, Dec. 9, 1986; Pitts and Krachmer, "Evaluation of Soft Contact Lens Disinfection," 470–72; Lippman, Gleason, and White, "Contact Lens and Solution Regulation"; Sariri, "Protein Interaction with Hydrogel Contact Lenses," 1–19; Schifrin with Rich, *Contact Lens Industry*, 1–6, 16–18, 31–33, 57–58, 60–61; McMahon and Zadnik, "Twenty-Five Years of Contact Lenses," 730–40; *AWN*, Dec. 1981, Sept. 1996; "Alcon Focusing on Its Ophthalmic Drug Business with Sale," *Pink Sheet*, Apr. 21, 1986; *Scope*, Dec. 1984.

46. Smick, "Evolution of Dual Disinfection; *AWN*, July 1983, Dec. 1990; *Spectrum*, Dec. 1985, Jan. 1987; Stein, Stark, and Randeri, "Comparison of Chemical and Thermal Disinfectant Regimens," 570–78; Product Listing, Nov. 17, 1999, Rebecca G. "Becky" Walker, AM. Randeri's team included Raj Bhatia, PhD, Ronald Quintana, PhD, Jerry Stein, PhD, Dana Sager, MS, and Masood Chowhan, PhD, and from Schlech's microbiology unit, Ruth Ann Rosenthal, MS, and Ronald L. Schlitzer, PhD.

47. Product Listing, Nov. 17, 1999, Walker, AM; *AWN*, July 1983, Mar. 1984, Aug. 1989; *Spectrum*, July–Aug., Sept., Nov. 1985, Jan.–Apr. 2004; *Eye on Tomorrow*, 1984; Sue Faro and Janet Campbell, July 23, 2019, AOH; Jerry Davidson, Dave Sattler, and David Sakamoto, Aug. 5, 2019, AOH; James Arno, June 28, 2019, AOH.

48. Krystel-Whittemore, Dileepan, and Wood, "Mast Cell"; Aoki and DeSantis, "Use of Lodoxamide to Treat Ophthalmic Allergic Conditions," US Patent, 1083; "Alcon/Genzyme Agreement," *Pink Sheet*, Apr. 21, 1986; Scholtz, "History of Ophthalmic Viscosurgical Devices"; Stark et al., "Reduction of Pupillary Constriction," 364–66; *Spectrum*, Spring 1991, May–Aug. 2004; Annita Verstap-

49. "Products with Approved NDAs and AADA/ANDAs (US)," Walker, AM; Jampel et al., "Apraclonidine," 1069–73; Lewis, Phillips, and Sassani, "Topical Therapies for Glaucoma,"1871–79; DeSantis, AOH; *AWN*, June 1988, Feb. 1989; *Update 1987: Alcon Today and Tomorrow*, 1986; *Spectrum*, July 1988.

50. *Spectrum*, July–Aug., Oct., Dec. 1985, May, June, July, Aug.–Sept., Nov. 1986, Feb.–Mar., June 1987, July 1988, Spring 1994; *AWN*, July 1986, Dec. 1987, Dec. 1988, Feb., Dec. 1989, Dec. 1990, Oct. 1991; Lightman, "Does Aldose Reductase Have a Role?" 7: 238–41; Kador, Kinoshita, and Sharpless, "Aldose Reductase Inhibitors," 841–49; Cagle, "Alcon Story."

51. Gregg Brown, "History of Alcon's Intellectual Property Operations, 1983–1987," TOM, AM; Arno, AOH; *AWN*, Nov. 1985, June 1988, Mar. 1996; *Alcon Today and Tomorrow*, 1986; *Alcon Today and Tomorrow*, 1990, ALC; *Eye on Tomorrow*, 1984; *Spectrum*, Nov. 1985, May, July 1996.

52. Corboy, AOH; Baldwin, AOH; Alcon Laboratories: Information Technology Group, HBS Retired Case Collection, box 186, folder 013, Baker Library Special Collections, Harvard Business School; Bob Brobst, Apr. 15, 2022, AOH.

53. *Spectrum*, July 1986, July 1987, Sept. 2002; *AWN*, July 1986, Aug. 1987; "Alcon R&D Technical Excellence Awards, BAS, AM. The 1985 awardees were Hans Moll, Bill Howe, Rajni Jani, Brenda Griffin, Mark DuPriest, Richard Dobbs; in 1986, Tai-Lee Ke, Louis DeSantis, Marjorie Lou, Larry Bruce; and in 1987, Michael Chandler, Betty Fortenberry House.

54. ARI Research Grant Recipients, Alcon Research Institute (website); Leibowitz, "Alcon Research Institute," 1039–40; Shuler, "Executive Profile: George Leone," 22–30; Leone, "Alcon Story"; *Spectrum*, Mar., 1986, Feb.–Mar. 1987, Sept.–Dec. 2004, 2006; *AWN*, June 1968, 1984, 1993, Oct. 1988, July 1990

55. *AWN*, Oct. 1997.

56. *Because All Skin Can Be Sensitive*, Allercreme brochure, AHR; *AWN*, Sept. 1981, 1982, Dec. 1982, July 1983; *Spectrum*, Oct. 1976; *Arkansas Gazette*, Oct. 29, 1978; *Alcon Today and Tomorrow*, 1986; Feik, AOH.

57. Steve Clark, July 22, 2019, AOH; *AWN*, Oct. 1983, Jan. 1986; Howell and Clynch, AOH.

58. *AWN*, Jan. 1986, 1992, July 1988, Feb. 1989, Feb. 1991; *Alcon*

pen to author, email, Apr. 12, 2022, TOM, AM.

Today and Tomorrow, 1986; *Update 1987: Alcon Today and Tomorrow*, 1986.

59. *AWN*, Aug. 1987, Mar. 1994; *Alcon Today and Tomorrow*, 1986; John Spruill, Alcon Hall of Fame Inductees, AHR; *Bryan Street Journal*, 1980, AHR; *Surgical Journal*, 1982; Kay Miles Spruill, Nov. 16, 2019, AOH. The American Academy of Ophthalmology and Otolaryngology divided in 1979, leaving the American Academy of Ophthalmology as the organization concerned with eye care.

60. A scholarly discussion of cataract surgery is found in Buratto and Packard, *History and Evolution of Modern Cataract Surgery*. One source for the layperson is Behrens, *Cataract Surgery*, Johns Hopkins Medicine (website).

61. Kelman, "Genesis of Phacoemulsification"; Kock, "Evolution of Phacoemulsification," 51–74, and Buratto, "History and Evolution of Nuclear Expression and Cortex Aspiration," 75–92; "Products with Approved NDAs and AADA/ANDAs (US)," Walker, AM; "NDAs, PMAs and 510(k)s for Alcon Laboratories, Inc. and Subsidiaries," Rebecca G. "Becky" Walker, AM; *Surgical Journal*, July 23, 1982, Feb. 18, Apr. 22, May 20, June 17, Oct. 21, Nov. 18, Dec. 16, 1983; *AWN*, July, Oct. 1983, Mar. 1984, Feb, 1991, Dec. 1993; *Alcon Today and Tomorrow*, 1986, 1990; *Eye on Tomorrow*, 1984.

62. Giorgio Vescovo to author, email, Feb. 1, 2022. One such meeting occurred at Nestlé in 1982, where Vescovo organized the meeting site and was invited by Schollmaier to attend. He heard the discourse between Schollmaier and Spruill on R&D resources for Surgical.

63. Boyle, "Foldable IOLs"; Sinskey, "Phacoemulsification and IOLs"; *Surgical Insights*, Feb., May–June, Sept.–Oct., Nov.–Dec. 1985, Jan.–Feb., Mar.–Apr., Sept. 1986, vols. 1, 5, 9, 1987, vol. 8, 1988, vol. 1, 1989, vol. 1, 1990; *Surgical Journal*, June 1981; *AWN*, Sept., Nov. 1985, Jan. 1986, Feb., June, Aug. 1987, Apr. 1988, Dec. 1990, Mar. 1994; *Alcon Today and Tomorrow*, 1986.

64. Kay Miles Spruill, AOH; Whitbeck and Grimm, AOH.

65. Blumenkranz, "Evolution of Laser Therapy in Ophthalmology," 12–25; *Surgical Insights*, vol. 5, 1987; *New York Times*, Feb. 20, 2022.

66. *Surgical Insights*, vols. 5, 7, 9, 1987, vols. 3, 5, 7, 1988; *Alcon Today and Tomorrow*, 1986; *AWN*, May 1986, Aug. 1987, June 1988, Sept. 1989; *Spectrum*, Dec. 1985, May 1986, July–Aug. 1987, Apr. 1988; Barrett, "New Hydrogel Intraocular Lens Design," 18–25.

67. Vern Feltner, May 7, 2021, AOH; Andy Lubrano, Aug. 2, 2019, AOH; *Surgical Journal*, Oct. 28, 1981, July–Aug. 1985; *Surgical Insights*, vol. 9, 1987.

68. *Surgical Journal*, Apr. 21, 1981, Apr. 22, Dec. 16, 1983; *Surgical Insights*, Feb., July–Aug., Sept–Oct.1985, Oct. 1986, vols. 3, 6, 1987; *AWN*, Sept. 1985. Primary members of Spruill's experienced Fort Worth staff included Daryl Dubbs, Jack Marshall, Peter Hatton, Kay Miles, Maury Rester, Henry Meadows, Eileen Devaney, Janet Supple, Nancy Hill, Johnnie Herndon, and Greg Booher.

69. *Bryan Street Journal*, 1980; *Surgical Journal*, 1981–83; *Surgical Insights*, 1984–87, vol. 10, 1988; Photos, Annual Sales Conferences, Surgical Scrapbooks, AHR.

70. *Alcon Update*, June 7, 1982, Surgical Scrapbooks, AHR.

71. *Scope*, Aug. 1983, Dec. 1985, AHR; *FWST*, Dec. 18, 1985; *Dallas Morning News*, Mar. 20, 1983.

72. *Scope*, June 1984, July 1985, AHR; Davidson, Sattler, and Sakamoto, AOH; Faro and Campbell, AOH; Rheiner, AOH.

73. Schifrin and Rich, "Contact Lens Industry," 39–46; Davidson, Sattler, and Sakamoto, AOH.

74. Davidson, Sattler, and Sakamoto, AOH; Goldin and Katz, "A Most Egalitarian Profession," 705–46; Carden, *Retail Innovations in American Economic History*, Independent Institute (website).

75. *Scope*, Apr. 1986, AHR; Sherry L. Cooper, "1971–2011," 64–73; Davidson, Sattler, and Sakamoto, AOH.

76. Schifrin and Rich, "Contact Lens Industry," 16–18; Buchanan, AOH; Koetting and Griebrok Jose, "Contact Lens Products," 249–58; *Spectrum*, July–Aug. 1985; *AWN*, Jan. 1985, Jan., May 1986; *Scope*, Apr., Sept. 1983, Dec. 1986, Sept. 1987; Annual Report, 1975.

77. *Spectrum*, July–Aug. 1985; *AWN*, May 1986, Feb. 1989, Dec. 1996; EHS, presentations to Nestlé management; Davidson, Sattler, and Sakamoto, AOH; Faro and Campbell, AOH; *Alcon Today and Tomorrow*, 1990; *Scope*, Dec. 1984, Mar., July 1988.

78. *Scope*, Aug. 1983, July 1985, AHR; *FWST*, Dec. 7, 1985; *AWN*, Dec. 1982, Jan. 1986, Dec. 1982, Feb. 1989, Oct. 1997; Milton Barley, Steve Clark, Herbert Kleiman, Blaise McGoey, Bill Rhue, Glenn Rickey, Len Schweitzer, Dick Sisson, Alcon Hall of Fame Inductees, AHR. These included Bill Rhue, Bob Grantham, Jim Bond, Roy Buchanan, Bob Nelson, Bob Grady, Sandy Howell, Rick

Johnson, Elizabeth Power, Ken Huff, Dick Hedlund, Glenn Rickey, Norb Walter, Bob Yates, Len Schweitzer, and Lee Wright

79. Bill Burns, Oct. 29, 2019, AOH; Cagle et al., "Topical Tobramycin and Gentamicin Sulfate," 523–34; Cagle, "Alcon Story."

80. *New Tobrex (Tobramycin 0.3%) Ophthalmic Solution* (product monograph), misc. promotional material, vol. 9.1, AHR; *AWN*, Dec. 1981, 1982.

81. *AWN*, July 1983, Mar., Sept., Nov. 1984, Jan. 1986, Feb., June 1987; Nelson, AOH; Johnson, AOH; *Alcon Today and Tomorrow*, 1986; *Update 1987*: *Alcon Today and Tomorrow*, 1986; *Scope*, Apr., Aug., Sept., Dec. 1983, Dec. 1984, Mar., July 1985, 1987, AHR; Video, V01a, R&D, Cagle, Schlech, Tobrex, Aug. 1984, BAS, AM.

82. *AWN*, July 1983, Mar., Sept., Nov. 1984, Jan. 1986, Feb., June 1987; *Scope*, Apr. Aug., Sept. Dec. 1983, Dec. 1984, Mar., July 1985, 1987.

83. Fraunfelder, Bagby, and Kelly, "Fatal Aplastic Anemia," 356–60; National Registry of Drug-Induced Ocular Side Effects (website); Jerry Cagle to author, email, Mar. 24, 2022, TOM, AM; Cagle, "Alcon Story." The National Registry of Drug-Induced Ocular Side Effects had been in operation for a few years. Chloramphenicol is a broad-spectrum antibacterial, so when reports of deaths due to aplastic anemia were flagged by the registry, the product was doomed.

84. *Scope*, Dec. 1983, May 1985; *AWN*, Apr. 1985; Rheiner, AOH; Johnson, AOH; McDonald, "Alcon Story"; Shuler, "Executive Profile: George Leone."

85. Shields and Hodapp, "Glaucoma 25 Years Ago"; Nelson et al., "Adverse Respiratory and Cardiovascular Events," 606–11; Polansky, "Comparison of Plasma Beta Blocking Activity," S17–S18. Between 1976 and 1985, the National Registry of Drug-Induced Ocular Side Effects reported 32 deaths and 450 serious respiratory and cardiovascular events attributed to Timoptic. The metabolic researcher was Jon Polansky, PhD, Department of Ophthalmology, University of California Medical Center, San Francisco.

86. *Scope*, Apr. 1986, AHR; *San Francisco Examiner*, Nov. 2, 1985; *Baltimore Evening Sun*, Oct. 28, 1985; *Memphis Commercial Appeal*, Dec. 14, 1985. Robert C. Allen, MD, of Emory University, Atlanta, and David Berry, MD, of the University of Colorado, Denver, joined Alcon R&D members Cagle, Larry Bruce, and Harold Beasley.

87. *Scope*, Dec. 1985, Apr. 1986, AHR; *AWN*, June 1987, Feb. 1989.

88. *AWN*, June 1987, Feb. 1989, 1990; *Scope*, Dec. 1986, July 1987, May 1988, AHR; Johnson, AOH; EHS, "Alcon Story"; Nelson, AOH.

89. *Update 1987: Alcon Today and Tomorrow*, 1986.

90. *Scope*, Apr., Dec. 1983, June, Dec. 1984, July, Dec. 1985, Apr., Dec. 1986, July 1987, Mar. 1988.

91. Allen Baker, June 18, 2022, AOH.

92. *AWN*, Dec. 1981, Mar., Sept., Nov. 1984, Jan. 1986, Aug. 1989, Apr. 1993, Aug. 1994, Sept. 1996; *Alcon Today and Tomorrow*, 1986; Gene Estes, May 30, 2019, AOH.

93. *AWN*, Nov. 1984, Jan. 1986, Aug., Oct. 1987, Dec. 1988; Helmut Horchler, "Alcon Story," Sept. 27, 2007; *Alcon Today and Tomorrow*, 1986.

94. *AWN*, May 1986, Feb. 1987, Dec. 1992.

95. Horchler, "Alcon Story"; *AWN*, Sept. 1985.

96. *AWN*, Dec. 1981, Mar., Sept., Nov. 1984, June 1985, May 1986, Oct., Dec. 1987, July 1988, Sept. 1989, Nov. 1994, July 1995, Sept. 1996; *Spectrum*, Aug. 1977; Vaucheret, "Alcon Story"; Enrique Chico, "Alcon Story," Oct. 25, 2004; Jan Somp, Apr. 22, 2021, AOH.

97. *AWN*, Sept. 1984; Giorgio Vescovo, emails, 2021, 2022, TOM, AM; LaMacchia, "Alcon Story"; LaMacchia, AOH.

98. *AWN*, Nov. 1985, July, Nov. 1986, June, Oct. 1987, June 1988, Feb. 1989; *Update 1987: Alcon Today and Tomorrow*, 1986. The ophthalmologists were Robert Weinreb, MD, and, from France, Philippe Demailly, MD; the pulmonologists were Robert Schoene, MD, and, from Belgium, Daniel DeVos, MD; with physiologist Jon Polansky, PhD, and Tom McDonald, PhD, head of Alcon Clinical Science, participating.

99. *AWN*, Jan. 1986, Aug. 1989; Sear, "Alcon Story"; Carlos Coscia, July 15, 2015, AOH; Leon de Chateauvieux, Dionisio A. Garcia, Carlos de Socio, Alcon Hall of Fame Inductees, AHR.

100. Coscia, AOH; Carlos Coscia, notes to author, Apr. 21, 2023, TOM, AM.

101. *AWN*, Dec. 1981, Sept. 1984, July 1986, Apr., July 1987, Feb., Aug. 1989, July 1995; Sear, "Alcon Story"; Coscia, AOH; Heer, *Nestlé*,

381; Dionisio Garcia, Arthur (Arturo) Hayton, MD (Oaxaca, Mexico, ophthalmologist), and Tom McDonald, conversations, 1979–1985, manufacture of Alcon products in Mexico and cost of Alcon prescription products in Mexico.

102. Coscia, AOH; Coscia, notes to author, Apr. 21, 2023; *AWN*, Aug. 1989; *Update 1987: Alcon Today and Tomorrow*, 1986; Sear, "Alcon Story"; "PAOF Board of Directors," Pan-American Association of Ophthalmology (website); Teresa Bradshaw, executive director, Pan-American Association of Ophthalmology, telephone conversation with author, June 14, 2021, TOM, AM. The author accompanied Mr. Conner to Lima, Peru, in October 1988.

103. *AWN*, Jan. 1986, Apr., July 1988, July 1990, Dec. 1992, July 1995; Sear, "Alcon Story"; Jeanne Lim Kah-Cheng, "Alcon Story," Oct. 25, 2004; T. J. Chen, Alcon Hall of Fame Inductees, AHR.

104. *AWN*, Jan. 1986, Apr., July 1988, July 1990, Dec. 1992, July 1995; *Update 1987: Alcon Today and Tomorrow*, 1986. The two physicians were Robert Schoene, a pulmonologist, and Robert Weinreb, an ophthalmologist. The R&D representative was Tom McDonald

105. *AWN*, Feb. 1987.

106. *AWN*, Jan. 1986, Apr., July 1988, July 1990, Dec. 1992, July 1995; *Update 1987: Alcon Today and Tomorrow*, 1986.

107. *AWN*, Jan. 1986, Aug. 1989, Apr. 1993; *Update 1987: Alcon Today and Tomorrow*, 1986.

108. Kologe, "Alcon Story"; Buhler, "Alcon Story"; Montgomery, AOH; *AWN*, Dec. 1981, Apr. 1993.

109. *AWN*, Nov. 1984, Dec. 1990, Aug. 1994; *Alcon Today and Tomorrow*, 1986; *Update 1987: Alcon Today and Tomorrow*, 1986; Montgomery, AOH; Charles Miller, May 24, 2021, AOH; Henry Meadows, Sept. 6, 2019, AOH; Rutherford, AOH.

110. *Alcon Today and Tomorrow*, 1986; *Update 1987: Alcon Today and Tomorrow*, 1986; Montgomery, AOH; *AWN*, June 1984, Feb. 1990; Beikman, Tsumpis, and Rao, AOH; Alcon Laboratories: Information Technology Group, HBS Retired Case Collection, box 186, folder 013, Special Collections, Baker Library, Harvard Business School; Brobst, AOH.

111. *AWN*, Dec. 1987; *Scope*, Sept. 1987, Mar., May 1988, AHR.

112. *AWN*, Mar. 1986, Feb., Dec. 1987, Mar., Dec. 1992; *Spectrum*, Feb. 1986, Fall 1990, Spring 1992; *Scope*, Dec. 1984, Apr., Dec.

1986, May, July 1988; *Surgical Insights*, vol. 2, 1985.

113. *AWN*, Dec. 1981, June 1984, Dec. 1987, Dec. 1998; *Surgical Insights*, vol. 7, 1987.

114. *AWN*, Mar. 1984, Jan., May, Nov. 1986, Apr., June 1987, July 1991; *Surgical Insights*, vol. 2, 1986, vol. 9, 1987.

115. *AWN*, July 1983, June 1985, Jan., Mar., July, Sept., Nov. 1986, Feb., Oct. 1987, July 1988, Dec. 1995; *Surgical Insights*, vol. 2, 1986, vols. 3, 10, 1987.

116. *AWN*, Apr. 1988; *Alcon Today and Tomorrow*, 1986; *Update 1987: Alcon Today and Tomorrow*, 1986; EHS, presentations to Nestlé management.

117. *Alcon Today and Tomorrow*, 1986; *Update 1987: Alcon Today and Tomorrow*, 1986; Nestlé, Annual Report, 1978, Nestlé Historical Archives. The exchange rate in December 1985 was $1 US, which equaled 2.1 Swiss francs.

118. *AWN*, Dec. 1987.

Chapter 6

1. Horchler, *Journey Well Traveled*, 227–65; Horchler, "Alcon Story"; Helmut Horchler to author, email, June 16, 2022, TOM, AM.

2. *AWN*, Aug. 1994, July 1996; Howell, "Alcon Story"; Howell and Clynch, AOH; Kathleen Knight, July 29, 2019, AOH; Shuler, "Executive Profile: George Leone," 22–30; A. J. Hiltenbrand, correspondence, May 2021, TOM, AM.

3. *AWN*, Nov. 1984, Oct. 1988, Feb., Apr. 1989.

4. *AWN*, Apr. 1997, Apr., Oct. 1988; *Alcon Today and Tomorrow*, 1986; Luttrell, HLP; Howard Luttrell, Curriculum Vitae (CV), HLP; *Alcon Today and Tomorrow*, 1990; "Bruce Coleman Rudy," Tribute Archive (website).

5. *Alcon Update*, Mar. 13, 1990, BAS, Alcon Records; *Alcon Today and Tomorrow*, 1990; William Hubregs, May 2, 2021, AOH.

6. EHS, "Alcon Story"; Cary Rayment, "Alcon Story," Apr. 25, 2006; Stevens, "Alcon Story"; *FWST*, Dec. 11, 1989; *San Francisco Chronicle*, Sept. 26, Nov. 26, 1988; *Alcon Today and Tomorrow*, 1989; *Surgical Insights* 3, 1989.

7. Rayment, "Alcon Story"; Stevens, "Alcon Story"; Allen Baker, AOH; Ardis Kvare, Mar. 30, 2021, AOH; Robert Stevens to

author, email, July 21, 2022, TOM, AM.

8. *Alcon Today and Tomorrow*, 1989; *AWN*, Apr. 1990, Aug. 1992, Sept., Dec. 1995, Sept. 1999; *Surgical Insights* 6, 1989, 1, 1990, 1, 1993; *Vision & Commitment*, 1998.

9. Merrill, "Alcon Story"; *Boston Globe*, Dec. 22, 1987, Dec. 15, 1992, Feb. 7, 1993; *Surgical Insights* 8, 1988, 1, 1993; *Update 1987: Alcon Today and Tomorrow*, 1986; *Athol (MA) Daily News*, Dec. 22, 1987; Van Damme, AOH.

10. *AWN*, Sept. 1990, Feb. 1991, Jan., Dec. 1992, July 1995, Aug. 1998; *Alcon Today and Tomorrow*, 1989, 1990; Daniel, AOH; Vogel, AOH; Clark, AOH; Pierre Vogel, "Ed Schollmaier, in Commemoration of Your Outstanding Leadership of Alcon Laboratories," June 9, 1998, EHS Papers, in possession of Taylor Schollmaier, Boulder, CO; Sear, "Alcon Story." These were Eric Noble, Australia; Carlos Taborda, Brazil and LACAR; and Marja Kaleva, UK and Germany.

11. *Vision & Commitment*, 1998, 2000; *AWN*, July, Sept. 1990, Feb. 1991; *Update 1987: Alcon Today and Tomorrow,* 1986; *Alcon Today and Tomorrow*, 1990; André Bens, "Alcon Story," Apr. 24, 2006.

12. *Alcon Today and Tomorrow*, 1990; *Scope*, July 1990; *Surgical Insights* 4, 1989, 3, 1990; *AWN*, Apr., Sept. 1990, Apr. 1997; *FWST*, Dec. 6, 1993.

13. *Scope*, July 1989; *Alcon Today and Tomorrow*, 1990; *AWN*, Apr. 1989; *FWST*, Aug. 22, 1988.

14. *Scope*, July–Aug. 1992; *Alcon Today and Tomorrow*, 1990.

15. *AWN*, Sept. 1996, Oct. 1997, May 1998; *Vision & Commitment*, 1998; *FWST*, Dec. 6, 1993; David McGlothin, July 7, 2022, AOH; Tran Trong, AOH; Walker, AOH.

16. *Surgical Insights* 4, 1992; *Vision & Commitment*, 1998; *Scope*, July 1989; *AWN*, Dec. 1988, Apr. 1997; *Alcon Today and Tomorrow*, 1990.

17. *Surgical Insights* 6, 1989; *Surgical Insights* 7, 1990; *AWN*, Sept. 1990, Feb. 1991.

18. *AWN*, Dec. 1988; *Scope*, July 1989.

19. *Scope*, July 1989; *AWN*, Dec. 1988; *Alcon Today and Tomorrow*, 1990.

20. *Scope*, Aug–Sept. 1991; *Surgical Insights* 1, 1992.

21. *AWN*, Feb. 1998, Jan.–Feb. 2000; *Vision & Commitment*, 1998.

22. *AWN*, Jan. 1992; *Vision & Commitment*, 1998; *Alcon Today and Tomorrow*, 1990.

23. *Vision & Commitment*, 1998; *AWN*, Sept. 1996; Tran Trong, AOH.

24. *Alcon Today and Tomorrow*, 1990; *Vision & Commitment*, 1996, 1998.

25. *AWN*, July 1991, Mar.–Apr. 2000; *Alcon Today and Tomorrow*, 1990; *Vision & Commitment*, 1996, 1998; Coscia, AOH; Carlos Coscia, notes to author, Apr. 21, 2023, TOM, AM.

26. *AWN*, Dec. 1995; *Vision & Commitment*, 1998; Keith Bell, Feb. 9, 2022, AOH; Tom McDonald to Roger Cowan, email, Feb. 3, 2022, TOM, AM.

27. Bell, AOH; Estes, AOH; Barley, AOH; *AWN*, Apr. 1989, June 1993, 1996; Bens, "Alcon Story"; *Surgical Insights* 1, 1993. André Bens to author, email, July 19, 2023, TOM, AM.

28. Luttrell, "My Journey," HLP; Howard Luttrell, "Key Events," HLP; Howard Luttrell, CV, HLP.

29. Luttrell, "My Journey," HLP; Howard Luttrell, "Alcon QA IT Chronology, 1969–2000," HLP; Luttrell, "Key Events," HLP; Luttrell, CV, HLP

30. Luttrell, "My Journey," HLP; Luttrell, "Alcon QA IT Chronology," HLP; Luttrell, interview, "Dr. Howard Luttrell Reviews Alcon History"; Luttrell, "Key Events," HLP; Luttrell, CV, HLP

31. *AWN*, Nov. 1994, Jan. 1995, July, Dec. 1996, May 1998; "Quality Management Systems," International Standards Organization (website); Robitaille, "Why ISO 9001 Still Matters"; Luttrell, "Key Events," HLP.

32. Luttrell, "My Journey," HLP; Howard Luttrell, "The QA Diaspora," HLP; Luttrell, "Key Events," HLP; *Alcon Today and Tomorrow*, 1986; Bens, "Alcon Story."

33. EHS, "Alcon Story"; Raval, AOH; Raval, "Alcon Story"; Gerald Cagle, "Alcon Story," Apr. 24, 2006.

34. EHS, presentations to Nestlé management, AHR; Alcon presentation to prospective CooperVision transferees, Spring 1989, AHR; Tom McDonald, "Alcon Story," Oct. 28, 2004; *Vision & Commitment*, 1996, 2000; *Alcon Today and Tomorrow*, 1990. R&D's annual budget was about 10 percent of that year's annual sales.

Raval's R&D organization was always in a state of flux; he moved personnel as issues and challenges appeared and were resolved. Tom McDonald, who always reported to Cagle, led the centralized Clinical Science group, and when Betty Fortenberry House, the Ophthalmic MSD, retired, he added that responsibility. About the same time, Barry Schlech moved from the head of Microbiology to lead the Pharmaceutical Science and Process Development groups; he reported to McDonald. Ralph Stone, PhD, the new MSD for Vision Care products, joined R&D, reporting to McDonald. During this time Robert Abshire, PhD, head of the Process Development group, transferred to Clinical Science to manage the Ciprofloxacin project, and then moved on to lead the Microbiology group until he retired. Joe Hiddemen, PhD, directed Technical Services, which included Robert Hackett, PhD, in charge of Toxicology; Ed Dorsey, PhD, Analytical Chemistry; and Barry Schlech and later Robert Abshire in Microbiology. These are just a small set of several dynamic organization changes Raval instituted to assure the best-qualified person was in the right position to deal with issues and challenges as they emerged.

35. Donn Lobdell, Feb. 25, 2021, AOH; Allen Baker, AOH; Raval, AOH; Raval, "Alcon Story"; Stevens to author, email, July 21, 2022.

36. Hubregs, AOH; Walker, AOH; Pencis, AOH; Roehrs, AOH; Alcon Hall of Fame Inductees, AHR; "Wiley Chambers, MD," Ophthalmology Innovation Source (website). Key members of his staff were Robert Roehrs, PhD, Mary Pencis, Michael Fitzpatrick, Michael Pfleger, Becky Walker, Terry Wiernas, Scott Kruger, and Mike Fenoglio

37. EHS, "Alcon Story"; Sisson, "Alcon Story"; Walker, AOH; Estes, AOH; AWN, Sept. 1996, Oct. 1997; Spectrum, Summer, 1994.

38. Hubregs, AOH; Pencis, AOH; Vilas-Boas and Tharp, "Drug Approval Process," 459–65. Brian Matthews was the former UK Medicines Commission member hired.

39. David Krapf, Aug. 27, 2019, AOH; Hubregs, AOH; Pencis, AOH; Vilas-Boas and Tharp, "Drug Approval Process," 459–65

40. Gregg Brown to author, email, Feb. 6, 2022, TOM, AM.

41. Spectrum, July–Aug., Oct. 1985; DeSantis, AOH; AWN, Apr., 1990, Dec. 1992, Mar.–May 2001; Alcon Today and Tomorrow, 1990. John Yanni, PhD, Thomas Dean, PhD, and Mark Hellberg, PhD, were examples of qualified employees brought into the Research department.

42. Alcon Today and Tomorrow, 1990; AWN, Dec. 1992, Mar.–May 2001; Spectrum, Nov. 1986; Eye on Tomorrow, 1984, ALC.

43. AWN, July 1999.

44. Spectrum, May–Aug., Sept.–Dec. 2004, May–Aug. 2005; Alcon Hall of Fame Inductees, AHR. Reporting to Hiddemen were Robert Hackett, PhD, Toxicology; Edwin Dorsey, PhD, Analytical Chemistry; and Barry Schlech, PhD, and later Robert Abshire, PhD, Microbiology.

45. Spectrum, Spring 1991; Scope, May–June 1991.

46. Spectrum, Spring 1991; Scope, May–June 1991; Alcon Hall of Fame Inductees, AHR; Cagle, "Alcon Story"; Rebecca G. Walker, AM.

47. AWN, Oct. 1991, Mar. 1994; Spectrum, Winter 1993; Walker, AM; Cagle, "Alcon Story"; Gerald "Jerry" Cagle to author, email, Apr. 1, 2022, TOM, AM; Alcon Hall of Fame Inductees, AHR; Abelson, Chambers, and Smith, "Conjunctival Allergen Challenge," 84–88; Dell et al., "Evaluation of Naphcon-A and Individual Constituents, 183.

48. AWN, Dec. 1993, Sept.–Oct. 2000; Spectrum, Winter 1993, Spring 1994; Walker, AM.

49. AWN, July, Sept., Dec. 1996; Surgical Insights 4, 1989; Walker, AM.

50. AWN, Oct. 1988, Nov. 1989; Scope, Oct. 1988; Robert Roehrs to author, email, Feb. 10, 2020, TOM, AM

51. Roehrs to author, email, Feb. 10, 2020; Walker, AM; AWN, Feb. 1990; Scope, May 1990.

52. Walker, AM.

53. Walker, AM; Rheiner, AOH; AWN, Dec. 1993; Scope, Jan. 1994.

54. Walker, AM; AWN, May 1998.

55. Walker, AM; AWN, July–Aug. 2000

56. Walker, AM; AWN, Mar. 1996.

57. Walker, AM; AWN, Mar. 1996; EHS, "Alcon Story"; Rheiner, AOH.

58. Barr, "Twenty Years of Contact Lenses"; Nalley, "Material Gains"; Smick, "Evolution of Dual Disinfection."

59. AWN, Oct. 1988, Apr. 1989, Feb. 1991, Sept. 1995, Dec. 1996,

July, Sept. 1999; *Alcon Today and Tomorrow*, 1990; *Scope*, Mar., July 1989, Nov. 1990, Mar., May–June, Oct.–Nov. 1991; *Spectrum*, Summer 1994; Walker, AM. The key team members were Masood Chowhan, PhD, Sally L. Buck, Ruth Ann Rosenthal, PhD, Bahram Asgharian, PhD, and David Meadows, PhD.

60. *AWN*, Dec. 1990, June 1994, Dec. 1996, Aug. 1998, Nov. 1999; *Spectrum*, Summer 1994; Walker, AM.

61. *AWN*, Dec. 1996, May, Oct. 1998, July 1999; Walker, AM.

62. *Alcon Today and Tomorrow*, 1989, 1990; *AWN*, Apr. 1989, Feb. 1991, June 1993; *Surgical Insights* 2, 1989, 7, 8, 1990, 8, 1991, 7, 1992.

63. *AWN*, Feb. 1989; Maloney, "Remarkable Evolution of Cataract Surgery."

64. *ANW*, July 1993, Apr. 1997; *Surgical Insights* 3, 4, 1993; Lobdell, AOH.

65. *Surgical Insights* 6, 1987, 1, 1990; *AWN*, Feb. 1998; Lobdell, AOH; *Alcon Today and Tomorrow*, 1989, 1990.

66. *Surgical Insights* 1, 7, 1990, 1, 1992, 1 1993; *Alcon Today and Tomorrow*, 1989, 1990; *AWN*, Apr. 1997, Nov. 1999.

67. *AWN*, June 1996; *Surgical Insights* 6, 1993; Walker, AM.

68. EHS, "Alcon Story"; Raval, "Alcon Story"; Stevens to author, email, July 21, 2022; Rayment, "Alcon Story"; Stevens, "Alcon Story"; *AWN*, Aug. 1998; Raval, AOH

69. "Alcon R&D Technical Excellence Awards," BAS, Alcon Records; Stevens to author, email, July 21, 2022.

70. *Surgical Insights* 4, 1990, 8, 1992, 1, 1993; *AWN*, Dec. 1995, June 1996; Southard, "History from an Ophthalmic Surgical Company Viewpoint," 231–51; Mike Southard, May 4, 2021, AOH.

71. *AWN*, Jan., Feb. 1995, June 1996.

72. *AWN*, Dec. 1992, Jan., Feb. 1995, June 1996; Southard, "History from an Ophthalmic Surgical Company Viewpoint," 231–51.

73. *AWN*, June 1996, Sept.–Oct. 2000; Southard, "History from an Ophthalmic Surgical Company Viewpoint," 231–51; Robert Stevens to author, email, Dec. 28, 2022, TOM, AM

74. Stevens to author, email, Dec. 28, 2022.

75. Gregg Brown, "History of Alcon's Intellectual Property Operations,

1983–1987," TOM, AM; James Arno, June 28, 2019, AOH; Lobdell, AOH.

76. Brown, "History of Alcon's Intellectual Property Operations," TOM, AM; Arno, AOH; Lobdell, AOH; *AWN*, Mar., Sept. 1996, May 1998.

77. "Alcon R&D Technical Excellence Awards," BAS, Alcon Records; *AWN*, June 1980, July 1990, June 1992, June 1993, Apr. 1997, Sept. 1999.

78. *AWN*, Feb., Apr. 1989; *Surgical Insights* 4, 1989, 1, 1990; *Alcon Today and Tomorrow*, 1986, 1989, 1990; *Update 1987: Alcon Today and Tomorrow*, 1986; Stevens, "Alcon Story"; *Vision & Commitment*, 1992; EHS, "Alcon Story."

79. Alcon presentation to prospective CooperVision transferees, Spring 1989, AHR; EHS, "Alcon Story"; Allen Baker, AOH; Rayment, "Alcon Story"; Meadows, AOH.

80. Allen Baker, AOH; Kvare, AOH; Kay Miles Spruill, Nov. 16, 2019, AOH; Meadows, AOH.

81. *Surgical Insights* 5, 6, 1990, 1, 1993. Rayment's marketing and sales staff included Peter Hatton, Bill Barton, David Eister, Joe Vonder-Haar, Mark Jeffers, Jack Marshall, Rick McLaughlin, Steve Brewer, Roger Williams, Mike Stropid, Joe Batal, Ed Peterson, Bob Yates, Tom Skiff, and Jerry Lindaman.

82. *Surgical Insights* 8, 1990, 1, 1993. Product managers were Joe Wolff, Bob Kling, Bob Painter, Bill George, Mark Summers, Larry Steiner, Peter Hyde, John Weymouth, and Cliff Southard. Henry Mitchell and David Lancaster served as surgical consultants.

83. *Surgical Insights* 4, 6, 7, 1990, 7, 8, 1991, 1, 2, 1992, 1, 4 1993, 1, 1994; *Surgical Journal*, Apr. 21, 1981; Meadows, AOH.

84. *Surgical Insights* 5, 1989, 6, 1990, 2–4, 6, 8, 1991, 1, 1992, 1–3, 1993, 1, 1994; *AWN*, Dec. 1990, Feb. 1991

85. *Surgical Insights* 3, 5, 1989, 5, 1990, 1, 6, 1993; *Alcon Today and Tomorrow*, 1990; *Vision & Commitment*, 1992, 1996, 1998, 2000.

86. *Surgical Insights* 6, 1987, 3, 1989, 1, 1990; *AWN*, Feb. 1998; Lobdell, AOH; *Alcon Today and Tomorrow*, 1989, 1990; *Vision & Commitment*, 1992, 1996, 1998, 2000.

87. *Surgical Insights* 3, 1989, 1, 7, 1990, 1, 1992, 1, 1993; *AWN*, Feb. 1998; Lobdell, AOH; *Alcon Today and Tomorrow*, 1989, 1990; *Vision & Commitment*, 1992, 1996, 1998.

88. *Update 1987: Alcon Today and Tomorrow*, 1986; *AWN*, Feb. 1989, Apr. 1990, Apr. 1993, Aug. 1997, Feb. 1998; *Vision & Commitment*, 1996; EHS, presentations to Nestlé management, AHR.

89. *FWST*, Feb. 5, June 9, 1994; *AWN*, Mar. 1994, Sept. 1999.

90. *AWN*, Dec. 1996; Faro and Campbell, AOH; Davidson, Sattler, and Sakamoto, AOH.

91. Faro and Campbell, AOH; *AWN*, Oct. 1998; *Vision & Commitment*, 1991.

92. Faro and Campbell, AOH; *Scope*, Mar. 1991.

93. *Scope*, Mar., July 1989; Faro and Campbell, AOH; *Alcon Today and Tomorrow*, 1990, 1991; *AWN*, Dec. 1990, Feb., Oct.–Nov. 1991.

94. *AWN*, Apr. 1989, Sept., Nov. 1990, July 1991, Mar. 1992, May–June 1993, June 1994, Mar. 1996; *Scope*, Mar., Oct.–Nov. 1991, Aug.–Sept. 1991, Jan.–Feb., Mar.–Apr., May–June 1992, Jan.–Feb., Mar.–Apr., May–June, July–Aug. 1993, Jan., Feb.–Mar. 1994.

95. *AWN*, Mar. 1994, Mar., Sept., Dec. 1996, Aug. 1998; *Scope*, Mar.–Apr. 1993, Feb.–Mar. 1994; Walker, AM; Davidson, Sattler, and Sakamoto, AOH.

96. *AWN*, Dec. 1990; *Scope*, Mar. 1988, Nov. 1990, Mar. 1991.

97. *AWN*, Apr. 1993, June 1994, Mar., Dec. 1996; *Scope*, June 1983, July, Sept. 1987, Mar. 1989, July 1990, Mar. 1991, Jan.–Feb. 1992, Mar.–Apr., Sept.–Oct. 1993; *Alcon Today and Tomorrow*, 1989, 1990; *Vision & Commitment*, 1992, 1996, 2000; Davidson, Sattler, and Sakamoto, AOH; Burns, AOH. Key members of the cadre included Bill Burns, David Sakamoto, Dave Sattler, Jerry Davidson, Kevin Buehler, George Neal, and Mike Hemric.

98. *Scope*, July 1988, July 1989, July 1990, Mar., Aug.–Sept. 1991, Jan.–Feb., Mar.–Apr. 1992, July–Aug. 1992; Mar.–Apr., July–Aug. 1993, Feb.–Mar. 1994; *AWN*, Feb. 1987, Apr. 1988, Feb. 1989, Dec. 1990, June, Aug. 1994, July 1995, July, Sept., Dec. 1996, Oct. 1997, May 1998; Howell and Clynch, AOH; Dave Sattler to author, email, Jan. 5, 2023, TOM, AM.

99. *AWN*, Apr. 1985, Jan., Mar., June, Dec. 1992; *Scope*, July, Sept. 1987, Oct. 1988, Mar. 1989, July 1990, Mar., Nov. 1991, Mar.–Apr., June 1992, Sept.–Oct., Mar.–Apr. 1993. Individuals who played prominent roles during these ten years included Len Schweitzer, Bill Burns, Rick Rheiner, Rick Johnson, Norb Walter, Bob Grantham, Bob Nelson, Elizabeth Powers, Tom Swift, Bill Rhue, Roy Buchanan, Diane Smith, Glenn Richey, Glenn Moro, Bill Barton, and Stuart Raetzman.

100. *AWN*, Mar., Dec. 1996, Dec. 1997, Aug. 1998; *Scope*, May–June 1992, July–Aug., Sept.–Oct. 1993; Walker, AM. Other members of Managed Care were Tom Skiff, Jerry Lindaman, Joe Czmarko, Sam Boswell, Kevin Fitzgerald, Jim Niewiarowski, Kurtis Klein, and Mike Hemric.

101. *Scope*, May 1988, Mar. 1989, May 1990, Feb.–Mar. 1994; *Alcon Today and Tomorrow*, 1991; *AWN*, Feb. 1990, Feb. 1991.

102. *Scope*, July 1989, May 1990, May–June, Aug.–Sept. 1991; *AWN*, Feb. 1990.

103. *Scope*, July 1989, May 1990, May 1991, Mar. 1994; *AWN*, Sept. 1989; *AWN*, Nov. 1999.

104. *AWN*, Dec. 1993; *Scope*, Jan. 1994; Walker, AM; Rheiner, AOH.

105. *AWN*, May 1998, Oct. 1998, Nov. 1999, July–Aug. 2000; Walker, AM; Rheiner, AOH.

106. Adamczyk and Jaanus, "Antiallergy Drugs and Decongestants," 245–61; *Scope*, Jan., Feb.–Mar. 1994; *AWN*, Mar. 1994.

107. *AWN*, Apr., Dec. 1997, July 1999; Walker, AM.

108. *AWN*, May 1998; Walker, AM.

109. *Scope*, May–June 1991; *AWN*, May 1990, Apr. 1993, Mar. 1996; *Alcon Today and Tomorrow*, 1991; Walker, AM.

110. *Scope*, May–June 1992, July 1996.

111. *AWN*, July, Sept. 1996, Apr. 1997.

112. *AWN*, Oct., Dec. 1988, Nov. 1989; *Scope*, Oct. 1988; Walker, AM; Barley, AOH.

113. *AWN*, Apr., Nov. 1989; *Scope*, July 1989, Mar.–Apr. 1992; *Alcon Today and Tomorrow*, 1990.

114. *AWN*, June 1993; *Scope*, May–June 1993.

115. *AWN*, Mar., Sept. 1996.

116. *AWN*, June 1993, June 1994, July 1995, Aug., Oct. 1997, May, Aug. 1998; *Scope*, July 1989, 1990, Mar. 1991, Mar.–Apr. 1992, Jan.–Feb. 1993, Feb.–Mar. 1994; Rheiner, AOH; Rick Johnson, Aug. 9, 2019, AOH; Burns, AOH; Nelson, AOH; Schweitzer, AOH; Grantham, AOH.

117. *Alcon Today and Tomorrow*, 1987, 1990; *Vision & Commitment*, 1992, 1995, 2000; *AWN*, Feb. 1991, Apr. 1993, Nov. 1999, Mar.–Apr., Sept.–Oct. 2000; *Scope*, Mar. 1989.

118. *Alcon Today and Tomorrow*, 1990, 1991; EHS, presentations to Nestlé management, AHR.

119. *AWN*, Jan., July 1986, Aug. 1989, Dec. 1990, June 1992, Apr. 1993, July 1995, Aug. 1997, Mar. 1999; *Alcon Today and Tomorrow*, 1990; Horchler, "Alcon Story"; Coscia, AOH; Horchler, *Journey Well Traveled*, 306–691; Hiltenbrand, correspondence, May 2021, TOM, AM; Bill Kwan, Dec. 28, 2021, AOH.

120. *AWN*, June 1987, Feb. 1989, Feb. Apr. 1990, Feb. 1991, Jan. 1992, Mar. 1994, July 1999; *Alcon Today and Tomorrow*, 1991; EHS, presentations to Nestlé management, AHR; Somp, AOH.

121. *AWN*, Oct. 1991, Jan., June 1992; Giorgio Vescovo to author, email, Mar. 27, 2021, TOM, AM; Somp, AOH.

122. *AWN*, Jan. 1996, Apr. 1997, Nov. 1999, Sept.–Oct. 2000; Southard, "History from an Ophthalmic Surgical Company Viewpoint," 231–51; Buratto and Southard, "Impact of IMPACT," 253–64; Southard, AOH; Beatrice Champeix, Apr. 6, 2021, AOH; Beatrice Champeix, "Alcon Story," Oct. 4, 2004; Vescovo to author, email, Apr. 3, 2021, TOM, AM.

123. *AWN*, Feb. 1991, Mar., Nov. 1994, Nov. 1999; Françoise Ganet, "The Beginning of Alcon History in Russia," Apr. 13, 2021, TOM, AM; LaMacchia, "Alcon Story"; LaMacchia, AOH; Somp, AOH.

124. *AWN*, Dec. 1992, July 1995, June 1996, July 1999; Coscia, AOH; "Board of Regents: Regent Emeritus William De La Peña, M.D.," University of California (website); Mike Southard to author, email, Jan. 13, 2023, TOM, AM; Coscia, AOH; Coscia, notes to author, Apr. 21, 2023.

125. *AWN*, Apr. 1993; *Alcon Today and Tomorrow*, 1987, 1991; Coscia, AOH; Coscia, notes to author, Apr. 21, 2023.

126. Coscia, AOH; Carlos Coscia, notes to author, Apr. 21, 2023; *AWN*, Sept. 1989.

127. *AWN*, Apr. 1993; Teresa Bradshaw, executive director, Pan-American Association of Ophthalmology to author, email, TOM, AM; *Alcon Today and Tomorrow*, 1987, 1991. These were Néstor Álvarez, Alejandro Edwards, Nelson Marques, and Roberto Quirós.

128. *Alcon Today and Tomorrow*, 1987; *Vision & Commitment*, 2000.

129. *Alcon Today and Tomorrow*, 1987; *Vision & Commitment*, 2000.

130. Horchler, *Journey Well Traveled*, 357–84, 497–525, 535–46, 666; *AWN*, June 1984, July 1995; Horchler, "Alcon Story."

131. Horchler, *Journey Well Traveled*, 382–412, 499–506, 559–72, 599–666; Horchler, "Alcon Story."

132. Horchler, *Journey Well Traveled*, 382–412, 499–506, 559–72, 599–666; *AWN*, July 1990; Horchler, "Alcon Story"; McDonald "Alcon Story." As head of the R&D Clinical Science department, the author participated in discussions with foreign regulatory agencies and represented R&D at most of its product launches overseas

133. Crewe, "Alcon Story"; Sear, "Alcon Story"; Kwan, AOH; Horchler, *Journey Well Traveled*, 416–29, 525–34, 546–59, 584–99; Horchler, "Alcon Story"; *AWN*, July 1990, June 1992, Dec. 1997.

134. Horchler, *Journey Well Traveled*, 336–56; Horchler, "Alcon Story"; *AWN*, June 1992, Oct. 1998; *AWN*, July 1990, June 1992.

135. Horchler, *Journey Well Traveled*, 469–84; Horchler, "Alcon Story"; *AWN*, Feb. 1990, Oct. 1991, Mar. 1992, Jan. 1995, June 1996, May, Oct. 1998; Hubregs, AOH; McDonald, "Alcon Story"; Cagle, "Alcon Story"; Sear, "Alcon Story"; *AWN*, Oct. 1983, Nov. 1984, Jan. 1986, Apr. 1997, Mar.–Apr. 2000; *Kansas City Business Journal*, Mar. 11, 2001. The five were Yasuhide Fukushima, Tashushi Tokunaga, Kazuo Okuhara, Kenichi Aoki, and Katsuhiko Nakajima.

136. *Alcon Today and Tomorrow*, 1987, 1990; *Vision & Commitment*, 1995, 2000.

137. *FWST*, Mar. 24, 1997; *San Francisco Examiner*, Mar. 13, 1992; *St. Louis Post Dispatch*, Mar. 24, 1994; *NYT*, Feb. 20, 2022; Cagle, "Alcon Story"; Raval, AOH; Horchler, *Journey Well Traveled*, 478–84; Allen Baker, AOH; Elaine Whitbeck to author, email, Jan. 18, 2023, TOM, AM.

138. *AWN*, July 1991, Aug. 1994, July 1996, Apr. 1997; Montgomery, AOH; Meadows, Sept. 6, 2019, AOH; Miller, AOH; Jackie Fouse, Apr. 10, 2021, AOH.

139. *AWN*, Aug. 1994; *Scope*, May–June 1993; *Surgical Insights* 3, 1990.

140. *AWN*, Aug. 1994.

141. *AWN*, Aug. 1994; Dennis Beikman, Nick Tsumpis, and Prakash Rao, June 22, 2019, AOH; Dennis Beikman to author, email, Sept. 19, 2023, TOM, AM; Nick Tsumpis to author, email, Sept. 19,

2023, TOM, AM.

142. *Scope*, July 1990, Oct.–Nov. 1991, May–June 1992, Jan.–Feb. 1993; *AWN*, Mar., Aug., Dec. 1992, July 2000; *Surgical Insights* 5, 1987; Daryl Dubbs, Jan. 17, 2023, AOH.

143. *AWN*, Jan. 1995, Dec. 1998

144. *AWN*, July 1990, Oct. 1991, Mar. 1992, Dec. 1998; *FWST*, Dec. 22, 1988, Jan. 8, 1989, Dec. 28, 1990, Oct. 1998.

145. *AWN*, Dec. 1987, Feb. 1991, Jan., Dec. 1995, Aug., Dec. 1998; *Scope*, May–June 1993; *Surgical Insights* 1, 2, 1989, 1, 1992, 1, 1993; *Spectrum*, Dec. 1988, Spring 1991, Spring, Winter 1992, Spring 1993.

146. *AWN*, Dec. 1992, Dec. 1993, Nov. 1994, Jan., July, Sept. 1995, June 1996, Dec. 1998.

147. *AWN*, Aug. 1988, Aug., Nov. 1989, July, Oct. 1991, Dec. 1990, Dec. 1992, Apr. 1993, Nov. 1994, Dec. 1995, June, Dec. 1996; *Scope*, Mar. 1988, Jan.–Feb. 1992, Sept.–Oct. 1993, Jan.–Feb. 1993; *Surgical Insights* 3, 1988, 5, 1989, 1, 5, 1990, 7 1991, 6, 1992, 1, 5, 1993; *Spectrum*, Dec. 1988, Fall 1990, Winter 1991, Summer 1992, Winter 1993, Winter 1994.

148. *AWN*, Feb., Aug. 1989, Feb. 1990, Feb. 1991, Aug., June, Dec. 1992, July 1993, Aug. 1994, July 1995, Dec. 1996, Feb. 1988; *Scope*, Aug.–Sept. 1991, May–June 1993, Mar. 1997, Feb. 1998; *Spectrum* 3, 2002.

149. *AWN*, Dec. 1996.

150. *Vision & Commitment*, 2000; *Alcon Today and Tomorrow*, 1987, 1990.

151. *AWN*, Feb. 1991.

Chapter 7

1. Allen Baker to author, email, Apr. 18, 2023, TOM, AM. The theme of the first two paragraphs arose from this email, which was expanded on in various discussions with other retired Alcon executives.

2. Sources are noted in chap. 1. For this and the subsequent five paragraphs, the author has followed Ed Schollmaier's oral narrative located in the Founders' Museum, Alexander Tower, Alcon, Fort Worth, Texas.

3. See chap. 2 for sources.

4. See chap. 3 for sources.

5. See chap. 4 for sources.

6. See chap. 5 for sources.

7. See chap. 6 for sources.

8. *AWN*, Sept. 1996, Apr., Oct. 1997, Aug. 1998.

9. *AWN*, Apr. 1982, 1988, Jun. 1985, Dec. 1997, Feb., Aug., Dec. 1998; Nestlé Annual Report, 1988, 1992, 1995, 1997, Nestlé Historical Archives.

10. Nestlé Annual Report, 2001, 2002, 2004, 2004, 2008, 2010, Nestlé Historical Archives; Alcon Annual Report, 2008, 2009, AHR; "Novartis Announces Intention to Seek Shareholder Approval"; Alcon, "Alcon Debuts as Independent, Publicly Traded Company"; *Alcon Annual Report, 2019*, https://s1.q4cdn.com/963204942/files/doc_financials/2019/ar/ALC-Annual-Report-2019.pdf, accessed May 14, 2023.

11. *Los Angeles Times*, June 8, 1991; *AWN*, Oct. 1983; *FWST*, July 28, 1983, June 6, 2002, Jan. 27, 2017; Feik, AOH; *FWST*, Oct. 16, 1990, Nov. 29, 2012; Buhler, "Alcon Story"; "Pharmaceutical Formulations Completes Acquisition of Konsyl Pharmaceuticals"; "Stuart Raetzman Appointed CEO"; "Biography: Jackie Fouse Ph.D.," Agios (website); "Adrienne Graves, PhD," Glaucoma Research Foundation (website); "Patricia Zilliox, PhD, President and CEO," Eyevensys (website); "Meet Our Team: Stella M. Robertson, PhD," Bios Partners (website); "Leader in Innovative Treatments," Nacuity Pharmaceuticals (website),; Joseph Spittler to author, email, May 22, 2023, TOM, AM.

12. *AWN*, Oct. 1988

13. "Alumnus of the Year Award; Dr. George F. Leone," p. 24; *FWST*, Sept. 23, 1990.

14. *AWN*, Aug. 1998; EHS, "Alcon Story."

15. *AWN*, Aug. 1998; EHS, "Alcon Story."

16. *AWN*, Aug. 1998; EHS, "Alcon Story"; *FWST*, Jun 10, 22, 1998

17. Taylor Schollmaier, Nov. 13, 2021, AOH; author's recollection of conversations with numerous Alcon retirees.

18. *FWST*, June 10, 1998, Jan. 13, 1999, Oct. 6, 2006, Apr. 21, May 4, 2007, Apr. 29, 2013, Aug. 12, Oct. 25, 2015, May 8, 2016, Sept. 28, Oct. 3, 2021; Calimbahin, "Ed Schollmaier, Former Alcon CEO

and TCU Donor, Dies at 87"; "Ed and Rae Schollmaier Arena," TCU Men's Basketball (website); "Message from Dean Valerio Ferme."

19. *AWN*, Apr. 1982, June 1987, Oct. 1988; Denny Alexander, Lane Anne Kimzey to author, emails, Apr. 13, 2023, TOM, AM; Leone, AOH; Leone, "Alcon Story"; Alexander Family Interview; EHS, "Alcon Story"; Sisson, "Alcon Story"; *Fort Worth News-Tribune*, Oct. 18, 1985; *Dallas Morning News*, May 9, 1982.

20. Alexander Family Interview; Alexander, Kimzey to author, emails, Apr. 13, 2023; *Fort Worth News-Tribune*, July 20, 1979, Aug. 13, 1982; *Dallas Morning News*, June 3, 1979; *FWST*, Jan. 18, 1980, Jan. 8, 1982, Oct. 12, 1985; *AWN*, Apr., 1982.

21. *FWST*, Apr. 8, 1984, Nov. 2, 1993, Sept. 17, 2003; Alexander Family Interview; Alexander, Anne Kimzey to author, emails, Apr. 13, 2023; *AWN*, Dec. 1982, June 1987, Mar. 1994; Daryl Dubbs, AOH, Jan. 17, 2023; Lale, "Catherine Alexander," p. 20.

22. *FWST*, June 3, 1979, Mar. 18, 1988, July 16, 2021; Alcon Annual Report, 1962, ALC; *FWST*, May 25, June 24, 1962; *William C. Conner Foundation: Educational Investment Fund, 2021 Annual Report.*

23. Conner Family Interview; Pan-American Association of Ophthalmology (website); William C. Conner, Curriculum Vitae (CV), ca. 1984, AHR; *FWST*, Jan. 14, 1992.

24. *Dallas Morning News*, May 9, 1982; *FWST*, May 2, June 3, 1979, Dec. 8, 1983, June 28, 1987, Mar. 18, Sept. 16, 17, 1988; Conner family interview.

Index

extraction of, 24, 65, 74, 224, 233, 237, 304, 307, 310-312, 348

products for, 88, 99, 226, 298, 343, 362-363

cattle, xv, xix, 21, 170

Center, Jack G., 169

Center Laboratories, 115, 119, 124, 136, 139, 145, 152, 169-170, 215, 275

Center, Thelma, 169

Central America, 85, 120, 177-178, 257

Cham, Switzerland, 252, 255, 256 f5.58

Chambers, Wiley A., 292, 297

Champeix, Beatrice, 341 f6.68, 343, 343 f6.69

Charoenvitvorakul, Siriwan, 349

Chateauvieux, Leon de, 175 f4.45, 178, 257

Chattanooga, Tennessee, 120

Chen, Jeanne, 260, 346 f6.71, 348

Chen, T.J., 260

Chicago, 14 f1.11, 43, 69, 72, 75, 85, 87-88, 119, 141, 167, 226, 245, 263

conferences in, 25, 26 f2.3, 30 f2.9, 33 f2.10, 40 f2.16, 57, 183

Chicago Pharmacal, 75. *See also* Conal

Chicago, University of, 121, 263

Chico, Enrique, 255

Chile, 177, 257, 345, 345 f6.70

China, 174, 198, 260-261, 346, 348, 349 f6.73, 363

Chowhan, Masood A., 301, 303, 417 n59

Christianity, 1, 3, 19, 101, 107, 378-380

Christmas, 50-51, 51 f2.21, 78, 109, 185, 235, 267, 356 f6.81, 357

Ciloxan, 297, 313, 317, 334, 335 f6.62, 336 f6.63, 337-338, 342, 344, 352, 362

Cincinnati, 58, 63, 377

City College of New York, 82

Clark, Steve, 231, 231f5.34, 247 f5.51, 248, 279

Clemmons, James Howard, 37, 40 f2.16, 43, 47, 52, 71, 77, 83

Clermont-Ferrand, France, 277, 315

Cleveland, 63

Clidiere, Thierry, 255, 342

Clynch, Marva, 83, 267, 355, 355 f6.80

Cobb, Dean, x

Cobb, Loral, x

Coben, Larry J., 208, 213 f5.19, 288

cocaine, 24

Collins, Alma, 109

Cologne, Germany, 289

Colombia, 43, 85-86, 85 f3.16, 177, 257, 268, 344-345

hot air balloon in, 259, 259 f5.65

Colorado, 43, 77

Colorado River, 7

Columbus, Ohio, 25

computers, 84, 130-131, 182, 225, 227-228, 327, 354

facilities for, 67

photographs of, 132 f4.8

Conal, 75, 86, 110, 114, 116-117, 141, 170, 258

manufacturing at, 94

Congo, 87. *See also* Zaire

Conner, BeBe, 5-7, 10, 11 f1.8, 14, 23 f2.2, 32, 35

Conner, Claire Crystelle, 6, 7 f1.4, 10, 17 f1.13, 32

Conner, James Clarence, 1-3, 1 f1.1

Conner, Laura Edna, 1-3, 1 f1.1, 5

Conner, Mary Frances, 35-36, 49

photographs of, 51 f2.21, 118 f4.1

Conner, William Clarence, ix, xv, 82, 105-110, 113, 116-117, 146, 259, 271, 274, 287, 345, 370

acquisitions and, 73-75, 108, 117, 119, 145, 168-169, 240, 262

advertising and, 150

airplane and, 102-103

Alcon Foundation and, 267

Alexander and, 10, 18-19, 53, 107, 114

at anniversary event, 184

awards and, 228

at barbecue, 183

board of directors and, 76-77, 85, 187-189

budget and, 33-34, 40, 375

buildings and, 27, 39, 51, 61, 89, 137

charter and, 37, 50

civic involvement of, 35, 107-109, 357, 367, 380

compensation plans and, 29

About the Author

Thomas O. "Tom" McDonald began his thirty-nine-year Alcon Research and Development career in December 1965 as a junior scientist, retiring as a vice president in 2004. He was inaugurated into the Alcon Hall of Fame in 2006.

McDonald spent his first decade at Alcon in the Toxicology department, becoming its director, where he profiled the safety for Miostat, Statrol, BSS, Avitene, Maxidex, Maxitrol, BSS PLUS, Pilopine HS, Fluorescite, and Tobrex. He collaborated in creating a new slit-lamp ocular scoring system that became the industry standard. He established the ophthalmic safe levels of ETO, ethylene chlorohydrin, and ethylene glycol, which were accepted by the FDA and published in the *Federal Register*. Thus, Alcon's reliance on ETO sterilization was preserved and continues to this day. In 1969, McDonald made Alcon R&D's first scientific presentation at the Association for Research in Vision and Ophthalmology (ARVO) annual conference and participated in the first R&D–supported product launch (BSS).

During an eighteen-month educational leave in 1977–78, McDonald earned his PhD in biology from Tulane University. His bachelor's and master's degrees are from Texas Christian University.

After returning from Tulane, McDonald spent the rest of his Alcon career in roles with increasing responsibility in R&D's Development section. During this time, he directed various Development groups and functions: the Worldwide Clinical Science department; the Ophthalmic and Consumer Products medical specialties groups; Generic Development; Pharmaceutical/Process Development; International Development; Japan Development; and Licensing/Theraputic Research. Successful products released included Betoptic (Alcon's first $100 million product), ProVisc, Alomide, Viscoat (Japan), AcrySof (Japan), Opti-Free (Japan), Naphcon-A, TobraDex, Ciloxan, Suprofen, Vexol, Emadine, Patanol, Opti-Free Express, and sixteen ophthalmic generic therapies.

During McDonald's four decades at Alcon, growth was explosive: R&D grew from 60 scientists to over 1,200 scientists and Alcon from 600 employees to 10,500. R&D's annual budget grew from nearly $1 million to $400 million and Alcon sales, from about $10 million to $4 billion.

After retiring, McDonald spent the next five years as a consultant for Nestlé Nutrition R&D, in Vevey, Switzerland, implanting Alcon's project management systems. Since then, McDonald, a seventh-generation Texan, has become a grassroots historian. His first book, *Texas Rangers, Ranchers, and Realtors: James Hughes Callahan and the Day Family in the Guadalupe River Basin*, published in 2021, explored social life and significant happenings in early Texas history. He is currently working on his third book—*Musings and Wanderlust of an Ophthalmic House Scientist*.

TOM MCDONALD, Ph.D.